Canadian Second Edition

BUSINESS
ESSENTIALS

Ronald J. Ebert
University of Missouri-Columbia

Ricky W. Griffin
Texas A & M University

Frederick A. Starke
University of Manitoba

Prentice Hall Canada Inc., Scarborough, Ontario

Canadian Cataloguing in Publication Data

Ebert, Ronald J.
       Business Essentials
2nd Canadian Edition
Includes index.
ISBN 0-13-083230-8

1. Industrial management - Canada. I. Griffin, Ricky W.
II. Starke, Frederick A., 1942- . III. Title.

HD70.C3E32   2000   658   C98-932950-X

ISBN 0-13-083230-8

Acquisitions Editor: Mike Ryan
Developmental Editor: Lesley Mann
Production Editor: Kelly Dickson
Copy Editor: Susan Broadhurst
Production Coordinator: Jane Schell
Photo Research: Susan Wallace-Cox
Cover and Interior Design: Mary Beth MacLean
Art Direction: Alex Li
Cover Image (Background): Greg Pease/Tony Stone Images; Insert Images: 1, 4:
       Digital Vision Ltd.; 2, 3: P. Crowther and S. Carter/Tony Stone Images
Page Layout: Joan M. Wilson

1 2 3 4 5   04 03 02 01 00

Printed and bound in the USA.

Visit the Prentice Hall Canada Web site! Send us your comments, browse our catalogues, and more
at **www.phcanada.com**. Or reach us through e-mail at **phcinfo_pubcanada@prenhall.com**.

Statistics Canada information is used with the permission of the Minister of Industry, as Minister
responsible for Statistics Canada. Information on the availabilty of the wide range of data from
Statistics Canada can be obtained form Statistics Canada's Regional Offices, its World Wide Web
site at http://www.statcan.ca, and its toll-free access number 1-800-263-1136.

CONTENTS IN

BRIEF

TABLE OF CONTENTS

PREFACE to the Canadian Second Edition

We didn't foresee that developing a new product could be so exciting! Indeed, following its introduction just three years ago, the enthusiastic reception for *Business Essentials* among instructors and students has stimulated this second edition of the book. For this revision, as with the first edition, we have conceived *Business Essentials* as a new product with a unique purpose. The book reflects more than just changes that are occurring in the practice of business. It also reflects the changing needs of students and teachers of business.

■ LISTENING TO THE CUSTOMER

The leading introductory business books all boast high-quality coverage and a wide variety of materials from which to pick and choose for each user's situations. "Each user," however, turns out to be a member of an increasingly diverse audience of both students and instructors.

Student Customers

Consider some of the different motivations for taking this course: Some students, for example, are working adults attending classes during off hours, while others are full-time students taking introduction to business as just one of many courses. While some students are studying business as a requirement of degree programs, others are taking the course simply to satisfy their curiosity.

To a growing number of these students, cost is a consideration in the course they select. Forced to weight limited financial resources against the increasing costs of attending school, students are increasingly adopting a critical consumer's perspective on educational "products." Questions such as "Am I getting my money's worth from this course?" mean that costs are being weighed against value received. Too often, the same reservations are being expressed when students leave their course saying, "Why did I have to buy this expensive book when we didn't use all of it? What a waste of money."

Instructor Customers

Instructors, too, face diverse needs in the differing settings in which learning takes place. Obviously, the business practitioner who takes time from other activities to teach an introductory course faces entirely different demands than the full-time instructor. Similarly, the custom of teaching a variety of courses and topics during a term places unique demands on every teacher. In addition, as instructors' interests and experiences lead to different orientations in their courses, they naturally pick and choose differently among the materials that they will emphasize. Finally, depending on an institution's timetable, an introductory course can range from 6 to 16 weeks in duration; naturally, that factor influences how much and which material can be covered.

In many instances, instructors must adopt long textbooks with comprehensive coverage that goes beyond their needs. In doing so, they pay a price on two counts. First, big books often require a big investment in preparation time: In designing courses, instructors must spend time deciding which material to emphasize, which to touch upon more lightly, and which to exclude entirely. Second, the instructor must answer to sometimes vocal students who want to know why so much material was omitted: "If it's important, why didn't we cover it? If it's not important, why did we have to pay for a book that has all that extra material in it? Isn't there a better book?"

■ MEETING THE CUSTOMER'S NEEDS

And so we come to the purpose of *Business Essentials*: It is an alternative for those who want a "no-nonsense" approach for the introduction to business course. It contains the "no-frills" essentials of business for those instructors who want focused coverage in a lower-priced book. And it does so with high-quality presentation. As such, it is an innovative product that responds to our customers' expressed desire for an option that is truly differentiated by both quality and price.

In creating *Business Essentials*, we naturally drew on our earlier experiences in developing *Business*. Through three successful editions, we have gained deep appreciation for the diversity of needs not only among the book's users but for the unmet needs of potential users. Much of the core material in *Business Essentials* is, of course, adapted from *Business*. It has, however, been thoroughly updated, and the organization and format of the book have been completely revised. Naturally, we have retained, adapted, or otherwise revamped the most valuable features of *Business*.

The *Business Essentials* project took advantage of many of the book's concepts for a team approach to product development, involving marketing, production, finance, product design, and business strategy to conceive and refine a product for a highly competitive market. In brief, the project enabled us to practise what we preach by addressing the significant but previously unmet needs of an important market segment. Prentice Hall, the authors, and the panel of advisers who teach business listened closely to our customers, both students and instructors, in creating an exciting new product.

Not surprisingly, the twofold mandate of *Business Essentials*—brevity and high quality—involved sometimes challenging, often difficult decisions about content and orientation. Very early in the project, we learned to appreciate the difficulties of being selective; deciding which subject matter to emphasize and which materials to exclude (you can't have a shorter book of high quality without cutting) was often painful. Ultimately, our decisions were guided by suggestions from teachers and students, as well as by our own experiences with the practice of business.

■ THE OBJECTIVES OF *BUSINESS ESSENTIALS*

This second Canadian edition of *Business Essentials* was guided by the fundamental objectives that we established for the book at the outset of this project:

- We wanted it to be an *affordable, lower-priced* alternative for students in the introductory course.
- We wanted it to be *reduced in length* while retaining high quality in its coverage of the essential facets of business.
- We wanted it to be *accurate*, with all statements of fact based on scientific research and/or managerial practice.
- We wanted it to be *current*, with illustrative examples and cases drawn from Canadian business stories that are still unfolding.

- We wanted it to be *readable* so that students could appreciate the experience of encountering and thinking about life in the world of business.

We believe we have met all the objectives. The price of *Business Essentials* is lower than that of other major, high-quality books designed for the introductory course. The length of the book is shorter than the other leading books, yet it offers significant coverage of business essentials, including both traditional topics and newer ideas. All of our examples are drawn from today's business world. Indeed, to make the book as current as possible, we added and updated information and examples right up to the moment we went to press in the spring of 1999.

■ THE THEMES OF *BUSINESS ESSENTIALS*

The 1990s have been a particularly exciting time to do business. But to be fully prepared for business in the third millennium, students need to be aware of the trends that will affect them as they start their careers. For this reason, we have concentrated on bringing several important themes to their attention.

- ***The Rise of International Business.*** Many businesspeople and observers of the business world see the globalization of the economy as the great challenge in the coming century. To keep students aware of this challenge, we have based many of the examples, boxes, and cases in this book on the experiences of global companies. Chapter 4, "Understanding International Business," provides full coverage of this important subject.

- ***The Significance of Small Business.*** Because we recognize that most students will not go to work for huge corporations, we have provided balanced coverage of both small and large companies throughout the text. Chapter 7, "Running the Small Business," is comprehensive. In addition, examples throughout the book deal with small businesses, and many chapters contain sections on how specific practices and issues apply to the special concerns of small businesses.

- ***The Growth of the Service Sector.*** The 1990s have witnessed the continued growth of the service sector around the globe. We stress the importance of this sector by giving it equal billing with manufacturing in Chapter 10, "Producing Goods and Services." Throughout, the book also provides prominent coverage of service businesses in the examples.

- ***The Need to Manage Information and Communications Technology.*** In our information-based society, the people and organizations that learn how to obtain and use information will be the ones that succeed. The explosive growth in information systems stems from the emergence of communications technologies such as multimedia communications systems. We cover this important topic in detail in Chapter 12, "Understanding Accounting and Information Systems," where the discussion has been completely reworked for accuracy and currency.

- ***The Role of Ethics.*** Business ethics and social responsibility, while not new topics, have been generating much discussion in recent years. We reflect the attention that these topics have generated by devoting a full chapter to them (Chapter 3, "Conducting Business Ethically and Responsibly"). And, of course, we treat issues of business ethics and social responsibility in our examples and cases.

- ***The Quality Imperative.*** Quality and productivity continue to be of special interest as we approach the year 2000. Chapter 11, "Increasing Productivity and Quality," was initiated in response to requests and suggestions of instructors. We also present productivity and quality considerations where they relate to other materials throughout the book.

- ***The Importance of Career Preparation.*** Most business students are naturally quite concerned about their careers. In response to these concerns, we have developed a special appendix, "Business Careers and the Job Search." Sections on the job outlook, guidelines for preparing cover letters and résumés and attending job interviews, as well as methods for assessing job offers, provide practical guidance for seeking employment and understanding the process.

■ FEATURES

A textbook, of course, is more than just ideas carefully presented in words. It must be packaged effectively and engagingly if it is to accomplish all its objectives. We have thus designed a number of devices to make this book as user-friendly as possible.

Part Opener

At the beginning of each of the six parts of the book is a brief outline introducing the material that will be discussed in that part. By revealing the rationale for the structure of the part, it gives students a glimpse of the "big picture" as they head into a new area of the business world.

Chapter Materials

Each *chapter* contains several features that are designed to increase student interest and understanding of the material being presented. These features are as follows:

- *Learning objectives.* A list of learning objectives is found near the beginning of each chapter. These guide students in determining what is important in each chapter.
- *Opening vignette.* Each chapter begins with a one-page description of an incident that happened in a real Canadian or international company. The subject matter of this opening case is relevant to the material being presented in that chapter. This helps the student bridge the gap from theory to practice.
- *Boxed inserts.* Each chapter includes one or more "Trends & Challenges" boxed inserts which describe activities in Canadian and international companies. These inserts are designed to clearly show students how theoretical concepts are put into actual practice by business firms.
- *Examples.* In addition to the boxed inserts, each chapter contains numerous examples of how businesses operate. These examples will further help students understand actual business practice in Canada and elsewhere.
- *Figures, tables,* and *photographs.* These illustrate a point or convey a message. The selective inclusion of these visuals increases the reader's involvement in the text. All photos are inspired by the text material; captions expand upon the text content.
- *Weblinks* in the margins of the text direct students to some of the most interesting and informative Websites available. All Weblinks are regularly updated in the "Destinations" section of the text's Companion Website at **www.prenticehall.ca/ebert**.

End-of-Chapter Material

Several important pedagogical features are found at the end of each chapter. These are designed to help students better understand the material that was presented in the chapter. The features are as follows:

- *Summary of learning objectives.* The material in each chapter is concisely summarized to help students understand the main points that were presented in the chapter.

- *Study questions and exercises.* There are three general types of questions here: questions for review (straightforward questions of factual recall), questions for analysis (requiring students to think beyond simple factual recall and apply the concepts), and application exercises (requiring students to visit local businesses or managers and gather additional information that will help them understand our business firms operate).

- *Building your business skills.* This new feature is an in-depth exercise that allows students to examine some specific aspect of business in detail. The exercise may ask the student to work individually or in a group to gather data about some interesting business issue and then develop a written report or a class presentation based on the information that was gathered.

- *Business Case study.* Each chapter concludes with a business case study which focuses on a real Canadian or international company. The case is designed to help students see how the chapter material can be applied to a real company that is currently in the news.

- *Take It to the Net.* A special feature of the Companion Website for *Business Essentials* is the *Take It to the Net* exercise for each chapter. The growing prominence of the Internet as an information medium has stimulated the introduction of this new feature, available online at **www.prenticehall.ca/ebert**. Students are directed towards Internet information sources and hands-on network activities that enhance and reinforce understanding of important topics in each chapter. As with *Building Your Business Skills*, the *Take It to the Net* exercises are specifically designed to foster in-depth involvement and problem solving. The format is hands-on, and activities are designed to accommodate both out-of-class preparation and in-class discussion. For example, here is a preview of the online exercise for Chapter 17, Financial Decisions and Risk Management:

Prentice Hall

COMPANION
WEBSITE

Many tools and resources are available on Canadian business Websites to help business managers improve financial decision making. One such Website is the Federal Business Development Bank of Canada (FBDB). Check out their Website at: **http://www.bdc.com**

1. What types of financing sources are available through the Federal Business Development Bank?

2. Visit the "Tools" section of the Website. Here you will find the "Ratio Calculator." What types of businesses would benefit most from this type of analysis tool? Why?

3. What does a "quick ratio" mean? Why and when would it be useful?

4. Which ratio(s) might be of most concern to an investor? A company sales manager? A company's creditors? A company's suppliers? The company's operations manager? An insurance underwriter? The company financial manager? Explain.

5. Evaluate the ratios as tools for making financial decisions. What are their strengths? What are their limitations?

Each *Take It to the Net* exercise also includes an annotated list of six to 10 other related Internet sites that students will find relevant and informative.

A proviso: although we waited until the last possible minute to finalize the installments in this feature, we understand that users will undoubtedly encounter problems in accessing some of the home pages and subdirectories we used in creating these exercises. The reason will almost always be the same: a content provider has exercised his or her option to make changes in material without incurring the costs of reworking printed material. Change and flexibility, in other words, are integral features of the Internet, and so while we aim to ensure URLs in our Companion Website are kept current and up-to-date, we urge everyone to be flexible and creative. There are numerous sources for most types of information, and both we and our colleagues have found that when faced with glitches, determined students not only find what they want but gain valuable experience in working with search engines. We are convinced that inventive students will not only locate alternative solutions to most exercise problems but will gain in enthusiasm in the process.

End-of-Part Material

Each part concludes with three video cases. CBC video cases are based on recent *Venture* episodes. (A videotape containing the 12 episodes that are summarized in the text is available for textbook adopters.) The instructor can show a CBC video in class and then either have class discussion using the questions at the end of the written case as a guideline, or ask students to turn in a written assignment which contains answers to the questions at the end of the case. This approach to teaching will add a major new dynamic to classes.

The ON LOCATION! Lands' End videos are found at the end of each part of the text (except for Part 6). Each segment focuses on a relevant aspect of operations at Lands' End Inc., a major catalogue retailer located in Dodgeville, Wisconsin. The purpose of these videos, which were shot on location and include interviews with managers and employees at Lands' End, is to anchor exercises focusing on the operations of a successful company that deals with both goods and services on a global scale. The authors and publisher wish to thank Coordinator of Public Relations Lisa Mullens and the other individuals at Lands' End who extended courtesy, cooperation, and resources in helping to create the *On Location!* video exercises.

■SUPPLEMENTARY MATERIAL

www.prenticehall.ca/ebert

- *Companion Website with Online Study Guide*: Our exciting new Website includes *Take It to the Net* exercises for each chapter of *Business Essentials*. It offers students a comprehensive online study guide with multiple choice and true/false review questions, as well as updated Internet destinations and search tools, CBC video case updates, and more. Instructors will be interested in our online syllabus builder and the password-protected Instructors button containing updates to the text and electronic versions of key supplements. (To obtain your password, please contact your Prentice Hall sales representative.) See **www.prenticehall.ca/ebert** and explore!

In 1981, Lands' End coined the term "direct merchant" to describe its approach to the retailing business. Since 1994, Lands' End has been the biggest catalogue company in North America with more than 8 million customers in 75 countries. "One thing we have learned over the years," says Managing Director Phil Young, "is that change is constant." Lands' End is the subject of the **On Location** *video exercises integrated into this edition of* **Business Essentials, Canadian Second Edition.**

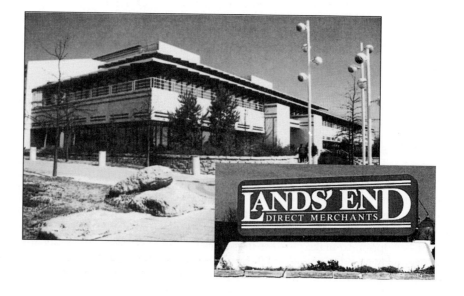

- *Instructor's Resource Manual and CBC Video Guide:* Prepared by Prof. Frederick A. Starke, the Canadian author of *Business Essentials*, this supplement contains extensive materials to aid instructors in effective use of the text. It includes a chapter synopsis and outline; teaching tips; suggestions on using the boxed inserts; answers to review, analysis, and application questions; answers for Building Your Business Skills and Business Case questions; answers to CBC and Lands' End video case questions; and answers to the Take It to the Net exercises on our Companion Website. (ISBN 0-13-084130-7)

- *Test Item File:* Containing nearly 3000 questions, prepared or adapted by Prof. Frederick A. Starke for the Canadian edition of this supplement, the Test Item File offers an average of 100 multiple choice, 50 true/false, and 15 essay questions per chapter. For each question Prof. Starke provides the correct answer with a page reference to the text, difficulty level (easy, moderate, or difficult), and classification (recall or application). (ISBN 0-13-084141-2)

- *PH Test Manager:* Utilizing our new Test Manager program, the computerized test bank for *Business Essentials* offers a comprehensive suite of tools for testing and assessment. Test Manager allows educators to easily create and distribute tests for their courses, either by printing and distributing through traditional methods or by online delivery via a Local Area Network (LAN) server. Once you have opened Test Manager, you'll advance effortlessly through a series of folders allowing you to quickly access all available areas of the program. Test Manager has removed the guesswork from your next move by incorporating Screen Wizards that assist you with such tasks as managing question content, managing a portfolio of tests, testing students, and analyzing test results. In addition, this all-new testing package is backed with full technical support, comprehensive online help files, a guided tour, and complete written documentation. Available as a CD-ROM for Windows 95. (ISBN 0-13-084144-7)

- *Electronic Transparencies in PowerPoint:* Expanded and improved for the Canadian second edition of *Business Essentials*, this supplement consists of approximately 600 electronic transparencies in PowerPoint 7.0. The transparencies illustrate key figures and concepts of the text, and include teaching notes and cross-references to related pages in *Business Essentials*. (ISBN 0-13-084142-0)

- *Colour Acetates:* Also expanded and improved, this full-colour set of transparencies presents approximately 100 graphic illustrations from the text. Lecture notes with a summary, questions for discussion, and page references to the text are included in the package. (Colour acetates are available in limited quantities to qualified adoptors only. Please contact your Prentice Hall sales representative for details.)

- *Prentice Hall/CBC Video Library:* In an exclusive partnership, the CBC and Prentice Hall Canada have worked together to develop an exciting video package consisting of 12 segments from the prestigious series *Venture*. At an average of seven minutes in length, these segments show students issues affecting real Canadian individuals and companies. Teaching notes are provided in *Instructor's Resource Manual and CBC Video Guide.* (Please contact your Prentice Hall sales representative for details. These videos are subject to availability and terms negotiated upon adoption of the text.)

- *ON LOCATION! Lands' End Videos:* Prepared exclusively for Prentice Hall, these six video segments focus on Lands' End Inc., a major catalogue retailer. The purpose of these videos, which were shot on location and include interviews with managers and employees at Lands' End, is to anchor exercises focusing on the operations of a successful American company that deals with both goods and services on a global scale. Each segment is eight to 10 minutes long. Written summaries with questions are provided at the end of Parts 1 to 5 in the text, and answers are discussed in the *Instructor's Resource Manual.* (Please contact your Prentice Hall sales representative for details. These videos are subject to availability and terms negotiated upon adoption of the text.)

■ACKNOWLEDGEMENTS

Although only three names appear on the cover of this book, we could never have completed the second edition of *Business Essentials* without the assistance of many fine individuals. Everyone who worked on the book was committed to making it the best that it could be. Quality and closeness to the customer are things that we read a lot about today. Both we and the people who worked with us took these concepts to heart in this book and made quality our watchword by listening to our users and trying to provide what they wanted.

We would like to thank all the professionals who took time from their busy schedules to review this edition of *Business Essentials* for us:

Drew Adams, Red River Community College

Tom Anger, Queen's University

Douglas Beatty, Lambton College

Robert Jakes, Saskatchewan Institute of Applied Science and Technology

Robert Jershy, St. Clair College

John Logan, Ryerson Polytechnic University

Grant Russell, University of Waterloo

John Scott, CGA

Joan Tripp, College of the North Atlantic

The supplements package for *Business Essentials*, Canadian Second Edition, also benefited from the able contributions of Dave Hunter, of Humber College, and Karen Blotnicky, of Mount Saint Vincent University. We would like to thank them both for their development of fine instructional and learning materials.

A superb team of professionals at Prentice Hall Canada made this book a pleasure to write. Authors often get the credit when a book is successful, but the success of this book must be shared with an outstanding group of people in Scarborough, Ontario. Mike Ryan (Acquisitions Editor) and Pat Ferrier (Publisher) have been true product champions and have improved both the book and its supplements in more ways than we can list. Lesley Mann, Senior Developmental Editor, and Kelly Dickson, Supervising Editor, also made outstanding contributions to the book on a day-to-day basis. (Incidentally, they are two of the nicest people we have ever worked with.)

Our colleagues at the University of Manitoba, Texas A&M, and the University of Missouri–Columbia also deserve recognition. Each of us has the good fortune to be a part of a community of scholars who enrich our lives and challenge our ideas. Without their intellectual stimulation and support, our work would suffer greatly.

Finally, our families. We take pride in the accomplishments of our wives, Ann, Glenda, and Mary, and draw strength from the knowledge that they are there for us to lean on. And we take joy from our children, Eric, Grant, Ashley, Dustin, Matt, and Kristen. Sometimes in the late hours when we're ready for sleep but have to get one or two more pages written, looking at their pictures keeps us going. Thanks to all of you for making us what we are.

Frederick A. Starke
Ricky W. Griffin
Ronald J. Ebert

■ABOUT THE AUTHORS

Ronald J. Ebert is Professor of Management at the University of Missouri–Columbia. He received his B.S. in Industrial Engineering from Ohio State University, his M.B.A. from the University of Dayton, and his D.B.A. from Indiana University, where he was a U.S. Steel Fellow. A member of and an active participant in the Academy of Management, the Institute of Management Sciences, the American Production and Inventory Control Society, and the Operations Management Association, Dr. Ebert has also served as the editor of the *Journal of Operations Management* and as Chair of the Production and Operations Management Division of the Academy of Management. In addition to *Business*, he is the co-author of three books: *Organizational Decision Processes*, *Production and Operations Management* (published in English, Spanish, and Chinese), and *Management*.

Dr. Ebert has held engineering and supervisory positions in quality management with the Frigidaire Division of General Motors Corporation. He has also done TQM and operations strategy consulting for the National Science Foundation, the United States Savings and Loan League, Kraft Foods, Oscar Mayer, Sola Optical USA, Inc., the City of Columbia, and the American Public Power Association. His research interests include manufacturing policy and strategy, engineering design processes in product development, statistical quality control, and subjective managerial judgments in strategy formulation.

Ricky W. Griffin was born and raised in Corsicana, Texas. He received his B.A. from North Texas State University and his M.B.A. and Ph.D. from the University of Houston. He served on the faculty of the University of Missouri–Columbia from 1978 until 1981, when he joined the faculty at Texas A&M. In 1990, he was named the university's Lawrence E. Fouraker Professor of Business Administration.

Dr. Griffin's research interests include leadership, workplace violence, and international management. He has done consulting in the areas of task design, employee motivation, and quality circles for such organizations as Baker-Hughes, Texas Instruments, Six Flags Corporation, Texas Commerce Bank, and AT&T. His research has won two Academy of Management Research Awards (both in the Organizational Behaviour division) and one Texas A&M University Research Award.

Dr. Griffin currently serves as the Director of the Center for Human Resource Management at Texas A&M. In addition to *Business*, he is the author or co-author of five books and more than 40 journal articles and book chapters.

Frederick A. Starke is Professor and Associate Dean of the Faculty of Management at the University of Manitoba. He received his B.A. and M.B.A. from Southern Illinois University and his Ph.D. from Ohio State University. He has served on the Faculty of Management at the University of Manitoba since 1968.

Dr. Starke's research interests include decision making, conflict management, and organizational politics. His research has been published in the *Academy of Management Journal*, the *Journal of Applied Psychology*, *Administrative Science Quarterly*, and the *Journal of Systems Management*. He has co-authored five books on management, organizational behaviour, and general business. He has taught extensively in executive development programs in both the public and private sector. He has also conducted management consulting projects for both public- and private-sector organizations.

The Prentice Hall Canada
companion Website...

Your Internet companion to the most exciting, state-of-the-art educational tools on the Web!

The Prentice Hall Canada Companion Website is easy to navigate and is organized to correspond to the chapters in this textbook. The Companion Website is comprised of four distinct, functional features:

1) **Customized Online Resources**

2) **Online Study Guide**

3) **Reference Material**

4) **Communication**

Explore the four areas in this Companion Website. Students and distance learners will discover resources for indepth study, research, and communication, empowering them in their quest for greater knowledge and maximizing their potential for success in the course.

A NEW WAY TO DELIVER EDUCATIONAL CONTENT

1) Customized Online Resources

Our Companion Websites provide instructors and students with a range of options to access, view, and exchange content.

- **Syllabus Builder** provides *instructors* with the option to create online classes and construct an online syllabus linked to specific modules in the Companion Website.

- **Mailing lists** enable *instructors* and *students* to receive customized promotional literature.

- **Preferences** enable *students* to customize the sending of results to various recipients, and also to customize how the material is sent, e.g., as html, text, or as an attachment.

- **Help** includes an evaluation of the user's system and a tune-up area that makes updating browsers and plug-ins easier. This new feature will enhance the user's experience with Companion Websites.

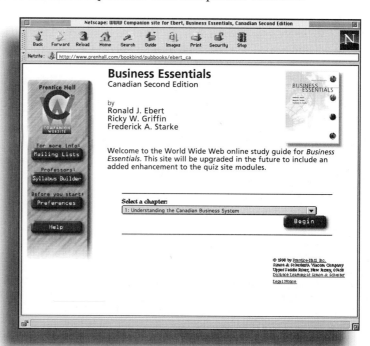

Prentice Hall

COMPANION WEBSITE

2) Online Study Guide

Interactive Study Guide modules form the core of the student learning experience in the Companion Website. These modules are categorized according to their functionality:

- True-False
- Multiple Choice
- Essay
- Internet Exercises

The True-False, Multiple Choice, Essay and Internet Exercise modules provide students with the ability to send answers to our grader and receive instant feedback on their progress through our Results Reporter. Coaching comments and references back to the textbook ensure that students take advantage of all resources available to enhance their learning experience. Essay answers can be sent to instructors for grading or be self-checked by students.

3) Reference Material

Reference material broadens text coverage with up-to-date resources for learning. **Web Destinations** provides a directory of Web sites relevant to the subject matter in each chapter. **NetNews (Internet Newsgroups)** is a fundamental source of information about a discipline, containing a wealth of brief, opinionated postings. **NetSearch** simplifies key term searches using Internet search engines. Downloadable material for teachers is provided in the password-protected *Instructors* area.

4) Communication

Companion Websites contain the communication tools necessary to deliver courses in a **Distance Learning** environment. **Message Board** allows users to post messages and check back periodically for responses. **Live Chat** allows users to discuss course topics in real time, and enables professors to host online classes.

Communication facilities of Companion Websites provide a key element for distributed learning environments. There are two types of communication facilities currently in use in Companion Websites:

- **Message Board** – this module takes advantage of browser technology, providing the users of each Companion Website with a national newsgroup to post and reply to relevant course topics.

- **Live Chat** – enables instructor-led group activities in real time. Using our chat client, instructors can display Website content while students participate in the discussion.

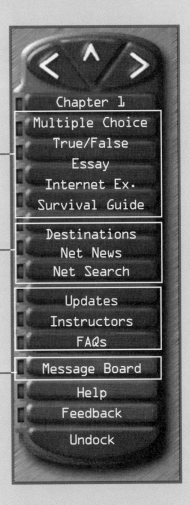

Chapter 1
Multiple Choice
True/False
Essay
Internet Ex.
Survival Guide

Destinations
Net News
Net Search

Updates
Instructors
FAQs

Message Board
Help
Feedback
Undock

Companion Websites are currently available for:

- Griffin: Business
- Starke: Contemporary Management in Canada
- Kotler: Principles of Marketing
- Evans: Marketing Essentials

Note: CW content will vary slightly from site to site depending on discipline requirements.

The Companion Websites can be found at:

PRENTICE HALL CANADA

1870 Birchmount Road
Scarborough, Ontario M1P 2J7

To order:
Call: 1-800-567-3800
Fax: 1-800-263-7733

For samples:
Call: 1-800-850-5813
Fax: (416) 299-2539
E-mail: phcinfo_pubcanada@prenhall.com

INTRODUCING THE CONTEMPORARY BUSINESS WORLD

In Chapters 1–4, you will read about four situations that may seem at first glance to have little in common: the Voisey's Bay mineral discovery, an employee buyout at Great Western Brewery, a dispute at the Toronto Better Business Bureau, and the international business strategy of Purdy's Chocolates.

The Better Business Bureau provides a service, while the other organizations provide a physical product. Great Western Brewery is a small firm, but the Voisey's Bay nickel mine will be very large. In spite of these and other differences, the four organizations have a fundamental similarity: they are all business organizations which must provide acceptable goods and services to their customers if they are to continue to exist. Each case tells part of the story of our contemporary business world.

Part One, Introducing the Contemporary Business World, provides a general overview of business today, including its economic roots, its legal structure, its ethical problems and opportunities, and its global reach.

- ■ We begin in **Chapter 1, Understanding the Canadian Business System,** by examining the role of business in the economy of Canada and other countries.
- ■ Then, in **Chapter 2, Setting Up Business in Canada,** we look briefly at the history of Canadian business and explore the various forms of business ownership in Canada.
- ■ In **Chapter 3, Conducting Business Ethically and Responsibly,** we examine how individual ethics and corporate social responsibility develop and affect the firm's environment, customers, employees, and investors.
- ■ In **Chapter 4, Understanding International Business,** we look at the major world marketplaces, how companies organize to operate internationally, and the development of free trade agreements.

CHAPTER 1

UNDERSTANDING THE CANADIAN BUSINESS SYSTEM

VOISEY'S BAY: FIELD OF DREAMS OR NIGHTMARE?

Here's a classic Canadian success story: In September 1993, Chris Verbisky and Al Chislett were flying in a helicopter over the rolling hills of northeast Labrador. Their company, Archean Resources Ltd., was doing diamond prospecting work for Vancouver-based Diamond Fields Resources (DFR) Inc. On that day, the two prospectors were returning from a three-month trip into the interior. Their search for diamonds had been completely unsuccessful, but their luck was about to change in a way that they never expected.

When they were only 10 kilometres from Voisey's Bay, they spotted a *gossan*—a rusty-coloured outcropping which is usually a good place to look for metals. As soon as they broke open the first rock, they knew they had stumbled onto something big. What they didn't know was that they had just discovered one of the world's richest base metals deposits.

Even though Verbisky and Chislett were impressed by their first "grab samples," it would still be 14 months before DFR really got interested in the discovery. In April 1994, DFR came up with $175 000 for a last-minute renewal of their option on the Voisey's Bay claim. It was not until October 1994 that the initial holes were drilled. Two sceptical engineers from a Toronto firm who came out to analyze the drill samples were dumbfounded at what they saw. The samples contained nearly 4 percent nickel content and 3 percent copper content (many mining companies are happy with 2 percent copper content). By the end of 1994, it was clear that DFR really had found something of immense value.

It is now estimated that the main body of ore contains reserves of about 150 million tonnes, which should translate into hundreds of millions of pounds of nickel annually and millions of pounds of copper. Annual revenues from this ore body alone will reach at least $400 million. Company profits will reach at least $150 million each year. The cost to develop the mine is expected to be about $500 million. Because the Voisey's Bay metals are very close to the surface and because the mine is close to Voisey's Bay, it should be very profitable.

DFR's stock, which was listed on the Toronto Stock Exchange, reflected the metal discovery. In October 1994, it was trading at about $4 per share. After the announcement of the discovery, the stock climbed steadily for the next few months, reaching $15 per share by early 1995. By April 1995, it had reached $33 per share.

The company finally gained instant credibility in April 1995 when Teck Corp. invested $108 million for a 10.4 percent share in DFR. That is more than DFR was worth before the Voisey's Bay discovery. Teck's investment has helped allay investor fears about the involvement of controversial mining promoter Robert Friedland, the co-chairman of DFR. In 1996 Inco bought controlling interest in DFR so that Inco would continue to be the dominant company in the world nickel mining industry. Inco paid $41 for each share of DFR stock.

Unfortunately, once Inco gained control of the deposit, things began to go wrong. Between March and November 1997, Inco's stock price dropped 50 percent because of declining world nickel prices, and because Inco had issued increased numbers of its shares to pay for the purchase of Voisey's Bay.

In September 1997, Inco announced that it would have to delay the proposed startup of the project because of a time-consuming and expensive environmental review process; by mid-1998, Inco had already spent $13 million on the environmental review. The government of Newfoundland also demanded that the company build a smelter in the province to smelt the ore it mined, even though it would have been more economically sound to send the ore elsewhere to be smelted. Then, a group called the Citizens Mining Council objected to the smelter on environmental grounds.

Inco is also having difficulties reaching agreement with aboriginal communities. The Innu Nation, for example, demanded a 3 percent smelter royalty, which would cost Inco $355 million based on anticipated production.

It was originally thought that development of Voisey's Bay would boost the economic growth of Newfoundland and Labrador by 15 to 25 percent. Of the 5 percent GDP growth that is predicted for the year 2003, a full percentage point was to have come from Voisey's Bay activity. But in March 1998, Goldman Sachs, a New York investment and banking firm, issued a report casting doubt on the economic viability of Voisey's Bay. The report said that even if outstanding aboriginal land claims could be resolved, the project is not worthwhile because nickel prices have dropped so low.

At the company's annual meeting in April 1998, chairman Michael Sopko had to cope with hostile questions from union and aboriginal leaders, shareholders, environmentalists, and political leaders. Rumours began circulating that Inco would have to take a massive writedown on the project. Is Voisey's Bay a field of dreams or a nightmare? Time will tell.

The forces of supply and demand that play such an important role in the financial future of companies like Inco and Diamond Fields Resources also dictate stories of success and failure for virtually every business enterprise. As you will see in this chapter, those forces define the Canadian market economy. You will also see that although the world's economic systems differ markedly, the standards for evaluating the success or failure of a system are linked to its capacity to achieve certain basic goals.

By focusing on the learning objectives of this chapter, you will better understand the Canadian business system and the mechanisms by which it not only pursues its goals but permits businesses large and small to pursue theirs. After reading this chapter, you should be able to:

1. Define the nature of Canadian *business* and its goals.
2. Describe different types of *economic systems* according to the means by which they control the *factors of production*.
3. Show how *demand* and *supply* affect resource distribution in Canada.
4. Identify the elements of *private enterprise* and explain the various degrees of *competition* in the Canadian economic system.
5. Explain the criteria for evaluating the success of an economic system in meeting its goals and explain how the federal government attempts to manage the Canadian economy.

■ THE IDEA OF BUSINESS AND PROFIT

What do you think of when you hear the word business? Does it conjure up images of huge corporations like Canadian Pacific and Alcan Aluminum? Smaller companies like your local supermarket? One-person operations like the barbershop around the corner?

business
An organization that seeks to earn profits by providing goods and services.

profit
What remains (if anything) after a business's expenses are subtracted from its sales revenues.

Royal Bank of Canada
www.royalbank.com

Imperial Oil
www.imperialoil.ca

economic system
The way in which a nation allocates its resources among its citizens.

factors of production
The resources used to produce goods and services: natural resources, labour, capital, and entrepreneurs.

natural resources
Items used in the production of goods and services in their natural state, including land, water, minerals, and trees.

labour
The mental and physical training and talents of people; sometimes called human resources.

capital
The funds needed to operate an enterprise.

entrepreneur
An individual who organizes and manages natural resources, labour, and capital to produce goods and services to earn a profit, but who also runs the risk of failure.

Indeed, each of these firms is a **business**—an organization that produces or sells goods or services in an effort to make a profit. **Profit** is what remains after a business's expenses have been subtracted from its revenues. Profits reward the owners of businesses for taking the risks involved in investing their money and time. The Royal Bank of Canada earned over $1 billion in profit in 1997, but most businesses will never earn anywhere near that much money.

Still, the prospect of earning profits is what encourages people to open and expand businesses. Today businesses produce most of the goods and services that we consume, and they employ many of the working people in Canada. Profits from these businesses are paid to thousands upon thousands of owners and shareholders. And business taxes help support governments at all levels. In addition, businesses help support charitable causes and provide community leadership.

In this chapter, we begin your introduction to Canadian business by looking at its role in our economy and society. Because there are a variety of economic systems found around the world, we will first consider how the dominant ones operate. Once you have some understanding of different systems, you can better appreciate the workings of our own system. As you will see, the effect of economic forces on Canadian businesses and the effect of Canadian businesses on our economy produce dynamic and sometimes volatile results.

■ GLOBAL ECONOMIC SYSTEMS

A Canadian business is different in many ways from one in China. And both are different from businesses in Japan, France, or Peru. A major determinant of how organizations operate is the kind of economic system that characterizes the country in which they do business. An **economic system** allocates a nation's resources among its citizens. Economic systems differ in who owns and controls these resources, known as the "factors of production."

Factors of Production

The basic resources a business uses to produce goods and services are called **factors of production**. They include natural resources, labour, capital, and entrepreneurs.[1] Figure 1.1 illustrates the factors of production.

Land, water, mineral deposits, and trees are good examples of **natural resources.** For example, Imperial Oil makes use of a wide variety of natural resources. It obviously has vast quantities of crude oil to process each year. But Imperial also needs the land where the oil is located, as well as land for its refineries and pipelines.

The people who work for a company represent the second factor of production, **labour.** Sometimes called *human resources*, labour is the mental and physical capabilities of people. Carrying out the business of such a huge company as Imperial requires a labour force with a wide variety of skills ranging from managers to geologists to truck drivers.

Obtaining and using material resources and labour requires **capital**, the funds needed to operate an enterprise. Capital is needed to start a business and to keep the business operating and growing. Imperial's annual drilling costs alone run into the millions of dollars. A major source of capital for most businesses is personal investment by owners. Personal investment can be made either by the individual entrepreneurs or partners who start businesses or by investors who buy stock in them. Revenues from the sale of products, of course, is another and important ongoing source of capital. Finally, many firms borrow funds from banks and other lending institutions.

Entrepreneurs are those people who accept the opportunities and risks involved in creating and operating businesses. They are the people who start new businesses and who make the decisions that allow small businesses to grow into larger ones. Murray Pezim, Conrad Black, and the Griffiths family are well-known Canadian entrepreneurs. The box "Raising Rhinos for Horns and Profit" describes the activities of entrepreneur Norman Travers.

TRENDS & CHALLENGES

Raising Rhinos for Horns and Profit

Norman Travers operates a game farm in Zimbabwe that contains a herd of endangered black rhinos. He does most of his business with tourists who pay to take photo safaris through his game farm. Some of his guests hunt game as well. Travers is part of an increasingly vocal African conservation movement that is driven by free-market thinking. He hopes someday to harvest rhino horns and sell them for profit. The removal of the horn does not hurt the animal and a new horn grows in to replace the old one. Travers can't do this yet because trading in rhino horns is banned by an international treaty designed to protect the dwindling rhino population. Travers and others argue that this approach to conservation is not working since poaching remains a serious problem. What is needed, he argues, is rhino ranching, which could supply the world demand for rhino horns while protecting the animals on game farms.

Travers is part of a growing group of game farmers who are privatizing and commercializing the wild game business in Africa. South Africa, for example, has 25 large private game reserves and many smaller ones. These game farms are so successful that animals such as buffalo, giraffe, impala, and wildebeest are regularly sold at animal auctions. All this activity provides jobs. The amount of land dedicated to game farming increased from 12 to 17 percent between 1986 and 1996.

In Zimbabwe, the Communal Areas Management Program for Indigenous Resources (CAMPFIRE) was started to help reduce complaints about marauding animals in villages that were close to national game parks. Indigenous residents were given permits to harvest game that came onto their lands. Villagers could either hunt the animals and use their meat, or sell their harvesting permits to safari operators who guided big-game hunters into the area. Either way, the villagers made money. Villages in northwestern Zimbabwe earned almost $500 000 in one three-year period under this program. Most striking, poaching in these areas dropped sharply, because the people living there now have an interest in preserving their local wildlife.

The move towards privatization has run into stiff opposition from Western conservation organizations and animal rights groups. They oppose the hunting of animals on moral grounds, and they object to reducing wild animals to simply an economic number. The CAMPFIRE program has been attacked by the Humane Society, which claims that CAMPFIRE is a stooge for safari operators and says that it is not necessary to kill animals in order to help the local people.

The clash of ideas is illustrated by the elephant situation in Zimbabwe. The government wants to repeal the international ban on trading in elephant ivory because there is a surplus of elephants and they want their poor rural populations to benefit from the selling of ivory. The country has about 64 000 elephants, but the government estimates that the carrying capacity of the land is only about 35 000. The "excess" elephants could be harvested, and their ivory and meat would be a big economic boost to the area.

Those who want the ivory ban lifted argue that groups like the Humane Society are simply practising "eco-colonialism." A game economist at the University of Zimbabwe says that it's easy for Westerners to view the problem from a distance and demand that elephants and other species be preserved, but that ignores the problems the people in the area are having. The economist asks this question: "Would citizens of industrialized countries choose the survival of, say, whales at the expense of their lives, or the education of their children, or their pensions?" Not likely. Yet that is what Westerners are asking Africans to do.

Types of Economic Systems

Different types of economic systems manage the factors of production in different ways. In some systems, ownership is private; in others, the factors of production are owned by the government. Economic systems also differ in the ways decisions are made about production and allocation. A **command economy**, for example, relies on a centralized government to control all or most factors of production and to make all or most production and allocation decisions. In **market economies**, individuals—producers and consumers—control production and allocation decisions through supply and demand. We will describe each of these economic types and then discuss the reality of the *mixed market economy*.

command economy
An economic system in which government controls all or most factors of production and makes all or most production decisions.

market economy
An economic system in which individuals control all or most factors of production and make all or most production decisions.

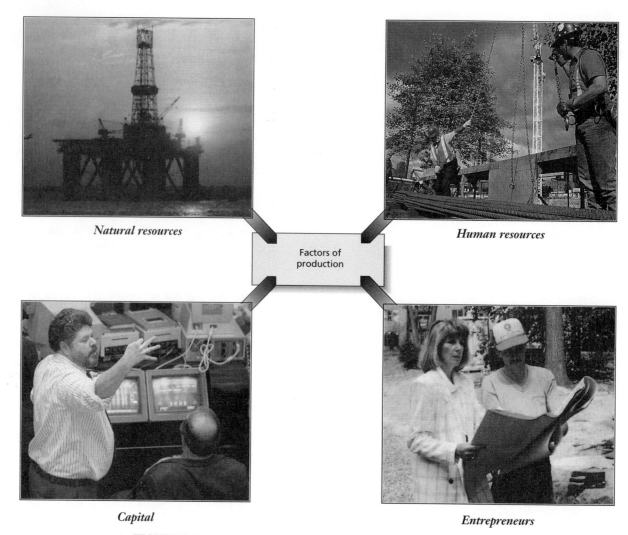

Natural resources

Human resources

Factors of production

Capital

Entrepreneurs

FIGURE 1.1

Factors of production are the basic resources a business uses to create goods and services. The four basic factors used are natural resources, human resources, capital, and entrepreneurs.

共產主義
communism
A type of command economy in which the government owns and operates all industries.

Command Economies.   The two most basic forms of planned economies are communism and socialism. As originally proposed by the 19th-century German economist Karl Marx, **communism** is a system in which the government owns and operates all sources of production. Marx envisioned a society in which individuals would ultimately contribute according to their abilities and receive economic benefits according to their needs. He also expected government ownership of production factors to be only temporary: Once society had matured, government would "wither away" and the workers would gain direct ownership.

Most Eastern European countries and the former Soviet Union embraced communist systems until very recently. During the early 1990s, however, one country after another renounced communism as both an economic and a political system. Today, Cuba, North Korea, Vietnam, and the People's Republic of China are among the few nations with avowedly communist systems. Even in these countries, however, command economic systems are making room for features of the free-enterprise system from the lowest to the highest levels. In Cuba, for example, special shops once reserved for diplo- 外交官 mats are now patronized by Cubans from all walks of life. Here, they can buy goods that the severely troubled government system cannot supply. Moreover, they use money earned from a variety of free-market activities (which are, technically, illegal). For example, the stores themselves are surrounded by paid bicycle parking lots, carwashes, and stalls selling home-grown produce and homemade handicrafts. All of this street-corner commerce reflects a rapid growth in private enterprise as a solution to problems that a centralized economy has long been unable to solve.[2]

In a less extensive command economic system called **socialism**, the government owns and operates only selected major industries. Smaller businesses such as clothing stores and restaurants may be privately owned. Although workers in socialist countries are usually allowed to choose their occupations or professions, a large proportion generally work for the government. Many government-operated enterprises are inefficient, since management positions are frequently filled based on political considerations rather than ability. Extensive public welfare systems have also resulted in very high taxes. Because of these factors, socialism is generally declining in popularity.[3]

socialism
A kind of command economy in which the government owns and operates the main industries, while individuals own and operate less crucial industries.

Market Economies. A *market* is a mechanism for exchange between the buyers and sellers of a particular good or service. To understand how a *market economy* works, consider what happens when a customer goes to a fruit stand to buy apples. Let's say that while one vendor is selling apples for $1 per kilogram, another is charging $1.50. Both vendors are free to charge what they want, and customers are free to buy what they choose. If both vendors' apples are of the same quality, the customer will buy the cheaper ones. But if the $1.50 apples are fresher, the customer may buy them instead. In short, both buyers and sellers enjoy freedom of choice.

Market economies rely on markets, not governments, to decide what, when, and for whom to produce. **Capitalism** provides for the private ownership of the factors of production. It also encourages entrepreneurship by offering profits as an incentive. Businesses can provide whatever goods and services and charge whatever prices they choose. Similarly, customers can choose how and where they spend their money.[4] Businesses that produce inefficiently or fail to provide needed or desired products will not survive. At least that is the theory in "pure" market economies.

capitalism
A market economy; an economic system in which markets decide what, when, and for whom to produce.

Mixed Economies. The economic systems we have described differ greatly from each other, but the fact is that no country in the world today has a purely communistic, socialistic, or capitalistic economy. For example, the People's Republic of China has begun encouraging some entrepreneurial activity. Both England and France maintain government control of some industries but allow free market operations in others. Government planners in Japan give special assistance to "sunrise industries"—those expected to grow. In Canada, the federal government regulates many aspects of business. And many utilities are owned by provincial governments. Thus, most of the world's countries have a **mixed economy** in which one of the basic economic systems dominates but elements of the other systems are present as well.

In recent years, government involvement in business has decreased because of deregulation and privatization. **Deregulation** means a reduction in the number of laws affecting business activity and in the powers of government enforcement agencies. In most cases, deregulation frees the corporation to do what it wants without government intervention, thereby simplifying the task of management. Deregulation is evident in many industries, including airlines, pipelines, banking, trucking, and communications.

Privatization refers to the transfer of activities from the government to the private sector. The federal government has sold several corporations, including Canadian National Railways, Air Canada, Teleglobe Canada, and Canadair Ltd. Provincial governments are also selling off businesses, for example, the Ontario Transportation Development Corp., Manitoba Oil and Gas Corp., Pacific Western Airlines (sold by the Alberta government), and Nova Scotia Power Inc. There is increasing talk about privatizing provincial hydroelectric utilities, particularly in Ontario, Quebec, and Newfoundland.[5]

Canada is not the only country where privatization is taking place. In Mexico, for example, 900 of the 1200 state corporations have been privatized.[6] Telephone companies in Mexico, New Zealand, and Argentina have also been privatized. In France, the government is privatizing 21 key state-controlled companies in an attempt to reduce the deficit and energize the economy. Firms to be sold include the nation's third largest bank,

mixed economy
An economic system with elements of both a command economy and a market economy; in practice, typical of most nations' economies.

deregulation
A reduction in the number of laws affecting business activity.

privatization
The transfer of activities from the government to the public sector.

Nova Scotia Power Inc.
www.nspower.com

Teleglobe Canada
www.teleglobe.ca

While we can identify different types of economies, the distinctions between them are becoming increasingly blurred. Previous command economies in Eastern Europe, for example, are moving towards a market system. The woman (top left) shown here is selling decorated eggs on the street. China still uses a command economy, but more and more elements of capitalism are becoming evident. In Canada, capitalism has always allowed farmers to decide what they would grow and how much to sell it for. Of course, capitalists aren't protected from failure, a concern that people in command economies seldom have to confront.

a large chemical company, and a large oil company. Privatization is a worldwide phenomenon, and it will lead to the dismantling of much of the government involvement in business that has developed during the 20th century. It is estimated that between 1993 and 1995 well over $100 billion were raised in equity markets by governments as they privatized some of their organizations.[7]

■ BASIS OF THE CANADIAN ECONOMIC SYSTEM

Understanding the complex nature of the Canadian economic system is essential to understanding Canadian businesses. In the next few pages, we will examine the workings of our market economy in more detail. Specifically, we look at markets, demand, supply, private enterprise, and degrees of competition.

A market is an exchange process between buyers and sellers of a particular good or service. For example, a customer exchanges money with a retail grocer for products such as breakfast cereal or toothpaste.

Markets, Demand, and Supply

In economic terms, a **market** is not a specific place, like a supermarket, but an exchange process between buyers and sellers. Decisions about production in a market economy are the result of millions of exchanges. How much of what product a company offers for sale and who buys it depends on the laws of demand and supply.

Basically, **demand** is the willingness and ability of buyers to purchase a product or service. **Supply** is the willingness and ability of producers to offer a good or service for sale. The **law of demand** states that buyers will purchase (demand) more of a product as its price drops. Conversely, the **law of supply** states that producers will offer more for sale as the price rises.

Demand and Supply Schedule. To appreciate these laws in action, consider the market for pizza in your town. If everyone in town is willing to pay $25 for a pizza (a relatively high price), the town's only pizzeria will produce a large supply. But if everyone is willing to pay only $5 (a relatively low price), the restaurant will make fewer pizzas. Through careful analysis, we can in fact determine how many pizzas will be sold at different prices. These results, called a **demand and supply schedule**, are obtained from marketing research and other systematic studies of the market. Properly applied, they help managers better understand the relationships among different levels of demand and supply at different price levels.

Demand and Supply Curves. The demand and supply schedule can be used to construct demand and supply curves for pizza in your town. A **demand curve** shows how many products—in this case, pizzas—will be *demanded* (bought) at different prices. A **supply curve** shows how many pizzas will be *supplied* (cooked) at different prices.

Figure 1.2 shows the hypothetical demand and supply curves for pizzas in our illustration. As you can see, demand increases as price decreases; supply increases as price increases. When the demand and supply curves are plotted on the same graph, the point at which they intersect is the **market price**, or **equilibrium price**—the price at which the quantity of goods demanded and the quantity of goods supplied are equal. Note in Figure 1.2 that the equilibrium price for pizzas in our example is $10. At this point, the quantity of pizzas demanded and the quantity of pizzas supplied are the same—1000 pizzas per week.

Surpluses and Shortages. But what if the restaurant chooses to make some other number of pizzas? For example, what would happen if the owner tried to increase profits by making more pizzas to sell? Or what if the owner wanted to reduce overhead, cut back on store hours, and reduce the number of pizzas offered for sale? In either case, the result would be an inefficient use of resources—and perhaps lower profits. For example, if the restaurant supplies 1200 pizzas and tries to sell them for $10 each, 200 pizzas will not be purchased. The demand schedule clearly shows that only 1000 pizzas will be demanded at this price.

market
An exchange process between buyers and sellers of a particular good or service.

demand
The willingness and ability of buyers to purchase a product or service.

supply
The willingness and ability of producers to offer a good or service for sale.

law of demand
The principle that buyers will purchase (demand) more of a product as price drops.

law of supply
The principle that producers will offer (supply) more of a product as price rises.

demand and supply schedule
Assessment of the relationships between different levels of demand and supply at different price levels.

demand curve
Graph showing how many units of a product will be demanded (bought) at different prices.

supply curve
Graph showing how many units of a product will be supplied (offered for sale) at different prices.

market price (or equilibrium price)
Profit-maximizing price at which the quantity of goods demanded and the quantity of goods supplied are equal.

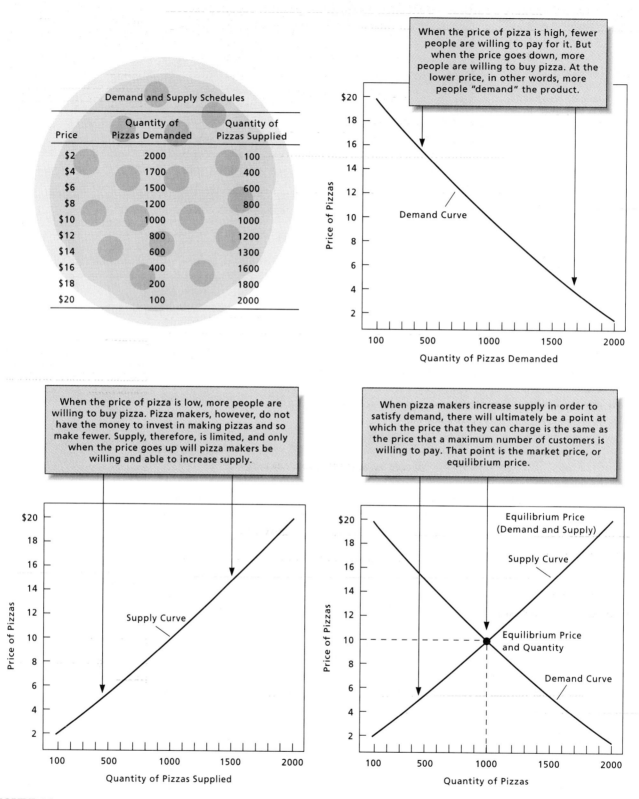

FIGURE 1.2
Demand and supply.

The pizza maker will have a **surplus**—a situation in which the quantity supplied exceeds the quantity demanded. The restaurant will thus lose the money that it spent making those extra 200 pizzas.

Conversely, if the pizzeria supplies only 800 pizzas, a **shortage** will result: The quantity demanded will be greater than the quantity supplied. The pizzeria will "lose" the extra money that it could have made by producing 200 more pizzas. Even though consumers may pay more for pizzas because of the shortage, the restaurant will still earn lower profits than it would have if it had made 1000 pizzas. In addition, it will risk angering customers who cannot buy pizzas. To optimize profits, therefore, all businesses must constantly seek the right combination of price charged and quantity supplied. This "right combination" is found at the equilibrium point.

This simple example, of course, involves only one company, one product, and a few buyers. The Canadian economy is far more complex. Thousands of companies sell hundreds of thousands of products to millions of buyers every day. In the end, however, the result is much the same: companies try to supply the quantity and selection of goods that will earn them the largest profits.

Private Enterprise

In his book *The Wealth of Nations*, first published in 1776, economist Adam Smith argued that a society's interests are best served by **private enterprise**—allowing individuals within that society to pursue their own interests without government regulation or restriction. He believed that because of self-interests, the "invisible hand of competition" would lead businesses to produce the best products they could as efficiently as possible and to sell them at the lowest possible price. Each business would unintentionally be working for the good of society as a whole.

Market economies have prospered in large part due to private enterprise. As Adam Smith first noted, private enterprise requires the presence of four elements: (1) private property rights, (2) freedom of choice, (3) profits, and (4) competition.[8]

Private Property.   Smith maintained that the creation of wealth should be the concern of individuals, not the government. Thus, he argued that the ownership of the resources used to create wealth must be in the hands of individuals, not the government. Individual ownership of property is part of everyday life in Canada. You or someone you know has bought and owned automobiles, homes, land, or stock. The right to **private property**—to buy, own, use, and sell almost any form of property—is one of the most fundamental aspects of capitalism. Most of us take private property for granted. Yet, in some countries you could not own a business even if you had the money to pay cash.

Freedom of Choice.   **Freedom of choice** means that you can try to sell your labour to whomever you choose. You can also choose which products to buy. Freedom of choice further means that producers of goods and services can usually choose whom to hire and what to make. Under normal circumstances, the government does not go to a manufacturing firm, for example, and tell it what kinds of products to make.

Profits.   What a company chooses to produce will, by definition, be affected by the *profits* it hopes to make. A business that fails to make a profit must eventually close its doors. The majority of small businesses fail within the first five years of their existence.[9] But the lure of profits leads some people to give up the security of working for someone else and assume the risks of entrepreneurship.

surplus
Situation in which quantity supplied exceeds quantity demanded.

shortage
Situation in which quantity demanded exceeds quantity supplied.

private enterprise
An economic system characterized by private property rights, freedom of choice, profits, and competition.

private property
The right to buy, own, use, and sell an item.

freedom of choice
The right to choose what to buy or sell, including one's labour.

competition 榜(增)争
The vying among businesses in a particular market or industry to best satisfy consumer demands and earn profits.

Competition.   If profits motivate individuals to start businesses, **competition** for resources and customers motivates individuals to operate their businesses efficiently. To gain an advantage over their competitors in the marketplace, businesses must produce their goods and services for as little as possible and sell them for as much as possible. However, if they are quite successful and their profits are unusually high, other firms will sense an opportunity and also enter the market. The ensuing competition between these firms will drive the prices down. To continue to make a profit, each business must constantly look for more efficient ways to make its products, as well as for new and/or improved products.

Degrees of Competition

Not all industries are equally competitive. Economists have identified four basic degrees of competition within a private enterprise system—pure competition, monopolistic competition, oligopoly, and monopoly. Table 1.1 describes these four degrees of competition.

pure competition
A market or industry characterized by a very large number of small firms producing an identical product so that none of the firms has any ability to influence price.

Pure Competition.   For **pure competition** to exist, firms must be small in size, but large in number. In such conditions, no firm is powerful enough individually to influence the price of its product in the marketplace.

First, in pure competition the products offered by each firm are so similar that buyers view them as identical to those offered by other firms. Second, both the buyers and sellers know the price that others are paying and receiving in the marketplace. Third, the firms involved in a purely competitive situation are small, which makes it relatively easy for a firm to go into or out of business.

Under pure competition, price is set exclusively by supply and demand in the marketplace. Sellers and buyers must accept the going price. Despite some government price-support programs, agriculture is usually considered to be a good example of pure competition in the Canadian economy. The wheat produced on one farm is essentially the same as wheat produced on another farm. Both producers and buyers are well aware of prevailing market prices. Moreover, it is relatively easy to get started or to quit producing wheat.

■ TABLE 1.1   Degrees of Competition

Characteristic	Pure Competition	Monopolistic Competition	Oligopoly	Monopoly
Example	Local farmer	Stationery store	Steel industry	Public utility
Number of competitors	Many	Many, but fewer than in pure competition	Few	None
Ease of entry into industry	Easy	Relatively easy	Difficult	Regulated by government
Similarity of goods or services offered by competing firms	Identical	Similar	Can be similar or different	No directly competing goods or services
Level of control over price by individual firms	None	Some	Some	Considerable

Monopolistic Competition.   In **monopolistic competition**, there are fewer sellers than in pure competition, but there are still many buyers. Sellers try to make their products at least appear to be slightly different from those of their competitors by tactics such as brand names (Tide and Cheer), design or styling (Ralph Lauren and Izod clothes), and advertising (as done by Coke and Pepsi).

Monopolistically competitive businesses may be large or small, because it is relatively easy for a firm to enter or leave the market. For example, many small clothing manufacturers compete successfully with large apparel makers. Product differentiation also gives sellers some control over the price they charge. Thus Ralph Lauren Polo shirts can be priced with little regard for the price of Eaton's shirts, even though the Eaton's shirts may have very similar styling.

Oligopoly.   When an industry has only a handful of sellers, an **oligopoly** exists. As a general rule, these sellers are almost always very large. The entry of new competitors is restricted because a large capital investment is usually necessary to enter the industry. Consequently, oligopolistic industries (such as the automobile, rubber, and steel industries) tend to stay oligopolistic.

Oligopolists have even more control over their alternatives than do monopolistically competitive firms. However, the actions of any one firm in an oligopolistic market can significantly affect the sales of all other firms. When one reduces prices or offers some type of incentives to increase its sales, the others usually do the same to protect their sales. Likewise, when one raises its prices, the others generally follow suit. As a result, the prices of comparable products are usually quite similar.

Since substantial price competition would reduce every seller's profits, firms use product differentiation to attract customers. For example, the four major cereal makers (Kellogg, General Mills, General Foods, and Quaker Oats) control almost all of the cereal market. Each charges roughly the same price for its cereal as do the others. But each also advertises that its cereals are better tasting or more nutritious than the others.[10] Competition within an oligopolistic market can be fierce.

Monopoly.   When an industry or market has only one producer, a **monopoly** exists. Being the only supplier gives a firm complete control over the price of its product. Its only constraint is how much consumer demand will fall as its price rises. Until 1992, the long-distance telephone business was a monopoly in Canada, and cable TV, which has had a local monopoly for years, will lose it when telephone companies and satellite broadcasters are allowed into the cable business.[11]

monopolistic competition
A market or industry characterized by a large number of firms supplying products that are similar but distinctive enough from one another to give firms some ability to influence price.

oligopoly
A market or industry characterized by a small number of very large firms that have the power to influence the price of their product and/or resources.

Kellogg Company
www.kelloggs.com

Quaker Oats Company
www.quakeroats.com

monopoly
A market or industry with only one producer, who can set the price of its product and/or resources.

Competition for shelf space in grocery stores is intense and this buyer has many brands to choose from. Is this a situation of pure competition, monopolistic competition or oligopoly?

natural monopoly
A market or industry in which having only one producer is most efficient because it can meet all of consumers' demand for the product. (without waste)

In Canada, laws such as the *Competition Act* forbid many monopolies. In addition, the prices charged by "natural monopolies" are closely watched by provincial utilities boards. **Natural monopolies** are industries where one company can most efficiently supply all the product or service that is needed. For example, like most utilities, your provincial electric company is a natural monopoly because it can supply all the power (product) needed in an area. Duplicate facilities—such as two nuclear power plants, two sets of power lines, and so forth—would be wasteful.

■ EVALUATING ECONOMIC SYSTEMS

Thus far we have noted that nations employ a variety of economic systems. We naturally think our economic system works better than those used in other countries. We point with pride to our high standard of living and to our general prosperity. Yet, leaders in other countries believe just as strongly that their systems are best. So how do we really know that our system works as well as we think? To assess the effectiveness of an economic system objectively, we must consider the society's goals, its record in meeting those goals, and the interaction of government and non-government forces within the economy.

Economic Goals

Nearly every economic system has as its broad goals stability, full employment, and growth. Economies differ in the emphasis they place on each and their approach to achieving them.

stability
A situation in which the relationship between the supply of money and goods, services, and labour remains constant

inflation
A period of widespread price increases throughout an economic system.

consumer price index
Changes in the cost of a basket of goods and services that the typical family buys.

Stability.   In economic terms, **stability** is a condition in which the balance between money available and goods produced remains about the same. As a consequence, prices for consumer goods, interest rates, and wages paid to workers change very little. Stability helps maintain equilibrium and predictability for businesspeople, consumers, and workers.

The biggest threat to stability is **inflation**, a period of widespread price increases throughout the economic system. The most widely known measure of inflation is the **consumer price index**, which measures changes in the cost of a "basket" of goods and services that a typical family buys. Figure 1.3 shows how inflation has varied over the last 20 years in Canada. The box "Coping with Inflation" describes some of the difficulties that several countries have faced because of high inflation.

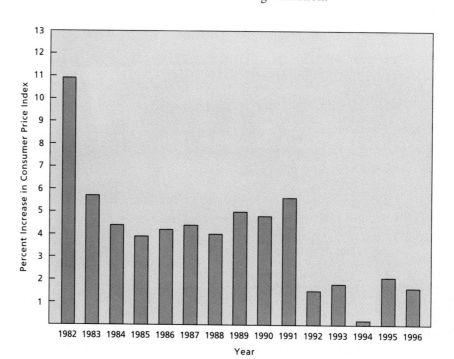

FIGURE 1.3
In the last few years the rate of price increases in Canada has dropped.

T R E N D S   &   C H A L L E N G E S

Coping with Inflation

For most of the 20th century, Canadians have taken for granted that inflation will not be a serious problem. While the annual inflation rate in Canada occasionally creeps up to 10 or 12 percent, this is nothing compared to the 500 percent experienced in Brazil in 1994, and the 4200 percent experienced in Argentina in 1989.

Argentina attempted to fight inflation by swapping its nearly worthless austral for a new peso valued at one to one with the U.S. dollar. By doing this, they hoped to develop a currency that Argentines could believe in. But conditioned as they were to high inflation, businesses initially continued to raise prices even after the new currency had been introduced. Over time, however, the inflation rate has gradually come down, and by 1994 was in the neighbourhood of 120 percent per year. Unfortunately, the new peso is overvalued by as much as 40 percent, and purchasing power is lower than it was before the plan was introduced. Many people who were formerly part of the middle class have been pushed into the lower class.

Brazil's annual inflation has exceeded 100 percent each year for the last decade. Recently, the rate has climbed even higher, exceeding 500 percent according to some indexes. These high rates have been caused primarily by chronic government deficits and excessive government spending. Individuals cope with these high rates using various strategies. One popular method is to pay by cheque and date the cheque as much as 10 days later. On the tenth day, the person takes the money from an interest-bearing account and puts it in an empty chequing account. But even these strategies may not help. Doctors note that the number of heart and stroke victims was up 20 percent in 1993, and they think that high inflation is the culprit because it increases the stress that people feel.

Like Argentina, Brazil is making a concerted effort to get inflation under control by introducing a new currency (the *real*, pronounced ray-AL) and tying it to the U.S. dollar. Unlike Argentina, there is no law guaranteeing convertibility of one real for one dollar, nor is there any law that forbids the central bank from printing money not backed by reserves. The expectations of Brazilians are crucial to the success of the plan. If they think the government will not back up the plan if the going gets tough, the country is likely to experience a new round of inflation soon.

These stories of high inflation in other countries may come as a surprise to Canadians. Inflation in Canada dropped to very low levels in the early 1990s, and by the middle of 1994 *deflation*—a decline in price levels—was experienced for the first time since 1955, as consumer prices fell by 0.2 percent. Lowered prices were caused in part by reductions in government tobacco taxes, and by the invasion of retail discounters like Wal-Mart into Canada.

Yet inflation is not necessarily bad. Stability can cause stagnation and a decline in innovation. The onset of inflation is usually a sign of growth. Initially, higher prices cause businesses to expand, hire new workers, pump more dollars into advertising, and introduce new and exciting products and services. New businesses also start up to take advantage of the prosperity.

Inflation is not the only threat to economic stability. Suppose that a major factory in your town closes. Hundreds or even thousands of workers would lose their jobs. If other companies in the area do not have jobs for them, these unemployed people will reduce their spending. Other local businesses will thus suffer drops in sales—and perhaps cut their own workforces. The resulting **recession**, characterized by a decrease in employment, income, and production, may spread across the province and the nation. A particularly severe and long-lasting recession, like the one that affected much of the world in the 1930s, is called a **depression**.

recession
The part of the business cycle characterized by a decrease in employment, income, and production.

Full Employment. Full employment means that everyone who wants to work has an opportunity to do so. In reality, full employment is impossible. There will always be people looking for work. These people generally fall into one of four categories.

Some people are out of work temporarily while looking for a new job, a situation known as *frictional unemployment*. A skilled engineer who has just quit her job but who will

depression
A particularly severe and long-lasting recession like the one that affected the world in the 1930s.

find a new job soon is in this category. Other people are out of work because of the seasonal nature of their jobs, a situation known as *seasonal unemployment*. Farm workers and construction workers, for example, may not work much in the winter. Sometimes people are out of work because of reduced economic activity, a situation known as *cyclical unemployment*. For example, many oil field workers in Alberta lost their jobs during the petroleum glut of the late 1980s. Some regained their jobs when stability returned, while many others moved to jobs in other industries. Finally, some people are unemployed because they lack the skills needed to perform available jobs, a situation known as *structural unemployment*. A steel worker laid off in a town looking for computer programmers falls into this category.

Because of the many reasons for unemployment, the rate of unemployment has varied greatly over the years, as Figure 1.4 shows. And because full employment is essentially impossible, our real goal is to minimize unemployment. High unemployment wastes talent and is a drain on resources that must be allocated to unemployment-associated welfare programs. Higher welfare costs, in turn, result in higher taxes for everyone.

growth
An increase in the amount of goods and services produced using the same resources.

Growth.   A final goal of our economic system is **growth**, an increase in the amount of goods and services produced by our own resources. In theory, we all want our system to expand—more businesses, more jobs, more wealth for everyone. In practice, growth is difficult without triggering inflation and other elements of instability. However, an extended period of no growth may eventually result in an economic decline—business shutdowns, a loss of jobs, a general decrease in overall wealth, and a poorer standard of living for everyone.

For many decades, Canada experienced growth rates in excess of most nations. More recently, however, countries such as South Korea, Taiwan, Japan, and Germany all had higher growth rates than Canada, in part because they became increasingly more efficient at producing goods and services.[12]

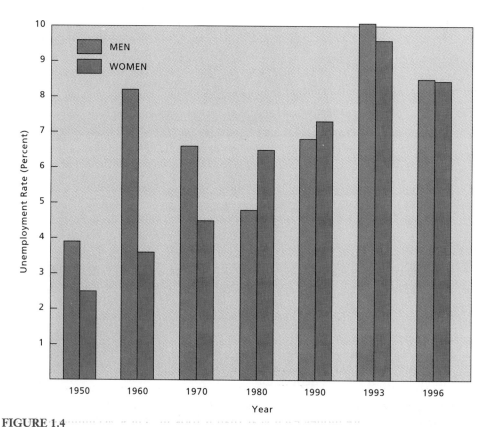

FIGURE 1.4

There has been a gradual upward trend in unemployment rates, with women having rates much closer to men in recent years.

Measuring Economic Performance

To judge how well an economic system is achieving its goals, economists use one or more of the following measures: standard of living, gross domestic product, productivity, the balance of trade, and national debt.

Standard of Living.   The **standard of living** is a measure of a society's economic well-being. It helps us to observe the change in a society's well-being over time and to compare one society's well-being with that of another. Canadians have become used to expecting their living standards to increase as time goes on. But we may be entering a period when living standards will not increase at all. Infometrica, an Ottawa-based economic consulting firm, predicts that in real terms, consumer disposable income will show no increase at all for the 1990s.[13]

standard of living
A measure of a society's economic well-being.

Gross Domestic Product.   If we add up the total value of all goods and services produced in Canada during a one-year period, that value is known as **gross domestic product (GDP)**. Canada's GDP in 1996 was $771 billion. Another figure that is often computed by economists is **gross national product (GNP)**. GNP includes the value of all goods and services produced by a country regardless of where the factors of production were located. For example, the profits earned by a Canadian company abroad are included in GNP, but not in GDP. Conversely, profits earned by foreign firms in Canada _are_ included in GDP.

gross domestic product (GDP)
The value of all goods and services produced in Canada during a one-year period.

gross national product (GNP)
The value of all goods and services produced by a country regardless of where the factors of production were located.

GDP and GNP are useful measures of economic growth because they allow us to track our economy's performance over time. But they may distort economic growth figures because they do not take account of the things that "nature" provides for free. Consider the GDP of, say, Indonesia. Using traditional measures, Indonesia's GDP grew 7.1 percent annually from 1971 to 1984. But if we calculate what was taken from nature to achieve this growth (tree cutting, soil depletion, mineral depletion), Indonesia's growth rate was only 4 percent.[14]

Per capita GDP allows us to compare GDP figures for different countries, taking into account their population size. Of the major industrial countries, Japan has the highest per capita GDP ($40 734), followed by Germany ($29 304), the U.S. ($26 225), France ($25 817), and Canada ($18 919).[15]

per capital GDP
Allows comparison of GDP figures for different countries, taking into account population size.

Productivity.   As a measure of economic growth, **productivity** describes how much is produced relative to the resources used to produce it. That is, if Mind Computers can produce a personal computer for $1000 but Canon needs $1200 to produce a comparable computer, Mind is more productive. Chapter 11 provides a detailed look at productivity. The box "Improved Productivity at Canadian National Railways" illustrates the importance of high productivity.

productivity
A measure of efficiency that compares how much is produced with the resources used to produce it.

Balance of Trade.   Another commonly used measure of economic performance is the balance of trade, the total of a country's exports to other countries minus its imports from other countries. A positive **balance of trade** is generally considered to be favourable because new money flows into the country from the sales of exports. A negative balance is less favourable because money is flowing out of the country from the purchase of imports. Canada has enjoyed a favourable balance of trade since the mid-1970s, but the balance is favourable only because Canada exports so much to the United States. Our balance of trade with most other countries is unfavourable.

balance of trade
The total of a country's exports (sales to other countries) minus its imports (purchases from other countries).

National Debt.   Like a business, the government takes in revenues (primarily in the form of taxes) and has expenses (military spending, social programs, and so forth). For many years, the government of Canada incurred annual **budget deficits**, that is, the government spent more money each year than it took in. These accumulated annual deficits have created a huge **national debt**—the amount of money that Canada owes its creditors.

budget deficit
The result of the government spending more in one year than it takes in during that year.

national debt
The total amount of money that Canada owes its creditors (presently over $550 billion).

TRENDS & CHALLENGES

Improved Productivity at Canadian National Railways

At its 1998 annual meeting, Canadian National Railways (CN) had good news for its shareholders. Revenues totalled $4.4 billion, and earnings per share rose from $3.49 in 1996 to $4.95 in 1997. CN is now North America's sixth largest railway. And CN's operating ratio—the amount of money it costs to generate $1 of revenue—is down to 81.5 percent. This means that it costs CN 81.5 cents to generate each dollar of revenue. The lower the operating ratio, the more efficient the company. In 1997, CN announced it would merge with Chicago-based Illinois Central Railway, the most efficient railway in North America, with an operating ratio of 62.3 percent. This should reduce CN's operating ratio even further.

These improvements have all come since CN changed its form of ownership from Crown corporation to public corporation. A decade ago, CN was one of the least competitive railways in North America, according to a special report produced by its own accounting department. In comparing CN to the typical large U.S. railway, the report said that CN had twice as many administrators, falling revenues, and labour expenses that ate up 45 per-

cent of each revenue dollar compared to U.S. railroads where labour expenses were taking only 28 percent.

There are some differences between Canadian and U.S. railroads that explain CN's former poor performance. For example, CN operates under difficult winter conditions that most U.S. railroads don't have to cope with. As well, CN operates more kilometres of track than most U.S. railroads, and much of this track does not get a lot of use.

One interesting fact: CN has far fewer train engineers than the typical U.S. railroad—6561 compared with an average of 9379 for U.S. railroads. It also has the smallest number of locomotives per train (2.56 versus 3.38 for U.S. railroads), and they pull the largest number of cars per locomotive.

As CN continues to pursue greater efficiency and a lower operating ratio, it will likely take some tough and unpopular actions. In fall of 1998, for example, CEO Paul Tellier announced that 3000 workers would be laid off, and that there might be additional layoffs in the future. He said that these actions were necessary to maintain CN's newfound productivity.

Managing the Canadian Economy

fiscal policies
Policies by means of which governments collect and spend revenues.

monetary policies
Policies by means of which the government controls the size of the nation's money supply.

The government manages the economic system through two sets of policies. **Fiscal policies** refer to the collection and spending of government revenues. Tax policies, for example, can function as fiscal policy to increase revenues. Similarly, budget cuts (for example, closing military bases) function as fiscal policy when spending is decreased.

Monetary policies focus on controlling the size of the nation's money supply. Working primarily through the Bank of Canada (the nation's central bank), the government can influence the ability and willingness of banks throughout the country to lend money. It can also influence the supply of money by prompting interest rates to go up or down. A primary goal in recent years has been to adjust interest rates so that inflation is kept in check.

The Bank of Canada
www.bank-banque-canada.ca

SUMMARY OF LEARNING OBJECTIVES

1. **Define the nature of Canadian *business* and its goals.** *Businesses* are organizations that produce or sell goods or services to make a profit. *Profits* are the difference between a business's revenues and its expenses. The prospect of earning profits encourages individuals and organizations to open and to expand businesses. The benefits of business activities also extend to wages paid to workers and to taxes that support government functions.

2. **Describe different types of** *economic systems* **according to the means by which they control the** *factors of production.* An *economic system* is a nation's system for allocating its resources among its citizens. Economic systems differ in terms of who owns and/or controls the four basic *factors of production:* natural resources, labour, capital, and entrepreneurs. In *command economies*, the government controls all or most factors. In *market economies*, which are based on the principles of *capitalism*, individuals control the factors of production. Most countries today have *mixed market economies* that are dominated by one of these systems but include elements of the others.

3. **Show how** *demand* **and** *supply* **affect resource distribution in Canada.** The Canadian economy is strongly influenced by markets, demand, and supply. *Demand* is the willingness and ability of buyers to purchase a product or service. *Supply* is the willingness and ability of producers to offer goods or services for sale. Demand and supply work together to set a *market* or *equilibrium price:* the price at which the quantity of goods demanded and the quantity of goods supplied are equal.

4. **Identify the elements of** *private enterprise* **and explain the various degrees of** *competition* **in the Canadian economic system.** The Canadian economy is founded on the principles of *private enterprise: private property rights, freedom of choice, profits,* and *competition.* Degrees of competition vary because not all industries are equally competitive. Under conditions of *pure competition*, a large number of small firms compete in a market governed entirely by demand and supply. In an *oligopoly*, there are only a handful of sellers. A *monopoly* exists when there is only one seller.

5. **Explain the criteria for evaluating the success of an economic system in meeting its goals and explain how the federal government attempts to manage the Canadian economy.** The basic goals of an economic system are *stability, full employment,* and *growth.* Measures of how well an economy has accomplished these goals include *standard of living, gross domestic product, productivity, balance of trade,* and *national debt.* The government uses *monetary policies* to control the size of the nation's money supply and *fiscal policies* to manage the effects of its spending and revenue collection.

STUDY QUESTIONS AND EXERCISES

Review Questions

1. What are the factors of production? Is one more important than the others? If so, which one? Why?

2. What are the major characteristics of a market economy? How does a market economy differ from a command economy?

3. Explain the differences in the four degrees of competition and give an example of each. (Do not use the examples given in the text.)

4. Why is productivity important? Why is inflation both good and bad?

Analysis Questions

5. Select a local business and identify the basic factors of production that it uses. Now identify the factors used by your college or university. What are the similarities and differences?

6. In recent years, many countries have moved from command economies to market economies. Why do

you think this has occurred? Can you envision a situation that would cause a resurgence of command economies?

7. Identify a situation in which excess supply of a product led to decreased prices. Identify a situation in which a shortage led to increased prices. What eventually happened in each case? Why?

Application Exercises

8. Choose a locally owned and operated business. Interview the owner to find out what factors of production the business uses and its sources for acquiring them.

9. Visit a local shopping mall or shopping area. List each store you see and determine what degree of competition it faces in that environment. How do other businesses compete to market goods or services?

10. Go to the library and read about 10 different industries. Classify each according to degree of competition.

BUILDING YOUR BUSINESS SKILLS

Goal

To encourage students to analyze the business challenges in moving from a command to a market economy.

Situation

An entrepreneur in Moscow wants to start a new business selling women's clothing. However, he is still adapting to the country's new economic and social environment, which is encouraging the development of free enterprise. As a result, he is uncertain how various economic factors will influence his chance for business success.

Method

Divide into groups of four or five people. The mission of each group is to brainstorm the entrepreneur's situation. In your discussion, analyze how each of the following factors is likely to influence business success. Remember to place yourself in the shoes of an entrepreneur whose country was communist until recently:

- Availability of startup capital.
- Availability of the raw materials needed in manufacturing.
- Availability of manufacturers skilled in clothing production.
- Adequacy of transportation network to move raw materials, supplies, and finished garments.
- Availability of skilled retail employees.

- Availability of bankers and other lenders who are willing to participate in continuing financing.
- The nature of government regulations of business.
- Consumer buying habits, attitudes, and tastes.
- Retailing environment and existing competition.

After your brainstorming session, work with group members to research the new market economies in Russia and other Eastern European countries. What do current articles in publications such as *The Globe and Mail*, *Canadian Business*, *Fortune*, and the *Wall Street Journal* tell you about the situation struggling entrepreneurs face?

Follow-Up Questions

1. Based on what you learned in this exercise, how does a command economy differ from a market economy?

2. What do you think are the biggest stumbling blocks in moving from a command to a market economy?

3. How did the conclusions you developed in your brainstorming session differ from what you learned in your research?

4. In the course of business, the entrepreneur will deal with creditors, suppliers, employees, government officials, consumers, and others. In what ways do the entrepreneur's relationships with each group in a market economy differ from those in a command economy?

BUSINESS CASE 1

At Last! Hibernia Starts Up

In 1959, a research geologist at Mobil Oil speculated that there might be oil off the coast of Newfoundland. Various wells were drilled over the next 20 years, but none were commercially viable. In 1979, however, a huge reserve of oil was discovered. Now, 40 years after the first tentative exploration efforts, the Hibernia project has finally begun pumping oil. A consortium of companies, including Mobil, Chevron, and Petro-Canada, are involved in the drilling.

Two other megaprojects are also in the works in the same general area off the coast of Newfoundland. The Terra Nova project (Petro-Canada) could begin pumping oil as early as 1999, and the Whiterose project (Husky Oil) by 2002. By 2002, production from these three projects could be as high as 350 000 barrels of oil a day. That is more than the combined output of Syncrude Canada and Suncor in northern Alberta's tar sands.

Hibernia's three biggest enemies were nature, politics, and economics. Although the area was known to contain oil, it was avoided for years because of major storms, and because it is in "iceberg alley." In 1982, the Ocean Ranger drilling rig sank in a winter storm, killing all 84 workers on it. That disaster motivated engineers to build a heavy platform that is anchored to the sea bottom. This platform will be able to withstand iceberg hits as well.

Federal and provincial squabbling about who owned the mineral rights also created uncertainty. Newfoundland claimed that it owned the rights, but the federal government argued that Newfoundland gave up those rights when it joined Canada in 1949. Eventually, all royalty rights were given to Newfoundland after then–prime minister Brian Mulroney intervened. Mulroney also demanded that the oil companies give at least some of the construction work associated with the project to Newfoundland companies.

Fluctuating oil prices were also a problem. High prices in the late 1970s made the project look economically sound. But by the late 1980s, oil prices had dropped to the point that the oil companies had decided to halt work on the project. The federal government then agreed to put up $1 billion in grants and $1.7 billion in loan guarantees to keep the project going. For its investment, the government received an 8.5 percent share in the project. In 1992, Gulf Canada suddenly pulled out of the consortium, creating another crisis. Gulf was replaced by Murphy Oil, which was also given loan guarantees by the federal government.

The federal government has adopted a policy that allows the companies in the consortium to recover some of their huge capital costs early; most royalties and corporate taxes won't come until some years later. It is doubtful whether the federal government will get any of the $1 billion in grant money back, but it does expect revenues from its 8.5 percent share.

The Hibernia project has made only a slight dent in Newfoundland's famous high unemployment rate. Critics say that the $1 billion grant translates into a cost of $172 400 for each of the 5800 jobs that were created during the peak construction time. Only about 650 workers will find permanent work because of Hibernia.

■ Case Questions

1. What is a "mixed economy"? How does the Hibernia project demonstrate Canada's mixed economy?

2. What incentives existed for oil companies to get involved in Hibernia? What incentives existed for the federal government to get involved?

3. Should the federal government have given $1 billion to the oil companies in order to keep them involved in the Hibernia project?

4. How did the forces of supply and demand affect the decisions of the oil companies and the federal government?

5. How are the factors of production evident in this case?

CHAPTER

2

SETTING UP BUSINESS IN CANADA

EMPLOYEE BUYOUTS—GOOD NEWS AND BAD NEWS

During the past few years, the idea of employee buyouts has become increasingly popular in both Canada and the U.S. In the U.S., for example, several of the largest firms in the commercial airline industry—United, TWA, and Northwest—recently became employee-owned. At United, the pilots and machinists unions now own 53 percent of the company. In exchange, they made concessions like agreeing to a no-strike clause.

In Canada, there are several prominent examples of employee buyouts. The most famous is probably the buyout of the Temiscaming, Quebec, forest products plant in 1972. International Paper sold the mill to the Quebec government, which kept a 40 percent stake and sold the rest to managers and an investment company. The mill has been profitable ever since. In 1991, the Ontario government facilitated a deal that allowed workers to save the Spruce Falls mill at Kapuskasing, Ontario. The workers paid $12.5 million for 52 percent ownership. Skeptics doubted whether the deal would be as successful as Temiscaming, but they were proved wrong. In its first quarter of operations, the mill made a profit of nearly $500 000. At Algoma Steel, employees bought a 60 percent ownership in the company as part of a bailout deal by the Ontario government.

Nova Corp. used to have a division that developed and manufactured magnetic bearings and gas seals for pipeline equipment. When it decided to shut down that division, it gave several managers the chance to form a separate compa-

ny to carry on the work. Each manager invested between $80 000 and $100 000 in the new venture, called Revolve Technologies Inc. Eighteen former Nova employees have also joined the new firm and have contributed between $10 000 and $50 000 apiece. Individuals who once worked for a large firm are now owner-managers of a much smaller one, with all the benefits (and problems) that go along with ownership.

An interesting, but less well-known case, is that of Great Western Brewery. In 1990, Molson Cos. Ltd. decided to close the Carling O'Keefe brewery in Saskatoon. The company offered to transfer workers to other plants, but Don Ebelher, the maintenance chief at the brewery, and 14 other workers bought the plant because they felt they would have more job security working for themselves. Each person put up between $50 000 and $100 000 for the 25 percent equity required. The rest of the money came from a loan through Saskatchewan's Economic Development Corp. Ebelher is now Great Western's CEO.

In this employee-owned company, employee initiative is high, consultation and teamwork are facts of life, the management structure is very flat, and everyone takes pride in their work because they own the company. The firm still needs managers, but they behave quite differently than their predecessors. They work much more closely with production workers and often discuss ways to improve the way that work is done. In a traditional organization, this typically wouldn't happen. The marketing manager at Great Western, Jack White, says that consultation with employees has made him a better manager. The company has four managers instead of the 12 it had when it was owned by Molson. The total number of employees has dropped from 65 to 55.

Interestingly, the workers are represented by a union. Why have a union in an employee-owned company? The local union president says that because Canadian brewing has traditionally been dominated by unions, there is still a competitive advantage to be gained by shipping products with a union label. But employees in this company have not demanded big wage increases because, as owners, they are keeping the financial health of the company in mind.

Problems exist in employee-owned firms, just as they do in traditionally owned businesses. At Great Western, for example, demand for the new company's product exceeded expectations, so workers felt they had to work long hours and scrape together leftover assembly line parts in order to increase production. Some employees routinely worked 60- or 70-hour weeks. But after these problems had been solved, the company's beer lost its novelty status in the marketplace, and its market share declined from its original 20 percent to 8 percent. At present, the plant is operating at less than 50 percent capacity.

At Algoma Steel, bonuses for top executives were cancelled in 1994 even though the company made a $16 million profit for the first quarter. Workers had given up $3 an hour as part of the original employee buyout plan, and the president felt that it would be inappropriate for him to take a large bonus after the workers had made big sacrifices. So he gave up his $400 000 bonus. A recent employee survey strongly favoured limiting the compensation of top executives. If lowered compensation makes it harder for the firm to attract top quality executives, company performance may decline.

Some employee-owned firms have found that they do not have the financial resources to achieve desired goals. Relcon Ltd., which makes electronic drives that regulate the speed of electric motors, became an employee-owned firm way back in 1960 when the founder of the firm died and the employees bought out his interest. Although the firm was profitable, it was never able to crack export markets because it didn't have the money to do so. But when it was taken over by Siemens AG, the German electronics giant, it suddenly had the necessary resources to become a player on the international scene.

Creative solutions to problems of business organization are becoming more common as firms struggle to enter markets or to remain competitive in rapidly changing markets. In this chapter, we examine the business structures that are open to both large and small businesses. By focusing on the learning objectives of this chapter, you will better understand the structural options open to Canadian businesses. After reading this chapter, you should be able to:

1. Trace the history of business in Canada.
2. Identify the major *forms of business ownership*.
3. Describe *sole proprietorships* and *partnerships* and explain the advantages and disadvantages of each.
4. Describe *corporations* and explain their advantages and disadvantages.
5. Describe the basic issues involved in creating and managing a corporation.
6. Identify recent trends and issues in corporate ownership.

■ A BRIEF HISTORY OF BUSINESS IN CANADA

Canadian business has not always had the variety of complex structures that currently exist in Canada. Indeed, a look at the history of business in Canada shows a steady development from sole proprietorships to the complex corporate structures of today. In this section, we will trace the broad outlines of the development of business in Canada. Table 2.1 highlights some of the specific events in Canadian business history.[1]

■ **TABLE 2.1 Some Important Dates in Canadian Business History**

1490	English fishermen active off the coast of Newfoundland		1896	First large pulp and paper mill in Canada opened at Sault Ste. Marie
1534	Account of first trading with native peoples written by Jacques Cartier		1897-1899	Klondike gold rush
1669	*Nonsuch* returns to London with a cargo of furs from Hudson Bay area		1907	First issue of *The Financial Post*
			1917-1922	Creation of Canadian National Railways
1670	Hudson's Bay Company founded		1920	First ship-plate steel mill in Canada opens in Sydney, Nova Scotia
1730-1740	Hat-making industry arises in Quebec and is stifled by French home officials		1926	U.S. replaces Great Britain as Canada's largest trading partner
1737	Compagnie des forges du St. Maurice formed to produce iron		1927	Armand Bombardier sells first "auto-neige" (forerunner of the snowmobile)
1779	North West Company formed		1927	Canadian Tire begins operations in Toronto
1785	Molson brewery opens		1929	Great stock market crash
1805	First Canadian paper mill built at St. Andrew's, Quebec		1929-1933	Great Depression
1809	First steamboat (the *Accommodation*) put into service on the St. Lawrence River by John Molson		1930	Canadian Airways Limited formed
			1932	Canadian Radio Broadcasting Corporation formed. (It became the CBC in 1936.)
1817	Bank of Montreal chartered		1935	Bank of Canada begins operations
1821	Hudson's Bay Company and North West Company merge		1937	Canadian Breweries Limited is formed
1830-1850	Era of canal building		1940	C.D. Howe appointed as Minister of Munitions and Supply
1836	First railroad train pulled by a steam engine		1945	Argus Corporation Limited formed
1850-1860	First era of railroad building		1947-1951	Early computer built at the University of Toronto
1855	John Redpath opens first Canadian sugar refinery in Montreal		1947	Leduc Number 1 oil well drilled in Alberta
1856	Railroad trains begin running between Toronto and Montreal		1949	A.V. Roe (Avro) makes Canada's first commercial jetliner
1857-1858	First oil well in Canada drilled near Sarnia, Ontario		1964	Volvo of Sweden begins assembling cars in Nova Scotia
1861	Toronto Stock Exchange opens		1965	Auto Pact signed with the U.S.
1869	Eaton's opens for business in Toronto		1969	Canada becomes world's largest potash producer
1879	National Policy implemented; raised tariffs on foreign goods to protect and encourage Canadian manufacturers		1980-1986	Dome, Canadair, and Massey-Ferguson receive financial assistance from the federal government
1880-1890	First western land boom		1989	Free trade agreement with U.S. comes into effect
1885	Last spike driven to complete the Canadian Pacific Railroad		1993	North American Free Trade Agreement comes into effect

The Early Years

Business activity and profit from commercial fishing were the motivation for the first European involvement in Canada. In the late 1400s, ships financed by English entrepreneurs came to the coast of Newfoundland to fish for profit. By the late 1500s, the Newfoundland coast was being visited by hundreds of fishing vessels each year.

Beginning in the 1500s, French and British adventurers began trading with the Indians. Items such as cooking utensils and knives were exchanged for beaver and other furs. One trading syndicate made over 1000 percent profit on beaver skins sold to a Paris furrier. Trading was aggressive and, over time, the price of furs rose as more and more Europeans bid for them. Originally the fur trade was restricted to eastern Canada, but by the late 1600s, *coureurs de bois* were travelling far to the west in search of new sources of furs.

European settlers who arrived in Canada in the 16th and 17th centuries initially had to farm or starve. Gradually, however, they began to produce more than they needed for their own survival. The governments of the countries from which the settlers 重商主義 came (notably England and France) were strong supporters of the mercantilist philosophy. Under *mercantilism*, colonists were expected to export raw materials like beaver pelts and lumber at low prices to the mother country. These raw materials were then used to produce finished goods like fur coats which were sold at high prices to settlers in Canada. Attempts to develop industry in Canada were thwarted by England and France, which enjoyed large profits from mercantilism. As a result, Canadian manufacturing was slow to develop.

The Factory System and the Industrial Revolution

British manufacturing took a great leap forward around 1750 with the coming of the **Industrial Revolution**. This revolution was made possible by advances in technology and by the development of the **factory system**. Instead of hundreds of workers turning out items one at a time in their cottages, the factory system brought together in one place all of the materials and workers required to produce items in large quantities, along with newly created machines capable of **mass production**.

Mass production offered savings in several areas. It avoided unnecessary duplication of equipment. It allowed firms to purchase raw materials at better prices by buying large lots. And most important, it encouraged **specialization** of labour. No longer did production require highly skilled craftspeople who could do all the different tasks required to make an item. A series of semiskilled workers, each trained to perform only one task and supported by specialized machines and tools, greatly increased output.

In spite of British laws against the export of technology and manufacturing in North America, Canadian manufacturing existed almost from the beginning of European settlement. Modest manufacturing operations were evident in sawmills, breweries, grist mills for grinding grain, tanneries, woollen mills, shoemakers' shops, and tailors' shops. These operations were so successful that by 1800, exports of manufactured goods were more important than exports of fur.

With the advent of steam power in the early 1800s, manufacturing activity began to increase rapidly. By 1850, more than 30 factories—employing more than 2000 people—lined the Lachine Canal alone. Exports of timber to England in 1850 were 70 times greater than what they were in 1800. The demand for reliable transportation was the impetus for canal building in the mid-1800s and then the railroad-building boom in the mid- and late 1800s.

Industrial Revolution
A major change in goods production that began in England in the mid-18th century and was characterized by a shift to the factory system, mass production, and specialization of labour.

factory system
A process in which all the machinery, materials, and workers required to produce a good in large quantities are brought together in one place.

mass production
The manufacture of products of uniform quality in large quantities.

specialization
The breaking down of complex operations into simple tasks that are easily learned and performed. (with machines capable of mass production)

The Entrepreneurial Era

One of the most significant features of the last half of the 19th century was the emergence of entrepreneurs willing to take risks in the hope of earning huge profits. Adam Smith in his book *The Wealth of Nations* argued that the government should not interfere in the economy, but should let businesses function without regulation or restriction. This *laissez-faire* attitude was often adopted by the Canadian government. As a result, some individuals became immensely wealthy through their aggressive business dealings. Some railway, bank, and insurance executives made over $25 000 per year in the late 1800s, and their purchasing power was immense. Entrepreneurs such as Joseph Flavelle, Henry Pellatt, and John MacDonald lived in ostentatious mansions or castles.

The size and economic power of some firms meant that other businesses had difficulty competing against them. At the same time, some business executives decided that it was more profitable to collude than to compete. They decided among themselves to fix prices and divide up markets. Hurt by these actions, Canadian consumers called for more regulation of business. In 1889, the first anti-combines legislation was passed in Canada, and legislation regulating business has increased ever since.

The Production Era

The concepts of specialization and mass production that originated in the Industrial Revolution were more fully refined as Canada entered the 20th century. The Scientific Management Movement focused management's attention on production. Increased efficiency via the "one best way" to accomplish tasks became the major management goal.

In the 18th century, the home crafts industry provided our young nation with clothing and foodstuffs. During the 19th century, machinery such as the cotton gin changed the way the world worked. Today, automation continues to alter our work lives and the types of products that are available to us.

Henry Ford's introduction of the moving assembly line in the U.S. in 1913 ushered in the **production era.** During the production era, less attention was paid to selling and marketing than to technical efficiency when producing goods. By using fixed work stations, increasing task specialization, and moving the work to the worker, the assembly line increased productivity and lowered prices, making all kinds of products affordable for the average person.

During the production era, large businesses began selling stock—making shareholders the owners—and relying on professional managers. The growth of corporations and improved production output resulting from assembly lines came at the expense of worker freedom. The dominance of big firms made it harder for individuals to go into business for themselves. Company towns run by the railroads, mining corporations, and forest products firms gave individuals little freedom of choice over whom to work for and what to buy. To restore some balance within the overall system, both government and labour had to develop and grow. Thus, this period saw the rise of labour unions and collective bargaining. We will look at this development in more detail in Chapter 10. The Great Depression of the 1930s and World War II caused the federal government to intervene in the economic system on a previously unimaginable scale.

Today, business, government, and labour are frequently referred to by economists and politicians as the three *countervailing powers* in our society. All are big. All are strong. Yet, none totally dominates the others.

production era
The period during the early 20th century when businesses focused almost exclusively on improving productivity and manufacturing methods.

The Sales and Marketing Eras

By the 1930s, business's focus on production had resulted in spectacular increases in the amount of goods and services for sale. As a result, buyers had more choices and producers faced greater competition in selling their wares. Thus began the so-called **sales era.** According to the ideas of this time, a business's profits and success depended on hiring the right salespeople, advertising heavily, and making sure products were readily available. Business firms were essentially production- and sales-oriented, and they produced what they thought customers wanted, or simply what the company was good at producing. This approach is still used by firms that find themselves with surplus goods that they want to sell (e.g., used-car dealerships).

Following World War II, pent-up demand for consumer goods kept the economy rolling. While brief recessions did occur periodically, the 1950s and 1960s were prosperous times. Production increased, technology advanced, and the standard of living rose. During the **marketing era,** business adopted a new philosophy on how to do business—use market research to determine what customers want, and then make it for them. Firms like Procter & Gamble and Molson were very effective during the marketing era, and continue to be profitable today. Each offers an array of products within a particular field (toothpaste or beer, for example), and gives customers a chance to pick what best suits their needs.

Procter & Gamble
www.pg.com

sales era
The period during the 1930s and 1940s when businesses focused on sales forces, advertising, and keeping products readily available.

marketing era
The period during the 1950s and 1960s when businesses began to identify and meet consumer wants in order to make a profit.

The Finance Era

In the 1980s, emphasis shifted to finance. In the **finance era** there was a sharp increase in mergers and in the buying and selling of business enterprises. Some people now call it the "decade of greed." As we will see in the next chapter, during the finance era there were many hostile takeovers and a great deal of financial manipulation of corporate assets by so-called corporate raiders. Critics charged that these raiders were simply enriching themselves and weren't creating anything of tangible value by their activity. They also charged that raiders were distracting business managers from their main goals of running the business. The raiders responded that they were making organizations more efficient by streamlining, merging, and reorganizing them.

finance era
The period during the 1980s when there were many mergers and much buying and selling of business enterprises.

The Global Era

The last few years have seen the continuation of technological advances in production, computer technology, information systems, and communication capabilities. They have also seen the emergence of a truly global economy. Canadians drive cars made in Japan, wear sweaters made in Italy, drink beer brewed in Mexico, and listen to stereos made in Taiwan. But we're not alone in this. People around the world buy products and services from foreign companies.

While it is true that many Canadian businesses have been hurt by foreign imports, numerous others have profited by exploring new foreign markets themselves. And domestic competition has forced many businesses to work harder than ever to cut costs, increase efficiency, and improve product and service quality. We will explore a variety of important trends, opportunities, and challenges of the global era throughout this book.

■ TYPES OF BUSINESS ORGANIZATIONS

All business owners must decide which form of legal organization—a sole proprietorship, a partnership, a corporation, or a cooperative—best suits them and their business. Few decisions are more critical, since the choice affects a host of managerial and financial issues, including income taxes and the owners' liability. In choosing a legal form of organization, the parties concerned must consider their likes, dislikes, and dispositions, their immediate and long-range needs, and the advantages and disadvantages of each form. Seldom, if ever, does any one factor completely determine which form is best.[2]

Sole Proprietorships

sole proprietorship
A business owned (and usually operated) by one person who is personally responsible for the firm's debts.

Eaton's
www.eatons.com

As the very first legal form of business organization, **sole proprietorships** date back to ancient times. They are still the most numerous form of business in Canada. Despite their numbers, however, they account for only a small proportion of total business revenues in this country.

Because most sole proprietorships are small, often employing only one person, you might assume that all are small businesses. However, sole proprietorships may be as large as a steel mill or as small as a lemonade stand. Some of Canada's largest companies started out as sole proprietorships. Eaton's, for example, was originally a one-man operation founded by Timothy Eaton. One of Canada's biggest sole proprietorships is the Jim Pattison Group, with sales of $3 billion and 15 000 employees (see the boxed insert on page 133).

Advantages.   Freedom is the most striking feature of sole proprietorships. Because they alone own their businesses, sole proprietors need answer to no one but themselves. They can also maintain a high level of privacy, since they are not required to report information about their operations to anyone.

Sole proprietorships are simple to form. Sole proprietors often need only put a sign on their door in order to go into business for themselves. They are also easy to dissolve. Rock concerts or athletic events may be organized as sole proprietorships by individuals who then dissolve the business entity when the event is over.

Low startup costs are yet another attractive feature of sole proprietorships. Legal fees are likely to be low, since some sole proprietorships need only register the business with the provincial government in order to make sure that no other business bears the same name. Some proprietorships do need to take out licences, however. For example, restaurants and pet shops need special licences.

Sole proprietorships also offer tax benefits for new businesses likely to suffer losses before profits begin to flow. Tax laws permit sole proprietors to treat the sales revenues and operating expenses of the business as part of their personal finances. Thus, a proprietor can cut taxes by deducting any operating losses from income earned from sources other than the business. Since most businesses lose money at the beginning, this tax situation is very helpful to entrepreneurs starting up.

Disadvantages.   One major drawback of sole proprietorships is their **unlimited liability**. A sole proprietor is personally liable for all debts incurred by the business. Bills must be paid out of the sole proprietor's own pocket if the business fails to generate enough cash. Otherwise, creditors can step in and claim the proprietor's personal possessions, including a home, furniture, and automobile. (Actually, the law does protect some of the proprietor's assets, but many can be claimed.) The impact of unlimited liability is described in the box "Unlimited Liability at Lloyd's of London."

Another disadvantage is lack of continuity. A sole proprietorship legally dissolves when the owner dies. The business can, of course, be reorganized soon after the owner's death if a successor has been trained to take over the business. Otherwise, executors or heirs must **liquidate** (sell the assets of) the business.

Finally, a sole proprietorship is dependent upon the resources of a single individual. If the proprietor has unlimited resources and is a successful manager, this characteristic is not really a problem. In most cases, however, the proprietor's financial and managerial limits constrain what the organization can do. Sole proprietors often find it hard to borrow money not only to start up, but also to expand. Banks often reject such applications, fearing that they will not be able to recover the loan if the sole proprietor becomes disabled. Often, would-be proprietors must rely on personal savings and loans from family for startup funds.

Partnerships

A partnership is established when two or more individuals agree to combine their financial, managerial, and technical abilities for the purpose of operating a company for profit. The partnership form of ownership was developed to overcome some of the more serious disadvantages of the sole proprietorship. There are several different types of partnerships, but our discussion focuses on the most common type—the **general partnership**.

Partnerships are often an extension of a business that began as a sole proprietorship. The original owner may want to expand, or the business may have grown too big for a single person to handle. Many professional organizations, such as legal, architecture, and accounting firms, are also organized as partnerships.

Advantages.   The most striking feature of general partnerships is their ability to grow by adding talent and money. Partnerships also have a somewhat easier time borrowing funds than do sole proprietorships. Banks and other lending institutions prefer to make loans to enterprises that are not dependent on a single individual.

Like a sole proprietorship, a partnership is simple to organize, with few legal requirements. Even so, all partnerships must begin with an agreement of some kind. It may be written, oral, or even unspoken. Wise partners, however, insist on a written agreement to avoid trouble later. This agreement should answer such questions as

- Who invested what sums of money in the partnership?
- Who will receive what share of the partnership's profits?
- Who does what and who reports to whom?
- How may the partnership be dissolved? In that event, how would leftover assets be distributed among the partners?
- How would surviving partners be protected from claims by surviving heirs if a partner dies?

Although it helps to clarify how partners relate to each other, the partnership agreement is strictly a private document. No laws require partners to file an agreement with some government agency. Nor are partnerships regarded as legal entities. In the eyes of the law, a partnership is nothing more than two or more persons working together. The partnership's lack of legal standing means that Revenue Canada taxes partners as individuals.

unlimited liability
A person who invests in a business is liable for all debts incurred by the business; personal possessions can be taken to pay debts.

liquidate
Sell the assets of a business.

Lloyd's of London
www.lloydsoflondon.co.uk

general partnership
A business with two or more owners who share in the operation of the firm and in financial responsibility for the firm's debts.

Revenue Canada
gopher://gopher.revcan.ca/

T R E N D S   &   C H A L L E N G E S

Unlimited Liability at Lloyd's of London

Lloyd's of London is one of the most famous insurance companies in the world. It began operations several centuries ago by insuring British merchant ships. The individuals who invest in Lloyd's are called "names." These names have unlimited liability, i.e., they are liable for any losses incurred by the company. Their liability for losses is not limited to their original investment, but rather to the amount of money they have. Thus, their personal property can be seized to pay off their liabilities.

Why would a person invest in a company like Lloyd's when they know they will have unlimited liability? Because historically such investments have yielded good returns. Traditionally, names have been wealthy people who could afford to take the occasional loss. But during the go-go 1980s, many new names were recruited who were not wealthy (but had dreams of wealth). When their involvement brought losses instead of profits, they lost everything they owned. The British press played up cases of names being forced to move out of expensive homes that had been in the family for generations, but many poorer people have also lost their homes.

Why has Lloyd's suddenly run into financial difficulty? The answer is that changing times are threatening the company. It is becoming clear that an insurance system designed in 1600 cannot cope with certain 20th-century realities—natural disasters, terrorism, pollution, industrial accidents, and a trend towards increasing litigation.

All of these factors have sent insurance claims sky-high. During one three-year period in the early 1990s, Lloyd's lost a total of $12 billion. In that same period, the number of names fell from 27 000 to 19 000. Several members who were part of a group of names that lost $800 million committed suicide. Another group of names from Canada sued the company, alleging fraud, to prevent Lloyd's from seizing their assets to make good on claims.

In April 1993, Lloyd's CEO David Rowland introduced a plan that would end the company's tradition of unlimited liability and allow corporations to become new members with limited liability. But existing names will continue to have unlimited liability. Late in 1994, the group suing Lloyd's won a lawsuit which said they had been the victims of negligence by professionals in the insurance market. In 1995, Lloyd's proposed a $6 billion settlement plan that was designed to end litigation and ensure the survival of the firm. The proposed settlement would forgive over $4 billion owed by names who simply can't repay it. In return, the names would be expected to drop their lawsuits against the company.

The deal was finally agreed to in September 1996. Past liabilities will be reinsured in a new company called Equitas Group.

Disadvantages.   As with sole proprietorships, unlimited liability is the greatest drawback of general partnerships. By law, each partner may be held personally liable for all debts incurred in the name of the partnership. And if any partner incurs a debt, even if the other partners know nothing about it, they are all liable if the offending partner cannot pay up. For example, right after two men formed a partnership to operate a car wash, their equipment severely damaged a customized van. The owner sued for damages. One partner lacked the funds to cover the loss, even though the partnership agreement specified that he was responsible for equipment liability claims. Fortunately, the other partner agreed to pay half the damages and to loan the money to his partner for the other half.

Another drawback is often lack of continuity. When one partner dies or pulls out, a partnership may dissolve legally, even if the other partners agree to stay. The dissolving of a partnership, however, need not cause a loss of sales revenues. If they wish, the surviving partners can quickly form a new partnership to retain the business of the old firm.

A related drawback is the difficulty of transferring ownership. No partner may sell out without the other partners' consent. Also, a partner who wants to retire or to transfer his or her interest to a son or daughter must receive the other partners' consent. Thus, the life of a partnership may depend on the ability of retiring partners to find someone compatible with the other partners to buy them out. Failure to do so may lead to forced liquidation of the partnership.

Finally, a partnership provides little or no guidance in resolving conflict between the partners. For example, suppose one partner wants to expand the business rapidly and the other wants it to grow slowly. If under the partnership agreement the two are equal, it may be difficult for them to decide what to do. Conflicts can involve anything from personal habits like smoking to hours of operation to managerial practices.

Corporations

Another very common form of business ownership is the **corporation**. Almost all larger businesses in Canada use this form.

When you think of corporations you probably think of giant businesses like General Motors of Canada or BCE. The very word *corporation* suggests bigness and power. Yet, the tiny corner newsstand has as much right to incorporate as does a giant oil refiner. And the newsstand and oil refiner have the same basic characteristics that all corporations share: legal status as a separate entity, property rights and obligations, and an indefinite life span.

A corporation has been defined as "an artificial being, invisible, intangible, and existing only in contemplation of the law."[3] As such, corporations may

- Sue and be sued.
- Buy, hold, and sell property.
- Make and sell products to consumers.
- Commit crimes and be tried and punished for them.

Corporations can be found in both the private and the public sector in Canada, although our emphasis is on the private sector.

Public Versus Private Corporations.   Some corporations are public, others private. A **public corporation** is one whose stock is widely held and available for sale to the general public. Anyone who has the funds to pay for them can go to a stockbroker and buy shares of Brascan, George Weston, or Canadian Pacific. The stock of a **private corporation**, on the other hand, is held by only a few people and is not generally available for sale. The controlling group may be a family, employees, or the management group. Eaton's was a private corporation for many years, but as part of its strategy to get out of financial difficulty, it "went public" in 1998 and began selling shares to any investor who wanted to buy them. Bata Shoes is still a private corporation.

Most new corporations start out as private corporations, because few investors will buy an unknown stock. As the corporation grows and develops a record of success, it may decide to issue shares to the public as a way to raise additional money. Apple Computer is just one example of a corporation that "went public." McCain Foods is a large private corporation that has been experiencing problems because of a feud between two of the McCain brothers, Wallace and Harrison. In 1994, they began serious discussions about how to take their company public.[4] Mutual Life Assurance Co. of Canada has also decided to go public, and several other Canadian life insurance companies are likely to do the same.[5] But some very large private corporations intend to stay private. For example, U.S. giant Cargill, with revenues of nearly $60 billion, intends to remain a private corporation. Because it does not have a lot of shareholders, it can invest in projects that show losses initially, but that might be very profitable in the long run. Shareholders might not be patient enough to allow this strategy if Cargill was a public corporation.[6] The box "Going Public" describes one manager's experience with going public.

Just as companies can "go public," they can also "go private"; that is, a public corporation can be converted to a private corporation. In 1997, Jim Pattison, a well-known Canadian entrepreneur, was involved in negotiations to convert three companies to private corporation status: Westar Group Ltd., Great Pacific Enterprises Inc., and B.C. Sugar Refinery Ltd.[7]

corporation
A business considered by law to be a legal entity separate from its owners with many of the legal rights and privileges of a person; a form of business organization in which the liability of the owners is limited to their investment in the firm.

public corporation
A business whose stock is widely held and available for sale to the general public.

private corporation
A business whose stock is held by a small group of individuals and is not usually available for sale to the general public.

McCain Foods Limited
www.mccain.com

TRENDS CHALLENGES

Going Public

At the first annual meeting of DataMirror Corp. in 1997, CEO Nigel Stokes acquired some new bosses—shareholders. These shareholders are just some of the people that Stokes will have to deal with now that he is heading a public corporation. Bay Street analysts, institutional investors, reporters, and others are now much more likely to hold him accountable for actions that he takes.

The biggest pressure he will have to deal with is the "pressure to perform," that is, the pressure to regularly show growth and profitability to investors. Stokes, who formerly owned 60 percent of privately held Nidak Associates, says that many private firms are low-growth, "lifestyle" companies where owners take pretty easy profits and employees are not under a lot of pressure to perform. In a public corporation, much more is expected of both managers and workers. And in a public company, workers often own shares of stock, so they feel more pressure to work harder in the hope that their shares will increase in value. Eighty percent of DataMirror employees bought stock in the company when it went public.

Stokes draws a relatively modest salary of $150 000. He hopes to make much more money from appreciation of the company's stock. DataMirror's stock price is already 50 percent higher than when it first began trading on the Toronto Stock Exchange in December 1996. Stokes believes in creating realistic expectations among investors so that when the company performs well the stock price will go up. In the company's first year, actual sales exceeded those forecast by 12 percent.

DataMirror
www.datamirror.com

Formation of the Corporation.   The two most widely used methods to form a corporation are federal incorporation under the *Canada Business Corporations Act* and provincial incorporation under any of the provincial corporations acts. The former is used if the company is going to operate in more than one province; the latter is used if the founders intend to carry on business in only one province.

Except for banks and certain insurance and loan companies, any company can be federally incorporated under the *Canada Business Corporations Act*. To do so, Articles of Incorporation must be drawn up. These articles include such information as the name of the corporation, the type and number of shares to be issued, the number of directors the corporation will have, and the location of the company's operations. All companies must attach the word "Limited" (Ltd./Ltée) or "Incorporated" (Inc.) to the company name to indicate clearly to customers and suppliers that the owners have limited liability for corporate debts. The same sort of rules apply in other countries. British firms, for example, use PLC for "public limited company" and German companies use AG for "Aktiengesellschaft" (corporation).

Provincial incorporation takes one of two forms. In certain provinces (British Columbia, Alberta, Saskatchewan, Manitoba, Ontario, Newfoundland, Nova Scotia, and the two territories), the registration system or its equivalent is used. Under this system, individuals wishing to form a corporation are required to file a memorandum of association. This document contains the same type of information as required under the *Canada Business Corporations Act*. In the remaining provinces, the equivalent incorporation document is called the letters patent. In Quebec, a corporation may be formed either by issuing a letters patent or by drawing up articles of incorporation. The specific procedures and information required vary from province to province. The basic differences between these incorporation systems is that the registration system forms corporations by authority of parliament, while the letters patent system forms corporations by royal prerogative.

corporate governance
The relationship between shareholders, the board of directors, and other top managers in the corporation.

Corporate governance refers to the relationship between shareholders, the board of directors, and other top managers in the corporation. We discuss each of these groups in the following paragraphs.

Shares of Stock and Shareholders' Rights.   Corporations can raise money by selling shares in the business—**stock**—to investors, who then are known as **shareholders**. Shareholders are the owners of a business. Business profits are distributed among shareholders in the form of **dividends**. Managers who run a corporation also serve at the discretion of the shareholders. The nature of the relationship between the shareholders, the board of directors, and management has been the focus of much recent discussion.[8]

Why do corporations sell stock? Besides the obvious reason already noted—to raise money—stock makes for an easy transfer of ownership in a corporation. Shareholders can sell their shares to anyone who is willing to buy them (unless the stock certificates say that shareholders must offer to sell them to the corporation first).

Corporate stock may be either preferred or common. **Preferred stock** guarantees those who own it a fixed dividend, much like the interest payment earned in a savings account. Preferred shareholders have priority, or preference, over common shareholders as to dividends and also to assets if a business liquidates, but usually do not have voting rights. Many major corporations issue preferred stock; few small corporations do.

In contrast, **common stock** usually pays dividends only if the corporation makes a profit. Holders of common stock have the last claim to any assets if the company folds. Dividends on common stock, like those on preferred stock, are paid per share. Thus, a shareholder with ten shares receives ten times the dividend paid a shareholder with one share. Unlike preferred stock, however, common stock *must* be issued by every corporation, big or small.

There are two types of common stock—Class A and Class B. Class A common shares always have voting rights, but Class B common shares usually do not. Shareholder rights advocates argue that Class B common shares prevent democracy from working in companies because controlling shareholders hold most of the Class A stock and sell non-voting Class B stock to the general public. If Class B shareholders don't like what is going on in the company, they can't vote out the board of directors.[9] For example, CanWest Global owned 35 percent of the Class B shares of WIC Communications and was the largest equity shareholder, but it didn't have any say in how WIC was run because its shares were all of the non-voting type.[10]

Public corporations are required by law to hold a shareholders' meeting each year. At these meetings, shareholders vote on a variety of motions, find out how their company is doing, and ask questions about the company's future plans. Most annual meetings are rather uninteresting, but occasionally some rather dramatic things happen. Consider the following:

* At the 1995 annual meeting of MacMillan-Bloedel Ltd., environmentalists who were opposed to the company's logging activities in B.C. dumped a truckload of manure at the hotel entrance where the meeting was being held; dissidents also dominated the question period, and one of them threw a bun at then-CEO Robert Findlay.

* At DuPont's 1992 annual meeting, Greenpeace members stormed the stage and roughed up the CEO; the meeting was cancelled after several top executives escaped out a side door on the stage.

* At the 1994 annual meeting of Hudson's Bay Co., several corporate officials told shareholders that they should not worry about the competitive threat Wal-Mart posed. This assurance was naive, and did not take into account Wal-Mart's market power.

* At the Cott Corp. annual meeting in 1993, CEO Gerald Pencer gave an emotional speech and then asked the shareholders to stand and sing together Dionne Warwick's 1985 hit, "That's What Friends Are For."

* The Royal Trustco Ltd. annual meeting in 1994 was a four-hour marathon where furious shareholders lambasted top managers about how they had ruined the company and left them without a cent.

When investors cannot attend a shareholders' meeting, they can grant to someone who will attend authority to vote the shares. This procedure, called voting by **proxy**, is the way almost all individual investors vote.

stock
A share of ownership in a corporation.

shareholders
Those who own shares of stock in a company.

dividend
A part of a corporation's profits paid out per share to those who hold its stock.

preferred stock
Shares whose owners have first claim on the corporation's assets and profits but who usually have no voting rights in the firm.

common stock
Shares whose owners usually have last claim on the corporation's assets (after creditors and owners of preferred stock) but who have voting rights in the firm.

proxy
A legal document temporarily transferring the voting rights of a shareholder to another person.

Corporations hold annual meetings with their shareholders. At such meetings, managers summarize what the corporation accomplished during the last year, announce plans for the coming year, and answer questions from individual shareholders. Shareholders also elect new members to the board of directors.

Ownership of common stock does not automatically give an individual the right to act for the corporation or to share in its management. (Many management personnel do own stock, however.) The only way that most shareholders can influence the running of a corporation is to cast their votes for the board of directors of the corporation once a year. In most cases, however, shareholders' votes are meaningless, since corporations offer only one slate of directors for election.

Even when shareholders have choices, the number of shareholders may mean little real power for individual owners. For example, Noranda has thousands of shareholders, but only a handful of them have enough votes to have any effect on the way the company is run.

board of directors
A group of individuals elected by a firm's shareholders and charged with overseeing, and taking legal responsibility for, the firm's actions.

The Board of Directors.   By law, the governing body of a corporation is its **board of directors**. The directors choose the president and other officers of the business and delegate the power to run the day-to-day activities of the business to those officers. The directors set policy on paying dividends, on financing major spending, and on executive salaries and benefits. For example, the board of directors can fire the CEO if the board does not agree with the CEO's business decisions. However, in most cases a board of directors will support the CEO.

Large corporations tend to have large boards with as many as 20 or 30 directors. Smaller corporations, on the other hand, tend to have no more than five directors. Usually, these are people with personal or professional ties to the corporation, such as family members, lawyers, and accountants.

inside directors
Members of a corporation's board of directors who are also full-time employees of the corporation.

Many boards have outside as well as inside directors. **Inside directors** are employees of the company and have primary responsibility for the corporation. That is, they are also top managers, such as the president and executive vice president. **Outside directors** are not employees of the corporation in the normal course of its business. Attorneys, accountants, university officials, and executives from other firms are commonly used as outside directors. The basic responsibility of both inside and

outside directors
Members of a corporation's board of directors who are not also employees of the corporation on a day-to-day basis.

outside directors is the same, however—to ensure that the corporation is run in a way that is in the best interests of the shareholders. Boards communicate with shareholders and other potential investors through the corporation's annual report, a summary of the company's financial health.

Directors also are legally responsible for the decisions they make, and they are increasingly being held responsible for their actions. For example, a group of shareholders sued the entire board of Microsoft Corporation because the company's failure to meet its profits projections caused the price of its stock to plummet.[11]

Officers.   Although board members oversee the corporation's operation, most of them do not participate in day-to-day management. Rather, they hire a team of top managers to run the firm. As we have already seen, this team, called *officers,* is usually headed by the firm's **chief executive officer**, or **CEO**, who is responsible for the firm's overall performance. Other officers typically include a *president*, who is responsible for internal management, and *vice presidents,* who oversee various functional areas like marketing or operations. Some officers may also be elected to serve on the board, and in some cases, a single individual plays multiple roles. For example, one person might serve as board chairperson, CEO, and president. In other cases, a different person fills each slot.

chief executive officer (CEO)
The person responsible for the firm's overall performance.

Advantages of the Corporation.   Limited liability is the most striking feature of corporations. That is, the liability of investors is limited to their personal investments in the corporation. In the event of failure, the bankruptcy courts may seize a corporation's assets and sell them to pay debts, but the courts cannot touch the personal possessions of investors. Limited liability may be the main reason that many businesses incorporate, but limited liability is meaningless in some cases. For example, if all your personal assets are tied up in a business, then limited liability offers you little protection.

Another advantage of a corporation is continuity. Because it has a legal life independent of its founders, a corporation can continue to exist and grow long after the founders have retired or died. In theory, a corporation can go on forever.

Most corporations also benefit from professional management. In a sole proprietorship, a single person typically owns and manages the business. In most corporations, on the other hand, professional managers run the company but do not necessarily own any part of it.

Finally, corporations have a relatively easy time raising money. By selling more stock, they can expand the number of investors. In addition, the legal protections afforded corporations and the continuity of such organizations tend to make bankers more willing to grant loans.

Disadvantages of the Corporation.   Ease of transferring ownership, one of the corporation's chief attractions, can also complicate the life of its managers. For example, one or more disgruntled shareholders in a small corporation can sell their stock to someone who wants to control the corporation and overthrow its top managers. Gaining control of a large corporation by this method is a complicated and expensive process, partially because of the large number of shareholders and partially because of the large sums of money involved. Amid the takeover environment of the 1980s, some shareholders of large firms succeeded. Philip Morris took over both General Foods and Kraft against their wishes and then combined them to form Kraft General Foods.[12] We discuss this interesting topic in more detail later in this chapter.

Forming a corporation also costs more than forming either a sole proprietorship or a partnership. The main reason is that someone who wants to incorporate must meet all the legal requirements of the province in which it incorporates. Corporations also need legal help in meeting government regulations. Corporations are far more heavily regulated than are proprietorships and general partnerships.

A corporation is subject to **double taxation** because it must pay income taxes on its profits and then shareholders must pay income taxes on the dividends they receive from the corporation. By contrast, sole proprietorships and partnerships are only taxed

double taxation
A corporation must pay taxes on its profits, and the shareholders must pay personal income taxes on the dividends they receive.

once, since their profits are treated as the owner's personal income. But remember that personal tax rates for proprietors and partners can be very high if they make a lot of profit in their business, so there may be tax advantages for a corporation once a business has achieved a certain amount of profit. Small *private* corporations also benefit from the small business tax rate, which is only 16 percent on the first $200 000 of net profit. Table 2.2 compares the various forms of business ownership using several different characteristics.

Cooperatives

cooperative
An organization that is formed to benefit its owners in the form of reduced prices and/or the distribution of surpluses at year-end

A **cooperative** is an organization that is formed to benefit its owners in the form of reduced prices and/or the distribution of surpluses at year-end. The process works like this: Suppose some farmers believe they can get cheaper fertilizer prices if they form their own company and purchase in large volume. They might then form a cooperative, which can be either federally or provincially chartered. Prices are generally lower to buyers and, at the end of the fiscal year, any surpluses are distributed to members on the basis of how much they purchased. If Farmer Jones bought 5 percent of all co-op sales, he would receive 5 percent of the surplus.

Voting rights are different from those in a corporation. In the cooperative, each member is entitled to one vote, irrespective of how many shares he or she holds. This system prevents voting and financial control of the business by a few wealthy individuals.

In numbers of establishments in Canada, cooperatives are the least important form of ownership. However, they are of significance to society and to their members; they may provide services that are not readily available or that cost more than the members would otherwise be willing to pay. The box "Mountain Equipment Co-op" describes a successful Canadian cooperative.

Mountain Equipment Co-op
www.mec.ca

■ SPECIAL ISSUES IN BUSINESS OWNERSHIP

Several issues in business ownership have arisen in recent years. Significant among these are acquisitions and mergers, divestitures and spin-offs, employee-owned corporations, strategic alliances, subsidiary and parent corporations, and institutional ownership.

Acquisitions and Mergers

acquisition
The purchase of a company by another, larger firm, which absorbs the smaller company into its operations.

Businesses today buy and sell other companies like farmers used to buy and sell produce. An **acquisition** occurs when one firm (usually the larger one) buys another (usually the smaller one). For example, Seagram acquired both Polygram and MCA. In contrast, a

■ **TABLE 2.2 A Comparison of Three Forms of Business Ownership**

Characteristic	Sole Proprietorship	Partnership	Corporation
Protection against liability for bad debts	low	low	high
Ease of formation	high	high	medium
Permanence	low	low	high
Ease of ownership transfer	low	low	high
Ease of raising money	low	medium	high
Freedom from regulation	high	high	low
Tax advantages	high	high	low

TRENDS CHALLENGES

Mountain Equipment Co-op

Mountain Equipment Co-op (MEC) is Canada's biggest outdoor gear cooperative. Its 1997 sales were $115 million, and it has one million members worldwide, each of whom pay $5 for the privilege. Two new retail outlets were opened in 1998, one in Toronto and one in Edmonton. The cooperative—which was originally called Alpine Fast Buck—was started in 1971 by a group of students at the University of British Columbia. It had sales of less than $100 000 in its first couple of years of operation, but it has grown steadily since then.

Competitive rivals like A.J. Brooks think the company has a competitive advantage simply because it is a cooperative. This makes it immune to some of the problems faced by business firms with more traditional structures (proprietorships, partnerships, or corporations). For example, the fact that MEC gets a steady stream of cash from people buying into the cooperative gives it some protection from market fluctuations. Membership is growing at the rate of 100 000 people per year.

Not having to make a profit also gives MEC a big public relations boost, which reduces its need to advertise, which, in turn, reduces its expenses. MEC is therefore able to charge lower prices than its competitors. Prices are pegged just high enough to provide revenue to cover salaries and overhead, and are often 40 percent lower than their competitors. MEC's current president, Bill Gibson, says that if a company focuses on providing a service, it will make a profit, but if it focuses simply on making a profit, it will go out of business.

MEC has another advantage: As a cooperative, it does not have to pay income tax because it strives to simply break even in its operations. Any profit that it does earn is redistributed to members. A typical surplus is 1 to 2 percent of annual sales. Surpluses are distributed to members on the basis of how much they purchased during the previous year.

---

merger is a consolidation of two firms that are more similar in size, and the arrangement is usually more collaborative. In 1998, two large bank mergers were proposed: the Royal Bank with the Bank of Montreal, and the Toronto-Dominion Bank with the Canadian Imperial Bank of Commerce. But permission to merge was denied by the federal government. Two large accounting firms—Coopers & Lybrand and Price Waterhouse—merged in 1998, as did automakers Chrysler and Daimler-Benz.

After a merger or acquisition, three things can happen. One possibility is that the acquired company will continue to operate as a separate entity. Even though Trilon Financial Corporation bought London Life Insurance, the insurance company has continued to operate autonomously. Another possibility is that the acquired business will be absorbed by the other and simply disappear. Finally, the two companies may form a new company. For example, when Warner and Time merged, they formed a new company called Time-Warner.

A merger or acquisition can take place in one of several different ways. In a **friendly takeover**, the acquired company welcomes the acquisition, perhaps because it needs cash or sees other benefits in joining the acquiring firm. But in a **hostile takeover**, the acquiring company buys enough of the other company's stock to take control, even though the other company opposes the takeover. Philip Morris's takeovers of General Foods and Kraft were both hostile.[13]

A **poison pill** is a defence management adopts to make a firm less attractive to a current or potential hostile suitor in a takeover attempt. The objective is to make the "pill" so distasteful that a potential acquirer will not want to swallow it. For example, a pill adopted by Inco gave shareholders the right to buy Inco stock or the acquirer's stock at a 50 percent discount if more than 20 percent of Inco stock were acquired by a group without approval of Inco's board of directors.

merger
The union of two companies to form a single new business.

PriceWaterhouseCoopers
www.pwcglobal.com

friendly takeover
An acquisition in which the management of the acquired company welcomes the firm's buyout by another company.

hostile takeover
An acquisition in which the management of the acquired company fights the firm's buyout by another company.

poison pill
A defence management adopts to make a firm less attractive to a hostile suitor in a takeover bid.

Divestitures and Spin-Offs

divestiture
A company sells part of its existing business to another company.

A **divestiture** occurs when a company decides to sell part of its existing business operations to another corporation. For example, Unilever—the maker of Close-Up toothpaste, Dove soap, Vaseline lotion, and Q-Tips—at one time owned several specialty chemical businesses it had set up to make ingredients for its consumer products. The company decided that it had to focus more on the consumer products themselves, so it sold the chemical businesses to ICI, a European chemical company. And Seagram sold Tropicana Products Inc. in order to generate funds to help pay for its acquisition of Polygram.

spin-off
A company sells part of its business to raise money.

In other cases, a company might decide to sell part of its operations to raise money. Kmart, for example, sold its profitable bookstore operations—Borders and Waldenbooks—in order to raise money to expand its discount chain. The actual sale was a new stock offering in a newly created corporation comprising bookstore chains. Such a sale is known as a **spin-off**. PepsiCo spun off Pizza Hut, KFC, and Taco Bell into a new, separate corporation called Tricon Global Restaurants.

Employee-Owned Corporations

As we saw in the opening case, corporations are sometimes owned by the employees who work for them. While many smaller corporations are owned by the individuals who founded them, there is a growing trend today for employees to buy significant stakes of larger corporations. The current pattern is for this ownership to take the form of **employee stock ownership plans** or **ESOP**.

employee stock ownership plan (ESOP)
An arrangement whereby a corporation buys its own stock with loaned funds and holds it in trust for its employees. Employees "earn" the stock based on some condition such as seniority. Employees control the stock's voting rights immediately, even though they may not take physicical possession of the stock until specified conditions are met.

An ESOP is essentially a trust established on behalf of the employees. A corporation might decide, for example, to set up an ESOP to stimulate employee motivation or to fight a hostile takeover attempt. The company first secures a loan, which it then uses to buy shares of its stock on the open market. A portion of the future profits made by the corporation is used to pay off the loan. The stock, meanwhile, is controlled by a bank or other trustee. Employees gradually get ownership of the stock, usually on the basis of seniority. But even though they might not have physical possession of the stock for a while, they control its voting rights immediately.

Strategic Alliances

strategic alliance
An enterprise in which two or more persons or companies temporarily join forces to undertake a particular project.

A **strategic alliance**, or joint venture, involves two or more enterprises cooperating in the research, development, manufacture, or marketing of a product. For example, the national oil company of Nigeria and Chevron Oil were both interested in building a new type of drilling platform to search for oil in swampy areas. The platform was so expensive, however, that the companies were afraid to build it on their own. They decided to each contribute half the costs and share in its use. In British Columbia, Babine Forest Products is a joint venture between forestry companies and an economic development company controlled by 21 native bands. One-third of the employees of the company are native.[14]

Toyota and General Motors recently agreed to jointly own and manage an automobile assembly plant in California. General Motors had not been able to operate the plant profitably alone, and had actually shut it down. But they eventually realized that they could learn more about the Japanese approach to management by working with Toyota. And the Japanese, in turn, got access to an assembly plant in the U.S. without having to invest millions of dollars in a new one.

Subsidiary and Parent Corporations

subsidiary corporation
One that is owned by another corporation.

parent corporation
A corporation that owns a subsidiary.

Still another important trend in business ownership is the growing number of subsidiary and parent corporations, three of which are listed in Table 2.3. A **subsidiary corporation** is one that is owned by another corporation. The corporation that owns the subsidiary, in turn, is called a **parent corporation**.

■ **TABLE 2.3   Parent/Subsidiary Relations**

p = parent, s = subsidiary

p Unilever	p Dylex	p Grand Met
s Lever Brothers	s Tip Top Tailors	s Pillsbury
s Lipton	s Harry Rosen	s Alpo
s Minnetonka	s Fairweather	s Heublein
s Chesebrough-Pond's	s Bi-Way	
	s Thrifty's	

Institutional Ownership

Most individual investors do not own enough stock to exert any influence on the management of big corporations. In recent years, however, more and more stock has been purchased by **institutional investors** such as mutual funds and pension funds. Because they control enormous resources, these investors can buy huge blocks of stock. Occasionally, institutional investors may expect to be consulted on major management decisions. Mutual funds are discussed in Chapter 18.

institutional investors
Organizations like mutual and pension funds that purchase large blocks of company stock.

SUMMARY OF LEARNING OBJECTIVES

1. **Trace the history of business in Canada.** Modern business structures reflect a pattern of development over centuries. Throughout much of the colonial period, sole proprietors supplied raw materials to English manufacturers. The rise of the factory system during the Industrial Revolution brought with it mass production and specialization of labour. During the entrepreneurial era in the 19th century, huge corporations—and monopolies—emerged. During the production era of the early 20th century, companies grew by emphasizing output and production. During the sales and marketing eras of the mid-1900s, businesses began focusing on sales staff, advertising, and the need to produce what consumers want. The most recent development has been towards a global perspective.

2. **Identify the major *forms of business ownership*.** The most common forms of business ownership are the *sole proprietorship*, the *partnership*, and the regular *corporation*. Each form has several advantages and disadvantages. The form under which a business chooses to organize is crucial because it affects both long-term strategy and day-to-day decision making. In addition to advantages and disadvantages, entrepreneurs must consider their preferences and long-range requirements.

3. **Describe *sole proprietorships* and *partnerships* and explain the advantages and disadvantages of each.** *Sole proprietorships*, the most common form of business, consist of one person doing business. Although sole proprietorships offer freedom and privacy and are easy to form, they lack continuity and present certain financial risks. For one thing, they feature *unlimited liability*. The sole proprietor is liable for all debts incurred by the business. *General partnerships* are proprietorships with multiple owners. Partnerships have access to a larger talent pool and more investment money than do sole proprietorships but may be dissolved if conflicts between partners cannot be resolved.

4. **Describe *corporations* and explain their advantages and disadvantages.** *Corporations* are independent legal entities that are usually run by professional managers. In some corporations, stock is widely held by the public; in other firms, stock is held by individuals or small, private groups. The corporate form is used by most

large businesses because it offers continuity and opportunities for raising money. It also features financial protection through *limited liability:* The liability of investors is limited to their personal investments. However, it is a complex legal entity subject to *double taxation:* In addition to taxes paid on corporate profits, investors must pay taxes on earned income.

5. **Describe the basic issues involved in creating and managing a corporation.** Creating a corporation generally requires legal assistance to file *articles of incorporation* and corporate *bylaws* and to comply with government regulations. Managers must understand shareholders' rights as well as the rights and duties of the *board of directors.*

6. **Identify recent trends and issues in corporate ownership.** Recent trends in corporate ownership include *acquisitions* (when one company buys another); *mergers* (when two companies combine to create a new one); *divestitures* (when a company decides to sell part of its existing operations to another corporation to narrow its own focus); *spin-offs* (when a company sells parts of its operations to another corporation in order to raise money); *employee stock ownership plans* (employees buy shares in the company that they work for); *strategic alliances* (two or more companies collaborate on an enterprise); *subsidiary and parent corporations* (one corporation—the parent—owns another corporation—the subsidiary); and *institutional ownership* (shares of a corporation are owned by mutual and pension funds).

STUDY QUESTIONS AND EXERCISES

Review Questions

1. What are the comparative advantages and disadvantages of the three basic forms of business ownership?

2. Why might a corporation choose to remain private? Why might a private corporation choose to go public?

3. What are the primary benefits and drawbacks to serving as a partner in a partnership?

4. Are joint ventures limited to corporations, or can individuals also enter into joint ventures?

5. Why is it important to understand the history of Canadian business?

Analysis Questions

6. Locate two annual reports and review them. Identify the specific points in the reports that the board of directors are communicating to the shareholders.

7. Go to the library and identify four major joint ventures beyond those discussed in the text. Is one of the parties likely to benefit more than the other?

8. How can you, a prospective manager during the global era, better prepare yourself now for the challenges you will face later in this decade?

Application Exercises

9. Interview a manager in a sole proprietorship or general partnership. Based on your talks, what characteristics of that business form led to the owner choosing it?

10. Interview the owner of a corporation. Based on your talks, what characteristics of that business form led to the owner choosing it?

BUILDING YOUR BUSINESS SKILLS

Goal

To help students analyze the implications of corporate acquisitions on individual stockholders.

Situation

You own 500 shares of Widget International (WI). Although you like the company's products, you are disappointed with the stock price. Analysts agree with you and warn that the company must drastically cut expenses or risk a takeover. Management begins to trim budgets, but its efforts are seen as too little too late. With the stock price continuing to drop, XYZ Corporation offers to buy WI. After successful negotiations, XYZ is set to acquire WI on January 1. When this happens, your 500 shares of WI will be converted into XYZ Corporation stock.

Method

Working in groups of four or five, analyze how this acquisition may affect your stock holdings. Research a similar corporate acquisition that took place in the past year as you consider the following factors:

- The nature of the acquiring company.
- The fit between the products or services of the two companies.
- The fiscal health of the acquiring company, as reflected in its own stock price.
- The stock market's long-term reaction to the acquisition. Does the market think it is a good move?
- Changes in corporate leadership as a result of the acquisition.
- Changes in the way the acquired company's products are produced and marketed.
- Announced budgetary changes.

Follow-Up Questions

1. After one company acquires another, what factors are likely to influence the stock market so that the stock price rises?
2. After one company acquires another, what factors are likely to influence the stock market so that the stock price drops?
3. Did your research identify any factors that are likely to trigger a corporate takeover?
4. In an acquisition, who is likely to be named CEO (the person in charge of the acquiring company)? Who is likely to be named CEO in a merger of equals? What factors are likely to influence this decision?
5. How is the board of directors likely to change as a result of an acquisition? A merger?

Prentice Hall

TAKE IT TO THE NET

Check out our Companion Website

for this chapter's Exploring the Net exercise, featuring the Website of the National Center for Employee Ownership and other intriguing, annotated destinations. You'll also find practice exercises, updated Weblinks from the text, links to newsgroups, updates, and more.

www.prenticehall.ca/ebert

BUSINESS CASE 2

Bargain Burials

When Rev. Eloi Arsenault came to Prince Edward Island to take over a Catholic parish, he was appalled at how much it cost a family to bury its loved ones. So, with help from the Knights of Columbus, a Catholic men's group, he set up the Palmer Road Funeral Co-operative. A local carpenter was hired to build simple caskets for $300. An embalming room was set up in the church basement, and bodies were moved using an old Ford station wagon. The goal was to provide funerals for about $1500, far less than the average price of $5000 being charged by the big funeral home chains.

Co-op interest in the death industry can be traced back to the 1930s, when "memorial societies" were first formed to get discounts for their members from local morticians. As the big funeral home chains began to dominate the industry, these memorial societies became more aggressive. In the past 10 years or so, their growth

has been considerable, and this growth is not limited to P.E.I. Similar co-ops are also springing up in the U.S. and Great Britain.

There are two main reasons for the recent growth of co-ops in the death industry. First, there has been a major consolidation in the funeral home business during the last decade, with fewer and fewer organizations owning more and more funeral homes. Two funeral home organizations—Service Corp. International (U.S.) and Loewen Group (Canada)—have become very large; the former has over 2000 funeral homes and the latter has almost 1000. A lot of people feel these corporate giants do not offer enough "warmth" when providing funeral services.

Second, the cost of an average funeral is now about $5000, a 25 percent increase just since the early 1990s. And this price does not include the cost of the cemetery plot, monument, or flowers, which can add several thousand dollars more. Even though industry consolidation should have lowered prices, that hasn't happened; instead, surveys show that large chains like Service Corp. and Loewen actually charge higher rates than independent funeral homes.

Funeral co-ops often operate with volunteer staff and do very little advertising. Yet their share of the market has increased to about 17 percent since the first one was formed in the mid-1980s. Traditional funeral homes have taken notice, and have fought back. For example, in P.E.I. they tried to persuade the Catholic bishop to transfer Father Arsenault off the island. When that failed, they tried to convince a Quebec casket manufacturer to stop supplying caskets to co-ops on the island. But that backfired when other co-ops in Quebec threatened to stop ordering caskets from the company unless it continued to supply the P.E.I. co-ops.

But success has had its price for the co-ops. Some people are worried that co-op funeral homes are becoming just like the big chains. The co-op started by Father Arsenault has abandoned its basement embalm-

ing room and Ford station wagon in favour of a more traditional funeral home and a hearse. And prices are creeping up; a co-op in Summerside sells funerals for about $5000.

■ Case Questions

1. What are the main differences between cooperatives and the other three forms of business ownership (sole proprietorships, partnerships, and corporations)?

2. Do these differences imply anything about the possible success of cooperatives versus the other three forms of business ownership? Why did cooperatives develop in the funeral business?

3. Compared to a corporation, why might a cooperative seem like a more appropriate form of ownership for a funeral home?

4. Cooperatives seem to be an appealing form of ownership, yet there are relatively few cooperatives in Canada. Why would this be so?

3

CONDUCTING BUSINESS ETHICALLY AND RESPONSIBLY

PROBLEMS AT THE BETTER BUSINESS BUREAU

Everyone has heard of the Better Business Bureau (BBB). Its mandate is to promote better business practices by warning consumers about everything from fly-by-night paving contractors to diamond mine scams.

The Toronto office has been the largest BBB in Canada for many years. Its president, Paul Tuz (shown in photo), worked tirelessly to build up the operation since he took the position in 1976. He pursued numerous business firms to become members of the BBB and got them to pay an annual membership fee. But problems began in the Toronto BBB's commission sales force in the late 1980s. These are the people who sign up the corporate memberships that are so critical to the BBB. One of the salespersons—a man by the name of James Peter Emms from Barrie, Ontario—eventually formed a group that challenged Tuz for leadership of the Toronto BBB.

Tuz originally praised Emms's sales skills. The average salesperson signs up four or five new members each week, but Emms signed up 14 per week on average. But Emms also had a talent for mobilizing dissent. Many people at the Toronto BBB had become so unhappy with Tuz that they wanted him out of the organization. Emms says that employees asked him to lead a task force to investigate complaints about the kind of money Tuz was taking out of the bureau.

During much of 1994, there were skirmishes between this task force (made up of several Barrie business firms) and the Toronto headquarters. Several of these were quite nasty. For example, Emms tried to get the Barrie police to investigate the BBB. Tuz retaliated by trying to have Emms arrested for parole violation (Tuz claimed that Emms came to the BBB after serving time in prison for fraud). Eventually, Tuz fired Emms.

By mid-1994, the task force was agitating to separate from the Toronto group. Then everyone started suing everyone else. A forensic accountant was hired to investigate task force complaints that Tuz had taken excessive pay and misappropriated money from the BBB. The accountant found that Tuz had been paid large sums of money, but that these payments had been approved by the BBB board.

When these findings hit the newspaper, the heat was turned up on the Toronto BBB, and they struck a deal with Emms and the Barrie task force. When *The Globe and Mail* obtained a copy of the agreement, it discovered that $325 000 had been paid by the Toronto BBB to Barrie; in return, the Barrie group agreed to drop Emms's wrongful dismissal lawsuits against the BBB and stop saying nasty things about Tuz. This was supposed to put an end to the infighting.

But in mid-1995, the national council said they would pull the Toronto bureau's licence unless its board of directors fired Tuz. Eventually Tuz resigned, as did the entire board. During this time, membership fees declined because good salespeople were leaving. The bureau ended up mortgaging its offices. It was also expelled from the Canadian Council of Better Business Bureaus.

Late in 1996, Tuz was arrested and charged with defrauding the BBB of $1.7 million. The charges dealt with issues about pay, pensions, expenses, and misappropriation of funds. In 1998, Tuz was cleared of all criminal fraud charges. Tuz's lawyer said that while his client had been legally exonerated, he had sustained major damage to his reputation and his personal finances.

This incident not only caused the Toronto BBB office to lose 75 percent of its dues-paying members, it has also raised questions about exactly what the BBB does, and, ironically, whether it has credibility as an organization. Further questions arose in 1998 when some details about the Calgary BBB office became public. The head of the Calgary office, Norm Haines, has been criticized because a management consulting company he operates also manages the BBB office. Other, competing management consulting firms are also members of the BBB. This means that Haines is in a position to make judgments about the marketplace activities of his competitors. There is no evidence that Haines has used his position to advantage, but critics see this as a potential conflict of interest.

In this chapter, we look closely at business ethics and social responsibility. At one time, these issues were not considered very important. But times have changed, and the practices of today's business firms are in the spotlight. As you will see, managers are faced with a variety of ethical dilemmas, and business firms must address many issues of social responsibility.

After reading this chapter, you should be able to:

1. Explain how individuals develop their personal *codes of ethics* and why ethics are important in the workplace.

2. Distinguish *social responsibility* from *ethics*.

3. Show how the concept of social responsibility applies to environmental issues and to a firm's relationships with customers, employees, and investors.

4. Identify three general *approaches to social responsibility* and describe the four steps a firm must take to implement a *social responsibility program*.

5. Explain how issues of social responsibility and ethics affect small businesses.

■ THE NATURE OF ETHICS IN THE WORKPLACE

ethics
Individual standards or moral values regarding what is right and wrong or good and bad.

Just what is ethical behaviour in business? You will find as many answers as people you ask, because **ethics**—standards or morals regarding what is right and wrong or good and bad—are highly personal.

Ethics vary greatly from person to person and from situation to situation. They are based on our society's ideas of right and wrong. Ethics vary from culture to culture. And within our cultural standards, we all develop our own personal "code of ethics" that accommodates differences within societal standards. For example, Western society generally considers stealing or bribery as "wrong" and patriotism and giving as "right." In other cultures, however, different ethical standards exist. It is important to realize, then, that what constitutes ethical and unethical behaviour is determined partially by the individual and partially by the cultural context in which it occurs.

Because ethics are both personally and culturally defined, differences of opinion can genuinely arise as to what is ethical or unethical. For example, many people who would be appalled at the thought of shoplifting a candy bar from a grocery store routinely take home pens and pads of paper from their offices, seeing these items almost as a part of their pay. Other people believe that if they find money on the sidewalk it is okay to keep it. Still other people view themselves as law-abiding citizens but have no qualms about using radar detectors to avoid speeding tickets. In each of these situations, people will choose different sides of the issue and argue that their views are ethical.

Influences on Ethics

Aside from situational factors, what makes different people's codes of ethics vary so much? The most common influences on an individual's ethics and behaviour are family, peers (and the values they convey), and experiences.

Families—especially parents—have the first chance to influence a child's ethics. Parents usually put a high priority on teaching their children certain values. In many families, these values include religious principles. Most parents also try to teach their children to obey society's rules and to behave well towards other people. The so-called *work ethic*—the belief and practice that hard work brings rewards—is learned in the home. Children who see their parents behaving ethically are more likely to adopt high ethical standards for themselves than are the children of parents who behave unethically. Teenagers are particularly likely to reject the verbal messages of parents who do not practise what they preach.

As children grow and are exposed more to other children, peers begin to have more influence on ethical behaviour. Indeed, the values of the group may become far more important than those of the larger society. Although such beliefs and behaviour are most talked about in the case of juvenile delinquent gangs, they also apply to the business world. Many unethical (and even criminal) business behaviours are fostered by a company environment in which such practices are acceptable (at least until the company gets caught).

Finally, experiences can increase or decrease certain types of ethical behaviour and beliefs about what is right and wrong. A child punished for telling lies learns that telling lies is wrong. Likewise, a company president who goes to jail for misrepresenting the company's financial position will probably have a new understanding of business ethics. But the manager who gets away with sexually harassing an employee will be more likely to see nothing wrong with it and do it again.

Company Policies and Business Ethics

In recent years, the general public has become increasingly concerned about the behaviour of Canadian business leaders. A 1990 survey by Decima Research showed that 45 percent of Canadians consider business leaders unprincipled. The comparable figure 10 years earlier was 20 percent.[1] As illegal and/or unethical activities by managers have caused more problems for companies, many firms are taking steps to encourage their employees to practise more acceptable behaviour.[2]

Perhaps the single most significant thing a company can do is to demonstrate top management's support for ethical behaviour. The importance of top management support is demonstrated in the box "To Bribe or Not To Bribe." Many companies have adopted written codes of ethics that clearly state the firm's intent to conduct business ethically. Levi Strauss has an "aspiration statement" that spells out the company's values-based formula for earning profits and making the world a better place. It declares that management will set an example for ethical behaviour that others in the company must follow.

A 1997 survey by KPMG found that two-thirds of Canada's largest corporations have codes of ethics (90 percent of large U.S. firms do). More and more regulatory and professional associations in Canada are recommending that corporations adopt codes of ethics. The Canada Deposit Insurance Corp., for example, requires that all deposit-taking institutions have a code of conduct that is periodically reviewed and ratified by the board of directors. The Canadian Competition Bureau, the Canadian Institute of Chartered Accountants, and the Ontario Human Rights Commission all are pushing for the adoption of codes of ethics by corporations.[3]

KPMG
www.kpmg.ca

Canadian Institute of Chartered Accountants
www.cica.ca

TRENDS CHALLENGES

To Bribe or Not To Bribe

Business executives occasionally must make difficult decisions that have important ethical implications. Consider the following situations:

- David Brink is the chairman of Murray & Roberts Holdings of South Africa. On one of its housing construction projects in the Sudan, the company experienced a problem when payments for work done didn't come through as expected. A government official indicated that he could start the money flowing again if the company would pay him a "commission." The company refused and took the matter to the World Court. Although it took 12 years to get a decision, the case was settled in the company's favour.

- Jean-Pierre van Rooy is president of Otis Elevator Co. of Farmington, Connecticut. When mobsters in St. Petersburg, Russia, approached the Otis operation and asked for "protection" money, the company refused, even though they knew that several other companies—including Coca-Cola and Pepsi—had had their operations firebombed after refusing to pay. Otis has a strict company policy of not paying bribes, so it has simply tightened security around its St. Petersburg plant and is hoping for the best.

The experiences of Brink and van Rooy are not unusual in the world of international business. While speaking at a conference on business ethics, the secretary general of Interpol, the world police intelligence network, noted that the tolerance for dishonesty is increasing in both the advanced and developing countries of the world. Managers are therefore likely to be faced at some point in their career with demands that they pay bribes to someone in order to facilitate work. Since corruption is common in international business, the main fear among managers is that they will lose important business contracts if they take a tough stand against paying bribes or commissions. But both Brink and van Rooy don't accept that argument. Brink says that while his company has lost some contracts because they wouldn't pay bribes, they are better off without that business; van Rooy also feels that

his company has not suffered because of its strict anti-corruption policy.

Some observers estimate that U.S. business firms lost more than $400 billion worth of business because of strict anti-corruption laws there. The U.S. *Foreign Corrupt Practices Act* bans all commissions and bribes, but it applies only to U.S.-based companies. Attempts are currently underway to get the 24-member Organization for Economic Cooperation and Development to support a stronger anti-corruption agreement, but there is considerable resistance in other countries to imposing rules like those by which U.S. corporations have to abide. Other critics say such a measure will not work because corruption is so common in much of the world.

One international banker advises his clients that bribes are a way of life in Russia, and if they want to do business there they will have to go along with paying bribes. Corruption was common under the old communist regime in Russia. For example, people paid bribes to get their children into good schools or to jump the line to buy a refrigerator. Surprisingly, things have gotten worse since the collapse of communism. In the first nine months of 1994, more than 70 000 bribery and extortion cases were opened. A presidential report said that one-third of all retail trade earnings goes for corrupt purposes. Russian consumers therefore pay a 33 percent "tax" for bribery. Nearly half the respondents in a recent poll said they had been forced to pay a bribe to a government official. Bribery has become so common that the newspaper *Komsomolskaya Pravda* compiled a price list of Moscow bribes (e.g., the bribe needed to obtain a Moscow residency permit and the right to purchase an apartment is around $35 000).

The greatest hope in raising the level of ethical behaviour lies with individual managers, particularly those at the top management level. If the chief executive sanctions anything illegal, this will send the wrong message to the firm's employees. Conversely, if the chief executive is high-profile about being very ethical, this not only models correct behaviour to employees, it may actually discourage bribe requests from outsiders because they know where the company stands.

■ THE NATURE OF SOCIAL RESPONSIBILITY

Ethics affect how an individual behaves within a business. But **social responsibility** affects how a business behaves as an entity on its own towards other businesses, customers, investors, and society at large. Like ethics, social responsibility is individualistic (for the firm, not a person), since it must attempt to balance different commitments. For example, to behave responsibly towards its investors, a company must try to maximize its profits. But a responsibility towards its customers means that it must produce safe goods or services. In their zeal to respond to investors, companies sometimes step over the line and act irresponsibly towards their customers. Hertz Rent-A-Car was recently charged with overcharging its corporate customers and filing bogus insurance claims for damages.

Just as an individual's personal code of ethics is influenced by many factors, so is a firm's sense of social responsibility. To a large extent social responsibility depends on the ethics of the individuals employed by a firm—especially its top management. But social responsibility can also be forced from outside by government and consumers. How a firm behaves is also shaped by how other firms in the same country and industry behave and by the demands of investors.

social responsibility
A business's collective code of ethical behaviour towards the environment, its customers, its employees, and its investors.

■ AREAS OF SOCIAL RESPONSIBILITY

In defining its sense of social responsibility—or having it defined—most firms must confront four issues. As Figure 3.1 shows, these issues concern an organization's responsibility towards its environment, its customers, its employees, and its investors.

Responsibility Towards the Environment

One critical area of social responsibility involves how the business relates to its physical environment. **Pollution** has been and continues to be a significant managerial challenge. Although noise pollution is attracting increased concern, air pollution, water pollution, and land pollution are the subjects of most anti-pollution efforts by business and governments.[4] The Kyoto Summit in 1997 was an attempt by various governments to reach agreement on ways to reduce the threat of pollution.

pollution
The injection of harmful substances into the environment.

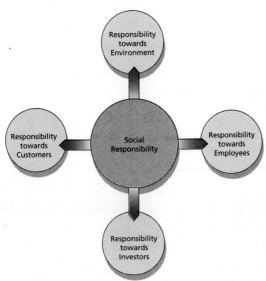

FIGURE 3.1
Four basic areas of social responsibility.

Air Pollution.   Air pollution results when a combination of factors converge to lower air quality. Large amounts of chemicals such as the carbon monoxide emitted by automobiles contribute to air pollution. Smoke and other chemicals emitted by manufacturing plants also help to create air pollution.

Legislation has gone a long way towards controlling air pollution. Under new laws, many companies have had to install special devices to limit the pollutants they expel into the atmosphere. Such clean-up efforts are not without costs, however. The bill to private companies for air pollution control devices runs into billions of dollars.

Even with these devices, however, acid rain remains a problem. **Acid rain** occurs when sulphur pumped into the atmosphere mixes with natural moisture and falls as rain. Much of the acid rain damage to forests and streams in the eastern United States and Canada has been attributed to heavy manufacturing and power plants in the midwestern United States.

Acid rain poses a dilemma in social responsibility for businesses. Current technologies to greatly reduce sulphur pollution are so costly that they would force many businesses to close. Such a move would cause major financial losses for investors and for laid-off employees, not to mention the loss of crucial services. The business challenge is to find ways to significantly reduce the sulphur—and thus the acid rain—without incurring costs that are too high to bear.

Water Pollution.   For years, businesses and municipalities dumped their waste into rivers, streams, and lakes with little regard for the effects. Thanks to new legislation and increased awareness on the part of businesses, water quality is improving in many areas. Millar Western Pulp Ltd. built Canada's first zero-discharge pulp mill at Meadow Lake, Saskatchewan. There is no discharge pipe to the river, no dioxin-forming chlorine, and next to no residue. Dow Chemical built a plant at Fort Saskatchewan that will not dump any pollutants into the nearby river.[5]

Land Pollution.   Two key issues are associated with land pollution. The first issue is how to restore the quality of land that has already been damaged. In 1998, five million cubic litres of toxic waste escaped from a holding pond at a zinc mine in Spain that was operated by the Canadian mining firm Boliden Ltd. Thousands of hectares of agricultural land were contaminated.[6]

acid rain
A form of pollution affecting the eastern United States and Canada as a result of sulphur expelled into the air by midwestern power and manufacturing plants.

Toxic waste spills such as the one that occurred at Boliden Ltd.'s mining operation in Spain can cause destruction of fish, wildlife, and agricultural land.

A second issue is how to prevent such problems in the future. Changes in foresting practices, limits on types of mining, and new forms of solid waste disposal are all attempts to address this issue, although such changes are often opposed. A whole new industry—**recycling**—has developed as part of increased consciousness about land pollution (see the box "Recycling Financial Results").

An especially controversial problem centres on toxic waste disposal. **Toxic wastes** are dangerous chemical and/or radioactive byproducts of various manufacturing processes. Because toxic waste cannot usually be processed into harmless material or destroyed, it must be stored somewhere. The problem is—where? Few people want a toxic waste storage facility in their town.

recycling
The reconversion of waste materials into useful products.

toxic waste
Pollution resulting from the emission of chemical and/or radioactive byproducts of various manufacturing processes into the air, water, or land.

TRENDS & CHALLENGES

Recycling Financial Results

Philip Services Corp. (PSC) is the largest metal recycling company in North America, with 1997 sales of $1.75 billion. It is an integrated waste management conglomerate with four divisions: (1) solid waste management (hauling and dumping industrial waste), (2) resource recovery (scrap metal recycling), (3) hazardous waste (oil and solvent recycling), and (4) environmental services (consulting services).

The company was started in the late 1970s by Allen and Philip Fracassi, who began by hauling sand and scrap steel out of Hamilton steel mills and foundries. The brothers wanted to change the view of waste management from a "haul-and-dump" mentality to a new focus on recycling and service. Their goal was to turn industrial waste into industrial fuel and raw materials.

Consider a typical example of PSC's current activity: PSC collects furnace dust—a reddish metallic powder that is a byproduct of steel mills—and hauls it to a transfer station, then shakes it through screens to remove any impurities like scrap iron, wood, or trash. The scrap iron is then sent to PSC's resource recovery division, while trash goes to the solid waste division. Then the dust is mixed with other additives to make it suitable for use in cement kilns.

PSC offers everything from consulting services and recycling to landfilling and emergency cleanup of toxic wastes. The business is more like manufacturing and processing than simply waste hauling. The company manufactures products from raw materials in the waste that is collected. The goal is to offer other companies one-stop-shopping for waste management, with an emphasis on recycling. PSC's contract with St. Lawrence Cement is illustrative of its approach. PSC sells the cement company waste oil and solvent, which St. Lawrence burns in its kilns. PSC also sends St. Lawrence sludge collected from, say, Redpath Sugars, as well as foundry sand and steel mill furnace dust which St. Lawrence uses in the production of cement.

The key to success is cross-selling the services of each PSC company to clients. For example, Waxman Resources, a PSC subsidiary, might send tin-plated copper scrap it picks up to Metal Recovery Industries (another PSC subsidiary) for de-tinning. Cross-selling allows PSC subsidiaries to sell clients on a wider range of services and keep the competitors away by stressing the one-stop-shopping approach.

PSC's rapid growth during the 1990s made it a favoured stock on the Toronto Stock Exchange. But on March 5, 1998, the company released its financial results for 1997, indicating that it had lost $95 million for the year. On April 1, those numbers were revised, with the loss being increased to $108 million. On April 23, the company restated its results for an unprecedented second time, saying that losses for 1997 were actually $143 million. An analyst at Standard & Poor's in New York said he had never seen a company restate its earnings downwards twice. The two restatements caused the company's stock—which had been selling for as high as $27 per share in mid-1997—to drop to about $12 per share in early 1998. A series of class-action lawsuits have been filed against the company by shareholders who claimed they were misled about the company's financial situation.

Company officials said that most of these losses were caused by problems in the metals recycling division. Originally, it was thought that $90 million of copper inventory was missing from two sites in Hamilton. Further investigation suggested that the losses might have been caused by the activities of a "rogue trader." Whatever the reason, investors were not happy to hear about the loss. Investors are also concerned that PSC's recent wave of acquisitions has not led to an increase in company profitability.

Canadian Standards Association
www.csa.ca

Many business firms are now acting to reduce various forms of pollution. However, the road to environmental purity is not easy. Under the Canadian and Ontario Environmental Protection Acts, liability for a business firm can run as high as $2 million per day. To protect themselves, companies must prove that they showed diligence in avoiding an environmental disaster such as an oil or gasoline spill.[7] The Environmental Choice program, sponsored by the federal government, licenses products that meet environmental standards set by the Canadian Standards Association. Firms whose products meet these standards can put the logo—three doves intertwined to form a maple leaf—on their products.[8]

Responsibility Towards Customers

Social responsibility towards customers generally falls into one of two categories: providing quality products and pricing those products fairly. As with the environment, firms differ in their level of concern about responsibility to customers. Yet unlike environmental problems, customer problems do not require expensive technological solutions. Most such problems can be avoided if companies obey the laws regarding consumer rights and illegal pricing practices.

consumerism
A social movement that seeks to protect and expand the rights of consumers in their dealings with businesses.

Rights of Consumers. Much of the current interest in business responsibility towards customers can be traced to the rise of consumerism. **Consumerism** is a form of social activism dedicated to protecting the rights of consumers in their dealings with businesses.

Consumers have several rights. First, they have the right to safe products. For example, when you buy a new paint sprayer, it must be safe to use for spraying paint. It must come with instructions on how to use it, and it must have been properly tested by its manufacturer. Dow Corning Corp. halted production of silicone breast implants after questions were raised about the product's safety. The box "What To Do in a Mad Cow Crisis" describes corporate concern about consumer safety.

Second, consumers have the right to be informed about all relevant aspects of a product. Food products must list their ingredients. Clothing must be labelled with information about its proper care. And banks must tell you exactly how much interest you are paying on a loan. Cereal companies have come under fire recently for some of the claims they have made about the oat bran content of their cereals, as well as its likely effects.

Kmart
www.kmart.com/

Third, consumers have a right to be heard. Many companies today have complaints offices. Retailers like Kmart offer a money-back guarantee if consumers aren't satisfied. On many of its products Procter & Gamble puts a toll-free number that consumers can call if they have questions or complaints. When companies refuse to respond to consumer complaints, consumer protection agencies such as the Better Business Bureau and consumer interest groups such as the Airline Passengers Association may intervene.

Finally, consumers have a right to choose what they buy. Central to this right is free and open competition among companies. In times past, "gentlemen's agreements" were often used to avoid competition or to divide up a market so that firms did not have to truly compete against each other. Such practices are illegal today and any attempts by business to block competition can result in fines or other penalties.

collusion
An illegal agreement among companies in an industry to "fix" prices for their products.

Interfering with competition can also mean illegal pricing practices. **Collusion** among companies—getting together to "fix" prices—is against the law. Polar Plastic Ltd. of Montreal pled guilty to conspiring to fix prices of disposable cups, glasses, and cutlery in the U.S. market. Although secret meetings and phone conversations took place between executives of competing companies as they tried to fix prices, the conspiracy was not successful.[9]

Responsibility Towards Employees

Organizations also need to employ fair and equitable practices with their employees. Later, in Chapter 9, we describe the human-resource management activities essential to a

TRENDS CHALLENGES

What To Do in a Mad Cow Crisis

The British public was jittery, and top executives at McDonald's and Burger King knew why. On March 21, 1996, the British government announced a possible link between bovine spongiform encephalopathy (BSE), or "mad cow disease," and Creutzfeld-Jakob disease, a fatal brain condition in humans. Fifty-five people in England had died from Creutzfeld-Jakob in 1994, including 10 people who had probably contracted the disease from beef contaminated with BSE. Coinciding with the increase in human deaths was a mad cow disease epidemic that had affected more than 162 000 animals since 1986.

To American fast-food restaurants doing business in Great Britain, the government announcement translated immediately into a business crisis. Customers' concerns about product safety and the need to maintain consumer confidence were uppermost on executives' minds. McDonald's was the first to act. Three days after the government announcement, the British division of the American fast-food giant suspended the sale of all British beef products. "Our customers expect us to take a lead and we have," declared Paul Preston, president of McDonald's United Kingdom division. "We believe that British beef is safe. However, we cannot ignore the fact that recent announcements have led to a growing loss of consumer confidence in British beef." McDonald's served nonburger selections for four days until its restaurants began receiving beef products from continental Europe.

Burger King acted seven days later to pull all British beef from its 382 restaurants. In making this decision, the firm cited the need to maintain consumer confidence in the safety of its products and the concern that it would be forced to close restaurants if it continued to use British beef. Burger King also announced that its burgers would be made from Italian, German, and French beef. The decision was well received. Burger King, confirmed company official Alan Randall, "has advertised extensively since this thing started and has been informing people that it imports all its meat. Because of that, our sales have not been hurt at all. People trust Burger King."

Many British food companies also took swift action. Bass Taverns, a chain of 2700 restaurants and pubs, withdrew all British beef and beef products from its menus four days after the crisis began. Monte's, an expensive private dining club in London, yielded to the concerns of diners who "can well afford the price of fine, imported cuts of meat." However, other British food companies took a different tack. Less concerned with consumer confidence than their U.S. counterparts, they continued to sell domestic beef and let customers make their own decisions about what not to eat. Many British firms seemed satisfied that the decision would not result in long-term sales drops. In fact, the first news of mad cow disease caused burger sales to decrease by half at restaurants, theme parks, and other food and beverage sellers. But, reports Maxine Donne, a food-service manager in Blackpool, "things quickly went back to normal. Everyone's aware of it now. I don't think anyone really cares." Colin Dawson, the managing director of a seaside resort park in Margate, agreed. "It's not that big a deal," argued Dawson. "The media has blown it out of proportion."

What influenced most the rapid decision of U.S. firms to pull British beef off their shelves? Was it an American culture that emphasizes health concerns? Or was it an equally American anxiety about litigation? No one can say for sure. It is certain, however, American fast-food chains placed great value on maintaining consumer confidence and trust. Perhaps the best indicator of whether these companies did the right thing is the collective reaction of their own consumers. If 20-year-old David Baker is typical, the choice to emphasize safety was on the mark: "I'm pretty wary of beefburgers now," volunteers Baker.

---

smoothly functioning business. These same activities—recruiting, hiring, training, promoting, and compensating—are also the basis for social responsibility towards employees. A company that provides its employees with equal opportunities for rewards and advancement without regard to race, sex, or other irrelevant factors is meeting its social responsibilities. Firms that ignore their responsibility to employees leave themselves open for lawsuits. They also miss the chance to hire better and more highly motivated employees.

The safety of workers is an important consideration for all organizations. The required use of hardhats, for example, is designed to protect workers from head injuries.

Royal Bank of Canada
www.royalbank.com

Bell Canada
www.bell.ca

Some progressive companies go well beyond these legal requirements, hiring and training the so-called hard-core unemployed (people with little education and training and a history of unemployment) and those who have disabilities. The Bank of Montreal, for example, sponsors a community college skills upgrading course for individuals with hearing impairments. The Royal Bank provides managers with discrimination awareness training. Rogers Cablesystems Ltd. has begun to provide individuals with mobility restrictions with telephone and customer-service job opportunities.[10] Bell Canada employs more than 1000 people with disabilities (2 percent of its permanent workforce). But, in Canada, over 50 percent of those with physical disabilities are still unemployed.[11]

In addition to their responsibility to employees as resources of the company, firms have a social responsibility to their employees as people. Firms that accept this responsibility make sure that the workplace is safe, both physically and emotionally. They would no more tolerate an abusive manager or one who sexually harasses employees than they would a gas leak.

Business firms also have a responsibility to respect the privacy of their employees. While nearly everyone agrees that companies have the right to exercise some level of control over their employees, there is great controversy about exactly how much is acceptable in areas like drug testing and computer monitoring. When Canadian National Railways instituted drug testing for train, brake, and yard employees, 12 percent failed. Trucking companies have found that nearly one-third of truckers who have been involved in an accident are on drugs.[12]

Respecting employees as people also means encouraging ethical behaviour. Too often, individuals who try to act ethically find themselves in trouble on the job. This problem is especially true for **whistle-blowers**, employees who detect an unethical, illegal, and/or socially irresponsible action within the company and try to end it.

In a socially responsible company, whistle-blowers can confidently report their findings to higher-level managers, who will act or forward the report to someone who can. However, in many firms, whistle-blowers are penalized for their efforts and find themselves demoted or even fired. A few of these individuals persist, taking their cases to the media or to government agencies. But employees in companies that discourage whistle-blowing more often choose to keep silent, to the loss of both business and society.

whistle-blower
An individual who calls attention to an unethical, illegal, and/or socially irresponsible practice on the part of a business or other organization.

Responsibility Towards Investors

It may sound odd to say that a firm can be irresponsible towards investors, since they are the owners of the company. But if the managers of a firm abuse its financial resources, the ultimate losers are the owners, since they do not receive the earnings, dividends, or capital appreciation due them. Managers can act irresponsibly in several ways.

Improper Financial Management.   Occasionally, organizations are guilty of financial mismanagement. In other cases, executives have been "guilty" of paying themselves outlandish salaries, spending huge amounts of company money for their own personal comfort, and similar practices. Creditors can do nothing. Even shareholders have few viable options. Trying to force a management changeover is not only difficult, it can drive down the price of the stock, a penalty shareholders are usually unwilling to assign themselves.

Cheque Kiting.   Other practices are specifically illegal. **Cheque kiting**, for instance, involves writing a cheque against money that has not yet arrived at the bank on which it is drawn. In 1993, E. F. Hutton and Co. was convicted of violating kiting laws on a massive scale: In a carefully planned scheme, company managers were able to use as much as $250 million every day that did not belong to the firm. Managers would deposit customer cheques for, say, $1 million into the company account. Knowing that the bank would collect only a percentage of the total deposit over the course of several days, they proceeded to write cheques against the total $1 million.

cheque kiting
The illegal practice of writing cheques against money that has not yet arrived at the bank on which the cheque has been written, relying on that money arriving before the cheque clears.

Insider Trading.   **Insider trading** occurs when someone uses confidential information to gain from the purchase or sale of stocks. Most of these cases have occurred in the United States. Ivan Boesky, a professional Wall Street trader, and Dennis Levine, an investment broker, worked together to make large profits. When Levine heard of an upcoming merger or acquisition, he passed the information along to Boesky. Boesky, in turn, bought and sold the appropriate stocks to make huge profits, which he then split with Levine. In one especially profitable instance, Boesky used Levine's information about Nestlé's plans to buy Carnation stock to earn over $28 million in profits.[13] In one highly publicized Canadian case, Veronika Hirsch, a mutual fund manager for AGF Management Ltd., bought shares in a mining company for herself weeks before she also bought the stock—at double the price—for the mutual fund she was managing. While technically not a case of insider trading, this was a violation of AGF's code of ethics since Hirsch did not inform AGF officials that she had purchased the stock.

insider trading
The use of confidential information to gain from the purchase or sale of stock.

Misrepresentation of Finances.   Irresponsible and unethical behaviour regarding financial representation is also illegal. All corporations are required to conform to generally accepted accounting practices in maintaining and reporting their financial status. Sometimes, though, managers project profits far in excess of what they truly expect to earn. When the truth comes out, investors are almost always bitter. Occasionally, companies are found guilty of misrepresenting their finances to outsiders.

■ IMPLEMENTING SOCIAL RESPONSIBILITY PROGRAMS

Thus far, we have discussed social responsibility as if consensus exists on how firms should behave in most situations. In fact, dramatic differences of opinion exist as to the appropriateness of social responsibility as a business goal. As you might expect, some people oppose any business activity that cuts into profits to investors. Others argue that responsibility must take precedence over profits.

Even people who share a common attitude towards social responsibility by businesses may have different reasons for their beliefs. Some opponents of such activity fear that if businesses become too active in social concerns, they will gain too much control over how those concerns are addressed. They point to the influence many businesses have been able to exert on the government agencies that are supposed to regulate their industries. Other critics of business-sponsored social programs argue that companies lack the expertise needed. They believe that technical experts, not businesses, should decide how best to clean up a polluted river, for example.

Supporters of social responsibility believe that corporations are citizens just like individuals and therefore need to help improve our lives. Others point to the vast resources controlled by businesses and note that since businesses often create many of the problems social programs are designed to alleviate, that they should use their resources to help. Still others argue that social responsibility is wise because it pays off for the firm.

Max Clarkson, formerly a top-level business executive, is now the director of the Centre for Corporate Social Performance and Ethics at the University of Toronto. He says that business firms that have a strong consciousness about ethics and social responsibility outperform firms that don't. After designing and applying a social responsibility rating system for companies, he found that companies that had the highest marks on questions of ethics and social responsibility also had the highest financial performance.[14]

Approaches to Social Responsibility

Given these differences of opinion, it is little wonder that corporations adopt a variety of postures when making decisions about social responsibility. Three common approaches are discussed below.

social-obligation approach
A conservative approach to social responsibility in which a company does only the minimum required by law.

Social-Obligation Approach.   The **social-obligation approach** is consistent with the argument that profits should not be spent on social programs. The company that uses this approach does the minimum required by government regulation and standard business practices, but nothing else.

Tobacco companies exemplify this approach. They did not put health warnings on their packages and did not drop television advertising until forced to do so by the government. In other countries that lack such bans, Canadian and American tobacco companies still advertise heavily and make no mention of the negative effects of smoking.

social-reaction approach
A moderate approach to social responsibility in which a company sometimes goes beyond the minimum required by law on request.

Social-Reaction Approach.   Firms using the **social-reaction approach** go beyond the bare minimums if specifically asked. For example, many companies will match employee contributions to approved causes. Others sponsor local hockey teams. But someone has to knock on the door and ask.

Social-Response Approach.   Firms that adopt the **social-response approach** actively seek opportunities to contribute to the well-being of society. McDonald's, for example, has worked with children's hospitals and local communities to establish Ronald McDonald Houses to provide lodging for families of seriously ill children hospitalized away from home.

social-response approach
A liberal approach to social responsibility in which a company actively seeks opportunities to contribute to the well-being of society.

Managing Social Responsibility Programs

Making a company truly socially responsible in the full sense of the social-response approach takes an organized and managed program. In particular, managers must take four steps to foster social responsibility.

Ronald McDonald House helps the families of children who are in hospital care. It is supported by McDonald's and is an excellent example of socially responsible behaviour by a business corporation.

In Bangladesh, contractors admitted they had been illegally hiring children to work in Levi Strauss plants. When the company learned of this, they struck a deal: the company would pay to send the children to school if contractors would continue to pay them wages and hire them when they turned 14. Levi Strauss thereby preserved its reputation as a conscientious Third World employer.

First, social responsibility must start at the top. Without this support, no program can succeed. Top managers must make the decision that they want to take a stronger stand on social responsibility and develop a policy statement outlining their commitment.

Second, a committee of top managers needs to develop a plan detailing the level of support to be directed towards social responsibility. Some companies set aside a percentage of profits for social programs. Levi Strauss, for example, has a policy of giving 2.4 percent of its pretax earnings to worthy causes. Managers also need to set specific priorities. Should the firm train the hard-core unemployed or support the arts, for example?

Third, one specific executive needs to be given the authority to act as director of the firm's social agenda. Whether this is a separate job or an additional responsibility, this individual must monitor the program and ensure that its implementation is consistent with the policy statement and the strategic plan.

social audit
A systematic analysis of how a firm is using funds earmarked for social-responsibility goals and how effective these expenditures have been.

Finally, the organization needs to conduct occasional social audits. A **social audit** is a systematic analysis of how a firm is using funds earmarked for its social-responsibility goals. Consider the case of a company whose strategic plan calls for spending $100 000 to train 200 hard-core unemployed people and subsequently to place 180 of them in jobs. If at the end of one year the firm has spent $98 000, trained 210 people, and placed 175 into jobs, an audit will confirm the program as a success. But if the program cost $150 000, trained only 90 people, and placed only 10 of them in jobs, the audit will reveal the program's failure. A failure should signal the director and the committee to rethink the program's implementation and/or their choice of priorities.

Social Responsibility and the Small Business

Although many of the examples in this chapter illustrate responses to social responsibility and ethical issues by big business, small businesses face many of the same questions.

As the owner of a garden supply store, how would you respond to a building inspector's suggestion that a cash payment would expedite your application for a building permit? As the manager of a nightclub, would you call the police, refuse service, or sell liquor to a customer whose ID card looks forged? Or as the owner of a small laboratory, would you actually call the board of health to make sure that it has licensed the company you want to contract with to dispose of the lab's medical waste? Is the small manufacturing firm justified in overcharging a customer by 5 percent whose purchasing agent is lax? Who will really be harmed if a small firm pads its income statement to help get a much-needed bank loan?

Can a small business afford a social agenda? Should it sponsor hockey teams, make donations to the United Way, and buy lightbulbs from the Lion's Club? Is joining the Chamber of Commerce and supporting the Better Business Bureau too much or just good business? Clearly, ethics and social responsibility are decisions faced by all managers in all organizations, regardless of rank or size. One key to business success is to decide in advance how to respond to these issues.

SUMMARY OF LEARNING OBJECTIVES

1. **Explain how individuals develop their personal *codes of ethics* and why ethics are important in the workplace.** Individual *codes of ethics* are derived from social standards of right and wrong. *Ethical behaviour* is behaviour conforming to generally accepted social norms concerning beneficial and harmful actions. The most common influences on ethics are situations, family and peers (and the values they convey), and experiences. Because ethics affect the behaviour of individuals on behalf of the companies that employ them, many firms are adopting formal statements of ethics. Unethical behaviour can result in loss of business, in fines, and even in imprisonment.

2. **Distinguish *social responsibility* from *ethics*.** *Social responsibility* refers to an organization's response to social needs, while *ethics* refers to an individual's perception of what is right and wrong.

3. **Show how the concept of social responsibility applies to environmental issues and to a firm's relationships with customers, employees, and investors.** Social responsibility towards the environment requires firms to minimize pollution of the air, water, and land. Social responsibility towards customers requires firms to price products fairly and to respect customers' rights. Social responsibility towards employees requires firms to respect workers both as resources and as people who are more productive when their needs are met. Social responsibility towards investors requires firms to manage their resources and to represent their financial status honestly.

4. **Identify three general *approaches to social responsibility* and describe the four steps a firm must take to implement a *social responsibility program*.** Companies approach social responsibility in many ways. The *social-obligation approach* emphasizes compliance with legal minimum requirements. Companies adopting the *social-reaction approach* go beyond minimum activities, if asked. The *social-response approach* commits a company to actively seeking to contribute to socially concerned projects. Implementing a *social responsibility program* entails four steps: (1) drafting a policy statement with the support of top management, (2) developing a detailed plan, (3) appointing a director to implement the plan, and (4) conducting social audits to monitor results.

5. **Explain how issues of social responsibility and ethics affect small businesses.** Managers and employees of small businesses face many of the same ethical questions as their counterparts at larger firms. Small businesses must confront the same areas of social responsibility and the same need to decide on an approach to social responsibility. The differences are primarily differences of scale.

STUDY QUESTIONS AND EXERCISES

Review Questions

1. What factors influence the development of an individual's personal code of ethics?

2. What are the major areas of social responsibility that organizations need to be concerned about?

3. List the four rights of consumers.

4. What are the three basic approaches to social responsibility that an organization might choose to adopt?

5. What is insider trading? Give an example.

Analysis Questions

6. What kind of wrongdoing would most likely prompt you to become a whistle-blower? What kind of wrongdoing would be least likely to prompt you? Why?

7. In what ways do you think your personal code of ethics might clash with the operations of some companies?

8. If you were a shareholder in a corporation, which of the three approaches to social responsibility would you like to see applied by company management? Why?

Application Exercises

9. Identify a local business and observe its operations. Identify the ways in which the firm is a potential or actual polluter and how the company addresses its pollution problems.

10. Using newspapers, magazines, and other business references, identify and describe one company that takes a social-obligation approach to social responsibility, one that takes a social-reaction approach, and one that takes a social-response approach.

BUILDING YOUR BUSINESS SKILLS

Goal

To encourage students to apply general concepts of business ethics to specific business situations.

Situation

As the head of human resources of a large bank, you are in the process of developing a corporate code of ethics that will be issued to every bank employee. Among the major sections in the document are those that deal with the following sensitive topics:

- Discrimination against minority employees.
- Discrimination against minority customers.
- Sexual harassment.
- Conflicts of interest.
- Accepting gifts from clients.
- Privacy and confidentiality.
- Accounting irregularities.
- Lying to clients and fellow employees.

Method

Step 1: Working with four other students, determine your company's ethical stance on each of the topics listed above. This part of the project may require additional research. In your analysis, be certain to distinguish between your company's *ethical* and *legal* responsibilities. For example, while discriminating against minority mortgage applicants on the basis of race is clearly illegal, lying to fellow employees may violate ethical, rather than legal, rules.

Step 2: Using the information gathered in your research, draft a corporate code of ethics that explains the bank's position in each area. The code should define what the bank will do in each of the following situations:

- A mortgage officer refuses to grant mortgages to qualified minority clients.
- A female employee is sexually harassed by a male supervisor.
- A lending officer grants a million-dollar loan to his wife's business associate even though the associate fails to meet appropriate qualifications.
- A supplier of computer equipment receives special treatment after she gives gifts to bank employees in charge of computer purchases.
- False data are included in accounting reports to stockholders.
- Employees are regularly caught lying to clients and fellow employees in order to enhance their own positions in the company.

Follow-Up Questions

1. Do your response to the ethics situations presented here have a common thread? If so, does this thread represent a values-based approach to corporate ethics? Explain.

2. What measures would you suggest for making your written code of ethics a living document that influences the way in which every employee conducts business?

3. In your opinion, is the need for corporate codes of ethics greater than it was five years ago? Explain your answer.

Prentice Hall

TAKE IT TO THE NET

Check out our Companion Website
for this chapter's Exploring the Net exercise, featuring the Website of The Body Shop and other intriguing, annotated destinations. You'll also find practice exercises, updated Weblinks from the text, links to newsgroups, updates, and more.

www.prenticehall.ca/ebert

COMPANION WEBSITE

BUSINESS CASE 3

Industrial Espionage

José Ignacio López de Arriortua did what millions of workers do each year—he changed jobs. But there was nothing ordinary about José López's job switch: Shortly after he left General Motors for Volkswagen, GM charged him with industrial espionage.

For nine months, López had headed GM's huge purchasing operation. Originally hired to slash $4 billion from GM's bill for automotive parts, he held a job that put him in the centre of key strategy decisions and financial forecasts. For one thing, José López handled

➤

on a daily basis the kind of top secrets that would in large part determine GM's success throughout the 1990s. Indeed, two days before announcing his resignation, López had attended an international strategy meeting at GM's Opel subsidiary in Germany. During the meeting, he was introduced to GM Europe's model plans, sales projections, and financial forecasts up to the year 2000. He also watched Opel prototypes being put through their paces on Opel's Dudenhofen track.

Fearing that López had taken confidential information away from the European strategy meeting, GM demanded written confirmation that López "had not taken any documents" with him "pertaining to [GM's] present and future corporate plans." Fuelling GM's deepest fears were Volkswagen's subsequent efforts to lure away other GM employees. With López's help, Volkswagen had indeed tried to recruit more than 40 managers at Opel and GM, often enticing them with offers of doubled salaries. Before an injunction put a stop to its recruiting forays, VW had succeeded in hiring away seven key GM executives.

Although VW has denied allegations of industrial espionage and corporate raiding, the charges have left both López and the German carmaker under a legal and ethical cloud. That cloud became heavier when the district attorney of Darmstadt, Germany, discovered confidential GM documents at the home of a former GM executive who had, like López, defected to VW. At stake for Volkswagen is the public's perception of company ethics—an intangible factor that could affect the firm's sales. When a German polling organization asked 1000 Germans what they thought of the López affair, 65 percent believed that there was "something to" the allegations, while only 7 percent deemed them unfounded. Although Volkswagen hired López to cut costs and help return the company to profitability, it may have set itself up for failure if consumers react negatively to perceived unethical conduct. It may be a classic case, says Ian I. Mitroff, head of the crisis-management unit at the University of Southern California, where "the solution to one difficulty puts you into even worse problems." The potential problem for Volkswagen is fairly clear—the loss of public trust.

Finally, there is at least one more irony in the López affair. During his nine-month tenure at General Motors, López is charged with having leaked proprietary information from one supplier to another—actions that were in fact tolerated by GM. Suppliers who had been given blueprints of top-secret technology were able to underbid companies that had spent millions on research and development. As a result of these actions, 110 key automotive suppliers have ranked GM last among its industry peers in professionalism, cooperation, and communication. That vote constitutes an astounding fall for a purchasing department once considered the most professional and ethical in the auto industry.

GM filed a civil suit against Volkswagen claiming that López stole GM's plans for new cars, parts lists, price lists, and plans for a secret manufacturing plant. It claimed that VW used this information to lower its costs and to gain market share at GM's expense.

In early 1997, Volkswagen agreed to give GM $100 million in cash and to purchase $1 billion in parts from GM over the next seven years. López also resigned from VW, and GM agreed to drop their civil suit against VW. Both companies issued a statement expressing satisfaction that the disagreement had been settled.

■ Case Questions

1. As a result of López's resignation, GM CEO John F. Smith Jr. decided to require all top officers to sign formal contracts restricting their ability to work for a competing company for three years after leaving GM. How do you feel about this contract provision?

2. In your opinion, does an employee have an ethical responsibility to maintain the confidentiality of information gained on the job with one company when taking a job with a competing firm?

3. Should Volkswagen be concerned with the public's reaction to the López affair?

4. GM allowed López to reveal suppliers' proprietary information in order to elicit lower bids. In effect, says Carnegie Mellon management professor Gerald C. Meyers, "when it's used for GM, it's a boon. When it's used against them, it's a terrible thing." Considering its behaviour, did GM demonstrate a double standard in its reaction to the López affair?

5. The ethics of both VW and GM were called into question by the López affair. How will the ethical misjudgments of both companies affect their relationship with customers, suppliers, and employees?

UNDERSTANDING INTERNATIONAL BUSINESS

PURDY'S GOES INTERNATIONAL

Purdy's Chocolates is a Vancouver-based gourmet chocolate maker that is run by Karen Flavelle. It is the largest manufacturer of chocolate in B.C., and has 44 stores in B.C. and Alberta. Sales revenues exceed $20 million a year, and the firm employs 600 people.

The Purdy brand is well-known in western Canada, but relatively unknown elsewhere. A couple of years ago Karen decided that Purdy's needed to break into some new markets if the firm had any hope of growing. She decided on Taipei, the capital of Taiwan, because the Taiwanese have a sweet tooth, and because Lei Mei How, a Taiwanese businesswoman, convinced her it would be a good idea.

Ms. How was so convinced that Purdy's Chocolates would be a hit in Taiwan that she paid for Neil Hastie, a vice president at Purdy's, to fly to Taiwan and personally conduct some market research. Among other things, he discovered that there is a fascination with North American products in Taiwan, and a well-organized retail sector that does a good job of showcasing new products.

After hearing these positive comments, Purdy's formed a partnership with Ms. How to set up shop in a high-end department store (Mitsukoshi) in Taipei. Purdy's began selling in October 1995, expecting first-year sales to be in the $200 000 to $250 000 range. But even that modest target wasn't reached because several unexpected roadblocks were encountered.

Purdy's discovered, for example, that getting chocolate onto store shelves in a tropical climate was a problem, particularly when the chocolate was melting in the cargo hold of a plane as it sat baking on the tarmac under the tropical sun. Hiring and managing staff from a distance was also a lot more difficult than it was close to the home base in Vancouver.

Purdy's also assumed that products that sold well to Asians in Vancouver would sell well in Taipei, but found that was not the case. For example, ice cream dipped in chocolate and rolled in nuts wasn't nearly as popular in Taipei as it was in Vancouver.

The company also discovered many "little" things that slowed it down. For example, the rectangular package that is so common for chocolate in Canada was not well received in Taipei. There, customers prefer packages that are circular or triangular, which necessitated changes in packaging.

These difficulties were serious enough that the profitability of the Asian venture was in serious doubt. Karen decided to sign an agreement with a distributor—Konig Foods Ltd. of Taipei. Konig arranges to have the product picked up at Purdy's factory and delivered to Konig's facility. Purdy's Chocolates now functions solely as a wholesaler and lets Konig deal with the retailers that sell Purdy's chocolate. In December 1998, the company filled its biggest order yet in Taiwan.

Like many other businesses. Purdy's is starting to adopt an international focus in its operations. Increasingly, Canadian firms will have to look beyond the domestic Canadian market in their business dealings.

By focusing on the learning objectives of this chapter, you will better understand the dynamics of international business management as well as some of the social, cultural, economic, legal, and political differences that make international trade a challenging enterprise. After reading this chapter, you should be able to:

1. Describe the rise of international business and identify the major world marketplaces.
2. Explain how different forms of *competitive advantage, import-export balances, exchange rates*, and *foreign competition* determine the ways in which countries and businesses respond to the international environment.
3. Discuss the factors involved in deciding to do business internationally and in selecting the appropriate *levels of international involvement* and *international organizational structure*.
4. Describe some of the ways in which *social, cultural, economic, legal*, and *political differences* act as barriers to international trade.
5. Explain how *free trade agreements* assist world trade.

■ THE RISE OF INTERNATIONAL BUSINESS

The total volume of world trade today is immense—around $7 trillion each year. As more and more firms engage in international business, the world economy is fast becoming a single interdependent system—a process called **globalization**. This interdependence becomes very obvious in the box "The Asian Crisis: A Worldwide Threat."

We often take for granted the diversity of goods and services available today as a result of international trade. Your television set, your shoes, and even the roast lamb on your dinner table may all be **imports**—that is, products made or grown abroad but sold in Canada. At the same time, the success of many Canadian firms depends in large part on **exports**—products made or grown domestically and shipped for sale abroad.

In this section, we examine some of the key factors that shape the global business environment. First, we identify and describe the major world marketplaces. Then we discuss some important factors that determine the ways in which both nations and their businesses respond to the international environment: the roles of different forms of *competitive advantage*, of *import-export balances*, and of *exchange rates*.

globalization
The integration of markets globally.

imports
Products that are made or grown abroad and sold in Canada.

exports
Products made or grown in Canada that are sold abroad.

Major World Marketplaces

The contemporary world economy revolves around three major marketplaces: North America, the Pacific Rim, and Western Europe. But business activity is not limited to these three markets. The World Bank notes, for example, that 77 percent of the world's people live in so-called "developing" areas. Economies in those areas are expanding 5 to 6 percent annually. There are 300 million consumers in Eastern Europe and another 300 million in South America. In India alone, estimates of the size of the middle class run from 100 million to 300 million.[1]

North America.   The United States dominates the North American business region. It is the single largest marketplace and enjoys the most stable and sound economy in the world. Many U.S. firms, such as General Motors and Procter & Gamble, have had successful Canadian operations for years, and Canadian firms like Nortel and Alcan Aluminum are major competitors.

Mexico has also become a major manufacturing centre. Cheap labour and low transportation costs have encouraged many foreign firms to build plants in Mexico. Both Chrysler and General Motors, for instance, are building new assembly plants, as are suppliers like Rockwell International Corp. Nissan opened an engine and transmission plant in 1983 and a car-making plant in 1992. Mexican forecasters expected 200 000 workers to be in the automobile industry by 1998.

Western Europe.   Europe is often divided into two regions. Western Europe, dominated by Germany, the United Kingdom, France, and Italy, has been a mature but fragmented marketplace for years. The evolution of the European Union in 1992 into a unified marketplace has further increased the importance of this marketplace. Major international firms like Unilever, Renault, Royal Dutch Shell, Michelin, Siemens, and Nestlé are all headquartered in this region.

Kellogg
www.kelloggs.com

Eastern Europe, which was until recently primarily communist, has also gained in importance, both as a marketplace and a producer. In May 1994, for example, Albania became the 197th country in which Coca-Cola is produced, as Coke opened a new $10 million bottling plant outside the capital city of Tirana. Meanwhile, Kellogg has opened a new plant in Riga, capital of the former Soviet republic of Latvia. Kellogg has also launched a vigorous campaign of television ads and in-store demonstrations to capitalize on one of the world's few remaining cereal frontiers.[2]

Foreign companies invested more than $8 billion in Poland in 1995–96, including $500 million from PepsiCo Inc. Also in 1995, Daewoo chose Poland as the centre of its new European operation, spending $1 billion for an auto plant near Warsaw.

The Pacific Rim.   The Pacific Rim consists of Japan, the People's Republic of China, Thailand, Malaysia, Singapore, Indonesia, South Korea, Vietnam, Taiwan, Hong Kong, the Philippines, and Australia. Fuelled by strong entries in the automobile, electronics, and banking industries, the economies of these countries grew rapidly in the 1970s and 1980s. In 1997–98, however, these countries ran into serious economic difficulties (see the box

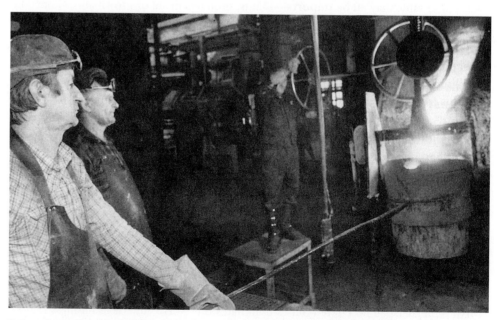

When Korean automaker Daewoo Group purchased this truck-making plant in Lublin, Poland, in 1995, it was a ramshackle collection of 14 overstaffed buildings with broken windows and 20-year-old equipment. Even today, molten steel for molding parts is poured by hand, and there is no computer system for keeping track of parts. Daewoo intends to change this state of affairs. Whereas demand for new cars is slowing in Western Europe, it's jumping in Central Europe, where Poland enjoys the largest economy.

entitled "The Asian Crisis: A Worldwide Threat"). Once these difficulties are overcome, Pacific Rim countries will once again be an important force in the world economy and a major source of competition for North American firms.

TRENDS & CHALLENGES

The Asian Crisis: A Worldwide Threat

During 1997 and 1998, serious economic and financial problems developed in several Asian countries, including Indonesia, Thailand, Malaysia, and South Korea. Even powerful Japan, once thought to be invincible, was mired in recession. As of mid-1998, Thailand, Indonesia, South Korea, and Japan were already in a recession, and Malaysia, Hong Kong, and Singapore were heading towards a recession. What caused the Asian crisis? Why were so many countries affected? What are the implications for Canada's economy?

Several interrelated factors caused the crisis— reduced economic growth rates in Asia, a sharp drop in the value of Asian currencies, high levels of foreign debt, high levels of bad debts, excess production capacity, a strategy to achieve economic growth by exporting more goods, and governments reluctant to take the steps necessary to resolve the crisis.

The first hint of the problems that lay ahead came in mid-1997, when the currencies of Indonesia, Malaysia, and Thailand began to decline in value. By mid-1998, these currencies had declined by as much as 70 percent against the U.S. dollar (the Canadian dollar declined about 8 percent during the same period). To achieve their high economic growth rates, Asian countries had borrowed large sums of money, and many of these loans were denominated in U.S. dollars. As the value of their currencies dropped, loan repayment costs skyrocketed and many companies became technically insolvent.

At that point, problems were still limited largely to the countries suffering the currency declines. But the effects soon spread to other countries. As the Indonesian *rupiah*, the Malaysian *ringgit*, and the Thailand *baht* declined in value, these countries found that they could export goods more easily because their products became cheaper on foreign markets. But other countries in Asia then became concerned that they would not be able to be competitive when exporting their goods because the values of the rupiah, ringgit, and baht were so low.

In this same general time period, the value of the South Korean *won* and the Japanese *yen* also dropped because those two countries had economic difficulties of their own. In Japan, for example, banks had loaned large amounts of money on questionable business ventures. Somewhere between half a billion and a billion dollars of bank loans are now thought to be uncollectible. Japan's bad-debt problem could amount to as much as 25 percent of its annual GDP. The same is generally true in South Korea.

As the value of the yen and the won dropped, Japan and South Korea became more competitive in exports, but they also put further downward pressure on the rupiah, ringgit, and baht. China has been able to resist most of these problems so far, but its banks also made many questionable loans. It may have to devalue its currency as well because it is intent on maintaining economic growth by exporting goods.

The International Monetary Fund (IMF) has tried to stabilize the Asian economies by granting multibillion dollar bailout deals. But the IMF typically grants these bailouts only if the country in question will do some very painful things like closing bankrupt companies and shutting down weak banks. These actions cause increases in unemployment, and governments of the Asian countries have avoided them because they are unpopular with their citizens.

Some critics of the IMF question whether its strategy of imposing austerity measures on these countries is wise. What is really needed, they argue, is acceptance of the fact that billions of dollars in bank loans that were made in the heady days of high economic growth will probably never be collected.

What impact will all this have on Canada? Each year, Canada exports billions of dollars in raw materials such as lumber and coal to Asia. But as those economies go into recession, demand for our raw materials declines. Hence, Canadian companies (who are also very export-oriented), will experience problems selling their products. And we are not alone. Fallout from the Asian crisis has affected family farms in New Zealand, fishers in Alaska, and petrochemical companies in Europe.

Australia, which has focused on exporting to Asia, has been particularly hard hit. Demand for Australian beef fell from 3800 metric tonnes in January 1997 to just 12 tonnes in January 1998. Asian orders for live Australian cattle fell from 31 000 head in January 1997 to zero one year later. That beef, which would have been sent outside Australia, now must be sold within the country, and the increase in supply has depressed beef prices in Australia.

It's a complicated world!

International Monetary Fund
www.imf.org

Japan, led by companies like Toyota, Toshiba, and Nippon Steel, dominates the region. In addition, South Korea (with such firms as Samsung and Hyundai), Taiwan (owner of Chinese Petroleum and manufacturing home of many foreign firms), and Hong Kong (a major financial centre) are also successful players in the international economy. China, the most densely populated country in the world, continues to emerge as an important market in its own right. In fact, the International Monetary Fund concluded in 1993 that the Chinese economy is now the world's third largest, behind the U.S. and only slightly behind Japan.[3] More than 120 Canadian firms have set up offices in China and tried to cash in on its rapid growth. But most of them have found the going quite difficult. A 1996 survey of 20 Canadian firms that had invested in China showed that less than half of them were profitable.[4]

Forms of Competitive Advantage

No country can produce all the goods and services that its people need. Thus countries tend to export those things that they can produce better or less expensively than other countries. The proceeds are then used to import things that they cannot produce effectively. However, this very general principle does not fully explain why nations export and import what they do. Such decisions hinge, among other things, on whether a country enjoys an absolute or a comparative advantage in the production of different goods and services.[5]

absolute advantage
A nation's ability to produce something more cheaply or better than any other country.

An **absolute advantage** exists when a country can produce something more cheaply than any other country. Saudi oil and Canadian timber approximate absolute advantage, but examples of true absolute advantage are rare. In reality, "absolute" advantages are always relative. Brazil, for instance, produces about one-third of the world's coffee. However, because its high-quality coffees are preferred by Canadians and Americans, the impact of Brazil's production is widely felt. Consider what happened when a severe frost in the winter of 1994 destroyed nearly half of the 1995–96 harvest. First, commodities prices—prices paid by producers, roasters, and speculators—jumped to their highest levels in 10 years. Then, the three largest coffee producers—Procter & Gamble, Kraft, and Nestlé—raised retail prices by 45 percent. With the threat to worldwide supplies, prices for lower-quality African coffees also went up. Forecasters predict that the prices paid by consumers will continue to reflect the damage to the 1995–96 Brazilian crop.[6]

comparative advantage
A nation's ability to produce some products more cheaply or better than it can others.

A country has a **comparative advantage** in goods that it can make more cheaply or better than other goods. For example, if businesses in a country can make computers more cheaply than automobiles, then computers represent a comparative advantage for its firms. The United States has a comparative advantage in the computer industry because of technological sophistication. Canada has a comparative advantage in farming because of fertile land. South Korea has a comparative advantage in electronics manufacturing because of efficient operations and cheap labour.

international competitiveness
The ability of a country to generate more wealth than its competitors.

International competitiveness refers to the ability of a country to generate more wealth than its competitors in world markets. Each year a *global competitiveness index* is published by the Swiss Institute for Management Development, which ranks the international competitiveness of a large number of countries. Canada ranked tenth in the 1998 survey; the U.S. was first, followed by Singapore and Hong Kong. Japan dropped from ninth to eighteenth.[7] A similar survey, produced by the World Economic Forum, ranks Canada fifth in the world.[8]

The Balance of Trade and the Balance of Payments

balance of trade
The difference in value between a country's total exports and its total imports.

A country's **balance of trade** is the difference in value between its total exports and its total imports. A country that exports more than it imports has a *favourable* balance of trade, or a surplus. A country that imports more than it exports has an *unfavourable* balance of trade, or a deficit.

Canada has enjoyed a favourable balance of merchandise trade since 1975. However, the trade balance is favourable only because Canada exports so much more to the U.S. than it imports from the U.S. Canada's trade balance with its other major trading partners (e.g., Japan, the U.K., and other European countries) is unfavourable. Our trade balance with all remaining countries of the world taken together as a group is also unfavourable (see Table 4.1).

A study by the World Trade Organization (WTO) found that Canada's economic dependence on the U.S. is growing, and this trend leaves Canada vulnerable. The U.S. accounts for 80 percent of Canada's merchandise exports and two-thirds of its imports. What's worse, only 50 companies operating in Canada account for nearly half of all merchandise exports, and these companies are often U.S. owned. Canada has too many of its eggs in one basket.[9]

Even if a country has a favourable balance of trade, it can still have an unfavourable balance of payments. A country's **balance of payments** is the difference between money flowing into the country and money flowing out of the country as a result of trade and other transactions. An unfavourable balance means more money is flowing out than in. For Canada to have a favourable balance of payments for a given year, the total of our exports, foreign tourist spending in this country, foreign investments here, and earnings from overseas investments must be greater than the total of our imports, Canadian tourist spending overseas, our foreign aid grants, our military spending abroad, the investments made by Canadian firms abroad, and the earnings of foreigners from their investments in Canada (see Figure 4.1). Canada has had an unfavourable balance of payments for about the last 20 years.

The Rate of Exchange

The **foreign exchange rate** is the ratio of one currency to another; it tells how much a unit of one currency is worth in terms of a unit of another currency. Canada's exchange rate has a significant effect on imports and exports. If the exchange rate decreases (that is, the value of the Canadian dollar falls in relation to other currencies), two things happen: our exports become less expensive to other countries, so they will want to buy more of what we produce; and prices of the goods other countries export to Canada will become more expensive, so we will buy less of them. If the exchange rate increases (that is, the value of the Canadian dollar increases), two things also happen: our exports become more expensive to other countries, so they will want to buy less of what we produce; and prices of the goods other countries export to Canada will become less expensive, so we will buy more of them.

World Trade Organization
www.wto.org

balance of payments
The difference between money flowing into and out of a country as a result of trade and other transactions.

foreign exchange rate
The ratio of one currency to another.

■ **TABLE 4.1   Canadian Exports to, and Imports from, Selected Countries, 1995**

Country	Exports to (billions)	Imports from (billions)
United States	$142.4	$113.6
Japan	8.4	10.7
United Kingdom	2.8	4.4
Germany	2.4	3.5
South Korea	1.7	2.2
France	1.2	2.3
Taiwan	1.0	2.6
Mexico	0.8	3.6
Hong Kong	0.6	1.1

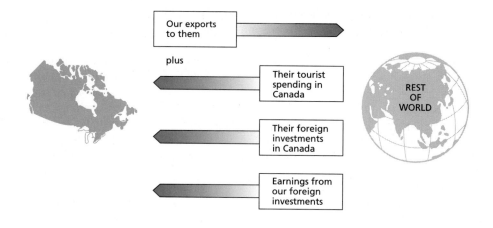

Total of above flows must be greater than

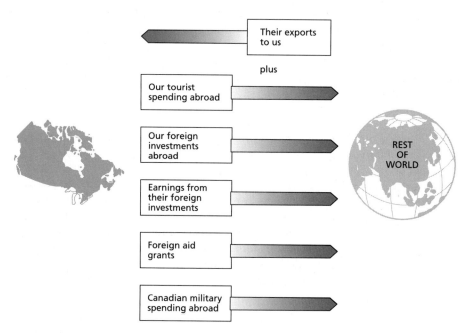

FIGURE 4.1

Requirements for Canada to have a favourable balance of payments. (The arrows indicate the direction of the flow.)

During the last 20 years, the value of the Canadian dollar has fluctuated a great deal in relation to the currencies of other countries, including the U.S. Since the U.S. is our biggest trading partner, the fluctuations of our currency compared to the U.S. dollar have a big impact on our economy. During the mid-1970s, the Canadian dollar was worth slightly more than the U.S. dollar. By the late 1970s, however, it started on a steady downward path that eventually led to a value of only $0.69 U.S. By 1990, it had risen substantially, and was worth about $0.89 U.S. More recently, it has declined again to $0.65.

The fluctuations in the Canadian dollar are small compared to fluctuations that other countries have experienced (see the box "A Tale of Three Currencies"). In 1997 alone, the value of the Malaysian *ringgit*, the Philippine *peso*, and the Thai *baht* dropped sharply as concerns were expressed about the sustainability of those countries' economies.

TRENDS & CHALLENGES

A Tale of Three Currencies

Canadians pay a lot of attention to the fluctuations of the Canadian dollar against the U.S. dollar. But these fluctuations are minor compared to the changes in value that have occurred in the Czech *koruna*, the Russian *ruble*, and the Mexican *peso*.

The Czech Republic. Until recently, the Czech Republic has been a favoured place for investment in the eyes of Westerners. But in 1997, its image became tarnished because of poor economic performance and political wrangling. Economic growth fell far short of forecasts, and the country ran a large trade deficit with some of its trading partners. Industrial production also dropped. Scandals in Czech financial markets, bank failures, and looted investment funds have all worked together to cause a sharp decline in the value of the Czech koruna.

At the beginning of 1997, each koruna was worth about 3.75 cents U.S. Faced with heavy pressure from currency speculators, the Czech central bank gave up supporting the koruna. When the bank made this decision, the koruna had already declined to about 3.25 cents; in the next month it declined even further to 3.0 cents. The total loss in 1997 alone was nearly 25 percent of the value of the currency. The drop in the value of the koruna led to a run on banks and currency exchanges, as the people of the Czech Republic tried to get their hands on more stable Western currencies.

Russia. During the many years of the communist regime, the value of the ruble was artificially controlled by the government. Although the ruble was used by Russians in everyday business activities, no one outside Russia wanted rubles because the currency was seen as worthless. Since the fall of communism, the weaknesses in the Russian currency have come to light. In 1992, the ruble was trading at about 1000 to a U.S. dollar. By the end of 1994, it had declined to about 3000 to a U.S. dollar. Then the real decline started. In just one day, the value of the ruble fell 27 percent, going from 3081 to 3926 to the U.S. dollar. In six weeks, the ruble lost 78 percent of its value.

These changes have had a big impact on Russian consumers. In the time it took one shopper to pick out a telephone and take it to the checkout, its price had increased from 75 000 to 100 000 rubles. On Moscow's subway, a ride that cost five one-hundredths of a ruble for the last 40 years has now increased to 250 rubles.

To put all this in perspective, a McDonald's hamburger now costs about 4900 rubles, up from 3 rubles when the first McDonald's restaurant opened in 1990. That is the equivalent of a hamburger in Canada increasing from $2.00 in 1990 to well over $2000 in 1994.

Mexico. In early 1994, it took about 3.1 pesos to purchase a U.S. dollar. During the first 11 months of 1994, the peso gradually declined in value to about 3.7 to the dollar. The decline was caused by a variety of things, including excessive borrowing by Mexico in foreign markets, increasing interest rates, and a rebel uprising in a southern province.

By December 1994, speculative pressure on the peso had become so great that the Mexican government reversed its long-standing policy of supporting the peso. The value of the peso immediately dropped about 13 percent in relation to the U.S. dollar. In 1995, the value declined even further; it now took 7.7 pesos to buy one U.S. dollar. At this point, the value of the peso had declined by more than 50 percent in just one year. This would be the equivalent of the Canadian dollar dropping from $0.72 U.S. to $0.36 U.S.

■ INTERNATIONAL BUSINESS MANAGEMENT

Wherever it is located, the success of any firm depends largely on how well it is managed. International business is so challenging because the basic management responsibilities—planning, organizing, directing, and controlling—are much more difficult to carry out when a business operates in several markets scattered around the globe.

It is not surprising, then, that business abounds with legends about managers who made foolish decisions because they failed to familiarize themselves with the foreign markets in which they hoped to do business. Estée Lauder, for example, launched an Italian cosmetics line with a picture of a model holding some flowers. The approach was conventional—and seemingly harmless. Unfortunately, the flowers chosen were the kind traditionally used at Italian funerals—hardly the image that Lauder intended to communicate.

Planning difficulties are compounded by difficulties in organizing, directing, and controlling. An organizational structure that works well in one country may fail in others. Management techniques that lead to high worker productivity in Canada may offend workers in Japan or the United Kingdom. Accounting and other control systems that are well-developed in Canada, may be unsophisticated or even nonexistent in developing nations. The internationalization of business also has an impact on individual managers, as the box "The Pleasures and Perils of International Business" shows.

"Going International"

The world economy is becoming globalized, and more and more firms are conducting international operations. This route, however, is not appropriate for every company. For example, companies that buy and sell fresh produce and fish may find it most profitable to confine their activities to a limited geographic area because storage and transport costs may be too high to make international operations worthwhile.

As Figure 4.2 shows, several factors enter into the decision to go international. One overriding factor is the business climate of other nations. Even experienced firms have

TRENDS & CHALLENGES

The Pleasures and Perils of International Business

John Aliberti is a middle manager at Union Switch & Signal in Pittsburgh, Pennsylvania. He handles the nuts and bolts of updating computerized rail systems for American cities. Aliberti was born and raised in Pittsburgh and studied computer science at the University of Pennsylvania. After university, he was hired by Union Switch and moved steadily up the ranks. But he didn't feel his job was particularly exciting.

In 1992, Union Switch needed someone to go to China to drum up business. Aliberti volunteered because he had technical expertise in the area required by the Chinese. By his second trip to China, he was hooked on his new work. In 1996, he made 10 trips to China, where he is treated with respect bordering on awe. He loves this part of his new job.

When in Beijing, Aliberti stays at the plush Shangri-La Hotel. The clerks on the executive floor know him well, since he spent nearly six months there in 1996. On this day, he is flying to Shanghai to negotiate a contract his company has won for the city's new subway system. On the way, he reminisces about a previous trip to Nanchang, where Union was building a rail yard. When he arrived, the Chinese welcomed him with a large banner at the factory gate that said "Welcome, Foreign Expert John Aliberti." Once in Shanghai,

Aliberti is picked up by a chauffeur-driven limousine and taken to a meeting with Chinese railway officials. When he enters the room, they rise respectfully. They say they have been waiting two days for him because they can't go ahead without him. After the negotiations are successfully concluded, the Chinese put on a 10-course banquet for him.

Aliberti has tremendous status and power in China. In Pittsburgh, his job is two rungs below the vice president, but in China he acts like a president. That turns him on. So does the knowledge that the rail systems his company is installing will dramatically improve the standard of living of the Chinese people. He feels that the same changes would hardly be noticed in Pittsburgh because the facilities are already so good there.

As more and more companies get involved in international business, managers like John Aliberti have tremendous opportunities for advancement in their companies. But opportunities are only part of the equation. As Aliberti's star rises at work, his ties to his family are becoming strained. His wife Cindy hates his trips to China because he is often gone at key family times like his daughter's birthday and Thanksgiving. Aliberti agrees, but he is drawn by the ground-breaking work he is doing in China. He sees himself as a pioneer, and that is exciting.

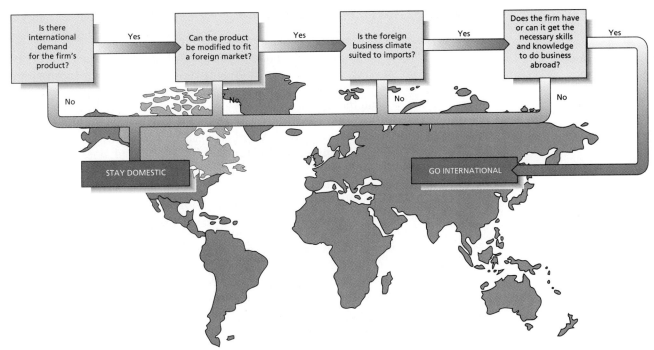

FIGURE 4.2
The decision to go international.

encountered cultural, legal, and economic roadblocks. (These problems are discussed in more detail later in this chapter.) In considering international expansion, a company should also consider at least two other questions: Is there a demand for its products abroad? If so, must those products be adapted for international consumption?

Gauging International Demand. Products that are seen as vital in one country may be useless in another. Snowmobiles, for example, are not only popular for transportation and recreation in Canada and the northern United States, but actually revolutionized reindeer herding in Lapland. But there would be no demand at all for this product in Central America. Although this is an extreme example, the point is quite basic to the decision to go international: namely, that foreign demand for a company's product may be greater than, the same as, or weaker than domestic demand.

Adapting to Customer Needs. If there is international demand for its product, a firm must consider whether and how to adapt that product to meet the special demands of foreign customers. For example, in Mexico, GM has raised the price of its Spanish-made Joy automobile because it has found that in a country where 60 percent of the population is under 25, there is a huge market of younger buyers who will pay for stylish, more powerful vehicles. In the Czech Republic, however, GM markets the same car—known as the Opel Corsa—to potential buyers in their 30s. Here, says GM's director of sales for Central Europe, "younger buyers can't even afford bicycles."[10]

■ LEVELS OF INVOLVEMENT IN INTERNATIONAL BUSINESS

Canadian business firms are involved in international business at many different levels, including importing and exporting goods and services, licensing agreements, establishing foreign subsidiaries, product mandating, strategic alliances, and as multinational firms. Each approach is discussed briefly in the following sections.

MacMillan Bloedel
www.mbpi.com

Exporting Goods and Services

Canadian business firms sell goods and services to many other countries. McCain Foods Ltd., for example, has become a formidable presence in Europe. It holds 75 percent of the "oven fries" market in Germany, and dominates the frozen french fry market in France and England.[11] MacMillan-Bloedel and Abitibi-Price sell newsprint and other forest products around the world. Small firms also export products and services. Seagull Pewter & Silversmiths Ltd., Magic Pantry Foods, and Lovat Tunnel Equipment Inc. have all recently won Canada Export Awards. Sabian Cymbals sells 90 percent of its products to 80 different countries outside Canada. Electrovert Ltd. does 95 percent of its business outside Canada. Other companies that export a large portion of their products include Canpotex Ltd. (100 percent), Canadian Wheat Board (89), Chrysler Canada (85), Pratt & Whitney Canada (84), Quno Corp. (82), Canfor Corp. (81), and Slocan Forest Products (74).[12] These companies have little in common with firms that concentrate on the Canadian market and then unload what is left somewhere else.[13]

Exporting increases sales volume and generates a flow of funds that can lead to profits. Exporting also reduces the unit cost of production because of the increased volume, allows for greater use of plant capacity, lessens the dependence on a single traditional market, offers some protection against a downturn in Canadian sales, and provides an opportunity to gain a knowledge of and experience with other products and potential markets. But there are also disadvantages to exporting, such as the expense required to develop export markets, the modifications to products necessary to meet government regulations, the acquisition of further financing, and the obligation to learn about the customs, culture, language, local standards, and government regulations of the new customers.

Improvements can be made in Canada's export record. Canada sells only 9 percent of its exports to developing countries. We export eight times as much to the U.S. alone as we do to *all* developing countries combined. In every developing area of the world, Canada ranks last among the G7 countries in exports.[14] Table 4.2 lists the top 10 importing and exporting countries of the world.

Importing Goods and Services

While many enterprises sell Canadian goods and services abroad, others are involved in buying goods and services in foreign countries for resale to Canadians. For example, Gendis Inc., a large Winnipeg-based corporation, distributes Sony electronic products throughout Canada. Locally, most large shopping malls have a retail outlet selling wicker goods, brass objects, carpeting, and similar products imported from India and various Far Eastern countries. Canadian importing businesses employ buyers who travel around the world seeking out goods that can be sold here. Foreign suppliers might have salespeople or representatives based in Canada to market these products.

Licensing Agreements

licensing agreement
An agreement by an owner of a process or product to allow another business to produce, distribute, or market it for a fee or royalty.

Licensing agreements exist when the owner of a product or process allows another business to produce, distribute, or market the product or process for a fee or royalty. Such agreements can mean a Canadian enterprise licenses another enterprise in a foreign country to produce, distribute, or market its products in that area. Or the agreement could work the other way, and foreign enterprises allow Canadian firms to produce, distribute, and market their products in Canada. For example, Can-Eng Manufacturing, Canada's largest supplier of industrial furnaces, exports its furnaces under licensing agreements with Japan, Brazil, Germany, Korea, Taiwan, and Mexico.[15]

Licensing agreements are used when a company does not wish to establish a plant or marketing network in another country. They avoid the need to manage operations in foreign countries, and allow the owner of the product or process to concentrate on further technological research and development, financed, in part, from the royalties received.

■ **TABLE 4.2   The Top 10 Importing and Exporting Countries, 1995**

	Exporting					Importing		
Rank	Country	$ Value (billions)	Share of World's Exports		Rank	Country	$ Value (billions)	Share of World's Imports
1	United States	584	11.7		1	United States	771	15.6
2	Germany	511	10.2		2	Germany	448	9.1
3	Japan	443	8.8		3	Japan	335	6.8
4	France	286	5.7		4	France	275	5.6
5	Britain	242	4.8		5	Britain	265	5.4
6	Italy	231	4.6		6	Italy	204	4.1
7	Netherlands	195	3.9		7	Hong Kong	192	3.9
8	**Canada**	**192**	**3.8**		8	Netherlands	176	3.6
9	Hong Kong	173	3.5		9	**Canada**	**168**	**3.4**
10	China	148	3.0		10	China	129	2.6
	All Others	2004	40.0			All Others	1966	39.9
	Total	5009	100.0			Total	4929	100.0

Establishing Subsidiaries

If the volume of business to be conducted is large and ongoing, Canadian enterprises may choose to establish subsidiary or branch operations in foreign countries through which they can market goods and services. Other reasons for establishing a subsidiary are that a foreign government requires it or it may increase sales because locally operated branches can respond more quickly to delivery and service requests. Sometimes branches are established by forming an operation where none previously existed. Another approach is to buy a business in the foreign country. Of course, this process works both ways, with foreign enterprises doing the same in Canada. The establishment of subsidiaries can lead to the sensitive issue of foreign ownership and the analysis of its benefits and drawbacks.

Product Mandating.   When a business operates branches, plants, or subsidiaries in several countries, it may assign to one plant or subsidiary the responsibility for researching, developing, manufacturing, and marketing one product or line of products. This approach allows the business to achieve optimum levels of efficiency because economies of scale are possible through specialization. The assignment of a product responsibility to a particular branch is known as **world product mandating**.

At Nortel, for example, the company's Belleville, Ontario, plant was chosen as the one to produce a new business telephone system designed for the world market. The plant won out in a competition with two other Nortel plants, one in Calgary and one in Santa Clara, California. The Belleville plant also has global mandates for several other product lines.

About 100 Canadian-based subsidiaries are now involved in some form of world product mandates. Some examples are:

- Pratt & Whitney Canada produces small gas turbine engines.

- Black and Decker Canada makes orbital sanders, the "Workmate" work bench, the "Workwheel" power stripper, and the "Workhorse" scaffold.

- Westinghouse Canada produces steam and gas turbines, airport lighting, and digital-video converters and displays.

world product mandating
The assignment by a multinational of a product responsibility to a particular branch.

Nortel
www.nortel.com

General Mills joined with Nestlé in 1989 to dramatically expand its international cereal business. Cereal Partners Worldwide (CPW) now features more than 40 distinctive cereal brands, including such familiar General Mills cereals as Honey Nut Cheerios and such Nestlé brands as Chocopic. With sales in more than 60 countries, CPW has quickly become the second largest cereal company outside North America.

Northern Telecom's manufacturing plant in Mexico. Note the Canadian, Mexican and U.S. flags on the back wall of the plant.

Strategic Alliances

strategic alliances
Two or more enterprises that cooperate in researching, developing, manufacturing, or marketing a product.

Strategic alliances involve two or more enterprises cooperating in researching, developing, manufacturing, or marketing a product. The relationship is more subtle than the usual supplier-customer relations, yet less formal than ownership. These relationships, which have become more popular in the last decade, take many forms and are also called cooperative strategies, joint ventures, strategic networks, and strategic partners. There are various reasons for entering into a strategic alliance, such as gaining access to new markets or customers, acquiring advanced or new technology, sharing the costs and risks of new ventures, obtaining financing to supplement a firm's debt capacity, and sharing production facilities to avoid wasteful duplication. Nortel, for example, has strategic alliances with several firms, including Daewoo (Korea), Tong Guang (China), and Ascom Hasler (Switzerland).

Multinational Firms

Multinational firms do not ordinarily think of themselves as having specific domestic and international divisions. Rather, planning and decision making are geared to international markets. Headquarters locations are almost irrelevant. Nortel, Royal Dutch Shell, Nestlé, IBM, and Ford are well-known multinational firms.

> **multinational firm**
> Controls assets, factories, mines, sales offices, and affiliates in two or more foreign countries.

The British firm Imperial Chemical Industries is one of the 50 largest industrial firms in the world, with nine major business units, four of which are headquartered outside of Britain. Until 1982, all 16 of its directors were British; today, the board includes two Americans, a Canadian, a Japanese, and a German. ICI has major operations in 25 different countries, and rather than managing businesses that are located and active within given countries, ICI managers are now in charge of business units that compete around the world.[16]

Fewer than 5000 of Nestlé Food Corp.'s 200 000-plus employees are stationed in its home country of Switzerland. The giant food-products company has manufacturing facilities in 50 countries and owns suppliers and distributors around the globe. Nestlé markets products worldwide by taking advantage of all possible levels of international involvement. In 1991, for instance, Nestlé entered a strategic alliance with the U.S. food-products company General Mills to create a new company called Cereal Partners Worldwide. General Mills initiated the joint venture with a European partner in an effort to cut into Kellogg's commanding lead in ready-to-eat cereals. For its part, Nestlé sees the venture as an opportunity to affirm its leadership in the $550 billion European food industry.

■ BARRIERS TO TRADE

Whether a business is selling to just a few foreign markets or is a true multinational, a number of differences between countries will affect its international operations. How a firm responds to and manages social, economic, and political issues will go a long way towards determining its success.

Social and Cultural Differences

Any firm involved in international business needs to understand something about the society and culture of the countries in which it plans to operate. Unless a firm understands these cultural differences—either itself or by acquiring a partner that does—it will probably not be successful in its international business activities.

Some differences are relatively obvious. Language barriers can cause inappropriate naming of products. In addition, the physical stature of people in different countries can make a difference. For example, the Japanese and French are slimmer and shorter on average than Canadians, an important consideration for firms that intend to sell clothes in these markets.

Differences in the average ages of the local population can also have ramifications for product development and marketing. Countries with growing populations tend to have a high percentage of young people. Thus, electronics and fashionable clothing would likely do well. Countries with stable or declining populations tend to have more old people. Generic pharmaceuticals might be more successful in such markets.

In addition to such obvious differences, a wide range of subtle value differences can have an important impact on international business. For example, many Europeans shop daily. To Canadians used to weekly trips to the supermarket, the European pattern may seem like a waste of time. But for Europeans, shopping is not just "buying food." It is also meeting friends, exchanging political views, gossiping, and socializing. The box "Faux Pas in Foreign Lands" describes how North Americans can make embarrassing mistakes in both business and politics when they are in a foreign country.

TRENDS & CHALLENGES

Faux Pas in Foreign Lands

Politicians and business executives in both Canada and the U.S. frequently find it necessary to go to a foreign country to transact business. On occasion, these people fail to "do their homework" and do not learn enough about the country to which they are travelling. Then they do something that creates embarrassment.

When U.S. president Bill Clinton travelled to Russia in 1994, his trip was generally a hit with the media and the folks back home. But at the end of one town-hall style meeting, a beaming Clinton gave the audience the North American high-sign, a circle made with the thumb and forefinger. Oops! That gesture would likely have started a brawl in a Moscow pub, because in Russia it is the equivalent of our middle finger salute. Former U.S. president George Bush had the same problem when he visited Australia a few years earlier. There, he gave a "thumbs-up" sign, which unfortunately is the Australian equivalent of the same middle finger salute.

These gaffes are not limited to visiting politicians. Business executives also have to be aware of local etiquette and how this impacts business negotiations. Consider these examples:

- Crossing your legs in a business meeting in Saudi Arabia is considered an insult, because when you do that you are showing the sole of your foot; this is an insult to the other people in the room.

- In Portugal, it is considered rude to discuss business during dinner.

- In Taiwan, tapping your fingers on the table is a sign of appreciation for a meal.

Because the difference between proper and improper behaviour can be so subtle, some companies hire local individuals to make sure that negotiations go smoothly. One such company is Dominion Bridge, which successfully concluded a deal to supply a subway/light rail system, a hydroelectric power station, and a cement plant in Chengdu, China. Interestingly, the man that Dominion hired also was working for the city of Chengdu. This would be considered a blatant conflict of interest in Canada, but not in China.

Business negotiation in China is a finely tuned waltz of etiquette and politics, and if everything doesn't go just right, the deal will fall flat. It is therefore important to have someone orchestrating all of the activities leading up to the signing of the deal. The president of Dominion Bridge says that it would take 100 years for a Canadian to develop the subtle understanding of the Chinese culture that their Chinese business agent has.

What implications does this kind of shopping have for firms selling in European markets? First, those who go shopping each day do not need the large refrigerators and freezers common in North America. Second, the large supermarkets one sees in Canada are not an appropriate retail outlet in Europe. Finally, the kinds of food Europeans buy differ from those Canadians buy. While in Canada prepared and frozen foods are important, Europeans often prefer to buy fresh ingredients to do their own food preparation "from scratch." These differences are gradually disappearing, however, so firms need to be on the lookout for future opportunities as they emerge. The box "The Cavalier Attitude Towards Murky Tea" gives examples of companies that had problems in foreign markets.

Economic Differences

Although cultural differences are often subtle, economic differences can be fairly pronounced. In dealing with economies like those of France and Sweden, for example, firms must be aware of when—and to what extent—the government is involved in a given

TRENDS CHALLENGES

The Cavalier Attitude Towards Murky Tea

Quaker Oats and General Motors share a common set of woes. Recently, both companies introduced home-grown American products into the Japanese market, and both encountered cultural and business turbulence that turned the trip abroad into an unpleasantly bumpy ride.

For Quaker Oats, the global marketing debacle involved its Snapple Beverage division, which manufactures fruit and iced-tea flavoured beverages. (As a result of marketing and distribution features at home and abroad, Quaker sold Snapple in 1997—for $1.4 billion less than it had paid for it three years earlier.) Although Snapple's arrival in Japan was heralded by ads declaring that "The Snapple Phenomenon Has Landed," Japanese consumers disliked Snapple's sweet fruit juice flavourings and the trade mark bits of fruit and granules of tea that Snapple likes to leave in its bottles. "The iced tea," volunteered at least one Japanese taster, "was murky looking."

Quaker's miscalculation of Japanese tastes, coupled with its refusal to adapt Snapple's formula and a poorly conceived marketing program, resulted in a dramatic drop in sales from 2.4 million bottles a month just after introduction in 1995 to a mere 120 000 bottles a month in 1996. Quaker decided to cut its losses in 1996 and stopped shipping Snapple to Japan. "Japan," eulogized the *Wall Street Journal*, "has given Snapple the raspberry."

General Motors also had high hopes when the Chevrolet Cavalier hit Japanese showrooms early in 1996—all decked out with a Toyota nameplate. The Cavalier was the first American car that Toyota had agreed to market on Japanese soil, and it was heralded by both companies as a model of U.S.–Japanese cooperation. The initial reaction of Japanese consumers was good, as it had been for Snapple. Within three months, sales reached the monthly goal of 1667 vehicles. By May, however, sales had dropped to just 472 cars a month.

What went wrong? Problems began popping up when GM was forced to make 150 changes to meet the requirements of the Japanese market. Some changes—such as moving the gas pedal forward—were needed because Japanese drivers are shorter than Americans. Other changes—such as placing the steering column on the right—were obviously more fundamental. Still others—such as covering the steering wheel and handbreak with leather—were merely attempts to satisfy finicky buyers. Whatever the reasons, costly redesigns left GM frustrated and complaining that unnecessary expenses were making competition inside Japan all but impossible. Meanwhile, Toyota regarded GM's stance as mere resistance to change.

Toyota also found the Cavalier to be plagued by an alarmingly high defect rate. According to some reports, as many as nine out of ten cars needed at least one repair before being accepted for sale in Japan. "Their vehicle defect rate is about 50 times that of Japanese vehicles," explained Naoki Yamaguchi, president of a regional Japanese dealer network. "If they would just put a little more effort into production control...." GM denies the severity of Cavalier's quality problem and points instead to what it says is a well-known Japanese strategy, namely, keeping foreign goods out of the home market by finding excessive fault with them.

Clearly, both Quaker Oats and General Motors learned the hard way that marketing American goods in Japan is far from easy. Although both companies undoubtedly expected cultural and business problems, neither was prepared for what it got. Unfortunately, in the opinion of some analysts, both marketing ventures may have been doomed from the start.

industry. The French government, for example, is heavily involved in all aspects of airplane design and manufacturing.

Similarly, a foreign firm doing business in a command economy must understand the unfamiliar relationship of government to business, including a host of idiosyncratic practices. General Motors, which entered a $100 million joint venture to build pickup trucks in China, found itself faced with an economic system that favoured state-owned companies over foreign investors. So, while its Chinese suppliers passed on inflation-based price increases for steel and energy, GM could not in turn pass increases on to Chinese consumers. With subsidized state-owned automakers charging considerably less per truck, GM had no choice but to hold its own prices—and lose money on each sale.

Legal and Political Differences

Closely linked to the structure of the economic systems in different countries are the legal and political issues that confront businesses as they try to expand internationally. These issues include tariffs and quotas, local-content laws, and business-practice laws. An awareness of differences in these areas can be crucial to a business's success.

Quotas, Tariffs, and Subsidies.   Even free-market economies often use some form of quota and/or tariff that affects the prices and quantities of foreign-made products in those nations. A **quota** restricts the total number of certain products that can be imported into a country. It indirectly raises the prices of those imports by reducing their supply.

The ultimate form of quota is an **embargo**: a government order forbidding exportation and/or importation of a particular product—or even all the products—of a particular country. For example, many countries control bacteria and disease by banning certain plants and agricultural products.

In contrast, a **tariff** is a tax charged on imported products. Tariffs directly affect the prices of products, effectively raising the price of imports to consumers who must pay not only for the products but also for the tariff. Tariffs may take either of two forms. A **revenue tariff** is imposed strictly to raise money for the government. But most tariffs in effect today are **protectionist tariffs** meant to discourage the import of a particular product.

Governments impose quotas and tariffs for a wide variety of reasons. For example, the U.S. government restricts the number of Japanese automobiles that can be imported into that country. Italy imposes high tariffs on imported electronic goods. Consequently, Sony Walkmans cost almost $150, and CD players are prohibitively expensive. Canada also imposes tariffs on many imported goods.

The duties that Canadians must pay to Canada Customs after shopping in the U.S. yield revenue for the federal government and may also deter Canadians from buying some goods in the U.S. But if prices are low enough in the U.S., consumers will shop there. In the late 1980s, price differentials became so great that cross-border shopping increased dramatically. Canadian retailers lowered prices in response. When Cineplex Odeon reduced general admission prices, attendance went up substantially. And Bata Shoes announced in 1991 that it would match any U.S. price on a comparable brand.[17]

A **subsidy** is a government payment to help a domestic business compete with foreign firms. Many European governments subsidize farmers to help them compete with U.S. grain imports. The U.S. argues that the Canadian government is actually subsidizing Canadian lumber companies by charging them unusually low fees to cut timber in certain areas.

Protectionism—the practice of protecting domestic business at the expense of free market competition—has both advocates and critics. Supporters argue that tariffs and quotas protect domestic firms and jobs. In particular, they protect new industries until they are truly able to compete internationally. Some claim that, since other nations have such measures, so must we. Still others justify protectionism in the name of national security. They argue that a nation must be able to produce goods needed for its survival in the event of war and that advanced technology should not be sold to potential enemies.

But opponents of protectionism are equally vocal. They note that protectionism reduces competition and drives up prices to consumers. They cite it as a cause of friction between nations. They maintain that, while jobs in some industries would be lost if protectionism ceased, jobs in other industries would expand if all countries abolished tariffs and quotas.

Local-Content Laws.   A country can affect how a foreign firm does business there by enacting local-content laws. **Local-content laws** require that products sold in a particular country be at least partly made in that country. These laws typically mean that firms seeking to do business in a country must either invest directly in that country or have a joint-venture partner from that country. In this way, some of the profits from doing business in a foreign country are shared with the people who live there.

---

quota
A restriction by one nation on the total number of products of a certain type that can be imported from another nation.

embargo
A government order forbidding exportation and/or importation of a particular product.

tariff
A tax levied on imported products.

revenue tariff
A tariff imposed solely to raise money for the government that imposes it.

protectionist tariff
A tariff imposed at least in part to discourage imports of a particular product.

subsidy
A government payment to help domestic business compete with foreign firms.

protectionism
Protecting domestic business at the expense of free market competition.

Canada Customs and Revenue Agency
www.rc.gc.ca

local-content laws
Laws requiring that products sold in a particular country be at least partly made in that country.

Many countries have local-content laws. In a fairly extreme case, Venezuela forbids the import of any product if a like product is made in Venezuela. Even when an item is not made in Venezuela, many companies choose to begin making their product in Venezuela both to drive out competitors and to prevent being forced out by local firms.

Local-content laws may even exist within a country; when they do, they act just like trade barriers. In Canada, for example, a low bid on a bridge in British Columbia was rejected because the company that made the bid was from Alberta. The job was given to a B.C. company. A New Brunswick window manufacturer lost a contract in Nova Scotia despite having made the lowest bid, and the job went to a Nova Scotia company.

The federal government of Canada is committed to removing such barriers. The 1994 Agreement on Internal Trade required all 10 provinces to remove barriers to agricultural trade by September 1997. But Quebec—which has a strong dairy lobby—still prohibits margarine that is coloured to look like butter. The province is therefore in violation of the agreement.[18]

Business-Practice Laws.   A final influence on how a company does business abroad stems from laws both abroad and in the firm's home nation. Sometimes, what is legal—and even accepted—business practice in one country is illegal in another. For example, in some countries it is perfectly legal to obtain business by paying bribes to government officials.

Transparency International, an organization devoted to stamping out global corruption, says that widespread bribery is devastating to developing countries. And the International Monetary Fund refused to lend money to Kenya until the government cleaned up its act.[19] In an attempt to create fairer competition among multinational companies, ministers from 29 member countries of the Organization for Economic Cooperation and Development (OECD) agreed in 1997 to criminalize bribery of foreign public officials.[20]

The formation of **cartels**—an association of producers whose purpose is to control supply and prices—gave the oil-producing countries belonging to the Organization of Petroleum Exporting Countries (OPEC) a great deal of power in the 1970s and 1980s. In 1994, the major aluminum producing countries, including Canada, worked out a deal to curb world production in an attempt to raise prices.[21] And in 1997, the 14-nation Association of Coffee Producing Countries (ACPC) agreed to extend their cartel-style export quotas to ensure that prices stayed up.[22] The diamond and shipping cartels have also been successful in keeping the prices they charge artificially high.[23]

Organization for Economic Cooperation and Development
www.oecd.org

cartel
Any association of producers whose purpose is to control supply of and prices for a given product.

A Quebec customs official seizing illegal butter-coloured margarine. The dairy industry in Quebec has been successful in maintaining the legislation that makes it illegal to make margarine the same colour as butter.

In 1998, the 29 members of the OECD agreed to toughen legislation designed to break up cartels. They also agreed to share information more extensively among themselves so they can more effectively prosecute cartels. The U.S. and Canada already coordinate their activity, and cartels in various industries—citric acid, marine transportation, explosives, and lysine—have been fined.[24]

dumping
Selling a product for less abroad than in the producing nation; illegal in Canada.

Many countries forbid **dumping**—selling a product abroad for less than the comparable price charged at home. In 1997, the Canadian International Trade Tribunal renewed anti-dumping duties on bicycle imports from Taiwan and China. Canadian manufacturers argued that the Canadian industry was being damaged by cheap foreign bicycles, and that China and Taiwan would continue to "dump" bicycles on the Canadian market if the duties were not continued.[25]

■ OVERCOMING BARRIERS TO TRADE

Despite the barriers described so far, world trade is flourishing. A number of world organizations and treaties have as their primary reason for being the promotion of international business.

Trade Agreements

General Agreement on Tariffs and Trade (GATT)
An international trade accord in which the 92 signatories agreed to reduce tariffs; often ignored by signatories.

Virtually every nation in the world has formal treaties with other nations regarding trade. One of the largest such treaties, the **General Agreement on Tariffs and Trade (GATT)**, was signed shortly after the end of World War II. But while the 92 countries that have signed GATT have agreed to reduce taxes on imported goods to 5 percent, not all have complied. One of the worst offenders is the United States.

European Union (EU)
An agreement among Western European nations to eliminate quotas and keep tariffs low on products traded among themselves, but to impose high tariffs and low quotas on goods imported from other nations.

Other GATT signatories who often do not live up to the terms of this treaty include the members of the **European Union.** The EU includes most Western European nations, most notably Belgium, Denmark, France, Greece, Ireland, Italy, Luxembourg, the Netherlands, the United Kingdom, and Germany. These nations continue to place quotas and high tariffs on goods imported from nonmember nations. But they have eliminated most quotas and set uniform tariff levels on products imported and exported within their group, encouraging intracontinental trade. In 1992, virtually all internal trade barriers were eliminated, making Western Europe the largest free marketplace in the world.

On January 1, 1995, the new World Trade Organization came into existence. It will oversee a one-third reduction in import duties on thousands of products that are traded between countries. The reductions will be phased in over the next few years. Canada, the U.S., and the European Union are founding members of the WTO.[26]

The Canada-U.S. Free Trade Agreement

Canada-U.S. Free Trade Agreement (FTA)
An agreement to eliminate over time tariffs on goods and services that move between the two countries.

The Canada-U.S. Free Trade Agreement (FTA) has as its goal the elimination over time of tariffs on products and services that move between the two countries. On January 1, 1989, tariffs were totally eliminated on about 15 percent of all goods traded between the U.S. and Canada. For the remaining 85 percent, tariffs were phased out over five or ten years, depending on the product. By January 1, 1998, tariffs were eliminated on almost all goods traded between the U.S. and Canada.

The North American Free Trade Agreement

North American Free Trade Agreement (NAFTA)
A trade agreement signed by Canada, the U.S., Mexico, and, later, Chile, whose purpose is to create a free trade area.

On January 1, 1994, the **North American Free Trade Agreement (NAFTA)** took effect. The objective of NAFTA is to create a free trade area for Canada, the U.S., and Mexico. It eliminates trade barriers, promotes fair competition, and increases investment opportunities. Canada later signed a separate free trade agreement with Chile.

Surveys conducted during the early 1990s showed that the majority of Canadians were opposed to both the FTA and NAFTA. They feared that jobs would be lost to other countries, and that Canada would be flooded with products manufactured in Mexico, where wages are much lower than they are in Canada. Supporters of NAFTA argued that the agreement would open up foreign markets for Canadian products.

What has *actually* happened since NAFTA took effect? Canada is shedding its image as a country whose people are "hewers of wood and drawers of water" and is becoming an exporting powerhouse. Trade between the U.S. and Canada has risen 37 percent since 1994, and Canada enjoyed a $22 billion trade surplus with the U.S. in 1996. Before free trade, exports accounted for about one-quarter of GDP, but now exports account for 40 percent. In the manufacturing sector, 60 percent of output is now exported, compared to just 30 percent in 1988. Canada is the most trade-intensive country in the G7 group. One job in three is now devoted to producing goods and services for export.[27]

Other Free Trade Agreements in the Americas

The Canada-U.S. Free Trade Agreement and NAFTA are the most publicized trade agreements in the Americas, but there has recently been a flurry of activity among other countries as well. On January 1, 1995, a free trade agreement known as Mercosur went into effect between Argentina, Brazil, Uruguay, and Paraguay. By 2005, tariffs will be eliminated on 80 percent of the goods traded between those four countries. Brazil has proposed enlarging Mercosur into a South American Free Trade Area (SAFTA), which might eventually negotiate with NAFTA to form an Americas Free Trade Area (AFTA).

SUMMARY OF LEARNING OBJECTIVES

1. **Describe the rise of international business and identify the major world marketplaces.** More and more business firms are engaged in international business. The term *globalization* refers to the process by which the world economy is fast becoming a single interdependent entity. The global economy is characterized by a rapid growth in the exchange of information and trade in services. The three major marketplaces for international business are *North America* (the United States, Canada, and Mexico), *Western Europe* (which is dominated by Germany, the United Kingdom, France, and Italy), and the *Pacific Rim* (where the dominant country, Japan, is surrounded by such rapidly advancing nations as South Korea, Taiwan, Hong Kong, and China).

2. **Explain how different forms of *competitive advantage, import-export balances, exchange rates*, and *foreign competition* determine the ways in which countries and businesses respond to the international environment.** With an absolute advantage, a country engages in international trade because it can produce a good or service more efficiently than any other nation. But more often countries trade because they enjoy comparative advantages, that is, they can produce some items more efficiently than they can produce other items. A country that exports more than it imports has a favourable balance of trade, while a country that imports more than it exports has an unfavourable balance of trade. If the exchange rate decreases (the value of the Canadian dollar falls), our exports become less expensive for other countries so they will buy more of what we produce. The reverse happens if the value of the Canadian dollar increases. Changes in the exchange rate therefore have a strong impact on our international competitiveness.

3. **Discuss the factors involved in deciding to do business internationally and in selecting the appropriate *levels of international involvement* and *international organizational structure*.** In deciding whether to do business internationally, a firm must determine whether a market for its product exists abroad, and if so,

whether the firm has the skills and knowledge to manage such a business. It must also assess the business climates of other nations to make sure that they are conducive to international operations.

A firm must also decide on its level of international involvement. It can choose to be an *exporter* or *importer*, to organize as an *international firm*, or to operate as a *multinational firm*. The choice will influence the organizational structure of its international operations, specifically, its use of *independent agents*, *licensing arrangements*, *branch offices*, *strategic alliances*, and *direct investment*.

4. **Describe some of the ways in which *social*, *cultural*, *economic*, *legal*, and *political differences* act as barriers to international trade.** *Social* and *cultural differences* that can serve as barriers to trade include language, social values, and traditional buying patterns. Differences in economic systems may force businesses to establish close relationships with foreign governments before they are permitted to do business abroad. *Quotas, tariffs, subsidies,* and *local-content laws* offer protection to local industries. Differences in *business-practice laws* can make standard business practices in one nation illegal in another.

5. **Explain how *free trade agreements* assist world trade.** Several *trade agreements* have attempted to eliminate restrictions on free trade internationally. The *General Agreement on Tariffs and Trade* (GATT) was instituted to eliminate tariffs and other trade barriers among participating nations. The *European Union* (EU) has eliminated virtually all trade barriers among the 12 principal Western European nations. The *North American Free Trade Agreement* (NAFTA) eliminates many of the barriers to free trade that exist among the United States, Canada, and Mexico.

STUDY QUESTIONS AND EXERCISES

Review Questions

1. Explain the difference between a nation's balance of trade and balance of payments.

2. What are the possible ways that Canadian firms can be involved in international business?

3. What are the advantages and disadvantages of multinational corporations?

4. How does the economic system of a country affect foreign firms interested in doing business there?

Analysis Questions

5. Make a list of all the major items in your bedroom. Identify the country in which each item was made. Give possible reasons why that nation might have a comparative advantage in producing this good.

6. Do you support protectionist tariffs for Canada? If so, in what instances and for what reasons? If not, why not?

7. Is the Canada-U.S. Free Trade Agreement good for Canada? Give supporting reasons for your answer.

8. The EU includes much of Western Europe, but some countries, such as Switzerland, have chosen not to join. Why might that be?

Application Exercises

9. Interview the manager of a local firm that does at least some business internationally. Identify reasons why the company decided to "go international," as well as the level of the firm's international involvement and the organizational structure it uses for its international operations.

10. Select a product familiar to you. Using library reference works to learn something about the culture of India, identify the problems that might arise in trying to market this product to India's citizens.

BUILDING YOUR BUSINESS SKILLS

Goal

To help students appreciate how high-context and low-context cultures influence global business communication. Low-context cultures use explicit written and verbal messages to communicate in business situations. Written agreements and written messages are important. High-context cultures communicate through both explicit messages and implicit context. Interpersonal relationships, and a high level of formality and etiquette, will affect the success of the communication.

Method

Step 1: A continuum of world cultures as defined by anthropologist Edward T. Hall is shown below. Use this information to develop a strategy for conducting meetings with businesspeople in Switzerland and Japan.

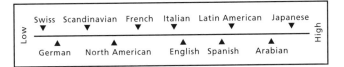

Step 2: Working in groups of four or five students, answer the following questions for each country: What should you do before you arrive in the country in order to increase your chance of success? If your meeting time is 1:00 p.m. on Tuesday, when should you arrive in order to

get the best results from your meeting? What title and position should you or another member of your team hold in order to achieve your business goals? How would your business style and the pace of your conversation differ in each country?

Follow-Up Questions

1. *Culture shock*—the inability to adapt to foreign cultures—is a problem that many Canadian businesspeople face when they work abroad. Based on this exercise, why do you think this is a problem?

2. How can management training seminars reduce *ethnocentrism*—the tendency to judge the cultures of foreign countries by Canadian standards?

3. Japan, Arab countries, and Latin American countries are high-context cultures. Do these countries share cultural patterns? How would you adapt your business style from country to country?

BUSINESS CASE 4

Microsoft Heads for the Wild, Wild East

There's a lot that Microsoft founder and CEO Bill Gates doesn't like about doing business in China—piracy, for example. Every year, factories in the People's Republic manufacture 54 million illegally copied software packages, robbing Microsoft and other firms of revenue that is rightfully theirs. So severe is the problem that a pirated version of Windows 95 was available months before the product's official launch—at just $5 a package.

Nevertheless, Microsoft views China as a huge marketing opportunity (and a 1996 U.S.–Chinese agreement banning the reproduction and sale of pirated intellectual property undoubtedly is helping to ease the company's concerns). With a population of 1.2 billion people, China is on the verge of mass computerization. Only 1 million computers were sold in 1995, but sales of 5 million are projected for the year 2000. Not surprisingly, Bill Gates is doing everything he can to make sure that these computers use Microsoft software.

Priming the Chinese computerization pump are government purchases. In Beijing, for example, officials are planning to levy new taxes and monitor their collection through a computerized network connected to a central database. The success of the plan depends on the purchase of 20 000 computers to link 3200 tax offices via Microsoft servers, Windows NT, and Windows 95. In another deal, the central bank of China is planning to install Windows-based PCs and servers in every one of its 10 000 branches. Thanks to purchases like these, Microsoft expects its annual sales in China of $20 million to skyrocket. "We're looking at 100-percent growth every year as far as we can see," beams Bryan Nelson, Microsoft's director for Greater China.

Forty-five percent of China's 1.2 billion population is under the age of 26. This younger generation of consumers is spending more than its parents on all

➤

than outsiders, define the standards for translating Chinese character fonts into computer language.

Microsoft's miscalculations were serious enough for the Chinese electronics industry to threaten a ban on the Taiwanese version of Windows. Bill Gates was advised that if he wanted to do business in China, he had better spend time there and "learn something from 5000 years of Chinese history." Gates did just that and, in the process, learned that Microsoft's success depends on a cooperative relationship with the Beijing government—one that sometimes places Microsoft in the back seat but that does ensure that it gets to go along for the ride.

■ Case Questions

1. To help control its exploding population, China enforces strict family planning. How do you think smaller families will affect consumer purchasing patterns in the emerging Chinese economy?

2. After its 1992 business miscalculation, Microsoft replaced its Chinese management team. Do you think this was a wise decision? Explain your answer.

3. The national average annual household income in China was just $684 in 1994. However, per capita income is rising at about 20 percent per year and is expected to reach $4000 by 2020. Why is Microsoft trying so hard to get a foothold in China if so few individuals and families can afford its products?

4. Why did the Chinese suggest that Microsoft's success depended on Bill Gates first-hand knowledge of their country?

consumer goods, including such electronic products as colour televisions, refrigerators, VCRs, telephones, and computers.

Tapping into this emerging consumer market requires that multinationals learn to deal effectively with local businesspeople and government officials, who often operate in distinctly non-Western ways. Microsoft learned the art of doing business in China the hard way when, in 1992, it contracted with a Taiwanese company to produce a Chinese-language version of Windows for use in mainland China. Government officials in Beijing rejected the product for various reasons. It was produced in Taiwan, which China does not recognize. The Chinese government also insisted that officials, rather

---

CBC VIDEO CASE I-1

Managed Care Ahead for Canada?*

"Foreign governments seeking to reduce the growing financial burden of social programs . . . pave the way for privatization and foreign investment."

—from a Liberty Mutual Annual Report

A very interesting sight awaits shoppers at the end of aisle 15 in one of Canada's new Wal-Mart stores, namely, a new private health insurance sales booth for U.S. company Liberty Health. As part of the insurance giant Liberty Mutual, Liberty Health finds its business exploding north of the U.S. border.

According to company representatives, about one-third of the costs of Canada's $24 billion health-care system are now covered by the private sector. This shift towards the private sector provides a real growth opportunity since, as Liberty Health's Gery Barry notes, "If you don't grow as an organization, you stop providing value." Liberty Health's parent company also sees Canada as a real growth opportunity, even mentioning it by name as a future growth market in a recent annual report.

Health-care consultant Michael Decter sees the possibility of substantial growth for companies such as Liberty

 ➤

Health. As medicare cuts back, it creates a real opportunity for the private sector to fill the gap in supplemental health coverage. Some observers are more cautious though, wondering if the trend to the private sector will also be accompanied by a shift towards increased pressures for cost savings. Private companies, notes industry observer Daphne Woolf, are motivated to reduce their liabilities in any way possible. Decter supports her assertion: "Managed care, as it's called in the U.S., is largely about costs, so it's really about squeezing costs, not about improving care."

Dan Smith, director of product design at Liberty Health, admits: "It is new to the Canadian marketplace where we don't just sit back and wait for the employee to go back to work. Traditionally, the marketplace has just let the employee get back to work. . . .We are working with the employee to force them back to work sooner." But some see Liberty Health's philosophy quite differently. Kathleen Connors, president of the Canadian Health Coalition, opposes the move towards privatization because health care is fundamentally different from "toasters or cars." According to Connors, "It's about people and if we start treating people like commodities then the caring and compassion that has been the fundamental part of the Canadian system will get lost."

STUDY QUESTIONS

1. What are the different types of economic systems? Which is closest to the way health care has operated in Canada until recently? Which is closest to the way Liberty Health does business?

2. What is a parent corporation? Who is Liberty Health's parent corporation?

3. What is social responsibility? How does Liberty Health appear to view its social responsibilities?

* Source: This case was written by Professor Reg Litz of the University of Manitoba. Video Resource: "Liberty Health," *Venture* #668 (November 11, 1997).

CBC VIDEO CASE I-2

The Power of the Few*

"Ultimately what a retailer does to us, that will put us out of business, they'll do to the next one, and the next one, and the one after that. And that's going to be your child, your husband, your relative that's going to be put out of work."

—*Canadian manufacturer*

Jack Berkovits looked up from his desk towards the wall in stunned disbelief. For over 20 years the Canadian retailer had served Zellers faithfully; in fact, the company had recently presented him with an award for excellence in service. The framed award hung on the wall a few feet from his desk. On his desk was another piece of paper from Zellers, however—this one quite intentionally not framed. It was a legal brief for a lawsuit Zellers was now filing against him and his company, D.G. Jewelry of Canada. As Zellers' sole ring supplier for over 20 years, he could not have even imagined the possibility of such a lawsuit only a few short years before. Recently Zellers had dictated new terms of sale to Jack—all stock would be brought in on consignment, rather than outright purchase, thus leaving the risk with Jack.

When $2 million of stock was subsequently returned, Jack decided that under these new terms he would have to look elsewhere, thus setting the stage for the Zellers suit. Even though the $2 million represented a comparatively minor inventory amount for a customer the size of Zellers, for a small firm such as D.G. Jewelry it represented life and death. As a result, Jack felt he had no choice but to look elsewhere for business. Now, to add insult to injury, his former "prized customer" was suing him!

The Zellers lawsuit signals a fundamental power shift in the Canadian marketplace. With a recent shake-out in Canadian retail, resulting in the closure of such firms as Consumers Distributing and Woodward's, only a half dozen large players remain. This shake-out only continues an earlier trend of consolidation in Canadian retail. From a high of 31 department stores in 1979, today there are but six; in the department store category, the "big three" of Eaton's, Sears, and the Bay dominate, while in the discount category, Zellers, Wal-Mart, and Kmart set the pace.

This allows the remaining retailers to place increased pressure on manufacturers to be faster and cheaper. More than one Canadian manufacturer has responded by simply going out of business. Other firms, with no choice but to "get along" in the new realities, find themselves increasingly integrated into a giant competitor's supply chain. Such "integration" includes using the retailer's computer system, and shipping quantity and quality according to the retailer's dictates, with the retailer having the option of shipping back if delivery specifications are violated in any way.

Perhaps most daunting for the small manufacturer is the prospect of penalties. When orders come in, the manufacturer must provide fast delivery, thus requiring the maintenance of huge inventories. If orders are not honoured, the supplier is vulnerable to huge penalties; being charged up to 10 percent for being two days late is not uncommon. The use of penalties was introduced by Wal-Mart and quickly embraced by other Canadian retailers. Some Canadian manufacturers wonder whether the penalties are viewed by the retailer as a profit centre, where a certain amount of penalty dollars are targeted for each quarter; retailers are quick to dismiss this as mere speculation.

STUDY QUESTIONS

1. What is profit? In what ways does the "power of the few" change who gets how much profit?

2. What are the different degrees of competition? How does this video case relate to the different degrees of competition?

3. What is a standard of living? What do the comments of some of the manufacturers suggest about the impact of the "power of the few" on the Canadian standard of living?

* Source: This case was written by Professor Reg Litz of the University of Manitoba. Video Resource: "Manufacturers Squeezed," *Venture* #666 (October 28, 1997).

LANDS' END VIDEO CASE I-3

Lands' End, Inc.: A Brief History

LEARNING OBJECTIVES
The purpose of this video exercise is to help students

1. Become better acquainted with a specific company currently conducting business as a public corporation.

2. Understand the path to growth taken by a company that has been in existence for less than four decades.

3. Understand more about the operations of a company that deals in both consumer goods and services.

BACKGROUND INFORMATION
Lands' End is a *mail order* (or *catalogue marketing*) retailer based in Dodgeville, Wisconsin. From its headquarters, the company mails out catalogues featuring high-quality merchandise that is competitively priced and backed by an unconditional guarantee. Lands' End catalogues specialize in casual and tailored clothing but include a variety of other products, including shoes, accessories, luggage, and items for the bed and bath.

Founded in Chicago in 1963, Lands' End originally specialized in sailing equipment; the first black-and-white catalogue featured no clothing at all. By 1977, clothing and luggage dominated the catalogue, and by 1979—the year of the move to Dodgeville—Lands' End had already recruited personnel in such areas as fabrics and clothing manufacture. The company now works directly with fabric mills and clothing manufacturers who are contracted to make products according to Lands' End's own specifications.

Lands' End introduced the term "direct merchant" to describe itself in 1981. In 1994, when sales surpassed those of L.L. Bean, it became the largest specialty catalogue retailer in the U.S. Today more than 1000 phone lines handle 50 000 calls a day (about 100 000 calls a day in the weeks just before Christmas). Toll-free lines (both to sales and customer service operators) are open 24 hours a day. In-stock orders are usually shipped from the distribution centre the day after they are received. Within the continental United States, standard delivery usually requires two business days.

THE VIDEO
Video Source. "Lands' End, Inc.: A Brief History," *Prentice Hall Presents: On Location at Lands' End*. This video introduces Lands' End by tracing the company's history from its origins as a small Chicago outlet in 1963 to its current position as the largest specialty catalogue company in the United States. In describing the firm's current operations, the video focuses on the emphasis Lands' End places on customer service and distribution efficiency.

DISCUSSION QUESTIONS

1. In general terms, describe the effect on Lands' End past, present, and/or future operations of each of the four factors of production (labour, capital, entrepreneurs, and natural resources).

2. In what ways do Lands' End's operations reflect patterns of demand and supply in its particular industry?

3. Lands' End operates in an industry characterized by pure competition. Which facets of the company's operations most clearly reflect conditions of pure competition? Which facets reflect the position currently enjoyed by Lands' End in its particular industry?

4. Lands' End became a public corporation in October 1986. In August 1987 and again in May 1994, shares were split two-for-one. If you were presented *today* with an opportunity to buy stock in Lands' End, would you buy some stock? Why or why not?

FOLLOW-UP ASSIGNMENT

To better understand the nature of Lands' End's industry and operations, familiarize yourself with the following concepts:

- Operations processes (Chap. 10)
- Service operations (Chap. 10)
- Quality control (Chap. 11)
- The marketing mix (Chap. 13)

- Pricing products (Chap. 15)
- Promoting products (Chap. 14)
- Direct mail (Chap. 15)
- Nonstore retailing (Chap. 15)
- Mail order marketing (Chap. 15)
- Physical distribution (Chap. 15)
- Distribution centre (Chap. 15)

FOR FURTHER EXPLORATION

Lands' End can be contacted on the Internet at
http://www.landsend.com

LANDS' END VIDEO CASE I-4

Doing Business Abroad the Lands' End Way

LEARNING OBJECTIVES

The purpose of this video exercise is to help students

1. Appreciate the difficulties experienced by a company when it decides to go international.

2. Understand how Lands' End responded to customer needs in markets as diverse as the United Kingdom and Japan.

3. Understand how Lands' End dealt with social, cultural, and economic differences as it expanded into international markets.

BACKGROUND INFORMATION

International sales are nothing new to Lands' End, which began selling to Canadian customers through regular mailings in 1987. But in the early 1990s, overseas expansion threatened to be a completely different matter:

- The company's first overseas venture—to the United Kingdom—was undertaken less than 10 years ago. Surprisingly, one of the first challenges the company encountered was language. Lands' End's copywriters worked in American English, but its new British customers wanted to hear about products in British English—and said so. Adjustments were made to Lands' End copy and by 1993, operations in the United Kingdom had been moved to a new home-based facility just outside London.

- In Japan, operations began in 1993, with the first Japanese catalogue issued in August 1994. In Japan, the main challenge turned out to be advertising media

and methods. Japanese customers are used to cluttered newspaper inserts; Lands' End has always worked to show individual products in the best possible light—a policy that doesn't lend itself to cluttered photography and advertising copy. Compromises were reached, and Lands' End discovered a formidable competitive tool in its iron-clad customer satisfaction guarantee.

THE VIDEO

Video Source. "Doing Business Abroad the Lands' End Way," *Prentice Hall Presents: On Location at Lands' End.* This video traces the history of Lands' End's foray into two overseas markets—the United Kingdom and Japan. Participants, including Vice President for International Operations Frank Buettner, recount some of the key challenges that faced the company as it adapted its approach to catalogue retailing to the demands of foreign customers.

DISCUSSION QUESTIONS

1. How would you describe Lands' End's level of international involvement? Which type of international organizational structure best applies to the company's approach to business in the United Kingdom and Japan?

2. List and describe some of the specific barriers to international trade that Lands' End has encountered. With which kinds of differences—social and cultural, economic, legal and political—does Lands' End seem to be most concerned? Why? In what ways have some of

➤

these differences affected Lands' End's international operations?

3. Why did Lands' End move so quickly to establish headquarters for its British operations inside the United Kingdom? What kinds of problems should be solved more easily because the company now has a "creative team of nationals" working at its home-based British facility?

4. Every company that markets its products in several countries faces a basic choice: (1) use a *decentralized approach* with a separate management for each country or (2) adopt a *global perspective* with a coordinated marketing program directed at one worldwide audience. Where would you place Lands' End on this spectrum? Is its approach primarily "decentralized"? Primarily "global"? If it reflects both options, why do you think this is so?

FOLLOW-UP ASSIGNMENT

At the conclusion of the video, Lands' End's three most important criteria for venturing into a foreign market are presented. All of these criteria concern a country's infrastructure: (1) the country must be economically stable, (2) it must have a good system for distributing goods, and (3) its telephone system must be dependable. You are also told that the company is now considering expansion into one of three countries—Germany, the Netherlands, or France. After your instructor has divided the class into groups of three to six people each, assign members to go to the library and gather current information on the infrastructure and economic conditions in these three countries. When each committee has collected its information, members should meet to compare notes and draw up a report that recommends that Lands' End select one country over the other two.

FOR FURTHER EXPLORATION

Lands' End can be contacted on the Internet at **http://www.landsend.com**

PART

2

MANAGING THE BUSINESS FIRM

Edgar Bronfman, William Stinson, and Lawrence Zepf are three of the people you will read about in the cases that open Chapters 5–7. These people all manage business organizations. Seagram and Canadian Pacific are very large, while Zepf Technologies is small. But the common thread among these managers is their ability to carry out the basic functions of management in a skillful and inventive way.

Part Two, Managing the Business Firm, provides an overview of business management today. It includes a look at the various types of managers, the special concerns of managing small businesses, the ways in which managers set goals for their companies, and how a business's structure affects its management and goals.

- We begin in **Chapter 5, Managing the Business Enterprise**, by examining corporate goals and strategy, the management process, and the different levels of management in the modern business organization.

- In **Chapter 6, Organizing the Business Enterprise**, we examine the different ways that business firms can structure themselves and the effects of these structures on corporate culture.

- Finally, in **Chapter 7, Running the Small Business**, we explore the role of small businesses and franchises in the Canadian economy—what they do, why they succeed or fail, and how they are owned and managed.

CHAPTER

5

MANAGING THE BUSINESS ENTERPRISE

PLANNING AND STRATEGY AT SEAGRAM

Montreal-based Seagram Co. is one of Canada's largest companies, with over 30 000 employees and annual sales of over $12 billion. The company was started in the 1920s by Sam Bronfman, who sold liquor by mail order. His son, Edgar Bronfman, Sr. became CEO in 1957. Until the early 1990s, the company's activities were focused largely on the production of wine, distilled spirits, and orange juice. But in the mid-1990s, the company, now led by Edgar Bronfman, Jr., began making some dramatic strategic moves. These moves have turned the company away from its traditional products and moved it towards the high-risk entertainment business.

The move into entertainment has occurred partly because Edgar Bronfman has both an artistic and a business temperament. He is friends with some well-known show-business types, including actor Michael Douglas, and he has long had a fascination with Hollywood. Bronfman is well aware that more than a few third-generation heirs have dissipated family fortunes, and he is determined that he will not make those mistakes. But he has also refused to simply make cautious investments; rather, he has embarked on a strategy that he thinks will make Seagram a stronger company.

Some of his decisions have startled company observers. For example, he paid more than $2 billion for 15 percent of Time-Warner in 1993, leading some to think that he might try a hostile takeover of that company. But he then unexpectedly sold those shares a short time later. He also sold a large block

of DuPont shares that Seagram had held for many years. In 1995, he bought MCA Inc. (now Universal) for $5.7 billion.

In 1997, Seagram decided to embark on an ambitious plan to process orange juice in China through its Tropicana Beverages Group. The plan was to form a joint venture with a Chinese organization to finance and build an orange juice processing plant. Seagram was also to build a technology centre and seedling nursery, and was to provide technical assistance to farmers who wanted to raise orange trees. But in 1998, Seagram indicated that it might sell shares in Tropicana as an initial public offering (IPO) that would help raise funds to pay for its Polygram acquisition. Market analysts thought that the IPO would raise between $3.5 and $4 billion. Seagram announced a few months later that it was simply selling Tropicana to PepsiCo Inc. for $3.3 billion in cash. The deal will allow PepsiCo to compete head-on with Coca-Cola (which owns the Minute Maid orange juice brand).

In 1998, Bronfman took a giant step into the world of entertainment with the $10.6 billion acquisition of Polygram NV, a company whose artists are as diverse as the Three Tenors, Elton John, and U2. With the acquisition of Polygram, Seagram instantly became the world's largest music company. The company thinks that Polygram's international music operations will fit perfectly with Universal's music business, which is strongest in North America. Seagram continues to focus on the entertainment industry, with the development of theme parks in the U.S., Japan, Spain, and China.

With its new initiatives, Seagram will be a $17 billion company that gets more than two-thirds of its sales revenue from entertainment. But are all these strategic changes a good idea? Industry observers note, for example, that the DuPont stock that Bronfman sold for $8.8 billion in 1995 would have been worth $20 billion in 1998 if the dividends had been reinvested. So far, Seagram's foray into the entertainment business has cost the Seagram family hundreds of millions in lost dividends. And critics of the Tropicana decision say that once again Seagram is waving goodbye to a steady source of income and trading it for the uncertain revenue of the music business.

If Edgar Bronfman is right about the music business, Seagram is going to be a global entertainment powerhouse. If he is wrong, Seagram will find itself heavily committed to a volatile industry where ups and downs are the order of the day. However, if this sounds like a dramatic departure from the company's past strategy, consider this: The history of Seagram reveals that the company has made several dramatic moves over the years. It was Edgar's grandfather, Sam Bronfman, who bootlegged booze into the U.S. during the 1920s, and it was also Sam who decided to get the company into the oil and gas business in the 1940s. And Edgar's father, Edgar Sr., actually controlled MGM briefly in the 1960s. So, maybe Edgar's strategy is not so dramatic after all.

Seagram
www.seagram.com

Edgar Bronfman is one of millions of managers worldwide who work in business firms. In this chapter, we explain how these managers differ from industrial engineers, accountants, market researchers, production workers, secretaries, and other people who work in business firms. Although we will focus on managers in business firms, managers are necessary in many other kinds of organizations—colleges and universities, charities, social clubs, churches, labour unions, and governments. The president of the University of Toronto, the prime minister of Canada, and the executive director of the United Way are just as much managers as the president of MacMillan Bloedel.

By focusing on the learning objectives of this chapter, you will better understand the nature of managing, the meaning of corporate culture, and the range of skills that managers like Edgar Bronfman need if they are to work effectively. After reading this chapter, you should be able to:

1. Explain the importance of setting *goals* and formulating *strategies* as the starting points of effective management.

2. Describe the four activities that constitute the *management process*.

3. Identify *types of managers* by level and area.

4. Describe the five basic *management skills*.

5. Describe the development and explain the importance of *corporate culture*.

■ SETTING GOALS AND FORMULATING STRATEGY

The starting point in effective management is setting **goals**, objectives that a business hopes (and plans) to achieve. Every business needs goals, and we begin by discussing the basic aspects of organizational goal setting. However, deciding what it *intends* to do is only step one for an organization. A company's managers must also make decisions about actions that will and will not achieve its goals. From this perspective, *strategy* is the broad program that underlies those decisions; the basic steps in formulating strategy are discussed later in the chapter.

goals
Objectives that a business hopes and plans to achieve.

Setting Business Goals

Goals are performance targets, the means by which organizations and their managers measure success or failure at every level. To properly motivate people to high achievement, goals should be specific, quantitative, challenging, and time-framed. In this section, we identify the main purposes for which organizations set goals, classify the basic levels of business goals, and describe the process by which goals are commonly set.

The Purposes of Goal Setting.   An organization functions systematically because it sets goals and plans accordingly. Indeed, an organization functions as such because it commits its resources on all levels to achieving its goals. Specifically, we can identify four main purposes in organizational goal setting:

1. *Goal setting provides direction, guidance, and motivation for all managers.* For example, each of the managers at Kanke Seafood Restaurants Ltd. is required to work through a goal setting exercise each year. Setting and achieving goals is the most effective form of self motivation.[1]

2. *Goal setting helps firms allocate resources.* Areas that are expected to grow, for example, will get first priority. Thus 3M allocates more resources to new projects with large sales potential than to projects with low growth potential.

3. *Goal setting helps to define corporate culture.* General Electric's goal, for instance, is to push each of its divisions to number one or number two in its industry. The result is a competitive, often stressful, environment and a culture that rewards success and has little tolerance for failure.

4. *Goal setting helps managers assess performance.* If a unit sets a goal of increasing sales by 10 percent in a given year, managers in that unit who attain or exceed the goal can be rewarded. Units failing to reach the goal will also be compensated accordingly.

Kinds of Goals.   Naturally, goals differ from company to company, depending on the firm's purpose and mission. Every enterprise, of course, has a *purpose*—a reason for being. Businesses seek profits, universities work to discover and transmit new knowledge, and government agencies exist to help in public activities. But every enterprise also has a mission and a **mission statement**—a statement of *how* it will achieve its purpose in the environment in which it conducts its business. By and large, a company's purpose is fairly easy to identify. Reebok, for example, attempts to make a profit by making and selling athletic shoes and related merchandise. IBM expresses the same purpose in selling computers and computer technology.

Consider the similarities and differences between Timex and Rolex. Both firms share a common purpose—to sell watches at a profit—yet they have very different missions. Timex sells low-cost, reliable watches in outlets ranging from department stores to corner drugstores. Rolex, on the other hand, sells high-quality, high-priced fashion watches through selected jewellery stores.

Regardless of a company's purpose and mission, however, every firm needs long-term, intermediate, and short-term goals:

- **Long-term goals** relate to extended periods of time—typically five years or more into the future. American Express, for example, might set a long-term goal of doubling the number of participating merchants during the next 10 years. Similarly, Kodak might adopt a long-term goal of increasing its share of the 35-mm film market by 10 percent during the next eight years.

- **Intermediate goals** are set for a period of one to five years into the future. Companies usually have intermediate goals in several areas. For example, the marketing department's goal might be to increase sales by 3 percent in two years. The production department might want to decrease expenses by 6 percent in four years. Human resources might seek to cut turnover by 10 percent in two years. Finance might aim for a 3 percent increase in return on investment in three years.

mission statement
Organization's statement of how it will achieve its purpose in the environment in which it conducts its business.

long-term goals
Goals set for extended periods of time, typically five years or more into the future.

intermediate goals
Goals set for a period of one to five years.

- Like intermediate goals, **short-term goals**—which are set for perhaps one year— are developed for several different areas. Increasing sales by 2 percent this year, cutting costs by 1 percent next quarter, and reducing turnover by 4 percent over the next six months are all short-term goals.

short-term goals
Goals set for the very near future, typically less than one year.

Who Sets Goals?   Within any company, managers at different levels are responsible for setting different kinds of goals. The firm's purpose is largely determined by the context in which it operates—that is, the environment in which it markets its products. The board of directors generally defines the firm's mission. Working in conjunction with the board, top managers then usually set long-term goals. These same managers typically work closely with middle managers to set intermediate goals. Finally, middle managers work with first-line managers to set and achieve short-term goals.

Formulating Strategy

Most managers must devote a great deal of attention (and creativity) to the formulation of business strategies—that is, ways of meeting company goals at all levels. **Strategy formulation** involves three basic steps:

1. setting strategic goals
2. analyzing the organization and its environment
3. matching the organization and its environment.[2]

strategy formulation
Creation of a broad program for defining and meeting an organization's goals.

Setting Strategic Goals.   **Strategic goals** are long-term goals derived directly from the firm's mission statement. For example, one of the first things new CEO George Fisher did at Kodak was to set several strategic goals. One strategic goal called for renewed emphasis on film marketing and processing, one called for eliminating several peripheral businesses, and still another stressed the need to speed up the introduction of new technology. When Wallace McCain took control of Maple Leaf Foods Inc., he set three strategic goals: make Maple Leaf a bigger company through acquisitions, build larger animal processing plants, and cut labour costs.[3]

strategic goals
Long-term goals derived directly from a firm's mission statement.

Maple Leaf Foods Inc.
www.mapleleaffoods.com

Analyzing the Organization and Its Environment.   **Environmental analysis** involves scanning the environment for threats and opportunities. New products and new competitors, for example, are both threats. So are new government regulations, imports, changing consumer tastes, and hostile takeovers. In formulating its new strategy, for instance, Kodak saw opportunities for growth in the film market and recognized that technology was changing so fast that it had to get that technology to market much faster than planned. It also saw increased competition from its biggest rival, the Japanese firm Fuji.

Meanwhile, managers also must undertake an **organizational analysis** to understand a company's strengths and weaknesses better. Strengths might include surplus cash, a dedicated workforce, an ample supply of managerial talent, technical expertise, or little competition. The absence of any of these strengths could represent an important weakness. Kodak, for example, saw that although it was doing fine in research and development, translating technological breakthroughs into new products was taking a long time.

environmental analysis
Process of scanning the environment for threats and opportunities.

organizational analysis
Process of analyzing a firm's strengths and weaknesses.

Matching the Organization and Its Environment.   The final step in strategy formulation is matching environmental threats and opportunities against corporate strengths and weaknesses. The matching process is the heart of strategy formulation: More than any other facet of strategy, matching companies with their environments lays the foundation for successfully planning and conducting business.[4] Kodak managers, for example, decided that the firm needed to concentrate on its core business, photographic equipment and supplies. Thus it began selling its other businesses, such as a software manufacturer and a consumer-credit division.

Kodak
www.kodak.com/homePage.shtml

A Hierarchy of Plans.   Figure 5.1 shows how plans can be viewed on three general levels: *strategic*, *tactical*, and *operational*. Each level reflects plans for which managers at that level are responsible. These levels constitute a hierarchy because implementing plans is practical only when there is a logical flow from one level to the next.

strategic plans
Plans that reflect decisions about resource allocations, company priorities, and steps needed to meet strategic goals.

tactical plans
Generally, short-range plans concerned with implementing specific aspects of a company's strategic plans.

operational plans
Plans setting short-term targets for daily, weekly, or monthly performance.

- **Strategic plans** reflect decisions about resource allocations, company priorities, and the steps needed to meet strategic goals. They are usually set by the board of directors and top management. Procter & Gamble's decision that viable products must be number one or number two within their respective categories is a matter of strategic planning.

- **Tactical plans** are shorter-range plans concerned with implementing specific aspects of the company's strategic plans. They typically involve upper and middle management. Coca-Cola's decision to increase sales in Europe by building European bottling facilities is an example of tactical planning.

- Developed by middle and lower-level managers, **operational plans** set short-term targets for daily, weekly, or monthly performance. McDonald's, for example, establishes operational plans when it explains precisely how Big Macs are to be cooked, warmed, and served.

Contingency Plans and Crisis Management

In 1994, the Walt Disney Company announced plans to launch a cruise line replete with familiar Disney characters and themes. The first sailing was scheduled for early in 1998, and the company began to book reservations a year in advance. However, the shipyard constructing Disney's first ship notified the company in October 1997 that it was behind

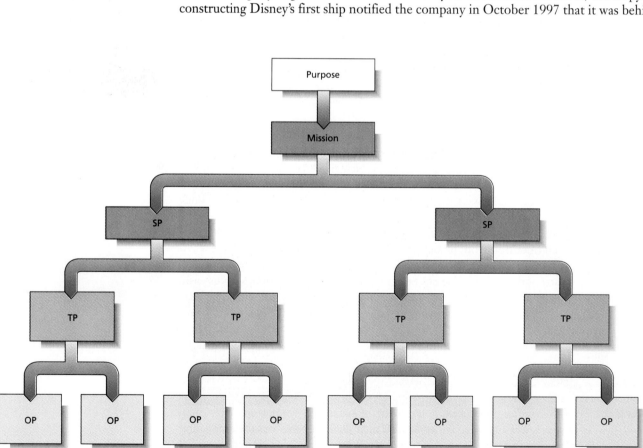

FIGURE 5.1
A hierarchy of plans.

schedule and that the ship would be delivered several weeks late. When similar problems befall other cruise lines, they can offer to rebook passengers on alternative itineraries. But because Disney had no other ship, it had no choice but to refund the money it had collected as prebooking deposits for its first 15 cruises. The 20 000 displaced customers were offered big discounts if they rebooked on a later cruise. However, many of them could not rearrange their schedules and requested full refunds. Moreover, quite a few blamed Disney for their problem, and a few expressed outrage at what they saw as poor planning by the entertainment giant.[5]

Because things change—often with little warning or indication—most managers recognize that plans may not be achieved as expected and that alterations may be necessary. Two common methods of dealing with the unknown and unforeseen are *contingency planning* and *crisis management*.

Contingency Planning.   Contingency planning takes into account the need to find solutions for specific aspects of a problem. By its very nature, a contingency plan is a hedge against changes that *might* occur. **Contingency planning**, then, is planning for change: It attempts to identify in advance important aspects of a business or its market that might change. It also identifies the ways in which a company will respond to changes. Today, many companies use computer programs for contingency planning.

contingency planning
Identifying aspects of a business or its environment that might entail changes in strategy.

Suppose, for example, that a company develops a plan to create a new business. It expects sales to increase at an annual rate of 10 percent for the next five years and develops a marketing strategy for maintaining that level. But suppose that sales have increased by only 5 percent by the end of the first year. Does the company abandon the business, invest more in advertising, or wait to see what happens in the second year? Any of these alternatives is possible. However, things will go more smoothly if managers have decided in advance what to do in the event of lower sales. Contingency planning can help them do exactly that.

Crisis Management.   A crisis is an unexpected emergency requiring immediate organizational response. **Crisis management** involves an organization's methods for dealing with emergencies. For example, when the oil tanker *Exxon Valdez* spilled millions of litres of oil off the coast of Alaska in March 1989, Exxon went into a crisis-management mode (albeit more slowly than some critics would have liked).

crisis management
An organization's methods for dealing with emergencies.

In the summer of 1996, there was concern that the e. coli. bacteria had gotten into some of the beef supply. This sign on a Burger King drive-through informed customers that it was not selling Whoppers or hamburgers while it carefully assessed the danger.

Johnson & Johnson
www.jnj.com/homepage.htm

A highly publicized case of effective crisis management involved the nonaspirin pain reliever Tylenol. Johnson & Johnson (J&J), the maker of Tylenol, has been widely praised for its response to two incidents in which Tylenol products were found to be tainted with cyanide. As soon as the company learned of the poisonings, it removed all Tylenol capsules from grocery and drugstore shelves. J&J management also made itself available to the media and embarked on an education program to inform the public of the steps being taken to correct the problem.

To prepare for emergencies better, many organizations maintain crisis plans. These plans, designed to enable employees to cope when disasters do occur, typically outline who will be in charge in different kinds of circumstances, how the organization will respond, and so forth. In addition, they typically lay out plans for assembling and deploying crisis-management teams.

■ THE MANAGEMENT PROCESS

management
The process of planning, organizing, leading, and controlling a business's financial, physical, human, and information resources to achieve its goals.

Management is the process of planning, organizing, leading, and controlling an enterprise's financial, physical, human, and information resources to achieve the organization's goals of supplying various products and services. Thus, the CEO of Walt Disney Productions, Michael Eisner, is a manager because he regularly carries out these four functions as films are being made. Actors like Bette Midler or Tom Selleck, while they may be the stars of the movies, are not managers because they don't carry out the four functions of management. The box "What Do Managers Actually Do?" gives some explanation of the dynamic nature of managerial jobs.

Planning

planning
That portion of a manager's job concerned with determining what the business needs to do and the best way to achieve it.

Determining what the organization needs to do and how to best do it or get it done means **planning**. Planning itself involves a series of activities by managers. First, managers need to determine the firm's goals. Next, they need to develop a comprehensive strategy for achieving those goals. After a strategy is chosen, managers must design tactical and operational plans for implementing it.

Organizing

organizing
That portion of a manager's job concerned with structuring the necessary resources to complete a particular task.

The second basic managerial activity, **organizing**, means determining how to best arrange resources and jobs to be done into an overall structure. Disney keeps each of its businesses somewhat independent and somewhat interdependent. Each business has its own management team, and the president of each business has considerable autonomy in running it. But many major decisions and those affecting several businesses (such as licensing Mickey Mouse T-shirts for sale at Disney World) are made at the corporate level. Groups such as the Imagineers also work for all Disney businesses. We will explore organizing in Chapter 6.

Disney
www.disney.com

Leading

leading
That portion of a manager's job concerned with guiding and motivating employees to meet the firm's objectives.

The activities involving interactions between managers and their subordinates to meet the firm's objectives are known as **leading** (or directing). By definition, managers have the power to give orders and demand results. Leading, however, goes beyond merely giving orders. Leaders attempt to guide and motivate employees to work in the best interests of the organization. For example, Michael Eisner's plans for Disney require tens of thousands of people to execute them. We discuss leadership more fully in Chapter 8.

TRENDS & CHALLENGES

What Do Managers Actually Do?

Henry Mintzberg of McGill University conducted a detailed study of the work of five chief executive officers and found the following:

1. Managers work at an unrelenting pace.
2. Managerial activities are characterized by brevity, variety, and fragmentation.
3. Managers have a preference for "live" action, and emphasize work activities that are current, specific, and well-defined.
4. Managers are attracted to the verbal media.

Mintzberg believes that a manager's job can be described as 10 roles that must be performed. The manager's formal authority and status give rise to three **interpersonal roles**: 1) *figurehead* (duties of a ceremonial nature, such as attending a subordinate's wedding); 2) *leader* (being responsible for the work of the unit); and 3) *liaison* (making contact outside the vertical chain of command). These interpersonal roles give rise to three **informational roles**: 1) *monitor* (scanning the environment for relevant information); 2) *disseminator* (passing information to subordinates); and 3) *spokesperson* (sending information to people outside the unit).

The interpersonal and informational roles allow the manager to carry out four **decision-making roles**: 1) *entrepreneur* (improving the performance of the unit); 2) *disturbance handler* (responding to high-pressure disturbances, such as a strike at a supplier); 3) *resource allocator* (deciding who will get what in the unit); and 4) *negotiator* (working out agreements on a wide variety of issues like the amount of authority an individual will be given).

Insight into what managers actually do can also be gained by looking at the so-called *functions* of management (planning, organizing, leading, and controlling). Consider the work of Patrick Ferrier, who is the Publisher, College Division, at Prentice Hall Canada, a publisher of textbooks for universities, community colleges, and high schools. His job is to manage the activities that are necessary to acquire and develop books in business, economics, science, math, and medicine for the Canadian college and university market. His work is at times intense, fragmented, rewarding, frustrating, and fast-paced. In short, he is a typical manager.

Ferrier carries out the *planning* function when he drafts a plan for a new book. He is *organizing* when he develops a new organization chart to facilitate goal achievement. He is *leading* when he meets with a subordinate to discuss that person's career plans. And he is *controlling* when he checks sales prospects for a book before ordering a reprint.

Some of Ferrier's activities do not easily fit into this "functions of management" model. For example, it is not clear which function he is performing when he negotiates the size of a reprint run with the manager of the sales division, or when he talks briefly with the president of his division about recent events in Ferrier's area of responsibility.

Controlling

The fourth basic managerial activity, **controlling**, means monitoring the firm's performance to make sure that it stays on track towards its goals. At Disney, Eisner's use of the Imagineers and the strategic management group and his decision to keep movie budgets low have kept the firm's profits growing.

Figure 5.2 shows the basic control process. The process begins with standards, or goals, the company wants to meet. For example, if the company wants to increase sales by 20 percent over the next 10 years, an appropriate standard might be an increase of around 2 percent each year. Managers must then measure actual performance regularly and compare this performance to the standard. If the two figures agree, the organization will continue its present activities. If they vary significantly, though, either the performance or the standard needs adjusting. For example, if sales have increased 2.1 percent at the end of the first year, things are probably fine. On the other hand, if sales have dropped by 1 percent, something needs to be done. The original goal may need to be lowered, more may need to be spent on advertising, and so forth.

controlling
That portion of a manager's job concerned with monitoring the firm's performance and, if necessary, acting to bring it in line with the firm's goals.

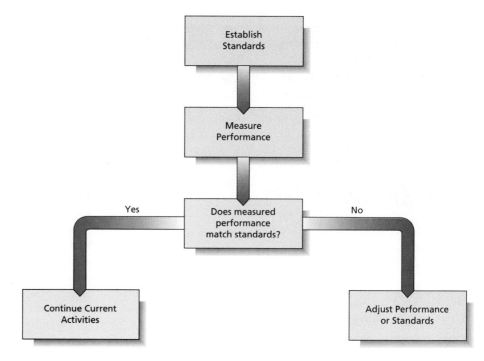

FIGURE 5.2
Steps in the control process.

The video case "Earth Buddy" on p. 146 clearly shows what happens when the controlling function is not properly carried out.

■ TYPES OF MANAGERS

Although all managers plan, organize, lead, and control, not all managers have the same degree of responsibility for each activity. Moreover, managers differ in the specific application of these activities. Thus we can divide managers by their *level* of responsibility or by their *area* of responsibility.

Levels of Management

The three basic levels of management are top, middle, and first-line management. As Figure 5.3 shows, in most firms there are more middle managers than top managers and more first-line managers than middle managers. Moreover, as the categories imply, the power of managers and the complexity of their duties increase as we move up the pyramid.

top managers
Those managers responsible for a firm's overall performance and effectiveness and for developing long-range plans for the company.

Top Managers.   The fairly small number of executives who guide the fortunes of most companies are **top managers**. Common titles for top managers include President, Vice President, Treasurer, Chief Executive Officer (CEO), and Chief Financial Officer (CFO). Michael Eisner is a top manager for Disney, and Edgar Bronfman is a top executive for Seagram. Top managers are responsible to the board of directors and shareholders of the firm for its overall performance and effectiveness. They set general policies, formulate strategies, oversee all significant decisions, and represent the company in its dealings with other businesses and government.[6]

middle managers
Those managers responsible for implementing the decisions made by top managers.

Middle Managers.   Although below the ranks of the top executives, **middle managers** occupy positions of considerable autonomy and importance. Titles such as Plant Manager, Operations Manager, and Division Manager are typical of middle-management slots. The

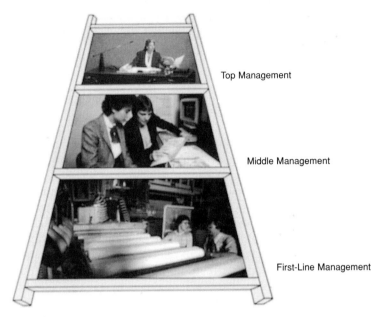

Top Management

Middle Management

First-Line Management

FIGURE 5.3
Most organizations have three basic levels of management.

producer of a Disney film is a middle manager. In general, middle managers are responsible for implementing the strategies, policies, and decisions of the top managers. For example, if top management decides to bring out a new product in 12 months or to cut costs by 5 percent, middle management will have to decide to increase the pace of new product development or to reduce the plant's workforce. With companies increasingly seeking ways to cut costs, however, the job of middle manager has lately become precarious in many large companies. Labatt's laid off 120 middle managers when it developed a new corporate strategy. Air Canada also recently dropped 400 managers.[7] See the box "The Downsizing Craze" for more information on this trend.

First-Line Managers.   At the bottom of the management hierarchy are **first-line managers** who supervise the work of employees. First-line managers hold titles such as Supervisor and Office Manager. The supervisor of Disney's animation department is a first-line manager. First-line managers tend to spend most of their time working with and supervising the employees who report to them. Some have entered the firm without a college or university degree or have been promoted from within the company.

first-line managers
Those managers responsible for supervising the work of employees.

Areas of Management

Within any large company, the top, middle, and first-line managers work in a variety of areas including marketing, finance, operations, human resources, and information. Figure 5.4 illustrates this relationship.

Marketing Managers.   Marketing includes the development, pricing, promotion, and distribution of a product or service. **Marketing managers** are responsible for getting products and services to buyers. Marketing is especially important for firms dealing in consumer products, such as Procter & Gamble, Coca-Cola, and Sun Ice. These firms often have large numbers of marketing managers at various levels. For example, a large firm will probably have a vice president for marketing (top manager), regional marketing managers (middle managers), and several district sales managers (first-line managers). A marketing person often rises to the top of this type of corporation.

marketing managers
Those managers responsible for developing, pricing, promoting, and distributing goods and services to buyers.

TRENDS CHALLENGES

The Downsizing Craze

By now, everyone has heard of downsizing—restructuring an organization and cutting large numbers of jobs in an attempt to improve profitability and productivity. Until recently, most firms that downsized were in financial trouble and needed to do something drastic to recover. But increasingly, organizations that are perfectly healthy are also downsizing. Bell Canada reduced staff by 3200, Inco laid off 2000 people, and Petro-Canada cut 564 jobs.

Even firms that are making record profits are downsizing. In 1995, General Motors of Canada reported record profits, yet it cut 2500 jobs during the year. The five largest banks in Canada reported total profits of over $6 billion in 1996, but they cut nearly 3000 jobs.

Normally when a recession hits, companies lay off people and then hire them back when business improves. But since the recession of 1990–92, companies have shown an unusual determination not to let staff levels increase. Why? Largely because they are very uncertain about what the future holds, and because increased global and domestic competition is motivating them to increase productivity while reducing costs. The top managers of most companies think that this can best be achieved by laying off workers.

Consider what is happening at Maritime Telephone and Telegraph Company Ltd. It cut 13 percent of its staff in 1995 and made further cuts in 1998. The reason is increasing competition in the long-distance market, which contributed to a profit decline of 33 percent in 1995. MT&T is relying on improved technology to provide better service to customers, even as it cuts its staff. In the maintenance department, for example, calls are now routed to a central computer that automatically tests the customer's line while a service person talks to the customer. This has allowed the company to cut the maintenance department by 23 employees.

The American Management Association analyzed the performance of 700 companies that had downsized between 1989 and 1994. They found that productivity rose in about a third of the companies and fell in another 30 percent of the companies. Profits rose in half of the companies and declined in about a third. In the vast majority of companies, morale dropped.

Whether downsizing is good or bad depends on your perspective. Politicians don't like it because they want lower unemployment levels. Employees certainly don't like it. But these are not the only groups that business managers must answer to. Another group—institutional and individual shareholders—often have a very big say in what management does. They often have a very

positive view of downsizing because they feel it will improve profits and increase the size of their dividend cheques. For example, the price of Petro-Canada stock rose from $8 per share in 1993 to $16.75 per share in 1996 after the company had cut 700 jobs.

Another example is Scott Paper Ltd. The company's low stock price had been causing complaints from the controlling shareholder (Scott Paper Co. of Philadelphia), so when Lee Griffith took over as president in 1995, he promised swift action to remedy the problem. Part of the strategy involved cutting jobs. During 1995, the stock price doubled.

One reason management is paying so much attention to shareholders is the increasing importance of pension and mutual funds. For example, the Ontario Teachers Pension Plan Board now holds about $12 billion in Canadian shares. Managers of pension and mutual funds are under pressure to achieve high returns for the pensioners and workers who invest in these funds, so they put pressure on company management to increase share value. One way to do this is downsizing, but managers of pension and mutual funds often don't care about staff levels in a company; they are more interested in the stock price.

Shareholder pressure on company management to downsize was illustrated at the 1995 annual meeting of National Trustco Inc. An institutional shareholder said the company was the worst-performing financial services company in North America. He said that the company needed a dramatic restructuring to reduce overhead, and layoffs had to be considered as part of that restructuring. He made this comment despite the fact that the company had already cut 400 jobs. National Trustco president Paul Cantor said that improvements had to be made, but he wasn't sure that downsizing was the answer.

Canadian politicians are very concerned about downsizing in the private sector because government is itself in the process of downsizing. The government had hoped that private-sector business firms would create new jobs at a time when government jobs would be harder to find, but now that appears unlikely.

Industry Minister John Manley has expressed concern that the downsizing trend is focusing attention too narrowly on profits and shareholder returns. He thinks Canadians want business to reinvest earnings into expansion to create new jobs. He is worried that downsizing is going to reduce consumer confidence in the economy, and that future growth prospects will be affected. He also thinks that shareholder concern about stock prices places too much emphasis on the short term, and not enough on the long-term health of the economy.

The trade-off between share value and job creation is a complicated question. One interesting study by the management consulting firm A.T. Kearney Inc. showed that 69 percent of U.S. managers considered share value a critical issue, but that only 43 percent of Canadian managers and 25 percent of European managers did. But employment has risen 7 percent in the United States since

1990, and only 5 percent in Canada. It has dropped 3 percent in Europe. Could it be that when all is said and done, downsizing creates more jobs than it destroys? Could it be that downsizing makes firms more profitable and productive, and that an economy made up of these healthier firms creates more new jobs? Perhaps, but this is little comfort to the thousands of individuals who have lost their jobs through downsizing and have had to cope with the trauma of finding a new place in the economy.

In contrast, firms that produce industrial products such as machinery and janitorial supplies tend to put less emphasis on marketing and to have fewer marketing managers. However, these firms do not ignore marketing altogether. In recent years, law firms, colleges, and universities have also come to recognize the value and importance of marketing. For a detailed look at marketing, see Chapters 13-15.

Bank of Montreal
www.bmo.com

Financial Managers.   Management of a firm's finances, including its investments and accounting functions, is extremely important to its survival. Nearly every company has **financial managers** to plan and oversee its financial resources. Levels of financial management may include a vice president for finance (top), division controller (middle), and accounting supervisor (first-line). For large financial institutions like the Bank of Montreal, First City Trust, and Burns Fry, effective financial management is the company's reason for being. No organization, however, can afford to ignore the need for management in this area. Chapters 16-18 treat financial management in detail.

financial managers
Those managers responsible for planning and overseeing the financial resources of a firm.

Operations Managers.   A firm's operations are the systems by which it creates goods and services. **Operations managers** are responsible for production control, inventory control, and quality control, among other duties. Manufacturing companies like Steelcase, Bristol Aerospace, and Sony need operations managers at many levels. Such firms typically have a vice president for operations (top), plant managers (middle), and foremen or supervisors (first-line). In recent years, sound operations management practices have also become increasingly important to service organizations, hospitals, colleges and universities, and the government. Operations management is the subject of Chapters 10-12.

operations managers
Those managers responsible for controlling production, inventory, and quality of a firm's products.

Human Resource Managers.   Every enterprise uses human resources. Most companies have **human resource managers** to hire employees, train them, evaluate their performances, decide how they should be compensated, and, in some cases, deal with labour unions. Large firms may have several human resource departments, each dealing with specialized activities. Imperial Oil, for example, has separate departments to deal with recruiting and hiring, wage and salary levels, and labour relations. Smaller firms may have a single department, while very small organizations may have a single person responsible for all human resource activities. Chapters 8 and 9 address issues involved in human resource management.

human resource managers
Those managers responsible for hiring, training, evaluating, and compensating employees.

Information Managers.   A new type of managerial position appearing in many organizations is **information manager**. These managers are responsible for designing and implementing various systems to gather, process, and disseminate information. Dramatic increases in both the amount of information available to managers and in the ability to manage it have led to the emergence of this important function. While relatively few in number now, the ranks of information managers are increasing at all levels. Federal Express, for example, has a Chief Information Officer. Middle managers engaged in information

information managers
Those managers responsible for the design and implementation of systems to gather, process, and disseminate information.

FIGURE 5.4

Organizations require managers from a wide variety of areas to be effective. The most common areas are marketing, finance, operations, human resources, and information.

management help design information systems for divisions or plants. Computer systems managers within smaller businesses or operations are first-line managers. Information management is discussed in Chapter 12.

Petro-Canada
www.petro-canada.ca

Other Managers. Some firms have more specialized managers. Chemical companies like CIL have research and development managers, for example, whereas companies like Petro-Canada and Apple have public relations managers. The range of possibilities is endless; the areas of management are limited only by the needs and imagination of the firm.

■ BASIC MANAGEMENT SKILLS

While the range of managerial positions is almost limitless, the success that people enjoy in those positions is often limited by their skills and abilities. Effective managers must possess several skills: *technical, human relations, conceptual, decision making,* and *time management skills.*

Technical Skills

technical skills
Skills associated with performing specialized tasks within a firm.

Skills associated with performing specialized tasks within a company are called **technical skills**. A secretary's ability to type, an animator's ability to draw a cartoon, and an accountant's ability to audit a company's records are all technical skills. People develop their technical skills through education and experience. The secretary, for example, probably took a keyboarding course and has had many hours of practice both on and off the job. The animator may have had training in an art school and probably learned a great deal from experienced animators on the job. The accountant earned a university degree and, possibly, professional certification.

As Figure 5.5 shows, technical skills are especially important for first-line managers. Most first-line managers spend considerable time helping employees solve work-related problems, monitoring their performance, and training them in more efficient work procedures. Such managers need a basic understanding of the jobs they supervise.

As a manager moves up the corporate ladder, however, technical skills become less and less important. Top managers, for example, often need only a cursory familiarity with the mechanics of basic tasks performed within the company. Michael Eisner, for example, freely admits that he can't draw Mickey Mouse or build a ride for Disney World.

Human Relations Skills

Hyatt Hotels
www.hyatt.com

A few years ago, Hyatt Hotels checked 379 corporate employees into the chain's 98 hotels. They were not, however, treated as guests. Rather, they were asked to make beds, carry luggage, and perform the other tasks necessary to make a big hotel function. Top management at Hyatt believes that learning more about the work of lower-level employees will allow executives to understand them better as human beings (and co-workers).

The Hyatt experiment was designed to test and improve the **human relations skills** of upper-level managers—that is, skills in understanding and getting along with other people. A manager with poor human relations skills may have trouble getting along with subordinates, cause valuable employees to quit or transfer, and contribute to poor morale.

human relations skills
Skills in understanding and getting along with people.

As shown in Figure 5.5, human relations skills are important at all levels. This is true because all managers in the hierarchy act as "bridges" between their bosses, their subordinates, and other managers at the same level in the hierarchy. Good communication skills are essential in achieving good human relations in an organization.

Conceptual Skills

Conceptual skills refer to a person's ability to think in the abstract, to diagnose and analyze different situations, and to see beyond the present situation. Conceptual skills help managers recognize new market opportunities (and threats). They can also help managers analyze the probable outcomes of their decisions. The need for conceptual skills

conceptual skills
Abilities to think in the abstract, diagnose and analyze different situations, and see beyond the present situation.

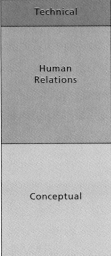

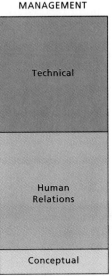

FIGURE 5.5
Different levels in an organization require different combinations of managerial skills.

differs at various management levels: top managers depend most on conceptual skills, first-line managers least. Although the purposes and everyday needs of various jobs differ, conceptual skills are needed in almost any job-related activity.

Decision-Making Skills

decision-making skills
Skills in defining problems and selecting the best courses of action.

Decision-making skills include the ability to define problems and select the best course of action. Figure 5.6 illustrates the basic steps in decision making.

1. *Define the problem, gather facts, and identify alternative solutions.* Current management at Schwinn recently realized that their predecessors had made some serious errors in assuming that mountain bikes were just a fad. The opposite proved to be true, and Schwinn's share of the bicycle market had dropped dramatically.

2. *Evaluate each alternative and select the best one.* Managers at Schwinn acknowledged that they had to take corrective action. They discussed such alternatives as buying a mountain bike maker, launching their own line of mountain bikes, or refocusing on other product lines. They chose to develop their own line of mountain bikes and did so in 1994.

3. *Implement the chosen alternative, periodically following up and evaluating the effectiveness of that choice.* Today Schwinn seems to be on track following its entry into the mountain bike market. Companywide sales and profits have begun to increase, and its new products are now attracting attention from the top mountain bike racers in the world.

Time Management Skills

time-management skills
Skills associated with the productive use of time.

Time management skills refer to the productive use that managers make of their time. In one recent year, for example, IBM CEO Louis Gerstner was paid $12.4 million in salary and bonuses. Assuming that he worked 50 hours a week and took two weeks' vacation, Gerstner earned $4960 an hour—about $266 per minute. Any time that Gerstner wastes clearly represents a large cost to IBM and its stockholders. Most managers, of course, receive much smaller salaries than Gerstner. Their time, however, is valuable, and poor use of it still translates into costs and wasted productivity.

To manage time effectively, managers must address three leading causes of wasted time:

1. *Paperwork.* Some managers spend too much time deciding what to do with letters and/or reports. Most documents of this sort are routine and can be handled quickly. Managers must learn to recognize those documents that require more attention.

2. *E-mail.* Electronic mail has become an important method of communication for managers in recent years. Some estimates place the number of e-mails the average manager receives each day between 170 and 180. Although this mode of communication can improve efficiency, it can also contribute to wasted time and effort.

3. *The telephone.* Experts estimate that managers get interrupted by the telephone every five minutes. To manage this time more effectively, they suggest having a secretary screen all calls and setting aside a certain block of time each day to return the important ones.

FIGURE 5.6
The decision-making process.

4. *Meetings.* Many managers spend as much as four hours a day in meetings. To help keep this time productive the person handling the meeting should specify a clear agenda, start on time, keep everyone focused on the agenda, and end on time.

■ CORPORATE CULTURES

What Is Corporate Culture?

Consider the following story, which details an interesting development in the relationship between employee behaviour and corporate values:

> In 1989, Microsoft programmer Wes Cherry wrote a software program duplicating the game solitaire. Originally designed to amuse people as they learned Microsoft's new Windows software, Solitaire became such a hit that since 1990 the company has packaged it with nearly 50 million copies of Windows. To the consternation of many companies, however, Solitaire has become a nuisance and even a threat to productivity. According to one survey, about 42 percent of office computer users admit to playing games at their desks. Some organizations have banned game playing, and some have even removed programs from company-owned computers. Meanwhile, other companies actually endorse computer games. Managers in these offices see them as contributing to productivity because they help to reduce stress.[8]

This story shows that just as every individual has a unique personality, so every company has a unique identity—its corporate culture. **Corporate culture** is the shared experiences, stories, beliefs, and norms that characterize an organization. Various corporate cultures can be effective. What is important to managers is establishing and maintaining a strong, clear culture.[9]

At Toyota's Cambridge, Ontario, plant, for example, the corporate culture stresses values, principles, and trust. It also emphasizes customer satisfaction. For each employee, the next person down the production line is the customer. The culture is one of continuous improvement *(kaizen).*[10]

corporate culture
The shared experiences, stories, beliefs, and norms that characterize a firm.

Mainframe Entertainment of Vancouver has one of the lowest turnover rates in the animation business. Its culture emphasizes giving young artists and designers opportunities to acquire new skills and develop leadership potential—opportunities not available in the bigger Los Angeles studios.

TRENDS CHALLENGES

Changing the Culture of a Manufacturing Plant

James Bonini was only 33 years old when he was named manager of Chrysler Corp.'s van plant in Windsor, Ontario. His key responsibility was to prepare for the introduction of a new van model. But in order to do this successfully, he concluded that he was going to have to change the culture at the plant, which was unfortunately characterized by numerous quality problems, managers who acted like drill sergeants, and workers who were demoralized. Bonini knew that he would have to win support for his ideas from the 84 managers at the plant, Canadian Auto Workers officials, and the 1800 workers at the plant.

Although he had degrees from Princeton and the University of California at Berkeley, Bonini had very little manufacturing experience. Yet in one year, he managed to introduce a major change in the culture at the plant. How did he do it?

Bonini knew that the first thing he had to do was deal with the disappointed individuals who thought they should have been given the plant manager's job. He acknowledged that he was inexperienced, and said he needed their help to institute the changes that were going to be necessary to make the new model a success. He also conducted meetings with workers to get their ideas and hear their gripes. He met with union officals as well, who advised him to talk individually with workers, some of whom had never met a plant manager before.

Initially, Bonini spent a lot of time on the production floor; this impressed both workers and union officials. He also promised that he would try to boost the sale of vans by making sure the plant was responsive to special customer orders. The plant had the reputation of being reluctant to fill such special orders, so this was a major change. After several special orders were successfully filled, van sales began creeping up for the first time in years.

Bonini also overhauled the plant's manufacturing system. A new way of thinking was introduced: when things go wrong, don't automatically blame the workers. Instead, look at the production system to see if it makes sense. Consistent with this idea was the notion that workers should be involved in decision making about how the plant would operate. The plant's antiquated body shop, for example, was divided into teams of workers who were given the job of developing standard operating procedures. For the first time ever, workers decided how production processes would be carried out. In the end, about 70 percent of the plant's operations were changed.

Within a year of coming to Windsor, Bonini was asked to manage a new engine plant that Chrysler was building in Latin America. When the workers heard this, they expressed the concern that all the good things that had been started at the Windsor plant would be lost if Bonini left. But that hasn't happened; Bonini's successor says that the cultural change that Bonini introduced was very powerful, and that any outsider who came into the plant understood how things were going to be done.

When two firms with different cultures merge, both have to adjust. For example, Baker-Lovick and McKim Advertising Ltd. were both purchased by BBDO Worldwide, a U.S. agency. But Baker-Lovick and McKim have completely different cultures. McKim is conservative and does not seek publicity, while Baker-Lovick loves the limelight. The new merged firm is likely to become more like Baker-Lovick in the future.[11] The box "Changing the Culture of a Manufacturing Plant" describes the change in culture that occurred *within* a factory when a new manager arrived on the scene.

Forces Shaping Corporate Culture

A number of forces shape corporate cultures. First, the values held by top management help set the tone of the organization and influence its business goals and strategies. For example, after Wozniak and Jobs founded Apple Computer, their laid-back approach and disdain for formality permeated the entire company. Even an older firm like Ford still bears traces of its founder. Most of Ford's top executives remain "car people," often engineers by training and background, rather than financial experts.

The firm's history also helps shape its culture. Championship banners line the Molson Centre, reinforcing the message that the Montreal Canadiens are winners. Maintaining a corporate culture draws on many dimensions of business life. Shared experiences resulting from norms sustain culture. Thus, working long hours on a special project becomes a shared experience for many employees. They remember it, talk about it among themselves, and wear it as a badge of their contribution to the company.

Stories and legends are also important. Walt Disney has been dead many years now, but his spirit lives on in the businesses he left behind. Quotations from Disney are affixed to portraits of him throughout the company's studios. And Disney's emphasis on family is still visible in corporate benefits such as paying for spouses to accompany employees on extended business trips. In fact, employees are often called "the Disney family."

Finally, strong behavioural norms help define and sustain corporate cultures. For example, a strong part of the culture at Hewlett-Packard Canada is that everyone wears a name tag and that everyone is called by his or her first name.

Communicating the Culture

To use the corporate culture for the betterment of the organization, managers must accomplish several tasks that all depend on effective communication:

- Managers themselves must have a clear understanding of the culture.
- Managers must transmit the culture to others in the organization. Communication is thus one of the aims in training and orientation for newcomers. Another way of communicating the culture is to develop a clear and meaningful statement of the organization's mission.
- Managers can maintain the culture by rewarding and promoting those who understand it and who work towards maintaining it.

SUMMARY OF LEARNING OBJECTIVES

1. **Explain the importance of setting *goals* and formulating *strategies* as the starting points of effective management.** *Goals*—the performance targets of an organization—can be *long-term*, *intermediate*, and *short-term*. They provide direction for managers, they help managers decide how to allocate limited resources, they define the corporate culture, and they help managers assess performance. *Strategies*—the methods that a company uses to meet its stated goals—involve three major activities: setting strategic goals, analyzing the organization and its environment, and matching the organization and its environment. These strategies are translated into *strategic*, *tactical*, and *operational plans*. To deal with crises or major environmental changes, companies develop *contingency plans* and plans for *crisis management*.

2. **Describe the four activities that constitute the *management process*.** *Management* is the process of planning, organizing, leading, and controlling an organization's financial, physical, human, and information resources to achieve the organization's goals. *Planning* means determining what the company needs to do and how best to get it done. *Organizing* means determining how best to arrange a business's resources and the necessary jobs into an overall structure. *Leading* means guiding and motivating employees to meet the firm's objectives. *Controlling* means monitoring the firm's performance to ensure that it is meeting its goals.

3. **Identify *types of managers* by level and area.** Managers can be differentiated in two ways: by level and by area. By level, *top managers* set policies, formulate strategies, and approve decisions. *Middle managers* implement policies, strategies, and decisions. *First-line managers* usually work with and supervise employees. Areas of managers include marketing, financial, operations, human resource, and information. Managers at all levels may be found in every area of a company.

4. **Describe the five basic *management skills*.** Most managers agree that five basic management skills are necessary for success. *Technical skills* are associated with performing specialized tasks ranging from typing to auditing. *Human relations skills* are associated with understanding and getting along with other people. *Conceptual skills* are the abilities to think in the abstract, to diagnose and analyze different situations, and to see beyond present circumstances. *Decision-making skills* allow managers to define problems and to select the best course of action. *Time management skills* refer to managers' ability to make productive use of the time available to them.

5. **Describe the development and explain the importance of *corporate culture*.** *Corporate culture* is the shared experiences, stories, beliefs, and norms that characterize an organization. A strong, well-defined culture can help a business reach its goals and can influence management styles. Culture is determined by several factors, including top management, the organization's history, stories and legends, and behavioural norms. If carefully communicated and flexible enough to accommodate change, corporate culture can be managed for the betterment of the organization.

STUDY QUESTIONS AND EXERCISES

Review Questions

1. What are the main purposes for setting organizational goals?

2. What are the four basic functions that all managers perform?

3. What are the major areas of management found in most organizations?

4. Relate the basic managerial skills to the four functions of management. For example, which skill(s) is (are) most important in leading?

5. What is corporate culture? What forces shape corporate culture?

Analysis Questions

6. Select any group of which you are a member (company, family, club, church, etc.). Explain how planning, organizing, leading, and controlling are practised in the group.

7. Identify managers by level and area at your college or university.

8. In what kind of company are technical skills for top managers more important than human relations or conceptual skills? Are there organizations in which conceptual skills are not important?

Application Exercises

9. Interview a manager of a local company. Identify that manager's job according to the level and area of management. Show how planning, organizing, leading, and controlling are part of his or her job. Inquire about the manager's education and work experience. Which management skills are most important for this job?

10. Compare and contrast the corporate cultures of two businesses in your community in the same industry (for example, a Sears department store and a Costco warehouse).

BUILDING YOUR BUSINESS SKILLS

Goal

To encourage students to use management skills to make important business decisions.

Situation

With five years of experience working in the corporate offices of one of the country's largest booksellers, you have just been assigned to be part of the team to develop a new chain of specialty bookstores. The idea behind the chain is that people want smaller bookstores that emphasize customer service, amenities, and product knowledge. They are tired of stores the size of supermarkets and clerks who know little about the books they sell. Your job is to work with team members to make key management decisions.

Method

Step 1: Working with four or five classmates, do library research on the bookselling business and particularly on the strengths and weaknesses of independent bookstores. Use what you learn to focus on the following factors. Brainstorm with team members to analyze the following issues:

- *The best markets for these stores:* Would specialized bookstores be likely to succeed in university towns, large cities, suburbs, or other areas?

- *The customer base:* Define your market in terms of socioeconomic status and educational level.
- *The best competitive environment:* Should you target locations that already have mega-booksellers or sites without them?

Step 2: Begin to define the business venture through the following management steps:

- Write a mission statement that defines your business purpose and strategy for achieving it.
- Define long-term and short-term goals by determining the markets you want to enter, the number of stores you want to open during the first year and within five years, the kind of books you want to stock, the ambiance and size of each store, and employee characteristics.
- Define how to differentiate your stores from the competition. For example, will you have a children's corner with a daily storytelling hour? Will you highlight prize-winning community interest books? Will

you have a book-ordering service that guarantees that customers receive requested books within 72 hours? Will you choose employees who are dedicated to customer service?

Follow-Up Questions

1. Why is an environmental analysis particularly important to the success of your venture?
2. Mega-booksellers are now online, including Amazon.com and Barnes & Noble. How is online commerce likely to affect your business?
3. Considering the competitive environment, do you think your venture will succeed? Why or why not?
4. Of all the management decisions you make, which do you consider the most important to the success of the business?
5. If the venture succeeds, what do you think the corporate culture will be like in five years?

Prentice Hall ◄ **T A K E   I T   T O   T H E   N E T**

Check out our Companion Website
for this chapter's Exploring the Net exercise, featuring the Kodak Website and other intriguing, annotated destinations. You'll also find practice exercises, updated Weblinks from the text, links to newsgroups, updates, and more.

COMPANION WEBSITE

w w w . p r e n t i c e h a l l . c a / e b e r t

BUSINESS CASE 5

No Longer Leading the League

Until July of 1997, Paul Beeston was the CEO of the Toronto Blue Jays. His associates thought that, like Tom Hanks in the movie *Big*, he walked a fine line between crazy kid and top-notch executive. Beeston, who was legendary for his commitment to the organization, started as the team's first full-time accountant and rose through the ranks to become president in 1989. He arrived at work between 7 a.m. and 7:30 a.m. each day and didn't take a vacation for years.

Until 1994, Beeston worked closely with Pat Gillick, the executive vice president and "master builder" of the club. Beeston handled the administration and balanced the books, while Gillick monitored the team's on-the-field performance. Big-name players like George Bell, Roberto Alomar, and Dave Winfield were signed to contracts. Beeston responded to fan concern about high player salaries by arguing that players need a good environment to work in.

Beeston was under constant pressure to win games and pennants. This is not a simple matter, since the club has 25 often temperamental ball players. It is necessary to continually find new players through the scouting system.

The ups and downs of professional sports franchises are well known. But until recently, the Toronto Blue Jays had been mostly up. From 1983 to 1993, the club had a winning record. It also won five divisional titles and, in 1992 and 1993, won back-to-back World Series titles. Attendance at Blue Jay games was high, the club was profitable, and the franchise was estimated to be worth nearly $200 million. Paul Beeston had indeed accomplished much as the club's CEO.

But since those good years, several problems have arisen. The baseball players strike in 1994 hurt all baseball teams, and in 1995 attendance at Blue Jay games dropped about 20 percent. These factors have caused a

►

reduction in the salary budget. When the Jays won the World Series in 1993, the total salary payroll was a league-high $50 million. In 1996, it was just $30 million. The Blue Jays have also lost some personnel, including players and managers. Pat Gillick left to join a competing team, the Baltimore Orioles; several key players like Roberto Alomar and Paul Molitor also left to join other teams.

In 1995, Beeston sent a letter to season ticket holders asking for their continued support and patience while the team tried to rebuild. He noted that it was not fun running an organization with the kinds of problems the Blue Jays had recently experienced.

But Beeston was not the kind of person to give up when problems arose. In late 1996, the Blue Jays acquired several new players, including Roger Clemens, Benito Santiago, and Carlos Garcia. The Jays' salary budget for 1997 was approximately US$55 million. The Jays have once again become big spenders, and they hope to be a pennant contender with this new talent.

In July 1997, Paul Beeston was named president and chief operating officer of Major League Baseball. In his new job, Beeston will be responsible for all phases of the central offices in New York City.

■ *Case Questions*

1. What management skills does Paul Beeston need to be effective? How did these skills change as he moved from accountant to CEO?

2. Briefly describe what each function of management involves in a position like Paul Beeston's.

3. Is being CEO of a baseball team much different from being CEO of a manufacturing firm? Explain.

CHAPTER
6

ORGANIZING THE BUSINESS ENTERPRISE

RESTRUCTURING AT CANADIAN PACIFIC

In November 1995, Canadian Pacific Ltd. announced a major restructuring. Under the plan, a new parent company will be set up, and it will wholly own six divisions: CP Rail System, CP Ships, PanCanadian Petroleum, Fording Coal, Marathon Realty, and Canadian Pacific Hotels. In the future, transportation and energy will be the two key elements in CP Ltd.'s overall corporate strategy.

As part of the reorganization, one of the six subsidiaries—CP Rail System Division—will move its headquarters from Montreal to Calgary. In the process, the division will cut 1450 management jobs and move another 730 jobs to Calgary. Most of the job losses will be felt in Montreal, although an eastern rail unit will still be located there. Shareholders must approve the proposed reorganization.

What motivated the move to Calgary? Since it was announced shortly after the Quebec referendum, some observers thought that it was politically motivated. But the CEO of CP Ltd., William Stinson, said that the referendum had nothing to do with the decision. He said it was strictly a business decision, and that it was necessary for railway management to be located where most of its revenues come from (80 percent of CP Rail Division revenues come from the west). Stinson also said that the reorganization would give CP Rail a

better management style, lower costs, and would bring the company closer to the customer.

Under the new structure, CP Rail will have considerable autonomy, and may eventually become a publicly traded company in its own right. It will have access to capital markets, whereas previously it had to rely on the parent company for funding. CP Rail will also be able to merge with another firm if it desires, or get involved in a joint venture, or even institute some form of employee ownership.

Observers of the rail industry think that competitive factors were a big consideration in the reorganization decision. For example, the privatization of Canadian National Railways in 1995 makes it more likely that it will be a more aggressive competitor in the next decade. In spite of the fact that CP Rail is one of the largest railways in the world (1994 sales were $3.7 billion), it made only $43 million in profit in 1994. By contrast, CN earned over $200 million in 1994. To maintain its competitiveness, CP Rail will have to become more efficient, and this reorganization is designed to achieve that goal.

This latest reorganization gives parent company CP Ltd. quite a different look than it had as recently as 10 years ago. Then, it was involved in all sorts of diverse businesses, including mining (Cominco), forest products (Canadian Pacific Forest

Products), airlines (Canadian Pacific Airlines), and communications (Unitel). All these business operations have been sold during the last decade.

Also as a result of the reorganization, the 11 layers of management in the company will be compressed to six. As well, costs will be cut by reducing the scale of activities in various locations around North America, including Toronto, Vancouver, Minneapolis, and Albany, New York. The reorganization will save the firm $100 million each year in administrative costs. Overall, industry analysts think the reorganization will give CP Ltd. a much clearer corporate strategy. It will also give CP Rail a tighter focus and greater earning power.

Canadian Pacific Ltd.
www.cprailway.com

The need to fit structure to operations is common to all companies, large and small. Whether a company employs five people or 500 000, it needs organization to function. In this chapter, we consider the nature of business organization and the structures that firms have traditionally chosen. By focusing on the learning objectives of this chapter, you will better understand the importance of business organization and the ways in which both formal and informal aspects of its structure affect the decisions a business makes. After studying this chapter, you should be able to:

1. Discuss the elements that influence a firm's *organizational structure*.
2. Describe *specialization* and *departmentalization* as the building blocks of organizational structure.
3. Distinguish between *responsibility* and *authority* and explain the differences in decision making in *centralized* and *decentralized organizations*.
4. Explain the differences between *functional*, *divisional*, *project*, and *international* organization structures.
5. Define the *informal organization* and explain its importance.

■ THE STRUCTURE OF BUSINESS ORGANIZATIONS

Exactly what do we mean by the term *organizational structure*? In many ways, a business is like an automobile. All automobiles have an engine, four wheels, fenders and other structural components, an interior compartment for passengers, and various operating systems including those for fuel, braking, and climate control. Each component has a distinct purpose but must also work in harmony with the others. Automobiles made by competing firms all have the same basic components, although the way they look and fit together may vary.

organizational structure
The specification of the jobs to be done within a business and how those jobs relate to one another.

Similarly, all businesses have common structural and operating components, each of which has a specific purpose. Each component must fulfill its own purpose while simultaneously fitting in with the others. And, just like automobiles made by different companies, how these components look and fit together varies from company to company. Thus, **organizational structure** is the specification of the jobs to be done within a business and how those jobs relate to one another.

Every institution—be it a for-profit company, a not-for-profit organization, or a government agency—must develop the most appropriate structure for its own unique situation. What works for Air Canada will not work for Revenue Canada. Likewise, the structure of the Red Cross will not work for the University of Toronto.

What accounts for the differences? An institution's purpose, mission, and strategy affect its structure. So do size, technology, and changes in environmental circumstances. A large manufacturing organization operating in a dynamic environment requires a different structure than a small service firm, such as a video rental store or barber shop.

organization chart
A physical depiction of the company's structure showing employee titles and their relationship to one another.

Most businesses prepare **organization charts** that illustrate the company's structure and show employees where they fit into the firm's operations. Figure 6.1 shows the organization chart for a hypothetical company. Each box represents a job within the company. The solid lines that connect the boxes define the **chain of command**, or the reporting relationships within the company. Thus, each plant manager reports directly to the vice president for production who, in turn, reports to the president. When the chain of command is not clear, many different kinds of problems can result.

An actual organization chart would, of course, be far more complex and include individuals at many more levels. Indeed, because of their size, larger firms cannot easily draw a diagram with everyone on it.

chain of command
Reporting relationships within a business; the flow of decision-making power in a firm.

■ THE BUILDING BLOCKS OF ORGANIZATIONAL STRUCTURE

Whether a business is large or small, the starting point in developing its organizational structure is determining who will do what and how people performing certain tasks can most appropriately be grouped together. Job specialization and departmentalization represent the basic building blocks of all businesses.

Specialization

The process of identifying the specific jobs that need to be done and designating the people who will perform them leads to **job specialization**. In a sense, all organizations have only one major "job"—say, making a profit by manufacturing and selling men's and boys' shirts. But this job, of course, is broken into smaller components. In turn, each component

job specialization
The use of individuals with specialized skills to perform specialized tasks within a business.

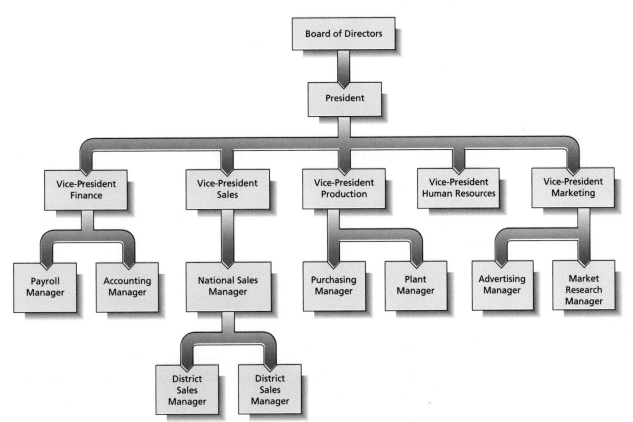

FIGURE 6.1
An organization chart shows key positions in the organization and interrelationships among them.

is assigned to an individual. Consider the manufacture of men's shirts. Because several steps are required to produce a shirt, each job is broken down into its component parts—that is, into a set of tasks to be completed by a series of individuals or machines. One person, for example, cuts material for the shirt body, another cuts material for the sleeves, and a third cuts material for the collar. Components are then shipped to a sewing room, where a fourth person assembles the shirt. In the final stage, a fifth person sews on the buttons.[1]

Mrs. Fields Cookies
www.imall.com/stores/
Mrs_Fields/Mrs_Fields.html

Specialization and Growth.   In a very small organization, the owner may perform every job. As the firm grows, however, so does the need to specialize jobs so that others can perform them. To see how specialization can evolve in an organization, consider the case of Mrs. Fields Cookies. When Debbi Fields opened her first store, she did everything herself: bought the equipment, negotiated the lease, baked the cookies, operated the store, and kept the records. As the business grew, however, Fields found that her job was becoming too much for one person. She first hired a bookkeeper to handle her financial records. She then hired an in-store manager and a cookie baker. She herself concentrated on advertising and promotions. Her second store required another set of employees—another manager, another baker, and some salespeople. While Fields focused her attention on other expansion opportunities, she turned promotions over to a professional advertising director. Thus the job that she once did all by herself was increasingly broken down into components and assigned to different individuals.

Job specialization is a natural part of organizational growth. It is neither a new idea nor limited to factory work. It carries with it certain advantages—individual jobs can be performed more efficiently, the jobs are easier to learn, and it is easier to replace people who leave the organization. On the other hand, if job specialization is carried too far and jobs become too narrowly defined, people get bored, derive less satisfaction from their jobs, and often lose sight of how their contributions fit into the overall organization.

Departmentalization

departmentalization
Process of grouping jobs into logical units.

profit centre
Separate company unit responsible for its own costs and profits.

After jobs are specialized, they must be grouped into logical units. This process is called **departmentalization**. Departmentalized companies benefit from the division of activities. Control and coordination are narrowed and made easier, and top managers can see more easily how various units are performing.

For example, departmentalization allows the firm to treat a department as a **profit centre**—a separate unit responsible for its own costs and profits. Thus, by assessing profits from sales in a particular area—say, men's clothing—Sears can decide whether to expand or curtail promotions in that area.

Computer maker Hewlett-Packard Co. recently reorganized its structure to increase customer responsiveness and improve decision making. Most of the firm's operations are now handled by teams, each of which functions with a great degree of autonomy from the others. Indeed, individual teams are virtually business owners. In the network-server division, for instance, top managers are responsible for their unit's overall costs. "Our profit-and-loss statement," reports marketing manager Jim McDonnell, "is like any other small company." Similarly, managers have the authority to reinvest their profits back into their own operating units. As decision makers, they need not wait for budget requests to percolate to the top of the corporate hierarchy and then filter back down. At the same time, however, they are responsible for contributions to companywide operations—supporting the firm's general research unit, for example, and paying the CEO's salary.[2]

Managers do not group jobs randomly. They group them logically, according to some common thread or purpose. In general, departmentalization may occur along *customer, product, process, geographic,* or *functional* lines (or any combination of these).

Customer Departmentalization.   Stores like Sears and The Bay are divided into departments—a men's department, a women's department, a luggage department, and so on. Each department targets a specific customer category (men, women, people who want to buy luggage). **Customer departmentalization** makes shopping easier by providing indentifiable store segments. Thus, a customer shopping for a baby's playpen can bypass Lawn and Garden Supplies and head straight for Children's Furniture. Stores can also group products in locations designated for deliveries, special sales, and other service-oriented purposes. In general, the store is more efficient and customers get better service—in part because salespeople tend to specialize and gain expertise in their departments.[3]

Product Departmentalization.   Both manufacturers and service providers often opt for **product departmentalization**—dividing an organization according to the specific product or service being created. A bank, for example, may handle consumer loans in one department and commercial loans in another. On a larger scale, 3M Corp., which makes both consumer and industrial products, operates different divisions for Post-it brand Tape Flags, Scotch-Brite scrub sponges, and the Sarns 9000 perfusion system for open-heart surgery.

Process Departmentalization.   Other manufacturers favour **process departmentalization**, dividing the company according to the production process used. Vlasic, a pickle maker, has separate departments that transform cucumbers into fresh-packed pickles, pickles cured in brine, or relishes.

Geographic Departmentalization.   Some firms may be divided according to the area of the country—or even the world—they serve. This is known as **geographic departmentalization**.

Functional Departmentalization.   Finally, many service and manufacturing companies develop departments based on a group's functions or activities—**functional departmentalization**. Such firms typically have a production department, a marketing and sales

Hudson's Bay Company
www.hbc.com

customer departmentalization
Departmentalization according to types of customers likely to buy a given product.

product departmentalization
Departmentalization according to products being created.

process departmentalization
Departmentalization according to the production process used to make a good.

geographic departmentalization
Departmentalization according to the area of the country or world supplied.

functional departmentalization
Departmentalization according to a group's functions or activities.

Whether they are produced manually or digitally, the drawings that comprise a full-length Walt Disney cartoon are the result of highly coordinated job specialization. A lead animator, for example, may provide a rough pencil sketch that is then refined by one or more artists. Other teams scan clean drawings into a computer and colour them according to a plan devised by the art director. Finally, to achieve hand-drawn movement, a team of so-called "in-betweeners" completes all the drawings needed to give fluid motion to one or two key frames drawn by the lead animator.

department, a personnel department, and an accounting and finance department. These departments may be further subdivided, as a university's business school may be subdivided into departments of accounting, finance, marketing, and management.

Because different forms of departmentalization offer different advantages, larger companies tend to adopt different types of departmentalization at various levels of the corporation. For example, the company illustrated in Figure 6.2 uses functional departmentalization at the top level. Its production department is divided along geographic lines, while its marketing unit is departmentalized by product group.

■ ESTABLISHING THE DECISION-MAKING HIERARCHY

A major question that must be asked about any organization is this: *Who makes which decisions?* The answer almost never focuses on an individual or even a small group. The more accurate answer usually refers to the decision-making hierarchy. The development of this hierarchy generally results from a three-step process:

1. *Assigning tasks:* determining who can make decisions and specifying how they should be made.
2. *Performing tasks:* implementing decisions that have been made.
3. *Distributing authority:* determining whether the organization is to be centralized or decentralized.

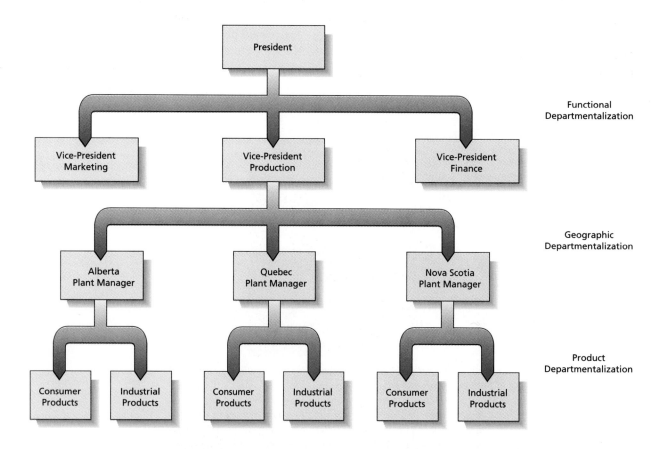

FIGURE 6.2
Most organizations use multiple bases of departmentalization. This organization, for example, is using functional, geographic, and product departmentalization.

Assigning Tasks: Responsibility and Authority

The question of who is *supposed* to do what and who is *entitled* to do what in an organization is complex. In any company with more than one person, individuals must work out agreements about responsibilities and authority. **Responsibility** is the duty to perform an assigned task. **Authority** is the power to make the decisions necessary to complete the task.

For example, imagine a mid-level buyer for The Bay who encounters an unexpected opportunity to make a large purchase at an extremely good price. Let's assume that an immediate decision is absolutely necessary—a decision that this buyer has no authority to make without confirmation from above. The company's policies on delegation and authority are inconsistent, since the buyer is *responsible* for purchasing the clothes that will be sold in the upcoming season but lacks the *authority* to make the needed purchases.

responsibility
Duty to accomplish assigned tasks.

authority
The right to make decisions necessary to accomplish certain tasks.

Performing Tasks: Delegation and Accountability

Trouble occurs when appropriate levels of responsibility and authority are not clearly spelled out in the working relationships between managers and subordinates. Here, the issues become delegation and accountability. **Delegation** begins when a manager assigns a task to a subordinate. **Accountability** falls to the subordinate, who must then complete the task. If the subordinate does not perform the assigned task properly and promptly, he or she may be reprimanded or punished, possibly even dismissed.

Subordinates sometimes cannot complete a task because their managers have not also delegated the necessary authority. Such employees face a dilemma: they cannot do what the boss demands, but that boss will probably still hold them accountable. Successful managers surround themselves with a team of strong subordinates and then delegate sufficient authority to those subordinates to get the job done. There are four things to keep in mind when delegating:

- decide on the nature of the work to be done
- match the job with the skills of subordinates

delegation
The assignment of a task, responsibility, and/or authority by a manager to a subordinate.

accountability
The liability of a subordinate in the event of non-performance of a task.

Manager delegating task to subordinate.

The Bank of Nova Scotia
www.scotiabank.ca

centralization
Occurs when top managers retain most decision-making rights for themselves.

decentralization
Occurs when lower- and middle-level managers are allowed to make significant decisions.

span of control
The number of people managed by one manager.

line authority
Organizational structure in which authority flows in a direct chain of command from the top of the company to the bottom.

line department
Department directly linked to the production and sales of a specific product.

- make sure the person chosen understands the objectives he or she is supposed to achieve
- make sure subordinates have the time and training necessary to do the task.

Distributing Authority: Centralization and Decentralization

In every organization, management must decide how to distribute authority throughout the hierarchy. **Centralization** occurs when top management retains the right to make most decisions that need to be made. In a highly centralized organization, the CEO makes most of the decisions, and subordinates simply carry them out. For example, Cedric Ritchie, the CEO of the Bank of Nova Scotia, knew all the details of the bank's operations and made many decisions that CEOs of other banks delegated to subordinates.[4]

Decentralization occurs when top managers delegate the right to make decisions to the middle and lower levels of the management hierarchy. At General Electric's Bromont, Quebec, plant, for example, every effort has been made to get employees involved in a wide range of decision making.[5] Traditional jobs like supervisor and foreman do not exist at the plant, and all hiring is done by committees made up of workers. Some workers spend only 65 percent of their time on production work; the other 35 percent is spent on training, planning, and in meetings. At Hymac Ltée., a Laval, Quebec, producer of pulp processing machinery, managers encourage employees to meet with customers to determine how Hymac can serve them more effectively.[6]

Span of Control. The distribution of authority in an organization also affects how many people work for any individual manager. The number of people managed by one supervisor is called the **span of control**. Employees' abilities and the supervisor's managerial skills help determine whether the span of control is wide or narrow. So do the similarity and simplicity of tasks performed under the manager's supervision and the extent to which they are interrelated. For example, by eliminating two layers of management, the president of the Franklin Mint recently increased his own span of control from 6 to 12.

When several employees perform either the same simple task or a group of interrelated tasks, a wide span of control is possible and often desirable. For instance, because all the jobs are routine, one supervisor may well control a whole assembly line. Moreover, each task depends on another: If one station stops, everyone stops. Having one supervisor ensures that all stations receive equal attention and function equally well. In contrast, when jobs are not routine, or when they are prone to change, a narrow span of control is preferable.

Not surprisingly, decentralized companies use wide spans of control and require few layers of management. The result is often called a *flat organizational structure*. On the other hand, centralized authority means that a firm relies on narrow spans of control, multiple layers of management, and a *tall organizational structure*.

Three Forms of Authority

In an organization, it must be clear who will have authority over whom. As individuals are delegated responsibility and authority in a firm, a complex web of interactions develops. These interactions may take one of three forms of authority: *line, staff,* or *committee and team*. In reality, like departmentalization, all three forms may be found in a given company, especially a large one.

Line Authority. **Line authority** is authority that flows up and down the chain of command (refer back to Figure 6.1). Most companies rely heavily on **line departments**—

departments directly linked to the production and sales of specific products. For example, Clark Equipment Corp. has a division that produces forklifts and small earth movers. In this division, line departments include purchasing, materials handling, fabrication, painting, and assembly (all of which are directly linked to production) along with sales and distribution (both of which are directly linked to sales).

Each line department is essential to an organization's success. Line employees are the "doers" and producers in a company. If any line department fails to complete its task, the company cannot sell and deliver finished goods. Thus, the authority delegated to line departments is important. A bad decision by the manager in one department can hold up production for an entire plant. For example, say that the painting department manager at Clark Equipment changes a paint application on a batch of forklifts, which then show signs of peeling paint. The batch will have to be repainted (and perhaps partially reassembled) before the machines can be shipped.

Staff Authority.   Most companies also rely on **staff authority**. Staff authority is based on special expertise and usually involves counselling and advising line managers. Common **staff members** include specialists in areas such as law, accounting, and human resource management. A corporate attorney, for example, may be asked to advise the marketing department as it prepares a new contract with the firm's advertising agency. Legal staff, however, do not actually make decisions that affect how the marketing department does its job. Staff members, therefore, aid line departments in making decisions but do not have the authority to make final decisions.

Suppose, for example, that the fabrication department at Clark Equipment has an employee with a drinking problem. The manager of the department could consult a human resource staff expert for advice on handling the situation. The staff expert might suggest that the worker stay on the job but enter a counselling program. But if the line manager decides that the job is too dangerous to be handled by a person whose judgment is often impaired by alcohol, that decision will most likely prevail.

Typically, the separation between line authority and staff responsibility is clearly delineated. As Figure 6.3 shows, this separation is usually shown in organization charts by solid lines (line authority) and dotted lines (staff responsibility). It may help to understand this separation by remembering that while staff members generally provide services to management, line managers are directly involved in producing the firm's products.

Committee and Team Authority.   Recently, more and more organizations have started to use **committee and team authority**—authority granted to committees or work teams that play central roles in the firm's daily operations. A committee, for example, may consist of top managers from several major areas. If the work of the committee is especially important, and if the committee will be working together for an extended time, the organization may even grant it special authority as a decision-making body that goes beyond the individual authority possessed by each of its members.

At the operating level, many firms today are also using *work teams*—groups of operating employees empowered to plan and organize their own work and to perform that work with a minimum of supervision. As with permanent committees, the organization will usually find it beneficial to grant special authority to work teams so that they may function more effectively.[7]

At Thermos, the well-known maker of insulated bottles, lunchboxes, and barbecue grills, interdisciplinary teams have largely replaced functions—marketing, engineering, and so forth—as the company's basic organizational principle. One team spent much of its time in the field learning about customers' cookout needs. The result was the Thermos Thermal Electric Grill, which uses entirely new technology to give food a barbecued taste while burning cleaner than gas or charcoal. The new grill, which also eliminates heavy propane tanks and messy cleanup, has already won numerous design awards

staff authority
Authority that is based on expertise and that usually involves advising line managers.

staff members
Advisers and counsellors who aid line departments in making decisions but do not have the authority to make final decisions.

committee and team authority
Authority granted to committees or work teams involved in a firm's daily operations.

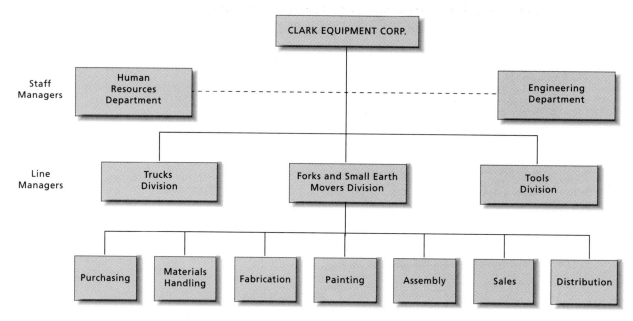

FIGURE 6.3
Line-and-staff organization: Clark Equipment Corp.

and is expected to raise Thermos's market share for electric grills from 2 percent to 20 percent over the next few years. "We need to reinvent our product lines," admits Thermos CEO Monte Peterson, and teamwork is doing it for us."[8]

■ BASIC ORGANIZATIONAL STRUCTURES

A glance at the organization charts of many organizations reveals what appears to be an infinite variety of structures. However, closer examination shows that most of them fit into one of three basic categories: functional, divisional, or project. As business has become more globalized, more and more firms are adopting an international organizational structure. These four structures are described below.

The Functional Structure

functional structure
Various units are included in a group based on functions that need to be performed for the organization to reach its goals.

The functional structure is the oldest and most commonly used. In the **functional structure**, the various units in the organization are formed based on the functions that must be carried out to reach organizational goals. The functional structure makes use of departmentation by function. An example of a functional structure is shown in Figure 6.1. The advantages and disadvantages of the functional structure are summarized in Table 6.1.

The Divisional Structure

divisional structure
Divides the organization into divisions, each of which operates as a semi-autonomous unit.

The functional structure's disadvantages can make it inappropriate for some companies. Many companies have found that the divisional structure is more suited to their needs. The **divisional structure** divides the organization into several divisions, each of which operates as a semi-autonomous unit and profit centre. In 1990, Alberta's Conservative government unveiled a new divisional structure and a new name for Alberta Government Telephones (AGT). The new organization is called Telus Corporation and is patterned after Montreal-based BCE. It oversees the telecommunications activity of seven operating companies, including AGT.

■ **TABLE 6.1   Advantages and Disadvantages of a Functional Structure**

Advantages	Disadvantages
1. Focuses attention on the key activities that must be performed.	1. Conflicts may arise among the functional areas.
2. Expertise develops within each function.	2. No single function is responsible for overall organizational performance.
3. Employees have clearly defined career paths.	3. Employees in each functional area have a narrow view of the organization.
4. The structure is simple and easy to understand.	4. Decision making is slowed because functional areas must get approval from top management for a variety of decisions.
5. Eliminates duplication of activities.	5. Coordinating highly specialized functions may be difficult.

As we saw earlier in this chapter, divisions in organizations can be based on products, customers, or geography. Whatever basis is used, divisional performance can be easily assessed each year because the division operates as a separate company. Firms with this structure are often called *conglomerates*.

The advantages and disadvantages of the divisional structure are summarized in Table 6.2.

Project Organization

A typical line or line-staff organization is characterized by unchanging vertical authority relationships. It has such a setup because the organization produces a product or service in a repetitive and predictable way. Procter & Gamble, for example, produces millions of tubes of Crest Toothpaste each year using standardized production methods. The company has done this for years and intends to do so indefinitely.

But some organizations find themselves faced with new product opportunities or with projects that have a definite starting and end point. These organizations often use a project structure to deal with the uncertainty encountered in new situations. **Project organization** involves forming a team of specialists from different functional areas of the organization to work on a specific project.[9] A project structure may be temporary or permanent; if it is temporary, the project team disbands once the project is completed and team members return to their regular functional area or are assigned to a new project.

Project organization is used extensively by Canadian firms, for example, in the construction of hydroelectric generating stations like those developed by Hydro-Québec on La Grande River, and by Manitoba Hydro on the Nelson River. Once the generating

project organization
An organization that uses teams of specialists to complete specific projects.

Hydro-Québec
www.hydro.qc.ca

Manitoba Hydro
www.hydro.mb.ca

■ **TABLE 6.2   Advantages and Disadvantages of a Divisional Structure**

Advantages	Disadvantages
1. Accommodates change and expansion.	1. Activities may be duplicated across divisions.
2. Increases accountability.	2. A lack of communication among divisions may occur.
3. Develops expertise in the various divisions.	3. Adding diverse divisions may blur the focus of the organization.
4. Encourages training for top management.	4. Company politics may affect the allocation of resources.

station is complete, it becomes part of the traditional structure of the utility. Project organization has also proven useful for coordinating the many elements needed to extract oil from the tar sands. Project management is also used in other kinds of tasks, including shipbuilding, construction, military weapons, aerospace, and health care delivery.[10] The box "Project Management at Genstar" describes how this form of organization works, and how authority issues are decided.

matrix organization
A project structure in which the project manager and the regular line managers share authority until the project is concluded.

Some companies use a **matrix organization**, which is a variation of project structure in which the project manager and the regular line managers share authority. When a project is concluded, the matrix is disbanded. IBM, for example, has a line-staff structure overall, but it used a matrix organization to develop the original PC. The matrix was disbanded when the PC succeeded.

TRENDS & CHALLENGES

Project Management at Genstar Shipyards Ltd.

Genstar Shipyards Ltd. is a Vancouver firm that specializes in the custom building and repair of icebreakers, research vessels, ferries, tugs, and barges. In peak periods, it delivers a new ship every two months. The value of the ships varies from a low of about $2 million for a small tugboat to a high of nearly $60 million for a state-of-the-art icebreaker. Construction periods for ships range from four months to two years.

Project management is really the only structure that makes sense for shipbuilding. Since time is of the essence in every construction contract, and since costs must be closely monitored, a project structure is necessary.

The shipyard has an operations manager who is responsible for the overall shipbuilding activity. Two project managers (PMs) report to the operations manager. Each ship the company builds is treated as a project, and the two PMs are responsible for seeing that projects are finished on schedule, to specification, and within budget. Some projects employ up to 400 people, so the PM's job may have a major administrative component.

The PM is responsible for the development of a master schedule for each vessel's design and construction. He or she identifies personnel and equipment that are necessary to complete the job, and interacts with all departments involved in the project. Once the master schedule has been set, the PM is responsible for seeing that the schedule and the budget are met. After the ship is built and launched, the PM oversees its trial run and delivery to the owner.

The PM has the authority to decide the construction sequence on the project as well as the number of workers that will be assigned to each phase of the project. These decisions are made after consulting the project plans. Workers on the project report to a supervisor. If the PM and the supervisor disagree about who should be assigned to a project, the PM can appeal to the superintendent (the supervisor's boss). The PM usually prevails on staffing issues.

Other areas of potential disagreement also exist. For example, a supervisor might think work on some part of a ship's construction ought to be done in one way, while the PM thinks it should be done in some other way. If the disagreement is a question of sequencing of the work, the PM will usually prevail; if the disagreement is about specific trade practices, the supervisor will generally win out. As another example, a supervisor may try to assign more tradespeople to a project than the PM thinks are necessary. The supervisor may be trying to create a cushion in meeting the construction schedule. In these cases, the PM usually wins out because the total project schedule and budget must be kept in mind, whereas the supervisor may be thinking only of the work that a particular crew is doing.

The PM does not have the authority to hire, lay off, or fire workers; this is the responsibility of the supervisor. The PM works with the supervisor to determine when the workforce should be increased or decreased. The PM also has the authority to approve payment to outside sources from which the company has purchased materials.

To be effective, the PM requires interpersonal skills (the ability to instill enthusiasm in workers), administrative skills (the ability to keep the project on schedule and within budget), and technical skills (the ability to communicate with the technically skilled people who are working on the project).

A problem with the matrix structure is that employees have two bosses—their regular line boss *and* the project manager. Employees may therefore receive conflicting orders. These and other problems have caused some firms that used to like the matrix structure to move away from it. For example, Digital Equipment Company's president, Robert Palmer, announced in 1994 that "matrix management at our company is dead."[11]

Digital Equipment Company
www.digital.com

International Organization

Many businesses today manufacture, purchase, and sell in the world market. Thus a number of variations on basic organizational structure have emerged. Moreover, as competition on a global scale becomes more complex, companies often find that they must experiment with the ways in which they respond.

For example, at Club Méditerranée, an international French-based firm that provides vacation sites (called "villages") around the world, each village manager used to report both to a country manager and to a number of different directors. Directors worked out of company headquarters, and each director had primary responsibility for some facet of Club Med operations and marketing. This structure, however, proved less than satisfactory. Club Med prides itself on providing village arrangements that reflect various *local* atmospheres—a difficult feat for directors to achieve from remote locations. To solve this problem, the company adopted a different form of organization. A major component of the new structure involved sending operations and marketing staff to specific geographic regions.

Club Med
www.world.net/clubmed/welcome.html

For similar reasons, other firms have developed a wide range of approaches to international organizational structure. Whirlpool, for example, purchased the appliance division of the Dutch electronics giant N.V. Philips and as part of its international organization structure now makes the cooling coils for its refrigerators at its new plant in Trento, Italy.[12] Other companies, such as Levi Strauss, handle all international operations through separate international divisions. Still others concentrate production in low-cost areas and then distribute and market globally. Some firms, such as Britain's Pearson PLC (which runs such diverse businesses as publishing, investment banking, and Madame Tussaud's Wax Museum), allow each of their businesses to function autonomously within local markets. Finally, some companies adopt a truly global structure in which they acquire resources (including capital), produce goods and services, engage in research and development, and sell products in whatever local market is appropriate, without any consideration of national boundaries.

■ THE INFORMAL ORGANIZATION

So far we have focused on the **formal organization** of businesses—the part that can be seen and drawn in chart form. But organization within any company is not limited to the organization chart and the formal assignment of authority. Frequently, the **informal organization**—the everyday social interactions among employees—alters a company's formal structure. At the New York Metropolitan Opera, for example, musicians and singers play poker during the intermissions. Hands are played quickly, with most pots in the $30 to $40 range. Luciano Pavarotti, the famed tenor, played once and lost big.[13]

One of the most powerful informal forces in any firm is the grapevine. The **grapevine** is an informal communications network that carries gossip and other information throughout the organization. As the box "Heard It Through the Grapevine" notes, the grapevine can be a useful source of information—if you take it with a grain of salt. See also the "Building Your Business Skills" exercise at the end of the chapter.

When its reports are accurate, the grapevine can serve a company by supplying information more rapidly than formal channels can. For example, if employees see an ambulance pull up to the plant, they will use the grapevine to find out if someone has had

formal organization
The specified relationships between individuals, their jobs, and their authority, as shown in the company's organization chart.

informal organization
A network of personal interactions and relationships among employees unrelated to the firm's formal authority structure.

grapevine
An informal communications network that carries gossip and other information throughout an organization.

TRENDS & CHALLENGES

Heard It Through the Grapevine

Faster than a speeding bullet—that's the office grapevine. But how accurate is it? Should you listen to it, or is it just so much gossip?

Today many experts advise tuning in to the grapevine's message. They note that the grapevine is often a corporate early warning system. Ignoring this valuable source of information can leave you the last to know that you're about to get a new boss, or that you have a potentially fatal image problem. Even personal information about co-workers and superiors can be useful in helping you interact positively with these individuals.

Do consider both the source and the message carefully, though. Most office gossip has at least some kernel of truth to it. But as "facts" get passed down from person to person, they can get twisted out of shape. In other cases, those passing on news will deliberately alter it, either to advance their own goals or to submarine someone else's chances. Experts also warn that listening to and passing on information damaging to someone's reputation can backfire, harming your credibility and making you a target for similar gossip.

In general, the more detailed the information, the less likely it is to be true. Likewise, beware the hush-hush "don't quote me on this" rumour. (Cynics claim that the better the news, the less likely it is to be true, too.) But the higher the source, the greater the likelihood that the grapevine has the real story. Don't reject information from "lower" sources, however. Many an executive secretary can provide valuable insights into a corporation's plans.

An interesting phenomenon of office communication occurs when individuals responsible for formal information systems, such as newsletters, press briefings, and memoranda, spread a somewhat different story on the grapevine. Which should you believe? Today it is so common for a corporate executive to publicly deny rumours of layoffs one day and hand out pink slips the next that no one even raises an eyebrow. The grapevine, unconcerned with public image and long-range schemes, cuts to the heart of the matter.

The grapevine is not infallible, however. In addition to miscommunication and attempts by some people to manipulate it for their own ends, it may carry rumours with absolutely no basis in fact. Such rumours are most common when there is a complete lack of information. Apparently, human nature abhors such a vacuum and fills it. Baseless rumours can be very hard to kill, however.

---

mentor
A manager who guides the careers of subordinates by offering them advice, providing them with training and expanded responsibility, and otherwise assisting them in gaining promotions.

an accident. Long before the personnel department can issue an announcement, the grapevine can supply the news that a pregnant worker had her baby early. Similarly, advance word of impending changes in the company's operations can help employees adjust mentally—and even physically (by getting a new job elsewhere, for example)—before the actual shift. The informal organization also facilitates networking and **mentoring**, which can enhance the career development of individuals and promote organizational effectiveness.

Some companies encourage the informal exchange of information.[14] For example, 3M sponsors clubs for 12 or more employees to try to enhance communication across departments. Other companies have physically arranged offices and other facilities to be more conducive to informal communications. One bank moved two departments to the same floor in an attempt to encourage intermingling of the employees. These companies believe informal communications can stimulate discussions that solve organizational problems.

On the down side, informal communications can also cause problems. They can play an instrumental role in office politics that put the interests of individuals ahead of those of the firm. Likewise, a great deal of harm can be caused if distorted or inaccurate information flows through the grapevine. For example, if the grapevine is carrying false information about impending layoffs, valuable employees may act quickly (and unnecessarily) to look for employment elsewhere.

The grapevine is a powerful informal communications network in most organizations. These workers may be talking about any number of things—an upcoming deadline on an important project, tonight's football game, the stock market, rumours about an impending takeover, gossip about forthcoming promotions, or the weather.

Intrapreneuring

Sometimes organizations actually take steps to encourage the informal organization. They do so for a variety of reasons, two of which we have already touched on. First, most experienced managers recognize that the informal organization exists whether they want it or not. Second, many managers know how to use the informal organization to reinforce the formal organization. Perhaps more important, however, the energy of the informal organization can be harnessed to improve productivity.

- To stimulate innovation, for example, 3M Corp. maintains a flat, decentralized organizational structure. As a rule, only a few levels of management bureaucracy are involved in approving new products. The corporate culture at 3M further supports innovation by encouraging researchers to spend 15 percent of their time exploring new ideas. Those who develop new products are rewarded both professionally and financially. As a result, 3M researchers usually develop about 200 new products each year. Among their most celebrated successes have been Post-it self-stick notes and a tape for mending broken bones.

3M
www.3M.com

- Through Xerox Technology Ventures, Xerox Corp. allocates $30 million to fund companies like QuadMark Ltd., an electronics development firm in which Xerox has a 60 percent stake. The purpose of XTV is to nurture internal technological innovations that, for various reasons, do not receive adequate attention from the parent company's development centre. For example, QuadMark developed a battery-operated copier that fits inside a briefcase next to a laptop computer. Another XTV-funded startup invented an advanced circuit board that could be inserted into an inexpensive PC and made to do the work of a $10 000 Xerox office workstation. Xerox deemed it wise to buy out the potential new competitor (for $15 million). Since 1989, XTV has generated 12 startups and now offers as much as 20 percent of the new companies' shares to successful founders.[15]

Xerox
www.xerox.com

intrapreneuring
Process of creating and maintaining the innovation and flexibility of a small business environment within the confines of a large organization.

Both 3M and Xerox are supporting a process called **intrapreneuring**—creating and maintaining the innovation and flexibility of a small business environment within the confines of a large, bureaucratic structure. The concept is sound. Historically, most innovations have come from individuals in small businesses (see Chapter 7). As businesses increase in size, however, innovation and creativity tend to become casualties in the battle for more sales and profits. In some large companies, new ideas are even discouraged, and champions of innovation have even been stalled in mid-career. In companies like 3M and Xerox, however, intrapreneuring is seen as an effective way of remaining as innovative as smaller firms that specialize in new products that the larger firms can bring to market quickly.

SUMMARY OF LEARNING OBJECTIVES

1. **Discuss the elements that influence a firm's *organizational structure*.** Every business needs structure to operate. Its *organizational structure* varies according to a firm's mission, purpose, and strategy. Size, technology, and changes in environmental circumstances also influence structure. In general, while all organizations have the same basic elements, each develops the specific structure that contributes to the most efficient operations.

2. **Describe *specialization* and *departmentalization* as the building blocks of organizational structure.** The building blocks of organizational structure are *job specialization* and *departmentalization*. As a firm grows, it usually has a greater need for people to perform specialized tasks (specialization). It also has a greater need to group types of work into logical units (departmentalization). Common forms of departmentalization are *customer*, *product*, *process*, *geographic*, and *functional*. Large businesses often use more than one form of departmentalization.

3. **Distinguish between *responsibility* and *authority* and explain the differences in decision making in *centralized* and *decentralized* organizations.** *Responsibility* is the duty to perform a task; *authority* is the power to make the decisions necessary to complete tasks. In a *centralized organization*, only a few individuals in top management have real decision-making authority. In a *decentralized organization*, much authority is delegated to lower-level management. In areas where both *line* and *line-and-staff systems* are involved, *line departments* generally have authority to make decisions, while *staff departments* have a responsibility to advise. In a *functional organization*, authority is usually distributed among such basic functions as marketing and finance.

4. **Explain the differences between *functional*, *divisional*, *project*, and *international* organization structures.** In the *functional structure*, the various units in the organization are formed based on the functions that must be carried out to reach organizational goals. In the *divisional structure*, the company is divided into divisions and each of these operate in a semi-autonomous fashion. In *project organization*, a company creates teams to address specific problems or to conduct specific projects. A company that has operations in many countries may require an additional level of *international organization* to coordinate those operations.

5. **Define the *informal organization* and explain its importance.** The *informal organization* is a system of personal relationships and interactions among employees that is unrelated to the formal organization shown in a firm's organization chart. A company's informal organization can have a major effect on its operations and must be taken into account by managers. Although the informal communication system known as the *grapevine* can help a business get information to its employees more quickly than formal channels, it can also be a source of disruption.

STUDY QUESTIONS AND EXERCISES

Review Questions

1. What is an organization chart? What purpose does it serve?

2. Explain the significance of size as it relates to organizational structure. Describe the changes that are likely to occur as an organization grows.

3. What is the difference between responsibility and authority?

4. Explain the basic features of the functional, divisional, project, and international structures.

5. Why is a company's informal organization important to its operations?

Analysis Questions

6. Is there an optimal span of control? Why or why not?

7. Identify the organizational structure of your college or university. Why does it have such a structure?

8. Explain how the functional, divisional, project, and international organization structures differ.

Application Exercises

9. Interview a manager of a local service business such as a fast-food restaurant. Identify what types of tasks are delegated. Is the appropriate authority also delegated in each case?

10. Using books, magazines, or personal interviews, identify an individual who has succeeded as an *in*trapreneur. In what ways did the structure of the intrapreneur's company help the person succeed? In what ways did the structure inhibit the person's success?

BUILDING YOUR BUSINESS SKILLS

Goal

To encourage students to understand the role of the grapevine in business firms, and to learn how to deal with rumours that spread through the grapevine.

Situation

Suppose that as a department manager, you learn that a rumour is spreading through the grapevine that the company is planning to close your facility at the end of the month, thereby laying off dozens of employees. The rumour is not true. You want to stop it but are not sure what to do.

Method

Evaluate the pros and cons of the following strategies for stopping the rumour.

Strategy 1: When you first hear the rumour, issue a formal memo denying everything but giving no additional information.

Strategy 2: As you happen to see them in the office, talk with employees and reassure them that the rumour is false. Rather than dealing with the rumour in detail, talk about it in general terms.

Strategy 3:

- When you first realize that a rumour is starting, try to track down its sources.

- Evaluate the damage being caused by the rumour.

- Plan a counterattack by gathering all the facts about the rumour and where it has spread.

- Confront the rumour by using concrete evidence to refute it; if necessary, bring in experts to support the refutation; directly state that the rumour is false and that spreading lies is damaging and unfair.

Follow-Up Questions

1. Which type of rumour is more difficult to contain—a rumour contained within an organization or one that has spread to competitors, customers, and other external groups?

2. Why do you think that the informal communications network holds such power in business organizations?

Prentice Hall T A K E   I T   T O   T H E   N E T

Check out our Companion Website
for this chapter's Exploring the Net exercise, featuring the Pinchot intrapreneurship Website and other intriguing, annotated destinations. You'll also find practice exercises, updated Weblinks from the text, links to newsgroups, updates, and more.

COMPANION WEBSITE   **w w w . p r e n t i c e h a l l . c a / e b e r t**

BUSINESS CASE 6

United Airlines Gives Managers the Power to Manage

Are long ladders a sign of a successful corporate reorganization? At United Airlines they are. Long ladders symbolize the company's new approach to management—an approach that often depends on teamwork to solve problems. A case in point: a team made up of pilots, ramp workers, and managers sat down together—for the first time—to figure out how to power planes idling at the gate with electricity instead of jet fuel. Electricity would save money, but because their short working ladders prevented ramp workers from plugging electrical cables into the aircraft, using electricity was literally out of reach.

Not surprisingly, the solution—longer ladders—was a no-brainer for team members, and not simply because several of them actually knew the situation first hand. What is surprising, perhaps, was the failure of traditional managers to see that when the problem is short ladders, the solution is probably longer ladders. At United, it seems, managers far removed from the loading gates had no way of assessing even the simplest problem. Worse yet, a stringent top-down management style prevented them from consulting with the right people—in this case, ramp workers at loading gates. According to Robert M. Sturtz, United's top fuel administrator, the company was able to identify the real problem only when management resorted to teamwork. In this instance, the result has been an annual savings of $20 million in fuel costs.

In 1994, United's 80 000 employees bought the carrier, creating one of the country's largest employee stock ownership plans (ESOP). Since then, United has been transformed from a top-driven hierarchical organization into one that values teamwork, initiative, and creativity. Chairman and CEO Gerald Greenwald has also reduced the number of management layers and removed many functional divisions in favour of a horizontal integration of resources that focuses on markets. "We are," he proclaims, "no longer a company that operates by command and control."

The key markets that now correspond to United's internal divisions are North America, international, cargo, shuttles, and new business development. Each division is headed by a senior vice president who reports directly to President and Chief Operating Officer John A. Edwardson. In addition, all operational groups, including on-board services and flight operations, report to the president. In short, authority has been decentralized, and divisional managers have the power to run their businesses.

Reorganization has also increased the authority of divisional and mid-level managers. Previously, such functional operations as airport services and reservations were worlds unto themselves, with their own organizational structures and chains of command. Because members of different areas rarely communicated, airline operations often suffered. According to James E. Goodwin, Senior Vice President for North America, United's Honolulu station nicely illustrated the poor coordination of the old system. "The sales organization," explains Goodwin, "reported to someone in Los Angeles, who then reported to someone in Chicago. The reservations function reported directly to Chicago. The airport manager reported to someone in San Francisco. In many cases, the people never even knew each other."

This arrangement led to open conflicts among departments. "The sales organization," recalls Goodwin, "would go out and make commitments to the customer that they couldn't deliver at the airport. All they could do is say, 'I only sell it. I don't make it.'" Worse yet, customer service problems had to be transferred to headquarters for resolution. When the new management discarded this function-based organizational structure, managers received both greater power and the resources needed to use it. To further speed decision making, unnecessary managerial levels were eliminated, thus creating a "flatter" organizational structure (the old one resembled a pyramid). Before that, recalls Edwards, "it wasn't uncommon to get a request for capital on my desk that had 13 to 14 signatures on it before it got to me."

What effect have these changes had on United's performance? Thanks in large part to improved productivity, United is taking market share away from rivals American and Delta and has solidified its position as America's number one air carrier. In addition, operating margins are fatter, the stock price has climbed, and knowledgeable outsiders have formed a favourable view of United's improved performance. Reports one industry analyst at Merrill Lynch, "United has hard statistics that show the company is working differently than in the past."

One of the most obvious signs of organizational change at United Airlines is the increased authority of mid-level managers to spend money. Before decentralization, vice presidents needed the president's approval for purchases over $4999—a situation that undermined their autonomy and their ability to make decisions.

➤

John A. Edwardson learned of the spending limit about a week after he took over as United's President and Chief Operating Officer: He received a purchase request from a vice president for $5000 worth of typing paper. Edwardson relates what happened next. "I walked over to his office and said, 'Is this a joke, or are you testing me?' And he said, 'I never test presidents, and I don't know you well enough to joke with you.'"

With the removal of United's rigid top-down organization, vice presidents can now spend up to $25 000 without seeking approval and have authority over about 95 percent of their budgets.

■ *Case Questions*

1. How have organizational changes at United affected the company's decision-making hierarchy?

2. Why did United's function-based organization fail?

3. How did reorganization affect managers' accountability and span of control?

4. Was increasing the spending authority of vice presidents a symbolic move, or did it have real organizational importance?

5. Why did a decentralized organizational structure work better at United than a top-down hierarchical structure?

CHAPTER

7

RUNNING THE SMALL BUSINESS

ZEPF TECHNOLOGIES INC.

Zepf Technologies Inc. (ZTI) of Waterloo, Ontario, is a good example of a small family business that has grown and plans to continue growing. Lawrence Zepf started the business in 1972 as a machine shop making automated packaging equipment for high-speed production lines. It was truly a family business as all seven of Zepf's sons and three of his five daughters were involved in the business. Since machinists were critical in the early years, Zepf made sure that his sons obtained their machinist's papers in the local three-year community college program.

Eventually, the family business grew and transformed. Innovative software, calculated risks, and personal commitment changed the business from a machine shop to a competitor in the international packaging industry. According to Zepf, the company's development and use of innovative technology was the driving force behind its success. In 1986, working with control specialists from West Germany, ZTI developed a unique, multi-axis bi-directional cutting lathe, affectionately named RAMBO. It was the only one of its kind in the world.

ZTI also developed the software Feedscrew Design System (FDS), which enabled it to design feedscrews that were extremely sophisticated and durable, resulting in the superior packaging and faster output of products. The company's success in new products was attributable to its contributing 10 to 12 percent of annual sales to R&D, and to substantial expenditures on employee training. The Zepfs believed that good management skills are a factor in growth, and that training is the key to adapting to growth. Rewarding employees is crucial, and in 1989 a profit sharing plan was introduced.

Recognizing the limited market in Canada, ZTI turned to European markets through a joint venture with a German firm to manufacture complete cams and specialty machinery. ZTI secured a contract in excess of $1 million with Jumex of Mexico to introduce the technology to that country. In 1989, the company won the Canada Awards for Business Excellence.

By 1992, the company had grown to about $4 million in sales and 40 employees. It was a reasonable size, but Larry Zepf, Lawrence's son and now president and chief executive of ZTI (pictured), was considering whether the company should remain with the status quo or attempt to grow. He wondered what the implications of growth would be for his family business.

Larry Zepf decided to grow, but he faced several challenges. First, growth requires capital, and his bank was unwilling to extend more financing. Zepf went searching for a more understanding account manager and found one. He felt that the Bank of Montreal had trained their managers to understand export-oriented manufacturing, which needs financing during a period of rapid growth.

ZTI's commitment to R&D during the 1980s provided a good basis for growth in the 1990s. As a result, ZTI was able to stay ahead of its competitors in packaging technology, enabling ZTI to enter export markets before their competitors. ZTI has grown internationally through exports sales, licensing agreements, and joint ventures in Scotland and the United States.

The type of employees ZTI needs has also changed. In the beginning, machinists were crucial to success, whereas now technologists are needed who can operate CAD/CAM design equipment. In the 1980s, there were three employees on the factory floor to one designer. Now the ratio is two designers per production employee. ZTI has difficulty finding highly skilled technologists and finds it expensive to do the training itself.

As the business has grown, so has the approach to management. In the past, family members were relied upon, but now professional managers from outside are being hired. The chief financial officer is not a family member, and others are likely to be hired to complement family talent. Even though financing was found through a bank, Zepf is now thinking about taking the company public, that is, selling shares to investors outside the family.

By 1995, ZTI had tripled sales to $11 million and employment had climbed to over 100. During this period, ZTI experienced many challenges typical of growth in small businesses: family succession, the need for debt and equity financing, the change in type of employees, and the hiring of nonfamily managers.

Every year, thousands of people like Lawrence Zepf launch new business ventures. These individuals, called entrepreneurs, are essential to the growth and vitality of the Canadian economic system. Entrepreneurs develop or recognize new products or business opportunities, secure the necessary capital, and organize and operate businesses.

In this chapter we first define the term "small business," describe the role of the entrepreneur, and note the advantages and disadvantages of owning a small business. Alternative approaches to becoming a small business owner (including franchising) are noted, as are the challenges facing entrepreneurs. The chapter concludes with a description of the various sources of assistance that are available to small business owners.

If you are aware of the challenges you will encounter as an entrepreneur, you are more likely to avoid the classic problems small business owners face. It is easy to start a business, but to operate one at a profit over a period of years requires the knowledge and application of the fundamentals of management. This chapter is designed to give you realistic expectations about small business management.

When you have completed this chapter, you should be able to:

1. Define *small business* and explain its importance to the Canadian economy.
2. Explain which types of enterprise best lend themselves to small business success.
3. Describe the startup decisions made by small businesses.
4. Identify the advantages and disadvantages of *franchising*.
5. Identify the reasons for the success and failure of small businesses.
6. Describe the sources of financial aid and management advice available to small businesses.

▪SMALL BUSINESS IN CANADA

The Canadian media pay considerable attention to the activities of large business enterprises but often neglect the fact that small businesses are thriving and are making a significant contribution to the economic well-being of Canadians. A small business may be a corporation, sole proprietorship, or a partnership. Small businesses include those operated by professionals, such as doctors, lawyers, and accountants, and self-employed

Statistics Canada
www.statscan.ca

owners, such as mechanics, television technicians, and restaurateurs. They are found in virtually every industry and are particularly prominent in the retail trade. In numbers, small business is the dominant type of business in Canada. According to Statistics Canada, small business enterprises account for about 98 percent of the 900 000 enterprises in Canada and for about 19 percent of total business revenue. The annual sales revenue for the average small business in 1996 was $284 000. Profits averaged $19 900, and the typical small business had 2.5 employees.[1]

The degree of small business varies across different industries. As shown in Figure 7.1, small business firms are dominant in the construction and retailing industries, but not so dominant in manufacturing. About six out of every ten Canadians employed in the private sector work in a firm with less than 500 employees.

History has shown that major innovations are as likely to come from small businesses or individuals as from big businesses. Small firms and individuals invented the personal computer, the stainless-steel razor blade, the transistor radio, the photocopying machine, the jet engine, and the self-developing photograph. They also gave us the helicopter, power steering, automatic transmissions, air conditioning, cellophane, and the ballpoint pen.

Small Business Defined

There are almost as many definitions of small business as there are books on the topic. Two approaches will be used here to define a small business: one based on characteristics and the other based on size. A **small business** is one that is independently owned and operated and is not dominant in its field of operations. It possesses most of the following characteristics:

small business
An independently owned and operated business not dominant in its field of operations.

- Management of the firm is independent. Usually the managers are also the owners.
- An individual or a small group supplies the capital and holds the ownership.
- The area of operations is usually local, and the workers and owners live in the same community. However, the markets are not always local.
- The enterprise is smaller than others in the industry. This measure can be in terms of sales volume, number of employees, or other criteria. It is free of legal or financial ties to large business enterprises.
- The enterprise qualifies for the small business income tax rate under the *Income Tax Act.*

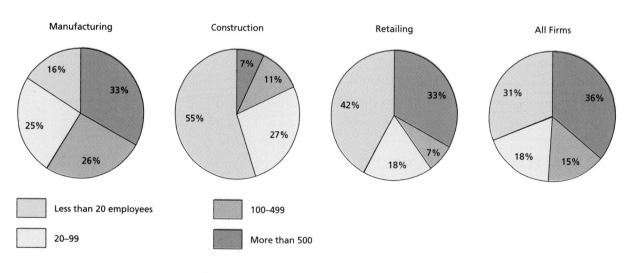

FIGURE 7.1
Employment distribution by enterprise size.

A common type of small business in Canada is the convenience store. It attracts customers from its immediate area with its long hours of operation and the product lines it carries.

The size of a small business is usually measured in terms of sales revenue or number of employees, but there is debate about what those numbers should be. For example, the Canadian government's Small Business Office defines a small business as one having less than $2 million in annual sales. Another government department defines a small business as one having less than 1500 employees, while other sources use a number as small as 50 employees. Given these differences, it is probably most useful to define a small business as one that has the five characteristics noted above. The video case "Earth Buddy" on p. 146 describes a typical small business in Canada.

■ENTREPRENEURSHIP

Although the concepts of *entrepreneurship* and *small business* are closely related, there are some important, though often subtle, differences between them. Many small businesspersons like to think of themselves as **entrepreneurs**—individuals who assume the risk of business ownership with the primary goal of growth and expansion. In reality, however, a person may be a small businessperson only, an entrepreneur only, or both. Consider an individual who starts a small pizza parlour with no plans other than to earn enough money from the restaurant to lead a comfortable lifestyle. That individual is clearly a small businessperson. With no plans to grow and expand, however, the person is not really an entrepreneur. In contrast, an entrepreneur may start with one pizza parlour and turn it into a national chain. Although this individual may have started with a small business, the growth of the firm resulted from entrepreneurial vision and activity.

The *Canadian Business* Entrepreneur of the Year award for 1997 went to Klaus Woerner, who started ATS Automated Tooling Systems in 1974 and built it into a company that currently has sales of $250 million annually and provides employment for over 2000 people.[2]

The typical entrepreneur is about 42 years old, as compared with the typical employee, who is about 34 years old. An increasing number of women are becoming entrepreneurs, and they now account for half the increase in new business owners each year. Women typically are more conservative than men in running a small business, and their failure rate is lower than for men.[3]

entrepreneur
Businessperson who accepts both the risks and the opportunities involved in creating and operating a new business venture.

Canadian Business
www.canbus.com

University of Western Ontario
www.uwo.ca

Dozens of studies have identified common traits among entrepreneurs. A researcher at the University of Western Ontario compiled a list of many of the characteristics identified by these studies, including assertive, challenge seeking, charismatic, coping, creative, improvising, opportunistic, preserving, risk taking, self-confident, tenacious, venturesome, and oriented towards achievement and action.[4] An Ontario government report, *The State of Small Business*, found that the main reasons for starting a business were:

- The need to achieve or the sense of accomplishment. Entrepreneurs believe that they can make a direct contribution to the success of the enterprise.
- The need to be their own boss and to control their time.
- The perceived opportunity in the marketplace to provide a product or service.
- The wish to act in their own way or have the freedom to adapt their own approach to work.
- The desire to experience the adventure of independence and a variety of challenges.
- The desire to make money.
- The need to make a living.[5]

The Jim Pattison Group
www.jimpattison.com

The motivations of successful entrepreneurs include having fun, building an organization, making money, winning in business, earning recognition, and realizing a sense of accomplishment.[6] The box "Jimmy Pattison—Canadian Entrepreneur Extraordinaire" describes the career of one of Canada's best-known entrepreneurs. Another well-known Canadian entrepreneur—stock promoter Murray Pezim—died in 1998. He was a flamboyant speculator and was involved in some of Canada's most famous gold finds.[7]

Entrepreneurship has both benefits and costs. On the positive side, entrepreneurs get a tremendous sense of satisfaction from being their own boss. They also enjoy successfully bringing together the factors of production (land, labour, and capital) to make a profit. Perhaps the greatest benefit, however, is that entrepreneurs can make a fortune if they have carefully planned what the business will do and how it will operate.

On the negative side, entrepreneurs can go bankrupt if their business fails. Customers can demand all sorts of services or inventory that small businesses cannot profitably supply. Entrepreneurs must work long hours and often get little in return in the first few years of operation. An entrepreneur may find that he or she is very good at one particular aspect of the business—for example, marketing—but knows little about managing the overall business. This imbalance can cause serious problems. In fact, poor management is the main reason businesses fail.

■ BECOMING A SMALL BUSINESS OWNER

Most people become involved in a small business in one of four ways: they take over a family business, they buy out an existing firm, they start their own firm, or they buy a franchise. There are pros and cons to each approach.

Taking Over a Family Business

Taking over and operating one's own family business poses both challenges and opportunities. One important challenge is dealing with family members who may consider a job, a promotion, and an impressive title their birthright, regardless of their talent or training. Mac Cuddy, the founder of Cuddy International Corp., had five sons who worked in the business, but he decided he needed to bring in outsiders for the top management positions because his sons did not have the management skills to run a large company. Eventually he fired two of his sons and a third left after being demoted. There was much conflict between family members in this situation.[8]

TRENDS CHALLENGES

Jimmy Pattison—Canadian Entrepreneur Extraordinaire

Most 65-year-old Vancouverites like to have a relaxed breakfast and read the newspaper. Not Jimmy Pattison, one of Canada's most famous entrepreneurs. It's 9 a.m., and he has been in his office since 6 a.m. He has already gone through his mail and phone messages, solved a potential crisis, and talked to a businessman from Thailand who wants to do a deal. In spite of his great wealth, Pattison has no intention of slowing down.

The Jim Pattison Group, one of Canada's largest sole proprietorships, has sales in excess of $3 billion and employs 17 000 people. Jimmy Pattison started out in the 1950s selling pots and pans door to door. He knew he could make enough money to live on if he sold just one set of pots and pans each day. He also learned that he could sell one set if he could just get three evening appointments to make his sales pitch. To get those three evening appointments, he had to knock on about 30 doors. Then he discovered that if he whistled while going door to door, he only had to make 22 house calls to get three appointments. So that's what he did.

In 1961, he began selling cars. Over the years he became involved in numerous other ventures. Now his one-man conglomerate owns 12 car franchises, a Caribbean bank, Ripley's Believe-It-Or-Not, Overwaitea

food stores, outdoor signs, Gold Seal fishery products, and Westar Group Ltd., to name just a few. The company's biggest investments in the next few years will be in B.C. and Alberta. Expansion into the U.S. is also planned. In the 1980s, the company did no business in the U.S., but now the U.S. accounts for 20 percent of company sales. Pattison is also thinking of expanding into Mexico.

Pattison is obviously in charge of the company. His inner circle includes six executives specializing in law, tax, accounting, insurance/administration, cash management, and deal-making. He says being a private company allows him to take a long-run perspective. He says that as long as he keeps his banker happy, things run smoothly. One of Pattison's biggest recent challenges has been to "renew" the company by recruiting a younger generation to replace his colleagues. Most of the new top executives come from the operating divisions. One is only 29 years old.

Pattison says he has only sales skills, but those have served him well throughout his career. He notes that sales requires hard work, and it forces you to relate to people. Those two elements are crucial for success. He also learned in selling that having the door slammed in your face teaches you to handle setbacks and disappointments. He learned not to take no for an answer.

Other family businesses are somehow able to avoid these succession squabbles. In seven generations of business activity (starting in 1788), the Wilson family of Nova Scotia has had no blowups or family spats. The family is unusual; about 70 percent of family businesses fail to continue from one generation to the next.[9] Figure 7.2 lists the key challenges facing the leaders of family-owned businesses.

A family business also has some unique opportunities. It can provide otherwise unobtainable financial and management resources because of the personal sacrifices of family members; family businesses often have a valuable reputation or goodwill that can result in important community and business relationships; employee loyalty is often high; and an interested, unified family management and shareholders group may emerge.

Buying an Existing Enterprise

Because a family-run business and other established firms are already operating, they have certain advantages for the purchaser: the clientele is established, financing might be easier because past performance and existing assets can be evaluated, experienced employees may already be in place, and lines of credit and supply have been established. An entrepreneur who buys someone else's business, however, faces more uncertainty about the exact conditions of the organization than a person who takes over his or her family's operation.

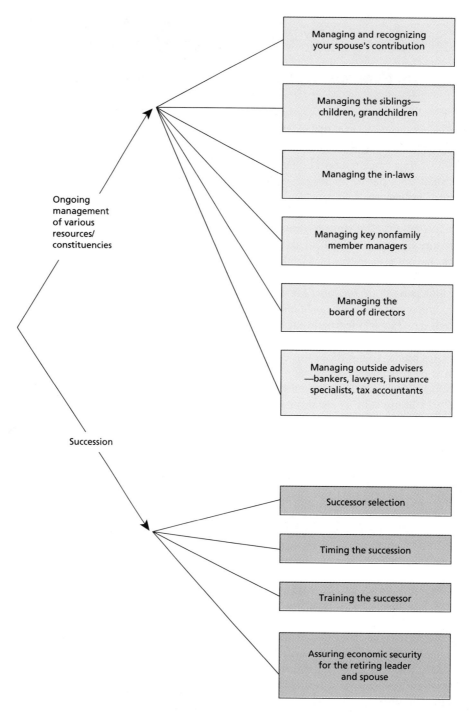

FIGURE 7.2
Family-owned business leader's key challenges.

The acquisition of an existing enterprise may have other drawbacks: the business may have a poor reputation, the location may be poor, and an appropriate price may be difficult to ascertain.

Starting a Business

This approach is likely the most challenging to becoming a small business owner, for there is no existing operation, no established customers, and no history in the form of financial or marketing records upon which to base decisions. Consequently, acquiring financing can be difficult; investors, either lenders or shareholders, have to be convinced of the enterprise's viability. Beginning a new enterprise usually means spending large amounts of money before sales or revenues materialize. Overall, new businesses pose a higher risk and greater uncertainty than established organizations since the business venture is unproven and the competence of the entrepreneur is most likely unknown.

A business plan is essential for those individuals who wish to start a small business. The contents of a business plan are described in Table 7.1.

■ TABLE 7.1   A Business Plan

The contents of a business plan vary depending upon the information required by the financial institutions or government agencies. Some entrepreneurs develop plans as a personal guide to check on where they are or want to be. The following are the components that might be included in such a plan:

Cover Page
Contains the enterprise's name, address, telephone numbers, and key contacts.

Table of Contents

Executive Summary
A brief statement, usually about one page long, summarizing the plan's contents.

Background/History of the Enterprise
A concise outline of when and how the enterprise got started, the goods or services it sells, and its major suppliers and customers.

Management
Background information on the entrepreneur and other employees, especially other managers (if there are any).

Marketing Assessment
Descriptions of the products or a service profile, the results of any market research, a market description and analysis, an identification of competition, and an account of the marketing strategy.

Production Assessment
A brief description of the production process, the technological process employed, quality requirements, location and physical plant, and details of machinery and equipment.

Financial Assessment
A review of the capital structure and the money needed to finance the business. Usually includes a projected balance sheet, profit and loss statement, and a cash flow forecast. Lenders may also require details of loan collateral and a repayment proposal.

Research and Development (R&D)
For many enterprises, R&D is important and a statement of what is planned would be included. There may also be an assessment of the risks anticipated with any new products or ventures.

Basic Data
Data on the enterprise's bankers, accountants, lawyers, shareholders (if any), and details of incorporation (if applicable).

Appendices
The following might be attached to a plan: detailed management biographies, product literature, evaluation of assets, detailed financial statements and cash flow forecast, and a list of major contracts.

The risks of starting a business from scratch are, not surprisingly, greater than those of buying an existing firm. Success or failure depends on identifying a genuine business opportunity—a product for which many customers will pay well but which is currently unavailable to them. To find openings, entrepreneurs must answer the following questions:

- Who are my customers?
- Where are they?
- At which price will they buy my product?
- In what quantities will they buy?
- Who are my competitors?
- How will my product differ from that of my competitors?

microenterprise
An enterprise that the owner operates part-time from the home while continuing regular employment elsewhere.

Many new businesses start as **microenterprises**—enterprises operated from the home part-time while the entrepreneur continues to work as a regular employee of another organization. Sometimes such a business is operated in partnership with others. The obvious advantage of beginning as a microenterprise is that the entrepreneur can test his or her idea before quitting regular employment. This approach is being used increasingly by Canadians.

Beginning a business from scratch has its benefits. An entrepreneur can create the image for the business he or she wants and is unrestricted by past reputation or policies. The owner has the flexibility to decide how big or small the operation is to be and has the chance to start small and grow at a manageable pace. Finally, an entrepreneur has the freedom to choose the location and building decor.

Buying a Franchise

Contrary to popular belief, franchising did not begin with the 1950s boom in fast-food franchises like McDonald's. Rather, its beginnings date back to the early 1800s. Not until 1898, however, when General Motors began franchising retail dealerships, did modern franchising begin in earnest. Similar systems were created by Rexall (pharmacies) in 1902, Howard Johnson (restaurants and, later, motels) in 1926, and many oil, grocery, motel, and fast-food franchisers in the early 20th century.

franchising
A contract between a manufacturer and a dealer that stipulates how a product or service will be sold.

One of the fastest ways to establish a business is to buy a franchise. Franchising has continued to increase in economic importance (see the box "Just Like Home"). **Franchising** involves drafting a contract between a manufacturer and a dealer that stipulates how the manufacturer's or supplier's product or service will be sold. The dealer, called a **franchisee**, agrees to sell the product or service of the manufacturer, called the **franchisor**, in return for royalties. Franchising organizations well-known in Canada include Holiday Inn, McDonald's, College Pro Painters, Weight Watchers, Kentucky Fried Chicken, Midas Muffler, and Canadian Tire.

franchisee
The dealer who agrees to sell the product or service.

Franchise purchase prices vary a great deal. A Fantastic Sam's hair salon franchise fee might be as little as $20 000, a McDonald's franchise might cost $750 000, and a professional sports team franchise like the Toronto Blue Jays will cost millions of dollars.

franchisor
The manufacturer of the product or service.

The franchising arrangement can be beneficial to both the franchisee and the franchisor. The franchisee enjoys the following benefits:

- *Recognition.* The franchise name gives the franchisee instant recognition with the public.
- *Standardized appearance of the franchise.* Customers know that consistency exists from one outlet to another.
- *Management assistance.* The franchisee can obtain advice on how to run the franchise effectively.

Canadian Tire Corporation
www.canadiantire.ca

TRENDS CHALLENGES

Just Like Home

It could be any Canadian city. On one corner sits a McDonald's restaurant. On another is a Kentucky Fried Chicken shop. Down the street is a 7-Eleven convenience store. A Budget Rent-A-Car outlet sits next to a Holiday Inn. Yes, it could be anywhere in Canada. But it's not. It's Tokyo, Japan.

Despite its reputation as an insular culture, Japan has embraced a number of franchising overtures. Probably the most successful chain to franchise in Japan is 7-Eleven stores, thanks largely to its major Japanese franchisee, Ito Masatoshi. He now operates 3800 7-Eleven stores. A savvy marketer, Masatoshi appealed to single urban residents stranded by the early closing hours of traditional Japanese grocery stores.

Japan is just one of many nations providing new markets for the franchise concept. Today, more and more franchisors are selling or opening operations from Fiji to France, from Moscow to Malaysia. Canada has more franchises than any nation outside the United States and most of these franchises are with U.S. firms.

U.S. franchisors like Kentucky Fried Chicken and McDonald's have dominated international markets for years. But NAFTA has created opportunities for Canadian franchisors to move into Latin America. Yogen Früz (frozen yogurt), Ceiling Doctor (home repairs), Pizza Pizza Ltd., and Cara Operations Ltd. have already gained some success in Mexico.

A common language is not enough to ensure success for franchises. Cultural differences have kept sales in the United Kingdom low. For example, ComputerLand has sold only 20 of 60 planned franchises in the U.K. British residents simply do not impulsively buy computers they see in store windows as their North American cousins do. Fast-food franchises have fared especially badly because most Britons prefer not to spend their spare cash eating out in such places.

Undeterred, many firms are looking closely at continental Europe for franchising opportunities. The new European Union rules will make it much easier for foreign firms to franchise their operations while still maintaining reasonable control over product offerings. The demise of communism in Eastern Europe and the dissolution of the Soviet Union also provide new areas for franchising. Formerly only joint ventures with the national governments were possible. Certainly franchising provides an excellent opportunity for citizens in these nations to gain expertise in marketing and other capitalist necessities. However, as some observers have noted, only the largest franchisors—those who can afford to accept a small initial fee and wait for the profits to come in—will be able to take advantage of this new franchising potential. Smaller franchisors will have to wait until the Eastern European countries develop stable economies, currencies, and individual entrepreneurs who have substantial cash to invest.

Those who have succeeded in international franchising offer a few basic rules. First, do your market research and make sure your product or service will fit into the culture. Gymboree, which franchises developmental play programs for preschoolers and their parents, has turned down Japanese investors because its centres require a great deal of space—something in short supply in Japan. Second, be patient. It may take 10 years for foreign stores to start showing a profit. Third, find a reliable partner. Toys 'R' Us entered into a joint venture with McDonald's to use the latter's expertise to open new toy stores in Japan. Finally, be prepared to be flexible. One frozen-yogurt maker found interest—and sales—picking up when it offered a green-tea flavour in Japan.

- *Economies of scale in buying.* The head office of the franchise buys in large volume and resells to the franchisee at lower prices than he or she could get buying alone.
- *Promotional assistance.* The head office of the franchise provides the franchisee with advertising and other promotional material.

Gymboree
www.gymboree.com

The franchisee is not the only party who gains in franchising. The franchisor enjoys the following benefits:

- *Recognition.* The franchisor is able to expand its area of operation by signing agreements with dealers in widely dispersed places.

Franchising is very popular in Canada. It offers individuals who want to run their own business an opportunity to establish themselves quickly in a local market.

- *Promotion savings.* The various franchisees can decide on local advertising efforts; this arrangement saves the franchisor money on wasted coverage in areas where it does not have a franchise.
- *Franchisee payments.* The franchisees pay the franchisor for the right to operate their franchises.
- *Attention to detail.* Since franchisees own their franchises, they are motivated to do a good job and to sell the franchisor's product or service aggressively.

Franchising has facilitated the growth of small business in Canada. The financial and management assistance franchisees can receive from the franchisor removes many of the risks that typically face small business owners. In fact, whereas about 80 percent of all small businesses fail within five years, less than 20 percent of franchises fail in the same period.

Franchising, however, does have its shortcomings. Not all of the franchises on the market are as successful as McDonald's. Many entrepreneurs are uninterested in becoming franchisees because the franchisor is able to regulate their behaviour too closely. They would rather start their own business and take whatever risks are necessary in return for the freedom to do what they want.

■ CHALLENGES FOR THE ENTREPRENEUR

Starting and operating a business enterprise is challenging: financing must be obtained, the enterprise must be carefully managed, and assistance must often be found.

Financing the Small Enterprise

The amount of capital needed to start a small business prevents some people from becoming entrepreneurs. However, sources of funding are available, and a list is given in Table 7.2. It should be noted that some sources are more likely than others to provide money. Lenders may or may not lend money to entrepreneurs, depending upon whether the enterprise is just beginning or is ongoing.

Funds for Starting a Business.   The most likely sources of financing are the personal funds of individuals, in particular, the entrepreneurs themselves. Some government agencies may provide assistance funds for startup and so might chartered banks if they think that the proposed business has promise.

Funds for an Ongoing Business.   After the enterprise has operated for some time, other services are more likely to be used, if a good financial reputation has been established. Sources include trade credit (that is, the delayed payment terms offered by suppliers), chartered banks, trust companies, and venture capitalists. Another source of funds is profits from the business. Entrepreneurs seldom pay themselves all the profits generated by the enterprise. Some profits are reinvested in the enterprise and are called **retained earnings.**

retained earnings
Profits reinvested in an enterprise.

Managing Funds.   In Table 7.2, each source is identified as debt or equity. **Debt** refers to borrowed funds that require interest payments and must be repaid. **Equity** refers to the money, or capital, invested in the enterprise by individuals or companies who become owners, and to profits reinvested. In the case of small enterprises, the entrepreneur is often the sole owner. The challenge for entrepreneurs is to keep the amount of funds borrowed and funds invested in ownership in balance. If an enterprise relies upon debt too heavily, interest payments might become burdensome and could lead to the failure of the enterprise.

Investors who invest equity obtain ownership and have some influence on the firm's operations. If investors own 51 percent or more of the firm's equity, they could control the enterprise. As enterprises require funds to grow, this diminishing of control frequently cannot be avoided.

debt
Borrowed funds that require interest payments and must be repaid.

equity
Money invested in the enterprise by individuals or companies who become owners.

■ TABLE 7.2   Principal Sources of Funds for Small Business Enterprises

Debt Sources

These are funds borrowed by the enterprise. They may come from:

- The entrepreneur who may loan money to the enterprise
- Private lenders, that is, individuals or corporations
- Financial institutions such as banks, credit unions, trust companies, and finance companies. Such borrowing may be by the enterprise but guaranteed by the entrepreneur or secured against other nonbusiness assets of the entrepreneur
- Trade credit, that is, the delayed payment terms offered by suppliers
- Government agencies, for example, the Federal Business Development Bank
- The selling of bonds or debentures (usually only done when the enterprise is larger)

Equity Sources

This money is invested in the enterprise and represents an ownership interest. It comes from:

- The entrepreneur's personal funds
- Partners, either individuals or corporations
- Family and friends
- Venture capitalists
- Governments
- The selling of shares to the public (usually only done when the enterprise is larger)
- Employees who may participate in a stock purchase plan or simply invest in the enterprise

Retained Earnings

Profits, that is, funds generated from the operation of the business, can be either paid to the owners in dividends or reinvested in the enterprise. If retained or reinvested, profits are a source of funds.

■ THE SURVIVAL OF SMALL BUSINESS

Numerous statistics on the survival rate of small businesses have been compiled. The following data are representative:

- About 13 to 15 percent of all business enterprises disappear each year.
- One half of new businesses fail in the first three years. After that the failure rate levels off.
- After 10 years, only 25 percent of businesses are still in existence.
- The average life span of small enterprises is 7.25 years.
- Female entrepreneurs have a survival rate about twice as high as that of males.[10]

The low survival rate need not be viewed as a serious problem, since failures are natural in a competitive economic system. In some cases, enterprises are poorly managed and are replaced by more efficient and innovative ones. In recent years, more enterprises have started than have failed, indicating the resiliency of small business and entrepreneurs.

Reasons for Success

Four factors are typically cited to explain the success of small business owners:

1. *Hard work, drive, and dedication.* Small business owners must be committed to succeeding and be willing to put in the time and effort to make it happen. Long hours and few vacations generally characterize the first few years of new business ownership.

2. *Market demand for the product or service.* If the area around a college has only one pizza parlour, a new pizzeria is more likely to succeed than if there are already 10 in operation. Careful analysis of market conditions can help small business people assess the reception of their products in the marketplace.

3. *Managerial competence.* Successful small business people have a solid understanding of how to manage a business firm. They may acquire competence through training (by taking courses in small business management at a local college), experience (by learning the ropes in another business), or by using the expertise of others.

4. *Luck.* Luck also plays a role in the success of some firms. For example, after one entrepreneur started an environmental clean-up firm, he struggled to keep his business afloat. Then the government committed a large sum of money for toxic waste cleanup. He was able to get several large contracts, and his business is now thriving.

Reasons for Failure

Small businesses collapse for a number of reasons (see Table 7.3). The entrepreneur may have no control over some of these reasons (for example, weather, fraud, accidents), but he or she can influence most items on the list. This is the main reason an entrepreneur should learn as much as possible about management.

■ ASSISTANCE FOR ENTREPRENEURS AND SMALL BUSINESS ENTERPRISES

In the Canadian economic system, the existence of small enterprises is considered desirable for a number of reasons, including the employment it provides, the innovations it introduces, and the competition it ensures. To help entrepreneurs through the hazards

■ TABLE 7.3   Causes of Small Business Failure

Poor management skills

poor delegation and organizational ability	entrepreneurial incompetence, such as a poor understanding of finances and business markets
lack of depth in management team	
lack of experience	

Inadequate marketing capabilities

difficulty in marketing product	too much competition
market too small, nonexistent, or declines	problems with distribution systems

Inadequate financial capabilities

weak skills in accounting and finance	inadequate costing systems
lack of budgetary control	incorrect valuation of assets
inadequate cash flow forecasts	unable to obtain financial backing

Inadequate production capabilities

poorly designed production systems	inadequate control over quality
old and inefficient production facilities and equipment	problems with inventory control

Personal reasons

lost interest in business	death
accident, illness	family problems

Disasters

fire	strikes
weather	fraud by entrepreneur or others

Other

mishandling of large project	difficulties with associates or partners
excessive standard of living	government policies change
lack of time to devote to business	

of starting up and operating a new business, substantial assistance is available. Government is the main source of assistance, but other sources are also available. Various sources of assistance are summarized in Table 7.4.

In spite of the numerous government assistance programs, small business owners are not happy with government involvement in small business. A 1993 *Financial Post* survey revealed that just 5 percent of small business owners felt that a government program had helped them start their business. By contrast, 46 percent felt that government policies and regulations (e.g., excessive paperwork requirements and red tape) have caused them to cut back their business operations. Small business owners also said that government assistance programs are not as effective as they used to be. Small business owners rank managerial competence as most important in promoting growth. Government assistance is ranked last.[11]

Financial Post
www.canoe.com

■ TABLE 7.4   Summary of Assistance for Small Business

Government Assistance

Industry Canada is the department in the federal government responsible for small business and has many programs to promote entrepreneurship. Provincial governments also have numerous programs.

The National Entrepreneurship Development Institute was established as a non-profit organization to serve as a clearing house for information about entrepreneurship.

Taxation policy allows small business to pay lower levels of taxes than other enterprises.

The Federal Business Development Bank (FBDB) administers the Counselling Assistance for Small Enterprises (CASE) program which offers one-on-one counselling by experienced people to thousands of entrepreneurs each year.

The *Small Business Loans Act* (SBLA) encourages the provision of term loan financing to small enterprises by private sector institutions by guaranteeing the loans.

The Program for Export Market Development shares the cost of efforts by business to develop export markets.

Incubators and technology centres operate across Canada. Incubators are centres where entrepreneurs can start their business with the assistance of counselling services. Federal government funds support technology centres that evaluate innovations under research and development.

Schools for Entrepreneurs funded by government but operated by the private sector prepare prospective entrepreneurs by training them in all aspects of small business. An example is the Regina Business and Technology Centre.

Private Sector

The Canada Opportunities Investment Network (COIN) is a computerized national investment matchmaking service operated through Chambers of Commerce. This service brings potential entrepreneurs together with people who might be willing to supply them with capital.

Banks and other financial institutions not only lend money but also provide advice to entrepreneurs.

Venture capitalists finance high-risk enterprises to which others are unwilling to lend money. Business angels are a special category of private venture capitalists who invest in new, high-risk enterprises that they feel should be supported even though no one else will.

Consultants and numerous publications exist to answer questions.

The Canadian Federation of Independent Business (CFIB) is the largest of the organizations formed to protect the interests of small business. It is a non-profit, nonpartisan group, or lobby, that represents the interests of about 75 000 small and medium-sized enterprises.

SUMMARY OF LEARNING OBJECTIVES

1. **Define *small business* and explain its importance to the Canadian economy.** A *small business* is independently owned and managed and does not dominate its market. Small businesses are crucial to the economy because they create new jobs, foster *entrepreneurship* and *innovation*, and supply goods and services needed by larger businesses.

2. **Explain which types of enterprise best lend themselves to small business success.** Services are the easiest operations for small business people to start because they require relatively low levels of resources. They also offer high returns on investment and tend to foster innovation. Retailing and wholesaling are more difficult because they usually require some experience, but they are still attractive to many entrepreneurs. New technology and management techniques are making

agriculture profitable once again for small farmers. As the most resource-intensive area of the economy, manufacturing is the area least dominated by small firms.

3. **Describe the startup decisions made by small businesses.** In deciding to go into business, the entrepreneur must choose between buying an existing business and starting from scratch. There are practical advantages and disadvantages to both approaches. A successful existing business, for example, has working relationships with other businesses and has already proved its ability to make a profit. New businesses, on the other hand, allow owners to plan and work with clean slates, but it is hard to make projections about the business's prospects.

4. **Identify the advantages and disadvantages of *franchising*.** *Franchising* has become a popular form of small business ownership because the *franchisor* (parent company) supplies the financial, managerial, and marketing assistance to the *franchisee*, who buys the right to sell the franchisor's product. Franchising also enables small businesses to grow rapidly. Finally, the risks in franchising are lower than those in opening a new business from scratch. However, the costs of purchasing a franchise can be quite high, and the franchisee sacrifices independence and creativity. In addition, franchises are no guarantee of success.

5. **Identify the reasons for the success and failure of small businesses.** There are four key factors that contribute to small business failure: *managerial incompetence or inexperience; neglect; weak control systems;* and *insufficient capital.* Similarly, four key factors contribute to small business success: *hard work, drive, and dedication; market demand for the products or services being provided; managerial competence;* and *luck.* Among the *entrepreneurial characteristics* that are also important are resourcefulness, a concern for positive customer relations, a willingness to take risks, and a strong need for personal freedom and opportunity for the type of creative expression that goes with running one's own company.

6. **Describe the sources of financial aid and management advice available to small businesses.** Financial and management advice for small businesses is available from several private and government sources. The private sources include the Canada Opportunities Investment Network, banks, venture capitalists, and the Canadian Federation of Independent Business. Government sources include Industry Canada, the Federal Business Development Bank, and incubators and technology centres.

STUDY QUESTIONS AND EXERCISES

Review Questions

1. Why has the number of small businesses in Canada increased?

2. What are the characteristics of a small business?

3. What are the characteristics of an entrepreneur?

4. What are the advantages and disadvantages of the following ways of becoming involved in a small business: taking over a family business, buying out an existing business, starting a business from scratch, and buying a franchise?

5. What are the causes of small business failure?

Analysis Questions

6. Why are small businesses important to the Canadian economy?

7. Why would a person want to become involved in a microenterprise instead of going into business full-time?

8. Why do small businesses fail despite all the assistance available? Should we be concerned about these failures?

Application Exercises

9. Interview a person who is involved in a family business to identify the management challenges he or she faces. Check your findings against the key challenges identified in Figure 7.2. Write the Canadian Association of Family Enterprises for more information at 10 Prince Street, 3rd Floor, Toronto, ON, M4W 1Z4.

10. Research a business that you are interested in and prepare a plan for starting it. Use the contents of a business plan listed in Table 7.1. Develop a complete, professional business plan using the EZ-Write Plan Writer disk that may be purchased separately.

BUILDING YOUR BUSINESS SKILLS

Goal

To encourage students to appreciate the value of networking to small business success and to develop a practical approach to finding and questioning networking sources.

Situation

Suppose that you and three partners have just started a small publishing company specializing in ethnic cookbooks. All of you have publishing backgrounds, but none of you has ever owned a company or run a business. You decide that one of the best ways to learn what it takes to operate a successful small business is to seek the advice of others.

Method

Step 1: Suggest six different networking sources—including professional and community organizations—that might be of value to a startup publishing company. Choose each source based on its ability to help you in a special way. For example, while one organization might place you in contact with qualified editorial workers, another might help you learn everything you need to know about running a company in your town. Make a list of the sources and describe their value to you.

Step 2: For each source, develop a list of questions, the answers to which might help your business in concrete ways. For example, in a networking meeting with the president of a professional editorial workers group, you might ask the following questions:

- Can I find copy editors and proofreaders through your organization?
- How much do they charge?
- Can you recommend an excellent photo researcher?

Step 3: Now sit down with three or four other students in your class to compare your networking sources and questions.

Follow-Up Questions

1. What is the most valuable networking source on your list and on the lists of other group members? Describe the reasons for your choices.
2. Sources of networking help can be long-term, short-term, or both. How would you classify each of the sources you identified?
3. What factors were responsible for the different approaches to networking that you found in your small group?

Prentice Hall TAKE IT TO THE NET

Check out our Companion Website
for this chapter's Exploring the Net exercise, featuring Industry Canada's Strategis Website for small business support and other intriguing, annotated destinations. You'll also find practice exercises, updated Weblinks from the text, links to newsgroups, updates, and more.

www.prenticehall.ca/ebert

BUSINESS CASE 7

Bumps in the Franchising Road

Franchising is a very popular form of business in Canada. But in the last few years, a recurring theme has been evident: conflict between franchisees and franchisors. Consider the difficulties at three franchises: Subway, Grower Direct, and Pizza Pizza.

Subway. Chris Downer, the owner of a Subway franchise in Etobicoke, Ontario, arrived one day at his store and found the locks changed and a security guard inside. Subway Franchise Systems had repossessed his store because he had missed a royalty payment of $4800. Downer broke a window to get in and sent the security guard home. He paid the money four days later, but was then hit with a $4600 legal bill from Subway to cover costs they had incurred when trying to get him to pay up.

➤

Some analysts feel that Subway has opened so many new outlets that existing franchisees are going to suffer. John Sotos, a Toronto franchise lawyer, fears that Subway's all-out expansion drive is putting franchisees at risk. He wonders what basis the Subway chain is using to reach the conclusion that it can sustain so many franchises. Ned Levitt, also a franchise lawyer, notes that the chain's low franchising fee ($10 000) may allow undercapitalized franchisees into the business. If they run into difficulty, these franchisees are more likely to be unable to keep up the necessary payments. Fred DeLuca, Subway's CEO, says the chain does not open new stores without taking current franchisees' well-being into account. If the chain determines that the opening of a new outlet will have severe impact on an existing franchisee, the new outlet will not be opened. He notes that about one-third of proposed new outlets are not opened because of objections from existing franchisees.

Grower Direct. This company is Canada's largest importer of roses, with sales of $25 million. It sells roses for $9.99 per dozen in stores across Canada. Owner Skip Kerr is able to sell roses at this low price because the firm is vertically integrated all the way back to the farm where the roses are grown. The company has grown rapidly by selling franchises for $20 000. In return, franchisees receive an exclusive territory.

While the franchising concept has allowed Grower Direct to rapidly increase its sales, there are problems. In Toronto and Vancouver, for example, several franchisees broke away from the company, claiming that they had to pay too much for their flowers from the franchisor and could buy them more cheaply in Toronto. But, as long as they were part of the franchise, they were forced to buy their flowers from Grower Direct.

Kerr agrees that franchisees can get flowers cheaper elsewhere, but he says these flowers are of much lower quality. One Toronto franchisee discovered that she could buy flowers on the local market for about half the price that Grower Direct was charging her as a franchisee. She now owns a non-franchised store.

One franchisee who owns 11 Grower Direct franchise outlets says being a franchisee is very restricting. Franchisees often have ideas about how to improve the business, but they must operate the way the franchisor dictates. Other franchisees accept the restrictions because they want to run a business outlet where they can be their own boss.

Pizza Pizza. Darlene Thiele owned two Pizza Pizza franchises. Because she had an outstanding balance of $28 000 with the franchisor, she was fearful that her stores would be taken away. In order to prevent a situation like the one facing Chris Downer, she hired a locksmith to change the locks on her store, and she slept in the store overnight. The next morning the police arrived at the front door, accompanied by two managers from Pizza Pizza headquarters. Soon after, the chain filed a lawsuit against Thiele, alleging breach of the franchise agreement. Then they stopped deliveries to her store.

Thiele was not alone in her run-ins with the franchisor. In 1992, several franchisees who had experienced difficulties with Pizza Pizza formed the Southern Ontario Pizza Franchisee Association (SOPFA). The franchisees began to grow bolder as they recognized that others had the same concerns they had. They eventually hired a lawyer who filed a $7.5 million lawsuit against Pizza Pizza, demanding that it produce certain financial statements, stop interfering with the regular operations of franchisees, and stop terminating franchise agreements without cause.

The case was eventually turned over to an arbitrator in the spring of 1994. He handed down a decision that supported some of the franchisees' claims, but didn't go as far as they would have liked. Pizza Pizza was told it owed the franchisees a total of $821 495. It paid this out in the summer of 1995. But more than one-third of the franchisees involved in the lawsuit were eventually terminated or bought out.

The province of Ontario introduced legislation in 1997 that will more closely regulate franchising. Alberta already has a law requiring franchisors to "deal fairly" with franchisees, and other provinces may follow suit. Lawyer Sotos says that regulation is needed prohibiting franchisors from doing things like increasing prices when they are the sole supplier, raising the amount of supplier rebates retained, discriminatory action against franchisees, and misuse of advertising funds.

■ *Case Questions*

1. Do franchisees really own their own businesses?

2. Do the benefits of being a franchisee outweigh the costs (e.g., restrictions put on franchisees by the franchisor)? Explain.

3. How might a franchisor address complaints from franchisees that they are being overly restricted in how they are allowed to operate?

Grower Direct
http://flowers.baynet.net/

CBC VIDEO CASE II-1

Earth Buddy*

Thoughts of bankruptcy, scandal, and personal disaster raced through Anton Rabie's mind as he faced the prospect that loomed before him. The buying office of the U.S. retail giant, Kmart, appeared to be having second thoughts about placing an order with Anton's fledging manufacturing company. The product Anton's company hoped to sell Kmart was a novelty product called Earth Buddy that Anton, together with four of his closest friends, had developed for the retail fad market.

The Earth Buddy was manufactured by stuffing sawdust and grass seed inside a nylon stocking. The stocking was then decorated with two eyes, glasses, a nose and mouth and placed in a colourful cardboard box. After purchasing an Earth Buddy the customer watered it and then watched as it sprouted its grassy toupee in the ensuing weeks.

To date Anton and his four business cohorts had sold thousands of Earth Buddies to several of the largest retail operations in Canada, including Zellers. Tremendous demand for the product had netted the company nearly $400 000 profit in only four short months of operation.

With this healthy momentum behind them, Anton and company had set their collective sights on even bigger targets south of border in the huge U.S. market. Combining persistence with panache, he had recently enticed Kmart U.S. to consider placing an order for 500 000 units. This order was several times larger than anything the company had handled to date.

The Kmart order was not without its problems, however. Foremost was Kmart's insistence on the order's timely delivery. This was a problem because of the comparatively small-scale runs the company was used to. Producing half a million buddies was almost inconceivable. Further complicating the demand for timely delivery was Kmart's unwillingness to make a firm written commitment to the order. This resulted in Anton's company having to begin the manufacture of the order on speculation that the written purchase order would be forthcoming.

Faced with these two uncertainties Anton and his friends decided to risk all and began manufacturing hundreds of thousands of Earth Buddies in the hope that the Kmart order would actually materialize. In order to realize their objective of 500 000 units, the company needed to produce about 16 000 units each day. This production objective required Michelle and Ben, the two manufacturing managers, to hire and train an additional 140 employees.

In the early weeks of manufacturing the order another problem had surfaced: raw material stockouts. Secure, sufficient, and balanced supplies of each of the key raw inputs were not always on hand. At one point, a shortage of sawdust had resulted in most of the company's production employees having to be sent home early and in a shortfall of several thousand finished buddies.

However, the worst problem associated with the Kmart order was its perpetual uncertainty. While Anton had been assured of a purchase order from the U.S. giant, he still had not received written confirmation of Kmart's commitment to the sawdust-based pals. With the majority of the order now complete, Anton felt both relieved and worried. What if the Kmart order fell through? Fresh out of business school, he had only limited experience in dealing with giant corporations and the giant orders they placed. What, if anything, could he do to secure the Kmart order?

STUDY QUESTIONS

1. What is a mission statement? How would you articulate the mission employed by the makers of Earth Buddy?

2. What is a contingency plan? How well do the makers of Earth Buddy appear to plan for possible contingencies?

3. What are the generic competitive strategies? Which of these best describes the Earth Buddy?

* Source: This case was written by Professor Reg Litz of the University of Manitoba. Video Resource: "Earth Buddy," *Venture* #518 (December 11, 1994).

CBC VIDEO CASE II-2

Diversifying with Jimmy*

"If you take a longer-term view of the world, which we tend to do in a private company, then all we have to do is concentrate on the growth of the business, what's best for the business. We don't have to worry about the security analysts, or the P/E ratios, or what the market is doing today."

—Jimmy Pattison

Canadian business legend and free enterprise evangelist Jimmy Pattison has quietly amassed one of Canada's largest private fortunes. His empire, which began out of a car dealership, is currently assessed at $3.4 billion and includes hundreds of companies in a dozen different countries. Being a privately held concern is very important to Jimmy. With no public shareholders to be accountable to, Pattison is free to pursue his penchant for acquisitions as and when he sees fit. He appears to "see fit" quite often; he bought 21 companies in a one-year period, or one almost every two weeks.

Today's trip on his private jet takes him and his senior management team to Cedar Grove, New Jersey, where he meets with representatives from four of his packaging companies. At every meeting the routine is the same; the divisional management team under review sits along one side of the conference table, Pattison's top management team along the other.

Pattison both observes and participates in the discussion as senior team members volley question after question at each division's team. Some might think that such a large and diverse empire would be difficult to control, but Pattison's monthly and quarterly reporting systems assure that he is kept abreast of everything and anything that might potentially affect operating results. Such a system is crucial. With operations in industries as diverse as fish marketing, outdoor billboard advertising, broadcasting, food retailing, and magazine publishing, many would be overwhelmed by the complexity. But, diverse as it is, it all makes sense to Jimmy. His theory of diversification is simple: Buy businesses you can relate to. Pattison explains: "We can put ourselves in the position of a consumer. . . . When I walk into a grocery store and I get treated a certain way, I can understand how the customer feels if she or he doesn't get treated very good.

I can't understand that sitting in a nuclear plant because I don't understand it."

Part of running a diversified empire is being willing to face the hard music of who's producing and who isn't. Pattison, who built his reputation on such practices as routinely firing his lowest-producing salesperson, keeps a watchful eye on key managers and how they deal with weak performers in his workforce of 17 000. He explains, "If people don't perform because they're either in the wrong spot in life, or they're lazy, or they lose interest, or they're better suited for something else, then we help them make up their mind."

He also demonstrates a realistic understanding of the seemingly unpredictable elements of business. He readily admits having "never owned a company that hasn't at some time . . . had some difficulties and had a winter season." Still, for all the bumps in the road, this self-made billionaire seems to know the art of managing.

STUDY QUESTIONS

1. What is entrepreneurship? To what extent does Jimmy Pattison meet the criteria for being an entrepreneur? Defend your answer.

2. What are the *functions* of management? Give several examples of the activities that would be evident as Jimmy Pattison carries out each of the functions of management.

3. What are the *skills* of management? Explain what Jimmy Pattison would do to effectively put into practice the various skills of management.

* Source: This case was written by Professor Reg Litz of the University of Manitoba. Video Resource: "The Gospel According to Jimmy," *Venture* #671 (December 2, 1997).

LANDS' END VIDEO CASE II-3

Planning in the Coming Home Division of Land's End

LEARNING OBJECTIVES

The purpose of this video exercise is to help students:

1. Appreciate the process whereby marketing managers develop practical plans to carry out the strategic decisions they make.

2. Understand the ways in which a specific company perceives its organizational strengths and uses them to seize marketplace opportunities.

3. Understand the relationship between product development and marketing as interrelated management areas.

BACKGROUND INFORMATION

The *Coming Home* catalogue, which specializes in products for bed and bath, was one of three specialty divisions launched by Lands' End in 1989. The decision to branch out into home textiles, says Managing Director Phil Young, came

➤

when marketers at Lands' End "recognized opportunity in the marketplace." Textile mills were either merging or closing, and those that stayed in business were stressing efficiency over quality. Lands' End thus saw an opportunity to enter the home-textiles market—especially in bedding—by introducing high-quality products backed by the company's unconditional guarantee and priced along its usual lines.

The process of developing such products as fitted sheets and folded baby blankets consists of several steps:

- The product development team identifies a need or opportunity in the marketplace.
- The strategy for designing the actual product reflects the company's mission—to develop the best product for the identified need.
- The competition is analyzed and the input of potential customers is collected.
- An appropriate supplier is selected.
- The product is tested, both in-house and among customers.

Young characterizes this approach to strategic planning as *SWOT analysis:* matching internal organizational Strengths and Weaknesses with external Opportunities and Threats.

THE VIDEO

Video Source. "Planning in the Coming Home Division at Lands' End," *Prentice Hall Presents: On Location at Lands' End.* The video focuses on the planning that underpins the product development process at the Coming Home division, which specializes in home textile products for bed and bath. Merchandising manager Rob Hayes discusses the approach that Lands' End marketers take to developing products that both meet carefully researched customer needs and satisfy the company's established quality standards.

DISCUSSION QUESTIONS

1. How would you characterize the overall approach of Lands' End management to the concept of matching the organization with its environment? Does it take risks, for example, or is it conservative?

2. According to Phil Young, the division's approach to the "'sheet that fits' . . . provides an edge for all Coming Home products—meeting the needs of the customer." How might this goal be translated into an item in the company's mission statement? Does the product development process described in the video suggest any particular strategic goals that might have been set by Lands' End management?

3. Judging from the management approach to product development at the Coming Home division, what can you say about the nature of managerial responsibility and organizational structure at Lands' End? Judging from the video, what can you say about corporate culture at Lands' End?

FOLLOW-UP ASSIGNMENT

At the conclusion of the video, the narrator poses the following question: *How does Lands' End fight against competitors using its ideas, like "the sheet that fits"?* To address this question, secure a *Coming Home* catalogue (phone, fax, or e-mail Lands' End). Next, consider the following comment made by Phil Young in 1996:

> One issue is always the "edge." Our just-completed SWOT analysis indicated that our competitors were catching up—chipping away at the "edge." So to identify all the elements of the edge, we listed the strengths and weaknesses that we have and what we *needed to do* to reinforce that edge. Then we set some specific goals in order to address everything we had to do in order to stay ahead of the competition.

Your instructor will divide you into groups of five or six people, with each acting as a "product development team." Each team should examine the descriptions of several different products in the *Coming Home* catalogue. Which products seem to be promoted most effectively? To which products would you attach an apparent marketing "edge"—some benefit or feature that, as a result of product development planning, looks as if it might help a given product to "stay ahead of the competition"? As a team, make recommendations for giving an "edge" to two or three products that seem to be in need of a competitive boost.

FOR FURTHER EXPLORATION

Visit Lands' End on the Internet at
http://www.landsend.com
On the Web page, scroll down to "The Company" and then down to the link to "The Company Inside and Out." To get a better idea of the areas in which the company tries to develop its organizational strengths, look at such features as "At Lands' End the Word 'Value' Rings True" and "Quality in the Apparel Business. . . ." According to Lands' End, in what ways does attention to quality furnish an "edge" in the development of its products? What role should "value" play in formulating a mission statement for Lands' End?

MANAGING HUMAN RESOURCES

You will read about timely and complex human resource management issues in the opening cases of the chapters in this section—motivating workers at MacMillan-Bloedel, and helping women break through the "glass ceiling" in business firms. In the difficult circumstances in which Canadian business firms have found themselves in the 1990s, it is important that the firm's human resources be managed effectively.

Part Three, Managing Human Resources, provides an overview of the relationship between managers and their employees, including managers' attitudes, the activities of managers responsible for human resources management, the special relationship between management and labour unions, and the role of the government in human resource issues.

■ We begin in **Chapter 8, Motivating, Satisfying, and Leading Employees**, by first examining the important concept of motivation, then describing several popular motivation theories, and then describing several strategies for enhancing employee job satisfaction.

■ Then, in **Chapter 9, Managing Human Resources and Labour Relations**, we describe the activities involved in recruiting, training, promoting, and compensating employees. We also look at labour unions, including the reasons they form, the collective bargaining process, and labour legislation in Canada.

CHAPTER

8

MOTIVATING, SATISFYING, AND LEADING EMPLOYEES

WORKING ON LONG-STANDING PROBLEMS

MacMillan-Bloedel Inc. (MacBlo) is Canada's biggest forest products company, with annual sales of $5 billion. In 1997, the company hired Thomas Stephens, a "turnaround specialist," as its new CEO in an attempt to respond to a continuing series of financial and human resource problems that have plagued the company for the last decade.

In January 1998, Stephens unveiled his plan for the future. It included downsizing the company (again), this time chopping one-fifth of its workforce in a bid to return to profitability. Half of these cuts were made in B.C. The company will now focus on wood products as its core business; it will also sell its paper business, and will likely get out of the packaging business as well.

In the 1980s, the company went through a traumatic time of downsizing, closing mills, shutting down machines, and reducing its workforce by 25 000 people. Despite all of its restructuring, the company continued to lose money and it suffered from competitive disadvantages. A Price-Waterhouse survey showed that the labour cost component of a tonne of pulp from the B.C. coast was $129, compared to $94 for eastern Canada and $84 for the southern U.S.

Labour relations had never been particularly good at the company. On three different occasions in the 1980s, the company experienced wildcat (unauthorized) strikes. Each time, the company sued the union for lost revenue, and each time they won cash awards and workplace concessions. Because of this, there was not a lot of trust between the union and com-

pany management. Further compounding the problem was a remark by the former president that the problems with the Canadian workforce meant that the company would be expanding operations only in the U.S.

To resolve its many problems, in 1993 the company embarked on a strategy to get its workers more involved in decision making. Several new ideas were introduced by management, including the following:

- production plans and financial data were shared with workers at regular intervals
- division managers took union reps on trips to competing mills to show them just how competitive the market had become
- joint union/management committees were set up to encourage suggestions from workers on how productivity could be improved
- workplace practices such as full flexibility were adopted when work was assigned to employees

In spite of these changes, distrust remained. At the Port Alberni mill, for example, management and workers struck a deal in which the company would spend $5 million to extend early retirement benefits, and the union would agree to the introduction of more flexible working arrangements. For example, in the past, if a millwright wanted to work on a pump and needed pipes disconnected, the millwright had to wait for a pipefitter to disconnect the pipes. Under the new arrangement, workers were supposed to do as much of a job as they were able to do. Unfortunately, the Port Alberni agreement fell apart because of poor communication and misunderstood goals. The workers were supposed to "pay back" the $5 million through increased productivity, but when these goals were not reached, the company announced that it would lay off another 200 workers. Finally, in 1997, management closed the mill. In January 1998, CEO Stephens invited Randy Sall, the union chief at Port Alberni, and the Port Alberni plant manager, Tony Sudar, to a meeting to discuss ways to reduce the high cost of lumber conversion. Stephens was impressed enough with the results that he allowed one shift to go back to work at the mill.

Stephens's belief in "comanagement" means that the union and management now have to work together to increase productivity. Randy Sall finds the new CEO's belief refreshing, and says that for the first time the union has some say in how the business is run. For his part, Stephens says his strategy is to get everyone around him committed to improvements.

Stephens has also introduced other changes. When informed that the corporate culture at MacBlo was seriously dysfunctional, he set up a voice mailbox and encouraged employees to leave questions for him. Stephens or another manager usually answers the questions within 24 hours. The idea was to deal with rumours before they got out of hand. Many of the voice mails indicated that there was poor communication within the company, and that employees did not know where the company was heading. Employees have gradually begun to understand that they can raise problems with top management, something they had been reluctant to do before.

Because a firm's human resources are its most important asset, managers must effectively motivate, lead, and satisfy employees. In this chapter, we will explore the reasons why satisfied employees are an asset to any company. We will also consider some of the approaches managers have taken to satisfy employees over the years. Increasingly, companies are looking for ways to enhance workers' job satisfaction and to develop managers with the leadership skills to meet both employee and corporate goals.

By focusing on the learning objectives of this chapter, you will better understand why employee morale and job satisfaction are important to businesses as large as MacMillan-Bloedel and as small as the corner grocery. After reading this chapter, you should be able to:

1. Discuss the importance of *job satisfaction* and *employee morale* and summarize their roles in *human relations* in the workplace.
2. Identify and summarize the most important theories of employee *motivation*.
3. Discuss different managerial styles of *leadership* and their impact on human relations in the workplace.
4. Describe some of the strategies used by organizations to improve employee motivation and satisfaction.

■ THE IMPORTANCE OF GOOD HUMAN RELATIONS IN BUSINESS

Human relations refers to the interactions between employers and employees and their attitudes towards one another. In this section, we will explore ways to define good human relations and some of the reasons they benefit businesses.

Job Satisfaction and Employee Morale

One way to assess human relations in a firm is by workers' job satisfaction. **Job satisfaction** is the pleasurable feeling experienced from doing your job well, whether you are a mail carrier, retail clerk, bus driver, or business executive. Employees with high job satisfaction are also likely to have high employee morale. **Morale** is the mental attitude that employees have about their workplace. It reflects the degree to which employees perceive that their needs are being met by the job.

human relations
Interactions between employers and employees and their attitudes towards one another.

job satisfaction
The pleasure and feeling of accomplishment employees derive from performing their jobs well.

morale
The generally positive or negative mental attitude of employees towards their work and workplace.

Companies can improve employee morale and job satisfaction in a variety of ways. Some large firms have instituted companywide programs designed specifically to address employees' needs. Some, such as Dow Chemical and Hewlett-Packard, sponsor special career-training programs for young students. These programs benefit both students and the sponsors, who ultimately benefit from a more educated, skilled, and committed workforce. Managers at Hyatt Hotels report that conducting frequent surveys of employee attitudes, soliciting employee input, and, most importantly, acting on that input gives their company an edge in recruiting and retaining productive workers. Meanwhile, small business managers realize that the personal touch can reap big benefits in employee morale and even devotion. About once a month, for instance, Anita Roddick of Body Shop cosmetics stores hosts a three-day party at her home in Scotland, where she, her husband, and about 20 franchise owners and employees "all cook together, talk, dance, and play music."[1]

What makes employees love the companies they work for? One survey by *Fortune* magazine found that three things are critical: a powerful, visionary CEO, a good physical work environment, and work that has a deep, rewarding purpose.[2]

Why Businesses Need Satisfied Employees

When workers are enthusiastic and happy with their jobs the organization benefits in many ways. Because they are committed to their work and the organization, satisfied workers are more likely to work hard and try to make useful contributions to the organization. They will also have fewer grievances and are less likely to engage in negative behaviours (e.g., complaining, deliberately slowing their work pace, etc.). Satisfied workers are also more likely to come to work every day and are more likely to remain with the organization. So, by ensuring that employees are satisfied, management gains a more efficient and smooth-running company.

empowerment
Motivating employees to produce high-quality products.

Empowerment of employees is the buzzword of the 1990s. It means motivating and energizing employees to create high-quality products and to provide bend-over-backwards service to customers so that the firm is more competitive. It means eliminating whole layers of traditional management that exist simply to control people. Properly used, it can reduce absenteeism and turnover and increase quality and productivity.[3] The box "Does Every Worker Want to be Empowered?" provides some interesting information on the idea of empowerment.

Just as the rewards of high worker satisfaction and morale are great, so are the costs of job dissatisfaction and poor morale. Dissatisfied workers, for example, are far more likely to be absent due to minor illnesses, personal reasons, or a general disinclination to go to work. Low morale may also result in high turnover. Some turnover is a natural and healthy way to weed out low-performing workers in any organization. But high levels of turnover have many negative consequences, including numerous vacancies, disruption in production, decreased productivity, and high retraining costs.

Job Satisfaction and Dissatisfaction Trends

The picture of Canadian industry shows mixed results when companies try to give employees what they want and to keep them on the job. Consider the following:

- A survey of 2300 workers by the Wyatt Co. of Vancouver found that three-quarters of Canadian workers are satisfied with the content of their job, but fewer than half are happy with the way they are managed. Workers felt that management did not show genuine interest in them and did not treat them with dignity. Managers, on the other hand, felt that they *did* treat workers with dignity. Perhaps most disconcerting of all, fewer than one-third of those surveyed felt that promotions were based on merit. The longer they had been with a company, the more cynical they were about this issue.[4]

TRENDS & CHALLENGES

Does Every Worker Want to be Empowered?

The empowerment movement involves several fundamental ideas: tapping into workers' brains *and* brawn, encouraging them to think on the job, encouraging them to be self-motivated and professional in their work, giving lower-level workers more responsibilities, and making workers feel that they are a real part of their company's success.

The South Bend, Indiana, manufacturing plant of the Eaton Corporation illustrates the empowered workplace. First, it is not easy to get hired at the plant. Only one applicant in 10 is offered a job, and promising candidates have to go through as many as 13 interviews before they are actually hired. The last interview is usually conducted by a group of workers from the factory.

The traditional factory hierarchy is avoided, and managers are called "vision supporters." Everyone wears the same blue uniforms. There are no time clocks; workers report their hours (including overtime) on an honour basis. Production statistics for each team—showing parts produced compared to pieces of scrap generated—are posted where everyone can see them. They clearly show which team has the strongest workers. Each work team is responsible for keeping its own members productive and

motivated. In practice, empowerment means having more authority, but it also means having some unpleasant responsibilities as well. When one group mistakenly passed through inspection a batch of 1200 faulty parts, the group's members went before all the other workers to explain what had happened.

Many workers are happy being empowered, but many others are not, preferring instead to have a low level of involvement with their job, and avoid the authority (and responsibility) that goes with being empowered. Beverly Reynolds, for example, liked the idea of being her own boss, but she didn't like the headaches that came with it—maintaining machines, having to learn a wide variety of jobs, and coping with the stress of knowing that her co-workers were always watching her to see how well she was performing. Mark Dixon, who was part of a team that fired one of its members for missing too many days of work, found the whole process very uncomfortable. He wished that a traditional manager could have dealt with the problem.

The plant manager says that empowerment is no panacea. Self-direction requires worker maturity *and* a desire to be empowered.

- Another survey of 1631 employees from 94 companies across Canada and the U.S. found that, while employees are optimistic and committed to their work, they also feel frustrated because they have no control over what happens in their job. Most employees feel that their abilities are not used to the fullest extent. They want direction and measurable goals.[5]

- Based on responses from 7000 private- and public-sector workers, a Conference Board of Canada survey found the following:
  - One-third of employees felt that caring for children or elderly parents limited their career advancement.
  - One-eighth had left an employer because of family responsibilities.
  - Seventeen percent had turned down promotions.
  - Twenty-five percent had turned down transfers.
  - Women were four times as likely as men to report conflicts in home and work responsibilities.[6]

Conference Board of Canada
www.conferenceboard.ca

All categories of employees—professional, clerical, management, and hourly—feel less secure in their jobs than just a few years ago. This pattern stems in part from cutbacks and layoffs experienced throughout industry in recent years. Many large corporations have announced plant closings, putting thousands of employees out of work. Not surprisingly, workers are likely to feel decreased commitment and job satisfaction.

Employees at small firms are generally more content with their lot. But it may be difficult to motivate some employees in family-owned firms—they know they will never control the firm because they are not part of the family.

Many workers are also dissatisfied with their salaries. Some, for example, do not think that pay is fairly distributed within their company. A large majority of nonmanagement employees do not believe that pay increases are linked directly to performance. Many workers think they are underpaid compared to people in other companies. The box "Workplace Blues" describes how many workers feel about their job and the company they work for.

■ MOTIVATION IN THE WORKPLACE

motivation
The set of forces that causes people to behave in certain ways.

Although job satisfaction and morale are important, employee motivation is even more critical to a firm's success. As we saw in Chapter 5, motivation is one part of the managerial function of directing. Broadly defined, **motivation** is the set of forces that cause people to behave in certain ways. For example, while one worker may be motivated to work hard to produce as much as possible, another may be motivated to do just enough to get by. Managers must understand these differences in behaviour and the reasons for them.

TRENDS & CHALLENGES

Workplace Blues

Lately, many business journals have reported on the demoralization of business managers. The low morale reported by so many middle managers in the 1990s is the result of job losses, a vastly increased workload for those who remain on the job, and a feeling that their work world is completely beyond their control.

Middle managers increasingly perceive that top management has no "game plan" other than to draw enormous salaries for themselves. The logical consequence is that many white-collar workers now have attitudes towards "the brass" that are more cynical than they were in the past.

"Loyalty between the corporation and its managers extends only as far as the next paycheque now," mourns one formerly committed manager. "In my career, I gave up a lot of personal plans—anniversary parties, vacations, and so on—for the sake of the company. I wouldn't do that today because I've realized all the loyalty and sacrifice was going one way only." Instead, more and more middle managers are turning to smaller companies, hoping not only to gain a real voice in operations, but also to escape the frenetic world of the large corporation.

Corporations benefit when demoralized managers move on. Low morale in the workplace has been linked to low productivity for reasons ranging from work avoidance (such as hanging out at the water cooler) to job avoidance

(such as calling in sick) to sabotage (both physical sabotage of company property and "emotional" sabotage of other workers).

What can a company with low morale do? The buzzword in business today is "empowerment"—giving workers at all levels a feeling that they *can* control things, that they *do* make a difference. One of the quickest ways to empower employees is to make them part owners of the business, a route many companies (including such industry giants as Avis) have taken successfully. Giving teams of employees full authority over meaningful projects from start to finish can also build commitment to the firm. Conducting frequent surveys of employee attitudes, soliciting employee input, and—most importantly—*acting on that input* have given companies such as Hyatt an edge in attracting and keeping valued staff.

In the long run, though, rebuilding morale will require rebuilding both trust and communication between upper management and those below. Those searching for the source of the current morale problem need look no further than the one place where few seem to realize there *is* a morale problem: the executive suite. Despite widespread press reports of low morale, 91 percent of CEOs at major companies said morale among middle managers in their companies was "excellent" or "very good." Is anybody up there listening?

Over the years, many theories have been proposed to address the issues of motivation. In this section, we will focus on three major approaches to motivation in the workplace that reflect a chronology of thinking in the area: *classical theory* and *scientific management*, *behaviour theory*, and *contemporary motivational theories*.

Classical Theory and Scientific Management

According to the so-called **classical theory of motivation**, workers are motivated solely by money. In his book *The Principles of Scientific Management* (1911), industrial engineer Frederick Taylor proposed a way for both companies and workers to benefit from this widely accepted view of life in the workplace.[7] If workers are motivated by money, Taylor reasoned, then paying them more would prompt them to produce more. Meanwhile, the firm that analyzed jobs and found better ways to perform them would be able to produce goods more cheaply, make higher profits, and thus pay—and motivate—workers better than its competitors.

Taylor's approach is known as **scientific management**. His ideas captured the imagination of many managers in the early 20th century. Soon, plants across Canada and the U.S. were hiring experts to perform **time-and-motion studies**. Industrial-engineering techniques were applied to each facet of a job in order to determine how to perform it most efficiently. These studies were the first "scientific" attempts to break down jobs into easily repeated components and to devise more efficient tools and machines for performing them.

As for compensation, Taylor's *differential percent system* was a new twist on the standard **piecework system** by which a worker was paid a set rate per piece completed. For example, a worker in a garment shop might receive 25 cents for each sleeve stitched. Under Taylor's system, however, workers who fell below a specified quota were paid at a certain level—a different percent—per piece. Those who exceeded the quota got higher pay, not just for the extra pieces but for all the pieces they completed.

Taylor's approach enjoyed much initial success among manual labourers. In many heavy industries, management was willing to pay greater wages for significant increases in productivity. Henry Ford, for example, was eventually able to build cars more rapidly and cheaply than any other automaker, in large part by paying his workers *more than double* the usual wage. Ultimately, however, the scientific management system began to show flaws resulting from its failure to see that factors other than money often contribute to job satisfaction.

The Hawthorne Studies

One of the first challenges to the classical theory of human relations management came about by accident. In 1925, a group of Harvard researchers began a study at the Hawthorne Works of Western Electric. Their intent was to examine the relationship between changes in the physical environment and worker output, with an eye to increasing productivity.

The results of the experiment at first confused, then amazed, the scientists. Increasing lighting levels improved productivity but so did lowering lighting levels. And against all expectations, raising the pay of workers failed to increase their productivity. Gradually they pieced together the puzzle. The explanation for the lighting phenomenon lay in workers' response to attention. In essence, they determined that almost any action on the part of management that made workers believe they were receiving special attention caused worker productivity to rise. This result, known as the **Hawthorne effect**, had a major influence on human relations management, convincing many businesses that paying attention to employees is indeed good for business.

But, as the scientists also found, the Hawthorne effect has limits. Even a pay raise is not enough to get people to work harder if they have an informal consensus that such behaviour is inappropriate. For example, they found that workers in a wiring room received constant criticism from their peers when they exceeded the group norm for

classical theory of motivation
A theory of motivation that presumes that workers are motivated almost solely by money.

scientific management
Analyzing jobs and finding better, more efficient ways to perform them.

time-and-motion studies
The use of industrial-engineering techniques to study every aspect of a specific job to determine how to perform it most efficiently.

piecework system
Paying workers a set rate for each piece of work produced.

Hawthorne effect
The tendency for workers' productivity to increase when they feel they are receiving special attention from management.

output. Eventually, most got the message and decreased their production to the established level. This result has led businesses to pay greater attention to the informal organization within their companies (see Chapter 6) and to recognize that human relations management is not a perfect solution.[8]

Contemporary Motivation Theories

Following the Hawthorne studies, managers and researchers alike focused more attention on the importance of good human relations in motivating employee performance. Stressing the factors that cause, focus, and sustain workers' behaviour, most motivation theorists are concerned with the ways in which management thinks about and treats employees. The major motivation theories include the *human-resources model*, the *hierarchy of needs model*, *two-factory theory*, *expectancy theory*, *equity theory*, and *good-setting theory*.

The Human-Resources Model: Theories X and Y.   In an important study, behavioural scientist Douglas McGregor concluded that managers had radically different beliefs about how best to use the human resources at a firm's disposal. He classified these beliefs into sets of assumptions that he labelled "Theory X" and "Theory Y."[9] As shown in Table 8.1, the two theories convey very different assumptions about people at work.

Theory X
A management approach based on the belief that people must be forced to be productive because they are naturally lazy, irresponsible, and uncooperative.

Theory Y
A management approach based on the belief that people want to be productive because they are naturally energetic, responsible, and cooperative.

Managers who subscribe to **Theory X** tend to believe that people are naturally lazy and uncooperative and must therefore be either punished or rewarded to be made productive. Managers who incline to **Theory Y** tend to believe that people are naturally energetic, growth-oriented, self-motivated, and interested in being productive.

McGregor generally favoured Theory Y beliefs. Thus he argued that Theory Y managers are more likely to have satisfied, motivated employees. Of course, Theory X and Y distinctions are somewhat simplistic and offer little concrete basis for action. Their value lies primarily in their ability to highlight and analyze the behaviour of managers in light of their attitudes towards employees.

The Hawthorne studies were an important step in developing an appreciation for the human factor at work. These women worked under different lighting conditions as researchers monitored their productivity. To the researchers' amazement, productivity increased regardless of whether the light was increased or decreased.

■ **TABLE 8.1** **Beliefs about People at Work**

Theory X	Theory Y
1. People are lazy.	1. People are energetic.
2. People lack ambition and dislike responsibility.	2. People are ambitious and seek responsibility.
3. People are self-centred.	3. People can be selfless.
4. People resist change.	4. People want to contribute to business growth and change.
5. People are gullible and not very bright.	5. People are intelligent.

Maslow's Hierarchy of Needs Model. Psychologist Abraham Maslow proposed that people have a number of different needs that they attempt to satisfy in their work. He classified these needs into five basic types and suggested that they are arranged in the hierarchy of importance shown in Figure 8.1. According to Maslow, needs are hierarchical because lower-level needs must be met before a person will try to satisfy those on a higher level.[10]

- *Physiological needs* are necessary for survival; they include food, water, shelter, and sleep. Businesses address these needs by providing both comfortable working environments and salaries sufficient to buy food and shelter.
- *Security needs* include the needs for stability and protection from the unknown. Many employers thus offer pension plans and job security.
- *Social needs* include the needs for friendship and companionship. Making friends at work can help to satisfy social needs, as can the feeling that you "belong" in a company.

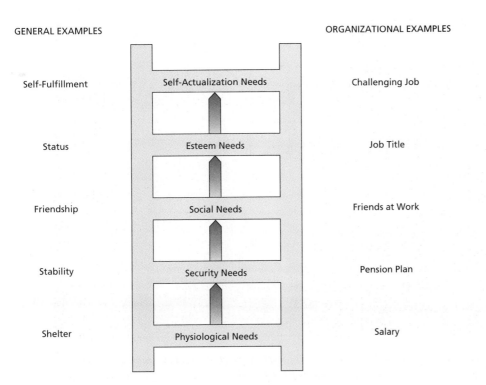

FIGURE 8.1

Maslow's hierarchy of human needs provides a useful categorization of the different needs people have.

- *Esteem needs* include the need for status and recognition as well as the need for self-respect. Respected job titles and large offices are among the things that businesses can provide to address these needs.

- Finally, *self-actualization needs* are needs for self-fulfillment. They include the needs to grow and develop one's capabilities and to achieve new and meaningful goals. Challenging job assignments can help satisfy these needs.

According to Maslow, once one set of needs has been satisfied, it ceases to motivate behaviour. This is the sense in which the hierarchical nature of lower- and higher-level needs affects employee motivation and satisfaction. For example, if you feel secure in your job, a new pension plan will probably be less important to you than the chance to make new friends and join an informal network among your co-workers. If, however, a lower-level need suddenly becomes unfulfilled, most people immediately refocus on that lower level. Suppose, for example, that you are seeking to meet your esteem needs by working as a divisional manager at a major company. If you learn that your division—and consequently your job—may be eliminated, you might very well find the promise of job security at a new firm as motivating as a promotion once would have been in your old company.

Maslow's theory recognizes that because different people have different needs, they are motivated by different things. Unfortunately, research has found that the hierarchy varies widely, not only for different people but across different cultures.

Two-Factor Theory.   After studying a group of accountants and engineers, psychologist Frederick Herzberg concluded that job satisfaction and dissatisfaction depend on two factors: *hygiene factors*, such as working conditions, and *motivating factors*, such as recognition for a job well done.[11]

Rewards and recognition are an important determinant of employee motivation. In 1998 the Financial Post recognized Theresa Butcher, its head librarian, as an Unsung Hero for all of her help to reporters and editors over many years.

According to **two-factor theory**, hygiene factors affect motivation and satisfaction only if they are *absent* or *fail* to meet expectations. For example, workers will be dissatisfied if they believe that they have poor working conditions. If working conditions are improved, however, they will not necessarily become *satisfied*; they will simply be *not dissatisfied*. On the other hand, if workers receive no recognition for successful work, they may be neither dissatisfied nor satisfied. If recognition is provided, they will likely become more satisfied.

Motivation factors lie along a continuum from *satisfaction* to *no satisfaction*. Hygiene factors, on the other hand, are likely to produce feelings that lie on a continuum from *dissatisfaction* to *no dissatisfaction*. While motivation factors are directly related to the work that employees actually perform, hygiene factors refer to the environment in which they perform it.

This theory thus suggests that managers should follow a two-step approach to enhancing motivation. First, they must ensure that hygiene factors—working conditions, clearly stated policies—are acceptable. This practice will result in an absence of dissatisfaction. Then they must offer motivating factors—recognition, added responsibility—as means of improving satisfaction and motivation.

Research suggests that two-factor theory works in some professional settings, but it is not as effective in clerical and manufacturing settings. (Herzberg's research was limited to professionals—accountants and engineers only.) In addition, one person's hygiene factor may be another person's motivating factor. For example, if money represents nothing more than pay for time worked, it may be a hygiene factor for one person. For another person, however, money may be a motivating factor because it represents recognition and achievement.

two-factor theory
A theory of human relations developed by Frederick Herzberg that identifies factors that must be present for employees to be satisfied with their jobs and factors that, if increased, lead employees to work harder.

Expectancy Theory.   **Expectancy theory** suggests that people are motivated to work towards rewards they want *and* they believe they have a reasonable chance—or expectancy—of obtaining.[12] A reward that seems out of reach, for example, is not likely to be motivating even if it is intrinsically positive. Consider the case of an assistant department manager who learns that a division manager has retired and that the firm is looking for a replacement. Even though she wants the job, she does not apply for it because she doubts that she would be selected. She also learns that the firm is looking for a production manager on a later shift. She thinks that she could get this job but does not apply because she does not want to change shifts. Finally, she learns of an opening one level higher—full department manager—in her own division. She may well apply for this job because she both wants it and thinks that she has a good chance of getting it.

Expectancy theory helps to explain why some people do not work as hard as they can when their salaries are based purely on seniority: Because they are paid the same whether they work very hard or hard enough to get by, there is no financial incentive for them to work harder. In other words, they ask themselves, "If I work harder, will I get a pay raise?" and conclude that the answer is no—that they expect not. Similarly, if hard work will result in one or more *undesirable* outcomes—say, a transfer to another location or a promotion to a job that requires travel—employees will not be motivated to work hard.

expectancy theory
The theory that people are motivated to work towards rewards they want and they believe they have a reasonable chance of obtaining.

Equity Theory.   **Equity theory** focuses on social comparisons—people evaluating their treatment by the organization relative to the treatment of others. This approach says that people begin by analyzing what they contribute to their jobs (time, effort, education, experience, and so forth) relative to what they get in return (salary, benefits, recognition, security). The result is a ratio of contribution to return. Then they compare their own ratios to those of other employees. Depending on their assessments, they experience feelings of equity or inequity.[13]

For example, suppose a new college graduate gets a starting job at a large manufacturing firm. His starting salary is $25 000 per year, he gets a compact company car, and he shares an office with another new employee. If he later learns that another new employee has received the same salary, car, and office arrangement, he will feel equitably

equity theory
The theory that people compare (1) what they contribute to their job with what they get in return, and (2) their input/output ratio with that of other employees.

treated. If the other newcomer, however, has received $30 000, a full-size company car, and a private office, he may feel inequity.

When people feel that they are being inequitably treated, they may do various things to restore fairness. For example, they may ask for raises, reduce their effort, work shorter hours, or just complain to their bosses. They may also rationalize their situation ("management succumbed to pressure to promote a woman"), find different people with whom to compare themselves, or leave their jobs altogether.

goal-setting theory
The theory that people perform better when they set specific, quantified, time-framed goals.

Goal-Setting Theory.   **Goal-setting theory** describes the kinds of goals that better motivate employees. In general, effective goals tend to have two basic characteristics. First, they are moderately difficult: While a goal that is too easy does little to enhance effort and motivation, a goal that is too difficult also fails to motivate people. Second, they are specific. A goal of "do your best," for instance, does not motivate people nearly as much as a goal like "increase profits by 10 percent." The specificity and clarity of this goal serves to focus attention and energy on exactly what needs to be done.[14]

An important aspect of goal setting is the employee's participation in the goal-setting process. When people help to select the goals that they are to work towards, they tend to accept them more readily and are more committed to achieving them. On the other hand, when goals are merely assigned to people with little or no input on their part, they are less likely to adopt them.

■ MANAGERIAL STYLES AND LEADERSHIP

leadership
Process of motivating others to work to meet specific objectives.

In trying to enhance morale, job satisfaction, and motivation, managers can use many different styles of leadership. **Leadership** is the process of motivating others to work to meet specific objectives. Leading is one of the key aspects of a manager's job. In this section, we begin by describing some of the basic features of and differences in managerial styles and then focus on an approach to managing and leading that understands those jobs as responses to a variety of complex situations.

Managerial Styles

managerial style
Patterns of behaviour that a manager exhibits in dealing with subordinates.

Early theories of leadership tried to identify specific "traits" associated with strong leaders. For example, physical appearance, intelligence, and public-speaking skills were once thought to be "leadership traits." Indeed, it was once believed that taller people made better leaders than shorter people. The "trait" approach, however, proved to be a poor predictor of leadership potential. Ultimately, attention shifted from managers' traits to their behaviours, or **managerial styles**: patterns of behaviour that a manager exhibits in dealing with subordinates. Managerial styles run the gamut from *autocratic* to *democratic* to *free-rein*. Naturally, most managers do not clearly exhibit any one particular style. But these three major types of styles involve very different kinds of responses to human relations problems. Under different circumstances, any given one—or any combination—may prove appropriate:

autocratic style
Managerial style in which managers generally issue orders and expect them to be obeyed without question.

- Managers who adopt an **autocratic style** generally issue orders and expect them to be obeyed without question. The military commander, of course, prefers and usually needs the autocratic style on the battlefield. Because no one else is consulted, the autocratic style allows for rapid decision making. It may therefore be useful in situations testing a firm's effectiveness as a time-based competitor.

democratic style
Managerial style in which managers generally ask for input from subordinates but retain final decision-making power.

- Managers who adopt a **democratic style** generally ask for input from subordinates before making decisions but retain final decision-making power. For example, the manager of a technical group may ask other group members to interview and offer opinions about job applicants. The manager, however, will ultimately make the hiring decision.

- Managers who adopt a **free-rein style** typically serve as advisers to subordinates who are allowed to make decisions. The chairperson of a volunteer committee to raise funds for a new library may find a free-rein style most effective.

free-rein style
Managerial style in which managers typically serve as advisers to subordinates who are allowed to make decisions.

Regardless of theories about the ways in which leaders ought to lead, the relative effectiveness of any leadership style depends largely on the desire of subordinates to share input or to exercise creativity. While some people, for example, are frustrated, others prefer autocratic managers because they do not want a voice in making decisions. The democratic approach, meanwhile, can be disconcerting both to people who want decision-making responsibility and to those who do not. A free-rein style lends itself to employee creativity—and thus to creative solutions to pressing problems. This style also appeals to employees who like to plan their own work. Not all subordinates, however, have the necessary background or skills to make creative decisions. Others are not sufficiently self-motivated to work without supervision.

Canadian vs. American Management Styles.   The management style of Canadian managers might look a lot like that of Americans, but there are several notable differences. Most fundamentally, Canadian managers are more subtle and subdued than American managers. Canadian managers also seem more committed to their companies, less willing to mindlessly follow the latest management fad, and more open to different cultures because of the multicultural nature of Canada. All of these characteristics may be advantageous for Canadian companies that will increasingly be competing in global markets.[15]

The Contingency Nature of Leadership

Because each managerial style has both strengths and weaknesses, most managers vary their responses to different situations. Flexibility, however, has not always characterized managerial style or responsiveness. For most of the 20th century, in fact, managers tended to believe that all problems yielded to preconceived, pretested solutions: If raising pay reduced turnover in one plant, for example, the same tactic would work equally well in another plant.

More recently, however, managers have begun to adopt a so-called **contingency approach** to managerial style: They have started to view appropriate managerial behaviour in any situation as dependent, or *contingent*, on the elements unique to that situation. This change in outlook has resulted largely from an increasing appreciation of the complexity of managerial problems and solutions. Pay raises, for example, may reduce turnover when workers have been badly underpaid. The contingency approach, however, recognizes that they will have little effect when workers feel adequately paid but ill-treated by management. This approach also recommends that training managers in human relations skills may be crucial to solving the problem in the second case.

contingency approach
Approach to managerial style holding that the appropriate behaviour in any situation is dependent (contingent) on the elements unique to that situation.

The contingency approach also acknowledges that people in different cultures behave differently and expect different things from their managers. A certain managerial style, therefore, is more likely to be successful in some countries than in others. Japanese workers, for example, generally expect managers to be highly participative and to give them input in decision making. In contrast, many South American workers actually balk at participation and want take-charge leaders. The basic idea, then, is that managers will be more effective when they adapt their styles to the contingencies of the situations that they face.[16]

■ STRATEGIES FOR ENHANCING JOB SATISFACTION

Deciding what motivates workers and provides job satisfaction is only part of the manager's battle. The other part is to apply that knowledge. Experts have suggested—and many companies have instituted—a wide range of programs designed to make jobs more interesting and rewarding and the work environment more pleasant. In this section, we will consider five of the most common types of programs: reinforcement and punishment, management by objectives, participative management, job enrichment and redesign, and modified work schedules.

Reinforcement and Punishment

B.C. Tel
www.bctel.com

National Hockey League
www.nhl.com

Many companies try to alter workers' behaviour through systematic rewards and punishment for specific behaviours. Rewards, or positive reinforcement, can be used to increase the frequency of desired behaviours. For example, paying large cash bonuses to salespeople who exceed their quotas will cause them to work even harder in the future to exceed their quotas again. New incentive reward systems at B.C. Tel, Drexis Inc., and the Toronto SkyDome all rely on positive reinforcement (see the box "Incentives and Motivation").

Punishment, on the other hand, is used to get people to change their behaviour by giving them unpleasant consequences. Employees who come to work late repeatedly may need to be suspended or have their pay docked to change their behaviour in the future. When the National Hockey League fines or suspends players found guilty of drug abuse, it is seeking to change their behaviour in the future.

Sometimes punishments may be necessary. Most managers dislike punishing unacceptable behaviour, in part because workers may respond with anger, resentment, hostility, or retaliation.

Extensive reinforcement works best when people are learning new behaviour, new skills, and new jobs. As they become more adept, rewards can become more infrequent. Managers generally like giving rewards and placing a positive value on a person's good behaviour, since these actions make for positive employer-employee relationships. Moreover, rewards are more likely to motivate workers and increase their job satisfaction than are punishments.

There are some limitations on using rewards to shape workers' behaviour. Rewards will only work if people:

- believe they can perform better by making an effort.
- believe that they will receive rewards for performing better.
- want the rewards the company offers for performing better.

Management by Objectives

One technique for managing the planning process is called *management by objectives*, or *MBO*. While MBO is mainly concerned with helping managers implement and carry out their plans, it can serve other purposes as well.

One very important benefit of using MBO is improved human relations. For example, when employees sit down with their managers to set goals for the coming year, they learn more about the organization's goals, come to feel that they are an important part of the team, and see how they can improve the company's performance by working towards their own goals.

The year-end assessment of goal attainment and rewards can also improve human relations. Assuming managers are using the MBO system properly, employees should come away from these meetings understanding the value of their contributions and with a fair and equitable reward. Thus, MBO can help employees satisfy a variety of needs and can also facilitate their perceptions of fairness. Investors Syndicate has enjoyed considerable success with its MBO program.

participative management
A method of increasing employees' job satisfaction by giving them a voice in how they do their jobs and how the company is managed.

Participative Management

Another popular technique for promoting human relations is **participative management.** Simply stated, participative management involves giving employees a voice in how they do

TRENDS CHALLENGES

Incentives and Motivation

Canadian companies have begun to realize that offering incentives beyond the normal benefits can result in creative ideas as well as large increases in employee productivity. These incentives may be monetary or nonmonetary. Consider the following:

- At B.C. Tel, a suggestion system was implemented that gives cash rewards to employees for ideas that generate revenue or save the company money. The employee receives 10 percent of the money saved or the revenue generated. Employees have received up to $20 000 for ideas.

- Drexis Inc. recently flew 12 employees and their families to Disney World as a reward for increasing sales by over 100 percent in one year.

- Proctor & Redfern Ltd., a consulting engineering firm, lets high achievers serve on committees with senior executives, represent the firm at outside functions, or enroll in development courses for which the company pays the bill.

- Avatar Communications Inc. sent employees on a weeklong Outward Bound expedition into the wilderness. The trip had both reward and motivational components.

- Pitney Bowes Canada Ltd. sent 60 of its top salespeople and their spouses to Hong Kong after they achieved 135 percent of their sales quota; salespeople who achieved 112 percent received a trip to San Diego.

- At Cloverdale Paint, employees who come up with innovative ideas to improve customer service receive a personal letter from the president and a coffee mug or T-shirt bearing the company logo. The best idea submitted each quarter earns the originator a restaurant gift certificate worth $50. The employee who makes the best suggestion of the year receives $200 and an engraved plaque presented at a workplace ceremony.

- Manitoba Telephone System instituted a suggestion system called IDEA$PLUS, which gives employees cash awards of up to $10 000 for good ideas.

- Employees at the Toronto SkyDome are given coupons for exceptional service, such as finding a lost child or repairing a broken seat. The coupons can be used to accumulate points that can be redeemed for prizes.

- Emery Apparel Canada Inc. conducts an annual "Oscar" awards ceremony. With great hoopla, the CEO asks for the envelope with the name of the winner of the top award. Last year, a 12-year employee won the award for figuring out (on her own time) how to satisfy a customer's difficult request.

- At Ford Motor Company, workers are rewarded for suggestions that save the company money. For example, when a metal press operator found a way to save on the amount of sheet metal used in floor panels, the company gave back to the worker $14 000 of the $70 000 saved. A recent study shows that activity like this has an effect—it takes workers at Ford one-third less time to build a car than workers at GM.

Incentives are important for top managers as well. The higher a manager is placed in a firm, the more likely it is that a good chunk of the manager's pay will be performance-based. A Conference Board of Canada study of executive compensation in Canada showed that up to 40 percent of top executives' total compensation comes in the form of incentives. For lower-level managers, the figure was 20 percent, and for other employees it was 10 percent. Top managers in the U.S. often receive up to 60 percent of their total compensation in the form of incentives. Most Canadian companies have set up some type of incentive plan for their senior executives.

Incentive systems must be carefully developed or they will not motivate employee behaviour in the desired direction. In addition to the usual sales and profit goals, firms are beginning to look at incentive systems that reward managers for achieving goals like effective downsizing, increasing environmental consciousness, and improving the corporate culture. A decision must also be made about whether the incentive system will be directed at individual employees or groups. Historically, incentives have been directed at individuals, but with the new emphasis on teamwork in organizations, this is changing. Now, a group may get an incentive if it gets a new product launched on time.

Incentive systems must be used with care because they may unintentionally motivate employees to engage in undesirable behaviour. For example, stockbrokers are often given bonuses for making sales of mutual funds. Super salespeople may be given trips to exotic locations in return for making their sales goals. This may motivate the salesperson to push a product or service that really doesn't meet the customers' needs.

their jobs and how the company is managed. Such participation should make employees feel more committed to the goals of the organization because they help shape them.

Some employees prefer a democratic, or supportive, leader. A survey at B.C. Telecom, for example, showed that people with a supportive boss missed less work, were less tense, felt more secure, and were more confident about their ability to get ahead in the company. Supervisors who got negative ratings usually were inflexible, supervised their workers too closely, and didn't communicate useful information to them.[17]

Japanese companies like Honda have been especially effective at practising participative management. And participative management has become more popular in recent years in Canada, partly from imitating the Japanese and partly as businesses and labour unions have become increasingly cooperative. At CP Express and Transport, for example, truck drivers were allowed to decide how to spend $8 million on new equipment.[18] The box "The Japanese Management System" describes some of the strong and weak points of that system.

At one level, employees may be given decision-making responsibility for certain narrow activities, such as when to take their lunch breaks, how to do their jobs, and so forth. At a broader level, employees are also being given a say in more significant issues and decisions. One popular technique to encourage participative management is the **quality circle**, a group of employees who meet regularly to consider solutions for problems in their work area. Great West Life, for example, has reported success with its quality circle program. Quality circles are explored in detail in Chapters 10 and 11.

While some employees thrive in participative management programs, they are not for everyone. The key is for managers to provide employees with opportunities to participate in decision making only to the extent that they want to participate. If employees really would prefer not to be involved, they should not be forced.

Job Enrichment and Redesign

While MBO programs and participative management can work in a variety of settings, job enrichment and job redesign programs can increase satisfaction only if a job lacks motivating factors to begin with.

Great West Life Assurance Company
www.gwl.ca

quality circle
A technique for maximizing quality of production. Employees are grouped into small teams that define, analyze, and solve quality and other process-related problems within their area.

These employees are part of a quality circle that is discussing ways to improve work methods and thereby increase productivity.

TRENDS & CHALLENGES

The Japanese Management System

In the 1980s, the Japanese management system was all the rage. At its most basic, the system contained the following elements:

1. *Lifetime employment.* Employees stay at one firm for their entire career instead of changing jobs as is common in Canada. Seniority is the basis for promotion.

2. *Temporary employees.* Large Japanese firms have many temporary employees, most of them female. If a downturn occurs, these employees are the first to be laid off. Women act as a buffer to protect men's jobs.

3. *Participative decision making.* When an important decision is to be made, everyone who will feel its impact is involved in the decision-making process. A decision is made only after a consensus is reached.

4. *Management training.* An emphasis on company loyalty underlies much management training in Japan. Training is oriented towards groups instead of individuals, and is designed to encourage team spirit.

5. *Other characteristics.* The Japanese management system also emphasizes daily exercise for employees at the work site, pep talks by supervisors, identical uniforms for workers and managers, no unions, non-specific job classifications, and company outings for employees and their families.

This system has served Japan well over the years. In fact, until recently it was thought that this system made Japan a formidable competitor in world markets. But things have changed dramatically in just a few short years. The 1990s have not been a happy time for Japanese managers and workers. During 1992–94, Japan found itself in a major recession, and industrial output declined for 23 consecutive months, the longest decline on record. Consumer confidence is weak, unemployment is rising, GNP is declining, and the lifetime employment and seniority ideas are coming under fire.

And now, another problem has appeared. In the past, most of the emphasis in Japanese companies was on training factory workers to carry out their tasks in an efficient manner. But in the process, not enough attention was paid to the productivity of *office workers*. Only a few office workers have personal computers, and it is not unusual for four or five workers to share a phone. The sense of order that pervades the factory is absent in the office.

When times were good in the 1980s, the excess office staff was not noticeable. But the deep recession of the 1990s has made the problem very clear. Japanese managers are now realizing that no amount of economizing in the factory can make up for overstaffed offices. One management consultant estimates that Japan's big public companies have 12 to 20 percent more middle managers than they need.

Japanese companies are beginning to address the problem of overstaffing. Many companies have reduced the hiring of college graduates, and are hoping that attrition will eventually solve the problem of overstaffing. Others are using the carrot-and-stick approach. At Honda Motors, for example, the seniority system is being replaced with a merit system. Employees will now be judged on the basis of how well they meet six-month goals set by their managers. Those who do not perform well will end up in lower-paying jobs.

Toyota Motor is trying to shock its white-collar workers into being more productive. Each department has been asked to give up 20 percent of its employees to task forces that will identify new business opportunities and explore ways to improve white-collar productivity.

Honda Motors
www.honda.com

Job Enrichment Programs.   Based on the two-factor theory discussed earlier, **job enrichment** attempts to add one or more motivating factors to a situation. For example, job rotation programs add to growth opportunities by rotating an employee through various positions in the firm. Workers gain new skills and a broader overview of their work that allows them to contribute to the firm in more ways.

Other job enrichment programs focus on increasing responsibility or recognition. At one company, a group of eight typists worked in isolated cubicles. Their job involved taking calls from any of dozens of field sales representatives and typing up service orders.

job enrichment
A method of increasing employees' job satisfaction by extending or adding motivating factors such as responsibility or growth.

They had no client contact; if they had a question about the order, for example, they had to call the sales representative. They also received little performance feedback. Interviews with these workers suggested that they were bored with their jobs and did not feel valued. As part of a job enrichment program, each typist was paired with a small group of designated sales representatives and became a part of their team. Typists were also given permission to call clients directly if they had questions about the order. Finally, a new feedback system was installed to give the typists more information about their performance. As a result, their performance improved and absenteeism decreased markedly.[19]

job redesign
A method of increasing employees' job satisfaction by improving the worker-job fit through combining tasks, creating natural work groups, and/or establishing client relationships.

Job Redesign Programs.   In some ways an extension of job enrichment, **job redesign** is even more application-oriented and recognizes that different people want different things from their jobs. By restructuring work to achieve a more satisfactory person-job fit, job redesign can motivate individuals who have a high need for growth or achievement.[20] Three typical ways of implementing job redesign are to combine tasks, to form natural work groups, and to establish client relationships.

Combining tasks enlarges a job and increases its variety, making workers feel that their work is more meaningful. In turn, workers are more motivated. For example, the job done by a computer programmer who maintains computer systems might be redesigned to include some system design and development work. The programmer is then able to use additional skills and is involved in the overall system package.

People who do different jobs on the same project are good candidates for *natural work groups*. On the one hand, these groups help employees get an overview of their jobs and see their importance in the total structure. On the other hand, these groups help management, and the firm in general, because the people working on a project are usually the most knowledgeable about it and are thus able to solve problems related to it. Quality circles are natural work groups.

One part of job redesign programs is to establish client relationships. This mechanic is explaining to a customer why she needs to have her air filter changed. Such personal contact often motivates employees to work harder because they can see how their work benefits customers.

To see how natural work groups affect motivation, consider a group where each employee does a small part of the job of assembling radios. One person sees his job as attaching red wires while another sees hers as attaching control knobs. The jobs could be redesigned to allow the group to decide who does what and in what order. The workers can exchange jobs and plan their work schedules. Now they all see themselves as part of a team that assembles radios.

A third way of redesigning a job is to *establish client relationships*—to let employees interact with customers. This approach increases the variety of a job. It also gives workers greater feelings of control over their jobs and more feedback about their performance. Lotus Development Corp. uses this approach as a means of granting necessary independence to creative employees: Instead of responding to instructions from marketing managers on how to develop new products, software writers are encouraged to work directly with customers. Similarly, software writers at Microsoft watch test users work with programs and discuss problems with them directly rather than receive feedback from third-party researchers.

Lotus Development Corp.
www.lotus.com/

Modified Work Schedules

As another way of increasing job satisfaction, many companies are trying out different approaches to working hours and the work week. Several types of modified work schedules have been tried, including flextime, the compressed workweek, telecommuting, and workshare programs.

Flextime.   Some modifications involve adjusting a standard daily work schedule. **Flextime** allows people to pick their working hours. Figure 8.2 illustrates how a flextime system might be arranged and how different people might use it. The office is open from 6 a.m. until 7 p.m. Core time is 9 a.m. until 11 a.m. and 1 p.m. until 3 p.m. Joe, being an early riser, comes in at 6 a.m., takes an hour lunch between 11 and 12, and finishes his day by 3 p.m. Sue, on the other hand, prefers a later day. She comes in at 9 a.m., takes a long lunch from 11 a.m. to 1 p.m., and then works until 7 p.m. Pat works a more traditional day from 8 a.m. until 5 p.m.

flextime
A method of increasing employees' job satisfaction by allowing them some choice in the hours they work.

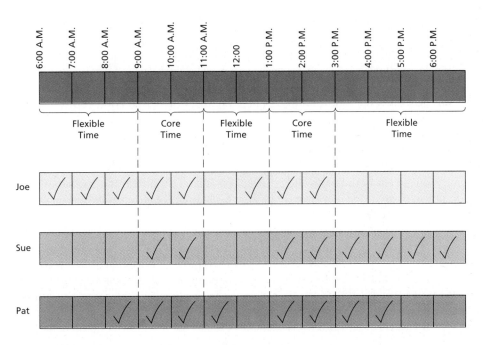

FIGURE 8.2

Flextime schedules include core time, when everyone must be at work, and flexible time, during which employees can set their own working hours.

Flextime programs give employees more flexibility in their professional and personal lives. Such programs allow workers to plan around the work schedules of spouses and the school schedules of young children, for example. The increased feeling of freedom and control over their work life also reduces individuals' levels of stress.

Companies can also benefit from flextime programs. In large urban areas, flextime programs reduce traffic congestion that contributes to lost work time. Companies benefit from the higher levels of commitment and job satisfaction among workers in such programs. 3M Canada and National Cash Register are among the companies that have adopted some form of flextime. A survey of 1600 Canadian companies showed that nearly half of them had some type of flextime program.

compressed workweek
Employees work fewer days per week, but more hours on the days they do work.

Bank of Montreal
www.bmo.com

The Compressed Workweek.   In the **compressed workweek**, employees work fewer days per week, but more hours on the days they do work. The most popular compressed workweek is 4 days, 10 hours per day, but some companies have also experimented with 3 days, 12 hours per day. The "weekend worker" program at 3M Canada in London, Ontario, offers workers 12-hour shifts on Saturdays and Sundays only, and pays them the same wage as if they had worked normal hours Monday through Friday. There is a long waiting list to transfer to weekend work.[21]

Tellers at the Bank of Montreal in Oakville Place work long days (up to 14 hours), but enjoy a short work week. Some tellers work 7 a.m. to 9 p.m. Thursday and Friday, and 7:30 a.m. to 5:30 p.m. Saturdays. Others work Monday to Wednesday for 14 hours each day. Employees like the system because it allows them to do personal errands during the day on the weekdays they do not have to be at work.[22]

telecommuting
Allowing employees to do all or some of their work away from the office.

Telecommuting.   A third variation in work design is **telecommuting**, which allows people to do some or all of their work away from their office. The availability of networked computers, fax machines, cellular telephones, and overnight delivery services makes it possible for many independent professionals to work at home or while travelling. More and more Canadian workers do a significant portion of their work outside their conventional offices.[23]

Telecommuting helps employees avoid driving a long way to work, but they often report feeling isolated and lonely. To avoid this problem, B.C. Tel and Bentall Development Inc. jointly developed a satellite telecommuting office in Langley, B.C. It allows workers who used to have to commute to Burnaby or Vancouver to reduce their travel time considerably and still be able to interact with other workers.[24]

But telecommuting may not be for everyone. Would-be telecommuters must ask themselves several important questions: "Can I meet deadlines even when I'm not being closely supervised? What will it be like to be away from the social context of the office five days a week? Can I renegotiate family rules, so my spouse doesn't come home expecting to see dinner on the table just because I've been home all day?"

Another obstacle to establishing a telecommuting program is convincing management that it will be beneficial for everyone involved. Telecommuters may have to fight the perception—from both bosses and co-workers—that if they are not being supervised, they are not working. Managers are often very suspicious about telecommuting, asking "How can I tell if someone is working when I can't see them?"

worksharing (job sharing)
A method of increasing employee job satisfaction by allowing two people to share one job.

NOVA Corp.
www.nova.ca

Workshare Programs.   A fourth type of modified work schedule, **worksharing** (also called **job sharing**), benefits both employee and employer. This approach allows two people to share one full-time job. For example, Kim Sarjeant and Loraine Champion, who are staff lawyers for NOVA Corp. in Calgary, share a position advising the human resources department. Sarjeant works Monday through Wednesday, and Champion works Wednesday through Friday.[25] A Statistics Canada survey showed that 8 percent of all part-time workers in Canada share a job with someone. People who share jobs are more likely to be women, to be university educated, and to have professional occupations like teaching and nursing. In addition, job sharers earned more than regular part-time workers.[26]

Short-run worksharing programs can help ease experienced workers into retirement while training their replacements. Worksharing can also allow students in university co-op programs to combine academic learning with practical experience.

Long-run worksharing programs have proven a good solution for people who want only part-time work. For example, five people might decide to share one reservationist's job at Air Canada with each working one day a week. Each person earns some money, remains in the job market, and enjoys limited travel benefits.

Air Canada
www.aircanada.ca

SUMMARY OF LEARNING OBJECTIVES

1. **Discuss the importance of *job satisfaction* and *employee morale* and summarize their roles in *human relations* in the workplace.** Good *human relations*—the interactions between employers and employees and their attitudes towards one another—are important to business because they lead to higher levels of *job satisfaction* (the degree of enjoyment that workers derive from their jobs) and *morale* (workers' overall attitude towards their workplace). Satisfied employees generally exhibit lower levels of absenteeism and turnover; they also have fewer grievances and engage in fewer negative behaviours.

2. **Identify and summarize the most important theories of employee *motivation*.** Views of employee motivation have changed dramatically over the years. The *classical theory* holds that people are motivated solely by money. *Scientific management* tried to analyze jobs and increase production by finding better ways to perform tasks. The *Hawthorne studies* were the first to demonstrate the importance of making workers feel that attention is being paid to their needs.

   The *human-resources model* identifies two kinds of managers: *Theory X managers*, who believe that people are inherently uncooperative and must be constantly reinforced, and *Theory Y managers*, who believe that people are naturally responsible and self-motivated to be productive.

   Maslow's *hierarchy of needs model* proposes that people have a number of different needs (ranging from physiological to self-actualization) that they attempt to satisfy in their work. People must fulfill lower-level needs before seeking to fulfill higher-level needs. *Two-factor theory* suggests that if basic *hygiene factors* are not met, workers will be dissatisfied; only by increasing more complex *motivating factors* can companies increase employees' performance.

   Expectancy theory holds that people will work hard if they believe that their efforts will lead to desired rewards. *Equity theory* says that employees compare the treatment they receive from the organization to the treatment received by others. *Goal-setting theory* says that employees who set quantified, difficult goals will outperform employees who don't set such goals.

3. **Discuss different managerial styles of *leadership* and their impact on human relations in the workplace.** Effective *leadership*—the process of motivating others to meet specific objectives—is an important determinant of employee satisfaction and motivation. Generally speaking, managers practise one of three basic managerial styles. *Autocratic managers* generally issue orders that they expect to be obeyed. *Democratic managers* generally seek subordinates' input into decisions. *Free-rein managers* are more likely to advise than to make decisions. Managers need to assess situations carefully, especially to determine the desire of subordinates to share input or exercise creativity.

4. **Describe some of the strategies used by organizations to improve employee motivation and satisfaction.** Managers can use several strategies to increase employee motivation and satisfaction. The principle of *reinforcement* holds that reward and punishment can control behaviour. *Rewards*, for example, are positive

reinforcement when they are tied directly to desired or improved performance. *Punishment* (using unpleasant consequences to change undesirable behaviour) is generally less effective. *Management by objectives* (a system of collaborative goal setting) and *participative management* (techniques for giving employees a voice in management decisions) can improve human relations by making employees feel like part of a team. *Job enrichment, job redesign*, and *modified work schedules* (including *flextime* and *workshare programs*) can enhance job satisfaction by adding motivating factors to jobs in which they are normally lacking.

STUDY QUESTIONS AND EXERCISES

Review Questions

1. Do you think most people are satisfied or dissatisfied with their work? Why?
2. Compare the hierarchy of human needs and the two-factor theory.
3. How can participative management programs enhance employee satisfaction?
4. In what type of situations might a manager be primarily autocratic (boss-centred)? In what type of situations might a manager be primarily democratic (subordinate-centred)?

Analysis Questions

5. Some evidence suggests that people fresh out of college or university initially show high levels of job satisfaction. Their job satisfaction drops dramatically in their late twenties, but gradually increases again as they get older. What might account for this pattern?
6. As a manager, how could you apply each of the theories of employee motivation discussed in this chap-

ter? Which would be easiest to use? Which would be hardest? Why?

7. Suppose you were an employee and realized one day that you were essentially dissatisfied with your job. Short of quitting, what might you do to improve things for yourself?
8. List five important Canadian managers of today who are also great leaders. Give reasons why you chose the five.

Application Exercises

9. Go to the library and research a manager and/or owner of a company in the early 20th century and a manager or owner of a company in the last decade. Compare the two in terms of their leadership style and their view of employee motivation.
10. Interview the manager of a local manufacturing company. Identify as many different strategies for enhancing job satisfaction at that company as you can.

BUILDING YOUR BUSINESS SKILLS

Goal

To encourage students to consider whether they could become successful telecommuters and to analyze the advantages and disadvantages of telecommuting.

Situation

You've worked for the same company for three years. Although you're satisfied with your job, your work schedule is a real problem. Your commute, by car, normally takes an hour, but if weather or traffic conditions are bad, the time can double. Life is too short for this, you tell yourself, and you are determined to try telecommuting. Your boss is willing, but you're still not sure whether it's the right decision for your personal life or your career.

Method

Step 1: Working alone, take the following test to judge whether you are a good candidate for telecommuting. Many of the answers require work experience, so you may have to ask a friend or family member for some on-the-job insights. Record your answers so you can share them with others:

1. Do you have the right personality for telecommuting?
   - Are you self-disciplined enough to work alone?
   - Are you a self-starter?
   - Would being isolated from other workers bother you?
   - Are you an effective time manager?

- Can you block out distractions and chores (e.g., cooking dinner, watching TV)?

2. What are the characteristics of an ideal telecommuting job? How do you think the following factors would affect your success? (If you are a full-time student, answer these questions based on the work you expect to do.)

- Do you interact with others all day or is most of your work independent?

- Are your work materials portable? Can you move them easily from office to home?

- Is most of your work computer- or telephone-based? Can you transmit your work electronically?

3. Do you understand the career risks of telecommuting, and are you willing to make adjustments for them?

- Why do you think it is important for telecommuters to keep a high profile at work?

- List three ways to maintain your visibility.

- Do you think it is important to continue to socialize with co-workers?

4. Are your working conditions right for telecommuting?

- How would you describe an appropriate at-home work space?

- What equipment would you need to set up a virtual office? Do you have a computer? Are you connected to the Internet? Do you have voice mail, a fax, and multiple phone lines to handle your various messages?

- If you have children, what child-care arrangements would you require?

Step 2: Come together with three or four other students to share and compare your answers. Based on your comparative analysis, can you identify critical differences in the way people view their suitability for telecommuting and the advantages and disadvantages of working in a virtual office?

Follow-Up Questions

1. What are the major advantages of telecommuting?

2. What are the major disadvantages?

3. How can a manager make telecommuting success more likely? How can he or she make it more difficult?

4. Many workers are struggling to achieve a work/life balance. Based on your responses and the responses of your classmates, is telecommuting a viable solution?

Prentice Hall ◄ **T A K E   I T   T O   T H E   N E T**

Check out our Companion Website

for this chapter's Exploring the Net exercise, featuring a British Website that surveys employee satisfaction and other intriguing, annotated destinations. You'll also find practice exercises, updated Weblinks from the text, links to newsgroups, updates, and more.

w w w . p r e n t i c e h a l l . c a / e b e r t

BUSINESS CASE 8

Has Levi's Lost Its Touch?

Levi Strauss & Co. is not only the world's leading maker of branded clothing and one of *Fortune* magazine's most admired companies. It is also a leader in creating a supportive work environment based on worker loyalty and trust.

The average length of service at the legendary blue jeans maker is more than 10 years, and management turnover at its headquarters in San Francisco is a mere 1.5 percent a year. Pay and bonuses are generous, and Levi's stock has risen with its fortunes, from U.S.$2.53 in

➤

1984 to U.S.$265 in 1996, a record most firms would envy. This is the firm that's paying children in Bangladesh to stay in school full-time until they are old enough to reclaim the guaranteed jobs in Levi's factories that await them when they turn 14. Under the leadership of CEO Robert Haas, whose great-great-granduncle started the firm, Levi's seems to have figured out how to be ethical and make money at the same time.

Employee motivation has been high during Haas's tenure, sustained by his vision of the firm. "I believe that if you create an environment that your people identify with, that is responsible to their sense of values, justice, fairness, ethics, compassion, and appreciation, they will help you be successful. There's no guarantee, but I will stake all my chips on this vision."

The company sets great store in its Aspirations Statement, which invokes teamwork, trust, diversity, recognition, and ethics, and is backed by required courses in leadership, diversity, and ethical decision making. Employees are assured that these values are real. Managers' bonuses, which can be as much as twice their salaries, depend directly on how well they achieve "aspirational behaviour," as judged by their subordinates and others. To compensate for ending its ESOP plan, Levi's has conscientiously promised an extra year's pay to each of its 37 000 employees if cash flow goals for 1997–2001 are met. Says Clive Smith, who works at the new plant in Cape Town, South Africa, "When we tell people what it's like working here, they think we're lying.... You'll have to fish the cops to get me out of here."

Yet the company is dealing with a possible threat to its sterling employee relations: a stunning layoff affecting 6000 jobs was announced in 1997. Partly the result of debt incurred in a massive buyback of company stock in 1996, the layoffs seem to go against everything the company had stood for in its dealings with employees, although job security was never promised. Ironically, another contributing factor to the loss of jobs was an expensive plan to improve Levi's service to retailers that depended on developing new computer systems and software, not the firm's core business. The effort failed.

Layoffs are not the only problem Levi's employees are facing. Workers in Levi's factories have traditionally been paid on a piece work system that pays them a certain amount of money for each zipper they sew or each belt loop they attach. In Levi's U.S. factories, this system has been replaced with a groupwork system where workers share tasks and are paid on the basis of how productive the *group* is. The company hoped this shift in emphasis from the individual to the group would relieve worker boredom and also reduce repetitive stress injuries that were caused by workers pushing themselves too hard to make piece work goals.

But the new system has created unanticipated problems. Skilled workers feel that their wages are being lowered because slower workers reduce the overall productivity of the team. Morale has dropped, there is infighting among employees, and faster workers have tried to banish slower workers from their teams. In one factory, when a team found out that one of its members was going to have hand surgery, they voted the worker off the team because they feared team productivity would suffer when she returned after her surgery. One executive said that Levi's has created a lot of pain and anxiety for its employees, and nothing positive has been accomplished.

■ Case Questions

1. How can Levi's minimize the damages its uncharacteristic actions might cause to employee morale and motivation? What specific strategies should management use?

2. CEO Haas has accepted responsibility for the situation that created the need for layoffs and plans to adhere to the firm's aspirational values. How can he use his position to focus employees on the positive aspects of working for Levi's?

3. Levi's president Peter Jacobi sees the company's unusual commitment to teamwork and trust as "a business strategy, pure and simple." Do you agree? Why or why not?

4. Jacobi also says, "We're not in business to create world peace." Can you think of any downside to the aspirational approach?

5. Do you think you would be satisfied working at Levi's. Why or why not?

CHAPTER

9

MANAGING HUMAN RESOURCES AND LABOUR RELATIONS

BREAKING THROUGH THE GLASS CEILING

Much has been written about the "glass ceiling" that prevents women from achieving top jobs in industry. Historically, most top jobs in the private and public sector have been held by men, and women were concentrated in the lower-paying clerical and secretarial positions. But times are changing, and women are gradually occupying more and more senior management positions. Recently there have been some major breakthroughs by women who have achieved top ranking jobs in major industrial firms. In the Canadian automobile industry, for example, the CEOs of two of the three domestic manufacturers are now women.

General Motors of Canada. Maureen Kempston Darkes (pictured), the president of General Motors of Canada Ltd., heads a company with a workforce of 35 000 people and 10 assembly and component plants. Although GM has the biggest automotive market share, that share has dropped over the years to about 33 percent. In the early 1990s, GM lost billions from its North American operations. Kempston Darkes has undertaken the task of improving GM's performance.

Dealing with overall manufacturing and marketing problems is a new experience for Kempston Darkes, who started with GM in 1975 and worked her way up through the legal and government affairs side of GM Canada. Along the way, she spent two years in the treasurer's office in New York, then returned to Oshawa and moved up through positions like vice president of public affairs and general counsel. Most CEOs at GM do not move up through this side of the business.

Ms Kempston Darkes's leadership style is to be accessible to subordinates. She is as likely to show up at a Pontiac/Buick dealership in Saskatoon as she is to be conducting a meeting in her office in Oshawa, Ontario. She has spent a great deal of time visiting dealerships across Canada. Sandy Williamson, the head of GM Canada's dealer council, says that she is by far the most accessible president that he can remember. One of her first acts as president was to personally write all of GM Canada's dealers and assure them that she supported the idea of a dealer-factory communication team that had been put together by her predecessor. The team's job is to keep the working relationships between dealers and GM smooth.

Kempston Darkes's management style appears to be flexible and collegial, but demanding. She has an open-concept office, and the sentries that usually guard a CEO's office are nowhere to be seen. When she visits one of the production plants, she drives herself to the site and unobtrusively walks in the front door like everyone else. She emphasizes that she is a team player.

Ford Motor of Canada Ltd. Bobbie Gaunt, the CEO of Ford Motor of Canada, was appointed in 1997. She heads a company that has 14 000 employees and several assembly and engine plants in Canada. Sales during 1996 were $25.5 billion. Gaunt is a 25-year veteran of Ford, and was formerly the director of marketing research for North American operations. She was also general sales manager for the Lincoln-

Mercury division. She is considered to be a world-class marketer, and is expected to boost sales for Ford Canada.

Gaunt says that change is happening in the industry, but it hasn't gone far enough or proceeded fast enough. She says that an industry as old and as large as the automobile industry will require a very long time to change.

Other CEO appointments. The changes at GM and Ford are not unusual. The Canadian CEOs of Home Depot, Xerox, General Foods, EDS, and Kraft are all women. And in the U.S., Jill Barad is the CEO of Mattel Inc., and the first woman to take over as head of a major industrial corporation.

Other top-level jobs just below the level of CEO are increasingly held by women in both Canada and the U.S. Gail McGovern is the head of AT&T's $26 billion consumer business, and Lois Juliber is the head of North American and European operations for Colgate-Palmolive. Both these women have a chance to become CEOs in a few years.

In spite of these high-profile cases, there is general agreement that much work remains to be done since women still make up only a tiny proportion of senior executives in business firms. In the automotive industry in particular, the perception persists that the industry is still a "boys' club." Recent discrimination and harassment lawsuits against Magna International and Mitsubishi Motor Corp. illustrate the problems that remain.

Ford Canada
www.ford.ca

GM Canada
www.gmcanada.com

The appointment of increasing numbers of women to top management jobs is no accident. Rather, it is the result of careful assessment of the human resources that a firm has available to it. The strategies used at Ford Canada and General Motors of Canada are typical of systems that businesses use to develop and maintain an effective workforce. These systems focus on defining the jobs that need to be done; ensuring that appropriate people are hired and oriented to their new jobs; training, appraising, and compensating employees; and providing appropriate human resource services to employees.

By focusing on the learning objectives, you will better understand some of the formal systems that companies use to manage their employees, as well as some of the key issues in contemporary labour relations. After reading this chapter, you should be able to:

1. Define *human resource management* and explain how managers plan for human resources.

2. Identify the steps involved in *staffing* a company.

3. Explain how organizations can develop workers' skills and manage workers who do not perform well.

4. Discuss the importance of *wages* and *salaries*, *incentives*, and *benefits programs* in attracting and keeping skilled workers.

5. Describe the major *laws governing labour-management relations*.

6. Identify the steps in the *collective bargaining process*.

■ FOUNDATIONS OF HUMAN RESOURCE MANAGEMENT

human resource management
The development, administration, and evaluation of programs to acquire and enhance the quality and performance of people in a business.

Human resource management involves developing, administering, and evaluating programs to acquire and enhance the quality and performance of people in a business. Human resource specialists—sometimes called personnel managers—are employed by all but the smallest firms. They help plan for future personnel needs. They recruit, train, and develop employees. And they set up employee evaluation, compensation, and benefits programs.

But in fact all managers are personnel managers. Managers of production, accounting, finance, and marketing departments choose prospective employees, train new workers, and evaluate employee performance. As you will see in this section, all managers must be aware of the basis of good human resource management—job-relatedness and employee-job matching.

Job-Relatedness and Employee-Job Matching

According to the principle of **job-relatedness**, all personnel decisions, policies, and programs should be based on the requirements of a position. That is, all criteria used to hire, evaluate, promote, and reward people must be tied directly to the job they perform. For example, a policy that all secretaries be young women would not be job-related since neither youth nor femaleness is essential in performing secretarial work. Such a policy represents poor human resource management because the company loses the chance to hire more experienced help and to consider skilled men for the position. On the other hand, a policy of hiring only young women to model teenage girls' clothing would be job-related and would thus reflect sound human resource management.

Fundamental to the concept of job-relatedness—and to human resource management in general—is the idea of matching the right person to the right job. The direct result of good human resource management is the close match of people, skills, interests, and temperaments with the requirements of their jobs. When people are well matched to their jobs, the company benefits from high rates of employee performance and satisfaction, high retention of effective people, and low absenteeism. All personnel activities relate in some fashion to the employee-job match. Job matching may not be easy, as shown in the box "Mismatch in Jobs and Skills."

job-relatedness
The principle that all personnel decisions, policies, and programs should be based on the requirements of a position.

■PLANNING FOR HUMAN RESOURCES

Just as planning for financial, plant, and equipment needs is important, so too is planning for personnel needs. As Figure 9.1 shows, such planning involves two types of activities by managers—job analysis and forecasting.

Job Analysis

Job analysis is the detailed study of the specific duties required for a particular job and the human qualities required to perform that job. For simple, repetitive jobs, managers might ask workers to create a checklist of all the duties they perform and the importance of each of those duties for the job. In analyzing more complex jobs, managers might combine checklists with interviews of job holders to determine their exact duties. Managers might also observe workers to record the duties they perform.

job analysis
A detailed study of the specific duties in a particular job and the human qualities required for that job.

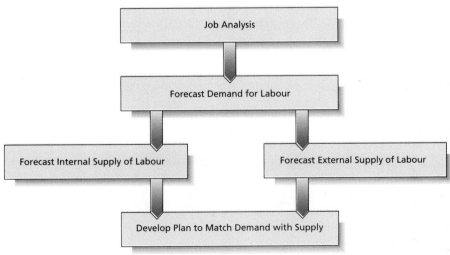

FIGURE 9.1
Planning for human resources.

TRENDS CHALLENGES

Mismatch in Jobs and Skills

There is a "mismatch" problem in Canada—people have skills the market no longer wants, and companies have needs that unemployed people cannot satisfy. The Canadian Labour Market and Productivity Centre estimates that 22 percent of the unemployed have skills that didn't match their former employers' needs. Interestingly, this figure is down from the 64 percent estimate in 1989. However, during the 1990s, the matching problem is likely to worsen again as companies become ever more demanding in what they want in employees.

The mismatch problem is obvious in a field like information technology. In an industry that relies almost solely on human brainpower and creativity, companies are in desperate need of computer programmers, software developers, and computer scientists. Canadian universities graduated one-third *fewer* computer scientists in 1990 than they did in 1986. Yet some graduates had difficulty finding employment because they were not trained to deal with computer networks, servers, workstations, and other new developments. During this same period, university enrollment increased 12 percent, with the number of students studying history increasing 59 percent, and sociology 31 percent. Neither of these areas are promising in terms of available jobs.

Why have students not become interested in information technology? Attitudes and perceptions probably play a negative role. Computer experts are often portrayed as socially inept individuals who are "nerds" or "geeks." There is still something in Canadians that allows people to dismiss careers in technology as uninteresting.

But this is only part of the reason that a mismatch problem exists. There is also a growing recognition that we must change the way people are trained. Education should be a lifetime experience, not merely something that ends when a person graduates from some school. Pressure to change and adapt comes from the workplace as companies adopt new technologies to deliver new services. Employees who were hired in the 1960s or 1970s may not want to adapt to the new realities.

Honeywell Ltd. is just one firm that has had to come to grips with some unpleasant new realities. Its Toronto plant, which makes instrumentation for heating and cooling equipment, found that customers were demanding that the firm be certified under the ISO 9000 international quality program. This meant that Honeywell would have to introduce just-in-time inventory, total quality management, and self-directed work teams. But when the company looked at its workforce, it found that only half had English as their first language, and that many had not finished high school.

Before the workers could cope with the new demands being imposed on the company, they needed to be trained. This gradually evolved into a "learning for life" program, which involved English, math, and computer courses. Employees were also trained in production and inventory management, total quality, and communication skills. Part of the training was provided at Humber College in Toronto. Each year, Humber sells about $30 million worth of education to private sector firms like Kodak Canada and John Labatt Ltd.

The mismatch problem will be solved when people on the job market have a total mix of characteristics—analytic abilities, practical skills, and flexibility—to encompass the full range of what companies are looking for. A recent Conference Board of Canada study asked employers what they were looking for in employees. Some of the things—teamwork, ability to think, ability to communicate—can be taught in school. But others—positive attitudes, responsibility, and adaptability—are more difficult to develop in educational programs.

One firm has taken advantage of this mismatch. Atlantic Computer Institute was founded on the idea that students often come out of universities over-educated and under-trained. The Institute trains them in computer technology in an intensive 11-month program. Graduates of the Institute find jobs in software writing, local area network support, and writing technical manuals.

Another way to cope with potential mismatches is a co-op program. Under this system, university students alternate between taking classes and working for a business firm. The University of Victoria, for example, operates a year-round schedule, alternating "job semesters" with traditional classes. When students graduate, they are often hired by the firm they worked for during the co-op program.

Using the job analysis, human resource managers can develop **job descriptions**. A job description outlines the objectives, responsibilities, and key tasks in a job. It also describes the conditions under which the job will be done, the relationship of the job to other positions, and the skills needed to do the job. The skills, education, and experience necessary to fill a position make up the **job specification**.

Job analysis and the resulting job descriptions and specifications are the foundations of effective human resource management. They serve as tools in hiring personnel for specific positions, as guides in establishing training programs, and as sources of comparison in setting wages. But most important, by defining job requirements objectively, they allow managers to make personnel decisions in keeping with the principles of job-relatedness.

job description
The objectives, responsibilities, and key tasks of a job; the conditions under which it will be done; its relationship to other positions; and the skills needed to perform it.

job specification
The specific skills, education, and experience needed to perform a job.

Forecasting

Once they have analyzed the nature of their needs, managers must forecast their needs. Managers need to forecast both their demand for employees of different types and the likely supply of such employees in the short term (less than one year), intermediate term (one to five years), and long term (over five years). Only then can they formulate specific strategies for responding to any potential employee surplus or shortage. As in any forecast, however, the manager's true purpose is to minimize major surprises, not to predict future needs exactly.

In forecasting *demand*, managers must take into account their businesses' plans for growth (if any). They must also figure in the normal rate of turnover and the number of older employees nearing retirement, among other factors. In forecasting *supply*, managers must consider the complexity of the job and which current employees could be promoted to fill higher positions. But they must also predict whether the labour market for a particular job will be in a state of surplus or shortage. In recent years, more and more companies are hiring short-term freelancers instead of long-term, career employees (see Business Case 9 at the end of this chapter).

■ STAFFING THE ORGANIZATION

Once managers have decided what positions they need to fill, they must find and hire individuals who meet the job requirements. Staffing of the corporation is one of the most complex and important aspects of good human resource management. In this section, we will consider how businesses fill positions from both outside and inside the organization. Sometimes personnel must be recruited and chosen from the outside. As well, decisions must be made about employee promotions to fill vacancies within the organization.

External Staffing

A new firm has little choice but to acquire staff from outside itself. Established firms may also turn to the outside to fill positions for which there are no good internal candidates, to accommodate growth, or as a way to bring in fresh ideas. Such external staffing can be divided into two stages: recruitment and selection.

Recruitment. In the first step, the company needs to develop a pool of applicants who are both interested in and qualified for the open positions. The purpose of **recruitment** is to generate a large number of potential employees. Thus, successful recruitment focuses only on the most basic qualifications of a job. For example, recruitment ads for a financial

recruitment
The phase in the staffing of a company in which the firm seeks to develop a pool of interested, qualified applicants for a position.

An in-depth interview with a prospective employee is often part of the recruiting process, particularly for managerial jobs.

Canadian Human Rights Act
Ensures that any individual who wishes to obtain a job has an equal opportunity to apply for it.

bona fide occupational requirement
When an employer may choose one applicant over another based on overriding characteristics of the job.

Canadian Human Rights Commission
www.chrc.ca

analyst might require applicants to hold an MBA degree with an emphasis on finance. But requiring a degree from a particular school will unnecessarily restrict the number of applicants. Recruitment specifications should always be clearly job-related.

When recruiting, firms must be careful not to violate anti-discrimination laws. The key federal anti-discrimination legislation is the **Canadian Human Rights Act** of 1977. The goal of this act is to ensure that any individual who wishes to obtain a job has an equal opportunity to compete for it. The act applies to all federal agencies, federal Crown corporations, any employee of the federal government, and business firms that do business interprovincially.

The *Canadian Human Rights Act* prohibits a wide variety of practices in recruiting, selecting, promoting, and dismissing personnel. The Act specifically prohibits discrimination on the basis of age, race and colour, national and ethnic origin, physical handicap, religion, gender, marital status, or prison record (if pardoned). Ambiguities in determining whether discrimination has occurred are sometimes circumvented by using the concept of **"bona fide occupational requirement."** An employer may choose one person over another based on overriding characteristics of the job in question. If a fitness centre wants to hire only women to supervise its women's locker room and sauna, it can do so without being discriminatory because it established a bona fide occupational requirement.

Enforcement of the federal act is carried out by the Canadian Human Rights Commission. The commission can either respond to complaints from individuals who believe they have been discriminated against, or launch an investigation on its own if it has reason to believe that discrimination has occurred. During an investigation, data are gathered about the alleged discriminatory behaviour and, if the claim of discrimination is substantiated, the offending organization or individual may be ordered to compensate the victim.

Each province has also enacted human rights legislation to regulate organizations and businesses operating in that province. These provincial regulations are similar in spirit to the federal legislation, with many minor variations from province to province. All provinces prohibit discrimination on the basis of race, national or ethnic origin, colour, religion, sex, and marital status, but some do not address such issues as physical handicaps, criminal record, or age. Provincial human rights commissions enforce provincial legislation.

The ***Employment Equity Act of 1986*** addresses the issue of discrimination in employment by designating four groups as employment disadvantaged—women, visible minorities, aboriginal people, and people with disabilities. Companies covered by the Act are required to publish statistics on their employment of people in these four groups.

Selection.   Once a pool of applicants has been identified, managers must sort through those individuals and select the best candidate for the job. **Selection** is by no means an exact science, since it is difficult to predict any given individual's behaviours and attitudes. Nevertheless, it is an important process. Hiring the wrong employee is costly to the firm and is unfair to that individual.

To reduce the element of uncertainty, personnel experts and other managers use a variety of selection techniques. The most common of these methods, as shown in Figure 9.2, are applications and résumés, screening interviews, ability and aptitude tests, reference checks, on-site interviews, and medical, drug, and polygraph tests. Each organization develops its own mix of selection techniques and may use them in any order.

The application form, used for almost all lower-level jobs, asks for information about the applicant such as background, experience, and education. A résumé is a prepared statement of the applicant's qualifications and career goals, and is commonly used by people seeking managerial or professional positions.

In many cases, companies receive several applications or résumés for a job opening. Human resource personnel must narrow the field, first on the basis of the applications and then by holding screening interviews. In these ways, clearly unqualified individuals

Employment Equity Act of 1986
Federal legislation that designates four groups as employment disadvantaged—women, visible minorities, aboriginal people, and people with disabilities.

selection
The process of sorting through a pool of candidates to choose the best one for a job.

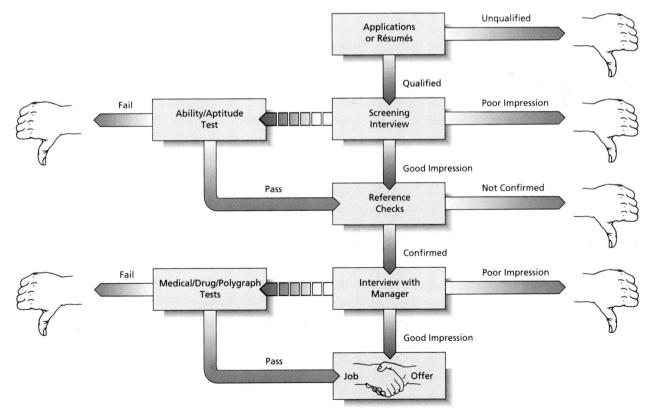

FIGURE 9.2
General steps in the selection process.

are weeded out, especially walk-in applicants for low-level jobs who simply do not have the required job skills. Line managers (those with hiring authority) then interview qualified applicants at greater depth. Other people in the hiring manager's department may also interview job candidates. In some companies, potential subordinates of the prospective employee are included in the interview process.

During both types of interviews, the interviewer asks questions about the applicant's background and qualifications. The interviewer must be careful to address only job-related issues. For example, a female applicant cannot be asked whether she plans to marry or have a family. Such questions can further sex discrimination. In addition to asking questions, interviewers also provide information about the company and answer any questions applicants may have.

For some positions, ability or aptitude tests may be part of the initial screening process.[1] When Toyota hired workers for its Cambridge, Ontario, plant, applicants were put through a series of tests to determine their math, verbal, and communication skills and their ability to work on a team. Even though most of the workers hired had never worked for an automobile firm before, they are now producing the highest-rated car in North America.[2] A new way to screen job applicants is described in the box "Screen Test."

Toyota
www.toyota.com

TRENDS & CHALLENGES

Screen Test

Finding, screening, and hiring new employees can be a big expense for companies. It can cost $5000–$10 000 to hire a clerical person, and much more to hire a top manager. In this cost-conscious era, companies are always ready to consider alternatives to the traditional hiring techniques.

One such promising new technique is video assessment. Potential new hires view videos that show a series of realistic work situations (portrayed by actors). For example, one scenario shows an assistant to a department manager who is trying to convince the supervisor of the word-processing pool to give his job top priority because the boss wants some last-minute changes made in a report. The supervisor refuses and the assistant goes back to the boss asking him to intercede. At the end of each situation the viewers choose one of four courses of action to resolve the problem shown in the video. The test administrator then uses the computer to score candidate choices (much like a college or university instructor would grade student exams).

Video assessment is fast, reliable, cheap, and versatile. It also lets managers screen more extensively for jobs at the lower levels in the organization. Improving selection at entry-level jobs should mean better customer service and greater chances for promotion from within. Video assessment can also give management greater insight into employee strengths and weaknesses before they are hired, and this can help the company solve long-standing problems like high turnover.

Video assessment evolved from assessment centres, which have been in use for more than 30 years (see the description later in this chapter). While assessment centres do get results, they are high-cost operations (up to $5000 for each person who is assessed). Videos are cheap by comparison. They take about an hour to complete and cost between $25 and $100. Canadian firms using video assessment include Weyerhaeuser, Reebok, Nortel, Eaton's, and B.C. Hydro.

But care must be taken when using video assessment. If a company simply buys a ready-made video from a consulting firm it may get lax about doing its homework—stating the specific knowledge, skills, and motivation needed to do various jobs. Mindlessly using video assessment could, for example, cause a company to hire a salesperson who is good at "cold calls" when what they really need is a salesperson who is good at maintaining existing accounts.

Another potential problem is that managers don't have a stake in selection criteria the way they do when they interview people. Some companies overcome these limitations by using multiple methods. Weyerhaeuser used both video assessment and an assessment centre to hire a supervisor for a sawmill. Some companies also use video assessment for ongoing training purposes. At Reebok, employees view the videos on a regular basis in training and development sessions.

Regardless of the type of test used, it must meet two conditions. First, the test must be job-related. A company cannot, for example, ask an applicant for a secretarial job to take a test on operating a forklift. It is clearly appropriate, however, to ask the person to take a typing test. The second requirement of an employment test is that it must be a valid predictor of performance. That is, there must be evidence that people who score well on the test are more likely to perform well in the job than are people who score poorly on the test. A test used for selection must not serve as a basis for discrimination against anyone for reasons unrelated to the job.

Another step used in employee selection is to check references. Reference checks often provide little useful information about an applicant's personality because applicants usually list as references only people likely to say good things about them. Even former employers may be reluctant to say negative things, fearing a lawsuit. But crosschecks can confirm information about an applicant's experience or education. For example, if you tell an interviewer that you graduated with a B. Comm. (Honours), a quick call to the student records office of your university can verify the truth of your statement.

Once a number of applicants have been interviewed and checked out, the manager will make a hiring decision. Before a job offer is actually made, however, some companies require an extra step—a physical exam, a polygraph test, and/or, increasingly, a drug test.[3] These tests are designed to protect the employer. For example, a manufacturer afraid of injuries from workers hurt on the job might require new employees to have a physical examination. The company gains some information about whether the employees are physically fit to do the work and what (if any) preexisting injuries they have. Polygraph (lie detector) tests are largely illegal now, and drug tests are also coming under fire. In 1998, for example, the Ontario Divisional Court decided that Imperial Oil Ltd.'s drug policy—which included preemployment drug testing that made offers of work conditional on a negative result—was unlawful because Imperial failed to prove that a positive drug test would indicate a failure to perform essential duties. Imperial's policy also required random drug and alcohol testing, and that was also judged to be discriminatory because the company could not prove that such testing was necessary to deter alcohol or drug impairment on the job.[4]

Internal Staffing: Promotions

No matter how careful it is, the selection process of new applicants cannot compare with a company's knowledge of its current employees. It is not surprising that many firms prefer to "hire from within"—to promote or transfer existing staff members—whenever possible.

Some firms that historically have practised promotion from within are rethinking that strategy. IBM, for example, has had only six CEOs in its history, all of whom were appointed after they had spent many years working their way up the hierarchy at IBM. But with the replacement of John Akers with outsider Louis Gerstner, the company will have an easier time breaking with tradition as it works to solve its massive problems.[5] Furthermore, promotion from within can cause disputes, especially in family-owned businesses.

IBM Canada
www.can.ibm.com

Women often face a "glass ceiling" in their quest to get promoted. They can see what it is like in upper management, but they are not allowed to go there. Some recent evidence suggests that the glass ceiling is developing some holes. A growing number of women who started their careers in the 1970s are now beginning to land top jobs in corporations. The Opening Case in this chapter describes several women who have broken through the glass ceiling. Another is Irene Rosenfeld, who is president of Kraft Foods Canada. In 1997 alone, several other high-profile top management positions were earned by women: Jill Barad (appointed CEO of Mattel Inc.), Gail J. McGovern (appointed head of the $26 billion consumer business of AT&T), and Lois Juliber (appointed head of North American and European operations for Colgate-Palmolive).[6] But there is still a long way to go. A 1996 survey by Catalyst showed that just 2 percent of senior executives at large corporations are women.

Jill Barad, CEO of Mattel.

closed promotion system
An internal promotion system in which managers choose the workers who will be considered for a promotion.

open promotion system
An internal promotion system in which all employees are advised of open positions and may apply for those positions if they want.

Handling of promotions and job changes varies from company to company. Some firms use **closed promotion systems** in which managers decide which workers will even be considered for a promotion. In such companies, promotion decisions tend to be made informally and subjectively and to rely heavily on the recommendations of an employee's supervisor. Closed systems remain popular, especially in small firms, because they minimize the time, energy, and cost of making promotion decisions.

Other firms maintain **open promotion systems** in which available jobs and their requirements are posted. Employees who feel they possess the qualifications fill out applications, take tests, and interview with managers, much as if they were outside applicants. Open systems allow individual employees to have more say in their career paths. The democratic nature of such systems may also contribute to higher employee morale. But an open system can be time-consuming and expensive. Resources must be spent processing, interviewing, and screening internal applicants.

■ DEVELOPING THE WORKFORCE

One of the first things that newcomers participate in is their orientation to the organization. It then falls to personnel experts and other managers to maintain and enhance the employee-job match and employees' performance on the job. Towards this end, some companies have instituted training and development programs on many levels. In addition, every firm has some system for performance appraisal and feedback that helps managers and employees assess the need for more training.

Orientation

orientation
The initial acquainting of new employees with the company's policies and programs, personnel with whom they will interact, and the nature of the job.

The purpose of the **orientation** is to help employees learn about and fit into the company. At one level, the orientation can focus on work hours, parking priorities, and/or pay schedules. People may simply watch films, read manuals, and be introduced to new co-workers. At another level, orientation can indoctrinate the worker into the corporate culture and provide valuable insights into how to succeed.

Employee Training and Development

After orientation, the new employee starts to work. However, both old and new employees may receive training or be enrolled in a development program. The reasons for training and development differ, as do the methods used. The most common methods are on-the-job training, off-the-job training, management development programs, networking/mentoring, and assessment centres.[7]

On-the-Job Training.   As the term suggests, **on-the-job training** is training that occurs while the employee is actually at work. Ford Motor trained 140 workers for a year to work in a new aluminum casting plant in Windsor, Ontario. Because workers need to know many jobs (e.g., melting aluminum and molding and cleaning engines), they needed a lot of training.[8] Much on-the-job training is unplanned and informal, as when one employee shows another how to use the new photocopier. Someone needs some help, so it is provided.

In other cases, on-the-job training is quite formal. For example, secretaries may learn to operate a new word-processing system at their desks. The advantages of on-the-job training are that it occurs in the real job setting and can be done over an extended period of time. The biggest disadvantage is that distractions on the job site may make training difficult.

Off-the-Job Training.   In contrast, **off-the-job training** is performed at a location away from the work site. It may be at a classroom within the same facility or at a different location altogether. For example, refresher courses are offered for managers of McDonald's 600 Canadian restaurants at the Canadian Institute of Hamburgerology; training videotapes are also shown to restaurant workers.[9] Coffee College is a two-week cram course run by Second Cup Ltd., Canada's largest retailer of specialty coffee. During their stay at Coffee College, franchisees and managers learn a lot of details about coffee. They also learn how to hire workers, keep the books, detect employee theft, and boost Christmas sales.[10]

Management Development Programs.   These programs are targeted specifically at current or future managers. In contrast to regular training, which focuses on technical skills, **management development programs** try to enhance conceptual, analytical, and problem-solving skills. Most large organizations have management development programs. Some programs are run in-house by managers or training specialists. Others take place at management development centres on university campuses. Still others require managers to get completely away from the workplace and study certain subjects intensively. For example, Decision Dynamics is a two-week management development program conducted at a resort hotel on Lake Winnipeg. A well-conceived strategy for developing managerial talent is almost mandatory if an organization is to prosper.

Networking and Mentoring.   In addition, some management development also takes place informally, often through processes known as networking and mentoring. **Networking** refers to informal interactions among managers for the purpose of discussing mutual problems, solutions, and opportunities. Networking takes place in a variety of settings, both inside and outside the office—for example, at conventions and conferences, meetings, business lunches, social gatherings, and so forth.

A mentor is an older, more experienced manager who sponsors and teaches younger, less experienced managers. The mentoring process helps younger managers learn the ropes and benefit from the experiences, insights, and successes (and failures) of senior executives. Networking and mentoring may be especially useful for female and/or minority managers: These individuals may have fewer role models and may be more likely to benefit from greater interaction with experienced managers.

Assessment Centres.   An **assessment centre** is a series of exercises in which management candidates perform realistic management tasks under the watchful eyes of expert appraisers. Each candidate's potential for management is assessed or appraised.

on-the-job training
Those development programs in which employees gain new skills while performing them at work.

off-the-job training
Those development programs in which employees learn new skills at a location away from the normal work site.

management development programs
Those development programs in which current and prospective managers learn new conceptual, analytical, and problem-solving skills.

networking
Informal interactions among managers for the purpose of discussing mutual problems, solutions, and opportunities.

assessment centre
A series of exercises in which management candidates perform realistic management tasks while being observed by appraisers.

A typical assessment centre might be set up in a large conference room and go on for two or three days. During this time, managers and potential managers might take selection tests, engage in management simulations, make individual presentations, and conduct group discussions. In a program like this the assessors look to see how each participant reacts to stress or to criticism by colleagues. They also watch to see which candidates emerge as leaders of the group discussions.

Performance Appraisal

performance appraisal
A formal program for comparing employees' actual performance with expected performance; used in making decisions about training, promoting, compensating, and firing.

Performance appraisals are formal evaluations of how well workers are doing their jobs. Every company assesses the performance of its employees in some way, even if it is only the owner telling the only employee, a receptionist, "Good job. You're getting a raise." In larger firms, the process is more extensive. A formal performance evaluation system generally involves a regularly scheduled written assessment. The written evaluation, however, is only one part of a multistep process.

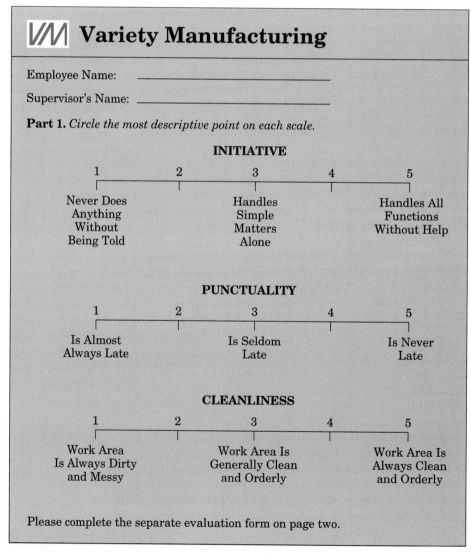

FIGURE 9.3

Graphic rating scales such as this one are common methods of performance appraisal.

The appraisal process begins when a manager makes job performance expectations clear to an employee. The manager must then observe the employee's performance. If the standards are clearly defined, a manager should have little difficulty with the next step—comparing expectations with actual performance. For some jobs, a rating scale like that illustrated in Figure 9.3 is useful. This comparison forms the basis for a written appraisal and for decisions about any raise, promotion, demotion, or firing of the employee. The final step in the appraisal process is for the manager to meet with the employee to discuss the appraisal.

When job performance expectations are based on the actual requirements of the job, formal appraisals benefit both the company and workers. The company is protected from lawsuits charging unfair treatment. It also has a reasonably objective basis on which to compare individuals for promotions. Workers benefit from clear goals to work towards and knowledge of how well they are doing. They often feel that such systems are fairer than subjective evaluations.

Terminating and Demoting Workers.   Written appraisals are especially important when a business must fire or demote employees. Most companies with formal systems have a step-by-step process of warnings and punishments leading up to dismissal. For the first warning, the manager might talk informally to the employee, expressing disappointment over the problem—poor job performance or attendance, for example. To protect itself from lawsuits, many companies require managers to give the offending employee a written warning. An employee causing a problem can also expect to hear about it during a formal appraisal. At that time, the manager will specify certain changes that the employee must make or lose the job. This system not only protects the company, it also lets employees know that their jobs are in jeopardy and offers them a chance to do better.

If a problem persists, a manager may have little choice but to discipline, demote, or dismiss the employee.

Demotions are most often used when managerial personnel fail to meet expectations. For example, a sales manager who is performing poorly may be demoted to sales representative. Demoted managers are often humiliated by this downgrading and seek jobs elsewhere.

In extreme cases, outright **termination** of the employee may be the only recourse. For example, a salesperson who continually falls far short of the established quota may be a drag on corporate profitability. Although firing is never pleasant, managers of companies with sound human resource policies can take some solace in knowing that, by the time such a dismissal takes place, the employee should be expecting it.

demotion
Reducing the rank of a person who is not performing up to standard.

termination
Firing an employee who is not performing up to standard.

■ COMPENSATION AND BENEFITS

A major factor in retaining skilled workers is a company's **compensation system**—what it offers employees in return for their labour. Wages and salaries are a key part of any compensation system, but most systems also include features such as incentives and employee benefits programs. We will explore each of these elements in this section. Bear in mind, however, that finding the right combination of elements is complicated by the need to make employees feel valued while simultaneously keeping company costs to a minimum. Thus, compensation systems are highly individualized, depending on the nature of the industry, the company, and the types of workers involved.

compensation system
What a firm offers its employees in return for their labour.

Wages and Salaries

Wages and salaries are the dollar amounts paid to employees for their work. **Wages** are dollars paid for time worked or for number of units produced. Workers who are paid by the hour receive wages. Canadian manufacturing workers are among the highest paid workers in the world. Only German workers receive higher wages.[11]

wages
Dollars paid based on the number of hours worked or the number of units produced.

salary
Dollars paid at regular intervals in return for doing a job, regardless of the amount of time or output involved.

Salary is the money an employee receives for getting a job done. An executive earning $100 000 per year may work five hours one day and fifteen the next. Such an individual is paid to get a job done rather than for the specific number of hours or days spent working. Salaries are usually expressed as an amount to be paid per year but are often paid each month or every two weeks.

In setting wage and salary levels, a company must consider several factors. First, it must take into account how its competitors compensate their employees. A firm that pays less than its rivals may soon find itself losing valuable personnel.

Within the company, the firm must also decide how wage and salary levels for different jobs will compare. And within wage and salary levels, managers must decide how much to pay individual workers. Two employees may do exactly the same job, but the employee with more experience may earn more, in part to keep that person in the company and in part because the experienced person performs better. Some union contracts specify differential wages based on experience. Note that the basis for differential pay must be job-related, however, not favouritism or discrimination.

Incentive Programs

incentive program
Any program in which a company offers its workers additional pay over and above the normal wage or salary level in order to motivate them to perform at a higher-than-normal level.

The term **incentive programs** refers to special pay programs designed to motivate high performance. The use of incentive programs increased in the 1980s, largely because of concern for productivity.

Sales bonuses are a typical incentive. Under such a program, employees who sell a certain number or dollar amount of goods for the year receive a special payment. Employees who do not reach this goal earn no bonus. Similarly, *merit salary systems* link raises to performance levels in non-sales jobs. For example, many baseball players have clauses in their contracts that pay them bonuses for hitting over .300, making the All-Star game, or being named Most Valuable Player. Executives commonly receive stock options and bonuses as an incentive.

gain-sharing plan
An incentive program in which employees receive a bonus if the firm's costs are reduced because of greater worker efficiency and/or productivity.

Some incentive programs apply to all employees in a firm. **Gain-sharing plans** distribute bonuses to all employees in a company based on reduced costs from working more efficiently. Palliser Furniture Ltd. introduced a gain-sharing plan that rewards employees for increasing production. Any profit resulting from production above a certain level is split 50-50 between the company and the employees.[12]

profit-sharing plan
An incentive program in which employees receive a bonus depending on the firm's profits.

Profit-sharing plans are based on profit levels in the firm. Profits earned above a certain level are distributed to employees. Stock ownership by employees serves as an incentive to lower costs, increase productivity and profits, and thus increase the value of the employees' stock.[13]

Comparable Worth

In spite of recent advances, the *average* woman still earns only about three-quarters of what the average man earns; *single* women, however, earn 99 percent of what single men earn. In 1969, women earned only 59 percent of what men earned. The most recent gains by women have occurred because men lost four of every five jobs that disappeared during the early 1990s. But most top jobs in the public and private sector continue to be held by men.[14] As well, women continue to have difficulty moving out of low-paying jobs. A 1998 Statistics Canada report showed that one-third of the men who had low-paying jobs in 1993 had been able to get a better paying job by 1995, but only 17 percent of the women were able to do so. Only 12 percent of *single-parent women* were able to get a better paying job.[15]

comparable worth
A legal idea that aims to pay equal wages for work of equal value.

Comparable worth is a legal concept that aims at paying equal wages for jobs that are of comparable value to the employer. This might mean comparing dissimilar jobs, such as those of nurses and mechanics or secretaries and electricians. Proponents of comparable worth say that all the jobs in a company must be evaluated and then rated in terms of basic dimensions such as the level of skill they require. All jobs could then be compared based on a common index. People in different jobs that rate the same on this index would be paid the same. Experts hope that this will help to reduce the gap between men's and women's pay.

Critics of comparable worth say that it ignores the supply and demand aspects of labour, and that forcing a company to pay people more than the open market price for their labour (which may happen in jobs where there is a surplus of workers) is not economically sound. A study prepared for the Ontario Ministry of Labour estimates that it will cost approximately $10 billion for the public and private sectors in Ontario to establish equitable payment for jobs of equal value.

In 1998, the Canadian Human Rights Tribunal ruled that the federal government must pay a total of about $2 billion to thousands of civil servants because it discriminated against workers in female-dominated job classifications. About 85 percent of these workers were women. The government is appealing the decision.

Canadian Human Rights Tribunal
www.chrt-tcdp.gc.ca

Benefits Programs

A growing part of nearly every firm's compensation system is **benefits** programs—compensation other than wages and salaries. Benefits now often comprise over half a firm's total compensation budget. Most companies are required by law to provide workers' compensation, holiday pay, and Canada Pension Plan and employment insurance contributions. Most businesses also voluntarily provide extended health, life, and disability insurance. Many also allow employees to buy stock through payroll deductions at a slightly discounted price. In the 1980s, many firms began to provide vision care and dental benefits to employees. Some even provide free legal services to employees.

As the range of benefits has grown, so has concern about containing their cost. Businesses are experimenting with a variety of procedures to cut benefits costs, while maintaining the ability to attract, retain, and maintain the morale of employees.[16] One

benefits
What a firm offers its workers other than wages and salaries in return for their labour.

Members of the Public Service Alliance of Canada celebrate the 1998 Canadian Human Rights Tribunal ruling that the federal government had discriminated against workers in female-dominated classifications and would have to reimburse them.

cafeteria benefits
A flexible approach to providing benefits in which employees are allocated a certain sum to cover benefits and can "spend" this allocation on the specific benefits they prefer.

new approach is the use of **cafeteria benefits**. These plans provide a set dollar amount in benefits and allow employees to pick among alternatives. Employees at Toyota's Cambridge, Ontario, plant are given the opportunity once each year to structure their benefits packages. For example, they can give more weight to dental coverage if they have young children, or to life insurance or disability coverage, depending on their circumstances.[17] More and more firms are using "temporary" workers on a long-term basis. Since they are not covered by most companies' benefits plans, temporary workers allow businesses to keep staff levels high and benefits costs low.

Employee Safety and Health.   Employee safety and health programs help to reduce absenteeism and labour turnover, raise productivity, and boost morale by making jobs safer and more healthful. In Canada, each province has developed its own workplace health and safety regulations. The purpose of these laws is to ensure that employees do not have to work in dangerous conditions. These laws are the direct result of undesirable conditions that existed in many Canadian businesses at the close of the 19th century. While much improvement is evident, Canada still has some problems with workplace health and safety. In one study of six Western industrialized nations, Canada had the worst safety record in mining and construction and the second worst record in manufacturing and railways.

Some industrial work—logging, construction, fishing, and mining—can put workers at risk of injury in obvious ways. But other types of work—such as typing or lifting—can also cause painful injuries. **Repetitive strain injuries** (RSIs) occur when workers perform the same functions over and over again. These injuries disable more than 200 000 Canadians each year and account for nearly half of all work-related time-loss claims.

repetitive strain injuries
Injuries that occur when workers perform the same functions over and over again.

Retirement.   Some employees are ready for retirement much earlier than others. But because most retirement plans are based on an employee's age, some workers who should retire earlier stay on the job while others, who are still useful workers, leave before they would like to. This policy is short-sighted. A compromise is to grant year-to-year extensions to productive employees who want to continue working but who have reached retirement age. Recently several workers in different locations across Canada have successfully challenged mandatory retirement rules. Their employers must allow them to work even though they are past the traditional retirement age.

In spite of these individual exceptions, Canadians generally are retiring earlier than they used to. In the period 1976–80, for example, the median retirement age in Canada was 64.9 years, but in the period 1991–95 that figure dropped to 62.3 years.[18] Two other interesting facts: Workers over age 65 are nearly four times as likely to die from work-related causes than younger workers, and older workers have double the health-care costs that workers in their forties do.[19]

Miscellaneous Services.   Human resource departments also provide many other services, which vary widely among firms. These range from setting policies to deal with allegations of sexual harassment on the job to helping employees arrange car pools.

■NEW CHALLENGES IN THE CHANGING WORKPLACE

As we have seen throughout this chapter, human resource managers face a number of ongoing challenges in their efforts to keep their organizations staffed with effective workforces. To complicate matters, new challenges arise as the economic and social environments of business change. More specifically, today's human resource managers must deal with workforces that are increasingly diverse and contingent.

Managing Workforce Diversity

An extremely important set of human resource challenges centres on **workforce diversity**: the range of workers' attitudes, values, beliefs, and behaviours that differ by sex, race, and ethnicity. The diverse workforce is also characterized by individuals of different ages and physical abilities. In the past, organizations tended to work towards homogenizing their workforces, getting everyone to think and behave in similar ways. Partly as a result of affirmative action efforts, however, many organizations are now creating workforces that are more diverse, embracing more women, more ethnic minorities, and more foreign-born employees than ever before.

workforce diversity
Range of workers' attitudes, values, and behaviours that differ by sex, race, and ethnicity.

Diversity as a Competitive Advantage.   Today, organizations are recognizing not only that they should treat everyone equitably, but also that they should acknowledge the individuality of each person they employ. They are also recognizing that diversity can be a competitive advantage. For example, by hiring the best people available from every single group rather than hiring from just one or a few groups, a firm can develop a higher-quality labour force. Similarly, a diverse workforce can bring a wider array of information to bear on problems and can provide insights on marketing products to a wider range of consumers. Says the head of workforce diversity at IBM: "We think it is important for our customers to look inside and see people like them. If they can't … the prospect of them becoming or staying our customers declines."

Levi Strauss adhered to this principle when it revised ads for 501 jeans. The original "501 Blues" spots aimed at and attracted hip, independent youngsters—mostly white. They did not appeal to Hispanics. Why not? Levi's own Hispanic employees provided an answer. The characters in the ads were depicted as hip and carefree, but they were always solitary figures. Because Hispanic culture places a higher value on day-to-day contact with friends and family, Levi's was advised to create ads that stressed camaraderie. Because Hispanics buy 50 percent more jeans than the average consumer, the company heeded the advice of its own employees and has been a much more successful marketer to Hispanic buyers.[20]

Diversity Training.   Another guideline calls for companies to use **diversity training**: programs designed to improve employees' understanding of differences in attitudes and behaviour patterns among their co-workers. However, there is no consensus yet on how to conduct such programs—on exactly what to teach and how to do it.

Many companies try to go beyond mere awareness training. DuPont, for example, offers a course for managers on how to seek and use more diverse input before making decisions. Sears offers what it calls diversity-friendly programs: bus service for workers who must commute from the inner city to the suburbs and leaves of absences for foreign-born employees to visit families still living overseas.[21] Finally, one consultant emphasizes that it is extremely important to integrate training into daily routines: "Diversity training," he says, "is like hearing a good sermon on Sunday. You must practise what you heard during the week."[22]

diversity training
Programs designed to improve employees understanding of differences in co-workers' attitudes and behaviours.

■ DEALING WITH ORGANIZED LABOUR

A special human-resource challenge faced by many firms is dealing with organized labour, or labour unions. A **labour union** is a group of individuals working together to achieve shared job-related goals, such as higher pay, shorter working hours, greater benefits, or better working conditions.[23]

labour union
Group of individuals working together formally to achieve shared job-related goals.

Why Do Workers Unionize?

Labour unions grew in popularity in Canada in the 19th and early 20th centuries. At that time, work hours were long, pay was minimal, and working conditions were often unsafe. Workers had no job security and received few benefits. Many textile mills employed large numbers of children and paid them poverty wages. If people complained, they were fired.

collective bargaining
Process by which labour and management negotiate conditions of employment for union-represented workers.

Collective Bargaining. Unions forced management to listen to the complaints of all workers rather than to just those few brave enough to speak out. Thus the power of unions comes from collective action. **Collective bargaining** is the process by which union leaders and managers negotiate common terms and conditions of employment for those workers represented by unions. Although collective bargaining does not often occur in small businesses, many medium-sized and larger businesses must engage in the process. We discuss the role of collective bargaining in more detail below.

Unionism Today

The growth of unions has slowed since the mid-1970s (see Figure 9.4). What has caused this change? Revelations of leadership corruption in the 1950s and 1960s tarnished the appeal of some unions. As well, since that time, foreign competition has prompted many heavily unionized industries, such as automobile and steel manufacturing, to cut back their workforces. The makeup of the workforce has also changed. Most union members used to be white males in blue-collar jobs. But the workforce is increasingly composed of women and minorities in white- or "pink"-collar (secretarial) positions.

At the same time, many nonunionized industries have developed strategies for avoiding unionization. Some companies have introduced new employee relations programs to keep their nonunionized facilities union-free. Some work to create a "family feeling," setting aside company land for gardens, tennis courts, and other family activities. Some have used carefully managed campaigns to persuade workers not to join unions. The box "What?! A Union at Wal-Mart?" describes one company's attempt to keep the union out.

Wal-Mart Canada
www.wal-mart.com

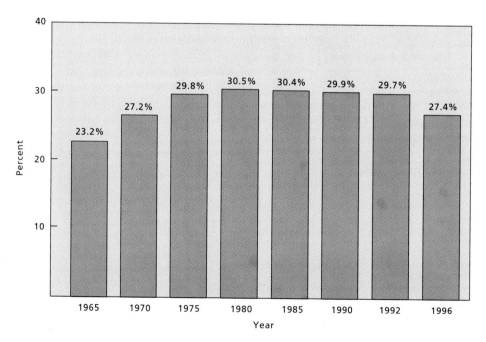

FIGURE 9.4
Union members as a proportion of the total workforce.

TRENDS CHALLENGES

What?! A Union at Wal-Mart?

Wal-Mart employees are supposed to be one big, happy family. And that family atmosphere is often cited as a key reason for Wal-Mart's phenomenal growth during the last decade (1996 sales were $93 billion). Wal-Mart has never had a union in any of its 2798 stores in the U.S., Canada, Argentina, Brazil, Mexico, or Puerto Rico. It has been able to resist unions partly by promoting its family-like culture. The company argues that forcing employees to work under a collective agreement will reduce their motivation and damage the company's successful formula for keeping consumers happy. The company has also resisted unionization in more direct ways. For example, when it purchased 122 Woolco stores in Canada a few years ago, it pointedly did not buy the nine Woolco stores that were unionized.

But in 1997, the Ontario Labour Relations Board (OLRB) certified a United Steelworkers Union local as the bargaining agent for employees at Wal-Mart's Windsor, Ontario, store in spite of the fact that the union lost the certification vote. And Wal-Mart employees at the store have been squabbling ever since.

How did Wal-Mart, which is famous for keeping unions out, lose this battle? Apparently, problems began on April 26, 1996, the day that management heard that a union was approaching employees about joining. Mr. Tino Borean, the district manager, came to the Windsor store the next day and spoke to employees at the "morning meeting" (this meeting is held every day and includes activities such as the store cheer and a discussion about store performance). While Borean's speech was not a violation of the labour act, it appeared that the union's organizing drive began faltering soon afterwards.

A few days later, an anti-union employee gave a speech at the morning meeting exhorting her fellow employees not to join the union. Pro-union employees who asked to respond to her speech were denied the right to do so. On May 2, the union filed its application for certification.

Employees were encouraged by management to ask questions about the union drive, but then the company decided to adopt a policy of refusing to answer employee questions, particularly the one about whether the store would close if the union vote was successful. This strate-

gy was carried out in spite of Wal-Mart's well-known practice of promptly answering employee questions about work-related matters.

On May 5, four days before the certification vote was held, the Windsor store manager told at least one employee that a union would mean a lot of changes at the store, and that employees might lose certain benefits that they currently had. When the certification vote was eventually held, the count was 151-43 against the union. This occurred in spite of the fact that the union had submitted 91 signed cards when it originally filed for certification. Since late April, support for the union had apparently dropped dramatically. The OLRB concluded that the company had violated the Ontario *Labour Relations Act* by giving employees the impression that the store would be closed if the union was certified, and decided to certify the union at Wal-Mart store 3115.

In April 1998, a majority of the workers at the store filed an application with the OLRB to have the union decertified. They claimed that there were voting irregularities in December 1997, when the workers were voting on their first collective agreement. The decertification application claims the union has had only minority support at the store.

Union activities at Wal-Mart are not an isolated phenomenon. A new wave of unionism may be about to sweep across Canada, and it may mean an increased presence for unions in service industries where they have historically had little representation. The movement may be fuelled by young people (including university graduates) who fear they will be stuck in low-wage jobs, and who hope that unions can help them avoid that fate. In 1997, unions were certified at nine Starbucks Coffee locations, and in 1998 the first union at a McDonald's was certified in Squamish, B.C.

Other changes are also occurring, including the increased numbers of women as union members. In 1967, women accounted for less than 20 percent of union membership in Canada, but by 1997, they represented nearly half of all union workers. These unionized women are highly concentrated in the public sector, which provides jobs for only 19 percent of the workforce, but accounts for 43 percent of all union members.

Nevertheless, labour unions remain a major factor in Canadian business. The labour organizations in the Canadian Labour Congress and independent major unions, such as the International Brotherhood of Teamsters and the Canadian Union of Public

Canadian Labour Congress
www.clc-ctc.ca

Jennifer Wiebe and Tessa Lowinger were instrumental in getting a union certified at a McDonald's outlet in Squamish, B.C. in 1998.

International Brotherhood of Teamsters
www.teamster.org

Canadian Union of Public Employees
www.solinet.org/cupe.html

Employees, can disrupt the economy by refusing to work. The votes of their members are still sought by politicians at all levels. And the concessions they have won for their members—better pay, shorter working hours, safer working conditions, and benefits such as extended health insurance—now cover nonunion workers as well.

■ THE LEGAL ENVIRONMENT FOR UNIONS IN CANADA

Political and legal barriers to collective bargaining existed until well into the 20th century. Courts held that some unions were conspirators in restraint of trade. Employers viewed their employees' efforts to unionize as attempts to deprive the employers of their private property. The employment contract, employers contended, was between the individual worker and the employer—not between the employer and employees as a group. The balance of bargaining power was very much in favour of the employer.

The employer/employee relationship became much less direct as firms grew in size. Managers were themselves employees. Hired managers dealt with other employees. Communication among owners, managers, and workers became more formalized. Big business had more power than workers. Because of mounting public concern, laws were passed to place the worker on a more even footing with the employer.

In 1900, government concern about labour disputes resulted in the passage of the *Conciliation Act*. The act was designed to help settle labour disputes through voluntary conciliation and was a first step in creating an environment more favourable to labour.

A more comprehensive law, the 1907 *Industrial Disputes Investigation Act*, provided for compulsory investigation of labour disputes by a government-appointed board before a strike was allowed. However, this act was later found to violate a fundamental provision of the *BNA Act*.

The current positive environment for labour did not come into being until 1943 when *Privy Council Order 1003* was issued. This order recognized the right of employees to bargain collectively, prohibited unfair labour practices on the part of management, established a labour board to certify bargaining authority, and prohibited strikes and lockouts except in the course of negotiating collective agreements. Approximately 45 years of dealings among labour, management, and government were required before the labour movement achieved its fundamental goal of the right to bargain collectively.

The Constitution Act (originally the *BNA Act*), passed in 1867, has also affected labour legislation. This act allocated certain activities to the federal government (e.g., labour legislation for companies operating interprovincially) and others to individual provinces (labour relations regulations in general). Thus, labour legislation emanates from both the federal and provincial governments but is basically a provincial matter. That is why certain groups of similar employees might be allowed to go on strike in one province but not in another.

Federal Legislation—The Canada Labour Code

The *Canada Labour Code* is a comprehensive piece of legislation that applies to the labour practices of firms operating under the legislative authority of parliament. The code is composed of four major sections:

Fair Employment Practices.   This section prohibits an employer from either refusing employment on the basis of a person's race or religion or using an employment agency that discriminates against people on the basis of their race or religion. These prohibitions apply to trade unions as well, but not to non-profit, charitable, and philanthropic organizations. Any individual who believes a violation has occurred may make a complaint in writing to Labour Canada. The allegation will then be investigated and, if necessary, an Industrial Inquiry Commission will be appointed to make a recommendation in the case. (Since 1982, fair employment practices have been covered by the *Canadian Human Rights Act*; they are also covered by the *Canadian Charter of Rights and Freedoms*.)

Standard Hours, Wages, Vacations, and Holidays.   This section deals with a wide variety of mechanical issues such as standard hours of work (eight-hour day and 40-hour week), maximum hours of work per week (48), overtime pay (at least one and a half times the regular pay), minimum wages, equal wages for men and women doing the same jobs, vacations, general holidays, and maternity leave. The specific provisions are changed frequently to take into account changes in the economic and social structure of Canada, but their basic goal is to ensure consistent treatment of employees in these areas.

Safety of Employees.   This section requires that every person running a federal work project do so in a way that will not endanger the health or safety of any employee. It also requires that safety procedures and techniques be implemented to reduce the risk of employment injury. This section requires employees to exercise care to ensure their own safety; however, even if it can be shown that the employee did not exercise proper care, compensation must still be paid. This section also makes provisions for a safety officer whose overall duty is to assure that the provisions of the code are being fulfilled. The safety officer has the right to enter any federal project "at any reasonable time."

Industrial Disputes Investigation Act (1907)
Provided for compulsory investigation of labour disputes by a government-appointed board before a strike was allowed.

Privy Council Order 1003 (1943)
Recognized the right of employees to bargain collectively.

Constitution Act, 1867
Divided authority over labour regulations between the federal and provincial governments.

Canada Labour Code
Legislation that applies to the labour practices of firms operating under the legislative authority of parliament.

Canada Industrial Relations Regulations. The final major section of the *Canada Labour Code* deals with all matters related to collective bargaining

Provincial Labour Legislation

Canada Labour Code
drhc.gc.ca/labour/labstand/
toc.html

Each province has enacted legislation to deal with the personnel practices covered in the *Canada Labour Code*. These laws vary across provinces and are frequently revised; however, their basic approach and substance is the same as in the *Canada Labour Code*. Certain provinces may exceed the minimum code requirements on some issues (e.g., minimum wage).

■ COLLECTIVE BARGAINING

Too often, people associate collective bargaining with the signing of a contract between a union and a company or industry. In fact, collective bargaining is an ongoing process involving not only the drafting but also the administering of the terms of a labour contract.

Reaching Agreement on the Contract's Terms

The collective bargaining process begins with the recognition of the union as the exclusive negotiator for its members. The *bargaining cycle* begins when union leaders meet with management representatives to agree on a new contract. By law, both parties must sit down at the bargaining table and negotiate "in good faith."

When each side has presented its demands, sessions focus on identifying the bargaining zone.[24] The process is shown in Figure 9.5. For example, although an employer may initially offer no pay raise, it may expect to grant a raise of up to 6 percent. Likewise, the union may initially demand a 10 percent pay raise while expecting to accept a raise as low as 4 percent. The bargaining zone, then, is a raise between 4 and 6 percent. Ideally, some compromise is reached between these levels and the new agreement is submitted for a ratification vote by union membership.

Most of the time this process will go smoothly. Sometimes, however, the two sides cannot—or will not—agree. Such an impasse is not illegal. How quickly and easily it is resolved depends in part on the nature of the demands made, the willingness of each side to use the weapons at its disposal, and the prospect for mediation or arbitration.

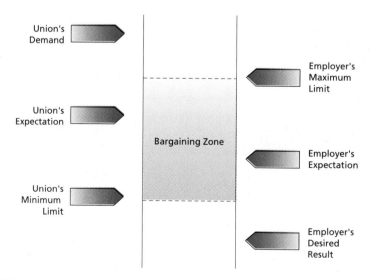

FIGURE 9.5
The bargaining zone.

Contract Demands.   Contract negotiations may centre on any number of issues. One common point of negotiation is compensation. For example, unions frequently fight for clauses ensuring a **cost-of-living adjustment** (COLA), especially during times of high inflation. Such a clause specifies that wages will increase automatically in proportion to increases in the cost of living, usually as reflected in the *consumer price index*, a measure of inflation.

Compensation was probably the dominant negotiation issue during the 1970s and 1980s. Business growth was producing large profits and labour wanted a portion of them. But as growth and inflation levelled off, compensation became a less critical part of most contract negotiations. In fact, givebacks have become a topic for negotiation in recent years.

Instead of pushing for more money or benefits, union negotiators have increasingly made job security an important agenda item. In some cases, job-security issues may take the form of the demand that the company not relocate.

The trend to reducing the workforce in return for job security is not restricted to North America. At British Steel Corp.'s Llanwern plant, the union agreed to a loss of 4454 jobs and the end of strict demarcations between jobs that prevented members of one union from doing the work of those in another union. In return, they received job security for the remaining workers at the plant. British Steel is now one of the lowest-cost producers of steel in the world.[25]

A final critical point of negotiation is management rights. Obviously, management wants as much control as possible over whom it hires, how it assigns work, and so forth. The union, on the other hand, often tries to limit management rights by specifying how hiring will be done, how work will be assigned, and other *work rules*. For example, at one automobile plant, the union contract specifies that three workers are to be used to change fuses in robots—a machinist to open the robot, an electrician to change the fuse, and a supervisor to oversee the process. Unions work to specify as many different job categories as possible. Workers in one category cannot perform work that falls into the domain of another category.

In general, the points bargained for may involve demands for mandatory and/or permissive items. *Mandatory items* are matters over which both parties must negotiate if either wishes to. Included in this category are wages, working hours, and benefits. *Permissive items* may be negotiated if both parties agree to do so. An example is a union demand to have veto power over the hiring and promotion of managerial personnel. In contrast, *illegal items* may not be legitimately brought to the negotiating table by either party. A management demand for a nonstrike clause would be an illegal item.

When Bargaining Fails

An impasse occurs when, after a series of bargaining sessions, management and labour fail to agree on a new contract or a contract to replace an agreement that is about to expire. Although it is generally agreed that both parties suffer when an impasse is reached and action is taken, each side can employ several tactics to support its cause until the impasse is resolved.

Union Tactics.   Unions can take a variety of actions when their demands are not met. Chief among these is the **strike**. When the United Auto Workers went on strike against General Motors in 1998, about 185 000 workers were off the job, including 12 000 workers in Canada. The strike by National Hockey League players in 1992, by Major League Baseball players in 1994, and by National Basketball Association players in 1998 were largely over economic issues.

During a strike, workers are not paid and the business is usually unable to produce its normal range of products and services. As the box "Strike Was No Ball for Business" demonstrates, the impact of a strike goes far beyond the company and its employees.

After a strike is over, employees may exhibit low morale, anger, increased absenteeism, and decreased productivity. In these situations, care must be taken to improve communications between management and workers.[26]

cost-of-living adjustment (COLA)
A contract clause specifying that wages will increase automatically with the rate of inflation.

United Auto Workers
www.uaw.org

strike
A tactic of labour unions in which members temporarily walk off the job and refuse to work in order to win concessions from management.

TRENDS & CHALLENGES

Strike Was No Ball for Business

When Major League Baseball players went on strike in 1994, many other organizations were affected. Brewing giant John Labatt Ltd. was particularly hard hit. Labatt owns 90 percent of the Toronto Blue Jays, 41 percent of the SkyDome where the team plays, and TSN (which broadcasts the games). The SkyDome alone was losing more than $100 000 per day during the strike. The strike also threatened Labatt's main product—beer—because baseball is such a high-profile arena for advertising this product.

But Labatt wasn't the only organization that suffered because of the strike. Broadcasters, advertisers, retailers, and restaurants had to scramble to save what remained of the summer after the strike began on August 12. Overall, the strike could have cost Toronto-area businesses more than $50 million in lost revenues of one sort or another. Montreal businesses could have lost $20 million.

Bitove Corp. is a hospitality company that handles catering at the SkyDome; it also operates food services at nearby restaurants, including Wayne Gretzky's and the Hard Rock Café. The company incurred substantial losses when games that were originally scheduled ended up not being played because of the strike. Well over 2000 jobs were lost at the SkyDome and Olympic Stadium as a result of the strike.

At CTV, losses approached $10 million because the network did not get to televise any post-season play. The losses were high because advertising rates for special events like the World Series are much higher than rates for regular movies or dramatic programs, which CTV had to substitute when there were no games to televise.

The bad news for baseball is sometimes good news for people operating other types of businesses. Video rental chains reported increases in sales after the strike began, and The Second City, a Toronto comedy club, played to a full house every night the week after the strike started. Formerly the club had experienced low turnouts whenever the Blue Jays played.

The lockout of National Hockey League players in 1994 caused the same kinds of problems as the baseball strike. Molson Cos. Ltd. owns the Montreal Canadiens, the Molson Centre, and the country's largest brewer, which advertises heavily at hockey games. Therefore they lost money on several ventures.

Maple Leaf Gardens also suffered during the strike. An entire season with no hockey would have resulted in a loss of $7 million. Layoffs and other cost-cutting measures would have been necessary, not only at Maple Leaf Gardens, but at every arena around the league.

The CBC was also hard hit because it had planned to start airing two hockey games instead of one in the fall of 1994 on *Hockey Night in Canada*. Saturday evening TV audiences, especially men, were down by as much as 50 percent during the lockout. While most of the money that was originally scheduled to be spent advertising hockey games was redirected, broadcasters worried that after the lockout ended they would have a tough time getting advertisers back.

Provincial governments stood to lose $75 million in profits because wagering on sports lotteries declined by as much as 50 percent during the hockey lockout. Ontario was the hardest hit because interest in sports betting is highest there. The Pro-Line lottery accounted for $65 million in 1993.

National Hockey League
www.nhl.com

Strikes may occur in response to an employer's unfair labour practices. A firm that refuses to recognize a duly certified union may find itself with a striking workforce and having to explain its refusal to the provincial labour relations board. Such strikes are rare, however.

Not all strikes are legal. *Sympathy strikes* (also called *secondary strikes*), where one union strikes in sympathy with strikes initiated by another labour organization, may violate the sympathetic union's contract. *Wildcat strikes*, strikes unauthorized by the union that occur during the life of a contract, deprive strikers of their status as employees and thus of the protection of labour laws.

Postal workers picket the mail-sorting plant in Toronto.

As part of or instead of a strike, unions faced with an impasse may picket or launch a boycott. **Picketing** involves having workers march at the entrance to the company with signs explaining their reasons for striking. A **boycott** occurs when union members agree not to buy the product of the firm that employs them. Workers may also urge other consumers to shun their firm's product. Another alternative to striking is a work **slowdown**: Instead of striking, workers perform their jobs at a much slower pace than normal. A variation is the "sickout," during which large numbers of workers call in sick.

Management Tactics.   Management can also respond forcefully to an impasse. To some extent, **lockouts** are the flip side of the strike coin. Lockouts occur when employers physically deny employees access to the workplace. Lockouts are illegal if they are used as offensive weapons to give the firm an economic advantage in the bargaining process. They might be used, for example, if management wants to avoid a buildup of perishable inventory or in similar circumstances. Lockouts, though rare today, were used by Major League Baseball team owners (without success) in 1990.

As an alternative to a lockout, firms faced with a strike can hire temporary or permanent replacements (**strikebreakers**) for the absent employees. When players in the National Football League went out on strike during the 1987 season, the team owners hired free agents and went right on playing. In 1992, National Hockey League owners planned to use minor league hockey players if they could not reach an agreement with striking NHL players. Laws forbid companies from permanently replacing workers who strike because of the firm's unfair labour practices.

More and more firms are contracting out work as a way to blunt their unions' effects. Instead of doing all the assembly work they used to do themselves, many firms now contract out work to nonunion contractors. This lessens the impact that the unions can have and results in fewer union workers.

Employers' associations are especially important in industries that have many small firms and one large union that represents all workers. Member firms sometimes contribute to a strike insurance fund. Such a fund could be used to help members whose workers have struck. They are similar in purpose to the strike funds built up by unions.

picketing
A tactic of labour unions in which members march at the entrance to the company with signs explaining their reasons for striking.

boycott
A tactic of labour unions in disputes with management in which members refuse to buy the products of the company and encourage other consumers to do the same.

slowdown
Instead of striking, workers perform their jobs at a much slower pace than normal.

lockout
A tactic of management in which the firm physically denies employees access to the workplace in order to pressure workers to agree to the company's latest contract offer.

strikebreaker
An individual hired by a firm to replace a worker on strike; a tactic of management in disputes with labour unions.

mediation
A method of settling a contract dispute in which a neutral third party is asked to hear arguments from both the union and management and offer a suggested resolution.

voluntary arbitration
A method of settling a contract dispute in which the union and management ask a neutral third party to hear their arguments and issue a binding resolution.

compulsory arbitration
A method of settling a contract dispute in which the union and management are forced to explain their positions to a neutral third party who issues a binding resolution.

Mediation and Arbitration.   Rather than using weapons on one another, labour and management can agree to call in a third party to help resolve the dispute. In **mediation**, the neutral third party (a mediator) can only advise—not impose—a settlement on the parties. In **voluntary arbitration**, the neutral third party (an arbitrator) dictates a settlement between two sides who have agreed to submit to outside judgment.

In some cases, arbitration is legally required to settle bargaining disputes. Such **compulsory arbitration** is used to settle disputes between government and public employees such as firefighters and police officers.

■ THE FUTURE OF UNIONISM IN CANADA

The union movement began in a period when the excesses of early capitalism placed the average worker at the mercy of the employer. For decades unions sought to bargain at arm's length with employers. This goal was met through legislation and the collective-bargaining process.

Many people considered unionism to be a worthwhile cause through the 1930s. But some people became critical of unions towards the end of the 1940s, and criticism has continued to mount. Unions are increasingly aware that they must cooperate with employers if they are both to survive. Critics of unions contend that excessive wage rates won through years of strikes and hard-nosed negotiation are partially to blame for the difficulties of large corporations. Others argue that excessively tight work rules limit the productivity of businesses in many industries. More and more often, however, unions are working with organizations to create effective partnerships in which managers and workers share the same goals—profitability, growth, and effectiveness with equitable rewards for everyone.

The future of unions depends on their ability to cope with the economic and social trends that threaten the labour movement. Some of these trends are

- the decline of the smokestack industries (e.g., steel, meat packing, chemicals, metals)
- employment growth in the service industries
- deregulation
- a more competitive business environment
- technological changes
- free trade

The Decline of the Smokestack Industries

Competition from abroad is causing many of these industries to seek ways to become more productive. The drive to make Canadian firms competitive internationally is a deep concern for Canadian labour leaders. They believe that management inevitably asks for concessions in its attempt to become more competitive.

Employment Growth in the Service Industries

The majority of Canada's labour force is now employed in the service industries. Except for government employees, these workers have never been highly unionized. Many work part-time, and the typical firm is small. These factors make it harder and more costly for unions to organize them than to organize full-time workers in large factories. However, unions are beginning to make progress in the service industries.

Deregulation

Deregulation continues to have an impact on unions. Deregulation of the airline, railway, and trucking industries has forced firms to become more competitive. Mergers, layoffs, givebacks, and new nonunionized firms in these and other deregulated industries challenge unions. Just as these firms have to learn to survive under deregulation, so will their employees' unions.

The Business Environment

As domestic and international competition becomes more intense, management has introduced changes to increase corporate efficiency. But these changes have caused conflicts between labour and management. United Parcel Service, for example, has been trying to capture more of the light-trucking market, so it raised its maximum package weight from 32 kilograms to 68 kilograms. But unionized drivers and sorters revolted when asked to lift the increased weights without protective health and safety guarantees. Employees are also unhappy about the way the company is pressuring them to do more work.[27]

UPS
www.ups.com

Technological Changes

Technology will continue to challenge labour unions. Some clerical and professional workers, for example, now work at home on computer terminals linked to their employers' office computers. Instead of having to commute to work by car, bus, or train, these workers telecommute. Some unions oppose the work-at-home concept because it makes organizing workers harder.

Free Trade

Finally, organized labour is concerned about the potentially negative impact of free trade agreements. Their fear is that products made in the U.S. or Mexico will be shipped tariff-free into Canada, and business firms will put pressure on Canadian workers to work for lower wages. At the worst, companies may simply move out of Canada altogether and do all their production in the U.S. or Mexico.

In 1994, for example, unionized workers at H.J. Heinz in Leamington, Ontario, signed a new collective agreement that contained concessions such as a wage reduction of 50 cents per hour and a reduction in paid holidays. Workers agreed to this in return for a guarantee of job security. In 1998, workers at the Maple Leaf plant in Burlington, Ontario, agreed to a contract that cut their wages by 40 percent. In return, the company agreed to guarantee 900 jobs.

SUMMARY OF LEARNING OBJECTIVES

1. **Define** *human resource management* **and explain how managers plan for human resources.** *Human resource management* is the development, administration, and evaluation of programs to acquire new employees and to enhance the quality and performance of people working in an organization. Planning for human-resource needs entails several steps. Conducting a *job analysis* enables managers to create detailed, job-related *job specifications*. After analysis is complete, they must forecast supply and demand for both the numbers and types of workers they will need. Only then do they consider strategies to match supply with demand.

2. **Identify the steps involved in *staffing* a company.** *External staffing*—hiring from outside the company—requires that a firm first *recruit* applicants and then *select* from among the applicants. Companies must ensure that they do not discriminate against candidates during the staffing process. The selection phase may include *interviewing, testing, and reference checking.* When possible, however, many companies prefer the practice of *internal staffing,* or filling positions by *promoting* existing personnel.

3. **Explain how organizations can develop workers' skills and manage workers who do not perform well.** If a company is to get the most out of its workers, it must develop those workers and their skills. Nearly all employees undergo some initial *orientation* process that introduces them to the company and to their new jobs. Many employees are given the opportunity to acquire new skills through *on-the-job* or *off-the-job training programs. Performance appraisals* help managers decide who needs training and who should be promoted. Appraisals also tell employees how well they are meeting expectations. Employees who continually fail to meet performance or behaviour expectations may be disciplined, demoted, or separated (terminated).

4. **Discuss the importance of *wages* and *salaries, incentives,* and *benefits programs* in attracting and keeping skilled workers.** Wages and salaries, incentives, and benefits packages may all be parts of a company's *compensation program.* By paying its workers as well as or better than competitors, a business can attract and keep qualified personnel. *Incentive programs*—for example, *bonuses, gain sharing,* and *profit sharing*—can also motivate personnel to work more productively. Although *benefits programs* may increase employee satisfaction, they are a major expense to business today.

5. **Describe the major *laws governing labour-management relations.*** In 1907, the *Industrial Disputes Investigation Act* was passed; it provided for compulsory investigation of labour disputes by a government-appointed board. *Privy Council Order 1003,* passed in 1943, recognized the right of employees to collectively bargain with their employer. The *Canada Labour Code* regulates employment practices, standard hours of work, safety for employees, and collective bargaining activities.

6. **Identify the steps in the *collective bargaining process.*** Once certified, the union engages in *collective bargaining* with the organization—that is, it negotiates with management on common terms and conditions of employment for the workers whom it represents. The initial step in collective bargaining is to reach agreement on a labour contract. Contract demands usually involve wages, job security, and/or management rights.

   Both labour and management have several tactics that can be used against the other if negotiations break down. Unions may attempt *strikes* or *boycotts* of employers or engage in work *slowdowns.* In some cases, employers may hire *strikebreakers* (replacement workers) or *lock out* workers (deny them access to the workplace). In extreme cases, *mediation* or *arbitration* may be used to settle disputes by bringing in neutral third parties.

STUDY QUESTIONS AND EXERCISES

Review Questions

1. Why is a good employee-job match important? Who benefits more, the organization or the employee? Why?

2. What are the advantages and disadvantages of internal and external staffing? Under what circumstances is each more appropriate?

3. What tactics can labour and management use to support their causes?

Analysis Questions

4. What benefits do you consider most and least important in attracting workers? In keeping workers? In motivating workers?

5. Select a job currently held by you or a close friend. Draw up a job description and job specification for this position.

6. Did you have to take a test to be admitted to school? If you did, how valid do you think your score was as a predictor of academic success? Explain.

7. Suppose you are a manager in a nonunionized company. You have just heard a rumour that some of your workers are discussing forming a union. What would you do? Be specific.

Application Exercises

8. Interview a human resource manager at a local company. Select a position for which the firm is currently recruiting applicants and identify the steps in the selection process.

9. Interview the managers of two local companies, one unionized and one nonunionized. Compare the wage and salary levels, benefits, and working conditions of workers at the two firms.

10. Obtain a copy of an employment application. Examine it carefully and determine how useful it might be in making a hiring decision.

BUILDING YOUR BUSINESS SKILLS

Goal

To encourage students to develop mechanisms for increasing the cohesiveness of a large, diverse workforce.

Situation

As the director of human resources at one of the country's leading banks, you realize that business success depends, in large part, on how effectively the firm's 40 000 employees work together. You convince the CEO and management committee that active steps are needed to make diversity a day-to-day corporate value.

Method

Work with three other students to translate the guidelines presented below into elements of a workable diversity program that fits the unique needs of your company:

- *Make diversity a specific management goal:* Write a short (one- to four-sentence) mission statement making diversity a corporate goal. The statement should link diversity with competitive success in an increasingly diverse marketplace.

- *Analyze compensation scales and be scrupulously fair in tracking individual careers:* Two years ago, your company merged with another bank, with the result that compensation for the same work varies widely, depending on the original employer. This is particularly problematic because the other firm tended to pay staff workers, many of whom are women and minorities, less than your firm does. Describe how you would correct this disparity, recognizing that it is impossible for a company to equalize everyone's pay at one time and that it is also unfair to freeze, for several years, the compensation of workers who have a higher wage base.

- *Continue to focus on diversity in the midst of downsizing:* With stock analysts criticizing the "fat" in the newly merged firm, the company must cut costs by eliminating 3000 jobs. Describe the specific steps you would take to ensure that women and minorities do not lose their jobs at a disproportionately high rate.

- *Contribute to the diversity of the workforce:* Briefly describe the criteria you would use to award scholarships to needy students. Would you award scholarships to young women who show promise in math and science, despite their economic backgrounds?

- *Celebrate diversity:* Write a one-page memo describing the activities planned during your company's Diversity Day.

- *Respond to the concerns of white males:* Make a list of five ways to increase the comfort of white males to prevent a diversity backlash. You may decide, for example, that men as well as women may be subject to sexual harassment and that appropriate actions will be taken against any man or woman who commits an act of harassment.

Follow-Up Questions

1. Which of these measures do you consider to be most important to the success of your corporate diversity program? Why?

2. After these measures are taken, do you think diversity training is necessary? If you do, describe the objectives of the training.

3. Can you think of any downside to emphasizing diversity?

BUSINESS CASE 9

Freelancing

When people think about careers, they usually think of going to work full-time for a company and, if they like it, staying at that company for many years. In fact, until recently the notion of "lifetime employment" was touted as the wave of the future. Even if a person didn't stay at one firm, the idea still was that the person would work full-time for a company for at least a few years.

But times are changing. A growing number of workers are becoming freelancers—individuals who contract with a company for a set period of time, usually until a specific project is completed. After the project is completed, the freelancer moves on to another project in the firm, or to another firm. Statistics Canada estimates that 30 percent of working adults are doing non-standard work such as freelancing.

Why is this happening? The main reason is that competitive pressures are forcing firms to reduce their costs and increase their productivity. The current buzzword is "flexibility" and this can often be achieved by hiring freelancers to solve specific company problems. This allows a firm to maintain a minimum number of full-time workers and then supplement them with freelancers.

Some people freelance because they can't get full-time work with one company, but others freelance by choice. Accomplished freelancers can control their own destiny, make above-average incomes, and have a strong sense of flexibility and freedom. Typically, freelancers don't get paid company benefits like full-time workers do, but pressures are building to change this. In 1994, the province of Saskatchewan became the first in Canada to require companies to pay contract and part-time workers at least some benefits.

Many banks and insurance companies have trouble seeing the needs of contract workers. To them, it may appear that the contract worker is not really employed on a steady basis because they work for so many different companies. Creative Arts Management Service is a firm that fills this void. It offers business advice, financial planning, budgeting, and legal services for contract workers. The firm takes the view that freelancing, if properly planned and executed, is the best security in the new economy of the 1990s.

While the work of technical or professional employees is often contracted out to freelancers, the management of various functions may also be contracted out. The Halifax District School Board contracted out the management of custodial services for the district's 42 schools to ServiceMaster Canada Ltd. The school district expects to save more than half a million dollars each year. And Manpower Temporary Services manages a packaging department for a pharmaceutical firm that sometimes numbers up to 130 people, and sometimes as few as 70, depending on demand. A Manpower manager is on site at the pharmaceutical firm; she recruits the temporary workers, does some of the necessary training, conducts performance appraisals of temporary workers, and handles the payroll.

Management experts predict that freelancing will increase in importance. With the massive layoffs that have been evident in recent years, workers are beginning to realize that job security is not provided by large firms. Rather, security comes from having confidence in your own knowledge and skills, and marketing yourself in innovative ways. Freelancing has been facilitated by the recent advances in information technology, since workers do not necessarily have to be at the workplace in order to do their work.

There are both positive and negative aspects to the idea of non-standard work. From the worker's perspective, those with marketable skills will find that non-standard work will result in high pay and satisfying work. For those without marketable skills, non-standard work will likely mean part-time work in low-paying service jobs. Those individuals who lack either the ability or interest to capitalize on non-standard work will find that there is much uncertainty in their careers.

➤

From the organization's perspective, a conclusion about the value of non-standard work means weighing the value of long-term employee loyalty and commitment against the benefits of the increased flexibility that is possible with part-time freelancers.

■ Case Questions

1. What kind of people are most likely to want freelance work?

2. What are the pros and cons of freelance work from the individual's perspective? From the organization's perspective?

3. Is it unethical to hire freelancers in order to avoid paying company benefits to them?

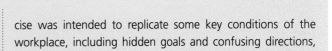

CBC VIDEO CASE III-1

Rocky Mountain Creativity*

Question: For what reason, besides the love of skiing, would executives from across Canada take 10 days out of their busy schedules and pay $4000 to come to Banff, Alberta, in the middle of winter?

Answer: To attend the Banff School of Management, one of Canada's most innovative executive training programs.

The Banff School of Management, situated in Canada's beautiful Rocky Mountains, is fast achieving a national reputation for its creative approach to management development. Managers come from across the country in search of something "extra" in leadership training.

The school's director, Doug Macnamara, advises students to "expect an intense experience." Macnamara claims that the school's training helps make managers into better leaders. One of the ways the school accomplishes this is by emphasizing creativity. The focus is not altogether surprising, given the school's home in the Banff Centre of Creative Arts. Doug sees the school's mission as helping bring creativity back to business. According to one student, the emphasis on creativity is essential, since "Creativity is a tool that a lot of businesses have not enhanced . . . they've actually depressed it."

The focus on encouraging creativity calls for a different pedagogical approach, since, according to Macnamara, people "can't figure out how to be creative by lecture." The course typically involves a wide variety of hands-on exercises emphasizing teamwork and collaborative problem solving. One class began its session with a semi-structured orienteering exercise carried out in the middle of the night. The exer-

cise was intended to replicate some key conditions of the workplace, including hidden goals and confusing directions, while encouraging cooperation and team-building.

Outdoor exercises comprise only part of the course though, with nearly half of it taking place in the classroom, where top-flight instructors from across the country provide a theoretical grounding for the practical side of management. Emphasis is on understanding personal behaviour, in this case both the student's and that of fellow team members, in order to understand basic principles of why people behave the way they do. Role playing is often used, as well as direct and sometimes confrontational feedback. For some, the program is too "touchy-feely." This route should not be interpreted as a substandard teaching mode, however. According to Macnamara, the Banff School seeks to "push people beyond their envelope." The director continues, arguing that "the best learning happens when you're active in it."

The course's training exercises range from yoga and ceramics to interpretative dance and improvisation. One reason for the inclusion of such "artsy" activities arises from the on-site presence of some of Canada's leading artists. The school doesn't hesitate to co-opt the artists into the program, since they are an excellent resource for alternative ideas, insights, and paradigms. According to Macnamara, "An excellent leader and excellent artist are actually very, very close to the same type." Therefore, since "we are called to be creative starting at 8:30 in the morning until whenever," it only makes sense to stimulate the creative juices using whatever is inherently creative and, in this case, readily accessible.

➤

1. What is the difference between on-the-job and off-the-job training? Which better describes the training that managers receive at the Banff School of Management?

2. What is empowerment? In what ways does the Banff School of Management seek to empower its students?

3. What is the difference between Theory X and Theory Y? Which theory better describes how the leaders of the Banff School of Management view their students?

* Source: This case was written by Professor Reg Litz of the University of Manitoba. Video Resource: "The Banff Experience," *Venture* #637 (April 6, 1997).

CBC VIDEO CASE III-2

Spirituality in the Workplace*

"Nations of people become wise once they've exhausted all the other possibilities."

—Abba Eban, former Israeli foreign minister

Spirituality and religious faith are becoming increasingly important in the corporate workplace. While in many cultures the practice of spirituality and prayer within the workplace is nothing new, the long-standing dichotomy between church and state in such Western cultures as Canada and the United States shows signs of being bridged in an increasing number of organizational environments.

In locations as "spiritual" as the office towers of Toronto's King and Bay Streets, Christians gather for Bible study and prayer. For some, the time is well spent, representing "an oasis in the middle of the week." Seminar leader Ian Percy reports never seeing such a widespread increase of interest in religion. Part of the reason for this interest may be a reaction to the fierce and cutthroat realities of modern day competition. Part of the reason may also be faddish, though—just one more float in the endless parade of quick fixes such as total quality and management by objectives. However, with the realities of downsizings and restructuring upon them, people appear to want something that endures and provides a transcendent meaning beyond the immediate moment. Ted Wayman of Organization Change Consultants also reports people desiring ethical principles grounded in spiritual principles that help in "coming to grips with our morality." For many, religious faith offers such a perspective.

The increased interest in religion can also be understood in a historical context. Wilfrid Laurier University history professor David Menault notes that the late 1800s were a period of massive change. One way to deal with the social dislocation of the new century was to focus beyond the present to the enduring meaning offered by religious faith. While Menault wonders whether last century's interest was more rhetorical than real, for some in this century the interest may indeed be genuine and enduring.

One company demonstrating the reality of its rhetoric is Service Master. The first of this company's four objectives is to honour God, followed by people development, pursuit of excellence, and finally, profitable growth. The company, founded in 1947, has racked up sales of over $4.5 billion and a 25 percent growth rate while holding to its God-centred creed. According to company management, the Biblical standards allow them to be good and prosper.

1. What is Maslow's hierarchy of needs? How does the increased attention on spirituality relate to the hierarchy?

2. What is the difference between hygienes and motivators in Frederick Herzberg's two-factor theory? Which does the increased focus on spirituality relate to?

3. What is meant by the term "human relations"? How does it relate to the increased interest in spirituality?

* Source: This case was written by Professor Reg Litz of the University of Manitoba. Video Resource: "Sprituality in Business," *Venture* #628 (February 2, 1997).

LANDS' END VIDEO CASE III-3

Some Secrets of the Much-Envied Work Climate

LEARNING OBJECTIVES

The purpose of this video exercise is to help students

1. See how a specific company has implemented its human resources policies

2. Understand the relationship between a company's overall "culture" and its approach to human resources

3. Understand how specific strategies for enhancing job satisfaction and morale can affect the attitudes and performance of a company's employees

4. Appreciate the importance of training as an element in both job satisfaction and productivity

BACKGROUND INFORMATION

According to Kelly Ritchie, Vice President for Human Resources at Lands' End,

> Turnover of our regular benefited group is in the single digits—very low for this industry. When people really like what they do, like who they do it with and for, work in facilities that are among the best around, and are fairly paid for their efforts, it would seem almost impossible not to be at least minimally satisfied.

In fact, Lands' End employees seem to be more than "minimally satisfied." Among the reasons is an 80 000-square-foot Activity Center that includes an Olympic-size swimming pool, a full-size gym, an indoor track, state-of-the-art exercise equipment, locker and shower rooms, and a not-for-profit cafeteria. The $8 million centre was donated by founder Gary Comer in 1987.

Lands' End employees also seem to be happy about the way their input is solicited during monthly feedback meetings and about the way CEO Michael Smith openly shares company information during all-company quarterly meetings. For its part, Lands' End considers its employees' job satisfaction a key element in one of its most important competitive strategies—keeping customers satisfied. Thus, the emphasis on what Ritchie describes as "our commitment to continuous, proactive training. . . . By spending the money up front," she reports, "we have much happier employees, we don't have to spend nearly as much money . . . on quality checks, and, most importantly, we have satisfied customers."

THE VIDEO

Video Source. "The Establishing and Maintaining of a Much-Envied Work Climate," *Prentice Hall Presents: On Location at Lands' End.* The video focuses on three aspects of human resources at Lands' End: the importance of open communications, both top-down and bottom-up; the importance of the Activity Center in maintaining job satisfaction and morale; and the importance of job training in maintaining a high level of customer service. Participants include Human Resources Manager Kelly Ritchie, who describes company policy, and two veteran phone operators, who talk about the practical effect of company policy.

DISCUSSION QUESTIONS

1. What strategies for enhancing motivation are evident at Lands' End? What strategies for enhancing job satisfaction and morale do you see at work?

2. Judging from the video, what can you say about the role played by human resources management in Lands' End's efforts to fulfill its organizational mission?

3. How would you describe the managerial style of CEO Michael Smith?

4. In what respect does the brand of human resources management practised at Lands' End reflect thinking about motivation and leadership in the 1990s?

FOLLOW-UP ASSIGNMENT

At the end of the video, the narrator asks whether you think there might be "other tools" Lands' End could implement to improve its human resources "culture." To address this question, your instructor will divide the class into "advisory teams" of five or six students each. Each member of the team should use the Internet to contact the Office of the American Workplace (OAW) at

http://www. fed.org/uscompanies/labor/

Here you will find detailed reports on the "best practices" of several high-performance companies singled out by the OAW. Each member of the team should examine the report on a specific company and provide the team with a brief overview of its human resources practices. Each team should then prepare a descriptive list of those practices that might be useful as "other tools" for human resources managers at Lands' End. The team should prepare a brief report summarizing its recommendations.

FOR FURTHER EXPLORATION

To find out more about what Lands' End itself has to say about its people and about the relationship between its human resources philosophy and its corporate culture, contact the company on the Internet at **http://www.landsend.com**

From the Home page, click on "The Library" to reach "In Persons," or click on "The Company" and then "The Company Inside" to reach "Out Our Way."

MANAGING PRODUCTION AND INFORMATION

Producing high-quality goods and services is at the heart of all business operations. The chapter opening cases in this section show how organizations like Toyota Motors, Dell Computer, and Canadian Steamship Lines have improved their production and information activities so that they are able to supply high-quality products and services to their customers on a timely basis.

Part Four, **Managing Production and Information**, provides an overview of three aspects of business important to a firm's existence: production of goods and services, increasing productivity and quality, and generating and using information to make business activities more effective.

- ■ We begin in **Chapter 10, Producing Goods and Services**, by examining how business firms produce both physical goods and intangible services, and how they plan, organize, and control the production process.

- ■ In **Chapter 11, Increasing Productivity and Quality**, we consider some of the approaches companies can take to improve the productivity and quality of their output, and thus their competitive position.

- ■ Finally, in **Chapter 12, Understanding Accounting and Information Systems**, we examine the role of accountants in gathering and presenting financial information about a company. We also consider the growing need for companies to manage information and how computers help in meeting this need.

CHAPTER
10

PRODUCING GOODS AND SERVICES

TOYOTA'S PRODUCTION SYSTEM: STILL THE STANDARD

Why do executives from Ford, Chrysler, and GM want to take plant tours of Toyota manufacturing facilities? To try to figure out how Toyota is able to make cars so efficiently, that's why. Toyota doesn't charge its competitors for these tours, and it doesn't keep anything secret from them. This seems odd; would Coke let Pepsi see its secret formula? But Toyota doesn't seem worried that competitors will see its operations close-up; it knows that those competitors have been trying (unsuccessfully) for years to match its productivity.

The Toyota Production System (TPS) is designed to mobilize all human and capital resources in such a way that peak efficiency, productivity, and quality will be achieved in the assembly of automobiles. Mercedes-Benz may have sophisticated engineering, Honda great engine technology, and Chrysler great styling, but Toyota has the most efficient production system.

The Big 3 domestic automobile manufacturers have all adopted parts of TPS, but none of them has been able to match the efficiency produced by the total TPS system. The system *looks* simple enough: maximize flow, eliminate waste, and respect people. But the implementation requires huge amounts of effort and insight. For example, lots of manufacturing plants have adopted the idea that any worker who sees something wrong can pull a cord and stop the production line. But Toyota is the only company that has actually been able to drive the right philosophies about quality down to the worker level.

A key aspect of TPS is consistent, smooth production. In many manufacturing plants, workers work hard the first few hours on the job to meet their quota, and then relax later in the day. This leads to uneven production. At Toyota, overproduction at any time is considered bad practice. Work flows are designed to move from process to process with no ups and downs. Another example: In the typical automobile plant, visitors will see stacks of half-finished parts and idle workers standing along assembly lines that are temporarily shut down for one reason or another. But at Toyota plants, workers are constantly in motion and almost look like dancers in a choreographed production.

TPS requires that experienced managers work with a highly motivated and well-trained workforce. The TPS system also involves dependence on outside suppliers who must run their own operations completely in sync with Toyota's. Because Toyota produces just 30 percent of the parts it needs (GM produces almost two-thirds of its own parts), suppliers are an integral part of Toyota's production system and often have an ownership stake in the company.

Toyota is famous for pioneering the just-in-time parts delivery system. Suppliers deliver parts up to eight times daily to Toyota factories, allowing the company to maintain inventory levels that are only one-quarter those at GM. Toyota's suppliers are also physically much closer to Toyota production plants than GM's suppliers are to its plants—an average of 100 kilometres for Toyota versus 700 kilometres for GM.

Suppliers are involved in all aspects of Toyota production so that they can be an effective part of the team that produces cars. If the supplier has problems, Toyota helps it to improve. Two Toyota engineers once spent seven months at a supplier improving its operations so it could meet Toyota's standards. All this took place while the supplier was under contract to a Toyota competitor.

The TPS system is not restricted to just the production line. It also works in important areas like new product development. With TPS, Toyota can develop a new car model in 18 months, a much shorter time than is typical in this industry. In 1996 and 1997, the company introduced 18 new or redesigned models. It also introduced a new engine—partly battery-powered—that gets 66 miles per gallon. The 120-

horsepower engine in the 1998 Corolla uses one-quarter fewer parts than its predecessor, making it lighter, cheaper, and more fuel-efficient.

With all this good news, are there any problems on the horizon for Toyota? Yes. The company will have to find more foreign markets for its cars because of limited demand within Japan. Unfortunately, Toyota has not been able to completely export its TPS system to its manufacturing facilities outside Japan. Its North American plants, for example, still require 30 to 50 percent more time to build a car than its Japanese plants do. These difficulties have arisen because of a lack of middle managers with TPS experience, and because so much time has to be spent bringing suppliers up to Toyota's standards.

Consider your first couple of hours on a typical weekday morning. Let's say you wake up to your favourite radio station. You prepare for your day, and shortly after you're out of the house, you stop at the corner newsstand for a newspaper on your way to the bus stop, where you catch the bus to work or school. The radio announcer, the newsstand clerk, the bus driver, and the teachers with whom you will interact at school are all workers in **service operations**: They provide you with intangible services such as entertainment, transportation, convenience shopping, and education. Other companies are engaged in **goods production**: They produce the tangible products—radios, newspapers, buses, textbooks—that you use so often.

Because more and more business activity is focused on the provision of services, it is often said that Canada is a **service economy**. In 1950, less than half of all Canadian workers were employed by service-producing companies, but by 1996 more than two out of every three workers were employed in a service-producing company. This trend towards services can be clearly seen in consumer expenditures. Between 1986 and 1997, the amount spent by consumers on services rose from 36 cents of each dollar to 41 cents.[1] Between 1986 and 1996, consumers increased their spending on services like new telephone technologies (up 40 percent), Internet and cellular phones (virtually unknown in 1986), and cablevision services (up almost 100 percent).[2]

By focusing on the learning objectives of this chapter, you will better understand the complexity of production processes for both goods and services. After reading this chapter, you should be able to:

1. Identify the characteristics that distinguish *service operations* from *goods production*.
2. Describe the factors involved in *operations planning* and *scheduling*.
3. Explain the activities involved in *operations control*, including *materials management* and the use of *production control tools*, and describe the special operations control problems of service operations.
4. Characterize the kinds of *automation* currently in use in production operations.

service operations
Business activities that provide intangible services.

goods production
Business activities that create tangible products.

service economy
A reference to the growing importance of services, rather than products, as the major contributor to the Canadian economy.

■ PRODUCTION MANAGEMENT: AN OVERVIEW

To understand the production processes of a firm, you need to understand the importance of products—both goods and services. Products provide businesses with both economic

utility
The power of a product to satisfy a human want; something of value.

time utility
That quality of a product satisfying a human want because of the time at which it is made available.

place utility
That quality of a product satisfying a human want because of where it is made available.

ownership (possession) utility
That quality of a product satisfying a human want during its consumption or use.

form utility
That quality of a product satisfying a human want because of its form; requires raw materials to be transformed into a finished product.

operations (production) management
The systematic direction and control of the processes that transform resources into finished goods and services.

results (profits, wages, goods purchased from other companies) and noneconomic results (new technology, innovations, pollution). And they provide consumers with what economists call **utility**—want satisfaction.

Four basic kinds of utility would not be possible without production. By making a product available at a time when consumers want it, production creates **time utility**, as when a company turns out ornaments in time for Christmas. By making a product available in a place convenient for consumers, production creates **place utility**, as when a local department store creates a "Trim-A-Tree" section. By making a product that consumers can take pleasure in owning, production creates **ownership (possession) utility**, as when you take a box of ornaments home and decorate your tree.

But above all, production makes products available in the first place. By turning raw materials into finished goods, production creates **form utility**, as when an ornament maker combines glass, plastic, and other materials to create tree decorations.

Because the term *production* has historically been associated with manufacturing, it has been replaced in recent years by *operations*, a term that reflects both services and goods production. **Operations** (or **production**) **management** is the systematic direction and control of the processes that transform resources into finished goods and services. Thus production managers are ultimately responsible for creating utility for customers.

As Figure 10.1 shows, production managers must bring raw materials, equipment, and labour together under a production plan that effectively uses all the resources available in the production facility. As demand for a good increases, they must schedule and control work to produce the amount required. Meanwhile, they must control costs, quality levels, inventory, and plant and equipment.

Not all production managers work in factories. Farmers are also production managers. They create form utility by converting soil, seeds, sweat, gas, and other inputs into beef cattle, tobacco, wheat, milk, cash, and other outputs.

Classifying Operations Processes

Whether they are independent farmers or employees of a multinational manufacturer, production managers must control the process by which goods are produced. We can classify production processes in four different ways:

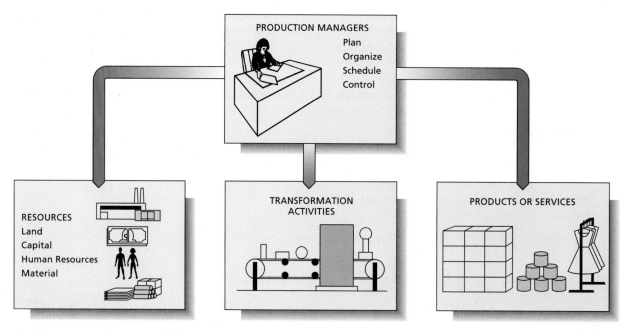

FIGURE 10.1
The transformation system.

- by the type of transformation technology used
- by whether the process is analytic or synthetic
- by the pattern of product flow during transformation
- by the extent of labour use

Transformation Technology.   Manufacturers use chemical, fabrication, assembly, transport, and clerical processes to transform raw materials into finished goods. In *chemical processes*, raw materials are chemically altered. Such techniques are common in the aluminum, steel, fertilizer, petroleum, and paint industries. In contrast, *fabrication processes* mechanically alter the basic shape or form of the product. Examples of fabrication abound in the metal-forming and machining industries, the wood-working industry, and the plastic-molding and plastic-forming industries.

As their name suggests, *assembly processes* involve putting together various components. These techniques are often used in the electronics, appliance, and automotive industries. *Transport processes*, in which goods acquire place utility by moving from one location to another, are also common in the appliance industry. For example, refrigerators are routinely moved from manufacturing plants to consumers through a series of regional warehouses and discount stores.

Finally, *clerical processes* transform information. Combining data on employee absences and machine breakdowns into a productivity report is a clerical process. One issue currently facing users of clerical transformation is whether too much information is being processed and presented.

Analytic versus Synthetic Processes.   A second way of classifying production processes is by the way resources are converted into finished goods. An **analytic process** breaks down the basic resources into components. For example, Alcan manufactures aluminum by extracting it from an ore called bauxite. The reverse approach, a **synthetic process**, combines a number of raw materials to produce a finished product such as fertilizer or paint.

analytic process
Any production process in which resources are broken down.

synthetic process
Any production process in which resources are combined.

Product Flow Pattern.   We can also classify production processes by how the plant is arranged and how the product moves through the plant.[3] In a **continuous process**, the flow is fairly smooth, straight, and continuous. A continuous-process pattern is usually found when a manufacturing operation is repetitive. Typically, such a plant turns out nearly identical finished products in production runs of several days, months, or even years. Toyota, Imperial Tobacco, and Labatt all use continuous processes.

In contrast, material in an **intermittent process** flows through a plant in a stop-and-go fashion and a seemingly scattered arrangement of equipment and departments. The jumbled flows occur because such plants produce short runs of custom-made products, each requiring a unique set of operations. Printing shops are an example. As various jobs are routed through the necessary departments, machines are shut down frequently in order to set up for other jobs.

One other major characteristic of this process is that each job passes through specialized departments. Intermittent processes usually group similar machines—grinders in one department and milling machines in another, for example. But a continuous process would place grinders or mills wherever they are needed along an assembly line.

continuous process
Any production process in which the flow of transformation from resources to finished product is fairly smooth, straight, and continuous.

intermittent process
Any production process in which the flow of transformation from resources to finished product starts and stops.

Labour Use.   Finally, processes vary in the amount of human input they need. **Labour-intensive processes** depend more on people than on machines. They are most likely to be used when labour is cheap or when there is an artistic element to the work. Many kinds of farming are still highly labour intensive. Producing cherries or lettuce is much more labour intensive than producing wheat or sugar beets.

Capital-intensive processes are those in which investment in machinery is great. A huge petroleum refinery is a classic example of a capital-intensive process. A refinery that may cost hundreds of millions of dollars to build and equip may operate with fewer than 100 employees.

labour-intensive process
Any process that depends more on people than on machines.

capital-intensive process
Any process in which investment in machinery is great.

Differences in the Service Focus

Service and manufacturing operations share several important features. For example, both transform raw materials into finished goods. In service production, however, the raw materials are not glass or steel. Rather, they are people who choose among sellers because they have either unsatisfied needs or possessions for which they need some form of care or alteration. In service operations, then, "finished products" are people with needs met and possessions serviced. There is, therefore, one very obvious difference between service and manufacturing operations: Goods are *produced*, but services are *performed*. Thus customer-oriented performance is a key factor in measuring the efficiency of a service company.

In many ways, the focus of service operations is more complex than that of goods producers. First, service operations feature a unique link between production and consumption. Second, services are more *intangible, customized,* and *unstorable* than most products. Finally, quality considerations must be defined—and managed—differently in the service sector than in manufacturing operations.

Focus on Process and Outcome.   Manufacturing operations focus on the *outcome* of the production process. The products offered by most service operations, however, are actually combinations of goods and services. Services, therefore, must focus on both the transformation *process* and its outcome—both on making a pizza and on delivering it to the buyer. Service operations thus require different skills than manufacturing operations. For example, local gas company employees may need the interpersonal skills necessary to calm and reassure frightened customers who have reported leaks. The job, therefore, can mean more than just repairing defective pipes. Factory workers who install gas pipes while assembling mobile homes are far less likely to need such skills.

Focus on Service Characteristics.   Service marketing plans always reflect that service products are characterized by three key qualities: *intangibility, customization,* and *unstorability*.

Intangibility.   Often, services cannot be touched, tasted, smelled, or seen. An important value, therefore, is the *intangible* value that the customer experiences in the form of pleasure, satisfaction, or a feeling of safety. For example, when you hire an attorney to resolve a problem, you purchase not only the intangible quality of legal expertise but the equally intangible reassurance that sympathetic help is at hand. Although all services have some degree of intangibility, some provide tangible elements as well.[4]

Customization.   When you visit a physician, you expect to be examined for *your* symptoms. Likewise, when you purchase insurance, get your pet groomed, or have your hair cut, you expect these services to be designed for *your* needs. Typically, therefore, services are *customized.*

Unstorability.   Services such as rubbish collection, transportation, child care, and house cleaning cannot be produced ahead of time and then stored. If a service is not used when available, it is usually wasted. Services, then, are typically characterized by a high degree of *unstorability.*

Focus on the Customer-Service Link.   Because they transform customers or their possessions, service operations often acknowledge the customer as part of the production process itself. For example, to purchase a haircut you must usually go to the barbershop or beauty salon.

As part of the production process, consumers of services have a unique ability to affect that process. In other words, as the customer, you expect the salon to be conveniently located, to be open for business at convenient times, to offer needed services at reasonable prices, and to extend prompt service. Accordingly, the manager adopts hours of operation, available services, and numbers of employees to meet the requirements of the customer.

A public transit system, which is an example of a high-contact system, provides the service of transportation.

Focus on Service-Quality Considerations.   Finally, consumers use different criteria to judge services and goods. Service managers must understand that quality of work and quality of service are not necessarily synonymous. For example, although your car may have been flawlessly repaired, you might feel dissatisfied with the service if you had been forced to pick it up a day later than promised.

In a drive to improve service quality, Ford's Parts and Service division thus changed its name to Customer Service in June 1993. It now focuses not on selling parts to dealers for profit but on acting as a consultant and technical trainer for dealer repair staffs. Because gaps in *product* quality have been closed by all carmakers, Ford's strategy is to transform its *service* operation into a more powerful competitive tool.[5]

To consider the extent of customer contact in service operations, think for a moment about your local public transit system. The service provided is transportation, and when you purchase transportation, you must board a bus or train. All public transportation systems are **high-contact systems**: To receive the service, the customer must be a part of the system. Other high-contact services providers include airlines, physicians, and car rental systems.

One way of classifying services is to ask if a given service can be provided without the customer being part of the production system. We can thus classify all services according to the extent of *customer contact*.[6]

In contrast to your public transit system, consider the cheque-processing operations at your bank. Workers sort the cheques that have been cashed that day and dispatch them to the banks on which they were drawn. This operation is a **low-contact system**: Customers are not in contact with the bank while the service is performed. Customers receive the service—their funds are transferred to cover their cheques—without ever setting foot in the cheque-processing centre. Gas and electric utilities, auto-repair shops, and lawn-care services are also low-contact systems.

high-contact system
Level of service-customer contact in which the customer receives the service as part of the system.

low-contact system
Level of service-customer contact in which the customer need not be part of the system to receive the service.

■ OPERATIONS PLANNING

Managers from many departments contribute to decisions about production management. As Figure 10.2 shows, however, no matter how many decision makers are involved, the process can be described as a series of logical steps. The success of any firm depends on the final result of this logical sequence of decisions.

The overall business plan developed by a company's top executives guides operations planning. This plan outlines the firm's goals and objectives, including the specific products and services that it will offer in the upcoming years. In this section, we will survey each of the major components of the business plan that directly affect operations planning. First, we will describe *forecasting* and then we will discuss the key planning and forecasting activities that fall into one of five major categories: *capacity, location, layout, quality,* and *methods planning*.

Forecasting

forecasts
Estimates of future demand for both new and existing products.

In addition to the business plan, managers develop the firm's *long-range production plan* through **forecasts** of future demand for both new and existing products. This plan covers a two- to five-year period. It specifically details the number of plants or service facilities, as well as labour, machinery, and transportation and storage facilities, that will be needed to meet demand. It also specifies how resources will be obtained.

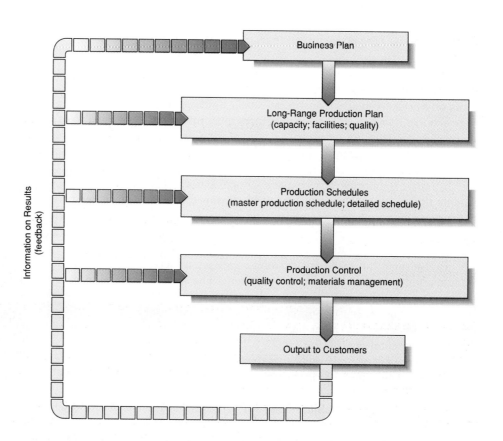

FIGURE 10.2
The steps in a production planning and control system ensure that production activities lead to customer satisfaction.

Forecasting uses both qualitative and quantitative methods. *Qualitative forecasts* may come from an expert or group of experts who basically use judgment and experience. *Quantitative forecasts* are statistical methods to project future demand from past demand patterns. For example, in developing a new line of Memorex videotapes, Memtek Products might use quantitative methods to calculate demand three years hence at 4 million cassettes per year. Its long-range production plan might translate this demand into a need to build three new plants, lease another warehouse, acquire four new tape-filling machines, and hire 2500 new employees.

Capacity Planning

The amount of a product that a company can produce under normal working conditions is its **capacity**. A firm's capacity depends on how many people it employs and the number and size of its facilities. Long-range planning must take into account both current and future capacity.

capacity
The amount of a good that a firm can produce under normal working conditions.

Capacity planning means ensuring that a firm's capacity just *slightly* exceeds the normal demand for its product. To see why this policy is best, consider the alternatives. If capacity is too small to meet demand, the company must turn away customers—a situation that not only cuts into profits but alienates both customers and salespeople. If capacity exceeds demand, the firm is wasting money by maintaining a plant that is too large, by keeping excess machinery online, or by employing too many workers.

When forecasts indicate a temporary business slowdown, companies plan for ways to use existing capacity. For example, when demand for farm machinery waned in the 1980s, John Deere found itself with excess production capacity. Rather than closing its plants, Deere used the extra capacity to make engines for companies producing air compressors and irrigation pumps as well as motor-home components for Winnebago. Capacity planning allowed Deere to use slack capacity while awaiting anticipated increases in demand for traditional farm products.[7]

Capacity Planning for Producing Services. In low-contact systems, maintaining inventory lets managers set capacity at the level of *average demand*. Orders that arrive faster than expected can be temporarily placed in inventory—set aside in a "to be done" file—to be processed during a slower period. For example, a catalogue-sales warehouse may hire enough order fillers to handle 1000 orders each day. When daily orders exceed average demand, some are set aside until a day when fewer than 1000 orders are received.

In high-contact systems, managers must plan capacity to meet *peak demand*. A supermarket, for instance, has far more cash registers than it needs on an average day. But on a Saturday morning or during the three days before Christmas, all registers will be running full speed.

Adjusting Capacity. Capacity adjustments are often made through the *make-versus-buy decision* for production components. If a firm chooses to manufacture (make) a needed item in its own facility, it will need *more* production capacity. If it chooses to purchase (buy) that item from another company, it will need *less* capacity. A clock maker, for example, can either make the hands for its products or buy hands already made by another company. If it decides to buy, it can adjust capacity downwards.

Instead of expanding capacity to meet peak demand, companies sometimes use pricing to shift peak demand to nonpeak periods. Golf club manufacturers, for example, will offer seasonal discounts to retailers during the winter to encourage early ordering. This practice sustains production during the winter months (an otherwise slow production period) and helps reduce the peak demand for production in springtime.

Ford
www.ford.com

Location Planning

Because facility location affects production costs and flexibility, sound location planning is crucial. Depending on the site of its facility, a company may either be capable of producing a low-cost product or may find itself at an extreme cost disadvantage. Such considerations weighed heavily on the decision-making process at Ford that resulted in the Mondeo—the so-called "world car" introduced in Europe in 1993 and (as the Ford Contour and Mercury Mystique) in the United States in 1994. Developed to be both manufactured and marketed around the world, the "world car" took advantage of design strengths in three separate engineering centres: Detroit (V-6 engine, automatic transmission, heating and air-conditioning units), London (four-cylinder engine, steering, suspension, electronics), and Cologne, Germany (basic structural engineering). To free its engineering workforce for other projects and facilities, Ford assigned a single 800-person team to design the Mondeo for both Europe and the United States and will employ identical production facilities to build the car at Genk, Belgium, and Kansas City, Missouri. By custom-building two production facilities on two continents, Ford has saved about 25 percent on customized factory machinery such as stamping dies and secured better prices for larger orders from its suppliers.[8]

Location Planning for Goods.   As we can see from Ford's "world car" strategy, managers must consider many factors in location planning. Location attractiveness is influenced by proximity to raw materials and markets, availability of labour, energy and transportation costs, local and provincial regulations and taxes, and community living conditions.

Some location decisions are now being simplified by the rise of industrial parks. Created by cities interested in attracting new industry, these planned sites come with the necessary zoning, land, shipping facilities, utilities, and waste-disposal outlets already in place. Such sites offer flexibility, often allowing firms to open new facilities before competitors can get started in the same area. The ready-made site also provides faster construction startups because it entails no lead time in preparing the chosen site.

Location Planning for Services.   Low-contact services are usually located near resource supplies, labour, or transportation. For example, post office mail-sorting facilities are usually located in downtown urban areas so that they are close to much of their supply (mail from downtown businesses). To facilitate both outgoing transport and incoming deliveries from suburban branches, they are often located near major roadways.

On the other hand, high-contact services must locate near customers, who are a part of the system. Meridian Bancorp, for example, operates a branch in Paradise, Pennsylvania, in the heart of Amish country. The facility thus features hitching posts for horse-drawn buggies. Similarly, have you ever noticed how the branches of several different banks are located next to one another? This pattern results from careful analysis of traffic flows, area businesses and schools, and income patterns of local residents.

Layout Planning

Once a site has been selected, managers must decide on plant layout. Layout determines whether a company can respond quickly and efficiently to customer requests for more and different products or if it finds itself unable to match competitors' production speed. Alternatives include *process, product, craft work, cellular,* and *fixed-position layouts.*

process layout
A way of organizing production activities such that equipment and people are grouped together according to their function.

Process Layouts.   In a **process layout**, equipment and people are grouped together according to function. In a custom-cake bakery, for instance, the blending of batters is done in an area devoted to mixing, baking occurs in the oven area, icing is prepared in the mixing area, and cakes are decorated on tables in a finishing area before boxing. The various tasks are each performed in specialized locations. Machine, woodworking, and dry cleaning shops usually feature process layouts.

Process layouts are well suited to *job shops*—firms that specialize in custom work. These companies do a variety of jobs for different customers. They rely on general-purpose machinery and skilled labour to respond to the needs of individual customers. For example, your local bakery can accommodate both your request for a wedding cake and your friend's request for a birthday cake.

Product Layouts.   In a **product layout**, resources move through a fixed sequence of steps to become finished goods. Equipment and people are set up to produce only one type of good and are arranged according to its production requirements. Product layouts often use **assembly lines**—a partially finished product moves step by step through the plant on conveyor belts or other equipment, often in a straight line, until the product is completed. Automobile, food-processing, and computer-assembly plants use product layouts.

Product layouts can be efficient and inexpensive because they simplify work tasks and use unskilled labour. They tend, however, to be inflexible because they require a heavy investment in specialized equipment that is hard to rearrange for new applications. In addition, workers are subject to boredom. Moreover, when workers at one end are absent or overworked, those farther down the line cannot help out.

Craft Work.   To address these problems, many Japanese companies have pioneered new ideas in job design on the assembly line. Both at home and in their Canadian and U.S. factories, NEC, Toyota, Sony, and other firms are finding alternatives to traditional conveyor belts and assembly lines. Instead of specialized jobs, workers are engaged in so-called "craft work" where each worker has the opportunity to assemble an entire product. Even when assembly lines are retained, as in automobile factories, employees are performing more tasks.

Cellular Layouts.   Closely related to craft work are **cellular layouts**, which are used when *families* of products can follow similar flowpaths. A clothing manufacturer, for example, may establish a "cell," or designated area, dedicated to making a family of clothing pockets—say, pockets for shirts, coats, blouses, trousers, and slacks. Although each type of

product layout
A way of organizing production activities such that equipment and people are set up to produce only one type of good.

assembly line
A type of product layout in which a partially finished product moves through a plant on a conveyor belt or other equipment.

NEC Computer Systems
www.nec.com

cellular layouts
Used to produce goods when families of products can follow similar flowpaths.

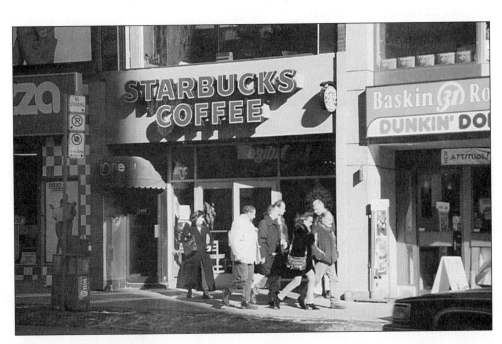

Location planning is an important part of service operations. Starbucks Coffee outlets are often located in areas close to competitors in order to take advantage of the high volume of consumer traffic.

pocket is unique in shape, size, and style, all go through the same production steps. Within the cell, therefore, various types of equipment (for cutting, trimming, sewing) are arranged close together in the appropriate sequence. All pockets pass, stage-by-stage, through the cell from beginning to end, in a nearly continuous flow. The cellular layout is similar to a product layout, except that product layouts usually are dedicated to single products instead of product families. Our clothing maker might also have cells for sleeves, collars, and so on. There may also be a separate area for final assembly.

Developments in Flexibility.   In addition to variations on the product layout, many companies have experimented with ways to make standard production lines more flexible. Some firms, for example, have adopted **U-shaped production lines**: Rather than stretching out in a straight line, machines are placed in a narrow U-shape, with workers operating them from within the U. Because machines are close together, in slow periods one worker can complete all the tasks needed to make a product by easily moving from one side of the U to the other. In busier times, more workers can be added until there is one worker per machine.

Another tool for production flexibility is the **flexible manufacturing system (FMS)**—using computer information systems, a single factory can produce a wide variety of products. Production is adapted rapidly to changes in customer demand, product-by-product, by integrating sales information with the factory's production activities.

But flexible manufacturing may soon be replaced by an even newer development. **Soft manufacturing** emphasizes computer software and computer networks instead of production machines. Soft manufacturing recognizes that complete automation of production processes may not be advisable and that humans are better at certain things than machines are.

Fixed-Position Layouts.   Sometimes, of course, the simplest layout is the most efficient. In a fixed-position layout, labour, materials, and equipment are brought to the work location. This layout is used in building ships, homes, skyscrapers, dams, and manufacturing facilities.

Layout Planning for Services

Service firms use some of the same layouts as goods-producing firms. In a low-contact system, for instance, the facility should be arranged to enhance the production of the service. A mail-processing facility at UPS or Federal Express, therefore, looks very much like a product layout in a factory: Machines and people are arranged in the order in which they are used in the mass processing of mail. In contrast, Kinko's Copy Centers use process layouts for diverse custom jobs: Specific functions as photocopying, computing, binding, photography, and laminating are each performed in specialized areas of the store.

High-contact service systems should be arranged to meet customer needs and expectations. For example, a cafeteria focuses both layout and services on the groups that constitute their primary market—families and elderly people. As shown in Figure 10.3, families enter to find an array of highchairs and rolling baby beds that make it convenient to wheel children through the line. Meanwhile, servers are willing to carry trays for elderly people and for those pushing strollers. (Notice, too, that customers must pass by the whole serving line before making selections. Not only does this layout help them make up their minds, but it also tempts them to select more.)

Quality Planning

In planning production systems and facilities, managers must keep in mind the firm's quality goals.[9] Thus any complete production plan includes systems for ensuring that goods are produced to meet the firm's quality standards. The issues of productivity and quality are discussed in more detail in Chapter 11.

U-shaped production lines
Machines are placed in a U-shape rather than a straight line so that a single worker can complete all the necessary tasks.

flexible manufacturing system (FMS)
A production system in which automatic equipment produces small batches of different goods on the same production line.

soft manufacturing
Emphasizes computer software and computer networks instead of production machines.

Kinko's
www.kinkos.com

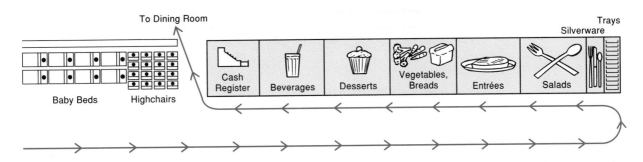

FIGURE 10.3
Layout of a cafeteria.

Methods Planning

In designing both production and service systems, managers must clearly identify every production step and the specific methods for performing them. In manufacturing, managers can also work to reduce waste and inefficiency by examining procedures on a step-by-step basis, an approach sometimes called *methods improvement.*

Similar procedures are useful in designing and evaluating low-contact service systems. At a bank, for example, the cash-management unit collects accounts receivable for corporate clients; the sooner cheques are collected and deposited, the sooner the client begins collecting interest. Thus delays—including the time required to check and adjust customer queries—are expensive, and speed and accuracy are of the essence.

In high-contact services, the demands of systems analysis are somewhat different. Here, for example, the steps to be analyzed include such operations as exchanging information or money, delivering and receiving materials, and even making physical contact. The next time you are at your dentist's office, for instance, notice the way dental hygienists "scrub up" and wear disposable gloves. They also scrub after patient contact, even if they intend to work on equipment or do paperwork, and they rescrub before working on the next patient. The high-contact system in a dental office, then, consists of very strict procedures designed to avoid contact that can transmit disease.

■ OPERATIONS SCHEDULING

Once plans identify the necessary resources and how to use those resources to reach a firm's quantity and quality goals, managers must develop timetables for acquiring the resources. This aspect of operations is called **scheduling**.

scheduling
Developing timetables for acquiring resources.

Scheduling Goods Operations

Scheduling occurs on many levels. A **master production schedule** shows which products will be produced, when production will occur, and what resources will be used during the scheduled time period. For example, the master schedule for Memtek might state that 70 000 Memorex tape cassettes will be produced in May, 60 000 in June, and 50 000 in July. Furthermore, the master schedule tells how many of the 70 000 cassettes produced in May should be standard videotapes, how many should be deluxe videotapes, and how many should be audio cassettes.

This information, however, is not complete. For example, manufacturing personnel must know on which days each type of cassette will be run. Machine startup and stop times must be assigned, and employees must be given scheduled work assignments.

master production schedule
Schedule showing which products will be produced, when production will take place, and what resources will be used.

Short-term *detailed schedules* answer questions like these on daily or weekly bases. These schedules use incoming orders and weekly sales forecasts to determine what size and variety of cassettes to make within a specified time period.

Scheduling Service Operations

Services scheduling may involve both work and workers. In a low-contact service, *work scheduling* may be based either on desired completion dates or on the time of order arrivals. For example, several cars may be scheduled for repairs at a local garage. Thus if your car is not scheduled for work until 3:30, it may sit idle for several hours even if it was the first to be dropped off. In such businesses, reservation and appointment systems can help to smooth demand.

On the other hand, if a hospital emergency room is overloaded, patients cannot be asked to make an appointment and come back later. In high-contact services, the customer is part of the system and must be accommodated. Thus precise scheduling of services may not be possible in high-contact systems.

In scheduling workers, managers must consider efficiency and costs. McDonald's, for example, guarantees workers that they will be scheduled for at least four hours at a time. To accomplish this goal without having workers idle, McDonald's uses *overlapping shifts:* The ending hours for some employees overlap the beginning hours for others. The overlap provides maximum coverage during peak periods. McDonald's also trains its employees to put off minor tasks, such as refilling napkin dispensers, until slow periods.

McDonald's
www.mcdonalds.com

■ OPERATIONS CONTROL

Once long-range plans have been put into action and schedules have been drawn up, the production manager's task is to control production activities so that they conform to plans. **Operations control** requires managers to monitor production performance, in part by comparing results with detailed plans and schedules. If schedules or quality standards are not met, corrective action is needed. **Follow-up**—checking to ensure that production decisions are being implemented—is an essential and ongoing facet of operations control.

Operations control features two major subareas: *quality control* and *materials management.* Both activities seek to ensure that schedules are met and that production goals are fulfilled, both in quantity and quality. In this section, we consider the nature of materials management and some important operations-control tools.

operations control
Managers monitor production performance by comparing results with plans and schedules.

follow-up
Checking to ensure that production decisions are being implemented.

Materials Management

Both goods-producing and service companies use materials. For some manufacturing firms, materials costs account for 50 to 75 percent of total product costs. For goods whose production uses little labour, such as petroleum refining, this percentage is even higher. Thus companies have good reasons to emphasize materials management.

Materials management involves not just controlling but also planning and organizing the flow of materials. Even before production starts, materials management focuses on product design by emphasizing materials **standardization**: the use, where possible, of standard and uniform components rather than new or different components. Ford's engine plant in Romeo, Michigan, for instance, builds several different engine models. To save costs, the plant now uses common parts for several models rather than unique parts for each. One kind of piston, therefore, is now used in different engines. When components were standardized, the total number of different parts was reduced by 25 percent. Standardization also simplifies paperwork, reduces storage requirements, and eliminates unnecessary materials flows.

materials management
Planning, organizing, and controlling the flow of materials from purchase through distribution of finished goods.

standardization
Using standard and uniform components in the production process.

Once the product is designed, materials management purchases the necessary materials and monitors the production process through the distribution of finished goods. The four major areas of materials management are *transportation, warehousing, inventory control,* and *purchasing* (see Figure 10.4).

Transportation includes the means of transporting resources to the company and finished goods to buyers. *Warehousing* refers to the storage of both incoming materials for production and finished goods for physical distribution to customers. Because inventory control and purchasing are more specialized operations, we will explain each process in more detail.

Inventory Control.   Inventory control includes the receiving, storing, handling, and counting of all raw materials, partly finished goods, and finished goods. Inventory control of raw materials and finished goods is primarily a warehousing task. Production managers generally spend more time and effort controlling *materials inventory*—the stock of items needed during the production process, which might include such items as small components to be used in final assembly. Inventory control ensures that enough materials inventories are available to meet production schedules.

Purchasing.   Most companies have purchasing departments to buy proper materials in the amounts needed, both at reasonable prices and at the right time. The importance of purchasing can be seen in the relationship between buying practices and certain

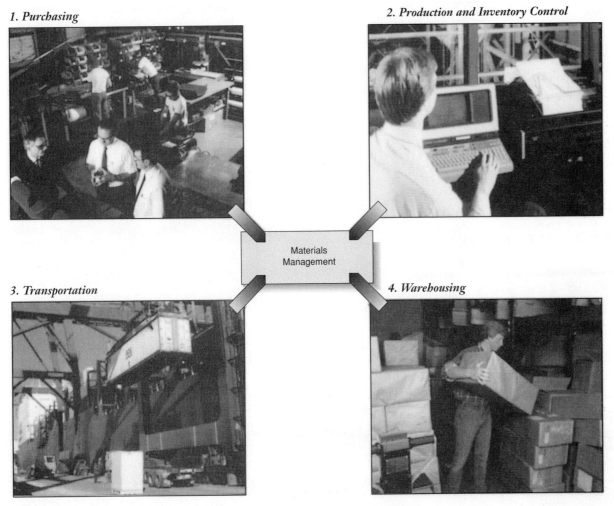

1. Purchasing

2. Production and Inventory Control

3. Transportation

4. Warehousing

Materials Management

FIGURE 10.4
Materials management begins with newly purchased materials and continues during production, transportation, and warehousing.

materials-management costs. For many years, purchasing departments practised *forward buying*: That is, they routinely purchased quantities of materials large enough to fill their needs for long periods. The practice was popular because it can save money by allowing a firm to purchase materials at quantity discounts. Thus it may be advantageous for a crate manufacturer to buy truckloads of nails to satisfy its need for several weeks.

At the same time, however, purchasing agents must balance the need to hold enough materials in stock with the need to avoid excess supplies. Excess supplies entail increased **holding costs**—the costs of keeping extra supplies or materials on hand. These include the real costs of storage, handling, insurance, and obsolescence of the inventory as well as *opportunity costs*—additional earnings that the company must pass up because of the funds tied up in inventory.

In response to today's rising holding costs, many purchasing departments have adopted a so-called *hand-to-mouth pattern*—placing small orders frequently. This practice also requires shorter **lead time**—that is, the gap between the customer's placement of an order and the seller's shipping of merchandise. For example, a radio maker who uses hundreds or thousands of standard components ranging from packaging materials to push buttons may significantly reduce holding costs by ordering only what it needs for the coming day or week.

Purchasing departments are responsible for **supplier selection**—finding and determining which suppliers to buy from.[10] Supplier selection typically follows a four-stage process. The purchaser first surveys possible suppliers. The purchaser then visits, evaluates, and narrows the list to the few suppliers who are best qualified to fill the company's needs. Purchaser and potential suppliers then negotiate terms of service, followed by the purchaser's final choice of a supplier. The fourth "stage" is actually an ongoing process: maintaining a continuing positive buyer-seller relationship. A good relationship ensures reliable and uninterrupted transactions that benefit both parties. Since maintaining relationships with multiple suppliers is expensive for the purchasing organization, most purchasers are working hard to reduce the number of their suppliers and vendors.

Tools for Operations Control

A wide variety of tools are available to help managers to make the necessary trade-offs for production control. Chief among these tools are just-in-time inventory systems, material requirements planning, quality control, and worker training.

Just-in-Time Inventory Systems.   To minimize trade-offs between setup and holding costs, some production managers are using a **just-in-time (JIT) inventory system**. JIT brings together all materials and parts needed at each production step at the precise moment when they are required for the production process. At Toyota's Cambridge, Ontario, plant, delivery trucks constantly pull up at the plant to unload tires, batteries, steering wheels, seats, and many other items needed in the just-in-time production system.[11]

When the Oshawa assembly plant of General Motors of Canada needs seats for cars, it sends the order electronically to a local supplier. The supplier has four hours to make the seats and ship them to the plant. The supplier loads the truck in reverse order so that the last seat loaded is the first one that will be used on the assembly line. The supplier knows, for example, that the plant will be making five four-door Luminas and then six two-door Monte Carlos.[12] As the box "Just-in-Time to the Hospital" shows, the JIT system is not limited to manufacturing plants.

JIT saves money by replacing a stop-and-go production approach with a smooth movement. Everything flows from the arrival of raw materials to subassembly, final completion, and shipment of finished products. JIT reduces the number of goods *in process* (not yet finished) to practically nothing. It also helps to assure reliable quality levels.

Material Requirements Planning.   Like JIT, **material requirements planning (MRP)** also seeks to deliver the right amounts of materials to the right place at the right time.

holding costs
Costs of keeping currently unsalable goods, or costs of money that could be otherwise invested.

lead time
The time between placing an order and actually receiving a shipment.

supplier selection
Finding and determining suppliers to buy from.

just-in-time (JIT) inventory system
A method of inventory control in which materials are acquired and put into production just as they are needed.

material requirements planning (MRP)
A method of inventory control in which a computerized bill of materials is used to estimate production needs so that resources are acquired and put into production only as needed.

TRENDS CHALLENGES

Just-in-Time to the Hospital

Mount Sinai Hospital in downtown Toronto buys about 600 different medical and surgical items from 60 different suppliers. Until recently, the narrow street behind the hospital was constantly clogged with suppliers' trucks delivering goods such as bandages, gloves, catheters, needles, and other supplies that hospitals need. These trucks caused traffic jams and interfered with cars bringing patients and visitors.

But things have changed dramatically. Now, one delivery truck comes to the hospital each evening at 11:00 p.m. This single delivery signifies the hospital's shift from the old system of keeping inventory to a new, stockless system of materials management.

Here's how it works. Individual suppliers no longer come to Mount Sinai to deliver the items they have sold the hospital. Rather, all suppliers deliver their products to Livingston Healthcare Services Inc. in Oakville. Livingston then stores these items and fills Mount Sinai's orders once each day. The orders are put into plastic boxes that are delivered to specific nursing stations at the hospital.

Formerly, the hospital spent about $33 million on supplies; of that, about 18 percent was for medical and surgical products. But only $28 million actually went to suppliers. The other $5 million was spent on salaries for hospital workers who managed the supplies once they got to the hospital.

A typical product, for example, was brought in, unpacked, and stored in the central store room. Then someone from one of the nursing stations would come to the store room, put the product on a cart, take it to the nursing station, unload it, and store it again. By the time the product was used on a patient, it might have been handled 20 times. The new system eliminates most of those steps. Now, all the items needed by a certain nursing station come in one bundle from Livingston.

The new system is highly computerized. Clerks carry scanners as they tour the stockrooms for each nursing station. Each product has a bar code and the computer indicates how many of that item are in stock. If more product is needed, the number is transmitted to the hospital's central computer. The computer assembles data from all the nursing stations and transmits a blanket order to Livingston's warehouse and distribution centre. If there is a crisis, Livingston can deliver within one hour.

How did Mount Sinai come up with the stockless system of materials management? Several years ago, when the hospital decided to overhaul its materials management system, it set up a committee to decide on a new system. That committee included everyone who was involved in ordering, handling, and paying for medical supplies—nurses, stockroom people, accountants, and ward clerks. The director of materials management says the new system was implemented smoothly because the people who had to use it had been involved in designing the system.

In the first year using the new system, Mount Sinai saved about $200 000. Seven full-time stocking employees were shifted to other work. The hospital also now has 5000 square feet of vacant space. This could mean additional savings of $750 000. The hospital is also looking at expanding the system to include food service, drugs, and laboratory testing.

MRP uses a **bill of materials** that is basically a "recipe" for the finished product. It specifies the necessary ingredients (raw materials and components), the order in which they should be combined, and the quantity of each ingredient needed to make one "batch" of the product (say, 2000 finished telephones). The recipe is fed into a computer that controls inventory and schedules each stage of production. The result is fewer early arrivals, less frequent stock shortages, and lower storage costs. MRP is most popular among companies whose products require complicated assembly and fabrication activities, such as automobile manufacturers, appliance makers, and furniture companies.

Manufacturing resource planning, also called **MRP II**, is an advanced version of MRP that ties together all parts of the organization into the company's production activities. For example, MRP inventory and production schedules are translated into cost requirements for the financial management department and personnel requirements for the human resources department; information on capacity availability for new-customer orders goes to the marketing department.

bill of materials
A "recipe" for production of a "batch" of a good that specifies the resources needed and the method of combining those resources.

MRP II (manufacturing resource planning)
An advanced version of MRP that ties together all parts of the organization into the company's production activities.

quality control
The management of the production process so as to manufacture goods or supply services that meet specific quality standards.

Toshiba
www.toshiba.co.jp/index.htm

Quality Control. Not all production control tools focus on inventory control. Also important is **quality control**: the management of the production process so as to manufacture goods or supply services that meet specific quality standards. McDonald's, for example, has been a pioneer in quality control in the restaurant industry since the 1950s. The company oversees everything from the farming of potatoes for french fries to the packing of meat for Big Macs. Quality-assurance staffers even check standards for ketchup sweetness and french fry length.

In their quest for quality control, many businesses have adopted *quality-improvement teams* (patterned after the Japanese concept of *quality circles*): groups of employees from various work areas who define, analyze, and solve common production problems. Teams meet regularly to discuss problems and to keep management informed of the group's progress in addressing various issues.

Many companies report that improvement teams have not only raised quality levels but increased productivity and reduced costs. They have also improved job satisfaction. But improvement teams also involve risks. Not all employees, for example, want to participate. Moreover, management cannot always adopt group recommendations, no matter how much careful thought, hard work, and enthusiasm went into them. The challenge for production managers, then, is to make wise decisions about when and how to use quality-improvement teams. (Quality control and quality-improvement teams are discussed in more detail in Chapter 11.)

Worker Training. Many experts point out that it is misleading—and potentially dangerous—to reduce productivity to quantitative measures. Productivity often depends on the effective use of a firm's human resources. At Japan's electronics giant Toshiba, for instance, President Fumio Sato saw the company's problem as a need to produce a greater variety of products on shorter production runs. At Toshiba's factory in Ome, therefore, workers on one production line are now trained to make nine different word processors, while workers on another line can make 20 different laptop computers. Although workers normally switch products after batches of 20, they are flexible enough to turn out lots as small as 10. In an industry in which the life cycle for a low-priced computer may actually be only months, this kind of flexibility is crucial in preventing overproduction and bloated inventories.[13]

When considering production control for services, it is important to remember that most services are delivered by people. In other words, service-system employees are both producers and salespeople. Naturally, human relations skills are vital for anyone who has contact with the public. If customer-contact employees lack the proper skills in direct communication, high-contact businesses such as airlines, employment agencies, and hotels will lose customers to competitors who have done a better job of training workers in those skills. In addition, an increasingly important human relations skill in today's marketplace is the ability to interact effectively with customers from different cultures.

In low-contact services operations, technical skills are more important than human relations skills. As a consumer, you probably do not care whether your local TV repairperson is very personable. But in high-contact service operations, human relations skills are more important. A student's counselling session, for example, is much more enjoyable when the academic counsellor is cheerful and pleasant. In most high-contact operations, a pleased customer is more likely to return.

Completing the Operations Management Process: Feedback

Production management does not stop when the goods go out the door or even when they are purchased. Feedback from consumers, the final phase, influences every other part of production management. Comments from users may lead managers to plan smaller or larger production runs. Consumer enthusiasm may dictate a speed-up in master schedules that calls for opening new plants or hiring more workers. Negative criticism of quality may cause managers to seek new production methods and to tighten controls. Because it is consumers—and their "dollar votes"—who determine the success or failure of a company, managers have little choice but to heed customer feedback.

■ THE FUTURE OF OPERATIONS MANAGEMENT

As Canadian businesses struggle to survive in fiercely competitive world markets, operations management becomes more and more crucial. Lagging productivity has put some Canadian industries at a disadvantage in pricing their goods for world markets. In their battle for lower production costs, higher productivity, and higher quality, more and more managers are turning to mechanization and automation of the operations process, especially with computers.

Mechanization and Automation

Using machines to do work previously done by people is the process of **mechanization**. Its natural extension is **automation**, performing mechanical operations with either minimal or no human intervention. These techniques are not new, of course. The Industrial Revolution began with huge spinning and weaving machines that soon rendered handmade fabric obsolete. Nearly every company in the world uses some machinery in place of hand labour. Some of the most advanced firms are using sophisticated robots in production. Many small firms have automated at least to the degree that personal computer systems monitor production outcomes.

The replacement of manual labour by machinery has been a source of ethical controversy for years. Advocates of labour, for example, contend that jobs are sometimes replaced unnecessarily. Critics have also charged that businesses sometimes use the threat of mechanization to gain wage concessions.

mechanization
The process of using machines instead of people to perform tasks.

automation
The process of performing mechanical operations with minimal or no human involvement.

Computers and Robotics

Computers stand at the forefront of modern automation. Companies use computers to construct detailed schedules, to monitor production, and to help determine raw material needs. In some firms, computers track customer orders as they move through the plant. Computers may also send production information to managers in various departments so that they know how much work is coming, what materials will be needed, and when each job must be completed. When Federal Express picks up a package, for example, the destination is read immediately by a portable scanner. This information then enters the Federal Express computer and is electronically transmitted to the central routing hub in Memphis. With this advance information, the facility can schedule its vehicles out of Memphis to other cities even before it receives incoming packages.

Federal Express
www.fedex.com

Robotics and Computer-Integrated Manufacturing.   Although Japanese companies pioneered their use, Canadian firms are becoming increasingly interested in **robotics**, the construction, maintenance, and use of computer-controlled machines in manufacturing operations. Automobile plants use robots to weld, assemble, paint, and inspect cars. Aircraft manufacturing plants are also using robotics to build planes faster and at less cost than humans can. Still, as the box "Robots: Mixed Success" discusses, robots have not yet found acceptance in many firms.

Robotics are only one part of a larger manufacturing automation system called **computer-integrated manufacturing (CIM)**. In addition to controlling robots, CIM can manage material requirements planning and just-in-time inventory systems.

robotics
The use of computer-controlled machines that perform production tasks.

computer-integrated manufacturing (CIM)
Computer systems that drive robots and control the flow of materials and supplies in the goods production process.

TRENDS & CHALLENGES

Robots: Mixed Success

Industrial robots are not the glamorous creations usually pictured in science fiction movies. Rather, they are machines that are programmed to repeat tirelessly the chores common in industry. At present, robots are used most frequently in the automobile industry for such tasks as welding, painting, and metalworking.

The first fully computerized robotic paint shop for railroad cars in North America was opened on October 5, 1988, at Canadian National Railway's Winnipeg Transcona shops. The system cleans and repaints CN's 11 500 covered hopper cars which transport bulk commodities like grain and potash. The shops process about 1100 cars per year, four times more than under the old manual system.

Harber Manufacturing, a Fort Erie, Ontario, manufacturer of wood-burning stoves, uses several different types of robots in its manufacturing processes. Five arc-welding robot systems—each costing over $100 000—join metal seams together in a continuous weld. Programmable platforms are also used to move raw materials within the reach of the arc-welding robots.

Robots were supposed to revolutionize the workplace, performing all the mundane and dangerous tasks from welding bolts to handling radioactive isotopes. Yet today, Canadian and American businesses employ only a fraction of the number used in Japan. Why so few electronic helpers? The answer lies in three problems: cost, complexity, and technical limitations.

Cost has kept robots out of many smaller enterprises. A hydraulic robot from Unimation, the leader in robotics, runs $30 000 to $200 000. Even smaller, less powerful robots from Japan can cost up to $40 000 each. With a price tag of $25 000 each, a HelpMate nurse's aid robot from TRC will pay for itself in two and a half years—if it's used 24 hours a day, seven days a week, 52 weeks a year.

Larger companies have often found that the initial purchase cost is the cheapest part of robotics. A company installing robotics needs computer scientists to program and reprogram robots. And before that, it needs to perform exhaustive studies to determine the precise task to be accomplished. As well, workers must be trained to operate and work with robots.

Human beings are still vastly superior to robots in a great many regards, especially in tasks requiring sensory input and adaptation. The most sophisticated robots today cannot read handwriting or pick a single right part out of a box of wrong ones. A few can recognize about 20 slightly different shapes as airplanes. Humans can identify thousands of slightly different shapes as planes. As one researcher notes, one human eye has about "100 million vision cells and four layers of neurons, all capable of doing about 10 billion calculations a second." In other words, the visual calculations of a one-eyed human being would take 100 000 supercomputers to imitate.

Perhaps one reason why Japanese businesses use more robots is that they expect less of them. In Japan, robots are used for the most simple, most mindless, most limited of tasks. The preponderance of such tasks in the auto industry (along with the enormous economic and technical resources of such companies) may explain why more than 50 percent of robots in use in Canada are in auto plants versus 10 percent in Japan.

The future of robotics in Canada may depend on recognizing where it can be most useful. Already, robots are making inroads into fields dangerous to humans. Submersible robots are replacing divers in offshore oil and gas operations. They toil for hours in areas of nuclear power plants where once humans worked in very short relays to minimize their exposure to radiation. Cyberworks Inc. is a Canadian manufacturer of robots. While the growth in demand for industrial robots has been slower than expected, the company believes robots will eventually be widely used in space exploration, undersea work, underground mining, and in nuclear waste facilities.

As they become more aware of the special capabilities of robots, more mundane businesses may be willing to take a chance. Robots never get a backache from stooping. Their arms and wrists can twist around completely. A robot watchguard with microwave vision can see through nonmetallic walls and spot an intruder 40 metres away in the dark. And those challenged had better give the right password. Robots still have no sense of humour.

Canadian National Railway
www.cn.ca

Computer-Aided Design and Manufacturing. The use of computers in manufacturing is not limited to robots and inventory control. Some of the most exciting uses of computers

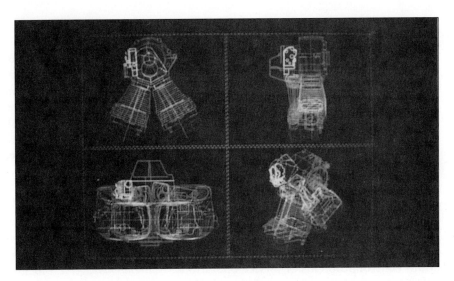

A CAD system displays four different views of this gasoline engine, allowing its design to be easily examined and modified.

in production are in the areas of computer-aided design (CAD) and computer-aided manufacturing (CAM), known collectively as CAD/CAM.

As its name suggests, **computer-aided design** uses computers to design new products. Through the use of sophisticated analysis methods and graphics, CAD allows users to create a design and simulate conditions to test the performance of the design, all within the computer. Engineers use CAD to design planes and cars. CAD systems let designers see the result of changes in design without having to create costly prototype models and test them under real-world conditions.

computer-aided design (CAD)
Computer analysis and graphics programs that are used to create new products.

In a direct offshoot of computer-aided design, **computer-aided manufacturing** uses computers to design and control the equipment needed in the manufacturing process. For example, CAM systems can produce tapes to control all the machines and robots on a production line. Overall, CAD/CAM is useful for engineers in a manufacturing environment to design and test new products and then to design the machines and tools to manufacture the new product.

computer-aided manufacturing (CAM)
Computer systems used to design and control all the equipment and tools for producing goods.

Decision Support Systems.   A new development in the evolution of *management information systems* has had an impact on manufacturing and production. Computer programs called **decision support systems (DSS)** give users easy access to decision models and data to help them make decisions on complicated problems. DSS allows users to investigate conveniently "What if?" questions. "What if the company decides to order twice as much raw material as needed—will we need more warehousing space?" "What if the company purchases 10 additional robots—will we be able to cut some of our present workforce?" "What if the company adds more flexible automation—will sales go up?"

decision support systems (DSS)
Computer systems used to help managers consider alternatives when making decisions on complicated problems.

SUMMARY OF LEARNING OBJECTIVES

1. **Identify the characteristics that distinguish *service operations* from *goods production*.**   Although the creation of both goods and services involves resources, transformations, and finished products, service operations differ from goods manufacturing in several important ways. Services are typically performed, but goods are produced. Services are largely *intangible* and *unstorable* and are more likely to be *customized* to meet the purchaser's needs. In addition, service production often requires the presence of the customer.

2. **Describe the factors involved in *operations planning* and *scheduling*.** *Operations planning* involves the analysis of five key factors. In *capacity planning*, the firm analyzes how much of a product to produce to stay just ahead of normal demand. *Location planning* for goods involves analyzing proposed facility sites in terms of proximity to raw materials and markets, availability of labour, energy and transportation costs, regulations and taxes, and community living conditions. Location planning for high-contact services involves locating the service near consumers. *Layout planning* involves designing a facility so as to enhance the production efficiency. In *quality planning*, systems are developed to ensure that products meet a firm's quality standards. Finally, in *methods planning*, specific production steps and methods for performing them are identified. Once plans identify needed resources and specify means of using them, production timetables are developed in the form of schedules.

3. **Explain the activities involved in *operations control*, including *materials management* and the use of *production control tools*, and describe the special operations control problems of service operations.** *Materials management* focuses on the control of *transportation, warehousing, inventory control*, and *purchasing*. These managers must also establish positive relationships with suppliers. To control inventory, they must balance *holding costs* with setup costs. Techniques such as *just-in-time (JIT) production systems* and *material requirements planning (MRP)* can assist managers in inventory control. The use of *quality circles* and worker training programs can assist in quality control. Special production control problems in service organizations derive from the unique characteristics of services, including the need for customization, the unstorability of services, and customer involvement.

4. **Characterize the kinds of *automation* currently in use in production operations.** *Automation* is the process of performing mechanical operations with either minimal or no human involvement. This process is changing the face of production operations in many areas. In a process called *computer-integrated manufacturing (CIM)*, computers drive *robots* to perform a variety of tasks and to control the flow of materials and supplies. CIM also integrates *computer-aided design (CAD)*, which uses computers to design new products, and *computer-aided manufacturing (CAM)*, which uses computers to design and control manufacturing equipment.

STUDY QUESTIONS AND EXERCISES

Review Questions

1. Explain how General Motors of Canada provides different forms of utility to its customers.

2. How does a process layout differ from a product layout? How does a fixed-position layout differ from a customer-oriented layout?

3. What is the difference between a high-contact and low-contact service?

4. What are the advantages of a flexible manufacturing system?

5. List and briefly describe several tools that are available to managers to assist them in production control.

Analysis Questions

6. Find examples of a synthetic production process and an analytic process. Then classify each according to whether it is chemical, fabrication, assembly, transport, or clerical. Explain your analysis.

7. Compare service and manufacturing operations.

8. Recall that there are three production-control problems inherent in service operations: customization, unstorability, and customer involvement. Choose three different services and analyze each in terms of these problems.

Application Exercises

9. Select two manufacturers, a large one and a small one, in your community and compare the methods they use to get good quality in their products. Contrast the kinds of problems they face in assuring high product quality.

10. Select a high-contact industry. Write an advertisement to hire workers for this business. Draw up a plan for motivating the hired workers to produce high-quality services for the firm.

BUILDING YOUR BUSINESS SKILLS

Goal

To encourage students to apply the concept of customization to an entrepreneurial idea.

Situation

Imagine that you are an entrepreneur with the desire to start your own service business. You are intrigued with the idea of creating some kind of customized one-on-one service that would appeal to baby boomers, who traditionally have been pampered, and working women, who have little time to get things done.

Method

Step 1: Come together with three or four other students to brainstorm business ideas that would appeal to harried working people. Among the ideas to consider are:

*   A concierge service in office buildings that would handle such personal and business services as arranging children's birthday parties and booking guest speakers for business luncheons.

*   A personal image consultation service aimed at helping clients improve their appearance, personal etiquette, and presentation style.

*   A mobile pet care network in which veterinarians and personal groomers make house calls.

Step 2: Choose an idea from these or others you might think of. Then write a memo explaining why you think your idea will succeed. Research may be necessary as you target:

*   A specific demographic group or groups. (Who are your customers and why would they buy your service?)

*   The features that make your service attractive to this group.

*   The social factors in your local community that would lead to success.

Follow-Up Questions

1. Why is the customization of and easy access to personal services so attractive as we approach the 21st century?

2. As services are personalized, do you think quality will become more or less important? Why?

3. Why does the trend to personalized, one-on-one service present unique opportunities for entrepreneurs?

4. In a personal one-on-one business, how important are the human relations skills of those delivering the service? Can you make an argument that they are more important than the service itself?

Prentice Hall

TAKE IT TO THE NET

Check out our Companion Website

for this chapter's Exploring the Net exercise, featuring product operations at Dofasco's Website and other intriguing, annotated destinations. You'll also find practice exercises, updated Weblinks from the text, links to newsgroups, updates, and more.

www.prenticehall.ca/ebert

BUSINESS CASE 10

Honda's "Global" Accord: A Customization Breakthrough

Even at the end of its four-year sales cycle, the 1997 model Honda Accord was still among the best-selling cars in North America, testimony to the brand's enormous and continuing popularity with baby boomers. Honda hopes to do even better with its newest Accord, which it will parlay into customized vehicles for several distinct global markets thanks to a revolutionary production change.

The Japanese automaker plans to base seven new Accords on a single innovative platform or frame (the most expensive part of any new car design) that can readily be shrunk or expanded to accommodate car bodies of varying sizes. The cars will range from a midsize American sedan to a sporty Japanese compact, a narrow European model, a minivan, a sport utility vehicle, and even two luxury cars. Honda's production breakthrough will allow it to differentiate each one of these cars from the others, inside and out.

By customizing the Accord, its maker hopes to increase market share worldwide, as it has already done in the United States. "Honda has come up with the best approach for going global," according to auto consultant Christopher Cedergren. "They can easily and inexpensively customize and design products for each market around the world." In the United States, Honda expects the customization to save about 20 percent of its production cost per vehicle, enabling it to keep the sticker price for the U.S. sedan at its current level (about U.S.$15 500) while increasing interior room and adding new features.

Other manufacturers have tried to capture a global market, but with a single car shipped around the world. Industry observers say Honda's advantage is in recognizing that North American drivers want different features than do Europeans—who don't want the same driving experience as Asians—and in coming up with a manufacturing solution to the problem of satisfying them all. Remarkably, the switchover to manufacturing the new model Accord was accomplished in 20 days (while the old model was still rolling off the production line) and required no layoffs or shutdowns.

With a much smaller research budget than its rival automakers ($2.1 billion compared to GM's $9 billion, for instance), Honda had a big incentive to innovate. Analysts think the bill for developing the new Accord may total $600 million, not bad compared with $2.6 billion for the Ford Taurus. So far, the gamble seems to be paying off.

■ Case Questions

1. How will Honda succeed in correctly customizing each of its new Accords? How can it ensure that it does not alienate trade-in customers who like the old model?

2. Toyota's Sienna minivan is based on the Camry chassis. Would you expect other competitors to try to adapt Honda's new production technology in their own bids for a global car? Why or why not?

3. What alternative strategies might competitors use instead of customization? What are their advantages and disadvantages?

4. North American automakers have been less successful at cutting costs than either Toyota or Honda. How can Honda promote its efficient cost management as a marketing strategy? Why might such a strategy also be dangerous?

11

INCREASING PRODUCTIVITY AND QUALITY

DELL SPEEDS ITS WAY TO QUALITY

Dell Computer is one of the fastest growing high-tech firms in North America. Starting from nothing in 1984, the company's sales revenues reached $3.5 billion in 1994 and $12 billion in 1997. How has this company grown so big so fast? Simple. It takes customer orders over the phone, then ships high-quality, low-priced computers within 48 hours of receiving the order. And the computers are custom-built to the customers' specifications (including the software the customer wants). Dell is able to do this in spite of the fact that it sells millions of computers each year.

Dell has never done business in quite the way that other computer makers have. Dell puts its capital and energy into activities that add value for its customers. It doesn't *produce* chips or monitors; rather, it buys them (and lots of other components) from other companies that specialize in making them. Dell focuses instead on high-efficiency *assembling* of components and creating custom-built computers for customers.

CEO Michael Dell stresses a few key production principles that drive productivity up and keep costs and inventories low. Perhaps the most important one is *speed*. Just-in-time manufacturing (see Chapter 10) has always been important in the firm, and Dell has recently extended this concept to its suppliers. It now requires its supply chain to warehouse most computer components within 15 minutes of its factories in Texas, Ireland, and Malaysia, and it has dropped suppliers who can't comply.

The key is to keep inventory moving quickly through the system. Maintaining a minimum supply of inventory is important in a field where rapid change is occurring. Suppose Dell has 10 days of inventory while a competitor has 50. When a new chip hits the market, Dell will be incorporating that new chip into its custom-built computers 40 days before its competitor will.

When Dell has a really reliable, high-quality supplier like Sony, it doesn't keep any inventory at all. It doesn't even test the monitor it uses. Dell just picks the monitors up from Sony at the rate it needs them. This helps Dell get the product from the end of Sony's production line to Dell's customers faster.

Because Dell doesn't even buy components until it receives an order for one of its computers, it realizes big savings on parts, whose prices can drop almost overnight. Speed also counts in receiving the customer's cash. Dell collects on sales faster than the competition, averaging 24 hours from order to cash. That's days sooner than its rivals Gateway and Compaq.

Close customer relations allow Dell to increase the value it delivers. Taking custom orders over the phone means that Dell knows exactly what kind of computer each customer has.

This is very useful if the customer calls in to ask a question about the computer. At Dell, the customer is in control. The company sees its job as taking the latest technology and applying it in such a way that the customer benefits. The company is not trying to develop new computer architecture; rather, it wants to improve the user's experience with computers. The Research and Development group at Dell therefore focuses on process and quality improvements in manufacturing.

Dell is also making a big splash on the Internet, writing up $3 million a day worth of orders from its Website. It is now the number one PC retailer on the Web, and sales are growing at the astounding rate of 20 percent a *month*. In fact, Dell has led the way to a whole new world of selling: Direct buyers of computers now account for a third of all new PC sales, double the number of just a few years ago.

Michael Dell says that speed is critical in the computer business, and that the company is setting the pace for the industry. With the firm's stock price continuing to climb, it seems that investors as well as customers agree that Dell has figured out how to achieve an enviable mix of productivity and quality.

Dell Computer Corporation
www.dell.com

It is no secret that *productivity* and *quality* are the watchwords of the 1990s. Companies are not only measuring productivity and insisting on improvements, they are also insisting that quality means bringing to market products that satisfy customers, improve sales, and boost profits.

By focusing on the learning objectives of this chapter, you will better understand the increasingly important concepts of productivity and quality. After reading this chapter you should be able to:

1. Describe the connection between *productivity* and *quality*.
2. Understand the importance of increasing productivity.
3. Explain *total* and *partial measures of productivity* and how they are used to keep track of national, industrywide, and companywide productivity.
4. Identify the activities involved in *total quality management* and describe four tools that companies can use to achieve it.
5. List six ways in which companies can compete by improving productivity and quality.

■ THE PRODUCTIVITY-QUALITY CONNECTION

productivity
A measure of efficiency that compares how much is produced with the resources used to produce it.

As we saw in Chapter 1, **productivity** is a measure of economic performance. It measures how much is produced relative to the resources used to produce it. The more we are able to produce the right things while using fewer resources, the more productivity grows and everyone—the economy, businesses, and workers—benefits.

Notice that productivity considers both the amounts and the quality of what is produced. By using resources more efficiently, the quantity of output will be greater. But unless the resulting goods and services are of satisfactory quality (the "right things"), consumers will not want them. **Quality**, then, means fitness for use—offering features that consumers want.

quality
A product's fitness for use in terms of offering the features that consumers want.

The importance of quality in productivity cannot be overstated. Poor quality has created competitive problems for Canadian firms that have focused only on efficiency (quantity). Businesses in other countries have emphasized both efficiency and quality and consequently have increased productivity more rapidly than Canadian companies.

■ MEETING THE PRODUCTIVITY CHALLENGE

Productivity is an international issue with major domestic effects. A nation's productivity determines how large a piece of the global economic resource pie it gets. A country with more resources has more wealth to divide among its citizens. A country whose productivity fails to increase as rapidly as that of other countries will see its people's standard of living fall relative to the rest of the world.

Nations also care about domestic productivity regardless of their standing versus other nations. A country that makes more out of its existing resources (increases its productivity) can increase the wealth of all its inhabitants if it so chooses. But a productivity decline shrinks a nation's available resources so that any one person's increase in wealth can come only at the expense of others in the society. In addition, investors, suppliers, managers, and workers are all concerned about the productivity of specific industries, companies, departments, and individuals.

Canadian workers, managers, and investors are particularly concerned about recent trends in Canadian productivity. For decades, Canadian products have done well in world markets. Recently, however, foreign competitors have made significant inroads.

Productivity Trends

The United States remains the most productive nation in the world. In 1996, for instance, the value of goods and services produced by each U.S. worker was $63 900. This current **level of productivity** is higher than that of any other country. In second place, French and Belgian workers produced $61 000 per worker, followed by Italian workers at $59 100. Canadian workers produced $56 700.[1]

level of productivity
Dollar value of goods and services relative to the resources used to produce them.

Slower Growth Rates.   Many Canadians are alarmed by the slowdown in our **growth rate of productivity**—the annual increase in a nation's output over the previous year. Canadian productivity has also slowed in comparison with that of other countries. The Conference Board of Canada released a report in 1997 showing that output per person in the U.S., for example, was one-third higher than output per person in Canada.[2] The report also noted that Canada's rate of productivity growth has been slow for 25 years.

growth rate of productivity
The increase in productivity in a given year over the previous year.

Difference Between the Manufacturing and Service Sectors.   Manufacturing productivity is higher than service productivity. Thus, manufacturing is primarily responsible for recent rises in the nation's overall productivity. With services growing as a proportion of Canadian businesses, productivity *must* increase more rapidly in that sector in the years ahead if Canada is to keep its edge. The box "Suggestions for Improving Canada's International Competitiveness" gives additional ideas for productivity improvements for Canada's industry in general.

Industry Productivity

In addition to differences between the manufacturing and service sectors, industries within these sectors differ vastly in terms of productivity. Agriculture is more productive in Canada than in many other nations because we use more sophisticated technology and superior natural resources. Technological advances have also given the computer industry a productivity edge in many areas. But investment in automated equipment—and thus productivity—in the automobile and steel industries has lagged behind that of other nations.

TRENDS & CHALLENGES

Suggestions for Improving Canada's International Competitiveness

In October 1991, Michael Porter, a business professor at Harvard University and an internationally recognized expert on competitiveness, released a report. In it he claims that Canada will have to stop living off its rich diet of natural resources and start emphasizing innovation and a more sophisticated mix of products if it hopes to be successful in international markets. He notes that one-third of Canada's total exports in 1989 were unprocessed or semiprocessed natural resources. In other words, Canadian industry has not upgraded or extended its competitive advantage into processing technology and the marketing of more sophisticated resource-based products. The proportion of Canadian exports based on resources is higher than in many industrialized countries, including the U.S., Japan, Germany, Britain, Korea, and Sweden.

Porter points out that nostalgic thinking about the "good old days" before free trade is not productive, and that rescinding the Canada–U.S. Free Trade Agreement will not make everything better. He says there can be no turning back and that old attitudes and practices inconsistent with international competitiveness will have to go.

The study criticizes Canadian business, government, and labour for their failure to abandon outdated ways of thinking regarding productivity and innovation. Porter makes the following recommendations to these groups:

To Business

- Compete based on innovation and cost, not simply cost.

- Concentrate on products with a lasting competitive edge.
- Spend more money on employee training.
- Finance university research to ensure that more of it is relevant.
- Base employee compensation on corporate performance.
- Stop relying on government assistance.

To Government

- Provide more training for the unemployed.
- Set higher national education standards.
- Finance university programs that are oriented towards competitiveness.
- Introduce stricter product standards to force Canadian companies to meet world product standards.
- Expand apprenticeship programs.

To Labour

- Recognize that, in the long run, the best guarantee of good wages is competitive corporate activities such as productivity enhancement programs.
- Help company management identify and remove barriers to productivity.
- Support broadening workers' skills.
- Take a more collaborative approach to union-management relations.

The productivity of specific industries concerns many people for different reasons. Labour unions need to take it into account in negotiating contracts, since highly productive industries can give raises more easily than can less productive industries. Investors and suppliers consider industry productivity when making loans, buying securities, and planning their own future production. Areas that have long depended on steel and auto plants have experienced economic and social devastation as a result of plant closings, layoffs, and closings of related businesses.

Company Productivity

High productivity gives a company a competitive edge because its costs are lower. As a result, it can offer its product at a lower price (and gain more customers), or it can make a greater profit on each item sold. Increased productivity also allows companies to pay workers higher wages without raising prices.

As a result, the productivity of individual companies is also important to investors, workers, and managers. Comparing the productivity of several companies in the same industry helps investors in buying and selling stocks. Employee profit-sharing plans are often based on the company's productivity improvements each year. And managers use information about productivity trends to plan for new products, factories, and funds to stay competitive in the years ahead.

Department and Individual Productivity

Within companies, managers are concerned with the productivity of various divisions, departments, workstations, and individuals. Improved productivity in any of these areas can improve a firm's overall productivity. An overemphasis on the performance of individuals and departments, however, tends to discourage working together as a team for overall company improvement. For this reason, many companies are cautious about using departmental and individual productivity measures.

■ MEASURING PRODUCTIVITY

To improve productivity, we must first measure it. Otherwise, we will not be able to tell whether a program has increased productivity.

Total and Partial Measures of Productivity

Every productivity measure is a ratio of outputs to inputs. The outputs are the value of goods and services produced. The inputs are the value of the resources used to create the outputs. In selecting a productivity measure, managers must decide which inputs are most important for their business. The choice of inputs (factors) determines the specific measure.

In some cases, all inputs are equally important, so managers use a **total factor productivity ratio**, which can be expressed as

$$\text{Productivity} = \frac{\text{Outputs}}{\text{Labour} + \text{Capital} + \text{Materials} + \text{Energy inputs}}$$

total factor productivity ratio
A measure of a firm's overall productivity calculated as outputs divided by all inputs.

If an insurance company sold $10 million in policies and used $2 million of resources to do so, its total factor productivity would be 5.

Total factor measures can become complicated because of the different inputs involved. It is difficult to find comparable measures for energy consumption, capital, labour, and material. For some purposes, **partial productivity ratios**—which ignore some factors—may be best. For example, **materials productivity** (a partial productivity ratio) may be a fairly good measure of overall productivity in non-labour-intensive industries. Expenditures for equipment are also a more significant cost in many of these firms. Materials and equipment, not labour, constitute over 90 percent of operating costs in highly automated oil refineries, chemical companies, and manufacturing plants.

partial productivity ratio
A measure of a firm's overall productivity based on the productivity of its most significant input; calculated as total outputs divided by the selected input.

materials productivity
A partial productivity ratio calculated as total outputs divided by materials inputs.

$$\text{Productivity} = \frac{\text{Outputs}}{\text{Materials}}$$

If a chemical plant uses eight tonnes of chemicals to produce two tonnes of insecticide, its materials productivity is 0.25.

National Productivity Measures

labour productivity
A partial productivity ratio calculated as total outputs divided ① by labour inputs for a company and as gross domestic product ② divided by the total number of workers for a nation.

gross domestic product (GDP)
The value of all goods and services produced by an economy.

At one time, partial ratios of labour productivity were the measure typically used by most nations. A country's **labour productivity** is usually calculated as

$$\frac{\text{Gross domestic product}}{\text{Total number of workers}}$$

The total number of workers in this equation represents the nation's total labour input. (Sometimes the total hours worked, not the number of workers, is used as the input in figuring labour productivity.) **Gross domestic product (GDP)**—the value of all goods and services produced in the economy—represents the nation's total output.

During the period 1982–97, Canada's overall labour productivity increased about 1.2 percent each year. In the goods-producing sector, the increase averaged 1.8 percent, while in the services-producing sector the increase averaged only 0.8 percent.[3]

Labour productivity measures are popular because they are easy to calculate and compare. Most governments keep records on gross domestic product and adjust them for inflation. The resulting constant-dollar data permit reliable year-to-year comparisons of national and international productivity changes. But as labour-intensive industries become less important, other measures, such as materials productivity, capital productivity, and even total factor productivity are coming into wider use.

Sector and Industry Productivity Measures

In addition to national productivity measures, we need to determine the productivity of various sectors and industries in order to isolate and solve productivity problems.

The rise in labour productivity among manufacturing workers does not necessarily mean that they are working harder or better than service workers, whose productivity is stagnating. More often, labour productivity increases because other, non-labour resources are added. The use of more capital—modernized trucks, machinery, and office equipment—often increases labour productivity by enabling fewer workers to accomplish more.

capital productivity
A partial productivity ratio calculated as total outputs divided by capital inputs.

Is the additional capital investment worth the cost? To see, we need to look at capital productivity. **Capital productivity** is the ratio of outputs (the value of all goods and services) divided by the capital inputs for all firms.

An employee observes a robot's movements at a nuclear laboratory. Properly used, robots can perform dangerous tasks more safely than humans.

Company Productivity Measures

Many companies have established productivity measures for individual divisions, plants, departments, and even jobs. Goals for productivity improvements are set in the areas of greatest importance. They serve as guidelines for workplace changes and performance evaluations. For example, an automated, petroleum-fuelled factory may place high priority on energy productivity. Its major goal, therefore, might be to raise the level of its sales per barrel of consumed fuel from $200 to $220. Employees would thus seek ways to conserve fuel while maintaining or increasing production and sales.

By contrast, a labour-intensive restaurant might use the dollar amount of food served per server as its main productivity measure. If it offers servers incentives to increase sales, they will encourage customers to order tempting (and highly profitable) specialties, drinks, and desserts.

Dividing a company's total profit by the number of employees it has gives us one measure of productivity, "profit per employee." In 1994, of the 50 largest companies in Canada in terms of employees, four firms exceeded $20 000 profit per employee. All of these were banks.[4]

■TOTAL QUALITY MANAGEMENT

It is no longer enough for businesses to simply measure productivity in terms of numbers of items produced. They must also take into account quality. But Canadian business has not always recognized the importance of quality.

In the decades after World War II, American business consultant W. Edwards Deming tried to persuade U.S. firms that they needed to improve quality at least as much as quantity. Like many a prophet, he was not honoured in his homeland. But his arguments won over the Japanese. Through years of meticulous hard work, Japan's manufacturers have changed "Made in Japan" from a synonym for cheap, shoddy merchandise into a hallmark of reliability.

Many of the quality assurance programs that are integral to the modern Japanese production system were Deming's brainchildren. And Japan's highest honour for industrial achievement is the Deming Award for Quality. It took the economic troubles of the 1970s and 1980s for Deming's ideas to gain acceptance in Canada and the United States.

In the automobile industry in the 1980s, Japanese firms held a big lead in quality. North American manufacturers have closed that gap, but the Japanese are ahead once again in the area of customer service. Nissan, for example, has formed a Satisfaction Department that coordinates training for their 4000 Canadian dealers, salespeople, and employees. It even determines bonuses based on customer satisfaction ratings rather than sales volume.[5]

European businesses have also recognized the importance of the quality message. In 1988, executives from Olivetti, Renault, and other companies established the European Foundation for Quality Management (EFQM). The stated mission of the organization is to increase quality awareness and to promote quality in goods and services throughout European enterprise. Today, EFQM has more than 160 member companies that all face the difficult challenge of producing high-quality products and services for customers across a continent with diverse languages, cultures, and economies.

European Foundation for Quality Management (EFQM)
www.euroqual.org/eqo/efqm/efqm.htm

Emphasis on quality manufacturing in Canada is increasing, as is evidenced by the Gold Plant Quality Award given to the workers of Toyota's Cambridge, Ontario, plant in 1991 and 1995. This award honours the plant as the top-quality producer of automobiles in North America. The award is proof of Toyota's emphasis on *kaizen* (the continual search for improvement) and *jidoka* (defect detection). But there is still room for improvement. In a recent survey of consumers in 20 different countries, Canada came in sixth in the overall quality of its products. Japan was first, Germany second, and the U.S. third.[6]

The perception of quality is also important. Canadian wines are turned back at European ports because the Economic Community maintains that Canada does not have a proper quality control system for its wines. This happens despite the recent prestigious award won by Inniskillen Wines Inc. at the Bordeaux Vin Expo against more than 4000 entries.[7]

Today, many Canadian companies recognize that quality products are a must. But they have found that producing quality goods and services requires an effort from all parts of the business. **Total quality management (TQM)** emphasizes that no defects are tolerable and that all employees are responsible for maintaining quality standards. At Toyota's Cambridge, Ontario, assembly plant, for example, workers can push a button or pull a rope to stop the production line when something is not up to standard.[8] The box "TQM at Standard Aero" shows how the concept was introduced at one Canadian company.

total quality management (TQM)
A concept that emphasizes that no defects are tolerable and that all employees are responsible for maintaining quality standards.

TRENDS & CHALLENGES

TQM at Standard Aero Ltd.

In 1991, the U.S. Air Force visited Standard Aero in Winnipeg, Manitoba. Standard had submitted a bid to overhaul aircraft that undercut its competitors by more than 50 percent, and the Air Force wanted to see the firm's factory before it signed the contract. They must have liked what they saw, because Standard got the contract. What the Air Force didn't know was that the impetus for the bid came not from Standard's managers (who were concerned about the size of the contract), but from shop floor employees.

Standard Aero has made TQM work where other companies have failed because it is dedicated to an often overlooked tenet of TQM: The only definition of quality that really counts is "what the customer wants." Standard employees talk to customers to find out exactly what they expect from the firm's work. Top management is also committed to TQM, has spent $13 million on the program to date, and has fired several top managers who would not commit to the program.

TQM became popular in the late 1980s, but has lately been greeted with increasing skepticism, with many companies being disappointed with the lack of fast results. Bob Hamaberg, CEO, says that there is nothing wrong with TQM; it has simply been applied badly in many companies.

The TQM process began at Aero in 1990 with the election of a "change council" consisting of Hamaberg and five senior managers. This council ensured that the TQM process received the money, equipment, and support necessary for success. A full-time "change manager" was appointed from within the company to make sure that the process didn't pull other managers from their regular duties.

Next, a nine-person task force was formed that consisted of employees who had done the full range of jobs on one of Standard's major overhaul contracts. Their first task was to find out what the customer wanted. To do this, the team designed a questionnaire and then visited customer plants around the world to gather information.

Even though the cost of this part of the process was about $100 000, much new information was gathered and many old beliefs about customers were shattered. For example, Standard found that in spite of free trade some U.S. firms were reluctant to deal with them because of complex cross-border paperwork. So Standard now does the paperwork for the customer. As a result of these actions, the task force picked up $7 million in new business.

The task force also worked within Standard to determine exactly how the company did its aircraft overhaul work. After weeks of analysis, the team was able to reduce the flow and complexity of work dramatically. For example, one gearbox had previously required 213 steps as it moved through the plant; the task force reduced the distance travelled by 80 percent, and cut the number of times the component changed hands by 84 percent. Also, by reducing paperwork involved in tracking the item they saved the company $150 000 per year.

Training is a major feature of the TQM program. Workers receive training in technical areas like statistics and machine operation, as well as in team building. The price tag at Standard has been about $1.5 million per year. Getting workers to be enthusiastic about TQM was not easy at first. Hamaberg's pep talks were crucial in getting workers to try it.

Hamaberg says that implementing TQM has been very hard, but that the results have been impressive. The task force members worked 12 to 14 hours per day, and he was concerned that they would burn out. He also notes that you can't do TQM all at once; it must be implemented step by step because people can't handle large amounts of immediate change.

Standard Aero
www.mts.net/standardaero

Any activity necessary for getting quality goods and services into the marketplace is a part of **quality assurance** (sometimes called quality management). Quality assurance is the management of the firm's quality efforts. Like any other management function, it involves planning, organizing, leading, and controlling.

quality assurance
Those activities necessary to get quality goods and services into the marketplace; also called quality management.

Planning for Quality

Planning for quality should begin before products are designed or redesigned. Managers need to set goals for both quality levels and quality reliability in the beginning. **Performance quality** refers to the features of a product and how well it performs. For example, Maytag gets a price premium because its washers and dryers offer a high level of performance quality. Customers perceive Maytags as having more advanced features and being more durable than other brands. (Everyone knows that the Maytag repairman is a lonely and idle person.)

performance quality
The overall degree of quality; how well the features of a product meet consumers' needs and how well the product performs.

Performance quality may or may not be related to quality reliability in a product. **Quality reliability** refers to the consistency or repeatability of performance. Toyota's small cars may not equal the overall quality level or have the luxury features of Rolls Royce; consequently, Toyota's prices are much lower. But Toyotas have high-quality reliability. The firm has a reputation for producing very few "lemons."

quality reliability
The consistency of quality from unit to unit of a product.

Some products offer both high-quality reliability and high performance quality. Kellogg has a reputation for consistent production of cereals made of good-quality ingredients. To achieve any form of high quality, however, managers must plan for production processes—equipment, methods, worker skills, and materials—that will result in quality products, as discussed in Chapter 10.

Organizing for Quality

Perhaps most important to the quality concept is the belief that producing quality goods and services requires an effort from all parts of the organization. The old idea of a separate "quality control" department is no longer enough. Everyone from the chairperson of the board to the part-time clerk—purchasers, engineers, janitors, marketers, machinists, and other personnel—must work to assure quality. In Germany's Messerschmitt-Boelkow-Blohm aerospace company, for example, all employees are responsible for inspecting their own work. The overall goal is to reduce eventual problems to a minimum by making the product right from the beginning. The same principle extends to teamwork practice at Heinz Co., where teams of workers are assigned to inspect virtually every activity in the company. Heinz has realized substantial cost savings by eliminating waste and rework.

At Motorola, the concept of teamwork as a key to organizational quality has resulted in an international event called the Total Customer Satisfaction Team Competition. Teams are composed of Motorola employees and also include customers and outside suppliers. Teams are judged on their success not only in promoting productivity but in sharing innovative ideas with people both inside and outside the company.

Motorola
www.mot.com

Although everyone in a company contributes to product quality, responsibility for specific aspects of total quality management is often assigned to specific departments and jobs. In fact, many companies have quality assurance, or quality control, departments staffed by quality experts. These people may be called in to help solve quality-related problems in any of the firm's other departments. They keep other departments informed of the latest developments in equipment and methods for maintaining quality. In addition, they monitor all quality control activities to identify areas for improvement.

Leading for Quality

Too often, firms fail to take the initiative to make quality happen. Leading for quality means that managers must inspire and motivate employees throughout the company to achieve quality goals. They need to help employees see how they affect quality and how quality affects their jobs and their company. Leaders must continually find ways to

quality ownership
The concept that quality belongs to each employee who creates or destroys it in producing a good or service; the idea that all workers must take responsibility for producing a quality product.

foster a quality orientation by training employees, encouraging their involvement and tying wages to quality of work. If managers succeed, employees will ultimately accept **quality ownership**—the idea that quality belongs to each person who creates or destroys it while performing a job.

General Electric Co. has recently embarked on a strong quality control initiative. Top management commitment to the program is assured by tying executive bonuses to actual implementation of the quality control program. The program involves training managers to be "Black Belts" in quality improvement. These Black Belts then spend their time in GE plants setting up quality improvement projects. Young managers have been told that they won't have much of a future at GE unless they become Black Belts. The company is investing millions in this project, and intends to have 10 000 Black Belts by the year 2000. The company is hopeful that the program can generate savings of $7 to $10 billion during the next decade.[9]

Controlling for Quality

By monitoring its products and services, a company can detect mistakes and make corrections. To do so, however, managers must first establish specific quality standards and measurements. Consider the following control system for a bank's teller services. Observant supervisors periodically evaluate transactions against a checklist. Specific aspects of each teller's work—appearance, courtesy, efficiency, and so on—are recorded. The results, reviewed with employees, either confirm proper performance or indicate changes that are needed to bring performance up to standards.

■TOOLS FOR QUALITY ASSURANCE

In managing for quality, many leading companies rely on assistance from proven tools. Often, ideas for improving both the product and the production process come from *competitive product analysis*. For example, Toshiba will take apart a Xerox photocopier and test each component. Test results help Toshiba's managers decide which Toshiba product features are satisfactory (in comparison to the competition), which product features need to be upgraded, or whether Toshiba's production processes need improvement.

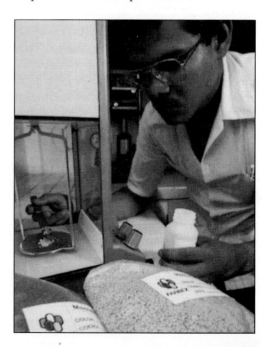

The quality control analyst at this plastics manufacturer is checking the weight of a sample of plastic pellets during the production process.

Methods such as value-added analysis, statistical process control, quality/cost studies, quality circles, benchmarking, cause-and-effect diagrams, ISO 9000, and re-engineering provide different routes to quality. Each of these approaches is discussed briefly below.

Value-Added Analysis

One effective method of improving quality and productivity is **value-added analysis**: the evaluation of all work activities, materials flows, and paperwork to determine the value that they add for customers. Value-added analysis often reveals wasteful or unnecessary activities that can be eliminated without harming (and even improving) customer service. When Hewlett-Packard, for example, simplified its contracts and reduced them from 20 pages to as few as two pages for all customers, computer sales rose by more than 18 percent.

value-added analysis
The evaluation of all work activities, material flows, and paperwork to determine the value they add for customers.

Statistical Process Control

Every business experiences unit-to-unit variations in its products and services. Although every company would like complete uniformity in its outputs, this is an impossible quest. Companies can gain better control, however, by understanding the sources of variation. **Statistical process control (SPC)** methods—especially process variation studies and control charts—allow managers to analyze variations in production data.

statistical process control (SPC)
Statistical analysis techniques that allow managers to analyze variations in production data and to detect when adjustments are needed to create products with high-quality reliability.

Process Variation.   Variations in a firm's products may arise from the inputs in its production process. As people, materials, work methods, and equipment change, so do production outputs. While some amount of **process variation** is acceptable, too much can result in poor quality and excessive operating costs.

Consider the box-filling operation for Honey Nuggets cereal. Each automated machine fills two 400-gram boxes per second. Even under proper conditions, slight variations in cereal weight from box to box are normal. Equipment and tools wear out, the cereal may be overly moist, machinists make occasional adjustments. But how much variation is occurring? How much is acceptable?

process variation
Any change in employees, materials, work methods, or equipment that affects output quality.

Information about variation in a process can be obtained from a **process capability study.** Boxes are taken from the filling machines and weighed. The results are plotted, as in Figure 11.1, and compared with the upper and lower **specification limits** (quality limits) for weight. These limits define good and bad quality for box filling. Boxes with over 410 grams are a wasteful "giveaway." Underfilling has a cost because it is unlawful.

Looking at the results of the capability study, we see that none of machine A's output violates the quality limits. In fact, most of the boxes from machine A are very close to the desired weight of 400 grams. In Figure 11.1, the shape of machine A's graph, high at the centre and dropping sharply at the margins, is typical of many production processes. Machine A, then, is fully capable of meeting the company's quality standards.

process capability study
A statistical process control method in which samples of the product are measured to determine the amount of process variation; shows the outputs' conformity with or deviation from specification limits.

But machines B and C have problems. In their present condition, they are "not capable." They cannot reliably meet Honey Nuggets' quality standards. The company must take special—and costly—actions to sort the good from the bad boxes before releasing the cereal for shipment. Unless machines B and C are renovated, substandard production quality will plague Honey Nuggets.

specification limits
Limits defining acceptable and unacceptable quality in production of a good or service.

Control Charts.   Knowing that a process is capable of meeting quality standards is not enough. Managers must still monitor the process to prevent its drifting astray during production. To detect the beginning of bad conditions, managers can check production periodically and plot the results on a **control chart**. For example, several times a day a machine operator at Honey Nuggets might weigh several boxes of cereal together to ascertain the average weight.

control chart
A statistical process control method in which results of test sampling of a product are plotted on a diagram that reveals when the process is beginning to depart from normal operating conditions.

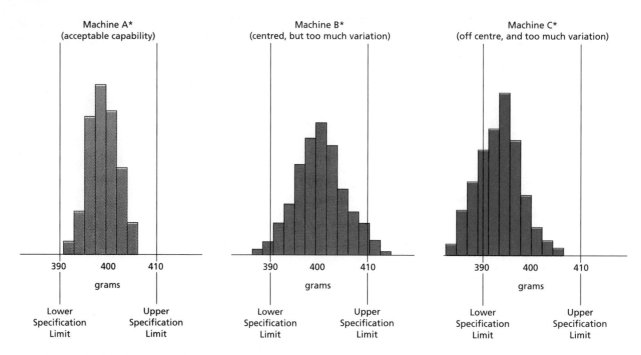

*Distribution of weights for 500 boxes from each machine

FIGURE 11.1
Process variation in box-filling for Honey Nuggets cereal.

Figure 11.2 shows the control chart for machine A, in which the first five points are randomly scattered around the centre line, indicating that the machine was operating well. However, the points for samples 5 through 8 are all above the centre line, indicating that something was causing the boxes to overfill. The last point falls outside the upper **control limit**, confirming that the process is out of control.

At this point, the machine must be shut down so that a manager and/or the operator can investigate what is causing the problem—equipment, people, materials, or work methods. Control is completed by correcting the problem and restoring the process to normal.

Quality/Cost Studies for Quality Improvement

Statistical process controls help keep operations up to *existing* capabilities. But in today's competitive environment, firms must consistently *raise* quality capabilities. Any improvement in products or production processes means additional costs, however, whether for new facilities, equipment, training, or other changes. Managers thus face the challenge of identifying those improvements that offer the greatest promise. **Quality/cost studies** are useful because they not only identify a firm's current costs but also reveal areas with the largest cost-savings potential.

Quality costs are associated with making, finding, repairing, or preventing defective goods and services. All of these costs should be analyzed in a quality/cost study. For example, Honey Nuggets must determine its costs for **internal failures**. These are expenses—including the costs of overfilling boxes and the costs of sorting out bad boxes—incurred during production and before bad products leave the plant. Studies indicate that many manufacturers incur very high costs for internal failures—up to 50 percent of total costs.

control limit
The critical value on a control chart that indicates the level at which quality deviation is sufficiently unacceptable to merit investigation.

quality/cost study
A method of improving product quality by assessing a firm's current quality-related costs and identifying areas with the greatest cost-savings potential.

internal failures
Expenses incurred during production and before bad products leave the plant.

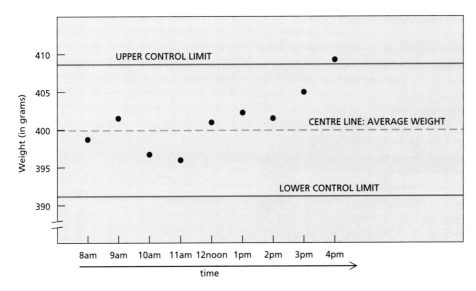

FIGURE 11.2
Honey Nuggets cereal process control chart for machine A.

Despite quality control procedures, however, some bad boxes may get out of the factory, reach the customer, and generate complaints from grocers and cereal eaters. These are **external failures** that occur outside the factory. The costs of correcting them—refunds to customers, transportation costs to return bad boxes to the factory, possible lawsuits, factory recalls—should also be tabulated in the quality/cost study.

external failures
Allowing defective products to leave the factory and get into consumers' hands.

The percentage of costs in the different categories varies widely from company to company. Thus every firm must conduct systematic quality/cost studies to identify the most costly—and often the most vital—areas of its operations. Not surprisingly, these areas should be targets for improvement. Too often, however, firms substitute hunches and guesswork for data and analysis.

Quality Circles

As we noted in Chapter 10, one proven technique for improving quality is the use of **quality circles**, groups of employees who work in teams to improve their job environment. Meeting on company time in the facility, quality circles are a forum for quality improvement. Although the format varies in different companies, circle members are deeply involved in initiating changes in their work environment.

quality circle
A technique for maximizing quality of production by grouping employees into small teams who define, analyze, and solve quality and other process-related problems within their area.

Quality circles organize their own efforts, choose a leader, and establish rules for discussion. Within the group, members identify aspects of their jobs that pose problems or are barriers to better quality and overall productivity. They gather data to evaluate the severity of problems and to identify improvement projects. The group's problem solving emphasizes brainstorming, group discussions, and tools such as process capability studies and cost analysis. Ultimately, the circle makes recommendations to management, identifying expected benefits, costs, and implementation timetables.

Perhaps the greatest benefit of quality circles, however, is not any direct cost savings, but their effect on employees' attitudes. Rather than viewing themselves as passive resources for production, employees develop a sense of self-worth and quality ownership. The talents and job knowledge of circle members are put to active, constructive use instead of lying dormant.

Benchmarking

benchmarking
Comparing the quality of the firm's output with the quality of the output of the industry's leaders.

An organization that uses **benchmarking** compares the quality of its output with the quality produced by the industry leaders. If differences are noted, the firm can figure out how the leaders are achieving their quality levels and then pursue the same strategy. Benchmarking can also be used to compare different departments or divisions in the same organization.

When Canon copiers first were sold in North America, they were priced below what it cost Xerox to make them. Canon could do this because it was far more efficient than Xerox. Xerox then embarked on a benchmarking exercise in order to regain its position as the most important company in the copier market. By using what it had learned about how other companies were making copiers, Xerox was able to cut its unit production cost in half and increase sales by 50 percent.[10]

Before Chrysler Corporation introduced its 1998 Dodge Ram pickup, it made improvements in nearly 100 features, including the introduction of the four-door, or quad cab design. This made the truck more competitive with trucks made by other companies.

Cause-and-Effect Diagrams

cause-and-effect diagram
Summarizes the four possible causes of quality problems—materials, human resources, methods, and machines.

A **cause-and-effect diagram** summarizes the four possible causes of quality problems—materials, human resources, methods, and machines. For example, if car bodies are being produced with rippled paint, the problem might be thin paint (materials), poor training (human resources), a defective sprayer (machines), or a layer of paint that is too thick (methods). The cause-and-effect diagram is used to identify the source(s) of the problem. Once the source is identified, actions can be taken to resolve the problem.

International Standards Organization
www.iso.ch

ISO 9000
A quality scorecard developed by the International Standards Organization.

ISO 9000

The International Standards Organization in Geneva, Switzerland, has developed a quality "scorecard" that is fast becoming a prerequisite for selling to the European Community. The aim of **ISO 9000** (pronounced ICE-O 9000) is to find the cause of product defects at the production-line level. The North American automobile industry adopted the standard in 1994 in order to measure the performance of its suppliers. After Toronto Plastics was awarded the designation, defects fell to 15 000 parts per million, down from 150 000 parts per million. About 600 Canadian firms have received the designation.[11] More information is contained in the box "ISO 9000: Seeking the Standard in Quality."

Re-engineering

re-engineering
The process of rethinking and redesigning business processes in order to achieve dramatic improvements in productivity and quality.

Re-engineering is the process of rethinking and redesigning business processes in order to achieve dramatic improvements in productivity and quality. In effect, those engaged in re-engineering ask, "If this were a new company, how would we run it?" The bottom line in every re-engineering process is redesigning systems to better serve the needs of customers.

A re-engineering process at IBM Credit Corp., a financing subsidiary of IBM, is typical. The firm exists to provide a service—financing computers and software. But each financing request had to go through a cumbersome series of steps, even though most customers needed an immediate answer. After two managers decided to "walk through" a typical request, they discovered that the actual approval work took only 90 minutes. The rest of the time was spent shuffling forms around between the various people who worked on the process. Their solution was to put one person in charge of all the steps. The result? A hundredfold increase in the number of requests handled.[12]

TRENDS & CHALLENGES

ISO 9000: Seeking the Standard in Quality

ISO 9000 standards enable firms to demonstrate that they follow documented procedures for testing products, training workers, keeping records, and fixing product defects. To become certified, companies must document the procedures that workers follow during every stage of production. They must also show that they have incorporated mechanisms to ensure that workers actually follow accepted practices. Not surprisingly, this approach leads to more reliable products with fewer defects. The purpose of ISO 9000 is "to ensure that a manufacturer's product is exactly the same today as it was yesterday, as it will be tomorrow." The goal of standardization is to guarantee that "goods will be produced at the same level of quality even if all the employees were replaced by a new set of workers."

Companies seeking ISO 9000 certification are audited by an elite group of quality-systems "registrars." These registrars focus on 20 different functions including design control, contract review, purchasing, inspection and testing, and training. For example, to pass order-processing requirements, a company must demonstrate procedures for guaranteeing on-time deliveries. Not surprisingly, the certification process is time-consuming and costly—it can take up to 18 months for a manufacturing plant employing 300 workers and cost more than $200 000.

Despite the interest in ISO 9000, however, it is not a cure-all for quality ailments. On the contrary, certification standards have little to do with customer satisfaction. Instead of imposing guarantee procedures, they focus on documenting a company's commitment to its *own* procedures. "With ISO 9000 you can still have terrible processes and products," complains Richard Buetow, director of corporate quality at Motorola. "You can certify a manufacturer that makes life jackets from concrete," says Buetow, "as long as those jackets are made according to the documented procedures and the company provides the next of kin with instructions on how to complain about defects. That's absurd."

Re-engineering is also underway at Novacor Chemicals in Sarnia, Ontario. Over the past 10 years, the company acquired four different businesses, each with its own style, technology, and processes. It is now rethinking how it produces about two million tonnes of petrochemicals each year. In the process, it is finding that it can save millions of dollars by having the four businesses operate in a coordinated fashion rather than as separate entities. For example, when plants were shut down for maintenance, each one hired its own maintenance team. Now, one team is hired and rotated among the four plants.[13]

In the mid-1990s, the re-engineering idea ran into difficulty, partly because it became too closely associated with downsizing.[14] What started out as a way to increase the efficiency of work processes ended up as a system that was used to rationalize downsizing. Some re-engineering efforts also failed because the changes that were introduced were not entrenched in the company's regular operations. As a result, after a few years it was hard to find any traces of the re-engineering that had supposedly been accomplished.[15]

Even major proponents of the idea such as Dr. Michael Hammer admit that somewhere along the way they lost sight of *people* and became too caught up in streamlining *processes*.[16] They also recognize that innovation comes from changing how people work, not simply from re-engineering.

■ COMPETING THROUGH PRODUCTIVITY AND QUALITY

While tools such as quality circles can help a firm improve product quality, they can enhance a company's ability to compete only when coupled with attention to all aspects of productivity. Both productivity and quality begin with attention to customers' needs. Also important are management's willingness to invest in innovation, its time perspective, its concern for quality of work life, how well it can streamline its service operations, and the size of the company.

Get Closer to the Customer

Many decaying businesses have lost sight of customers as the driving force for all business activity. With misplaced intentions, they waste resources designing products customers do not want. They ignore customers' reactions to existing products. They fail to keep up with changing consumer tastes, or they go beyond consumers' tastes. In contrast, the most successful businesses keep close to their customers and know what they want in the products they consume.

At Greyhound Lines of Canada, marketing and operations vice president John Munro wanted to make a point about the importance of clean restrooms to customers. He warned regional managers that he would visit bus depots on one hour's notice to see if the restrooms were clean enough to eat dinner in them. Within weeks, photos of regional managers having dinner in the spotless restrooms began pouring into Munro's office.[17]

Greyhound Lines of Canada
www.greyhound.com

Invest in Innovation and Technology

Once companies know what their customers want, managers must find efficient ways to produce it. Investment in research and development in Canada has lagged behind that in Europe and Japan. Rather than creating new products, more and more companies are choosing to copy innovations and market similar products to save innovation costs. Firms that have continued to invest in truly innovative technology have kept their productivity rising, along with their incomes. But firms that have merely copied the automation they see others using have not been as productive.[18]

Adopt a Long-Run Perspective

Part of the decline in innovation among Canadian firms reflects a common short-run perspective. Shareholders prefer short- and intermediate-term (less than five years), "sure thing" paybacks. Many companies reward managers with salaries and bonuses based on their quarterly or yearly performance. With owners and managers unwilling to wait for financial returns, many buildings, tools, and equipment have become old or obsolete. Canada is still a creative hothouse, but many businesses are shying away from long-term risks and are failing to convert their good new ideas into actual products.

By contrast, instead of emphasizing short-run results, many quality-oriented firms are committed to a long-run perspective for **continuous improvement**—the ongoing commitment to improving products and processes, step by step, in pursuit of ever-increasing customer satisfaction. Motorola is a good example of a company that emphasizes continuous, long-run improvement. In 1981, the firm adopted a five-year goal of a tenfold reduction of errors. In 1986, it extended that goal to a hundredfold reduction of errors by 1992. Despite initial hopes, however, Motorola missed its goal for 1992: At the start of that year, defects still ran at 40 per one million parts. Motorola managers had to be satisfied with the reminder that five years earlier, the defect rate had been 6000 per one million parts. Moreover, Motorola continues to plan for still greater improvement. By 2001, say company officials, Motorola quality will be an unimaginable one defect per one *billion* parts. The focus on continuous improvement at another company is described in the box "SABRE-Toothed Tiger of the Skies."

continuous improvement
The ongoing commitment to improve products and processes, step by step, in pursuit of ever-increasing customer satisfaction.

TRENDS & CHALLENGES

SABRE-Toothed Tiger of the Skies

SABRE is the computerized reservation service of American Airlines. Most Canadians first heard about it when American Airlines offered to invest $246 million in troubled Canadian Airlines International if CAI would become part of SABRE. However, CAI was already a partner with Air Canada in the Gemini reservation system; therefore, it needed approval to join SABRE because doing so would doom Gemini.

SABRE has over 85 000 terminals in 47 countries. It allows travel agents to make reservations on virtually any airline and to book hotel rooms, rental cars, and even theatre tickets in many places. The system is just the latest development in American's ongoing dedication to continuous improvement.

The system got its start in the late 1950s, when reservations for American's flights exceeded the old system's (file cards and blackboards) capacity to handle them. By 1963, the original SABRE was in place, handling 85 000 phone calls, 40 000 confirmed reservations, and 20 000 ticket sales in its first year. (Today the system handles nearly 2000 messages *per second* during peak season.) By keeping track of passengers and passenger miles, SABRE also enabled American to launch the first comprehensive "frequent flier" program in the industry. By the mid-1970s, the system was also tracking spare parts, scheduling crews, and developing flight plans. In addition, the system enables the firm to maximize its revenues by shifting fares on each flight as necessary.

In 1976, SABRE moved beyond American's offices and into the offices of travel agents, enabling them not only to make reservations instantly but also to provide their clients with seat assignments (and even boarding passes) prior to their flights. Before SABRE, less than 40 percent of airline tickets were booked through travel agents. Today 80 percent are. On an average day, 40 000 new or changed fares are entered into the system. When "fare wars" break out, that number zooms to 1.5 million per day!

American continued to make changes in SABRE throughout the 1980s. Some of these changes, such as making the screen formats of all airlines' listings the same so that American was not unfairly favoured, were the result of government regulations. But other changes—especially American's decision to sell copies of its software programs to anyone interested in buying them—came from within. Why? As the cost of developing and refining such software has risen, American wants to recoup some of its investment as quickly as possible. Moreover, the firm is convinced that it will still have an edge on its competition because it is better at interpreting and using the information that SABRE provides.

What lies ahead? Continued expansion worldwide is likely. But computer experts at American also argue that the current centralized system must be decentralized and that the system's reliance on the mainframe computer must be reduced if the system is to grow. American has also joined with a variety of other firms in the travel industry to create InterAAct, a system designed to list hotel and rental car options as methodically and comprehensively as SABRE does airline seats. If it succeeds, American will have another weapon against the competition.

Emphasize Quality-of-Work-Life Factors

Positive employee attitudes in small businesses have certainly made productivity growth better than it would otherwise have been. But big corporations represent so large a part of total national output that the reactions of their workers are central to improving productivity. Large firms can make their employees' jobs more challenging and interesting by enhancing their workers' physical and mental health through recreational facilities, counselling services, and other programs.

Many firms are replacing the environments of yesterday, based on management-directed mass production, with worker-oriented environments that foster loyalty, teamwork, and commitment. As we saw in Chapter 8, firms using this approach have found success in the concept of **employee empowerment**: the principle that all employees are

employee empowerment
Principle that all employees are valuable contributors to business and should be entrusted with certain decisions regarding their work.

Operators at Dofasco monitor the production of steel products with the latest in high-technology monitoring devices.

valuable contributors to a business and should be entrusted with certain decisions regarding their work. Such confidence in employee involvement contrasts sharply with the traditional belief that managers are the primary source of decision making and problem solving.

Employee Training.   For employee involvement to be effective, it must be implemented with preparation and intelligence. Training is one of the proven methods for avoiding judgments and actions that can lead to impaired rather than improved performance. In a recent survey, for example, insufficient training was the most-mentioned barrier encountered by work teams.

Improve the Service Sector

As important as employee attitude is to goods production, it is even more crucial to service production, since employees often *are* the service. The service sector has grown rapidly but this growth has often come at a cost of high inefficiency. Many newly created service jobs have not been streamlined. Some companies operate effectively, but many others are very inefficient, dragging down overall productivity. As new companies enter these markets, however, the increased need to compete should eventually force service producers to operate more productively.

Quality begins with listening to customers in order to determine what services they want. Companies in the temporary-services industry, for example, have long emphasized the needs of clients for clerical and light-industrial employees. More recently, however, temp services have realized the need for high-skilled, specialized temps like nurses, accountants, and scientists.

In trying to offer more satisfactory services, many providers have discovered five criteria that customers use to judge service quality:[19]

- *Reliability*: Perform the service as promised, both accurately and on time.
- *Responsiveness*: Be willing to help customers promptly.
- *Assurance*: Maintain knowledgeable and courteous employees who will earn the trust and confidence of customers.
- *Empathy*: Provide caring, individualized attention to customers.
- *Tangibles*: Maintain a pleasing appearance of personnel, materials, and facilities.

Smaller Can Be Better than Bigger

One bright spot in the productivity picture is small business. Many giant corporations have found themselves overextended. One department does not know what another is doing. Unnecessary duplication leads to wasted resources. By offering their customers higher product quality and tailored services, smaller companies have improved their overall productivity and have become more competitive.

In terms of job satisfaction, small businesses offer features that large ones cannot. Employees in small firms lag well behind their corporate counterparts in pay and benefits. But small companies offer employees more challenging, interesting work than do big firms. They give their employees more respect and greater chances of having their ideas adopted.

SUMMARY OF LEARNING OBJECTIVES

1. **Describe the connection between *productivity* and *quality*.** *Productivity* is a measure of economic performance: It compares how much is produced with the resources used to produce it. *Quality* is a product's fitness for use. However, an emphasis solely on productivity or solely on quality is not enough. Profitable competition in today's business world demands high levels of both productivity and quality.

2. **Understand the importance of increasing productivity.** During the 1980s, the growth rate of Canadian productivity slowed down. In recent years, Canada's growth rate of productivity has lagged behind that of countries like Japan, South Korea, and France.

3. **Explain *total* and *partial measures of productivity* and how they are used to keep track of national, industrywide, and companywide productivity.** *Total factor productivity* includes all types of input resources: labour, capital, materials, energy, and purchased business services. *Partial productivity measures* do not use as many input factors. *Labour productivity* is the most common national productivity measure. Many companies develop their own measures for partial and total productivity.

4. **Identify the activities involved in *total quality management* and describe four tools that companies can use to achieve it.** *Total quality management (TQM)* refers to the planning, organizing, leading, and controlling of all the activities needed to get quality goods and services into the marketplace. Managers must set goals for and implement the processes needed to achieve high quality and reliability levels. *Statistical process control* methods such as *process capability studies* and *control charts* can help keep quality consistently high. *Quality/cost studies*, which identify potential savings, can help firms improve quality. *Quality improvement teams* also can improve operations by more fully involving employees in decision making. Finally, *benchmarking*—studying the best practices of other companies and using the knowledge to improve a company's own products and services—has become an increasingly common TQM tool.

5. List six ways in which companies can compete by improving productivity and quality. A business must first and foremost stay close to customers to better know their needs and wants. To increase quality and productivity, businesses must invest in innovation and technology. They must also adopt a long-run perspective for continuous improvement. In addition, they should realize that smaller can be better: Many smaller businesses have succeeded because they provide quality service and job satisfaction. Finally, placing greater emphasis on the quality of work life can also help firms compete. Satisfied, motivated employees are especially important in increasing productivity in the fast-growing service sector.

STUDY QUESTIONS AND EXERCISES

Review Questions

1. What is the connection (relationship) between productivity and quality?

2. Why do labour unions care about the productivity of an industry?

3. How do total factor productivity ratios differ from partial factor ratios?

4. What activities are involved in quality assurance?

5. How do the purposes of statistical process controls and quality/cost studies differ?

Analysis Questions

6. How would you suggest the service sector increase productivity?

7. Some people argue that, while quality circles work well in Japan, Canadians lack the team orientation and management-labour trust to make them viable here. Do you agree or disagree? Why?

Application Exercises

8. Using a local company as an example, show how you would conduct a quality/cost study. Identify the cost categories and give some examples of costs in each category. Which categories do you expect will have the most and least costs? Why?

9. Select a company of interest to you and analyze it for productivity and quality improvements. Which of the "six suggestions for competing" detailed in the chapter apply to this company? What additional suggestions would you make to help this company improve its overall productivity?

BUILDING YOUR BUSINESS SKILLS

Goal

To encourage students to understand how benchmarking can help improve quality and productivity.

Situation

As the director of maintenance for a regional airline, you are disturbed to learn that the cost to maintain your 30-plane fleet is skyrocketing. A major factor in this cost escalation is repair time: When maintenance or repairs are required, work often proceeds slowly, with the result that additional aircraft are required to meet the schedule. You decide to do a benchmarking study to learn how other companies have managed similar problems. Your goal is to apply the best practices to your own maintenance and repair operation.

Method

Step 1: Working with three or four other students, choose your benchmarking target from among the following choices:

- The maintenance and repair operation of a competing airline

- The pit crew operation of an Indianapolis 500 race car team

- The maintenance and repair operation of a nationwide trucking company

Write a memo explaining the reasons for your choice.

Step 2: Write up a list of benchmarking questions that will help you learn the best practices of your targeted company. Your goal is to ask questions that will help you improve your own operation. These questions will be asked during on-site visits.

Step 3: As part of a benchmarking project, you will be dealing with your counterparts in other companies. You have a responsibility to prepare for these encounters and to understand that what you learn during benchmarking is privileged information. Based on this, describe what steps you would take before your first on-site visit and how you would define your benchmarking code of ethics.

Follow-Up Questions

1. Why is benchmarking an important method for improving quality?

2. Why did you make your benchmarking choice? Explain why the company you selected holds more promise than other companies in helping you solve your internal maintenance problems.

3. What kind of information would help you improve the efficiency of your operation? Are you interested in management information, technical information, or both?

4. In an age of heightened competition, why do you think companies are willing to benchmark with each other?

Prentice Hall

TAKE IT TO THE NET

Check out our Companion Website

for this chapter's Exploring the Net exercise, featuring information on Canadian productivity and quality from the National Quality Institute and other intriguing, annotated destinations. You'll also find practice exercises, updated Weblinks from the text, links to newsgroups, updates, and more.

www.prenticehall.ca/ebert

BUSINESS CASE 11

Samsung Takes to the Road

Already a powerhouse in finance, machinery, chemicals, and especially electronics, Samsung, the huge South Korean manufacturer, is planning on getting into the auto business. Although there is a worldwide glut of new cars, Samsung's chairman Lee Kun Hee is determined to produce a car good enough to vault the firm into the world's top 10 automakers in the next dozen years. With production plans to build 1.5 million cars a year, Samsung must succeed at the expense of its entrenched competitors. As one analyst put it, "There's no logical opening in the marketplace where Samsung can step in and fill a vaccum. Its sales will have to come out of someone else's hide."

Despite its advantage in electronics, which accounts for more and more of the inner workings of today's new cars, Samsung faces a difficult road test. It has never manufactured a car before, and the global market's perception of the quality of Korean autos tends to be low. Its Korean competitors have apparently convinced their parts suppliers not to sell to their new rival, so Samsung is getting parts from a number of manufacturers as new to the car industry as itself.

The new venture is also costly: The bill has run to $3.5 billion so far, almost a third more than planned. And Jeong Ju Wha, the firm's head of production, will conduct nearly a year's worth of expensive trial production runs before releasing the first model for sale. "It's the only way we can win," he says.

But Samsung has one or two other forces working in its favour. First, it has very deep pockets for new ventures, having already succeeded in another supposedly saturated industry, semiconductors. Second, it adheres to the Korean tradition of preserving jobs and creating new industries to provide them. So committed is the firm to this philosophy of work that its 160 000 workers have been promised no one will be laid off.

➤

Its expertise in electronics will undoubtedly also weigh in Samsung's favour as features such as satellite navigation systems become more common in cars. And finally, Samsung has the unusual benefit of assistance from Nissan, the Japanese auto manufacturer, which is providing production expertise, design input, worker training, and even an aluminum engine plant. Samsung will pay Nissan a fee for its help and turn over 2 percent of the factory price of each car sold, which Nissan hopes will bring it up to $1 billion in revenues.

Samsung still faces a big marketing challenge: It has to distinguish its new product in a seriously crowded market, and then it has to convince drivers around the world to buy it.

■ *Case Questions*

1. How do you think Samsung can achieve quality in its new venture?

2. How can Samsung measure the quality of its products? What would a comparison with Canadian products tell the firm? How should Samsung make such a comparison?

3. What productivity measures can Samsung rely on?

4. How can Samsung identify problems in quality and productivity when they arise? What solutions do you suggest?

5. What is the upside of Samsung's extensive quality testing? How might the firm promote that to its advantage?

6. One of the marketing strategies under consideration at Samsung is the purchase of one of its rival car makers, the Korean firm Kia Motors, which recently sold 770 000 cars in one year with earnings of $8.2 million. How would such a purchase affect Samsung's quality control procedures? What impact might it have on productivity?

C H A P T E R

12

UNDERSTANDING ACCOUNTING AND INFORMATION SYSTEMS

INFORMATION PROCESSING UNDER PRESSURE

The ore carrier *Nanticoke*, owned by Canadian Steamship Lines (CSL), was working its way through the dangerous American Narrows on the St. Lawrence River when it suddenly encountered a fog bank. The fog was so dense that Captain Joe Sahni couldn't see the bow of the boat just 200 metres ahead. How could he stay in the narrow, safe channel and avoid running aground?

The answer was the ship's new Canadian-designed and developed Electronic Chart Precise Integrated Navigation System (ECPINS). The system displayed the *Nanticoke's* position on a computer screen showing the Thousand Islands waterway. The ship's position was updated twice a second using the U.S. military's global positioning satellite. This allowed Captain Sahni to determine where he was within five metres. The system provided so much detail that Sahni could actually see the bow of the ship change position on the screen as the ship drifted sideways. The ship successfully navigated the fog bank.

The next day, Captain Sahni phoned the director of navigation for the company and told him the investment in ECPINS had just paid for itself. The *Nanticoke* was the first ship outfitted with the system, which is produced by Offshore Systems International Ltd. of Vancouver. Now, Canadian Steamship Lines has installed ECPINS on 11 more of its ships that sail the Great Lakes and the eastern seaboard. CSL also plans to outfit its deep-ocean vessels with the system. Each unit costs about $100 000.

Massive changes are taking place in the shipping business. Raymond Johnston, who became CEO of CSL in 1991, moved into high-tech information processing initially to cut costs and to keep customers happy. But the changes that were eventually implemented weren't limited to ship navigation. Johnston also made the management decision that control over spending should be in the hands of the ships' masters rather than the financial and accounting people in Montreal.

Under the old system, a ship would order more supplies than it needed because orders were regularly cut by head office and delivery was unreliable. The solution to this problem lay in computers, not just for guiding ships through fog, but for a whole list of important functions. Now, ships order electronically directly from their suppliers, payroll is completed on board, and maintenance plans are computerized.

These major changes have had to be carefully introduced. Many of the people working on the ships did not have much experience with computers, and some of them were quite apprehensive about this new way to process information. The changes have also required CSL to invest in computer hardware and employee training. So far, the company has spent about $3 million on hardware and about $1.5 million on training and software.

But the new system is paying off. In tandem with traditional radar, ECPINS should help avoid collisions and running aground, two common problems ships face. In the first two years using ECPINS, CSL has had no significant groundings or collisions. This has saved about $2 million annually. Additional savings are evident because ships that cost $35 000 per day to operate don't have to wait at anchor for fog to clear. The time lost to breakdowns and accidents used to be about 2 percent of total fleet operating time; now it is less than one-half of 1 percent. Computers and the ECPINS system are turning sea dogs into information workers.

In today's complex range of business environments, the need to manage information efficiently and quickly is crucial. This is especially true for accountants, who are responsible for compiling and issuing the basic financial information about a company's economic activity. Among other things, accountants are information managers. In most businesses, moreover, accountants play a role in almost all activities.

By focusing on the learning objectives of this chapter, you will be able to describe the activities of accountants and the concepts and rules that govern them. Because the computer stands at the forefront of information management, we also explore some of the ways in which companies manage information with computers. After reading this chapter, you should be able to:

1. Explain the role of accountants and distinguish between the three types of professional accountants found in Canada.
2. Explain how the following three concepts are used in *record-keeping: accounting equations, double-entry accounting,* and *T-accounts* for debits and credits.
3. Describe two important *financial statements* and show how they reflect the activity and financial condition of a business.
4. Explain how computing key *financial ratios* can help in analyzing the financial strengths of a business.
5. Identify the role played in computer systems by *databases* and *application programs.*
6. Classify *computer systems* by size and structure.
7. List some trends in the application of computer technology to business information management.

■ WHAT IS ACCOUNTING?

accounting
A comprehensive system for collecting, analyzing, and communicating financial information.

Accounting is a comprehensive information system for collecting, analyzing, and communicating financial information. As such, it is a system for measuring business performance and translating those measures into information for management decisions. Accounting also uses performance measures to prepare performance reports for owners, the public, and regulatory agencies. To meet these objectives, accountants keep records of such transactions as taxes paid, income received, and expenses incurred, and they analyze the effects of these transactions on particular business activities. By sorting, analyzing, and recording thousands of transactions, accountants can determine how well a business is being managed and how financially strong it is. Accounting information is also important in helping managers interpret and extrapolate information for planning purposes.

accounting system
An organized procedure for identifying, measuring, recording, and retaining financial information so that it can be used in accounting statements and management reports.

Because businesses engage in many thousands of transactions, ensuring consistent, dependable financial information is mandatory. This is the job of the **accounting system**: an organized procedure for identifying, measuring, recording, and retaining financial information so that it can be used in accounting statements and management reports.

The system includes all the people, reports, computers, procedures, and resources for compiling financial transactions.[1]

Users of Accounting Information

Noranda Inc.
www.noranda.com

In 1997, Noranda Inc., Canada's biggest natural resource company, announced plans to refocus on the mining and metals side of its activities by selling its forest products and oil and natural gas interests. In preparation for the announcement, corporate officers relied on accounting to provide information for everyone who might be interested in the firm's activities. Its 49 percent ownership of Norcen Energy Resources Ltd. will be sold. Its oil and gas subsidiary, Canadian Hunter Exploration Ltd., will be distributed as a dividend to Noranda shareholders, as will its interest in Noranda Forest Inc., a forest products company. A statement issued to shareholders and the public will show clearly how much each of the three segments contributed to Noranda's overall sales, expenses, and earnings. Current and potential stockholders will also be told how the new stock shares will be distributed.[2]

Noranda accountants must tabulate financial projections for the separation because stakeholders have important questions about the soon-to-be three companies: Do the business prospects indicate that as separate companies they are good credit risks? As investments, will they pay sufficient financial returns to owners? Have adequate arrangements been made for employee retirement funds and benefits? Do their business prospects look healthy enough to support current employment levels? Upon receiving accounting answers to questions such as these, different information users (owners, employees, regulatory agencies, lenders, and the public) are better prepared to make decisions for themselves and for their organizations.

As the Noranda example illustrates, there are numerous users of accounting information:

- *Business managers* use accounting information to set goals, develop plans, set budgets, and evaluate future prospects.

- *Employees and unions* use accounting information to get paid and to plan for and receive such benefits as health care, insurance, vacation time, and retirement pay.

- *Investors and creditors* use accounting information to estimate returns to stockholders, determine a company's growth prospect, and determine whether it is a good credit risk before investing or lending.

- *Tax authorities* use accounting information to plan for tax inflows, determine the tax liabilities of individuals and businesses, and ensure that correct amounts are paid on time.

- *Government regulatory agencies* rely on accounting information to fulfill their duties. The Toronto Stock Exchange, for example, requires firms to file financial disclosures so that potential investors have valid information about a company's financial status.

■ WHO ARE ACCOUNTANTS AND WHAT DO THEY DO?

At the head of the accounting system is the **controller**, who manages all the firm's accounting activities. As chief accounting officer, the controller ensures that the accounting system provides the reports and statements needed for planning, controlling, and decision-making activities. This broad range of activities requires different types of accounting expertise specialists. In this section we will begin by distinguishing between the two main fields of accounting: financial and managerial. Then we will discuss the different functions and activities of certified public accountants and private accountants.

controller
Person who manages all of a firm's accounting activities (chief accounting officer).

Financial Versus Managerial Accounting

In any company, two fields of accounting (financial and managerial) can be distinguished by the different users they serve. As we have just seen, it is both convenient and accurate to classify users of accounting information as users outside the company and users inside the company. This same distinction allows us to categorize accounting systems as either financial or managerial.

financial accounting system
Field of accounting concerned with external users of a company's financial information.

Financial Accounting.   A firm's **financial accounting system** is concerned with external users of information: consumer groups, unions, stockholders, and government agencies. It prepares and publishes income statements and balance sheets at regular intervals, as well as other financial reports that are published for shareholders and the general public. All of these documents focus on the activities of the company as a whole, rather than on individual departments or divisions.

In reporting data, financial accountants must conform to standard reporting formats and procedures imposed by both the accounting profession and government agencies. This requirement helps ensure that users can clearly compare information, whether from many different companies or from the same company at different times. The information in such reports is mostly historical; that is, it summarizes financial transactions that have occurred during past accounting periods.

managerial (or management) accounting
Field of accounting that serves internal users of a company's financial information.

Managerial Accounting.   In contrast, **managerial** (or **management**) **accounting** serves internal users. Managers at all levels need information to make decisions for their departments, to monitor current projects, and to plan for future activities. Other employees also need accounting information. Engineers, for instance, want to know the costs for materials and production so that they can make product operation improvements. To set performance goals, salespeople need data on past sales by geographic region. Purchasing agents use information on material costs to negotiate terms with suppliers.

Reports to these users serve the company's individual units, whether departments, projects, plants, or divisions. Internal reports may be designed in any form that will assist internal users in planning, decision making, and controlling. Furthermore, as projections and forecasts of both financial data and business activities, internal reports are an extremely important part of the management accounting system. They are forward-looking rather than historical in nature.

Canadian Institute of Chartered Accountants
www.cica.ca

Certified General Accountants' Association of Canada
www.cga-canada.org

chartered accountant (CA)
An individual who has met certain experience and education requirements and has passed a licensing examination; acts as an outside accountant for other firms.

certified general accountant (CGA)
An individual who has completed an education program and passed a national exam; works in private industry or a CGA firm.

Professional Accountants

Users of financial statements want to be confident that the accountants who have prepared them have a high level of expertise and credibility. Three professional accounting organizations have developed in Canada to certify accounting expertise.

The Canadian Institute of Chartered Accountants grants the **Chartered Accountant (CA)** designation. To achieve the designation, a person must earn a university degree, then complete an educational program and pass a national exam.[3] About half of all CAs work in CA firms who offer their accounting services to the public; the other half work in government or industry. CA firms typically provide audit, tax, and management services. CAs focus on external financial reporting, that is, certifying for various interested parties (shareholders, lenders, Revenue Canada, etc.) that the financial records of a company accurately reflect the true financial condition of the firm. The Certified General Accountants' Association of Canada grants the **Certified General Accountant (CGA)** designation. To achieve the designation, a person must complete an education program and pass a national exam. Some CGAs work in private industry and others work in CGA firms. CGAs also focus on external financial reporting, and emphasize the use of the computer as a management accounting tool.

TRENDS CHALLENGES

Who Can We Blame for This Mess?

The accounting profession has come under increased pressure during the 1990s, partly as a result of fallout from the unexpected failures of the Canadian Commercial Bank and the Northland Bank in the 1980s. It now seems that every time a business firm fails, there is talk of suing the public accounting firm that audited its books. The average person simply does not understand how a business firm can suddenly fail right after it has just been audited by a public accounting firm, particularly after the firm certifies that the business adhered to generally accepted accounting principles.

Some people think that auditors should expand their reports or clarify their language so that readers of financial statements will have a better idea of how a company is doing before they invest in it. Others suggest that auditors should give more consideration to the users of financial statements, and perhaps provide specific financial reporting for different user groups. Perhaps auditors should be charged with detecting fraud and reporting it when they find it.

Individuals in the accounting profession recognize that there is a "chummy" relationship between public accounting firms and their clients. There is also considerable elasticity in the application of generally accepted accounting principles. Some critics argue that business firms should be required to change their auditors every five years to prevent these relationships from developing.

One of the outcomes of several visible business failures in Canada and the U.S. is a sharp rise in the liability insurance premiums that are being paid by the big accounting firms. Insurance premiums have increased tenfold in the past two years, coverage has been reduced, and deductability limits have been increased. Interestingly, the smaller accounting firms have not faced

big increases, mainly because they do not generally audit the books of large firms (the ones who get sued for megabucks).

Big firms attract big clients, and when a big firm is sued, the suit frequently names the firm's auditor as well. At the end of 1992, for example, outstanding claims against the six biggest accounting firms in the U.S. totalled $30 billion. The most notable Canadian case involved Coopers & Lybrand, with claims against that firm totalling $500 million.

In 1993, the Canadian Life & Health Insurance Compensation Corp. (better known as Comp-Corp.), which was set up to protect holders of policies issued by insolvent companies, sued the public accounting firm of Mallette Maheu for negligence. It claimed Mallette made errors that forced Comp-Corp. to pay over $93 million in claims to policyholders of Les Cooperants, the failed insurance company. Comp-Corp. claimed that Mallette employees made errors that allowed Les Cooperants Insurance Group to report a profit of over $3 million in 1989, whereas the company actually lost $21 million. Mallette Maheu said the suit was frivolous and unfounded.

There are interesting legal ramifications of these lawsuits. In the simplest case, both a corporation and its auditor may be sued. But even if they are both found negligent, and if the courts decide that the auditor is 20 percent responsible, the accounting firm may have to pay the entire bill if the business firm has no money (which is likely, since it went bankrupt). And its gets worse. In theory, since accounting firms are partnerships, the partners have unlimited liability. In a big settlement, the partners' personal assets could be seized to pay the legal judgment. For this reason, there is increasing discussion of ways to limit the legal liability for audit firms.

The Society of Management Accountants of Canada grants the **Certified Management Accountant (CMA)** designation. To achieve the designation, a person must complete an education program. Unlike CAs or CGAs, CMAs typically work in industry and focus on internal management accounting, that is, they provide information for management decision making within a firm. CMAs emphasize the role of accountants in the planning and overall strategy of the firm in which they work.

Business firms employ specialized accountants with various professional designations in many different areas, including budgeting, financial planning, internal auditing, payroll, and taxation. In small businesses, one person may handle all accounting tasks.

certified management accountant (CMA)
An individual who has completed an education program; works in industry and focuses on internal management accounting.

A financial report is an integral component of the financial accounting system.

audit
An accountant's examination of a company's financial records to determine if it used proper procedures to prepare its financial reports.

generally accepted accounting principles (GAAP)
Standard rules and methods used by accountants in preparing financial reports.

Auditing.   Professional accountants are responsible for auditing a company's financial records. In an **audit**, an accountant examines a company's accounting system to determine whether it fairly reflects the firm's financial operations. Companies normally must provide audited financial reports when applying for loans or when selling stock. One of the auditor's responsibilities is to make sure the company's accounting system adheres to generally accepted accounting principles. **Generally accepted accounting principles (GAAP)** are a body of theory and procedure indicating the practices accountants should follow when making assessments of a company's financial records. The box "Who Can We Blame for This Mess?" describes some of the practical problems in auditing.

■ TOOLS OF THE ACCOUNTING TRADE

Accountants, whether public or private, rely on record-keeping. All accountants use journals and ledgers to enter and keep track of business transactions for their company. Underlying these records are the two key concepts of accounting: the accounting equation and double-entry bookkeeping.[4]

Record-Keeping with Journals and Ledgers

As Figure 12.1 shows, record-keeping begins with initial records of the firm's financial transactions. Examples include sales orders, invoices for incoming materials, employee time cards, and customer payments on installment purchases. Large companies receive and process tens of thousands of these documents every day. But unless they are analyzed and classified in an orderly fashion, managers cannot keep track of the business's progress.

journal
A chronological record of a firm's financial transactions along with a brief description of each transaction.

Notations of the sorted records are entered into a journal, an intermediate form of record, as the initial records are received. A **journal** is just a chronological record of financial transactions along with a brief description of the transaction. Some companies keep only a single (general) journal. Others keep specialized journals for cash receipts, sales, purchases, and the like. For centuries, journals were kept by hand but, today, many firms use computers for their record-keeping.

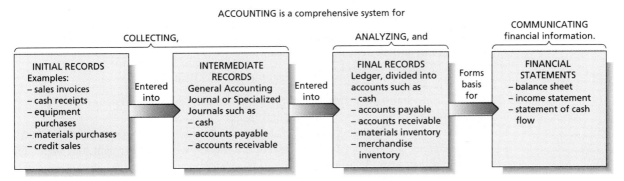

FIGURE 12.1
Accounting and record-keeping.

Transactions from a company's journal(s) are brought together and summarized, usually monthly, in final records called **ledgers**. Ledgers are divided into categories (accounts) similar to those of specialized journals. Unlike journals, accounts in a ledger contain only minimal descriptions of transactions. But they do contain an important additional column, labelled "Balance," as shown in Figure 12.4 (see page 261). (We will explore the meaning of the debit and credit columns shortly.) Because of this column, ledgers enable managers to tell at a glance where the company stands. If the balance is unexpectedly high or low, accountants and other managers can track backwards to the corresponding journal entry to see what has caused the unexpected balance.

ledger
Summations of journal entries, by category, that show the effects of transactions on the balance in each account.

Finally, at the end of the year, accountants total up all the accounts in a firm's ledger and assess the business's financial status. This summation is the basis for annual financial reports. With the preparation of financial reports, the old *accounting cycle* ends and a new cycle begins.

To clarify this record-keeping process, consider Figure 12.2, which illustrates a portion of the process for Perfect Posters, Inc. Notice how the cheque from Eye Poppers (an initial record) has been entered in the firm's general accounting journal (an intermediate record). As you can see, this entry eventually turns up in Perfect Posters' ledgers (a final record). And as we will discuss in the next section, these ledger entries are ultimately reflected in the financial reports that Perfect Posters needs for its shareholders and bank.

Eye-Poppers, Inc. 702 Willow St. Don Mills, Ontario	**CHEQUE NUMBER** **09006**

September 29 , 19 *98*

Pay to the
Order of _____*Perfect Posters Inc.*_____ $ __245.00__

Two Hundred forty-five and ————— $\frac{xx}{100}$ **Dollars**

BANK

_____   *Joan Little*
Authorized Signature
: 200 5268474 264 1223   **Ivan Itsch, Treasurer**

FIGURE 12.2

Record-keeping at Perfect Posters, Inc. traces the path of every financial transaction, such as this cheque from a customer, showing how it affects each financial category.

The Accounting Equation

At various points in the year, public and private accountants balance the data in journals and ledgers by using the following accounting equation:

$$\text{Assets} = \text{Liabilities} + \text{Owners' equity}$$

To understand why this equation is important, you must first understand what accountants mean by assets, liabilities, and owners' equity.

You are probably familiar with the first two terms in their general sense. Charm and intelligence are often said to be "assets." Someone who cannot swim may be a "liability" on a boat trip. Accountants apply these terms more narrowly, focusing on items with quantifiable value. Thus an **asset**, in the accounting sense, is anything of economic value owned by the firm. Examples include land, buildings, equipment, inventory, and payments due the company. In contrast, a **liability** is a debt owed by the firm to others.

Finally, you may have heard people speak of the "equity" they have in their home, meaning the amount of money they would get if they sold the house and paid off the mortgage. Similarly, **owners' equity** refers to the amount of money a firm's owners would receive if they sold all the company's assets and paid off all its liabilities (*liquidated* the company). We can rewrite the accounting equation to show this definition:

$$\text{Assets} - \text{Liabilities} = \text{Owners' equity}$$

If a company's assets exceed its liabilities, owners' equity is positive: If the company goes out of business, the owners will receive some cash (a gain) after selling assets and paying off liabilities. If liabilities outweigh assets, however, owners' equity is negative: There are insufficient assets to pay off all debts. If the company goes out of business, the owners will get no cash and some creditors will not be paid. Finally, owners' equity is also a meaningful number of both investors and lenders. For example, before lending money to owners, lenders want to know the amount of owners' equity existing in a business.

Owners' equity consists of two sources of capital:

- the amount that the owners originally invested
- profits earned by and reinvested in the company.

For example, when a company operates profitably, its assets increase faster than its liabilities. Owners' equity, therefore, will increase if profits are kept in the business instead of paid out as dividends to shareholders. Owners' equity can also increase if owners invest more of their own money to increase assets. However, owners' equity can shrink if the company operates at a loss or if the owners withdraw assets.

Double-Entry Accounting

If your business purchases inventory with cash, you do *two* things: (1) decrease your cash and (2) increase your inventory. Similarly, if you purchase supplies on credit, you (1) increase your supplies and (2) increase your accounts payable. If you invest more money in your business, you (1) increase your cash and (2) increase your owners' equity. In other words, *every transaction affects at least two accounts.* Accountants thus use a **double-entry accounting system** to record the *dual effects* of financial transactions.

Recording dual effects ensures that the accounting equation always balances. As the term implies, the double-entry system requires at least two bookkeeping entries for each transaction. This practice keeps the accounting equation in balance.

Debits and Credits: The T-Account

Another accounting tool uses *debits* and *credits* as a universal method for keeping accounting records. To understand debits and credits, we first need to understand the

asset
Anything of economic value owned by a firm or individual.

liability
Any debt owed by a firm or individual to others.

owners' equity
Any positive difference between a firm's assets and its liabilities; what would remain for a firm's owners if the company were liquidated, all its assets sold, and all its debts paid.

double-entry accounting system
A bookkeeping system, developed in the 15th century and still in use, that requires every transaction to be entered in two ways—how it affects assets and how it affects liabilities and owners' equity—so that the accounting equation is always in balance.

T-account. The format for recording transactions takes the shape of a **T** whose vertical line divides the account into two sides. The **T** format for Perfect Posters' General Accounting Journal is shown in Figure 12.3.

In bookkeeping, *debit* and *credit* refer to the side on which account information is to be entered: The left column of any T-account is called the *debit* side, and the right column is the *credit* side:

debit = left side
credit = right side

When an asset increases, it is entered as a **debit**. When it decreases, it is entered as a **credit**. Thus when Perfect Posters received payment from Eye Poppers, it received more cash—an asset. It thus debited the General Accounting Journal (Figure 12.4) by placing $245 on the left side of that T-account.

Figure 12.5 shows how the rules of the T-account are consistent with the terms of the accounting equation. Debits and credits provide a system of checks and balances. Every debit entry in a journal must have an offsetting credit entry elsewhere (not shown here). If not, the books will not balance because some error (or deliberate deception) has been introduced in the record-keeping. To ensure accurate financial records, accountants must find and correct such errors.

T-account
An accounting format that divides an account into a debit and a credit side.

debit
In bookkeeping, any transaction that increases assets or decreases liabilities or owners' equity; always entered in the left column.

credit
In bookkeeping, any transaction that decreases assets or increases liabilities or owners' equity; always entered in the right column.

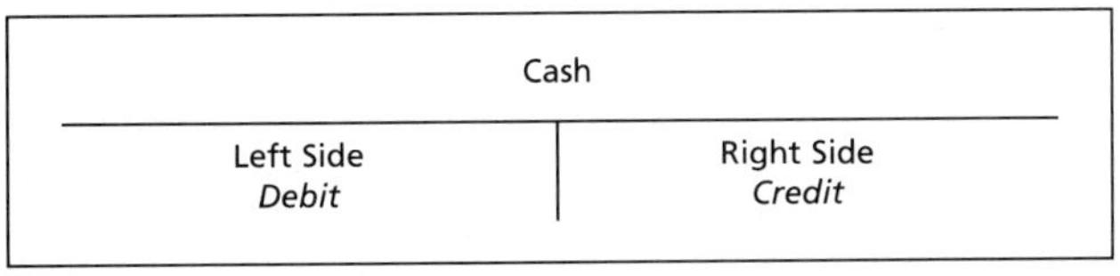

FIGURE 12.3
This unnumbered/unlabelled general accounting journal T format divides an account into two sides.

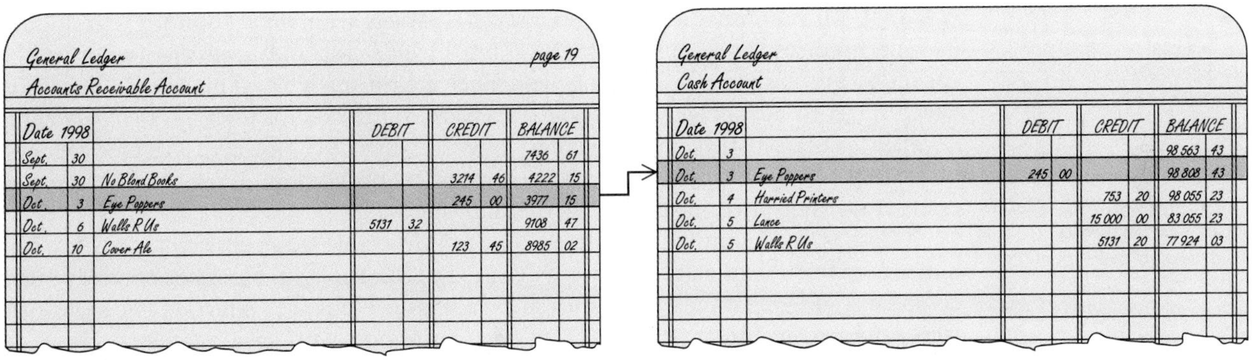

General Ledger — page 19
Accounts Receivable Account

Date 1998			DEBIT		CREDIT		BALANCE	
Sept.	30						7436	61
Sept.	30	No Blond Books			3214	46	4222	15
Oct.	3	Eye Poppers			245	00	3977	15
Oct.	6	Walls R Us	5131	32			9108	47
Oct.	10	Cover Ale			123	45	8985	02

General Ledger
Cash Account

Date 1998			DEBIT		CREDIT		BALANCE	
Oct.	3						98 563	43
Oct.	3	Eye Poppers	245	00			98 808	43
Oct.	4	Harried Printers			753	20	98 055	23
Oct.	5	Lance			15 000	00	83 055	23
Oct.	5	Walls R Us			5131	20	77 924	03

FIGURE 12.4
Under the double-entry accounting system, this cheque from a customer increases the Cash Balance and decreases the Accounts Receivable Balance.

Accounting Equation	Assets		=	Liabilities		+	Owner's Equity	
Rules of the T-Account	Debit for Increase	Credit for Decrease		Debit for Decrease	Credit for Increase		Debit for Decrease	Credit for Increase

FIGURE 12.5
In both the T-account and the accounting equation, debits and credits provide a system of checks and balances.

The double-entry system, therefore, provides an important method of accounting control: At the end of the accounting cycle, debits and credits must balance. In other words, total debits must equal total credits in the account balances recorded in the general ledger. An imbalance indicates improper accounting that must be corrected. "Balancing the books," then, is a control procedure to ensure that proper accounting has been used.

■ FINANCIAL STATEMENTS

financial statement
Any of several types of broad reports regarding a company's financial status; most often used in reference to balance sheets, income statements, and/or statements of cash flows.

As we noted earlier, the primary purpose of accounting is to summarize the results of a business's transactions and to issue reports that can help managers and others make informed decisions. Some of the most important reports, called **financial statements**, fall into several broad categories: balance sheets, income statements, and statements of cash flows. Balance sheets are sometimes called statements of financial position because they show the financial condition of a firm at one time. Other financial statements summarize the economic activities that have occurred during a specified period, usually one year. Together, these statements provide a picture of a business's financial health: what it is worth, how much it earns, and how it spends its resources.[5] Misleading financial statements can be very costly to investors.

Balance Sheets

balance sheet
A type of financial statement that summarizes a firm's financial position on a particular date in terms of its assets, liabilities, and owners' equity.

At one time, the only financial statement released to external users (such as shareholders and lenders) was the **balance sheet**. Early balance sheets provided sketchy information. Today, balance sheets supply a considerable amount of information including detailed, technical descriptions of complex accounts and transactions. Balance sheets present the accounting equation factors: a company's assets, its liabilities, and its owners' equity. Figure 12.6 shows a balance sheet for Perfect Posters.

current assets
Cash and other assets that can be converted into cash in the following year.

Assets.   Most companies have three types of assets from an accounting standpoint: current, fixed, and intangible. **Current assets** include cash and assets that can or will be converted into cash in the following year. They are normally listed in order of **liquidity**, which refers to how quickly they can be converted into cash or used up. Business debts normally can be satisfied only through payments of cash. A company that cannot generate cash easily as needed (in other words, a company that is not liquid) may be forced to sell assets at sacrifice prices or even to go out of business.

liquidity
The ease and speed with which an asset can be converted to cash; cash is said to be perfectly liquid.

Cash is, by definition, completely liquid. Marketable securities are slightly less liquid but can be sold quickly if there is a need for additional cash. Stocks or bonds of other companies and government securities such as treasury bills are all marketable securities. **Accounts receivable** are amounts due from customers who have purchased goods on credit. Most businesses expect to receive payment within 30 days of a sale.

accounts receivable
Amounts due to the firm from customers who have purchased goods or services on credit; a form of current asset.

Following accounts receivable is merchandise inventory, the cost of merchandise that has been acquired for sale to customers but is still on hand. Merchandise inventory is two steps removed from cash: first the inventory must be sold, generating accounts receivable, and then the accounts receivable must be collected to obtain cash.

fixed assets
Assets that have long-term use or value to the firm such as land, buildings, and machinery.

The final current asset listed is prepaid expenses. Included in this category would be supplies on hand and rent paid for the period to come. In all, Perfect Posters' current assets as of December 31, 1998, totalled $57 210.

amortization
Distributing the cost of a major asset over the years in which it produces revenues; calculated by each year subtracting the asset's original value divided by the number of years in its productive life.

Normally, the next major balance sheet classification is **fixed assets**. Items in this category have long-term use or value, for example, land, buildings, and equipment. Because buildings and equipment do eventually wear out or become obsolete, however, the accountant has amortized them. **Amortization** means calculating the useful life of the asset, dividing its worth by that many years, and then subtracting the resulting amount each year. That is, the asset's remaining value on the books goes down each year. In Figure 12.6, Perfect Posters has fixed assets of $107 880 after depreciation.

Perfect Posters, Inc.
555 Riverview, Toronto, Ontario

Perfect Posters, Inc.
Balance Sheet
As of December 31, 1998

Assets

Current Assets:		
Cash		$7,050
Marketable securities		2,300
Accounts receivable	$26,210	
Less: Allowance of doubtful accounts	(650)	25,560
Merchandise inventory		21,250
Prepaid expenses		1,050
Total current assets		**$57,210**
Fixed Assets:		18,000
Building	65,000	
Less: Accumulated depreciation	(22,500)	42,500
Equipment	72,195	
Less: Accumulated depreciation	(24,815)	47,380
Total fixed assets		**107,880**
Intangible Assets:		
Patents	7,100	
Trade marks	900	
Total intangible assets		**8,000**
Total assets		**$173,090**

Liabilities and Owners' Equity

Current Liabilities:		
Accounts payable	$16,315	
Wages payable	3,700	
Taxes payable	1,920	
Total current liabilities		**$21,935**
Long-term Liabilities:		
Notes payable, 8% due 2003	10,000	
Bonds payable, 9% due 2007	30,000	
Total long-term liabilities		**40,000**
Total liabilities		**$61,935**
Owners' Equity:		
Common stock, $5 par	40,000	
Additional paid-in capital	15,000	
Retained earnings	56,155	
Total owners' equity		**111,155**
Total liabilities and owners' equity		**$173,090**

FIGURE 12.6
Perfect Posters, Inc., balance sheet as of December 31, 1998.

Despite their name, intangible assets are not without monetary value, although their worth is hard to set. **Intangible assets** usually consist of the cost to obtain rights or privileges such as patents, trade marks, copyrights, and franchise fees. Another intangible asset, *goodwill*, can be recorded only when a business is being bought. It is the amount paid for an existing business over and above the value of its other assets because the firm has a particularly good reputation or good location. Perfect Posters has intangible assets of $8000 in patents for specialized equipment it designed to store posters vertically in the warehouse and for trade marks it owns.

Liabilities. Like assets, liabilities are separated into different categories, in this case, current liabilities and long-term liabilities. **Current liabilities** are debts that must be paid within the year. They include unpaid bills to suppliers for materials (**accounts payable**) as well as wages and taxes that will have to be paid in the coming year. Note in Figure 12.6 that Perfect Posters has current liabilities of $21 935.

Debts that are not due within one year are called **long-term liabilities**. They normally represent borrowed funds on which the company must pay interest. Perfect Posters' long-term liabilities are $40 000.

Owners' Equity. The final section of the balance sheet shows owners' equity broken down into common stock, paid-in capital, and retained earnings. When Perfect Posters was formed, the declared legal value of stock was $5 per share. By law, this $40 000 ($5 × 8000

intangible assets
Nonphysical assets such as patents, trade marks, copyrights, and franchise fees, which have economic value but whose precise value is difficult to calculate.

current liabilities
Any debts owed by the firm that must be repaid within the year.

accounts payable
Amounts due from the firm to its suppliers for goods and/or services purchased on credit; a form of current liability.

long-term liabilities
Any debts owed by the firm that need not be repaid within the year.

shares) cannot be distributed as dividends. Paid-in capital is additional money invested in the firm by the owners.

A company's net profits less dividend payments to shareholders are its **retained earnings**. Retained earnings accumulate when profits, which could have been distributed to shareholders, are instead kept for use by the company. Perfect Posters has total paid-in capital of $15 000 (from common stock plus additional paid-in capital) and retained earnings of $56 155.

retained earnings
A company's net profits less any dividend payments to shareholders.

Income Statements

income (profit-and-loss) statement
A type of financial statement that describes a firm's revenues and expenses and indicates whether the firm has earned a profit or suffered a loss during a given period.

Perhaps the most popular form of financial statement is the **income statement**. It is sometimes called a **profit-and-loss statement** because its description of a company's revenues and expenses results in a figure of the firm's profit or loss. That is,

$$\text{Revenues} - \text{Expenses} = \text{Profit (or Loss)}$$

An income statement enables the reader to assess how effectively management is using the resources entrusted to it. Figure 12.7 shows an income statement for Perfect Posters.

revenues
Any monies received by a firm as a result of selling a good or service or from other sources such as interest, rent, and licensing fees.

Revenues.   The first major category shown on an income statement is revenues. **Revenues** are the value of the resources that flow into a business from selling products or providing services. The $250 a law firm receives for preparing a will and the $65 a supermarket receives from a customer for groceries are both revenue. Perfect Posters reported revenues of $256 425 from the sale of the art prints and other posters it supplies to retailers.

cost of goods sold
Any expenses directly involved in producing or selling a good or service during a given time period.

Cost of Goods Sold.   The next section of the income statement details expenses involved in producing goods—the **cost of goods sold**. This category shows the costs of obtaining materials to make the products that were sold during the year. Perfect Posters, for example, started the year with posters valued at $22 380 in the warehouse. During the year it bought $103 635 more of these posters for a total of $126 015 worth of merchandise available to sell during 1998. By the end of the year it had sold all but $21 250 of the posters, which remained as "merchandise inventory" on December 31. So the firm's cost to obtain the goods it sold was $104 765.

gross profit (gross margin)
A firm's revenues (gross sales) less its cost of goods sold.

Subtracting cost of goods sold from revenues gives us **gross profit** (or **gross margin**). Perfect Posters' gross profit was $151 660 ($256 425 – $104 765).

Operating Expenses.   In addition to costs directly related to acquiring the goods it sells, every company has general operating expenses, ranging from erasers to the president's

Coca-Cola
www.cocacola.com

Fixed assets at this Coca-Cola bottling plant include the building and equipment that fills the bottles and moves them through production.

□□□□□□□□□□□   **Perfect Posters, Inc.**
555 Riverview, Toronto, Ontario

Perfect Posters, Inc.
Income Statement
Year ended December 31, 1998

Revenues (gross sales)		**$256,425**
Costs of goods sold:		
Merchandise inventory,		
January 1, 1998	$22,380	
Merchandise purchases		
during year	103,635	
Goods available for sale		$126,015
Less: Merchandise inventory,		
December 31, 1998		21,250
Cost of goods sold		104,765
Gross profit		**151,660**
Operating expenses:		
Selling and repackaging expenses:		
Salaries and wages	49,750	
Advertising	6,380	
Depreciation—warehouse and		
repackaging equipment	3,350	
Total selling and repackaging		
expenses		59,480
Administrative expenses:		
Salaries and wages	55,100	
Supplies	4,150	
Utilities	3,800	
Depreciation—office equipment	3,420	
Interest expense	2,900	
Miscellaneous expenses	1,835	
Total administration expenses		71,205
Total operating expenses		**130,685**
Income before taxes		20,975
Income taxes		8,390
Net income		**$12,585**

FIGURE 12.7
Perfect Posters, Inc. income statement for year ended December 31, 1998.

salary. Like cost of goods sold, **operating expenses** are resources that must flow out of a company for it to earn revenues. Perfect Posters had operating expenses of $59 480 in selling and repackaging expenses and $71 205 in administrative expenses for a total of $130 685.

Subtracting operating expenses and income taxes from gross margin yields **net income** (also called **net profit** or **net earnings**). As Figure 12.7 shows, in 1998, Perfect Posters' net income was $12 585. Remember that the net income figure can only be computed after many assumptions have been made and much data analyzed.

The Budget: An Internal Financial Statement

In addition to financial statements, managers need other types of accounting information to aid in internal planning, controlling, and decision making. Probably the most crucial *internal* financial statement is the budget. A **budget** is a detailed statement of estimated receipts and expenditures for a period of time in the future. Although that period is usu-

operating expenses
Costs incurred by a firm other than those included in cost of goods sold.

net income
(net profit or net earnings)
A firm's gross profit less its operating expenses and income taxes.

budget
A detailed financial plan for estimated receipts and expenditures for a period of time in the future, usually one year.

Procter & Gamble
www.pg.com

key ratio
A value obtained by dividing one value on a financial statement by another value.

Dun & Bradstreet
www.dnb.com

liquidity ratios
Measures of a firm's ability to meet its immediate debts; used to analyze the risks of investing in the firm.

current ratio
A form of liquidity ratio calculated as current assets divided by current liabilities.

ally one year, some companies also prepare budgets for three- or five-year periods, especially when considering major capital expenditures.

Budgets are also useful for keeping track of weekly or monthly performance. Procter & Gamble, for example, evaluates all its business units monthly by comparing actual financial results with monthly budgeted amounts. Discrepancies in "actual versus budget" totals signal potential problems and initiate action to get financial performance back on track.

■ ANALYZING FINANCIAL STATEMENTS

The financial statements discussed above present a great deal of information. But what does it all mean? How can these statements help investors decide what stock to buy or managers to decide whether to extend credit to another firm? By using statistics and ratios, we can analyze and compare financial statements from various companies and help answer these questions. We can also check a firm's progress by comparing its current and past statements.

A **key ratio** is a value obtained by dividing one value on a financial statement by another value. A business firm's financial condition can be assessed by comparing several important key ratios of items from its financial statements with key ratios for similar types of firms. Dun & Bradstreet Canada publishes key ratios for a variety of industries, including retail trade, wholesale trade, manufacturing, construction, services, and so on.

Ratios are normally grouped into four major classifications based on what they measure. These groups are (1) short-term solvency ratios, (2) long-term solvency ratios, (3) profitability ratios, and (4) activity ratios. Solvency ratios estimate risk; profitability ratios measure potential earnings; and activity ratios reflect management's use of assets. Depending on the types of decisions to be made, a user may apply none, some, or all the ratios in a particular group.

Short-Term Solvency Ratios

In the short run, a company's survival depends on its ability to pay its immediate debts. As noted earlier, such payments require cash. Short-term solvency ratios measure a company's relative liquidity. The higher a firm's **liquidity ratios**, the lower the risks involved for investors. The two most commonly used liquidity ratios are the current ratio and the quick (or acid-test) ratio.

Current Ratio.   This ratio has been called the bankers' ratio because it is used by those concerned with a firm's creditworthiness. By dividing current assets by current liabilities, the **current ratio** measures a company's ability to meet its current obligations out of its current assets. It reflects a firm's ability to generate cash to meet obligations through the normal, orderly process of selling inventories and collecting accounts receivable.

As a rule of thumb, a current ratio of 2:1 is satisfactory. A larger current ratio may imply that assets are not being used productively and should be invested elsewhere, rather than in current assets. A smaller current ratio may indicate that a company will have difficulty paying its bills.

How does Perfect Posters measure up? Judging from its current assets and liabilities at the end of 1998, we see that

$$\frac{\text{Current assets}}{\text{Current liabilities}} = \frac{\$57\ 210}{\$21\ 935} = 2.61$$

The firm may be holding too much cash, but it is a good credit risk.

Quick (Acid-Test) Ratio.   The current ratio represents a company's ability to meet expected demands for cash. In contrast, the **quick ratio**, or **acid-test ratio**, which divides quick assets by current liabilities, measures a firm's ability to meet emergency demands for cash. *Quick assets* include cash and assets just one step removed from being converted into cash: marketable securities and accounts receivable. Inventory is excluded from this measure because it can be liquidated quickly only at sacrifice prices. Thus, the quick ratio is a more stringent test than is the current ratio. As a rule of thumb, a quick ratio of 1.0 is satisfactory.

If we again consider Perfect Posters' position at the end of 1998, we see that

$$\frac{\text{Quick assets}}{\text{Current liabilities}} = \frac{\$7050 + 2300 + 26\,210 - 650}{\$21\,935} = 1.59$$

quick ratio (acid-test ratio)
A form of liquidity ratio calculated as quick assets (cash plus marketable securities and accounts receivable) divided by current liabilities.

In an emergency, the firm apparently can pay off all current obligations without having to liquidate its inventory.

Long-Term Solvency Ratios

If a company is to survive in the long run, it must be able to meet both its short-term (current) and long-term liabilities. These debts, as we have seen, usually involve interest payments. A firm that cannot meet these payments is in serious danger of collapse or takeover—a risk that makes creditors and investors alike very cautious. To measure this risk, we use long-term solvency ratios—**debt ratios**—like the debt-to-owners'-equity ratio.

debt ratios
Measures a firm's ability to meet its long-term debts; used to analyze the risks of investing in the firm.

The Debt-to-Owners'-Equity Ratio.   Calculated as debt (total liabilities) divided by owner's equity, the **debt-to-owners'-equity ratio** describes the extent to which a firm is financed through borrowings. This ratio is commonly used in industry financial statistical reports so that a reader can compare a company's ratio with industry averages. Companies with debt-to-owners'-equity ratios above 1 are probably relying too much on debt.

In the case of Perfect Posters, this ratio works out to

$$\frac{\text{Debt}}{\text{Owners' equity}} = \frac{\$61\,935}{\$111\,155} = .56$$

debt-to-owners'-equity ratio
A form of debt ratio calculated as total liabilities divided by owners' equity.

If this firm developed disastrous business difficulties and had to liquidate, all of the creditors would be protected. The owners' equity is more than sufficient for meeting all debts.

Sometimes, however, a fairly high debt-to-owners'-equity ratio may be not only acceptable but desirable. Borrowing funds gives companies or individuals **leverage**, the ability to make a purchase they otherwise could not afford. You have probably read about a "leveraged buyout" (LBO) in the newspapers. In these instances, firms have borrowed (taken on debt) in order to buy another company. When the purchased company allows the buying company to earn profits that exceed the cost of the borrowed funds, leveraging makes sound financial sense, even if it raises the debt-to-owners'-equity ratio. Unfortunately, many LBOs have gotten into financial trouble when actual profits fell short of anticipated levels or interest payments ballooned due to rising rates.

leverage
Using borrowed funds to make purchases, thus increasing the user's purchasing power, potential rate of return, and risk of loss.

Profitability Ratios

Although it is important for investors to know that a company is solvent in both the long and short term, safety or risk alone is not an adequate criterion for investment decisions. To decide which company's stock to buy, investors also need to have some measure of what returns they can expect. Return on investment and earnings per share are three commonly used **profitability ratios**.

profitability ratios
Measures of a firm's overall financial performance in terms of its likely profits; used by investors to assess their probable returns.

return on investment (return on equity)
A form of profitability ratio calculated as net income divided by total owners' equity.

Return on Investment.   Owners are interested in how much net income the business earns for each dollar invested by the owners. **Return on investment** (sometimes called **return on equity**) gives them the desired measure by dividing net income by total owners' equity.

For Perfect Posters, the ratio in 1998 was

$$\frac{\text{Net income}}{\text{Total owners' equity}} = \frac{\$12\ 585}{\$111\ 155} = 11.3\%$$

Is this figure good or bad? There is no set answer. If the firm's ratio for 1998 is higher than for previous years, then owners and potential investors should be encouraged. But if 11.3 percent is lower than the ratios of other companies in the same industry, they should be concerned.

earnings per share
A form of profitability ratio calculated as net income divided by the number of common shares outstanding.

Earnings per Share.   This ratio is one of the most quoted financial statistics. Defined as net income divided by the number of shares of common stock outstanding, **earnings per share** determines how large a dividend a company can pay its shareholders. It also indicates how much the company can reinvest in itself instead of paying dividends—that is, how much it can grow. Investors watch this ratio and use it to decide whether to buy or sell the company's stock. Often, a company's stock will lose market value when its latest financial statements report a decline in earnings per share.

If we assume that Perfect Posters has only one class of stock, we can calculate its earnings per share as

$$\frac{\text{Net income}}{\begin{array}{c}\text{Number of common}\\ \text{shares outstanding}\end{array}} = \frac{\$12\ 585}{8000} = \$1.57 \text{ per share}$$

Earnings per share is easy to calculate in the abstract. But in real life the computation is quite complex, in part because of the many classes of stock available.

Activity Ratios

Obviously, the efficiency with which a firm uses resources is linked to profitability. As a potential investor, then, you want to know which company "gets more mileage" from its resources. **Activity ratios** measure this efficiency. For example, say that two firms use the same amount of resources or assets. If firm A generates greater profits or sales, it is more efficient and thus has a better activity ratio.

activity ratios
Measures of how efficiently a firm uses its resources; used by investors to assess their probable returns.

By the same token, if a firm needs more resources to make products comparable to its competitors', it has a worse activity ratio. In June 1994, for instance, the consulting firm of Harbour & Associates Inc. released a study showing that in order to match Ford's efficiency, General Motors would have to cut 20 000 workers. According to the report, production inefficiency at its plants costs GM $2.2 billion annually in excess labour costs. On the upside, however, GM is making substantial progress. A similar report issued two years earlier had concluded that GM needed to cut 70 000 workers because excess labour costs were $4 billion.[6]

inventory turnover ratio
An activity ratio that measures the average number of times inventory is sold and restocked during the year.

Inventory Turnover Ratio.   Perhaps the most widely used typical activity ratio is the **inventory turnover ratio**. This ratio measures the average number of times inventory is sold and restocked during the year. It is expressed as the cost of goods sold divided by the average inventory. A high ratio means efficient operations—a smaller amount of investment is tied up in inventory. The company's funds can then be put to work elsewhere, earning greater returns.

Inventory turnover rates must be compared with earlier years and with industry averages. An inventory turnover rate of 5 might be excellent for an auto-supply store, but it would be disastrous for a supermarket, where a ratio of about 15 is common.

Perfect Posters' inventory turnover ratio for 1998 was

$$\frac{\text{Cost of goods sold}}{\text{Average inventory*}} = \frac{\$104\ 765}{(\$21\ 250\ +\ \$22\ 380)/2} = 4.8 \text{ times}$$

Average Inventory is the average of inventory value on
January 1, 1998, and December 31, 1998.

The firm's new merchandise replaces old merchandise every 76 days (365 days/4.8). This ratio of 4.8 is below the average of 7 for comparable wholesaling operations, indicating that the business is slightly inefficient. So, although Perfect Posters is highly profitable and low risk, it is not truly a "perfect" company!

■ MANAGING INFORMATION WITH COMPUTERS

Accounting information is obviously a vital element in modern business. Business information, however, can take many forms in addition to the financial: information about customers' locations and order patterns, information about supplies and finished goods on hand, information about workers' pay and productivity, information about products in development, and information about competitors and customers, for example.[7] The list is endless. Not surprisingly, the computer is at the forefront of contemporary information management. In this section, we explore the ways in which companies manage information with computers. First, however, to understand information management, you must understand what information is and what it is not. Only then can you appreciate what computers do and how they do it.

Information Management: An Overview

Businesspeople today are bombarded with facts and figures. Modern communications enable businesses to receive daily—and even hourly—information from remote plants, branches, and sales offices. To find the information they need to make critical decisions, managers must often sift through a virtual avalanche of reports, memos, magazines, and phone calls. How can businesses get useful information to the right people at the right time?

Most businesses regard their information as a private resource—an asset that they plan, develop, and protect. It is not surprising, then, that companies have information-management departments, just as they have production, marketing, and finance departments. Information management is an internal operation that determines business performance and outcomes.

Data versus Information.   Although businesspeople often complain that they get too much information, what they usually mean is that they get too many data. **Data** are raw facts and figures. **Information**, although based on data, is better defined as the meaningful, useful interpretation of data.

For example, consider the following *data:*

- 20 million tubes of toothpaste were sold in Canada last year
- the birth rate is rising
- 18 million tubes of toothpaste were sold the year before last
- advertising for toothpaste increased 17 percent last year
- a major dentists' group recently came out in favour of brushing three times a day

data
Raw facts and figures.

information
The meaningful, useful interpretation of data.

If all these data were put together in a meaningful way, they might produce *information* about what, in general, sells toothpaste and whether, in particular, toothpaste manufacturers should construct new plants to meet increasing demand. The challenge for businesses, then, is to turn a flood of data into manageable information.

Management Information Systems.   One response to this challenge has been the growth of **management information systems (MIS)**—systems for transforming data into information that can be used in decision making. Those charged with running a company's MIS services must first determine what information will be needed. Then, they must gather the data and, finally, provide ways to convert data into the desired information. They must also *control* the flow of information so that it goes only to people who need it.

■ DATABASES AND APPLICATIONS PROGRAMS

As noted earlier, all computer processing is the processing of data. This processing is carried out by **programs**, instructions the computer reads and according to which it performs specified functions. In this section, we begin by briefly describing the nature of computer data and databases. We then discuss a couple of the specialized *applications programs* designed for business use.

Data and Databases

Computers convert data into information by organizing it in some meaningful manner. With a computer system, chunks of data—numbers, words, and sentences—are stored in a series of related collections called *fields, records,* and *files.* Taken together, all the files constitute a **database**—a centralized, organized collection of related data.

Once data are entered into the database, they can be *processed*—manipulated, sorted, combined, and/or compared. In **batch processing**, data are collected over some time period and then processed as groups or batches. Payrolls, for example, are usually run in batches: Because most employees get paid on either a weekly or a biweekly basis, the data (the hours worked) are accumulated over the pay periods and processed at one time.

Batch processing was once the only type of computer processing. Although it is still widely used, companies today have choices such as **real-time processing**, in which data are entered and processed immediately. This system is always used when the results of each entry affect subsequent entries. For example, if you book seat F6 on Airfree Flight 253 on December 23, the computer must thereafter keep other passengers from booking the same seat.

Applications Programs

Inexpensive technology has made automation an option for businesses of all types and sizes. Programs are also available for a huge variety of business-related tasks. Some of these programs—Accpac, Great Plains, Simply Accounting, WISPR, and TAXPREP—address common accounting problems. Other programs have been developed for application to specialized needs. Three important application programs used by businesses are *word processing, spreadsheets,* and *database management.*

Word-Processing Programs.   Popular **word-processing programs** such as Word, Word for Windows, and WordPerfect basically allow computers to act as sophisticated typewriters. Sentences or paragraphs can be added or deleted without retyping or restructuring an entire document, and mistakes are easily corrected.

---

management information systems (MIS)
Systems for transforming raw data into information that can be used in decision making.

program
Set of instructions used by a computer to perform specified activities.

database
Centralized, organized collection of related data.

batch processing
Method of collecting data over a period of time and then processing by computer as a group or batch.

real-time processing
Method of entering data and processing them by computer immediately.

word-processing program
Application program that allows computers to store, edit, and print letters and numbers for documents created by users.

Spreadsheet Programs. Worksheets called **electronic spreadsheets** spread across and down a page in columns and rows. The user enters data, including formulas, at row and column intersections, and the computer automatically does the calculations. Balance sheets, income statements, and a host of other financial reports can be prepared using these programs.

Spreadsheets are also a useful planning tool, because they allow managers to see how changing one item will affect other related items. For example, a manager can insert various operating cost percentages, tax rates, or sales revenues. The computer will automatically recalculate all of the other figures and determine net profit.

Database Management Programs. **Database management programs** can keep track of a firm's relevant data. They can then sort and search through data and integrate a single piece of data into several different files. Companies can use programs such as dBaseIV and R-Base to create their own "home-grown" or *primary databases*. They may also use *secondary databases* that are created and sold by other businesses. Secondary databases cover a huge range of information. ABI/INFORM, for example, is a secondary database of abstracts and indexing to business articles from over 800 magazines and newspapers. Other databases are specialized. Dow Jones News/Retrieval, for instance, offers financial news; Lexis compiles legal materials.

■ TYPES OF COMPUTER SYSTEMS

Although all computer systems share basic common elements, they vary dramatically in size, capacity, and cost.

Categorizing Computer Systems by Size

Grouping computer systems by cost, capacity, and capability results in four basic categories:

- *Microcomputers.* Most of the computers that you see sitting on desks are **microcomputers** (also called **personal computers**, or PCs). The convenience and power of microcomputers like the IBM PC, the Apple Macintosh, and the Compaq have shifted the balance of computer power to smaller systems.
- *Minicomputers.* Larger, faster, and more sophisticated than microcomputers, **minicomputers** can process over a million instructions per second (MIPS). They can also support multiple users and provide much more storage than micros.
- *Mainframes.* Still bigger and faster than minicomputers are **mainframes.** Costing $1 million or more, they can store and access billions of characters and process tens of millions of instructions per second. Mainframes are most often found in banks and other commercial organizations where large volumes of data must be processed.[8]
- *Supercomputers.* The largest, fastest, and most expensive of all computers, **supercomputers** are used mainly in scientific applications in which huge numbers of complex calculations need to be performed very quickly. In part because of their cost—over $5 million—there are at present fewer than 150 of these systems in operations.

Systems Architecture

Although differences in computer capacity and ability are shrinking, systems *architecture* has remained a fairly constant feature. **Systems architecture** refers to the location of the various parts of the system: its data-entry and data-processing operations, database, data output, and computer staff. Systems architecture is classified according to the organization of the system's parts:

electronic spreadsheets
Application programs that allow the user to enter categories of data and determine the effect of changes in one category (e.g., sales) on other categories (e.g., profits).

database management program
Application program for creating, storing, searching, and manipulating an organized collection of data.

Dow Jones & Company
www.dowjones.com

microcomputer (or personal computer)
Smallest, slowest, least expensive form of computers.

minicomputer
Computer whose capacity, speed, and cost fall between those of microcomputers and mainframes.

mainframe
Computer whose capacity and speed enable it to service many users simultaneously.

supercomputer
Largest, fastest, most expensive form of computers.

systems architecture
Location of a computer system's elements—data-entry and data-processing operations, database, data output, and computer staff.

Performing in seconds calculations that would take a human being working nonstop for 24,000 years, graphics workstations like this one at Ford's Studio 2000X in Dearborn, Michigan, add a new dimension (actually, several new dimensions) to computer-graphics imagery. Using programs from companies like Silicon Graphics and Evans & Sutherland, Ford engineers can transform a designer's sketched lines into rotating mathematical models of a vehicle's entire surface.

centralized system
Form of computer system architecture in which all processing is done in one location through a centralized computer, database, and staff.

decentralized system
Form of computer-system architecture in which processing is done in many locations by means of separate computers, databases, and personnel.

computer network
Group of interconnected computer systems able to exchange information with one another from different locations.

wide area network
Network of computers and workstations linked by telephone wires or by satellite.

local area network (LAN)
Network of computers and workstations, usually within a company, linked together by cable.

- *Centralized systems.* In a **centralized system,** most of the processing is done in one location. For example, a bank's branch teller machines all need the same information. Thus they are all hooked up to the main office's mainframe, which houses all customer information files in a central database. Centralized systems do have drawbacks: For example, when the central computer fails or communications lines to the central computer go down, all the branches go down.

- *Decentralized systems.* In a **decentralized system,** each location determines the needs of its own system: physical components, programs, databases, personnel, and so forth. Plants are independent of centrally located mainframes and communication links between locations. A drawback arises when different locations independently adopt incompatible components and/or programs. It may become difficult or impossible for systems at separate locations to share important data.

- *Networks.* At the same time, however, computer *networking* now allows computers to exchange data quickly and easily. A **computer network** is a group of interconnected computer systems that can exchange information among several different locations. Networks may link computers nationwide through telephone wires or satellites, as in **wide area networks.** Wal-Mart, for example, invested more than US$20 million on a satellite network that links its nearly 2000 retail stores to its Bentonville, Arkansas, headquarters.

  Internal networks may link computers through cables, as in **local area networks (LANs).** The computers in internal networks share processing duties, software, storage areas, and data. On television's Home Shopping Network, for example, hundreds of operators seated at monitors in a large room are united via a LAN for entering call-in orders from customers. This arrangement allows the use of a single computer system with one database and software system. Combination systems using local and wide area networks are also possible. Separate plants or offices might handle orders locally while electronically transmitting sales summaries to a corporate office. Computer networks thus give companies the advantages of both centralized and decentralized processing.

Many companies today are finding their old mainframe systems outmoded. Over the years, components and features were simply added on, increasing capacity without meeting the need for greater flexibility. Systems have become overcustomized, and reprogramming mainframes to respond to new formats is expensive and time-consuming. To construct systems that will support such innovative management techniques as just-in-time inventory and total quality management, many companies are thus "downsizing"—switching from mainframe to network systems: Connected workstations called "clients" communicate quickly with "servers" (computers that hold databases and database programs). At Motorola, for instance, networking "rings" in three LANs now route data requests from 1000 workstation "clients" through 30 minicomputer "servers." Cost of the company's MIS has dropped from 3.7 percent to 1.2 percent of sales.[9] Another computer problem is described in the box "Can You Believe It?"

TRENDS CHALLENGES

Can You Believe It?

An interesting and, to some, unbelievable problem has arisen in computer systems. It seems that the arrival of the year 2000 will cause a lot of companies serious problems. Most computers use only the last two digits in a year to keep track of dates (e.g., "99" for 1999). They do this because in the bygone days of punched-card computer programs, which had only 80 columns for data, using only the last two digits saved space. When more modern software was developed, the issue was never revisited, perhaps because nobody thought that programs written back then would still be in use today. But they are, and when the year 1999 ends and the year 2000 begins, computers will become very confused.

Some computers will assume that "00" means 1900, while others will pick a year at random. Still others will not know what to do and will do nothing. Organizations that do calculations in which dates are critical will be most affected. For example, banks (interest rates), government agencies (employment insurance), insurance companies (insurance policies), and utilities (monthly bills) will all have this problem. Paul Raymond of CGI Information Systems in Montreal says that a person could conceivably get a telephone bill for 100 years when the century turns.

To appreciate the magnitude of this problem, consider these facts: large organizations have an average of 8000 computer programs, and each program averages 1500 lines of code. Assuming a cost of $1 per line to revise codes, it will cost a large organization about $12 million to solve this problem. At Allstate Insurance, for example, there are 100 full-time programmers working on the problem. The company will eventually spend $40 million to make its computers ready for the year 2000. A company that started working on the problem in 1996 would have had to allocate 27 full-time people to fix all of its codes before the year 2000. The Gartner Group, a technology research firm, estimates that worldwide expenditures could total $600 billion.

Insurance companies encountered the problem first. In 1993, they discovered that they could not compute the maturity date of seven-year policies. They resolved the problem by entering seven-year policies as six-year policies and doing the remaining year's calculations on paper. In 1994, they entered seven-year policies as five-year policies and did paper calculations for the last two years. But this system is becoming unworkable as the year 2000 approaches. Banks discovered the problem in 1994 when they realized that it was the last year for which they could calculate five-year mortgage rates.

The problem is significant enough that some organizations are already working on resolving it. Laurentian Bank spent six months fixing their mortgage system, just one of many systems the bank has. The trick is to develop software that recognizes that the year 2000 immediately follows 1999. To the average person, this may sound easy, but it is not.

Perhaps the biggest problem at the moment is getting management to recognize that a problem exists. Banks and insurance companies understand the date problem because they are already experiencing it, but many other firms are not yet aware of the difficulties they will face. These companies may discover the problem in 1999 and find that they simply do not have enough time to fix it. Various studies have shown that large software development projects are almost always problematic. One-quarter of such projects are cancelled before they are finished, and three-quarters do not work as planned. If these findings hold true, businesses that wake up to the problem in 1999 may find that their very existence is threatened.

This problem is not limited just to business firms. A 1997 report by the Auditor-General warned that crucial government public services like search and rescue operations, employment insurance payments, and commercial cargo clearance could be severely disrupted unless the federal government takes immediate and aggressive action to solve the problem.

A crisis for one organization may be an opportunity for another. Those who will capitalize on this opportunity are technology consultants and computer programmers. Ottawa-based Progestic International Inc. has developed a system for fixing the year 2000 problem without having to tamper with the software programs in a computer system. It was chosen by the province of Ontario as one of the firms that will help solve its year 2000 problems.

Bob Bemer, the man who created the "escape sequence" (the "Esc" button on your computer keyboard) is now working on a way to solve the year 2000 problem. Basically, his approach is to attack the problem at the fundamental level where computers operate in ones and zeros (called machine code). His method is too complex to describe here, but expert programmers that have looked at his patented material agree that it will work for many companies. However, they think it is very risky because it requires tampering with source code and stored data, and that simply isn't done. But as time runs out, it may be the only alternative available to businesses who have waited until the last minute.

Progestic International
www.progestic.com/index.htm

■ THE FUTURE OF INFORMATION MANAGEMENT

Although computing is constantly evolving, some of its foundational elements are already here: artificial intelligence, expert systems, office information technologies, executive information systems, operation information systems, data communication networks, and multimedia communication systems. The most powerful vehicle for using these elements to their full potential is the marriage of computers to communication technologies. Thanks to lower-cost, higher-capacity networks, the joining of computers, communication, and the mass media is already in its first stages.

Artificial Intelligence

artificial intelligence (AI)
Construction and programming of computers to imitate human thought processes.

Artificial intelligence (AI) can be defined as the construction and programming of computers to imitate human thought processes. In developing components and programs for artificial intelligence, computer scientists are thus trying to design computers capable of reasoning so that computers, instead of people, can perform useful activities. Robotics, for example, is a category of AI:

- An AI system developed by Hitachi allows an automated subway in Sendai, Japan, to brake more swiftly and smoothly than if a human were at the controls.

- Designed to serve giant companies that must store immense amounts of information, IBM's Tape Library Dataserver stores 42 trillion bytes of data. Data requests can be made from terminals in various departments. Cameras mounted on each robotic "band" locate one out of almost 19 000 numbered tape cartridges. The robot then loads the cartridge into a reader that projects the information on the personal computer screen of a manager needing data on inventory, transactions, employees, or customers.[10]

With their "reasoning" capabilities, robots can "learn" repetitive tasks such as painting, assembling components, and inserting screws. Furthermore, they avoid repeating mistakes by "remembering" the causes of past mistakes and, when those causes reappear, adjusting or stopping until adjustments are made.

Computer scientists are also designing AI systems that possess sensory capabilities (vision with lasers, hearing, feeling) and that can process natural languages. When machines can process natural languages, humans will be able to give instructions and ask questions without learning special computer languages. When machines can reason on the basis of natural-language inputs, they may be able to learn from experience and apply their learning to solving new problems.[11]

Expert Systems

A special form of artificial intelligence programs, **expert systems** try to imitate the behaviour of human experts in a particular field. Expert systems thus make available the rules that an expert applies to specific types of problems. In effect, they supply everyday users with "instant expertise."

Many firms already use expert systems for training and analysis:

- The Digital Equipment sale force uses a system called Xcon to match customer needs with the most appropriate combination of computer input, output, and memory devices: Almost as if they were accompanied by expert sales advisers, sales-people receive one-of-a-kind equipment suggestions that the system has tailored to each customer's specific requirements.[12]

- Nortel Networks uses a system called Engineering Change Manager to simplify and speed up product design changes. The system considers factors such as a component's strength requirements, shape, appearance, and cost. It then creates the suggested redesigns to meet all the requirements. The new designs are then given to engineers, who can compare them with their own designs for better, faster product improvements.[13]

Office Information Technologies

Office information technologies (OIT) are the computer-based devices and applications whose function is to enhance the performance and productivity of general office activities. In this section we will survey three of the most solidly entrenched innovations in today's automated office: fax machines, voice mail, and e-mail.

Fax machines (short for *facsimile-transceiver machines*) can transmit text documents, drawings, and photograph images over telephone lines in a matter of seconds, thus permitting written communication over long distances. Fax machines are popular with both large and small firms because of speed and low cost.

Voice mail is a computer-based system for receiving and delivering incoming telephone calls. Incoming calls are never missed because a voice responds to the caller, invites a message, and stores it. A company with voice mail has each employee's phone networked for receiving, storing, and forwarding calls.

An **electronic mail** (or **e-mail**) system electronically transmits letters, reports, and other information between computers, whether in the same building or in another country. It is also used for voice transmission and for sending graphics and videos from one computer to another. E-mail thus substitutes for the flood of paper and telephone calls that threatens to engulf many offices.

Executive Information Systems

Executive information systems (EIS) are quick-reference, easy-access information clusters specially designed for instant access by upper-level managers. Business planning strategy sessions, and competitive evaluations depend on convenient information retrieval by senior-level managers, who do not typically possess technical computer skills. An EIS is easily accessible with simple keyboard strokes or even voice commands.

Operation Information Systems

Computer technology is having a major impact on production and manufacturing through the use of **operation information systems** which includes computer-aided design (CAD), computer-aided manufacturing (CAM), and computer operation control.

expert system
Form of artificial intelligence that attempts to imitate the behaviour of human experts in a particular field.

Digital Equipment
www.digital.com

fax machine
Machine that can transmit copies of documents (text and graphics) over telephone lines.

voice mail
Computer-based system for receiving and delivering incoming telephone calls.

electronic mail (e-mail)
Computer system that electronically transmits letters, reports, and other information between computers.

executive information system (EIS)
Easy-access information cluster specially designed for upper-level managers.

operation information system
Computer system used to manage production and manufacturing operations.

CAD assists in designing products by simulating the real product and displaying it in three-dimensional graphics. Immersion's MicroScribe-3D software (www.immerse.com), for example, uses a penlike tool to scan the surface of any three-dimensional object, such as a football helmet, and electronically transforms it into a 3D graphic. The helmet designer can then try different shapes and surfaces for the helmet in the computer and observe the new designs on the video monitor.[14] For many design applications, CAD creates faster designs at lower cost than manual modelling methods.

Data Communication Networks

data communication network
Global network (such as the Internet) that permits users to send electronic messages and information quickly and economically.

Gaining popularity on both home and business computers are public and private **data communication networks**: global networks that carry streams of digital data (electronic messages, documents, and other forms of video and sound) back and forth quickly and economically on telecommunication systems. The most prominent networks, the Internet and the World Wide Web, have emerged as powerful communication technologies.[15]

Internet
Global data communication network serving thousands of computers with information on a wide array of topics and providing communication flows among certain private networks.

The Internet.   The **Internet** (or the Net, for short) is the largest public network, serving thousands of computers with information on business, science, and government and providing communication flows among certain private networks, including CompuServe and MCI Mail. Originally commissioned by the Pentagon as a communication tool for use during war, the Internet allows personal computers in virtually any location to be linked together by means of large computers known as network servers. The Net has gained in popularity because it makes available an immense wealth of academic, technical, and business information. Another major attraction is its capacity to transmit e-mail. For thousands of businesses, therefore, the Net is joining—and even replacing—the telephone, the fax machine, and express mail as a standard means of communication.

The Net continues to grow because it offers new opportunities for computing enhancements. Consider Java by Sun Microsystems Inc. Java is a software language that can be used by software developers on any type of PC. By instantaneously connecting software writers with software users on the Internet, it provides an entirely new, convenient way of creating, selling, delivering, and using software. Software writers like it because they can create a new tool and then send it on the Net to users. When the program arrives it automatically loads itself and runs on the requestor's PC. Thus, the user avoids having to install a big program. Suppose you want to create a Website and you are not a programmer. Just use Java to call up "Webra" and you'll get assistance. If you want to create animation for your Website, use Java to call up "Dimension X" and you get programs to create animation with just a few mouse clicks. Each time the program is needed you call up Java and it comes across the Net, then leaves when you're finished. As with the Java example, these applets (short application or mini-programs) can be retrieved from many suppliers' Websites; they perform a specific function, then disappear after the user is finished. One danger is that when you import these just-in-time programs they may carry viruses that infect users' systems, so security is a problem.[16]

World Wide Web
Subsystem of computers providing access to the Internet and offering multimedia and linking capabilities.

World Wide Web.   Thanks to a subsystem of 7000 computers known as the **World Wide Web** (WWW, or simply the Web), the Internet is easier to use than ever before. It has made the Internet usable to a general audience, rather than just to technical users. The Federal Express Website, for example, gives customers access to the FedEx package-tracking database. Each day up to 12 000 customers look through the FedEx Web pages and find out the status of their packages without any help from FedEx employees. This customer self-help saves FedEx up to $2 million each year.

The computers linked by the Web are known as Web servers. They are owned by corporations, colleges, government agencies, and other large organizations. There are now well over 200 000 such sites serving up tens of millions of pages of publicly accessible information.[17] The user can connect with the Web by means of **browser** software (such as Netscape, Netcruiser, WebExplorer, and Mosaic). Browsers support the graphics and linking capabilities needed to navigate the Web.

Among the most successful enterprises to take advantage of the Web are those that operate search engines. Companies such as InfoSeek, Lycos, and Yahoo maintain free-to-use public directories of the Web's ever-increasing content. These indexes constantly scan the Web to stay up to date. A search engine may respond to approximately 10 million inquiries per day. It is thus no surprise that search engines are packed with paid ads placed by companies such as Honda and AT&T.

Intranets.   The success of the Internet has led some companies to extend the Net's technology internally, for browsing internal Websites containing information throughout the firm. These private networks, or **intranets**, are accessible only to employees via entry through electronic firewalls. At Compaq Computer Corp., the intranet allows employees to shuffle their retirement savings among various investment funds. Ford Motor Co.'s intranet, with links to design centres in Asia, Europe, and the United States, helped engineers design the 1996 Taurus. A major advantage of these intranets is their use of a more standardized electronic system for information storage and access. The revolutionary new information links were previously impossible among departments and offices separated by distance or by incompatible software, computers, and databases. The new technology uses a more standardized system based on the same structure used in the Internet.[18]

Multimedia Communication Systems

Today's information systems include not only computers but also **multimedia communication systems**: connected networks of communication appliances such as faxes, televisions, sound equipment, cell phones, printing machines, and photocopiers that may also be linked with such mass media as TV and radio broadcast programming, news and other print publications, and library collections. Not surprisingly, the integration of these elements is already changing the ways we live our lives and manage our businesses. A good example is T. Rowe Price's TeleAccess, a customer service in which investors make their own financial transactions by interacting with a computer on the phone, or use their home computers to track their investments and electronically change their portfolios.

Multimedia communication technology is profoundly expanding the applications of PCs. Today's programs incorporate sound, animation, and photography as well as ordinary graphics and text. Communication power has multiplied through online information services such as Prodigy and CompuServe that provide instant access to financial and news data. Electronic discussion groups and business meetings display interactive dialogue on screens for the benefit of conference callers in widespread locations. America Online, for example, has some 14 000 chat rooms that allow PC users to exchange electronic messages in real time.[19] Today's PCs have built-in TV circuits so that you can tune in your favourite TV show on the computer monitor, watch movies from CD-ROMs, and listen to your favourite music.

browser
Software supporting the graphics and linking capabilities necessary to navigate the World Wide Web.

intranet
Private network of internal Websites and other sources of information available to a company's employees.

Compaq Computer Corp.
www.compaq.com

multimedia communication system
Connected network of communication appliances (such as faxes or TVs) that may be linked to forms of mass media (such as print publications or TV programming).

SUMMARY OF LEARNING OBJECTIVES

1. **Explain the role of accountants and distinguish between the three types of professional accountants found in Canada.** By collecting, analyzing, and communicating financial information, accountants provide business managers and investors with an accurate picture of a firm's financial health. *Chartered Accountants*

(CAs) and *Certified General Accountants* (CGAs) provide accounting expertise for client organizations who must report their financial condition to external stakeholders. *Certified Management Accountants* (CMAs) provide accounting expertise for the firms that employ them.

2. **Explain how the following three concepts are used in *record-keeping: accounting equations, double-entry accounting*, and *T-accounts* for debits and credits.** The *accounting equation* (assets = liabilities + owners' equity) is used to balance the data in both *journals* and *ledgers*. *Double-entry accounting* acknowledges the dual effects of financial transactions and·ensures that the accounting equation always balances. Using the *T-account*, accountants record financial transactions in the shape of a T, with the vertical line dividing the account into *debit* and *credit* columns. These tools enable accountants not only to enter but to track transactions.

3. **Describe two important *financial statements* and show how they reflect the activity and financial condition of a business.** The *balance sheet* summarizes a company's assets, liabilities, and owners' equity at a given point in time. The *income statement* details revenues and expenses for a given period of time and identifies any profit or loss.

4. **Explain how computing key *financial ratios* can help in analyzing the financial strengths of a business.** Drawing upon data from financial statements, ratios can help creditors, investors, and managers assess a firm's finances. The *current, liquidity, and debt-to-owners'-equity ratios* all measure solvency, a firm's ability to pay its debt in both the short and long runs. *Return on sale, return on investment*, and *earnings per share* are all ratios that measure profitability. *Inventory turnover ratios* show how efficiently a firm is using its funds.

5. **Identify the role played in computer systems by *databases* and *application programs*.** Through computer sequences of instructions called *programs*, computers are able to process data and to perform specific functions. Once *data* (raw facts and figures) are centralized and organized into meaningful *databases*, they can be manipulated, sorted, combined, and/or compared according to program instructions. The most popular business *applications programs* are *word processing, spreadsheets*, and *database management*.

6. **Classify *computer systems* by size and structure.** Computers can be categorized according to cost, capacity, and capability. The smallest, slowest, and least expensive computers are *microcomputers*. The largest, fastest, and most expensive are *supercomputers*. *Minicomputers* and *mainframes* fall in between, but all these distinctions are beginning to blur. In contrast, computer systems differ sharply in architecture. In *centralized systems*, most processing is done from one location, using a centralized database. In *decentralized systems*, each location handles its own processing from its own database. Computer *networks* allow branch computers to communicate, offering some of the advantages of both centralized and decentralized systems.

7. **List some trends in the application of computer technology to business information management.** The next generation of computers promises exciting developments in information management. Advances in *artificial intelligence, expert systems, office information technologies, executive information systems, operation information systems, data communication networks*, and *multimedia communication systems* continue to offer businesspeople assistance in making decisions and solving problems.

STUDY QUESTIONS AND EXERCISES

Review Questions

1. What are the three kinds of accountants found in Canada? How are they different?

2. What are the basic kinds of financial statements? What major information does each contain?

3. What are the four major classifications of financial statement ratios? Give an example of one ratio in each category.

4. Describe three important types of specialized computer application programs designed for business use.

5. Describe microcomputers, minicomputers, mainframes, and supercomputers according to cost, speed of processing, and capacity.

Analysis Questions

6. Suppose Inflatables, Inc., makers of air mattresses for swimming pools, has the following transactions in a typical week:

    • sale of three deluxe mattresses to Al Wett (paid cash, $75) on July 16

    • received cheque from Ima Flote in payment for mattresses bought on credit ($90) on July 13

    • received new shipment of 200 mattresses from Airheads Manufacturing (total cost $2000) on July 17

    Construct a journal for Inflatables, Inc.

7. If you were planning to invest in a company, which of the three types of financial statements would you most want to see? Why?

8. Describe the types of activities for which a local department store might choose to use batch processing. For what activities would it prefer real-time processing?

Application Exercises

9. Interview an accountant at a local manufacturing firm. Determine what kind of budgets the firm uses, and the process by which budgets are developed. Also determine how budgeting helps managers plan their business activities? Give specific examples.

10. Describe the computer system at your college or university. Identify the system's components and describe its capacity/speed and architecture.

BUILDING YOUR BUSINESS SKILLS

Goal

To encourage students to understand the difference between World Wide Web directories and search engines and to compare the usefulness of each tool in a research project.

Background

The World Wide Web is jam-packed with information. The challenge is to access sites that have the information you need. Among the most useful mechanisms for navigating the Web are search engines and directories. Whereas search engines index every word at a Website, directories catalogue information into subject categories, subcategories, and subsubcategories. Search engines pull up the largest number of sites, but are more difficult to use because of the sheer volume of material.

Yahoo! (http://www.yahoo.com) and the Britannica Information Guide (http://www.ebig.com) are directories, whereas altavista (http://altavista.digital.com), excite (http://www.excite.com), hotbot (http://www.hotbot.com), infoseek (http://www. infoseek. com), and lycos (http://www.lycos.com) are search engines.

Method

Step 1: Divide into groups of four or five people. Then choose a business-related research topic that interests every group member. It could be a company such as Coca-Cola or CBC, a business leader such as Microsoft CEO Bill Gates, or a current issue such as business ethics, Internet marketing, or product liability. Working with group members, narrow your topic so it is manageable. For example, you might choose to investigate product liability cases related to automobile air bags or the changes in corporate leadership at Coca-Cola after the death in 1997 of chairperson and CEO Roberto C. Goizueta.

Step 2: Go to the directories and search engines listed in this exercise. Start by reading through each site's help section for search advice. Focus on advanced search commands that will help narrow results. For example, you will learn that using quotation marks around a phrase means that the directory or search engine will look for the phrase instead of the separate words that make up the phrase.

Step 3: Type your topic into the directories and search engines listed in this exercise. Working with group members, analyze each response list to determine where you got the most useful results.

Follow-Up Questions

1. Which site gave you the most useful information?
2. What differences did you notice between the broad categories of directories and search engines?
3. What differences did you notice between specific directories and among specific search engines?
4. What mechanisms did you discover to help you conduct successful future searches?
5. What directory or search engine would you go to first with your next research question? Why?
6. How has the World Wide Web changed the nature of business research?

Prentice Hall **T A K E   I T   T O   T H E   N E T**

Check out our Companion Website

for this chapter's Exploring the Net exercise, featuring information on the year 2000 problem from Industry Canada's Strategis Website and other intriguing, annotated destinations. You'll also find practice exercises, updated Weblinks from the text, links to newsgroups, updates, and more.

COMPANION WEBSITE

w w w . p r e n t i c e h a l l . c a / e b e r t

BUSINESS CASE 12

Is Your Computer a Television? Or Is Your TV a Computer?

Picture yourself watching the World Series on TV and using a wireless keyboard to open a window on the television screen. Now you can download the pitcher's career stats from the team's home page on the Internet without even missing an out.

There is little doubt in most observers' minds that some day soon the functions of the family television and the home office computer will be joined in a single machine. Whether that machine will be a computer that picks up TV feeds from the Internet, or a TV with computer and Internet capabilities, is a question that threatens to shake up both the computer and television manufacturing industries, with broadcasters caught in the middle.

In an escalating series of news conferences, product unveilings, and sweeping statements about the future as they see it, executives of consumer electronics firms and computer makers have been squaring off for several years. Neither has had much success breaking into the other's market yet, but neither is giving up any time soon. Gateway 2000 Inc., which makes PCs, also

sells a big-screen computer television under the brand name Destination. Several electronics firms have marketed Web TV devices that allow users to access the Internet on conventional TVs. Sales of both products have been disappointing.

Most Canadian and U.S. households own one or more TVs, and about 40 percent own a personal computer. Both industries are assuming that with the arrival of digital or high-definition television technology, people will have to begin replacing their TVs before the scheduled end of conventional broadcasting in 2006. With the prospect of $150 billion in revenues just from sales of the new sets, the stakes are high for what may be the biggest market stakeout of the computer age.

PC makers want to produce their television pictures in a format incompatible with the one that broadcasters use, which uses 525 lines per screen but gets higher resolution than normal with extra channel capacity. TV manufacturers, anticipating the announced plans of major broadcasters who lobbied hard for—and secured—the right to broadcast HDTV,

▶

expect to produce high-definition TVs or PC/TVs that accept 1080 lines per screen. The Federal Communication Commission (FCC) in the U.S. has urged an agreement over technology and doesn't want to arbitrate the coming clash.

The computer industry is counting on the decline of television viewing and the rise of the Internet to change the way people use their TVs. It's already clear that most browsing on the Net is occurring during television's traditional prime time hours. And "we think it is much easier to have a PC do television than to add personal computing capabilities to TVs," says Intel executive Rob Siegal. "The PC has just got to migrate from the home office to the family room. In fact, within the next year, every new PC sold in the United States will include a digital TV receiver as standard equipment, and computer industry executives expect to sell a million PCs with digital TV decoders by 2002.

Consumer electronics firms, even while they explore the interactive potential, defend the simplicity and single function of their traditional product, the television set. "I think people will buy these (digital) TVs for entertainment—a great high-definition picture on a big screen," says Richard Kraft, president of Matsushita Electric's U.S. subsidiary, which make the Panasonic and Quasar brands. And broadcasters have slowed their drive towards HDTV as well. Says Michael Jordan, chairperson of Westinghouse Electric Corp. which owns CBS, "All of a sudden we got this thing approved, and nobody has a clue what they are going to do."

Those in the computer camp counter that with the new digital technology, the "PC theatre," a computer that combines traditional TV programming with computer functions, will be transparently easy to use. But is it what the customer ordered? Jim Meyer, vice president of Thomson Consumer Electronics, which makes the RCA and Proscan brands, doesn't think so. He says that he is not convinced that interactivity is going to be the service that drives this product. "Interactivity may be popular in Silicon Valley, but it may not be popular elsewhere."

■ Case Questions

1. The combination of broadcast and computing functions in a single machine is known in the communication industry as convergence. Do you think convergence is an idea whose time has come? Why or why not?

2. Do you think consumers place greater value on simplicity of use or functionality? Which do you prefer?

3. Television networks are concentrating on perfecting digital high-definition programming and getting it on the air by 1999, as mandated by the FCC in the U.S. For now they are not planning any of the kind of interactive programming that computer makers want to offer with their PC/TVs. How might a change in the networks' plans affect the computer and consumer electronics industries? How do you think the networks should use whatever power they have to influence the outcome?

4. Do you foresee any way in which computer and television makers can successfully divide the consumer computing and entertainment markets between them? What would this mean for the consumer?

5. Why might the FCC be unwilling to mandate a solution to the problem of incompatible technologies? Do you agree with the FCC's decision to force the market to choose?

CBC VIDEO CASE IV-1

ISO 9000: Management Fad or New Competitive Reality?*

Global competition brings with it a whole new set of benefits and costs. Benefits include expanded markets for both supply and demand; costs include jet lag, making sure you get paid, and differences in quality standards across countries. One way to deal with the quality problem is to have a standard that is internationally recognized and conformed to. In recent years, for manufacturers that standard has been ISO 9000.

ISO 9000 is a certification process that involves being internationally recognized for conforming to certain stan-

➤

dards of quality in all aspects of operation. Up front, the process seems rather simple—just satisfy the demands of an 11-page booklet of guidelines. Typically, the process involves documenting what the company does and how it does it with the help of a certified consultant. Once the documentation is complete, the company is audited by an ISO representative to see if it actually conforms to its own written standards. It is then either given a passing grade or rejected. Once the company successfully passes the audit, it is "in" as an ISO-certified company.

However, as the experiences of one Ontario company testify, the realities can be much more complex than might at first appear. Genesis Microchip, a small firm specializing in digital image manipulation, reports spending about $160 000 and a year and a half of company time in the certification process.

For some non-certified companies, the question of whether ISO certification really adds anything comes up frequently. Everyone aspires to quality, their line of reasoning goes, so what is added by going through the ordeal of certification? One respected quality-driven company, Motorola, supports this contrarian view. According to Vice President for Quality Richard Budo, ISO 9000 in and of itself has had very little impact on the end product. Perhaps, he continues, ISO's biggest contribution is to bring the adherent's paperwork up to standard. Motorola has gone so far as to release a public statement indicating that Motorola is "critical of how ISO is being used and misrepresented." The suspicion also arises from the

heavy reliance on consultants, who some see as getting into the ISO business as a way to make a quick buck. Recently, business cartoon Dilbert articulated this skepticism in a strip that satirized the ISO process as a sham.

One ISO advocate, Susan Lores, sees ISO differently. According to her, ISO is a reflection of the new global basis of competition. According to Lores, being ISO certified "enhances Canadian business competing in global markets." If you want to do business in a certain market, this line of counter-argument continues, you have to be ISO certified. This is particularly the case for Canadian businesses seeking to do business with firms in many European countries. ISO is dominant in Europe, where it emerged from a set of British standards. With 150 000 companies already registered worldwide, the trend towards registration has just hit Canada.

STUDY QUESTIONS

1. What is quality? How does ISO 9000 aid in achieving worldwide quality standards?

2. What is process variation? How can ISO 9000 aid in managing process variation?

3. What is quality ownership? Does ISO 9000 guarantee that quality ownership occurs?

* Source: This case was written by Professor Reg Litz of the University of Manitoba. Video Resource: "ISO 9000," *Venture* #561 (October 8, 1995).

CBC VIDEO CASE IV-2

Surfing Through Peach Orchards?*

"The image we're working on here ... is not just about selling more product, but just about getting the image right."

Advertising is as much about selling a feeling as selling a product. For the advertising manager that means making a connection between a feeling—whether that feeling is freedom, happiness, or fear—and a client's product or service. One way that Regina photographer Douglas Alker has been able to make that connection is through the use of composite photography. Alker, referred to as the "king of image makers," has established himself on the forefront of this form of photographic imagery. He makes imaginative use of diverse and seemingly unrelated images.

Composite photography is a comparatively new technique. It involves blending digital photos into one overriding image. The technique is not cheap and can cost upwards of $10 000 per day. The high cost is a result of the nature of the technique, since finding the right image can potentially take the photographer almost anywhere.

The task of finding the "perfect" location recently took Alker to Hood River, Oregon, as he searched for the right image for an allergy-treatment product. His idea was to combine peach blossoms with a kayak race. His search took him to a peach orchard where the natural lighting at sunset was ideal. Alker's intent was to use the pollen-rich environment of the orchard to convey the "chained to a tissue box" sensation people feel when hit by a bout of allergic reactions.

The production schedule for this kind of shooting is extremely tight, both in terms of dollars and time. The day's shots get express-couriered to New York City, where they are scanned by the advertising agency that hired Alker. Given their final responsibility for the product, the New York agency screens, and either approves or rejects, Alker's daily production. Such tight control is part of the work package for Alker. Since he's really working for his client's client, it's crucial that the intermediary, in this case the New York agency, be kept informed of what's happening and be happy with the results. Since Alker only works on about 20 campaigns each year, such close supervision doesn't present a problem.

On this particular shoot things apparently went well; the New York agency gave its approval the first time through. The next stop for the shoot was Hawaii. Alker's

purpose? To find the right location for a surfer image that he might overlay on the Oregon peach orchard. After three nights, the background shot begins to emerge and shooting is scheduled to begin the next morning. Production recommences the next morning at 5 a.m.

STUDY QUESTIONS

1. What is utility? What are the different kinds of utility? What kind of utility is Alker providing his clients?

2. What are the different kinds of product layouts? Which of these best describes Alker's production system?

3. What is the difference between a high-contact and a low-contact service production system? Which best describes Alker's work?

* Source: This case was written by Professor Reg Litz of the University of Manitoba. Video Resource: "Photo Boy," *Venture* #663 (October 7, 1997).

LANDS' END VIDEO CASE IV-3

From a Functional to a Team Approach at Lands' End

LEARNING OBJECTIVES

The purpose of this video exercise is to help students:

1. Understand the purpose and function of formal teamwork within a larger organizational structure

2. Assess the ways in which organizational structure can affect employee attitudes and productivity

3. Appreciate some of the factors that affect a company's decisions about how to organize its operations

BACKGROUND INFORMATION

In March 1994, certain key operations at Lands' End underwent a significant change. Up until then, different departments had been organized along functional lines: in other words, people who specialized in certain business functions—marketing, finance, quality control, and so on—were grouped with people performing "like" functions. But, says Joan Brown, Vice President for Quality Assurance, "while we were expected to work together as teams, it really wasn't working very well." Consequently, Lands' End changed the operations of its product development personnel. It shifted from a functional to a truly team-oriented approach.

Reorganization, of course, meant upheaval, both physical and psychological. Work space was reconfigured to accom-

modate the team concept, and team members had to adjust their attitudes towards both work space and privacy. Although the precise benefits in effectiveness and efficiency cannot yet be measured, the new team approach appears to be addressing the three main problems that it was designed to address. "Time to bring a new product to market has been reduced," reports Brown, "and communication has significantly improved. Even more importantly, everyone associated with the product now has the same goals."

THE VIDEO

Video Source. "Product Development at Lands' End: From a Functional to a Team Approach," *Prentice Hall Presents: On Location at Lands' End*. The video focuses on the sleepwear and swimwear team to show how teamwork has been integrated into product development operations at Lands' End. Members of the team recall the adjustments they had to make in order to adapt to the new form of organization and explain the advantages that it has brought to them in their jobs.

DISCUSSION QUESTIONS

1. Briefly describe what you understand to be the key responsibility of each member of the sleepwear and swimwear team (copywriter, inventory manager, art

director, quality assurance specialist, team manager, and team assistant).

2. In what ways does the change from functional to team approach probably affect each member's level of responsibility and authority?

3. Of the three types of organizational change—structural, technological, and people—people change is generally regarded as the hardest to implement. Judging from the video, how would you assess the effectiveness of this change at Lands' End?

4. In what ways does team organization probably contribute to quality planning and quality control? To inventory control? To improvements in system design? To worker motivation and quality of work life? To overall productivity?

FOLLOW-UP ASSIGNMENT

"None of our goals blended," recalls Joan Brown. "Inventory's goal, for example, was to get the product in the building and out the door to the customer. Quality, on the other hand, would stop anything from going out that did not meet its expectations—which ran headlong against the inventory manager's goal."

Your instructor will divide the class into product development teams like the one described in the video. First, each team will decide on the consumer product that it is developing: it can be anything that is of interest to everyone. On each team, members will assume the following roles: inventory manager, copywriter, art director, quality assurance specialist, and team manager. Your quality assurance specialist will meet briefly with your instructor to identify some quality control problem in the team's selected product; he or she will then explain the problem to the team. One team member should be appointed to take minutes. With all members contributing, the team will work to find a solution to its problem. Working from the minutes of its meeting, each team will report to the class on its meeting and its solution to its problem.

FOR FURTHER EXPLORATION

Visit Lands' End on the Internet at
http://www.landsend.com

Scroll down from the "Home" page to the link to "The Company." From there, take a trip to the "Internet Store," where you can select from such product categories as "Kids," "Men's Casual," and "Women's." To get a better idea of how teamwork is ultimately reflected in the copywriter's description of company products, browse the descriptions of several products. In what ways does the copywriter promote quality as a key function of a given Lands' End product?

MANAGING MARKETING

What is the first thing you think of when you hear the names Coffee Crisp, Post-it, Crest, and Eno? If you grew up in Canada, you probably didn't hesitate at all before picturing candy, little slips of paper with one sticky edge, toothpaste, and something to calm your stomach. Your rapid association of company names and the goods or services they provide is a tribute to the effectiveness of the marketing managers of the firms that produce these goods. These and many other names have become household words because companies have developed the right products to meet customers' needs, have priced those products appropriately, have made prospective customers aware of the products' existence and qualities, and have made the products readily available.

Part Five, **Managing Marketing**, provides an overview of the many elements of marketing, including developing, pricing, promoting, and distributing various types of goods and services.

- ■ We begin in **Chapter 13**, **Understanding Marketing Processes and Consumer Behaviour**, by examining the ways in which companies distinguish their products, determine customer needs, and otherwise address consumer buying preferences.

- ■ Then, in **Chapter 14**, **Developing and Promoting Goods and Services**, we explore the development of different types of products, the effect of brand names and packaging, how promotion strategies help a firm meet its objectives, and the advantages and disadvantages of several promotional tools.

- ■ Finally, in **Chapter 15**, **Pricing and Distributing Goods and Services**, we look at the strategies firms use to price their products. We also consider the various outlets business firms use to distribute their products, and we discuss the problems of storing goods and transporting them to distributors.

CHAPTER

13

UNDERSTANDING MARKETING PROCESSES AND CONSUMER BEHAVIOUR

HOW GOOD IS MARKET RESEARCH INFORMATION?

Exactly how much confidence can companies place in the market research they purchase? Consider what happened in two interesting cases.

National Research Group Inc (NRG). This organization conducts consumer research for firms like Paramount, Twentieth Century Fox, MGM, TriStar, and Walt Disney. NRG recruits audiences to view soon-to-be-released films and then analyzes their reactions through the use of questionnaires. Summaries of audience reactions are sent to the movie studio, which can then alter the film or change the ending depending on what the market research shows. The movie studios pay NRG for developing this data.

In 1993, about two dozen former employees of NRG claimed that it was falsifying audience data about films, and that it prevented people who didn't like a film from being in focus groups that discussed it (see p. 300 for a discussion of focus groups). NRG also does phone surveys of moviegoers, and the former employees claim there are shady activities in this part of the business as well. For example, they claim that phone-room personnel routinely fill out unfinished questionnaires, and that test results are made up for movies when they can't find enough people to fill out questionnaires.

NRG disputes these claims and says that it would be impossible to falsify data because there is only a half hour between the time a test screening ends and the time preliminary data are conveyed to movie studio heads. The company also argues that if it were falsifying data, it would be much less accurate in its predictions of how much revenue a film will generate. NRG says its forecasts of box office receipts are within 10 percent of those actually collected about 80 percent of the time.

Nielsen Media Research. This famous company has reported on the television viewing habits of North Americans for many years. In all that time, there seemed to be widespread acceptance that its market research was accurate. But suddenly in 1996, Nielsen reported a significant drop in the number of people watching television; as a result, broadcast networks might end up owing advertisers a lot of money because the networks are not delivering as large an audience as they promised when advertising rates were set.

How did the networks react to the latest Nielsen data? They claimed it was unreliable, and that the numbers were being generated from a sample of households that was different from those used in the past (Nielsen recently expanded the number of households it gathers data from).

It is a fact that gathering data on peoples' television viewing habits is becoming more difficult. In some markets, the system used involves an electronic meter attached to a TV set that determines what channel is being watched. A "people meter" is also part of this system; it tells who is watching. Viewers must punch in a preassigned number on their remote control whenever they start or stop watching. Critics say people forget to do this and so the data are inaccurate. In other markets, the classic "paper diary" is used to gather information. Viewers note their viewing habits for each quarter-hour, including the station they are watching, the channel number, and who is watching. This is a lot of work, and in some markets, less than one-quarter of the targeted homes send in their diaries. Worse, one study showed that these diaries contained many errors.

Both NBC and Fox are considering a lawsuit against Nielsen after the ratings for NFL football dropped 7 percent. They also want changes made in their agreement with Nielsen before they renew it. Several networks are also spending $40 million to test a new market research system that will challenge Nielsen's within a few years. The work is being done by Statistical Research Inc., a company the networks have used in the past to check the accuracy of Nielsen's ratings.

Certain businesses rely heavily on organizations like the National Research Group and Nielsen Media Research to provide data about their customers. But all businesses need information about their customers, and this important aspect of marketing will be explored in the next three chapters. We begin in this chapter by exploring the nature of marketing. As you will see, the marketing process is complex, requiring marketers to understand the nature of their product (and its place in the market) and the nature of their customers. The special problems of marketing internationally and of marketing for the small business are also addressed.

Nielsen Media Research
www.nielsenmedia.com

By focusing on the learning objectives of this chapter, you will gain a better understanding of marketing activities and the ways in which marketing influences consumer purchases. After reading this chapter, you should be able to:

1. Define *marketing* and explain its functions.
2. Explain market *segmentation* and show how it is used in *target marketing*.
3. Explain the purpose and value of *market research*.
4. Describe the key factors that influence the *consumer buying process*.
5. Explain how international and cultural differences affect marketing strategies.
6. Identify potential problems and opportunities in the marketing activities of small businesses.

■ THE NATURE OF MARKETING

What do you think of when you think of marketing? If you are like most people, you probably think of advertising for something like detergent or soft drinks. But marketing is a much broader concept. **Marketing** is "the process of planning and executing the conception, pricing, promotion, and distribution of ideas, goods, and services to create exchanges that satisfy individual and organizational objectives."[1] In this section, we will dissect this definition to see what it encompasses.

marketing
Planning and executing the development, pricing, promotion, and distribution of ideas, goods, and services to create exchanges that satisfy both buyers' and sellers' objectives.

Marketing: Goods, Services, and Ideas

Marketing of tangible goods is obvious in our everyday life. You walk into a department store and a woman with a clipboard asks if you'd like to try a new cologne. A pharmaceutical company proclaims the virtues of its new cold medicine. Your local auto dealer

consumer goods
Products purchased by individuals for their personal use.

industrial goods
Products purchased by companies to use directly or indirectly to produce other products.

offers an economy car at an economy price. These **consumer goods** are products that you, the consumer, buy for personal use. Firms that sell their products to the end user are engaged in *consumer marketing*.

Marketing is also applied to industrial goods. **Industrial goods** are items that are used by companies for production purposes or further assembly. Conveyors, lift trucks, and earth movers are all industrial goods, as are components and raw materials such as transistors, integrated circuits, coal, steel, and plastic. Firms that sell their products to other manufacturers are engaged in *industrial marketing*.

Marketing techniques can also be applied to services. *Service marketing* has become a major area of growth in the Canadian economy. Insurance companies, airlines, investment counsellors, clinics, and exterminators all engage in service marketing to consumers. Some firms market their services to other companies, for example, security guards, janitors, and accountants.

Finally, marketing can be applied to *ideas* as well as to goods and services. Television advertising and other promotional activities have made "participaction" a symbol of a healthy lifestyle.

Relationship Marketing

relationship marketing
Strategy that emphasizes lasting relationships with customers and suppliers.

Harley-Davidson
www.harley-davidson.com

Although marketing often focuses on single transactions for products, services, or ideas, a longer-term perspective has become equally important for successful marketing. Rather than emphasizing a single transaction, **relationship marketing** emphasizes lasting relationships with customers and suppliers. Not surprisingly, stronger relationships, including stronger economic and social ties, can result in greater long-term satisfaction and retention of customers. Harley-Davidson offers social incentives through the Harley Owners Group (H.O.G.), the largest motorcycle club in the world, with nearly 300 000 members and approximately 900 dealer-sponsored chapters worldwide. H.O.G., explain Harley marketers, "is dedicated to building customers for life. H.O.G. fosters long-term commitments to the sport of motorcycling by providing opportunities for our customers to bond with other riders and develop long-term friendships."[2]

Planning and Executing Marketing Strategy

marketing managers
Responsible for planning and implementing all the marketing activities that result in the transfer of goods or services to customers.

marketing plan
A detailed strategy for gearing marketing activities to meet consumer needs and wants.

As a business activity, marketing requires management. Although many individuals also contribute to the marketing of a product, a company's **marketing managers** are typically responsible for planning and implementing all the marketing activities that result in the transfer of goods or services to its customers. These activities culminate in the **marketing plan**: a detailed and focused strategy for gearing marketing activities to meet consumer needs and wants. Marketing, therefore, begins when a company identifies a consumer need and develops a product to meet it. One way of identifying those needs, market research, is explored later in this chapter. Here, however, we begin by noting two important aspects of the larger market-planning process: developing the marketing plan and setting marketing goals.

Developing the Marketing Plan.   Marketing managers must realize that planning takes time. Indeed, the marketing-planning process may begin years before a product becomes available for sale. For example, the Dutch electronics firm Philips (its major label is Magnavox) developed such products as VCRs and compact discs years before these products actually hit the market. And although Philips has recently invested $1 billion in the planning and development of advanced semiconductor memory chips, the company is not assured of success. Without such planning and preparation, however, the electronics line would have little or no chance of success in a highly competitive market.[3]

Philips
www.philips.com

Each of these advertisements provides information about a specific product, service, or idea. The President's Choice line, for example, is a consumer food product that can be consumed. The advertisement for the Metro Toronto Zoo promotes a service that can be enjoyed. The safer sex advertisement promotes the idea of changing behaviour as a way of combatting sexually transmitted diseases.

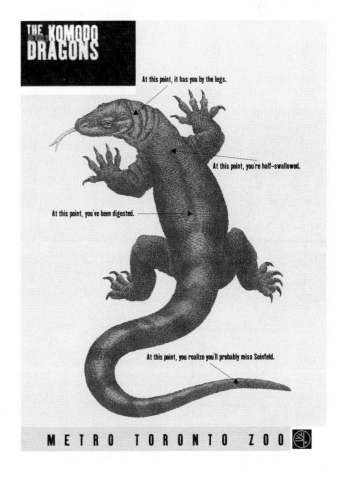

Setting Goals for Performance.   Marketing managers—like all managers—must set objectives and goals and then establish ways to evaluate performance. An insurance company, for example, might establish the goal of increasing sales by 10 percent in its western and central Canadian sales districts. The district sales managers' performances will be evaluated against that goal. Or, a consumer products company might set a goal to reduce by 30 percent the time it takes to bring a new product to market.

The Marketing Concept

Increased competition and the growth of consumer discretionary income has given added impetus to an idea that had its beginnings early in the 20th century. This idea or philosophy, known as the **marketing concept**, means that the whole firm is coordinated to achieve one goal—to serve its present and potential customers and to do so at a profit. This concept means that a firm must get to know what customers really want and to follow closely the changes in tastes that occur. The various departments of the firm—marketing, production, finance, and human resources—must operate as a system, well coordinated and unified in the pursuit of a common goal—customer satisfaction.

The importance of customer satisfaction has been recognized at IBM, which introduced a scheme that influences the pay of 350 managers. Up to 15 percent of their pay is tied to how satisfied their customers are. Bell Canada has a similar scheme; team awards are based partly on customer satisfaction.[4] Japan Air Lines' 747s are equipped with video monitors in the armrests so that passengers may choose exactly what they want to watch from a movie library. At Air France, a passenger who purchases a first-class ticket to Paris can upgrade to the Concorde at no extra cost.[5]

The Marketing Mix

In planning and implementing their marketing strategies, managers rely on the four principal elements of marketing. These four elements, often called the Four Ps of marketing, are *product* (including developing goods, services, and ideas), *pricing*, *promotion*, and *place* (distribution).[6] Together, these elements are known as the **marketing mix**, depicted in Figure 13.1.

There are many possible combinations of the four elements in the marketing mix. Price might play a large role in selling fresh meat but a very small role in selling newspapers. Distribution might be crucial in marketing gasoline but not so important for lumber. Promotion could be vital in toy marketing but of little consequence in marketing nails. The product is important in every case but probably less so for toothpaste than for cars.

Product.   Clearly, no business can undertake marketing activities without a **product**—a good, service, or idea that attempts to fulfill consumers' wants. The conception or development of new products is a continual challenge. Businesses must take into account

marketing concept
The idea that the whole firm is directed towards serving present and potential customers at a profit.

Bell Canada
www.bell.ca

marketing mix
The combination of product, pricing, promotion, and distribution strategies used in marketing a product.

product
A good, service, or idea that satisfies buyers' needs and demands.

| Product choices determine basic design of the product offered to consumers. | + | Price choices determine how much consumers pay for the product. | + | Promotion choices determine the visibility and image of the product to consumers. | + | Place choices determine where and when the product is available to consumers. | = | CUSTOMER SATISFACTION and BUSINESS PROFITABILITY |

FIGURE 13.1
Choosing the marketing mix for a business.

changing technology, consumer wants and needs, and economic conditions, among other factors. A 1997 Statistics Canada study showed the percentage of Canadian households that owned the following items: VCR (85 percent), microwave oven (86.3 percent), compact disc player (25 percent), personal computer (33 percent), and dishwasher (48.5 percent). Most of these products did not even exist 25 years ago.[7]

Statistics Canada
www.statcan.ca

Having the product that consumers desire may mean changing existing products. For example, in the clothing industry, manufacturers must be alert to changes in fashion, which often occur rapidly and unpredictably. And as computer technology changes, so must many computer products, such as application programs.

Companies are also trying harder to provide products that satisfy very specific needs of consumers. Formerly, companies manufactured thousands of identical products and then sold them to as many different customers as they could. Customers therefore had to buy products that didn't meet their exact requirements. Now, more and more businesses are pursuing a strategy of **mass customization**—providing thousands of customers with exactly the products they want. Dell Computer is perhaps the most well-known company pursuing this strategy (refer back to the opening case in Chapter 10).

mass customization
Providing customers with products that have exactly the features that each customer wants rather than providing the same product to all customers.

Manufacturers may also develop new products and enter markets in which they have not previously competed. Consumer food giants such as Kraft Inc., General Mills, Sara Lee, and Quaker Oats have entered the institutional and restaurant food-service markets. They have modified consumer food mixes for the mass production needed in prisons, hospitals, schools, and restaurants.

Producers may develop new or "improved" goods and services for the sake of product differentiation. **Product differentiation** is the creation of a product or product image that differs enough from existing products to attract consumers. Product differentiation does not always mean a change in how a product functions. But when successful, it always means a change in how customers react. For example, early kitchen and laundry appliances were available only in white. Frigidaire capitalized on this situation, offering comparably priced and performing appliances, but in colours. Procter & Gamble is a master at product differentiation, working to make its products not only different from those of other firms but also from its own competing goods.

product differentiation
The creation of a product or product image that differs enough from existing products to attract consumers.

Services can also be sources of differentiation. One company has developed a computer system so that its customers at retail home centres and lumber yards can custom-design decks and shelving. As a result, the company has differentiated its commodity two-by-fours by turning them into premium products. We discuss product development in Chapter 14.

Pricing.   **Pricing** a product—selecting the most appropriate price at which to sell it—is often a balancing act. On one hand, prices must support a variety of costs: the organization's operating, administrative, and research costs as well as marketing costs, such as advertising and sales salaries. On the other hand, prices cannot be so high that consumers turn to competing products. Obviously, successful pricing means finding a profitable middle ground between these two requirements. For Dell Computer, for instance, price is a competitive weapon: Dell's extraordinary growth stems from selling its computers at prices lower than its competitors can offer. Rock-bottom prices are possible by selling directly to customers (90 percent of which are other businesses and organizations), and Dell builds the PCs only after they've received the customer's order.[8]

pricing
That part of the marketing mix concerned with choosing the appropriate price for a product to meet the firm's profit objectives and buyers' purchasing objectives.

Both low or high price strategies may be appropriate for a company under various situations. Low prices will generally lead to a larger volume of sales. High prices will usually limit the size of the market, but will increase a firm's profits per unit. In some cases, however, high prices may actually attract customers by implying that the product is especially good or rare. We will discuss pricing in more detail in Chapter 15.

Promotion.   The most visible component of the marketing mix is **promotion**, those techniques designed to sell a product to consumers. Promotional tools include advertising, personal selling, sales promotions, and public relations. Chapter 14 explores the promotion of products in more depth.

promotion
That part of the marketing mix concerned with selecting the appropriate technique for selling a product to a consumer.

advertising
Any promotional technique involving paid, nonpersonal communication used by an identified sponsor to persuade or inform a large number of people about a product.

personal selling
A promotional technique involving the use of person-to-person communication to sell products.

sales promotion
A promotional technique involving one-time direct inducements to buyers (such as coupons, sales displays, and contests) to purchase a product.

public relations
Any promotional activity directed at building good relations with various sectors of the population of buyers.

publicity
A promotional technique that involves nonpaid communication about a product or firm and that is outside the control of the firm.

distribution
That part of the marketing mix concerned with getting products from the producer to the buyer, including physical transportation and choice of sales outlets.

In marketing terms, **advertising** is any form of paid, nonpersonal communication used by an identified sponsor to persuade or inform certain audiences about a good, service, or idea. Advertising may be done through television, radio, magazines, newspapers, billboards or any other type of broadcast or print media.

Automobiles, appliances, and stereo equipment are often promoted through the use of **personal selling**—person-to-person sales. However, the bulk of personal selling occurs with industrial goods. Purchasing agents and other members of a business who require information about a product's technical qualities and price are usually referred to the selling company's sales representatives.

Less expensive items are often marketed through the use of **sales promotions**. Sales promotions can take many forms. Premiums (gifts included with the product), trading stamps, coupons, and package inserts are all sales promotions meant to tempt consumers to buy more of a product. Free samples, exhibits, and trade shows give customers an opportunity to try the product or talk with company representatives. The prevalence of self-service retail outlets has led marketers to think about package design—the "silent seller"—as an important sales promotion.

Public relations includes all promotional activities directed at building good relations with various sectors of the population. Many public relations activities are good deeds paid for by companies. Sponsorship of softball teams, Special Olympics, and automobile racing teams are examples of public relations efforts. Companies may also use public relations activities to boost employee morale.

Publicity also refers to a firm's efforts to communicate to the public, usually through mass media. Publicity, however, is not paid for by the firm, nor does the firm control the content of publicity. Publicity, therefore, can sometimes hurt a business. For example, Dun & Bradstreet received considerable negative publicity when newspapers and magazines reported that it was billing its customers for financial reports they did not need.

Place (Distribution).   Getting a product into a retail store requires transportation, decisions about direct sales, and a number of other **distribution** processes. Transportation options include moving merchandise by air, land, or pipeline, and, more specifically, by railroad, truck, air freight, or steamship.

Decisions about direct sales can affect a firm's overall marketing strategy. Many manufacturers sell their products to other companies who, in turn, distribute the goods to retailers. Some companies sell directly to major retailers such as Sears, Kmart, and Safeway. Still others sell directly to the final consumer. Chapter 15 presents more detail on distribution decisions.

Marketing: Creating Exchanges

exchange
Any transaction in which two or more parties trade something of value.

The last part of the definition of marketing focuses on the exchange process. An **exchange** is any transaction in which two or more parties trade things of value. In marketing, the typical exchange involves a business providing a good or service in return for payment from a buyer.

Although the exchange process always includes payment, the payment does not always involve money. It may involve barter, the trading of goods of equal value. Many people assume that barter survives as a means of exchange only in undeveloped economies, but it has become increasingly common throughout the world. Among companies, bartering takes several forms. In *countertrading*, multinational companies swap goods with companies in less developed countries. For example, Coca-Cola sold Coke to Eastern Europe and Asian countries and was paid in bathtubs and honey.

Another popular form of bartering occurs when companies with excess inventories of products trade them for advertising. Casio Inc., for example, disposed of surplus products (watches, calculators, musical keyboards) worth $25 million in return for advertising opportunities for its main products.[9] Although bartering may seem unusual, it is mutually satisfying to both parties and sometimes provides even better returns than cash sales.

Satisfaction and Utility.   One requirement of the exchange process, therefore, is that it should satisfy both buyers and sellers. If marketing managers provide an attractive mix of product, price, promotion, and placement, then sellers should earn satisfactory profits. Customers, meanwhile, should be getting satisfaction from the utility that the purchased product provides. If both buyers and sellers are satisfied, marketing operations will have contributed to the success of the exchange.

Recall from Chapter 10, for example, that production operations create *utility*, especially form and time utility, by transforming raw materials into products when buyers want them. Similarly, marketing operations create *time, place,* and *possession utilities*: Buyers not only obtain the product *when* and *where* they want it but receive the right to *use* it as they want. Figure 13.2 illustrates this relationship. Note that although it is convenient to distinguish between the roles of production and marketing management, product utility serves a common purpose: creating value for buyers

The need for the exchange process to satisfy both sellers and buyers underscores the importance of the marketing concept. To earn profits consistently, sellers must attempt to supply buyers' wants. Coca-Cola learned this lesson the hard way. In the 1980s, the firm tried to withdraw its original formula Coke and substitute a new formula it believed would have greater appeal. The company reckoned without its traditional customers, however. Their outcry eventually led Coca-Cola's management to reintroduce the original version as "Classic Coke."

■ TARGET MARKETING AND MARKET SEGMENTATION

Marketing managers long ago recognized that they cannot be "all things to all people." People have different tastes, different interests, different goals, different lifestyles, and so on. The marketing concept's recognition of consumers' various needs and wants led marketing managers to think in terms of target marketing. **Target markets** are groups of people with similar wants and needs.

Target marketing clearly requires **market segmentation**, dividing a market into categories of customer types or "segments." For example, Mr. Big-and-Tall sells to men who are taller and heavier than average. Certain special-interest magazines are oriented towards people with specific interests. Once they have identified market segments, companies may adopt a variety of product strategies. Some firms decide to provide a range of

target market
Any group of people who have similar wants and needs and may be expected to show interest in the same product(s).

market segmentation
Dividing a market into categories according to traits customers have in common.

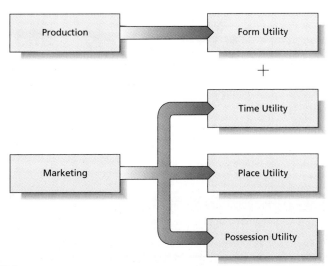

FIGURE 13.2
Production and marketing create utility for customers.

Geographic segmentation: Marketers at Absolut Vodka realize Canadians have strong regional ties. This first regional ad used by Absolut appeared in Atlantic Progress, *an East Coast business magazine.*

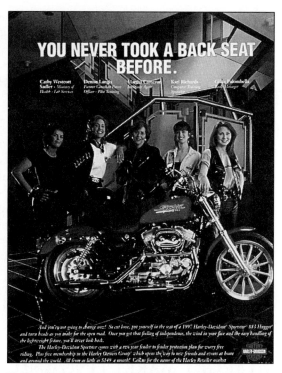

Demographic segmentation: Harley owners are typically men, but this advertisement, commissioned by the Canadian division of Harley-Davidson, focuses on moderate- to high-income women as Harley owners, and stresses the themes of independence, strength, and freedom.

Geographic segmentation: Johnson & Johnson targets children with Band-Aid Sesame Street Bandages; Big Bird and Cookie Monster "help turn little people's tears into great big smiles."

Psychographic segmentation: This Nokia advertisement explicitly appeals to customers' motives, attitudes, interests, and individual needs.

products to the market in an attempt to market their products to more than one segment. For example, General Motors of Canada offers compact cars, vans, trucks, luxury cars, and sports cars with various features and prices. Their strategy is to provide an automobile for nearly every segment of the market.

In contrast, some businesses restrict production to one market segment. Rolls-Royce, for example, understands that only a relatively small number of people are willing to pay $310 000 for exclusive touring limousines. Rolls, therefore, makes no attempt to cover the entire range of possible products; instead, it markets only to a very small segment of the total automobile buyers market.

Identifying Market Segments

By definition, the members of a market segment must share some common traits or behaviours that will affect their purchasing decisions. In identifying market segments, researchers look at geographic, demographic, psychographic, and product-use variables.

Geographics.   In some cases, where people live affects their buying decisions. The heavy rainfall in British Columbia prompts its inhabitants to purchase more umbrellas than do those living in Arizona's desert. Urban residents have less demand for four-wheel-drive vehicles than do their rural counterparts. Sailboats sell better along both coasts than they do in the prairie provinces.

These patterns affect marketing decisions about what products to offer, at what price to sell them, how to promote them, and how to distribute them. For example, consider marketing down parkas in rural Saskatchewan. Demand will be high, price competition may be limited, local newspaper advertising may be very effective, and the best location may be one easily reached from several small towns.

Demographics.   Demographics include traits such as age, income, gender, ethnic background, marital status, race, religion, and social class. Many marketers, for example, have discovered that university and community college students are an important market segment. Students across Canada have discretionary income totalling $4–$5 billion. Ford Motor of Canada has marketed to students since the mid-1980s, and gives graduates a $750 rebate on their first-time purchase of a car. Table 13.1 lists some demographic market segments. Note that these are objective criteria that cannot be altered. Marketers must work with or around them.

Brenda Laurel of Purple Moon discovered that boys and girls show wide differences in their computer game preferences. While working at Interval Research Co. in California, Laurel spent the years between 1992 and 1995 researching those gender differences. She put her findings into action via Purple Moon, a spinoff of Interval Research that creates and markets adventure software for girls 8–12. Purple Moon's first two titles, *Rockett's New School* and *Secret Paths in the Forest*, quickly made their way into the top 20 best-selling children's software titles for 1997.

Purple Moon
www.purple-moon.com

Demographics affect how a firm markets its product. For example, marketing managers may well divide a market into age groups such as 18–25, 26–35, 36–45 and so on. A number of general consumption characteristics that can be attributed to these age groups help marketing managers develop specific plans. For example, managers at Binney & Smith Canada Ltd., the makers of Crayola crayons, discovered that the number of children 3–7 years of age—the top users of crayons—was declining. They also noticed that the size of the age group 8–12 was increasing. This group, called "tweens" by demographers because they are between the ages of children and teenagers, is much more sophisticated and brand-conscious than younger children. They have very distinct preferences, and don't like crayons much, viewing them as "babyish." Tweens prefer coloured pencils, so Binney & Smith introduced a new line of coloured pencils called "Crayola IQ" aimed at the tween group. In a radical departure from past practice, they abandoned the famous yellow-and-green Crayola package and replaced it with a new all-green package. Sales jumped 44 percent.[10]

Binney & Smith Canada
www.crayola.com

■ **TABLE 13.1**   **Demographic Market Segmentation**

Age	Under 5; 5–11; 12–19; 20–34; 35–49; 50–64; 65+
Education	Grade school or less; some high school; graduated high school; some college or university; college diploma or university degree; advanced degree
Family life cycle	Young single; young married without children; young married with children; older married with children under 18; older married without children under 18; older single; other
Family size	1, 2–3, 4–5, 6+
Income	Under $9000; $9000–$14 999; $15 000–$24 999; $25 000–$34 999; $35 000–$45 000; over $45 000
Nationality	Including but not limited to African, Asian, British, Eastern European, French, German, Irish, Italian, Latin American, Middle Eastern, and Scandinavian
Race	Including but not limited to Inuit, Asian, Black, and White
Religion	Including but not limited to Buddhist, Catholic, Hindu, Jewish, Muslim, and Protestant
Sex	Male, female
Language	Including but not limited to English, French, Inuktitut, Italian, German, and Ukrainian

The box "Teenagers: An International Market Segment" describes similarities across countries in the 13–19 age group.

psychographics
A method of market segmentation involving psychological traits that a group has in common, including motives, attitudes, activities, interests, and opinions.

Psychographics.   Members of a market can also be segmented according to **psychographic** (mental) traits such as their motives, attitudes, activities, interests, and opinions. Psychographics are of particular interest to marketers because, unlike demographics and geographics, they can be changed by marketing efforts.

For example, many companies have succeeded in changing at least some consumers' opinions by running ads highlighting products that have been improved directly in response to consumer desires. General Motors used this approach in the development and promotion of Saturns. GM gained an improved image by advertising its intended new design in conjunction with consumer-preferred features such as a one-price policy, careful selection of employees, high product quality, emphasis on quality, customer convenience during servicing, and extensive warranty coverage.

Product-Use Variables.   This fourth way of segmenting looks at how group members use a good or service, their brand loyalty, and why they purchase the product. A women's shoe maker, for example, might find three segments—athletic, casual, and dress shoes. Each market segment is looking for different benefits in a shoe. A woman buying an athletic shoe will probably not care much about its appearance, but she will care a great deal about arch support, traction offered by the sole, and sturdiness. In contrast, a woman buying a casual shoe will want it to look good but be comfortable, while a woman buying a dress shoe may require a specific colour or style and accept some discomfort and a relatively fragile shoe.

Market Segmentation: A Caution

Segmentation must be done carefully. A group of people may share an age category, income level, or some other segmentation variable, but their spending habits may be quite different. Look at your friends in school. You may all be approximately the same age, but you have different needs and wants. Some of you may wear cashmere sweaters

TRENDS CHALLENGES

Teenagers: An International Market Segment

We all know that trends spread rapidly through the ranks of teenagers. But that tendency is now accelerating internationally. Teens around the world have amazingly similar preferences for consumer products. BSB Worldwide, an advertising agency, videotaped teenagers' rooms in 25 different countries. From the items on display, it was hard to tell whether the room was in Mexico City, Tokyo, or Los Angeles.

The biggest beneficiary of this trend appears to be U.S. companies. The hot new trends in the U.S. often pop up in many other countries as well. Because the populations of Asia and Latin America are much younger than the population of North America, the teen market is big business. For example, the total number of 10- to 19-year-olds in Brazil, Argentina, and Mexico is 57 million; in the U.S., the total is only 35 million.

The most unifying force among teenagers is television. Satellite TV is helping to unify patchworks of domestic markets, and companies can mount Europe- or Asia-wide campaigns. No network is more popular than MTV, which is a monster hit in Europe and is watched by more households there than in the U.S. It broadcasts news and socially conscious programming, and is creating a Euro-language of simplified English.

MTV also promotes little-known European musicians and has the power to make them big stars in other countries. For example, it helped the Danish group Aqua sell over 12 million copies of its album worldwide and have a top-ten hit in countries such as Australia, Switzerland, Belgium, and Malaysia. MTV has a roster of 200 advertisers, including Levi Strauss, Procter & Gamble, Johnson & Johnson, Apple Computer, and Pepsi Cola. These firms advertise on MTV because it reaches the market segment they want.

MTV may cause a revolution in worldwide marketing. At present, it is difficult to sell the same products to 35-year-olds in different countries because they never were exposed to anything but products from the country where they were raised. Not so for the upcoming generation of teenagers. They see (and buy) products from various countries and will probably continue to do so as they get older. Two famous brand names, Coke and Pepsi, are already competing vigorously to attract international teens to use their product.

Fashion fads are also spreading around the world. Hip-hop, first popularized by African-Americans, means wearing loose-fitting urban street wear, baggy jeans, sweat shirts, hiking boots, athletic shoes, and baseball caps (worn backwards). Within this fashion category, certain brands have become very popular. Levi jeans, Nike or Reebok athletic shoes, and Timberland boots are some of the brands that have profited.

Sports is the other universal language of teenagers. Basketball stars like Michael Jordan and Shaquille O'Neal have high name recognition overseas. In a poll of Chinese students in rural Shaanxi province, Michael Jordan tied with former Chinese premier Zhou En-lai for the title "World's Greatest Man." Not surprisingly, testimonial advertisements by big-name sports stars have a big impact on potential buyers. It is not uncommon for students to own multiple pairs of Nike Air Jordans.

Teen tastes in consumer electronics are also similar across countries. Kodak is developing an advertising campaign directed specifically at teenagers in the hope that when they have their own children they will use Kodak products to take pictures of them. Teens are also more comfortable with personal computers than their parents are. So, even if the parents are buying the machine, the teen determines what brand is purchased.

MTV
www.mtv.com

while others wear sweatshirts. The same holds true for income. University professors and truck drivers frequently earn about the same level of income. However, their spending patterns, tastes, and wants are generally quite different.

In Canada, the two dominant cultures—English and French—show significant differences in consumer attitudes and behaviour. Researchers have found, for example, that compared to English Canadians, French Canadians are more involved with home and family, attend ballet more often, travel less, eat more chocolate, and are less interested in convenience food. Obviously, prudent marketers should take these differences into account when developing marketing plans. This is, however, easier said than done.

It is one thing to know that consumers in Quebec buy large quantities of certain products; it is quite another to capitalize on these differences. One problem is that differences may not continue over time. Change is continually occurring in consumption patterns across Canada, and data may quickly become outdated. Another problem is that consumption patterns differ from region to region in Canada even where culture is not the main cause. The buying behaviour of Quebec and Ontario consumers may be more similar than the behaviour of British Columbia and Newfoundland consumers.

■ MARKET RESEARCH

market research
The systematic study of what buyers need and how best to meet those needs.

Market research can greatly improve the accuracy and effectiveness of market segmentation.[11] **Market research**, the study of what buyers need and how best to meet those needs, can address any element in the marketing mix. One marketer might study how consumers respond to an experimental paint formula. Another might explore how potential buyers will respond to a possible price reduction on calculators. Still another marketer might check audience response to a proposed advertising campaign with a humourous theme. A company manager might also try to learn whether customers will be more likely to buy a product in a store, a mall, or a special discount shop.

Most companies will benefit from market research, but they need not do the research themselves. O-Pee-Chee Co. Ltd. of London, Ontario (the bubble gum and candy manufacturer), does no market research and no product testing, yet it continues to be successful in a market where products change at a dizzying pace. By signing a licensing agreement with two U.S. giants, O-Pee-Chee simply has to look at what's hot in the U.S. and then start manufacturing those lines in Canada.[12]

The importance of selling products in today's international markets is expanding the role of market research into new areas. For example, when companies decide to sell their goods or services in other countries, they must decide whether to standardize products or to specialize them for new markets.

Consider the case of PepsiCo when it entered a joint venture to market Cheetos in Guangdong province, China. Originally, Cheetos—crispy cheese-puff snacks—did not "test well" in China. The Chinese, it seems, do not eat cheese and did not care for Cheetos' taste. PepsiCo tested more than 600 flavours (including Roasted Cuttlefish) on more than 1000 Chinese consumers before arriving at two—Savoury American Cream and Zesty Japanese Steak. Chinese packaging will bear the Chinese characters "qui duo," pronounced "CHEE dwaugh." "Luckily," explains the general manager of PepsiCo Foods International, "the translation is 'new surprise,' instead of some phrase that might offend people."

Honda Motor Co. Ltd. traditionally had its new product research and development centralized at Honda R&D Ltd. in Japan, with a desire for a single global design. Now, however, international differences in customers' desires are requiring a whole new way of doing business for Honda: the company has turned over more of its decision making to its regional R&D operations in response to massive new product demands worldwide. North America needed 10 new models for the years 1997–99, Europe 7, and Japan 15. Honda sales are also growing in Latin America, but the market is not yet big enough to justify an independent product design centre. Honda also plans to expand into India and Vietnam.[13]

The box "Romancing the Profits" describes the experience of Harlequin Enterprises in doing market research on customers in foreign countries.

The Research Process

Market research can occur at almost any point in a product's existence. Most commonly, however, it is used when a new or altered product is being considered.

TRENDS CHALLENGES

Romancing the Profits

The largest romance publisher on earth occupies an uninspired office building in Toronto. Harlequin Enterprises Ltd., which started in Winnipeg in 1949, now has sales revenue exceeding $400 million annually. Its profits accounted for 83 percent of the total profits of its parent, Torstar Corp., the publisher of the *Toronto Star*. With the emergence of the women's liberation movement in the 1970s, skeptics predicted that romance novels were finished, but it hasn't worked out that way. Romance novels now account for 44 percent of all mass-market paperbacks sold in North America, and Harlequin controls 80 percent of that market.

The company also has a strong presence in overseas markets. By 1995, it sold 45 million books in Eastern Europe alone; it also plans to start selling romances in China. Harlequin offers translations in 24 languages, and prints its books in 16 regions around the world. Interestingly, the book covers remain pretty much the same worldwide, including the emphasis on Caucasians.

When deciding whether to enter a foreign country, Harlequin looks for three things: First, there must be a distribution system already in place because it is prohibitively expensive to set one up. Second, there must be access to TV and print media so that demand can be stimulated through advertising. Third, the company must be able to convert the money it receives for books into dollars. The company has been reluctant to enter Russia because it does not really satisfy any of these criteria. In China, however, where the free market system is growing daily, the company has big plans.

How has Harlequin managed to achieve such success? A major reason is its emphasis on market research. The average reader is around 40, and half have a college education. Over half are employed. Research has shown

that readers abroad have the same interests as North American readers. Focus groups and major surveys of North American consumers are a key part of Harlequin's strategic planning.

Readers of romance novels are not a demographic group to be trifled with. They want plot-driven books with lots of action. In all the romance books, the focal couple first meet, then have a misunderstanding, and then make up by the end of the book. Readers know there will be no violence and there will always be a happy ending.

The company has experienced some frustrations in gathering market research data. Because bookstores and other retail outlets take books on consignment, they can return any they don't sell. Thus, the publisher may ship products to retailers, but there is no guarantee of sales. Worse, it takes many months to determine how well a book is doing, and if it is selling particularly well or poorly. Executives at Harlequin say that if book sales could be accurately counted from week to week, Harlequin's books would take all 10 spots on the *New York Times* bestseller list.

Harlequin has developed new products by expanding into TV, and has signed a 50-50 partnership agreement with Alliance Communications Corp., Canada's largest independent film producer. Harlequin supplies the editorial work and Alliance produces the films. In the fall of 1998, for example, several Harlequin movies appeared on The Movie Channel, including *Loving Evangeline*, *Broken Lullaby*, and *Recipe for Revenge*.

Harlequin
www.romance.net

The process begins with a *study of the current situation*. In other words, what is the need and what is being done to meet it at this point? Such a study should note how well the firm is or is not doing in meeting the need.

The second step is to *select a research method*. As you will see shortly, marketing managers have a wide range of methods available. In choosing a method, marketers must bear in mind the effectiveness and costs of different methods.

The next step is to *collect data*. **Secondary data** are information already available as a result of previous research by the firm or other agencies. For example, Statistics Canada publishes a great deal of data that are useful for business firms.

Using secondary data can save time, effort, and money. But in some cases secondary data are unavailable or inadequate, so **primary data**—new research by the firm or its

secondary data
Information already available to market researchers as a result of previous research by the firm or other agencies.

primary data
Information developed through new research by the firm or its agents.

agents—must be obtained. Hostess Frito-Lay, the maker of Doritos, spent a year studying how to best reach its target market—teenagers. The researchers hung around shopping malls, schools, and fast-food outlets to watch teenagers.[14]

Once data have been collected, marketers need to *analyze the data*. As we shall see later, data are not useful until they have been organized into information.

Marketing personnel then need to share their analysis with others by *preparing a report*. This report should include a summary of the study's methodology and findings. It should also identify alternative solutions (where appropriate) and make recommendations for the appropriate course of action.

Research Methods

The four basic types of methods used by market researchers are observation, survey, focus groups, and experimentation. Probably the oldest form of market research is simple **observation** of what is happening. A store owner notices that customers are buying red children's wagons, not green. The owner reorders more red wagons, the manufacturer's records show high sales of red wagons, and marketing concludes that customers want red wagons. Today, computerized systems allow marketers to "observe" consumers' preferences rapidly and with tremendous accuracy. For example, electronic scanners in supermarkets enable store owners to see what is and is not selling without having to check the shelves. Observation is also a popular research method because it is relatively low in cost, often drawing on data that must be collected for some other reason, such as reordering, anyway.

Sometimes, however, observation of current events is not enough. In many cases, marketers need to ask questions about new marketing ideas. One way to get answers is by conducting a **survey**. The heart of any survey is a questionnaire that is mailed to individuals for their completion or is used as the basis of telephone or personal interviews. Surveys can be expensive to carry out and may vary widely in their accuracy. Because no firm can afford to survey everyone, marketers must be careful to get a representative group of respondents. They must also construct their questions so that they get honest answers that address the specific issue being researched.

Some companies have their workers contact consumers directly to get information about how they feel about the company's product. Honda's "E.T. Phone Home Project" involved factory workers calling over 47 000 owners to find out if they were happy with the car and to get ideas for further improvements. The changes that were suggested appeared in the 1995 and 1996 Honda Accords. At Hewlett-Packard, every bit of customer feedback is assigned to an "owner" who must act on the information and report back to the consumer who called. For example, if a complaint about a printer is received, an employee checks the company's database to see if the complaint is widespread and what the company is doing about it.[15]

Many firms also use **focus groups**, where 6 to 15 people are brought together to talk about a product or service. A moderator leads the group's discussion, and employees from the sponsoring company may observe the proceedings from behind a one-way mirror. The people in the focus group are not usually told which company is sponsoring the research. The comments of people in the focus group are taped, and then researchers go through the data looking for common themes.

Union Gas Ltd. and Levi Strauss have set up focus groups to ask employees about their needs. John Deere uses focus groups of farmers to discuss its tractors. From these discussions have come many specific suggestions for changes in the product (for example, turning off the tractor with a key, different ways to change the oil filter, and making the steps up to the tractor cab wider).[16]

At their best, focus groups allow researchers to explore issues too complex for questionnaires and can produce creative solutions. But because a focus group is small, its responses may not represent the larger market. Focus groups are most often used as a prelude to some other form of research.

observation
A market research technique involving viewing or otherwise monitoring consumer buying patterns.

survey
A market research technique based on questioning a representative sample of consumers about purchasing attitudes and practices.

Hewlett-Packard
www.canada.hp.com/home/
home/htm

focus group
A market research technique involving a small group of people brought together and allowed to discuss selected issues in depth.

Deere & Company
www.deere.com

The last major form of market research, experimentation, also tries to get answers to questions that surveys cannot address. As in science, **experimentation** in market research attempts to compare the responses of the same or similar individuals under different circumstances. For example, a firm trying to decide whether or not to include walnuts in a new candy bar probably would not learn much by asking people what they thought of the idea. But if it made up some bars with nuts and some without and then asked people to try both, the responses could be very helpful. Experimentation is, however, very expensive. In deciding whether to use it or any other research method, marketers must carefully weigh the costs against the possible benefits.

experimentation
A market research technique in which the reactions of similar people are compared under different circumstances.

■ UNDERSTANDING CONSUMER BEHAVIOUR

Market research in its many forms can be of great help to marketing managers in understanding how the common traits of a market segment affect consumers' purchasing decisions. Why do people buy VCRs? What desire are they fulfilling? Is there a psychological or sociological explanation for why consumers purchase one product and not another? These questions and many others are addressed in the area of marketing known as consumer behaviour. **Consumer behaviour** focuses on the decision process by which customers come to purchase and consume a product or service.

consumer behaviour
The study of the process by which customers come to purchase and consume a product or service.

Influences on Consumer Behaviour

According to the not-so-surprising title of one classic study, we are very much "social animals."[17] To understand consumer behaviour, then, marketers draw heavily on the fields of psychology and sociology. The result is a focus on four major influences on consumer behaviour: *psychological, personal, social,* and *cultural*. By identifying the four influences that are most active, marketers try to explain consumer choices and predict future purchasing behaviour:

- *Psychological influences* include an individual's motivations, perceptions, ability to learn, and attitudes.
- *Personal influences* include lifestyle, personality, economic status, and life-cycle stage.
- *Social influences* include family, opinion leaders (people whose opinions are sought by others), and reference groups such as friends, co-workers, and professional associates.
- *Cultural influences* include culture (the "way of living" that distinguishes one large group from another), subculture (smaller groups, such as ethnic groups, with shared values), and social class (the cultural ranking of groups according to criteria such as background, occupation, and income).

All these factors can have a strong impact on the products that people purchase—often in complex ways.

The purchase of some products is not influenced by psychosocial factors. Consumers with high brand loyalty are less subject to such influences—they stick with the brand of their preference. However, the clothes you wear, the food you eat, and the dishes you eat from often reflect social and psychological influences on your consuming behaviour.

The Consumer Buying Process

Researchers who have studied consumer behaviour have constructed models that help marketing managers understand how consumers come to purchase products. Figure 13.3 presents one such model. At the base of this and similar models is an awareness of the

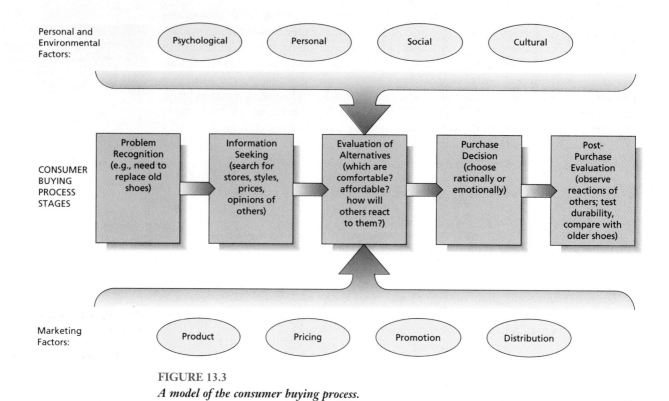

FIGURE 13.3
A model of the consumer buying process.

psychosocial influences that lead to consumption. Ultimately, marketing managers use this information to develop marketing plans.

Problem Recognition.   The buying process begins when a consumer becomes aware of a problem or need. After strenuous exercise, you may recognize that you are thirsty and need refreshment. After the birth of twins, you may find your one-bedroom apartment too small for comfort. After standing in the rain to buy movie tickets, you may decide to buy an umbrella.

Need recognition also occurs when you have a chance to change your purchasing habits. For example, the income from your first job after graduation will let you purchase items that were too expensive when you were a student. You may also discover a need for professional clothing, apartment furnishings, and cars. Visa and The Bay recognize this shift and market their credit cards to graduates.

Information Seeking.   Having recognized a need, consumers seek information. This search is not always extensive. If you are thirsty, you may ask where the soda pop machine is, but that may be the extent of your information search. Other times you simply rely on your memory for information.

Before making major purchases, however, most people seek information from personal sources, marketing sources, public sources, and experience. For example, if you move to a new town, you will want to find out who is the best local dentist, physician, hair stylist, butcher, or pizza maker. To get this information, you may check with personal sources such as acquaintances, co-workers, and relatives. Before buying an exercise bike, you may go to the library and read the latest *Consumer Reports*—a public source of consumer ratings—on such equipment. You may also ask market sources such as the salesclerk or rely on direct experience. For example, you might test-ride the bike to learn more before you buy.

Consumer Reports
www.consumerreports.org

Some sellers treat information as a value to be added to their products. For example, Body Shop International, a cosmetics manufacturer and retailer with no marketing or advertising department, has nevertheless been cited as a model of how to sell in the 1990s. The company's philosophy includes giving the customer product information rather than the traditional sales pitch. What makes this strategy work? The typical Body Shop customer is a skeptical consumer who generally distrusts advertising and sales hype, demands more product information, and is loyal to companies that, like the Body Shop, are perceived to be socially and environmentally responsible.[18]

Evaluation of Alternatives.   The next step in the consumer decision process is to evaluate your alternatives. If you are in the market for a set of golf clubs, you probably have some idea of who produces clubs and how they differ. You may have accumulated some of this knowledge during the information-seeking stage and combined it with what you knew before. Based on product attributes such as colour, taste, price, prestige, quality, and service record, you will decide which product meets your needs most satisfactorily.

Purchase Decision.   Ultimately, you make a purchase decision. You may decide to defer the purchase until a later time or you may decide to buy now. "Buy" decisions are based on rational and emotional motives. **Rational motives** involve a logical evaluation of product attributes: cost, quality, and usefulness. By definition, **emotional motives** lead to irrational decisions. Many spur-of-the-moment decisions are emotionally driven, though not all irrational decisions are sudden. Emotional motives include fear, sociability, imitation of others, and aesthetics. You might buy mouthwash to avoid ostracism. You might buy the same brand of jeans as your friends. And you might buy a chocolate milkshake because you like the taste.

Note that by "irrational" we do not mean insane or wrong, merely a decision based on nonobjective factors. Gratifying a sudden urge for ice cream may not require much thought and may produce lots of enjoyment. But in some cases, irrational decisions are bad. We have all purchased items, taken them home, and then wondered, "Why in the world did I buy this thing?"

Body Shop International
www.the-body-shop.ca

rational motives
Those reasons for purchasing a product that involve a logical evaluation of product attributes such as cost, quality, and usefulness.

emotional motives
Those reasons for purchasing a product that involve nonobjective factors.

Body Shop International, which has no marketing or advertising department, is viewed by its loyal customers as socially and environmentally responsible.

Post-Purchase Evaluations.   Marketing does not stop with the sale of a product or service, but includes the process of consumption. What happens *after* the sale is very important. A marketer wants consumers to be happy after the consumption of the product so that they will buy the product again. In fact, since consumers do not want to go through a complex decision process for every purchase, they often choose a product they have used and liked.

Not all consumers are satisfied with their purchases, of course. Dissatisfied consumers may complain, file a lawsuit, or publicly criticize the product and the company. They are unlikely to purchase the product again. In addition, dissatisfied customers are much more likely to speak about their experience with a product than are satisfied customers. Dissatisfied customers can have a very negative impact on a company's marketing effort. In fact, word-of-mouth can be the most influential marketing tool and also the most devastating, since businesses cannot control it.[19]

purchase anxiety
A fear on the part of people who have made a purchase that their selection was wrong.

Doubts about the rationality of a purchase decision can cause **purchase anxiety**, sometimes called buyer's remorse. If you feel purchase anxiety after remodelling your home, you probably will not buy the services of the same interior designer again. Doing so would only perpetuate your anxiety. Reduction of purchase anxiety is important to marketers, particularly for expensive items like furniture and major appliances.

■ THE INTERNATIONAL MARKETING MIX

Marketing products internationally means mounting a strategy to support global business operations. Obviously, this is no easy task. Foreign customers, for example, differ from domestic buyers in language, customs, business practices, and consumer behaviour. When they decide to go global, marketers must thus reconsider each element of the marketing mix: product, pricing, promotion, and place.

International Products

Some products, of course, can be sold abroad with virtually no changes. Budweiser, Coca-Cola, and Marlboros are exactly the same in Toronto, Tokyo, and Timbuktu. In other cases, firms have been obliged to create products with built-in flexibility—for instance, electric shavers that adapt to either 115- or 230-volt outlets.

At times only a redesigned—or completely different—product will meet the needs of foreign buyers, however. To sell the Macintosh in Japan, for example, Apple had to develop a Japanese-language operating system. Whether they are standard domestic products or custom-made products for foreign markets, however, the most globally competitive products are usually reliable, low-priced products with advanced features.

International Pricing

When pricing for international markets, marketers must handle all the considerations of domestic pricing while also considering the higher costs of transporting and selling products abroad. Some products cost more overseas than in Canada because of the added costs of delivery. Due to the higher costs of buildings, rent, equipment, and imported meat, a McDonald's Big Mac that sells for $2.99 in Canada has a price tag of over $10 in Japan. In contrast, products like jet airplanes are priced the same worldwide because delivery costs are incidental; the huge development and production costs are the major considerations regardless of customer location.

International Promotion

Some standard Canadian promotional devices do not always succeed in other countries. In fact, many Europeans believe that a product must be inherently shoddy if a company does *any* advertising.

International marketers must also be aware that cultural differences can cause negative reactions to products that are advertised improperly. Some Europeans, for example, are offended by television commercials that show weapons or violence. Advertising practices are regulated accordingly. Consequently, Dutch commercials for toys do not feature the guns and combat scenes that are commonplace on Saturday morning television in North America. Meanwhile, cigarette commercials that are banned from Canadian and U.S. television are thriving in many Asian and European markets.

Symbolism, too, is a sometimes surprising consideration. In France, for instance, yellow flowers suggest infidelity. In Mexico, they are signs of death—an association made in Brazil by the colour purple. Clearly, product promotions must be carefully matched to the customs and cultural values of each country. The box "Pitfalls in Global Promotion" describes some difficulties companies have had when promoting their product in foreign markets.

TRENDS CHALLENGES

Pitfalls in Global Promotion

Marketing products internationally can provide big payoffs to those who do their homework. As many firms have learned, careful research of both idiomatic nuances and cultural norms is critical to global success.

Some early attempts by Chinese marketers underscore this point. China had several products it wanted to market in the United States. But, as the manufacturers learned too late, brand names such as White Elephant batteries, Maxipuke playing cards, and Pansy brand men's underwear did not attract many U.S. customers.

But even careful research is not a guarantee of success. Japan's giant Toyota ran afoul in China with a marketing campaign targeted specifically to Chinese culture. Toyota launched an advertising campaign based on the old Chinese proverb, "When you get to the foot of the mountain, a road will appear." Toyota added: "Wherever there is a road, there is a Toyota." In China, however, truth in advertising is taken very seriously. The Chinese hold to this tenet in their own advertising and expect foreign companies to do the same. A year after the slogan was used in print and TV ads, Chinese authorities told Toyota that it constituted false advertising. Toyota had to drop the campaign.

Ads sometimes backfire from miscalculating a country's sense of humour. Take the case of Luis Nasr, creative director of an ad agency in Ecuador, who designed an ad for a hair-growth product called Regenal Forte. The ad featured a picture of Mikhail Gorbachev with the caption, "He didn't use Regenal Forte in time." The Russian ambassador was not amused. The uproar soon subsided, however, and the ad subsequently won a prize at the New York Print Festival.

Marketing managers are trying to avoid these kinds of problems with *global advertising*, a strategy in which the same basic ad campaign—with minor alterations from country to country—is used throughout the world. Peter S. Sealey, senior vice president and director of global marketing for Coca-Cola, puts it this way: "There is global media now, like MTV. And there is a global teenager. The same kid you see at the Ginza in Tokyo is in Picadilly Square in London, in Pushkin Square, at Notre Dame." So why not create an advertisement that will appeal to the universal teenager (or universal parent or universal businessperson)?

International Distribution

Finally, international distribution presents several problems. In some industries, delays in starting new distribution networks can be costly. Therefore, companies with existing distribution systems often enjoy an advantage over new businesses. Several companies have gained advantages in time-based competition by buying existing businesses. Procter & Gamble, for example, saved three years of startup time by buying Revlon's Max Factor and Betrix cosmetics, both of which are well established in foreign markets. P&G can thus immediately use these companies' distribution and marketing networks for selling its own brands in the United Kingdom, Germany, and Japan.

Other companies contract with foreign firms or individuals to distribute and sell their products abroad. Foreign agents may perform personal selling and advertising, provide information about local markets, or serve as exporters' representatives. But having to manage interactions with foreign personnel complicates a marketing manager's responsibilities. In addition, packaging practices in Canada must sometimes be adapted to withstand the rigours of transport to foreign ports and storage under conditions that differ radically from domestic conditions.

Given the need to adjust the marketing mix, success in international markets is hard won. Even experienced firms can err in marketing to other countries. International success requires flexibility and a willingness to adapt to the nuances of other cultures. Whether a firm markets in domestic or international markets, however, the basic principles of marketing still apply. It is only the implementation of those principles that changes.

■ SMALL BUSINESS AND THE MARKETING MIX

As we noted in Chapter 7, far more small businesses fail than succeed. Yet many of today's largest firms were yesterday's small businesses. McDonald's began with one restaurant, a concept, and one individual (Ray Kroc) who had foresight. Behind the success of many small firms lies a skillful application of the marketing concept and careful consideration of each element in the marketing mix.

Small Business Products

Some new products—and firms—are doomed at the start simply because few consumers want or need what they have to offer. Too often, enthusiastic entrepreneurs introduce products that they and their friends like, but they fail to estimate realistic market potential. Other small businesses offer new products before they have clear pictures of their target segments and how to reach them. They try to be everything to everyone, and they end up serving no one well. In contrast, sound product planning has paid off for many small firms. "Keep it simple" is a familiar key to success—that is, fulfill a specific need and do it efficiently.

Small Business Pricing

Haphazard pricing that is often little more than guesswork can sink even a firm with a good product. Most often, small business pricing errors result from a failure to project operating expenses accurately. Owners of failing businesses have often been heard to utter statements like "I didn't realize how much it costs to run the business!" and "If I price the product high enough to cover my expenses, no one will buy it!" But when small businesses set prices by carefully assessing costs, many earn very satisfactory profits—sometimes enough to expand or diversify.

Small Business Promotion

Many small businesses are also ignorant when it comes to the methods and costs of promotion. To save expenses, for example, they may avoid advertising and rely instead on personal selling. As a result, too many potential customers remain unaware of their products.

Successful small businesses plan for promotional expenses as part of startup costs. Some hold down costs by taking advantage of less expensive promotional methods. Local newspapers, for example, are sources of publicity when they publish articles about new or unique businesses. Other small businesses have succeeded by identifying themselves and their products with associated groups, organizations, and events. Thus a custom-crafts gallery might join with a local art league and local artists to organize public showings of their combined products.

Small Business Distribution

Problems in arranging distribution can also make or break small businesses. Perhaps the most critical aspect of distribution is facility location, especially for new service businesses. The ability of many small businesses—retailers, veterinary clinics, gourmet coffee shops—to attract and retain customers depends partly on the choice of location.

In distribution, as in other aspects of the marketing mix, however, smaller companies may have advantages over larger competitors, even in highly complex industries. They may be quicker, for example, in applying service technologies. Everex Systems Inc. sells personal computers to wholesalers and dealers through a system the company calls "Zero Response Time." Phone orders are reviewed every two hours so that the factory can adjust assembly to match demand.

SUMMARY OF LEARNING OBJECTIVES

1. **Define *marketing* and explain its functions.** *Marketing* is "the process of planning and executing the conception, pricing, promotion, and distribution of ideas, goods, and services to create exchanges that satisfy individual and organizational objectives."

2. **Explain market *segmentation* and show how it is used in *target marketing*.** *Market segmentation* is the process of dividing markets into categories of customers. Businesses have learned that marketing is more successful when it is aimed towards specific *target markets*—groups of consumers with similar wants and needs. Markets may be segmented by *geographic, demographic, psychographic,* or *product-use variables.*

3. **Explain the purpose and value of *market research*.** *Market research* is the study of what buyers need and of the best ways to meet those needs. This process involves a study of the current situation, the selection of a research method, the collection of data, the analysis of data, and the preparation of a report that may include recommendations for action. The four most common research methods are *observation, survey, focus groups,* and *experimentation.*

4. **Describe the key factors that influence the *consumer buying process*.** A number of personal and psychological considerations, along with various social and cultural influences, affect consumer behaviour. When making buying decisions, consumers first determine or respond to a problem or need and then collect as much information as they think necessary before making a purchase. *Post-purchase evaluations* are also important to marketers because they influence future buying patterns.

5. **Explain how international and cultural differences affect marketing strategies.** Because consumer behaviour, languages, and customs of other nations differ from those of Canada, *international marketing*—the use of marketing strategy to support global, rather than just domestic, business operations—often requires marketers to reconsider the marketing mix. New products, prices that reflect higher transportation costs, culture-specific advertising, and the use of foreign distribution firms may all be necessary.

6. **Identify potential problems and opportunities in the marketing activities of small businesses.** Small businesses face special marketing challenges if they are to survive and grow. Every aspect of the marketing mix should be addressed and planned for prior to the startup of a new business. Small businesses should be aware of their market potential, should price carefully, should plan on promotional costs as part of startup costs, and should choose feasible locations.

STUDY QUESTIONS AND EXERCISES

Review Questions

1. What are the similarities and differences between consumer marketing and industrial marketing?

2. Explain how and why market segmentation is used in target marketing.

3. Identify the steps in the consumer buying process.

4. What elements of the marketing mix may need to be adjusted to market a product internationally? Why?

Analysis Questions

5. Using examples of everyday products, explain why marketing plans must consider the marketing mix.

6. Pick an everyday product such as books, dog food, or shoes. Using your product as an example, show how different versions of it are aimed towards different market segments. Show how the marketing mix differs for each of the segments.

7. Select a readily available product and describe the steps you would expect to find in the consumer decision process about buying that product.

8. If you were starting your own new small business, what are the major pitfalls you would try to avoid as you put together your marketing plans?

Application Exercises

9. Interview the marketing manager of a local business. Identify the degree to which this person's job is oriented towards each of the eight marketing functions.

10. Select a product made by a foreign company and sold in Canada. Compare it to a similar product made domestically in terms of its product features, price, promotion, and distribution. Which one of the two products do you believe will be more successful with Canadian buyers? Why?

BUILDING YOUR BUSINESS SKILLS

Goal

To encourage students to assess how their own buying behaviour differs for major and minor purchases and to understand how their buying behaviour compares with that of others.

Method

Step 1: Keep a diary of the purchases you make during the next two weeks. Include both small purchases (a toothbrush, for example, or a can of tennis balls) and large ones (a computer, a mountain bike, a leather jack-

et). If you make no major purchases during this period, think back to several purchases you have made recently (perhaps within the past six months). In thinking about each purchase, identify and describe the steps involved in each—recognizing a problem or need, seeking information about competing products, evaluating alternative products, making the decision to purchase a specific product, and evaluating the purchase after it has been made.

Step 2: Pair off with another student and take turns analyzing the five stages in each other's purchasing decisions.

Follow-Up Questions

1. Looking at your own consumer buying process, how would you say that it differs for major and minor purchases? Conduct the same analysis for your partner's purchases.

2. List and explain the important differences between the ways you and your partner handle the consumer purchase process.

3. What factors influenced the different ways in which you and your partner approached consumer purchases? Analyze the effects of psychological, economic, social, and cultural differences.

4. For minor purchases—a new cap, for example— were the information-seeking and evaluation of alternatives steps always performed quickly? If not, analyze why they took longer than the purchase probably warranted.

Prentice Hall

TAKE IT TO THE NET

Check out our Companion Website

for this chapter's Exploring the Net exercise, featuring the General Electric Website and other intriguing, annotated destinations. You'll also find practice exercises, updated Weblinks from the text, links to newsgroups, updates, and more.

www.prenticehall.ca/ebert

BUSINESS CASE 13

Which Washer Is Best?

There are basically two types of washing machines— top loaders and front loaders. The former dominate the market in Canada and the U.S., and the latter dominate the market in Europe. In front loaders, clothes spin around a horizontal axis, with the clothes tumbling in and out of a pool of detergent-rich water. The clothes are rinsed repeatedly. By contrast, North American top loaders swirl clothes around in a tub of water that dilutes the detergent.

Europeans argue that front loaders are better because:

- they get clothes cleaner
- they use less water and are more energy-efficient
- they are easier on clothes because there is no centre shaft for the clothes to hit during the wash cycle
- they spin more water out of the clothes during the wash cycle, which means that the time in the dryer is reduced

North Americans see several disadvantages of front loaders:

- they take three times as long to complete the wash cycle

- they are much more expensive than top loaders because they must have watertight doors
- clothes cannot be added during the wash cycle as they can in top loaders
- front loaders don't have the capacity of top loaders
- front loaders are not as easy to load as top loaders

In spite of these back-and-forth arguments, front loaders may be getting a foothold in North America. In 1997, both Maytag and Amana announced that they would begin producing front loaders. At the moment, front loaders have only a 2 percent market share in North America. The key reasons are price (front loaders sell for as much as $3000, while top loaders often go for as little as $500) and efficiency (front loaders take much longer to complete the wash cycle).

The marketing strategy used by Europeans is to tout their washers as upscale products like fancy cars. Producers often try to get home builders to install them as a home is being built, and then the homeowner adds the price to the mortgage.

➤

■ *Case Questions*

1. Consider the detailed activities that must be carried out when washing clothes. What would the typical consumer find attractive about front loaders? About top loaders?

2. What would the typical consumer find unattractive about front loaders? About top loaders?

3. What kind of consumers in Canada and the U.S. are likely to purchase a front-loading washing machine?

4. How can the perceived (and real) disadvantages of front loaders be overcome by manufacturers? Be specific.

CHAPTER
14

DEVELOPING AND PROMOTING GOODS AND SERVICES

PROMOTING ATHLETES AND SALES

More and more businesses are doling out corporate sponsorship money to Olympic athletes in the hopes of catching the public's eye. At the 1998 Winter Olympics in Nagano, Japan, corporate sponsorship was very much in evidence, with Nike Canada supporting Canada's snowboarding and hockey teams, Labatt Brewing Co. and Ford Motor Co. supporting curling, and the Bank of Montreal supporting figure skating. And these were just a few of the companies that were involved. They all hope that their support of amateur athletes will help them be recognized as good corporate citizens and nice companies to do business with, and that millions of consumers will buy their products.

There is also a very practical side to this support, since government budget cuts have forced Olympic athletes to look for assistance from the corporate sector. The Canadian Olympic Association (COA) raised $19 million in corporate sponsorships during 1997, the first year of its four-year fund-raising cycle. That figure was about 50 percent more than the COA raised in the entire previous four-year period. The increase was attributed to both a booming economy and more aggressive marketing by the COA.

Roots Canada's involvement in the 1998 Winter Olympics illustrates what corporate sponsorship is all about. Roots struck a deal with the COA to provide the official jackets for the Canadian Olympic team, which allowed it to put the Roots logo on *all* Canadian athletes' clothing during

medal presentations. Roots has also struck a separate sponsorship deal with figure skater Elvis Stojko, and is selling Olympic-themed merchandise at its stores. The company has also been successful in getting other high-profile individuals who have nothing to do with the Olympics to wear its products. At the Asia-Pacific Economic Cooperation group summit in 1997, Canada's Finance Minister Paul Martin was seen wearing a Roots jacket in a publicity photo.

Other companies were active in the 1998 Winter Olympics as well. Imperial Oil, for example, supported both men's and women's hockey teams at the Olympics. The company did so to demonstrate its support of Canadian athletes, but also because it thought that hockey would have a very large audience, and the Imperial logo would be seen by millions of Canadians.

There are two categories of support that companies can provide. The first is to become an *official sponsor* of the Olympics by contributing a minimum of $1 million to the COA. In return, a company is allowed to use the famous five-ring Olympic symbol in its advertising. Imperial Oil was an official sponsor. A company can also become an *official supplier* to the Olympics. This requires a contribution of about $300 000 in products or services, and also gives the company the right to use the Olympic symbol, but fewer benefits than official sponsors have. In 1998, there was even an official employee assistance provider; Warren Shepell Consultants sent a delegation to Japan to provide psychological counselling to Olympic athletes and coaches.

Sponsorship requirements can be quite specific. For example, members of Canada's snowboarding team wore outfits bearing Nike's famous "swoosh" logo during actual competition, but at pre-Olympic competitions, they displayed the Panasonic Canada Inc. logo. And at the opening and closing ceremonies, they were required to wear jackets made by Roots Canada Inc.

In the last chapter, we introduced the four components of the marketing mix: product, promotion, price, and distribution. In this chapter, we will look more closely at the first two of these components. In particular, we will look at the complex issue of what a *product* is and how it can best be *promoted* to customers.

By focusing on the learning objectives of this chapter, you will better understand new product development and promotion. After reading this chapter, you should be able to:

1. Identify a *product* and distinguish between *consumer* and *industrial products*.
2. Trace the stages of the *product life cycle* and explain the *growth-share matrix*.
3. Discuss the importance of *branding* and *packaging*.
4. Identify the objectives of *promotion* and discuss the considerations involved in selecting a *promotional mix*.
5. Describe the various *advertising media* available to marketing managers.
6. Identify the different types of *sales promotions* and explain the uses of *publicity* and *public relations*.
7. Understand the importance of international promotional strategies in an increasingly global market.

■ WHAT IS A PRODUCT?

In developing the marketing mix for any products—whether ideas, goods, or services—marketers must consider what consumers really buy when they purchase products. Only then can they plan their strategies effectively. We will begin this section where product strategy begins—with an understanding of product *features* and *benefits*. Next, we will describe the major *classifications of products*, both consumer and industrial. Finally, we will discuss the most important component in the offerings of any business—its *product mix*.

Features and Benefits

Customers do not buy products simply because they like the products themselves—they buy products because they like what the products can *do* for them, either physically or emotionally. As one marketing expert has observed, "Consumers don't buy quarter-inch drills; they buy quarter-inch holes." This observation goes to the heart of any effort to analyze products and product success: Companies must base the approach to products (quarter-inch drills) on providing consumers with products that *do* what customers want *done* (drill quarter-inch holes).

To succeed, then, a product must include the right features and offer the right benefits. Product features are the qualities, tangible and intangible, that a company "builds into" its products, such as a 12-horsepower motor on a lawn mower, an improved accounting system, pH balance in a shampoo, or a 60-40 fibre blend in a shirt. To be saleable, however, a product's features also must provide *benefits*: The mower must provide an attractive lawn; the accounting system, better information for making decisions; pH balance, clean and healthy hair; and a 60-40 blend, a good-looking, easy-care shirt.

Obviously, features and benefits play extremely important roles in the pricing of products. Products are much more than just *visible* features and benefits. In buying a product, consumers are also buying an image and a reputation. The marketers of Swatch Chrono watch, for example, are well aware that brand name, packaging, labelling, and after-purchase service are also indispensible parts of their product. Advertisements remind consumers that such "real" features as shock and water resistance, quartz precision, and Swiss manufacture come hand-in-hand with Swatch's commitment to three "concept" features: young and trendy, active and sporty, and stylistically cool and clean.

Swatch
www.swatch-art.com

Classifying Goods and Services

One way to classify a product is according to expected buyers. Buyers fall into two groups: buyers of *consumer* products and buyers of *industrial* products. As we saw in Chapter 13, the consumer and industrial buying processes differ significantly. Not surprisingly, then, marketing products to consumers is vastly different from marketing them to other companies.

Classifying Consumer Products.   Consumer products are commonly divided into three categories that reflect buyers' behaviour: convenience, shopping, and specialty products.

- **Convenience goods** (such as milk and newspapers) and **convenience services** (such as those offered by fast-food restaurants) are consumed rapidly and regularly. They are relatively inexpensive and are purchased frequently and with little expenditure of time and effort.

- **Shopping goods** (such as stereos and tires) and **shopping services** (such as insurance) are more expensive and are purchased less frequently than convenience goods and services. Consumers often compare brands, sometimes in different stores. They also may evaluate alternatives in terms of style, performance, colour, price, and other criteria.

- **Specialty goods** (such as wedding gowns) and **specialty services** (such as catering for wedding receptions) are extremely important and expensive purchases. Consumers usually decide on precisely what they want and will accept no substitutes. They will often go from store to store, sometimes spending a great deal of money and time to get a specific product.

convenience goods/services
Relatively inexpensive consumer goods or services that are bought and used rapidly and regularly, causing consumers to spend little time looking for them or comparing their prices.

shopping goods/services
Moderately expensive consumer goods or services that are purchased infrequently, causing consumers to spend some time comparing their prices.

specialty goods/services
Very expensive consumer goods or services that are purchased rarely, causing consumers to spend a great deal of time locating the exact item desired.

Classifying Industrial Products.   Depending on how much they cost and how they will be used, industrial products can be divided into two categories: *expense items* and *capital items*.

Expense items are any materials and services that are consumed within a year by firms producing other goods or supplying services. The most obvious expense items are industrial goods used directly in the production process, for example, bulkloads of tea processed into tea bags. In addition, *support materials* help to keep a business running without directly entering the production process. Oil, for instance, keeps the tea-bagging machines running but is not used in the tea bags. Similarly, *supplies*—pencils, brooms, gloves, paint—are consumed quickly and regularly by every business. Finally, *services* such as window cleaning, equipment installation, and temporary office help are essential to daily operations. Because these items are used frequently, purchases are often automatic or require little decision making.

Capital items are "permanent"—that is, expensive and long-lasting—goods and services. All these items have expected lives of more than a year—typically up to several years. Expensive buildings (offices, factories), fixed equipment (water towers, baking ovens), and accessory equipment (computers, airplanes) are capital goods. Capital services are those for which long-term commitments are made. These may include purchases for employee food services, building and equipment maintenance, or legal services. Because capital items are expensive and purchased infrequently, they often involve decisions by high-level managers.

expense items
Relatively inexpensive industrial goods that are consumed rapidly and regularly.

capital items
Expensive, long-lasting industrial goods that are used in producing other goods or services and have a long life.

The Product Mix

product mix
The group of products a company has available for sale.

The group of products a company has available for sale, be they consumer or industrial, is known as the firm's **product mix**. Black and Decker, for example, makes toasters, vacuum cleaners, electric drills, and a variety of other appliances and tools. 3M makes everything from Post-its to laser optics. And Nike, famous for its footwear, has introduced a whole line of sports-related products like baseball gloves and bats, hockey sticks, basketballs, and in-line skates.[1]

Most companies begin with a single product. Over time, successful companies may find that the initial product does not suit all consumers shopping for the product type. So they often introduce similar products designed to reach other consumers. Apple computer introduced the first successful personal computer. Shortly thereafter, Apple produced a range of personal computers for various applications—for example, the Apple 2C, 2E, 2GS, Macintosh Plus, and Macintosh SE. A group of similar products intended for a similar group of buyers who will use them in similar fashions is known as a **product line**.

product line
A group of similar products intended for a similar group of buyers who will use them in a similar fashion.

Companies also may extend their horizons and identify opportunities outside of their existing product line. The result—multiple (or diversified) product lines—is evident in firms like Procter & Gamble. This firm began by making soap, but it now also produces paper products, foods, coffee, and baby products. Multiple product lines allow a company to grow more rapidly and minimize the consequences of slow sales in any one product line.

■ DEVELOPING NEW PRODUCTS

To expand or diversify product lines—indeed, just to survive—firms must develop and successfully introduce streams of new products. Faced with competition and shifting consumer preferences, no firm can count on a single successful product to carry them forever. Even basic products that have been widely purchased for decades require nearly constant renewal. Consider the unassuming facial tissue. The white tissue in the rectangular box has been joined (if not replaced) by tissues of many different colours and patterns. They arrive in boxes shaped and decorated for nearly every room in the house, and they are made to be placed or carried not only in the bathroom but in the purse, the briefcase, and the car.

The New Product Development Process

General Electric
www.ge.com

In January 1990, General Electric announced its five-year program for the revolutionary GE90, a cleaner, quieter jet engine. GE had already spent its $2 billion development budget and, in 1993, celebrated the maiden flight of its test engine. Still, GE did not know when the engine would be certified for use in commercial jets.[2]

Automobile manufacturers face an even longer time horizon as they go about developing a new engine to replace the internal combustion engine that has powered automobiles for over 100 years. The need to increase fuel economy and reduce emissions has motivated companies like Ford to invest $420 million in an alliance with Daimler-Benz and Canadian fuel cell maker Ballard Power Systems to produce cars powered by fuel cells by 2004.[3]

High-definition television (HDTV) is another example of a new product that has taken a long time to develop. Because HDTV gives much improved picture quality, it was thought that it would quickly be accepted by consumers. But HDTV is off to a very slow start because of a classic chicken-and-egg problem: broadcasters haven't decided to offer high-definition programs (because they require special transmitters and cameras), and manufacturers of HDTVs have been holding back because they don't know if broadcasters are going to produce high-definition programs for consumers to watch.[4]

Bombardier Inc.
www.bombardier.com

In 1989, discussions about the possibility of manufacturing a new long-range executive jet began at Bombardier Inc. of Montreal. Over the next few years, the company spent millions of dollars developing the product, which finally became available in 1998 (see the box "Developing and Promoting a New Product"). There are no guarantees that the plane will be successful, but the opportunity is potentially great.

TRENDS & CHALLENGES

Developing and Promoting a New Product

When you think of new product development, you often think of toothpaste, computers, or automobiles. But how about airplanes? Two new airplanes, aimed at the most elite market in the world, will be flying before the year 2000. They are long-range corporate jets, and they will be able to carry eight passengers from New York to Tokyo in 13 hours without refuelling. Only 350 to 800 of these planes will be sold, likely at a price of about $30 million each. The customers are multinational companies, a few billionaires, and a few heads of state.

Only two companies are developing this new product. One is a world-famous U.S. firm (Gulfstream) and the other is Bombardier Inc. of Montreal. This is going to be a David-and-Goliath struggle, but there is a big surprise: the Goliath is Bombardier. With annual sales of nearly $5 billion, 36 500 employees, manufacturing operations in eight countries, and markets in more than 60, Bombardier is the sixth largest aviation company in the world, and a major force in international transportation. The company has grown from its beginnings as a maker of snowmobiles to its present size by acquiring several firms, including Canadair, Learjet, Short Brothers PLC, and de Havilland. By contrast, Gulfstream is a small player and makes only top-of-the-line corporate jets. Its new jet is called the Gulfstream V.

In a football-field-size room at its Montreal headquarters, a team of 250 Bombardier engineers sit at computer screens designing the new plane (called the Global Express). Part of the team is responsible for the wings and fuselage. Another part is building the engine. Next door, in a building so big its corridors have street names so that workers won't get lost, other parts of the new product development plan are being carried out.

The idea for an intercontinental business jet costing $30 million started in 1989 when CEO Laurent Beaudoin called vice president John Holding from his car phone and suggested that they leapfrog the competition. Bombardier's strategy has been to be a leader in selected market niches, and company executives agreed that with the increasing globalization of business, a global business jet was needed. In spite of the increased emphasis on electronic communication and corporate efficiency, Bombardier is betting that it will continue to be necessary to conduct business face-to-face, particularly when new international deals are being put together. Hence, it will market the new jet on the basis that it economizes on the executive's most precious commodity—time.

Bombardier conducted market research on the new product by asking potential customers which pair of cities they most frequently travelled between. They found that New York–Tokyo was the key. Bombardier next asked customers if they would pay $28 million for a plane that could travel 12 000 kilometres at 850 kilometres per hour. They said yes. By the end of 1993, the company had 30 orders in hand, so the final go-ahead was given. Bombardier will break even when it sells the 100th plane.

Compared to the Gulfstream V, the Global Express has the edge. It will be faster, enabling it to get to Tokyo an hour sooner. And it is roomier inside, with a higher, wider cabin that has 19 percent more floor area. The Gulfstream's advantage is that it will be on the market two years sooner. Because this is a critical new product for Gulfstream's future success, it is already aggressively competing against the Global Express. In late 1993, it took out a full-page advertisement in *The Wall Street Journal* offering a $250 000 discount on its new plane to anyone who cancelled an order for the Global Express. But nobody took up the offer.

Promoting a product like an executive jet is nothing like selling toothpaste. The emphasis here is on personal selling in the most extreme sense of the term. Those individuals or companies that are considered "serious buyers" get regular personal visits from executives of both Bombardier and Gulfstream. Customers of Gulfstream are offered free rides on the plane anywhere in the world. They also get a tour of the plane's cockpit, which is loaded with the latest electronic gadgets.

The sales pitches made for both planes are convincing (and conflicting). Bombardier's pitch is that the Gulfstream V is simply a warmed-over version of its last jet, the Gulfstream IV, and that the Global Express is a faster and bigger plane with a longer range. Gulfstream counters with the fact that its plane will be available before the Global Express; they also claim that Bombardier will not be able to live up to the performance claims it is making for the Global Express.

In the end, it may not be the sales pitch that sells the airplane. Most buyers say the choice is a very subjective one. Both planes are very good products, and industry analysts think there is room in the market for each one.

The high *mortality rate* for new ideas means that only a few new products eventually reach commercialization. Moreover, as in the case of the GE90, *speed to market* with a product is often as important as care in developing it. Product development is a long and complex (and expensive) process. Companies do not dream up new products one day and ship them to retailers the next. In fact, new products usually involve carefully planned—and sometimes risky—commitments of time and resources. The box "Predicting the Success of New Products" identifies some of the factors that are needed to make a new product a success.

Product Mortality Rates.   Typically, new products move through a series of stages, beginning with the search for ideas and culminating in introduction to consumers. At each stage of this process, potential products fall from further consideration as the company pursues more attractive alternatives. In fact, it is estimated that it takes 50 new product ideas to generate one product that finally reaches the marketplace. Even then, of course, only a few of those survivors become *successful* products. Many seemingly great *ideas* have failed as *products*. Indeed, creating a successful new product has become more and more difficult.

TRENDS & CHALLENGES

Predicting the Success of New Products

What does it take to make a new product or service successful? Why do certain products or services flop, while others are wildly successful? Although predictions about which new product ideas will be successful are somewhat risky, there are certain "success factors" that are helpful in predicting success. The more success factors a product or service has, the higher the probability that it will be demanded by consumers.

Some of these success factors are as follows:

1. *Time*—If the product idea helps consumers save time or control time it is more likely to be successful. The four new product champions of recent times—fax machines, VCRs, microwave ovens, and automatic teller machines—all save customers time.

2. *Convenience*—If a product makes it easier to do something, consumers will want it. Cellular phones and the appearance of ATMs in shopping malls are examples of this factor.

3. *Government regulation*—If regulations help a product, it is more likely to be successful; if not, it is more likely to fail. For example, U.S. and European governments have been slow to approve the technical standards necessary for high-definition televi-

sion (HDTV). Thus, Japanese TV manufacturers have had difficulties selling HDTV sets.

4. *Existing technology*—The technology used to produce regular TV picture resolution is much cheaper than the technology needed for HDTV. And the picture that is produced is pretty good. It is therefore unlikely that consumers would pay a lot more money for HDTV.

5. *Human nature*—New products that require people to change the way they behave are less likely to be successful than those that don't. Personal computer usage in homes grew slowly during the 1980s because they required large behavioural changes in people. The use of debit cards, on the other hand, has increased rapidly because they are easy to use.

6. *Cost*—The less a product costs, the more likely people are to buy it. Car phones cost $4000 in the early 1980s and there weren't many buyers. Now they cost less than $100 and demand is skyrocketing.

Companies that develop new product and service ideas that maximize these success factors are more likely to achieve success than companies that ignore these factors.

Speed to Market. The principle is quite simple: The more rapidly a product moves from the laboratory to the marketplace, the more likely it is to survive. By introducing new products ahead of competitors, companies quickly establish market leaders. They become entrenched in the market before being challenged by late-arriving competitors.

How important is **speed to market**—that is, a firm's success in responding to customer demand or market changes? One study has estimated that a product that is only three months late to market (that is, three months behind the leader) sacrifices 12 percent of its lifetime profit potential. A product that is six months late will lose 33 percent.

speed to market
The rate at which a business firm responds to consumer demands or market changes.

The Seven-Step Development Process. To increase their chances of developing a successful new product, many firms adopt some variation on a basic seven-step process (see Figure 14.1).

1. Product ideas. Product development begins with a search for ideas for new products. Product ideas can come from consumers, the sales force, research and development people, or engineering personnel. The key is to actively seek out ideas and to reward those whose ideas become successful products.

FIGURE 14.1
The new product development process.

2. Screening.   This second stage is an attempt to eliminate all product ideas that do not mesh with the firm's abilities, expertise, or objectives. Representatives from marketing, engineering, and production must have input at this stage.

3. Concept testing.   Once ideas have been culled, companies use market research to solicit consumers' input. In this way, firms can identify benefits that the product must provide as well as an appropriate price level for the product.

4. Business analysis.   This stage involves developing an early comparison of costs versus benefits for the proposed product. Preliminary sales projections are compared with cost projections from finance and production. The aim is not to determine precisely how much money the product will make but to see whether the product can meet minimum profitability goals.

5. Prototype development.   At this stage, product ideas begin to take shape. Using input from the concept-testing phase, engineering and/or research and development produce a preliminary version of the product. Prototypes can be extremely expensive, often requiring extensive hand crafting, tooling, and development of components. But this phase can help identify potential production problems.

6. Product testing and test marketing.   Using what it learned from the prototype, the company goes into limited production of the item. The product is then tested internally to see if it meets performance requirements. If it does, it is made available for sale in limited areas. This stage is very costly, since promotional campaigns and distribution channels must be established for test markets. But test marketing gives a company its first information on how consumers will respond to a product under real market conditions.

7. Commercialization.   If test-marketing results are positive, the company will begin full-scale production and marketing of the product. Gradual commercialization, with the firm providing the product to more and more areas over time, prevents undue strain on the firm's initial production capabilities. But extensive delays in commercialization may give competitors a chance to bring out their own version.

■ THE PRODUCT LIFE CYCLE

product life cycle (PLC)
The concept that the profit-producing life of any product goes through a cycle of introduction, growth, maturity (levelling off), and decline.

Products that reach the commercialization stage begin a new series of stages known as the product life cycle. **Product life cycle (PLC)** is the concept that products have a limited profit-producing life for a company. This life may be a matter of months, years, or decades, depending on the ability of the product to attract customers over time. Strong products such as Kellogg's Corn Flakes, Coca-Cola, Ivory soap, Argo corn starch, and Caramilk candy bars have had extremely long productive lives.

Stages in the Product Life Cycle

The product life cycle is a natural process in which products are born, grow in stature, mature, and finally decline and die. The life cycle is typically divided into four states through which products pass as they "age" on the market:

1. *Introduction.* The introduction stage begins when the product reaches the marketplace. During this stage, marketers focus on making potential consumers aware of

the product and its benefits. Because of extensive promotional and development costs, profits are nonexistent.

2. *Growth.* If the new product attracts and satisfies enough consumers, sales begin to climb rapidly. During this stage, the product begins to show a profit. Other firms in the industry move rapidly to introduce their own versions.

3. *Maturity.* Sales growth begins to slow. Although the product earns its highest profit level early in this stage, increased competition eventually leads to price cutting and lower profits. Towards the end of this stage, sales start to fall.

4. *Decline.* During this final stage, sales and profits continue to fall. New products in the introduction stage take away sales. Companies remove or reduce promotional support (ads and salespeople) but may let the product linger to provide some profits.

Figure 14.2 shows the four stages of the cycle—not yet complete—for VCRs. The product was introduced in the late 1970s and is, of course, widely used today. (Notice that profits lag behind sales because of the extensive costs of developing new products.) If the market becomes saturated, sales will begin to decline. Sales will also fall if new products, such as laser discs, send the VCR the way of the eight-track audio player.

The Growth-Share Matrix.   Companies with multiple product lines typically have various products at each point in the PLC. To decide how best to market each product, many marketers rely on the growth-share matrix, which classifies products according to market share and growth potential.

- Most products start as *question marks*—low market share, high growth potential—because they are entering new markets that may grow but have not yet captured consumers' attention. A company will likely "invest" in these products, hoping that they will eventually perform well in the market.

- During the growth stage, products may become *stars* with high market share and high growth potential. Stars have large shares of still-growing markets, and companies will normally "hold" these products because they will eventually profit from them.

- In the maturity stage, products can serve as *cash cows*—high market share, low growth potential—because their large market share makes them profitable even though market growth is slow. Companies "harvest" the profits from these products.

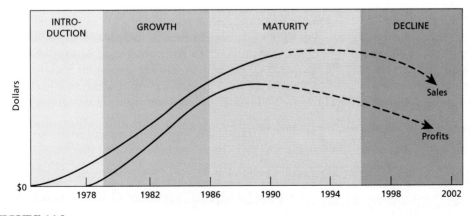

FIGURE 14.2
The product life cycle for VCRs. Note that profits lag behind sales due to the extensive development ment costs to create the new product.

- Products in the decline stage are *dogs*—low market share, low growth potential—whose profits and sales signal that the life cycle is nearly complete. At some point, companies "kill" these products and no longer devote any energy to them.

When developing marketing plans, managers must consider not only the product's location on the growth-share matrix but also the direction in which it is moving. For example, while a question mark with increasing market share may be headed for stardom, a question mark with decreasing market share may require major changes or elimination.

In addition, companies always seek balance and continuity in the product mix. A company loaded with cash cows, for example, has a great present but may have a questionable future. Because they require a lot of attention, a firm loaded with stars may be focusing its managers' energies too narrowly. On the other hand, a firm with mostly cash cows and stars, some question marks, and a couple of unavoidable dogs has developed a strong product pipeline and a balanced product mix.

■ IDENTIFYING PRODUCTS

As noted earlier in the chapter, developing the features of a product is only part of a marketer's battle. Identifying that product in consumers' minds through the use of brand names, packaging, and labelling is also important.

Branding Products

brand names
Those specific names of products associated with a manufacturer, wholesaler, and/ or retailer that are designed to distinguish products from those of competitors and are promoted as part of the product.

An especially important component of product development is deciding on a name for the product. **Brand names** were introduced to try to simplify the process of product selection for consumers. Customers try a product, remember its name, and go back to it next time. Millions of dollars have been spent developing names like Noxzema, Prudential, and Minute Maid and attaching meaning to them in consumers' minds.

The key in coming up with a brand name for a product is to keep the name simple. As few letters and numbers as possible make the name sound "good" and easy to remember. The brand must also be consistent with current lifestyles. Post recently changed the name of Sugar Smacks to Honey Smacks and its mascot from Sugar Bear to Honey Bear. In today's health-conscious market, a honey cereal is viewed more favourably than a sugar-coated one.

An issue of growing importance in branding strategy is faced by firms that sell products internationally. They must also consider how product names will translate in various languages. In Spanish, for example, the name of Chevrolet's now-defunct Nova simply became *no va*—"it does not go." Sales were particularly poor in South America. Similarly, Rolls-Royce was once going to name a new touring car "Silver Mist." Rolls changed the name to "Silver Shadow" when it discovered that *mist* is German for "manure."[5] Naturally, foreign companies hoping to sell in Canada must be equally careful. The box "Building Brands at Nestlé" describes that company's brand strategy.

trade mark
The exclusive legal right to use a brand name.

Trade Marks, Patents, and Copyrights.   Because brand development is very expensive, a company does not want another company using its name and confusing consumers into buying a substitute product. Many companies apply to the Canadian government and receive a **trade mark**, the exclusive legal right to use a brand name. Trade marks are granted for 15 years and may be renewed for further periods of 15 years, but only if the company continues to protect its brand name.

Just what can be trade marked is not always clear, however. If the company allows the name to lapse into common usage, the courts may take away protection. Common usage occurs when the company fails to use the ® symbol for its brand. It also occurs if the company fails to correct those who do not acknowledge the brand as a trade mark.

TRENDS & CHALLENGES

Building Brands at Nestlé

Nestlé is the world's most successful international food company. It is the market leader in instant coffee in Australia (71 percent), France (67 percent), Japan (74 percent), and Mexico (85 percent). In powdered milk, it is the leader in the Philippines (66 percent) and Brazil (58 percent). In Chile, Nestlé has 73 percent of the cookie market and 70 percent of the soups and juices market.

Although Nestlé is a global company, it lives on local brands. It achieves much of its growth in developing countries simply by getting there before other companies do. Once in a country, it builds both a manufacturing and a political presence. Nestlé already gets one-quarter of its worldwide sales from the Far East and Latin America. About one-third of company profits come from products sold outside developed countries.

Nestlé owns nearly 8000 brands worldwide, but you won't see hundreds of their brands in a store near you. Only about 750 are registered in more than one country, and only 80 brands are registered in more than 10 countries. Nestlé thus rejects the "one-world, one-brand" school of marketing that companies like Coca-Cola and PepsiCo embrace.

In the developed world, Nestlé pursues a strategy of acquiring well-known brands. For example, it owns Stouffer's, Perrier, and Carnation. In developing countries, it grows by building up brand loyalty to a local brand—for example, Bear Brand condensed milk in Asia. By developing only a few brands in each country, Nestlé is able to highly focus its advertising money and thereby achieve big market shares. The executive vice president in charge of marketing says the company does not believe in life cycles for brands; he says that a well-managed brand will outlive any manager.

Nestlé's experience selling coffee in Thailand demonstrates its attitude towards brand development. How does a Swiss company sell a hot beverage in the tropics? The general manager of Nestlé Thailand decided that coffee was the perfect product to capitalize on the growth that Thailand was experiencing in the late 1980s. He and his team decided to forget advertising coffee based on traditional taste and aroma. Instead, the advertisements emphasized coffee as a stress reducer and as a promoter of romance. When one of the team members saw a Nestlé promotion on cold coffee from Nestlé Greece, they quickly adopted that idea. Coffee sales jumped from $25 million in 1987 to $100 million in 1994.

An extreme example of Nestlé's strategy of local brand development is found in China. After 13 years of talks, Nestlé was finally invited into China in 1987 because the government wanted to increase milk production. Nestlé opened a powdered milk plant in 1990, but then it had a tough choice to make: use the overburdened local network of trains and roads to collect milk, or build its own roads. It chose the latter, even though it was very costly. Farmers now follow Nestlé's "milk roads" when they bring their milk to the chilling centres for weighing and analysis.

Nestlé pays the farmers promptly, something the government didn't always do, so farmers now have an incentive to produce more milk (the district cow population increased 50 percent in 18 months). Nestlé also brought in experts to train farmers in animal health and hygiene. In its first year, the factory produced 316 tonnes of powdered milk; by 1994 it produced 10 000 tonnes. Nestlé now has exclusive rights to sell the product across China for 15 years. The company predicts that sales will reach $700 million by the year 2000.

Windsurfer, a popular brand of sailboards, lost its trade mark, and the name can now be used by any sailboard company. The same thing has happened to other names that were formerly brand names—trampoline, yo-yo, thermos, snowmobile, kleenex, and aspirin. But companies like Xerox, Coke, Jell-O, and Scotch tape have successfully defended their brand names.

Companies want to be sure that both product brands and new product ideas are protected. A **patent** protects an invention or idea for a period of 20 years. The cost is $1000 to $1500; it takes nine months to three years to secure a patent from the Canadian Patent Office.[6]

Copyrights give exclusive ownership rights to the creators of books, articles, designs, illustrations, photos, films, and music. Computer programs and even semicon-

patent
Protects an invention or idea for a period of 20 years.

ductor chips are also protected. Copyrights extend to creators for their entire lives and to their estates for 50 years thereafter. Copyrights apply to the tangible expressions of an idea, not to the idea itself. For example, the idea of cloning dinosaurs from fossil DNA cannot be copyrighted, but Michael Crichton, the author of *Jurassic Park*, could copyright his novel because it is the tangible result of the basic idea.

Brand Loyalty. Companies that spend the large amount of money it takes to develop a brand are looking for one thing from consumers: **brand loyalty**. That is, they want to develop customers who, when they need a particular item, will go back to the same brand and buy the company's products.

Brand loyalty is measured in three stages. First, the company wants *brand recognition.* By putting the brand in front of consumers many times and associating it with a type of product, the producer hopes that consumers will become aware of its existence.

Recognition is not enough, however. The owner of the brand wants consumers to start showing *brand preference* when they make a purchase. Brand preference requires not only awareness that the brand exists but also a favourable attitude towards the ability of the brand to provide benefits.

Finally, because a brand may be unavailable in a store from time to time, companies seek *brand insistence*. Brand insistence is highly valued by brand owners, but it is very difficult to achieve. For all convenience and many shopping products, consumers will freely substitute another brand when they need a product. Usually, only specialty products have much potential for developing brand insistence in a large group of consumers. For example, a family wanting to buy or sell a home might insist on using a trusted local realtor.

Packaging Products

With a few exceptions, including fresh fruits and vegetables, structural steel, and some other industrial products, products need some form of **packaging** in which to be carried to the market. A package also serves as an in-store advertisement that makes the product attractive, clearly displays the brand, and identifies product features and benefits.

A growing number of companies are shifting their promotional spending from advertising to packaging. The trend is to lighter, brighter colours that stand out more on grocery store shelves. The package is the marketer's last chance to say "buy it" to the consumer.[7]

Packaging reduces the risk of damage, breakage, or spoilage, and it increases the difficulty of stealing smaller products. But once a product is opened and used, expensive packaging may become waste.

Labelling Products

Every product has a **label** on its package. Packaging and labelling can help market the product. In Canada, the information on package labels is regulated by the federal government. The ***Consumer Packaging and Labelling Act*** has two main purposes: to provide a comprehensive set of rules for packaging and labelling of consumer products, and to ensure that the manufacturer provides full and factual information on labels. All prepackaged products must state in French and English the quantity enclosed in metric and imperial units. The name and description of the product must also appear on the label in both French and English.

In recent years labels have begun to display the Universal Product Code (UPC) bar code. This series of bars of various lengths and widths and spaces helps identify and keep track of merchandise. It also enables retailers to speed up the checkout process by using special bar-code scanners.

brand loyalty
Customers' recognition of, preference for, and insistence on buying a product with a certain brand name.

packaging
The physical container in which a product is sold, including the label.

label
That part of a product's packaging that identifies the product's name and contents and sometimes its benefits.

Consumer Packaging and Labelling Act
A federal law that provides comprehensive rules for packaging and labelling of consumer products.

■ PROMOTING PRODUCTS AND SERVICES

It is no secret to anyone who watches television, reads magazines, or even surveys the urban landscape that businesses rely on advertising, publicity, and other techniques in the battle to attract the attention of customers and maintain their loyalty. In many businesses, promotion can be the key either to establishing a new product or to keeping an established product in the public eye.

In free market systems, a business uses promotional methods to communicate information about itself and its products to consumers, industrial buyers, or both. The purpose, of course, is to influence purchase decisions. From an *information* standpoint, promotions seek to accomplish four things with potential customers:

- make them *aware* of products
- make them *knowledgeable* about products
- *persuade* them to like the products
- persuade them to *purchase* products

Promotional Objectives

The ultimate objective of any promotion is to increase sales. However, marketers also use promotion to communicate information, position products, add value, and control sales volume.[8]

Communication of Information.   Consumers cannot buy a product unless they have been informed about it. Information can advise customers about the availability of a product, educate them on the latest technological advances, or announce the candidacy of someone running for a government office. Information may be communicated in writing (newspapers and magazines), verbally (in person or over the telephone), or visually (television, a matchbook cover, or a billboard). Today, the communication of information regarding a company's products or services is so important that marketers try to place it wherever consumers may be. If you are an average consumer, you come in contact with approximately 1500 bits of promotional communication a day![9]

Product Positioning.   Another objective of promotion, **product positioning**, is to establish an easily identifiable image of a product in the minds of consumers. For example, by selling only in department stores, Estée Lauder products have positioned themselves as more upscale than cosmetics sold in drugstores. With product positioning, the company is trying to appeal to a specific segment of the market rather than to the market as a whole.

product positioning
The establishment of an easily identifiable image of a product in the minds of consumers.

Adding Value.   Today's value-conscious customers gain benefits when the promotional mix is shifted and when it communicates value-increased products. Burger King, for example, shifted its promotional mix by cutting back on advertising and using those funds instead for customer discounts. Similarly, Compaq Computer countered increased pressure from low-priced competitors by introducing its own lower-priced desktop computers with enhanced capabilities.[10] In addition to adding value, promotion is the main way to establish a product's perceived value. It means creating communications and directing them to value-conscious customers.

Compaq Computer
www.compaq.com

Controlling Sales Volume.   Sales volume control is also an objective of promotions. Many companies, such as Hallmark Cards, experience seasonal sales patterns. By increasing its promotional activities in slow periods, the firm can achieve a more stable sales volume throughout the year. As a result, it can keep its production and distribution systems running evenly.

Promotional Strategies

push strategy
A promotional strategy in which a company aggressively pushes its product through wholesalers and retailers, who persuade customers to buy it.

pull strategy
A promotional strategy in which a company appeals directly to customers, who demand the product from retailers, who demand the product from wholesalers.

Once a firm's promotional objectives are clear, it must develop a promotional strategy to achieve these objectives. Promotional strategies may be of the push or pull variety. A company with a **push strategy** will aggressively "push" its product through wholesalers and retailers, who persuade customers to buy it. In contrast, a company with a **pull strategy** appeals directly to customers, who demand the product from retailers, who in turn demand the product from wholesalers. Advertising "pulls" while personal selling "pushes."

Makers of industrial products most often use a push strategy, and makers of consumer products most often use a pull strategy. Many large firms use a combination of the two strategies. For example, General Foods uses advertising to create consumer demand (pull) for its cereals. It also pushes wholesalers and retailers to stock these products.

The Promotional Mix

promotional mix
That portion of marketing concerned with choosing the best combination of advertising, personal selling, sales promotions, and publicity to sell a product.

As we noted in Chapter 13, there are four basic types of promotional tools: advertising, personal selling, sales promotions, and publicity and public relations. The best combination of these tools—the best **promotional mix**—depends on many factors. The company's product, the costs of different tools versus the promotions budget, and characteristics in the target audience all play a role. Figure 14.3 shows different combinations of products, promotional tools, and target consumers.

■ ADVERTISING PROMOTIONS

What candy bar is "one of life's sweet mysteries"? What soap is "99 and 44/100 pure"? What product is "only available in Canada—Pity." What is the store where "the lowest price is the law"? If you are like most Canadians, you can answer these questions because of advertising. (The answers are Caramilk, Ivory soap, Red Rose tea, and Zellers.)

Advertising Media

advertising medium
The specific communication device—television, radio, newspapers, direct mail, magazines, billboards—used to carry a firm's advertising message to potential customers.

In developing advertising strategies, marketers must consider the best **advertising medium** for their message. IBM, for example, uses television ads to keep its name fresh in consumers' minds. But it also uses newspaper and magazine ads to educate consumers on products' abilities and trade publications to introduce new software.

An advertiser selects media with a number of factors in mind. The marketer must first ask: Which medium will reach the people I want to reach? If a firm is selling hog breeding equipment, it might choose *Playboar*, a business magazine read mostly by hog farmers. If it is selling silverware, it might choose a magazine for brides. If it is selling toothpaste, the choice might be a general audience television program or a general audience magazine such as *Reader's Digest* (or *Sélection*, for exposure to a similar audience of francophones).

Each advertising medium has its own advantages and disadvantages. The relative importance of different media is shown in Figure 14.4.

Newspapers.   Newspapers remain the most widely used advertising medium. They offer excellent coverage, since each local market has at least one daily newspaper, and many people read the paper every day. This medium offers flexible, rapid coverage, since ads can change from day to day. It also offers believable coverage, since ads are presented side by side with news. Newspapers, however, do not usually allow advertisers to target their audience well.

Goods Promotion: House (real estate)
Tool: Personal selling
Consumer: House buyer

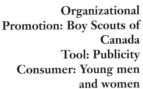

Organizational
Promotion: Boy Scouts of
Canada
Tool: Publicity
Consumer: Young men
and women

Service Promotion: Weight-loss program
Tool: Sales promotion (coupon)
Consumer: Overweight person

Event Promotion: Rock concert
Tool: Advertising
Consumer: Cheering fan

Person or Idea
Promotion: Candidate for premier
Tool: Publicity/advertising/personal sales
Consumer: Voter

FIGURE 14.3
Each promotional tool should be properly matched with the product being promoted and the target customer.

Television.   Television allows advertisers to combine sight, sound, and motion, thus appealing to almost all the viewer's senses. Information on viewer demographics for a particular program allows advertisers to promote to their target audiences. National advertising is done on television because it reaches more people than any other medium.

One disadvantage of television is that too many commercials cause viewers to confuse products. Most people, for example, can't recall whether a tire commercial was sponsored by Firestone, Goodyear, or B.F. Goodrich. In addition, VCR viewers often

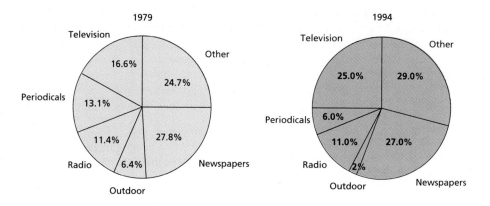

FIGURE 14.4
Relative importance of various media; 1979 and 1994.

fast-forward past the ads of TV shows that they have recorded. Moreover, because "commercial spots" last only a short time (usually 30 seconds), the impact of the commercial is lost if the viewer is not paying attention. The brevity of TV ads also makes television a poor medium in which to educate viewers about complex products. Finally, television is the most expensive medium in which to advertise. A 30-second commercial during the NFL Super Bowl costs about $1 million.

direct mail
Printed advertisements, such as flyers, mailed directly to consumers' homes or places of business.

Canada Post
www.canpost.ca

Direct Mail.   **Direct mail** involves flyers or other types of printed advertisements mailed directly to consumers' homes or places of business. Direct mail allows the company to select its audience and personalize its message. Although many people discard "junk mail," targeted recipients with stronger-than-average interest are more likely to buy. Although direct mail involves the largest advance costs of any advertising technique, it does appear to have the highest cost-effectiveness. Particularly effective have been "fax attacks," in which advertisers send their "mail" messages electronically via fax machines and get higher response rates than they would if they used Canada Post.

The rise of mailing lists and the high cost of developing them have led to a thriving industry: the swapping and selling of mailing lists and consumer data among businesses for use in direct-mail advertising. Such practices present an ethical question for many businesses, whose customers resent having their names and addresses bought and sold or their fax machines tied up. As a result of consumer protests, many companies now promise not to sell a customer's name if the customer asks them not to.

Radio.   A tremendous number of people listen to the radio each day, and radio ads are inexpensive. In addition, since most radio is programmed locally, this medium gives advertisers a high degree of customer selectivity. For example, radio stations are already segmented into listening categories such as rock and roll, country and western, jazz, talk shows, news, and religious programming.

Like television, however, radio ads are over quickly. And radio permits only an audio presentation. As well, people tend to use the radio as "background" while they are doing other things, paying little attention to advertisements.

Magazines.   The many different magazines on the market provide a high level of consumer selectivity. The person who reads *Popular Photography* is more likely to be interested in the latest specialized lenses from Canon than is a *Gourmet* magazine subscriber. Magazine advertising allows for excellent reproduction of photographs and artwork that not only grab buyers' attention but may also convince them of the product's value. And magazines allow advertisers plenty of space for detailed product information. Magazines have a long life and tend to be passed from person to person, thus doubling and tripling the number of exposures.

One problem with magazine advertising is that ads must be submitted well in advance to be included in a certain issue. Often there is no guarantee of where within a magazine an ad will appear. Naturally, a company prefers to have its advertisement appear near the front of the magazine or within a feature article.

Outdoor.   Outdoor advertising—billboards, signs, and advertisements on buses, taxis, and subways—is relatively inexpensive, faces little competition for customers' attention, and is subject to high repeat exposure. Unfortunately, companies have little control over who will see their advertisements. Because roadside billboards are prohibited on some major Ontario arteries, Moving Impressions Inc. has introduced "rolling billboards"— advertisements attached to the sides of large freight trucks. The truck companies get a piece of the action.[11]

Word-of-Mouth.   Consumers form very strong opinions about products as a result of conversations with friends and acquaintances. If **word-of-mouth** says that a product is good, higher product sales are very likely. Of course, word-of-mouth will also spread bad news about a product.

word-of-mouth
Opinions about the value of products passed among consumers in informal discussions.

Some companies rely heavily on word-of-mouth advertising. Big Rock Brewery does no advertising, but relies on word-of-mouth to expand its market share. It already has a 7 percent share of Alberta's draft beer market, and its exports to the U.S. are increasing rapidly.[12]

Electronic Commerce.   A new and rapidly growing approach to advertising involves the Internet. **Electronic commerce** refers to the buying and selling of goods through electronic means. Consumers can log on to various Websites, examine the products available, and then decide which ones to purchase. Canadian companies spent about $10 million on Internet advertising in 1997.[13]

electronic commerce
The buying and selling of goods through electronic means.

Some well-known direct sellers (see Chapter 15) such as Tupperware, Electrolux, Amway, and Mary Kay do not allow their sales reps to create Websites or sell over the Internet. These companies are concerned that the Internet does not provide the kind of service that is beneficial to their customers.[14]

This Chapters website is typical of the many new websites that have come into existence in the last few years as electronic commerce has grown.

But Internet shopping can benefit both the buyer and the seller. The company does not have to maintain a physical outlet with all its accompanying costs, yet it is able to reach a global market. The consumer understands that Internet shopping is an efficient way to gather information and make comparisons among competing products. Internet advertising does have limitations. Unless Websites are very interesting, most consumers probably will not pay much attention to them. Consumers may also be reluctant to wade through thousands of electronic pages looking at details on hundreds of different products. This type of advertising will nevertheless develop rapidly in the next few years; in 1997, worldwide sales on the Internet totalled just $13.1 billion, but by 2002 they are predicted to exceed $400 billion.[15]

Other Advertising Channels.   A combination of many additional media, including catalogues, sidewalk handouts, *Yellow Pages*, skywriting, telephone calls, special events, and door-to-door communications, make up the remaining advertisements to which Canadians are exposed. Each of these media is specialized and used selectively, often locally by small businesses, political campaigners, and special-interest groups.

■ PERSONAL SELLING PROMOTIONS

Virtually everyone has done some selling. Perhaps you had a lemonade stand or sold candy for the drama club. Or you may have gone on a job interview, selling your abilities and service as an employee to the interviewer's company. In personal selling, a salesperson communicates one-to-one with a potential customer to identify the customer's need and match that need with the seller's product.

Personal selling—the oldest form of selling—provides the personal link between seller and buyer. It adds to a firm's credibility because it provides buyers with someone to interact with and to answer their questions. Because it involves personal interaction, personal selling requires a level of trust between the buyer and the seller. When a buyer feels cheated by the seller, that trust has been broken and a negative attitude towards salespeople in general can develop. Consider the image of the sleazy used car dealer. To counteract this reputation, many companies are emphasizing customer satisfaction and generally striving to improve the effectiveness of whatever personal selling they undertake.

Personal selling is the most expensive form of promotion per contact because presentations are generally made to one or two individuals at a time. Personal selling expenses include salespeople's compensation and their overhead, usually travel, food, and lodging. The average cost of an industrial sales call has been estimated at nearly $300.[16]

telemarketing
The use of the telephone to carry out many marketing activities, including sales and research.

Such high costs have prompted many companies to turn to **telemarketing**: using telephone solicitations to carry out the personal selling process. Telemarketing can be used to handle any stage of the personal selling process or to set up appointments for outside salespeople. For example, it saves the cost of personal sales visits to industrial customers. Each industrial buyer requires an average of nearly four visits to complete a sale; some companies have thus realized savings in sales visits of $1000 or more. Not surprisingly, such savings are stimulating the growth of telemarketing.

■ SALES PROMOTIONS

sales promotion
Short-term promotional activities designed to stimulate consumer buying or cooperation from distributors and other members of the trade.

Sales promotions are short-term promotional activities designed to stimulate consumer buying or cooperation from distributors, sales agents, or other members of the trade. They are important because they increase the likelihood that buyers will try products. They also enhance product recognition and can increase purchase size and amount. For example, soap is often bound into packages of four with the promotion, "Buy three and get one free."

To be successful, sales promotions must be convenient and accessible when the decision to purchase occurs. If Harley-Davidson has a one-week motorcycle promotion and you have no local dealer, the promotion is neither convenient nor accessible to you, and you will not buy. But if The Bay offers a 20-percent-off coupon that you can save for use later, the promotion is convenient and accessible.

Types of Sales Promotions

The best-known sales promotions are coupons, point-of-purchase displays, purchasing incentives (such as free samples, trading stamps, and premiums), trade shows, and contests and sweepstakes.

Coupons.   Any certificate that entitles the bearer to a stated savings off a product's regular price is a **coupon**. Coupons may be used to encourage customers to try new products, to attract customers away from competitors, or to induce current customers to buy more of a product. They appear in newspapers and magazines and are often sent through direct mail. A **rebate** is a type of coupon that entitles the buyer to a price reduction if the buyer sends the coupon to the company that sold the product. Only 5 to 10 percent of customers ever bother to send in a rebate coupon.[17]

coupon
A sales-promotion method featuring a certificate that entitles the bearer to a stated savings off a product's regular price.

Point-of-Purchase Displays.   To grab customers' attention as they walk through a store, some companies use **point-of-purchase (POP) displays**.[18] Displays located at the end of the aisles or near the checkout in supermarkets are POP displays. POP displays often coincide with a sale on the item(s) being displayed. They make it easier for customers to find a product and easier for manufacturers to eliminate competitors from consideration. The cost of shelf and display space, however, is becoming more and more expensive.[19]

rebate
A type of coupon that entitles the buyer to a price reduction if the buyer sends the coupon to the company that sold the product.

point-of-purchase (POP) display
A sales-promotion method in which a product display is so located in a retail store as to encourage consumers to buy the product.

Purchasing Incentives.   Purchasing incentives such as free samples, trading stamps, and premiums are used by many manufacturers and retailers. Free samples allow customers to try a product for a few days without any risk. They may be given out at local retail outlets or sent by manufacturers to consumers via direct mail.

Although the use of free samples is commonplace in Canada, it is very unusual in some other countries, especially those that are changing over to free-market economies. Procter & Gamble's marketing team was greeted with thanks and even tears when it gave free shampoo samples to grateful shoppers in Warsaw, who were stunned at getting a valued product without having to pay for it or even wait in a long line.[20]

Some retail outlets offer trading stamps as a bonus for patronizing a particular store. Finally, **premiums** are gifts, such as pens, pencils, calendars, and coffee mugs, that are given away to consumers in return for buying a specified product. Retailers and wholesalers also receive premiums for carrying some products.

premium
A sales-promotion method in which some item is offered free or at a bargain price to customers in return for buying a specified product.

Trade Shows.   Periodically, industries sponsor **trade shows** for their members and customers. Trade shows allow companies to rent booths to display and demonstrate their products to customers who have a special interest in the products or who are ready to buy. Trade shows are relatively inexpensive and are very effective, since the buyer comes to the seller already interested in a given type of product. International trade shows are becoming more important.

trade shows
A sales-promotion method in which members of a particular industry gather for displays and product demonstrations designed to sell products to customers.

Contests and Sweepstakes.   Customers, distributors, and sales representatives may all be persuaded to increase sales of a product through the use of contests. Distributors and sales agents may win a trip to Hawaii for selling the most pillows in the month of March. Although sweepstakes cannot legally require consumers to buy a product to enter, they may increase sales by stimulating buyers' interest in a product.

■ PUBLICITY AND PUBLIC RELATIONS

Much to the delight of marketing managers with tight budgets, *publicity* is free. Moreover, because it is presented in a news format, consumers see publicity as objective and highly believable. However, marketers often have little control over publicity.

For example, in 1995 Silken Laumann and her rowing teammates were stripped of their gold medals at an international competition because Laumann had inadvertently used a little-known product called Benadryl that contained a banned substance. The maker of Benadryl, Warner Wellcome, suddenly saw its product mentioned prominently on national newscasts, and it didn't have to pay a cent for the advertising. However, the company is not sure that it wants its product to be associated with an unfortunate incident.

The Miss Canada International organization also received negative publicity when the 1996 beauty contest winner was stripped of her title after being involved in a fight with a woman in a Newfoundland bar. Then, the first runner-up was denied the title because the pageant's organizer claimed she was not performing her duties. The first runner-up disputed these claims and accused the pageant's organizer of lying about her. All of this negative publicity was widely reported in newspapers across Canada.[21]

On a more positive note, the hottest-selling toy in 1996 was Tickle Me Elmo, a doll that says, "That Tickles" when you press on its chest. The craze started partly because a publicist at Freeman Public Relations sent one of the dolls to the son of TV personality Rosie O'Donnell. Two hundred Elmos were also sent to the show's producers. One day on her show, O'Donnell said she would toss an Elmo into the audience each time one of her guests used the word "wall." After that publicity, retail sales of the doll skyrocketed, and Tyco sold more than twice as many Elmos as they had predicted.[22]

In contrast, *public relations* is company-influenced publicity. It attempts to establish a sense of goodwill between the company and its customers through public-service announcements that enhance the company's image. For example, a bank may announce that senior citizens' groups can have free use of a meeting room for their social activities.

United Way of Canada
www.uwc-cc.ca

Most large firms have a department to manage their relations with the public and to present desired company images. As well, company executives may make appearances as guest speakers representing their companies at professional meetings and civic events. They also may serve as leaders in civic activities like the United Way campaign and university fund-raising. Through PR offices, many companies produce audiovisual materials about company activities and make them available to interested groups, other companies, or the general public.

Companies can also take steps to exercise some control over publicity by press releases and press conferences. A *press release* is a written announcement sent to news agencies describing a new product, an event, or information about the company that may be of interest to the general public. In a *press conference*, a firm's representative meets face-to-face with the press to communicate information that the media may then publish or broadcast publicly.

■ INTERNATIONAL PROMOTIONAL STRATEGIES

As we saw in Chapter 4, recent decades have witnessed a profound shift from "home-country" marketing to "multi-country" and now to "global" marketing. Nowhere is this rapidly growing global orientation more evident than in marketing promotions, especially advertising.

Growth of Worldwide Advertising

In the mid-20th century, companies began exporting to other countries when domestic sales stagnated. Advertising played a key role in these efforts because it was the best tool for creating product awareness in each country—that is, for stimulating sales by explaining a product's benefits to new consumers.

Today, worldwide advertising is a large part of many companies' promotional expenditures. Collectively, the 50 top advertisers spend more than $15 billion annually for worldwide advertising. For example, taking advantage of advertising's broad cross-cultural reach, the Anglo-Dutch firm Unilever advertises soap and health-care products in more than 25 countries in the Middle East, South America, Europe, North America, Asia, Central America, and South Africa. Included in the top-50 list of global ad spenders are 29 Japanese companies and 10 from the United States, along with several European firms.

Emergence of the Global Perspective

Every company that markets its products in several countries faces a basic choice: use a *decentralized approach* with separate marketing management for each country or adopt a *global perspective* with a coordinated marketing program directed at one worldwide audience. The **global perspective**, therefore, is actually a company philosophy that directs marketing towards a worldwide rather than a local or regional market.

global perspective
Company's approach to directing its marketing towards worldwide rather than local or regional markets.

The truly global perspective means designing products for multinational appeal—that is, genuinely *global products*. Brands like Coca-Cola, McDonald's, Revlon, Rolex, and Xerox, which are approaching global recognition in a huge variety of countries and cultures, are thus becoming truly *global brands*. Not surprisingly, then, globalization is affecting many firms' promotional activities. In effect, they have already posed the question "Is it possible to develop global advertising?" Certainly one universal advertising program would be more efficient and cost-effective than developing different programs for each of many countries. For several reasons, however, global advertising is not feasible for most companies. There are four factors that make global advertising a difficult proposition: *language differences*, *product variations*, *cultural receptiveness*, and *image differences*.

Language Differences. Perhaps the most obvious barrier to the global ad is language. Compared with those in other languages, for example, ads in English require less print space and air time because English is an efficient language with greater precision of meaning than most. More importantly, translations from one language to another are often inexact and lead to confusion and misunderstanding.

Product Variations. Even if a basic product has universal appeal, at least modest *product variations*—slightly different products—are usually preferred in different cultures. In order to communicate product variations and their features (and of course their advantages), advertising must reflect these differences. For example, MasterCard International has created a worldwide TV ad with video "windows" placed at three strategic points at which regional marketers can insert footage appealing to local tastes in credit card agreements.[23]

Cultural Receptiveness. Another variable is cultural receptiveness to alien ideas and products. For example, there is considerable difference across nations regarding the acceptability of mass advertising for "sensitive" products or those that cause social discomfort (for instance, underwear, condoms, feminine-hygiene products), not to mention those for which advertising may be legally restricted (pharmaceuticals, alcohol, cigarettes). Generally speaking, European countries have more liberal advertising environments than countries in North America, Asia, the Middle East, and Latin America. For worldwide advertising, magazines are the most popular medium for sensitive products because clear messages can be demographically targeted.

Image Differences. Each company's overall *image* can vary from nation to nation, regardless of any advertising appeals for universal recognition and acceptance. For example, a recent study comparing well-known global brands in the United States and the United Kingdom found that American Express, IBM, and Nestlé had higher-ranking images in the U.S. than in the U.K. In contrast, Heinz, Coca-Cola, and Ford had higher-ranking images in the U.K.[24]

Firms that are concerned about image and visibility use advertising to present desirable corporate images and to boost public awareness of them. For example, Philips Electronics, the Dutch firm, has embarked on a worldwide campaign to make a more prominent connection between its product brands and its corporate name. Similarly, following two years of market research, Texas Instruments Inc. decided on some image updating. In order to inform consumers of its diversified operations and products and to overcome its traditional image as a semiconductor-chip maker, TI launched a $10 million worldwide advertising campaign in seven languages.[25]

Heinz
www.heinz.com

SUMMARY OF LEARNING OBJECTIVES

1. **Identify a *product* and distinguish between *consumer* and *industrial products*.** *Products* are a firm's reason for being: *Product features*—the tangible qualities that a company builds into its products—offer *benefits* to buyers whose purchases are the main source of the companies' profits. In developing products, firms must decide whether to produce *consumer goods* for direct sale to consumers or *industrial goods* for sale to other firms. Marketers must recognize that buyers will pay less for common, rapidly consumed *convenience goods* than for less frequently purchased *shopping* and *specialty goods*. In industrial markets, *expense items* are generally less expensive and more rapidly consumed than such *capital items* as buildings and equipment.

2. **Trace the stages of the *product life cycle* and explain the *growth-share matrix*.** New products have a life cycle that begins with *introduction* and progresses through stages of *growth*, *maturity*, and *decline*. Profits rise through the early maturity period; sales rise through late maturity period. In the *growth-share matrix*, products are classified according to market share and growth potential. *Question marks* are new products with low market share but high potential. *Stars* have both high market share and high potential, while *dogs* rate low in both categories. *Cash cows* are mature products with high market share but low potential.

3. **Discuss the importance of *branding* and *packaging*.** Each product is given an identity by its brand and by the way it is packaged and labelled. The goal in developing *brands*—symbols to distinguish products and to signal their uniform quality—is to increase the preference consumers have for a product with a particular brand name. *Trade marks* grant exclusive legal rights to a brand name. *Packaging* provides an attractive container and advertises features and benefits.

4. **Identify the objectives of *promotion* and discuss the considerations involved in selecting a *promotional mix*.** The chief objectives of *promotion* are communicating information about products, positioning products, adding value, and controlling sales volume. To meet these objectives, marketers must choose a *push strategy* (marketing aggressively to channel members) or a *pull strategy* (appealing directly to consumers). They must also select the best combination of tools—advertising, personal selling, sales promotion, and/or publicity and public relations—for the *promotional mix*.

5. **Describe the various *advertising media* available to marketing managers.** Marketers may use various *advertising media*, or specific communication devices for transmitting a seller's message to potential buyers. The most common media—*newspapers, television, direct mail, radio, magazines, outdoor advertising*, and *electronic commerce*—differ in their cost and their ability to segment target markets. The combination of tools chosen by a company is called the *media mix*.

6. **Identify the different types of *sales promotions* and explain the uses of *publicity* and *public relations.*** *Sales promotions*—such as *coupons, point-of-purchase (POP) displays, free samples, trading stamps, premiums, trade shows*, and *contests*—increase the chances that customers will recognize or try products. *Publicity*—general mass media information about a company or product—differs from other types of promotions in being free (although often uncontrollable) and is useful in ensuring the broad dissemination of a message. *Public relations* is company-influenced publicity.

7. **Understand the importance of international promotion strategies in an increasingly global market.** A truly global perspective means designing products for multinational appeal. Factors that make global advertising difficult include language differences (inexact translations must be avoided), product variations (different cultures prefer different variations of a product), cultural receptiveness (advertising of some products is considered inappropriate in some cultures), and image differences (an advertisement's effectiveness is influenced by the image of the company that is doing the advertising).

STUDY QUESTIONS AND EXERCISES

Review Questions

1. What are the various classifications of consumer and industrial products? Give an example of a good and a service for each category different from the examples given in the text.

2. Describe the differences between the push and pull promotional strategies. Why would a company choose one rather than the other?

3. Compare the advantages and disadvantages of the different advertising media.

4. What is the advantage of personal selling over the other communication tools?

5. Is publicity more or less readily available to small firms than to large ones? Why?

Analysis Questions

6. How would you expect the naming, packaging, and labelling of convenience, shopping, and specialty goods to differ? Why? Give examples to illustrate your answers.

7. Take a look at some of the television advertising that is being done by small local businesses in your area. What differences can you see between those commercials and the ones done by large national companies?

8. Pick a consumer product and trace the steps in the personal selling process for this item. Do the same for an industrial product.

9. Find some examples of publicity about some local and national businesses. Do you think the publicity had positive or negative consequences for the businesses? Why?

Application Exercises

10. Interview a manager of a local manufacturing firm. Identify the company's products according to where they stand in the product life cycle.

11. Choose a product sold nationally. Identify as many media used in its promotion as you can. Which medium is used most? Why? Do you believe the promotion is successful? Why or why not?

12. Interview the owner of a local small business. Identify the promotional objectives and strategies of the firm as well as the elements in the promotional mix. What (if any) changes would you suggest? Why?

BUILDING YOUR BUSINESS SKILLS

Goal

To encourage students to evaluate advertising from the standpoint of industry professionals.

Situation

Bob Garfield is the advertising critic for *Advertising Age* magazine, which should be available in your college or local library. (An electronic edition can be found on Prodigy.) He discusses various advertising issues and evaluates new ads, awarding ratings that range from one star (*) to four stars (****). Garfield has recently discussed ads for Magnavox (27-inch colour TV infomercial), IBM ("Solutions for a Small Planet"), and Coors (Coors Light Channel).

Method

Step 1: Working individually or in small groups, identify one of the campaigns criticized by Bob Garfield (your instructor may provide them for you, or you may get the information through library research).

Step 2: Evaluate and critique one or more ad campaigns individually or with a group. How would you rate a given ad?

Analysis

Compare your critique with Garfield's. What factors did you take into consideration when you evaluated the campaign? What was the rationale for your rating compared with Garfield's?

Follow-Up Questions

1. In evaluating an ad, what issues appear to be most important to Garfield? How do they compare with the criteria you used in your evaluation?

2. Were you surprised by some of the information contained in Garfield's reviews, such as the size of the budgets for individual advertising campaigns? Why? Did such information prompt you to rethink your opinion about a campaign?

Prentice Hall ◄ **TAKE IT TO THE NET**

Check out our Companion Website

for this chapter's Exploring the Net exercise, featuring the *i*QVC electronic home shopping Website and other intriguing, annotated destinations. You'll also find practice exercises, updated Weblinks from the text, links to newsgroups, updates, and more.

COMPANION WEBSITE

w w w . p r e n t i c e h a l l . c a / e b e r t

BUSINESS CASE 14

Charting the Air Jordan Route

With a 37-percent share of the nearly $7 billion worldwide sneaker market, Nike is the clear winner in the race to dominate the athletic footwear market. Nowhere is Nike's dominance more evident than in the marketing strategy it uses to sell its biggest single product—Air Jordan sneakers. Endorsed by basketball superstar Michael Jordan, 12 different versions of Air Jordans have enjoyed the power of Nike's marketing muscle since 1985. The result, according to John G. Horan, publisher of *Sporting Goods Intelligence*, is that "over time, there's been nothing even remotely close to the Air Jordan. It's that extra zing that Michael Jordan brings to the party."

Not surprisingly, the introduction of a new Air Jordan product has the power to ignite the action at athletic footwear retailers. Fuelling this ignition is Nike's deliberate, carefully crafted marketing strategy: control supply and increase demand while at the same time generating enough excitement among target customers—teenagers—to convince them to pay $115 (U.S.) a pair. Because of this strategy, customers are willing to pay for the Michael Jordan name—and, of course, state-of-the-art sneakers with carbon-fibre spring plates, herringbone traction inserts, air insoles, and 16 stitching-reinforced lace eyelets.

➤

The strategy is implemented by means of hype, which begins when the company issues a release date for a new Air Jordan model. In Step 2, Nike deliberately manufactures too few shoes to meet expected demand. Customers learn of the release date not through advertising, but through a word-of-mouth network that connects them with shoe salespeople. The result of this combination of hype and operations control is a kind of self-perpetuating demand for Air Jordan sneakers. And make no mistake about it—demand issues from the star power of the Michael Jordan name. The Chicago Bulls superstar regularly wears the latest Air Jordan in one or two National Basketball Association play-off games, but Nike's advertising strategy is otherwise decidedly low key.

By stark contrast, there is nothing low key about the scene at stores on opening day for retail sales. Teenage customers arrive hours before the store opens, and many buy the latest Air Jordans even if they own six other Air Jordan models in good condition. Why? Because the sneakers are Jordans and because the shoes give them status among their peers. Because Nike's marketing strategy does not include meeting current demand, the unlucky may have little choice but to wait for the next Air Jordan model and the next bout of hype and purchasing frenzy.

Riding high on the sale of Air Jordan sneakers and propelled by a marketing strategy that limits supply in the face of increasing demand, Nike's relationship with small, independent retailers is often strained. For one thing, these outlets receive their product shipments after national chains. Even so, they realize that they are getting an eminently saleable product, and despite some frustration, many small retailers believe that late inventory shipments cost them relatively little in lost sales of Air Jordans. As one retailer explains, "I know I can sell them—before the [release] date or after." At the same time, however, Nike's practice of maintaining strict control over product allocation makes small retailers nervous, especially when products not related to Jordan are involved. "Nobody," volunteers one store owner, "likes to be told that they can't maximize their business."

In spite of its success, Nike cannot afford to rest on its laurels. Sneaker sales are, in fact, stagnant so Nike has a new game plan. Under a program called "Alpha"—which began late in 1998—Nike markets its most expensive sportswear, sporting goods, and sneakers as a unit. Advertisements feature well-known sports figures like Tiger Woods wearing a Nike watch, Nike sunglasses, a Nike jacket, and Nike sneakers.

■ *Case Questions*

1. Air Jordan sneakers continue in the growth stage of the product life cycle. Is this trend likely to continue after Michael Jordan retires from basketball? (Research the impact on sneaker sales during Jordan's temporary retirement in 1994–95.)

2. The latest Air Jordan model does not have the Nike swoosh symbol emblazoned on its side. How do you think the decision to remove it will affect brand recognition? Why do you think Nike decided to market a sneaker without the company's trade mark symbol?

3. Describe the elements in Nike's promotion of Air Jordan sneakers. Why is advertising such a small part of the promotional mix?

4. Why is Michael Jordan's endorsement so important to product success?

Nike
www.nike.com

15

PRICING AND DISTRIBUTING GOODS AND SERVICES

BIG CHANGES AT CANADA'S MOST FAMOUS RETAILER

Timothy Eaton immigrated to Canada from Ireland in the 19th century and built a retailing empire by promising to refund money if the customer found the goods to be unsatisfactory. In that era, such a guarantee was unheard of. But it worked, and over the next few decades, Eaton's prospered. By the 1950s, Eaton's accounted for more than half of all department store spending in Canada.

Eaton's is a company that is rich in family tradition. Timothy Eaton passed the presidency on to his son John Craig Eaton, who was in turn succeeded by his cousin Robert Young Eaton. John David Eaton (John Craig's son) became president in 1942 and dominated the firm until the 1970s. John Craig Eaton II is the great-grandson of Timothy—a fourth-generation Eaton.

Their emphasis on tradition has, on occasion, led to an inability to change in response to changing markets. In the 1970s, for example, Eaton's refused to get rid of its in-store drug sections in spite of strong evidence that competitors like Shoppers Drug Mart had stolen this market from them. As well, suggestions that some small-town stores should be closed because they were a drain on the company's profitability were ignored.

Massive changes in Canadian retailing during the last decade (including the entry of large U.S. competitors) have caused a sharp decline in Eaton's fortunes. Because Eaton's is a private corporation, it is not required to publish its financial statements and has been famous for being tight-lipped about its financial condition. In response to speculation about the

company's financial state, John Craig Eaton II had said only that it was making money. However by the early 1990s, the first rumours were heard that Eaton's was in trouble. A 1996 article in *Canadian Business* speculated that Eaton's was in a tough race to see if it could cut costs fast enough to stay ahead of plunging sales. From 1992–97, annual sales revenue declined from $2.1 billion to $1.6 billion. The firm lost $80 million in 1995, and $120 million in 1996.

All the speculation ended in February 1997 when Eaton's shocked the industry by announcing that it was seeking bankruptcy protection under the *Companies' Creditors Arrangement Act* (CCAA). This act gives judges a lot of discretion as they seek ways to save the company. Filing for bankruptcy under the CCAA has become a fashionable alternative to the *Bankruptcy and Insolvency Act* (BIA), because the CCAA doesn't contain as many financial requirements. For example, if a company files for bankruptcy under the BIA, any dividends paid out a year or less before the filing can be taken back if the company was insolvent at the time (Eaton's paid out $10 million in dividends late in 1996).

The changes that are sweeping through retailing in the 1990s are going to make it difficult for Eaton's to prosper. Competition is coming from the so-called big-box stores like Price-Costco, from the so-called category killers like Toys Я Us, from television shopping, and from stores like Wal-Mart, Kmart, and Zellers. Each of these competitors is going to pose a significant problem for Eaton's.

It is unclear how committed the Eaton family is to maintaining its presence in retailing. At one time, the company controlled real estate worth about $1 billion, but it sold much of that in 1995. It also launched a takeover bid for Baton Broadcasting in January 1996. But the firm has maintained that it will continue to be a presence in retailing. Its commitment to retailing can be seen in its expenditures on store facelifts, upgrades in technology, and improved logistics.

In 1992, the Eaton's warehouse outside Toronto was operating with outdated equipment and procedures. As a result, deliveries to Eaton's retailers across Canada were often held up. Distribution managers were bluntly told that they weren't meeting the needs of customers and that things had to change. In just a few years, major changes were introduced. The warehouse is now a modern distribution facility. Arriving goods are taken off trucks and moved through the warehouse on an automated conveyor system. Bar-code readers scan labels and automatically send products down conveyers to trucks that take them to the appropriate Eaton's store. Now, a customer who orders a mattress will have it within 48 hours. In 1992, items were kept in a warehouse for an average of eight days.

Eaton's also changed the way it deals with suppliers, who must now comply with packaging, labelling, and shipment accuracy rules. For example, the company now deals with only four suppliers of brand-name ladies wear, whereas it formerly dealt with 20. Each of the four suppliers is rewarded with bigger sales volume.

But is all this change enough to ensure Eaton's place in retailing? A 1997 study by CIBC Wood Gundy estimates that Sears now controls 42.4 percent of the department store market, The Bay 33.3 percent, and Eaton's 24.4 percent. Eaton's lost four percentage points of market share between 1996 and 1998.

The Eaton family is looking at possible new frontiers. One of the most interesting is in broadcasting. The company already has a long history in this field as the majority owner of Baton Broadcasting. With money from the sale of its real estate holdings, Eaton's can buy up additional television stations. Perhaps retailers like Eaton's will one day sell merchandise through "virtual stores" that consumers will browse through via cable-TV channels.

In September 1997, Eaton's creditors approved a $419 million restructuring plan that may allow the company to return to profitability by 1999. Eaton's decided to go public in 1998, and sold 11.7 million shares of its stock to the public. Proceeds from the sale will be used to finance store renovations.

In this chapter, we complete our look at the marketing function by examining the role of pricing and distribution. The opening case describes how one Canadian retailer is trying to meet the challenges of competition and changes in consumer tastes.

The first part of the chapter examines the pricing objectives of business firms, as well as the various methods they use to decide what to charge for the goods and services they produce. The second part of the chapter describes how producers get their goods and services into consumers' hands. Should the company sell directly to consumers? Or should some type of intermediary like a retailer be used? How will the merchandise be moved from the factory to the consumer?

By focusing on the learning objectives of this chapter, you will consider questions like these and better understand the importance of distribution in the marketing process. After reading this chapter, you should be able to:

1. Identify the various *pricing objectives* that govern pricing decisions and describe the tools used in making these decisions.

2. Discuss *pricing strategies* and tactics for existing and new products.

3. Identify the different *channels of distribution* and explain different *distribution strategies*.

4. Explain the differences between *merchant wholesalers* and *agents/brokers*.

5. Identify the different types of *retail stores*.

6. Describe the major activities in the *physical distribution process*.

7. Compare the five basic forms of *transportation* and identify the types of firms that provide them.

■ PRICING OBJECTIVES AND TOOLS

pricing
Deciding what the company will receive in exchange for its product.

In **pricing**, managers decide what the company will receive in exchange for its products. In this section, we first discuss the objectives that influence a firm's pricing decisions. Then we describe the major tools that companies use to meet those objectives.

Pricing to Meet Business Objectives

Companies often price products to maximize profits. But other objectives can also be involved. Some firms, for example, are more interested in dominating the market or securing high market share than in maximizing profits. Pricing decisions are also influenced by the need to survive in competitive marketplaces, by social and ethical concerns, and even by corporate image.

Profit-Maximizing Objectives.   Pricing to maximize profits is tricky. If prices are set too low, the company will probably sell many units of its product. But it may miss the opportunity to make additional profit on each unit—and may indeed lose money on each exchange. Conversely, if prices are set too high, the company will make a large profit on each item but will sell fewer units. Again, the firm loses money. In addition, it may be left with excess inventory and may have to reduce or even close production operations. To avoid these problems, companies try to set prices to sell the number of units that will generate the highest possible total profits.

In calculating profits, managers weigh receipts against costs for materials and labour to create the product. But they also consider the capital resources (plant and equipment) that the company must tie up to generate that level of profit. The costs of marketing (such as maintaining a large sales staff) can also be substantial. Concern over the efficient use of these resources has led many firms to set prices so as to achieve a targeted level of return on sales or capital investment.[1]

Market-Share Objectives.   In the long run, of course, a business must make a profit to survive. Nevertheless, many companies initially set low prices for new products. They are willing to accept minimal profits—even losses—to get buyers to try products. In other words, they use pricing to establish **market share**: a company's percentage of the total market sales for a specific product. Even with established products, market share may outweigh profits as a pricing objective. For a product like Philadelphia Brand Cream Cheese, dominating a market means that consumers are more likely to buy it because they are familiar with a well-known, highly visible product.

market share
A company's percentage of the total market sales for a specific product.

Other Pricing Objectives.   Profit-maximizing and market-share objectives may not be appropriate in some instances. During difficult economic times, many firms go out of business. Loss containment and survival replace profit maximization when a company in distress attempts to right itself. In the mid-1980s, John Deere priced its agricultural equipment for survival in a depressed farm economy. (ex: new medicine introduced)

Social and ethical concerns may also affect pricing for some types of products. In 1987, drugmaker Burroughs Wellcome received approval to begin selling AZT, the first drug shown to help in combating AIDS. A storm of protest erupted when Burroughs announced that a year's supply of AZT would cost $10 000. After months of relentless pressure, Burroughs reduced the price to about $3000.[2]

Pricing decisions may also reflect a company's image. Retailers such as Braemar and Holt-Renfrew will not sell a $10 shirt or $20 dress, and Kmart will not carry $500 men's suits, regardless of quality.

Price-Setting Tools

Whatever the company's pricing objective, managers must measure the business impact before they can set prices. Three basic tools are used for this purpose: economic demand-supply comparisons, cost-oriented pricing, and break-even analysis. Rarely is one of these tools sufficient. Most often, they are used together to identify prices that allow the company to reach its objectives.

Economic Demand-Supply Comparisons.   Economic theory helps firms maximize profits. This approach looks at the total market for a product, identifying the amount that consumers will demand and producers will supply at various prices.

Figure 15.1 compares demand for and supply of movie tickets at various prices. As prices go up, the number of tickets sought goes down, causing the downward-sloping demand curve. But theatre owners would be willing to supply more tickets when prices are higher, as shown in the upward-sloping supply curve.

Considering the two curves together tells us the best (profit-maximizing) price for movie tickets: $5.00. At this price, the number of tickets demanded and the number of tickets supplied are the same. According to economic theory, in the long run, the market price will *always* settle where the demand and supply curves meet.

Cost-Oriented Pricing.   The major weakness of the demand-and-supply approach to pricing is that it focuses entirely on identifying a market price for a product. It does not consider whether companies can make money at this price. As well, it treats the products of all suppliers as identical, which is not always true. In contrast, cost-oriented pricing takes into account the firm's need to cover its costs of producing the product. The box "How Much Should a Movie Ticket Cost?" presents an interesting case where costs are not considered in pricing.

A music store manager would begin using the cost-oriented approach to pricing records by calculating the cost of making compact discs (CDs) available to shoppers. Included in this figure would be store rent, sales clerks' wages, utilities, CD displays,

(a) Demand-and-Supply Schedules for Movie Tickets

Price (dollars)	Tickets Demanded (units of tickets)	Tickets Supplied (units of tickets)
$1.00	108	10
3.00	80	32
5.00	60	60
7.00	35	87
9.00	10	110

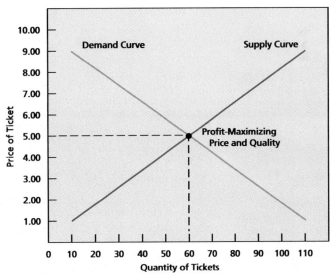

FIGURE 15.1

Demand-and-supply schedules for movie tickets (a) and demand-and-supply curves for movie tickets (b).

TRENDS & CHALLENGES

How Much Should a Movie Ticket Cost?

Think about this: When you go to a first-run movie theatre, you pay the same price for each film you see. But it may cost as little as $2 million or as much as $200 million to make a film. Shouldn't the admission price be based on how much the film cost to make? After all, you pay a lot more for a Lincoln Continental than you do for a Ford because the Lincoln costs more to make. Shouldn't the same pricing system apply to Hollywood?

Edgar Bronfman, CEO of Seagram Co. Ltd. (which owns Universal Studios), thinks so. At an entertainment industry conference in 1998, Bronfman argued that the movie industry's current pricing model makes no sense. He made the case for a new approach to pricing, and openly said that movie studios must look at ways to increase revenues in order to cope with the skyrocketing cost of movie production. In 1997, the average price for producing a Hollywood movie was a record $53.4 million; distribution costs added another $22.2 million to the final studio outlay.

It is interesting that Bronfman's pricing idea met with a very cool reception from movie industry people. Tom Sherak, chairman of Twentieth Century Fox, said Bronfman's ideas will not work in the movie business. Sherak also feared that Bronfman's idea would cause filmmakers to demand that their films be priced higher at the box office so they could make more expensive films like *Titanic*.

---

markup
The amount added to the cost of an item to earn a profit for the retailer or wholesaler.

insurance, and the cost of the CDs. Assume that the cost of a CD comes to $9.00. If the store sold the CD for this price, it would not make any profit. The manager must add in an amount for profit called **markup**. A markup of $6.00 over cost in this case would result in a selling price of $15.00.

Profit is usually evaluated based on a percentage of the selling price. The manager calculates the markup percentage as follows:

$$\text{Markup percentage} = \frac{\text{Markup}}{\text{Sales price}}$$

$$\text{Markup percentage} = \frac{\$6.00}{\$15.00} = 40.0\%$$

variable costs
Those costs that change with the number of goods or services produced or sold.

That is, out of every dollar taken in, 40 cents will be gross profit for the store. However, out of this profit still must come store rent, utilities, insurance, and all those other costs.

Another way to express the markup is as a percentage of cost instead of a percentage of sales price. The $6.00 markup is 66.7 percent of the $9.00 cost of a CD ($6.00 ÷ $9.00). Some retailers prefer to express the markup using this cost-based method. Others, however, prefer the sales-price approach.

fixed costs
Those costs unaffected by the number of goods or services produced or sold.

break-even analysis
An assessment of how many units must be sold at a given price before the company begins to make a profit.

Break-Even Analysis: Cost-Volume-Profit Relationships. A company that uses cost-oriented pricing can count on covering its **variable costs** (materials and labour primarily) for each item sold. It will also make some money towards **fixed costs** such as equipment, rent, management salaries, and insurance. But without a **break-even analysis**, the company does not know how many units it must sell before all its fixed costs are covered and it truly begins to make a profit.

break-even point
The number of units that must be sold at a given price before the company covers all its variable and fixed costs.

Continuing with the music store example, suppose the variable costs for each CD (basically, the cost of buying the CD from the producer) are $8.00. Fixed costs for keeping the store open for one year are $100 000. The **break-even point**, the number of

CDs that must be sold to cover both fixed and variable costs and thus for the store to start to make some profit, will be 14 286 CDs, calculated as follows:

$$\text{Break-even point (in units)} = \frac{\text{Total fixed costs}}{\text{Price} - \text{variable cost}}$$

$$= \frac{\$100\ 000}{\$15.00 - \$8.00}$$

$$= 14\ 286\ \text{CDs}$$

Figure 15.2 shows the break-even point graphically. Note that if sales are below 14 286 CDs, the store loses money for the year. If sales exceed 14 286 CDs, profits grow by $7.00 for each CD sold.

In reality, managers calculate break-even points for each of several possible price levels. As the price per CD increases, the number of units that must be sold before the break-even point is reached decreases. As prices fall, the number of units that must be sold before the break-even point is reached increases. Table 15.1 shows this relationship for a variety of prices. Prices below $8.00 are not considered because, if the price does not exceed the item's variable cost, the break-even point will never occur.

The music store owner would certainly like to hit the break-even quantity as early as possible so that profits will start rolling in. Why not charge $20.00 per CD, then, and reach break-even earlier? The answer lies in the downward-sloping demand curve we discussed earlier. At a price of $20.00 per CD, sales at the store would drop. In setting a price, the manager must consider how much CD buyers will pay and what the store's local competitors charge.

■ PRICING STRATEGIES AND TACTICS

The pricing tools discussed in the previous section provide a valuable guide for managers trying to set prices on specific goods. But they do not provide general direction for managers trying to set a pricing philosophy for their company. In this section, we discuss *pricing strategy*—that is, pricing as a planning activity that affects the marketing mix. We then describe some basic *pricing tactics*—ways in which managers implement a firm's pricing strategies.

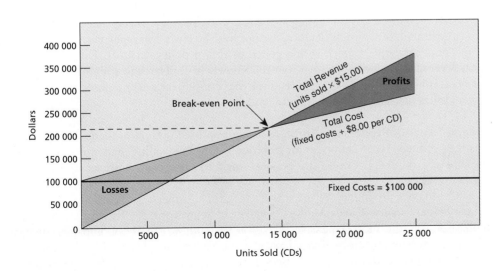

FIGURE 15.2
Break-even analysis: 14 286 CDs is the break-even point.

■ **TABLE 15.1 Comparison of Break-Even Quantities for Various Price Levels**

Price ($)	Number of CDs for Break-Even Quantity	Total Cost and Revenue at Break-Even Quantity
$ 8.00	*	*
$10.00	50 000	$500 000
$12.00	25 000	$300 000
$14.00	16 667	$233 340
$15.00	14 286	$214 290
$16.00	12 500	$200 000
$18.00	10 000	$180 000
$20.00	8 333	$166 660

*Does not exist at this price.

Pricing Strategies

Let's begin this section by asking two questions. First: Can a manager really identify a single "best" price for a product? The answer is: probably not. For example, a study of prices for popular nonaspirin pain relievers (such as Tylenol and Advil) found variations of 100 percent.[3] In this market, in other words, some products sold for twice the price of other products with similar properties. Granted, such differences may reflect some differences in product costs. The issue, however, is a little more complex. Such wide price differences reflect differing brand images that attract different types of customers. In turn, these images reflect vastly different pricing philosophies and strategies.

Our second question is this: Just how important is pricing as an element in the marketing mix? As we have already seen, it is a mistake to try to isolate any element in the marketing mix from the others. Nevertheless, because pricing has a direct and visible impact on revenues, it is extremely important to overall marketing plans. Moreover, it is a very flexible tool. It is certainly easier to change prices than to change products or distribution channels. In this section, we will focus on the ways in which pricing strategies for both new and existing products can result in widely differing prices for very similar products.

Whatever price strategy a company is using, it must be clearly communicated to buyers. Wal-Mart clearly communicates a low price strategy to consumers, but Eaton's strategy, with all its recent difficulties, has not been so clear. For many years, Eaton's had a high-price strategy, coupled with a generous return policy. In 1991, Eaton's switched to an "everyday low price" strategy, but then slowly drifted back to a high-price strategy with occasional sales. Industry experts think that consumers were confused by this strategy, and that this added to Eaton's problems.[4]

Pricing Existing Products. A firm basically has three options available in pricing its existing products. It can set prices for its product above prevailing market prices charged for similar products. It can set prices below market. Or it can set prices at or near the market price.

Companies pricing above the market play on customers' beliefs that higher price means higher quality. Curtis Mathes, a maker of televisions, VCRs, and stereos, promotes itself as the most expensive television set "but worth it." Companies such as Godiva chocolates and Rolls-Royce have also succeeded with this pricing philosophy.

In contrast, both Budget and Discount car rental companies promote themselves as low-priced alternatives to Hertz and Avis. Ads for Suave hair-care products argue that "Suave does what theirs does—for a lot less." Pricing below the prevailing market price can succeed if the firm can offer a product of acceptable quality while keeping costs below those of higher-priced options.

Budget Rent a Car
www.budgetrentacar.com

A company can use different strategies for different customers. Airlines, for example, use a technique called *yield management* to predict precisely how many last-minute business travellers will want to get on a flight and be willing to pay a very high price. As a result, prices for leisure travel (which must be booked weeks in advance) are much lower than prices for business travel.[5] The price of a last-minute ticket from Chicago to Phoenix, for example, is $1404 while a "cheap seat" booked in advance costs only $238. This type of pricing system has allowed airlines to boost their profits significantly.

Finally, in some industries, a dominant firm establishes product prices and other companies follow along. This is called **price leadership**. (Don't confuse this approach with *price fixing*, the illegal process of producers agreeing among themselves what prices will be charged.) Price leadership is often evident in products such as structural steel, gasoline, and many processed foods. These products differ little in quality from one firm to another. Companies compete through advertising campaigns, personal selling, and service, not price.

price leadership
The dominant firm in the industry establishes product prices and other companies follow suit.

Pricing New Products: Skimming and Penetration Pricing.   Companies introducing new products into the market have to consider two contrasting pricing policy options: coming in with either a very high price or a very low one. The former is known as a **price-skimming strategy** and the latter is a **penetration-pricing strategy**.

Skimming may allow a firm to earn a large profit on each item sold. This cash is often needed to cover product development and introduction costs. But skimming is possible only as long as the company can convince consumers that the product is truly different from existing products on the market. Eventually, the initial high profits will attract competition. Microwave ovens, calculators, and VCRs were introduced at comparatively high prices and prices fell as new companies entered the market.

On the other hand, the low initial prices of a penetration-pricing strategy seek to generate consumer interest and stimulate trial purchases of the new product. New food products—convenience foods, cookies, and snacks—are often promoted at special low prices that stimulate brisk early sales of the product. Penetration pricing provides for minimal, if any, profit. This strategy can only succeed if the company can raise its price as consumer acceptance grows. Such price increases must be managed carefully to avoid alienating future customers.

price-skimming strategy
The decision to price a new product as high as possible to earn the maximum profit on each unit sold.

penetration-pricing strategy
The decision to price a new product very low to sell the most units possible and to build customer loyalty.

Pricing Tactics

No matter what philosophy a company uses to price existing or new products, its managers may adopt one or more pricing *tactics* such as price lining or psychological pricing. Managers must also decide on what, if any, discounting tactics to use.

Sears Canada
www.sears.ca

Price Lining.   Companies selling multiple items in a product category use price lining. For example, a department store carries literally thousands of products. To set a separate price for each brand and style of suit, plate, or couch would take many hours. By using **price lining**, the store can predetermine three or four price points at which a particular product will be sold. For men's suits, the price points might be $175, $250, and $400. All men's suits in the store will be priced at one of these three points. Buyers for the store must choose suits that can be purchased and sold profitably for one of these three prices.

Price lining requires managers to set each price level with a specific type of customer in mind and to display and sell the products accordingly. For example, Sears offers three lines of power tools, batteries, and appliances. "Sears Good" is for novice or occasional users. "Sears Better" is for avid users. And "Sears Best" is for professional users.

price lining
The practice of offering all items in certain categories at a limited number of predetermined price points.

psychological pricing
The practice of setting prices to take advantage of the non-logical reactions of consumers to certain types of prices.

Psychological Pricing.   Another pricing tactic, **psychological pricing**, takes advantage of the fact that customers are not completely rational when making buying decisions.[6] **Odd-even psychological pricing** proposes that customers prefer prices that are not stated in even dollar amounts. That is, customers see prices of $1000, $100, $50, and $10 as

odd-even psychological pricing
A form of psychological pricing in which prices are not stated in even dollar amounts.

These teens are as concerned with the price tag as with the style of the clothing they might buy on this shopping trip.

threshold pricing
A form of psychological pricing in which prices are set at what appears to be the maximum price consumers will pay for an item.

discount
Any price reduction offered by the seller in order to persuade customers to purchase a product.

cash discount
A form of discount in which customers paying cash, rather than buying on credit, pay lower prices.

seasonal discount
A form of discount in which lower prices are offered to customers making a purchase at a time of year when sales are traditionally slow.

trade discount
Discount given to firms involved in a product's distribution.

quantity discount
A form of discount in which customers buying large amounts of a product pay lower prices.

distribution mix
The combination of distribution channels a firm selects to get a product to end-users.

much higher than prices of $999.95, $99.95, $49.95, and $9.95, respectively. One common explanation for this widely recognized process is that the consumer looks at the whole dollar figure, ignores the cents, and rounds down.

Closely related to odd-even pricing, **threshold pricing** argues that consumers set maximum prices they will pay for a particular item. Many gift shops, for example, will carry a supply of gifts in the $20-or-under price range. The feeling is that gift-givers often place an upper limit of $20 on gifts they buy.

Discounting.   The price that is eventually set for a product is not always the price at which all items are sold. Many times a company has to offer a price reduction—a **discount**—to stimulate sales. Cash, seasonal, trade, and quantity discounts are the most common forms.

In recent years, **cash discounts** have become popular, even at retail stores. Stores may offer **seasonal discounts** to stimulate the sales of products during times of the year when most customers do not normally buy the product. Travellers can find low prices on summer trips to tropical islands and July shoppers can get sale prices on winter coats thanks to seasonal discounts. **Trade discounts** are available only to those companies or individuals involved in a product's distribution. Thus, wholesalers, retailers, and interior designers pay less for fabric than the typical consumer does. Related to trade discounts are **quantity discounts**—lower prices for purchases in large quantities. Case price discounts for motor oil or soft drinks at retail stores are examples of quantity discounts.

■ THE DISTRIBUTION MIX

We have already seen that a company needs an appropriate product mix. But the success of any product also depends in part on its **distribution mix**: the combination of distribution channels that a firm selects to get a product to end-users. In this section, we will consider some of the many factors that enter into the distribution mix. First, we will explain the need for *intermediaries*. We will then discuss the basic *distribution strategies*. Finally, we will consider some special issues in channel relationships—namely, conflict and leadership.

Intermediaries and Distribution Channels

Once called *middlemen*, **intermediaries** are the individuals and firms who help to distribute a producer's goods. They are generally classified as *wholesalers* or *retailers*. **Wholesalers** sell products to other businesses, who resell them to final consumers. **Retailers** sell products directly to consumers. While some firms rely on independent intermediaries, others employ their own distribution networks and sales forces. The decision normally hinges on three factors:

- the company's target markets
- the nature of its products
- the costs of maintaining distribution and sales networks

We examine these factors more closely below by describing some of the distribution decisions that go into the marketing of consumer products.

Distribution of Consumer Products

Figure 15.3 shows six primary **distribution channels** aimed at different target audiences and product types. Note that *all* channels *must* begin with a manufacturer and end with a consumer or an industrial user. Channels 1 through 4 are most often used for the distribution of consumer goods and services.

Channel 1. In this **direct channel**, the product travels from the producer to the consumer with no intermediaries. Companies such as Avon, Fuller Brush, Tupperware, and many encyclopedia distributors use this channel. Direct channel distribution is also popular with craftspeople who sell their wares through word-of-mouth reference or from booths at local flea markets or craft shows. Roadside vegetable stands also use the direct channel.

Channel 2. In this channel, manufacturers distribute their products through retailers. Goodyear Tire and Rubber has set up its own system of retail outlets. The perfume and fragrance industry uses its own sales force to sell many of its products to retailers who, in turn, sell them across the counter to consumers.

intermediary
Any individual or firm other than the producer who participates in a product's distribution.

wholesalers
Intermediaries who sell products to other businesses, who in turn resell them to the end-users.

retailers
Intermediaries who sell products to the end-users.

distribution channel
The path that a product follows from the producer to the end-user.

direct channel
A distribution channel in which the product travels from the producer to the consumer without passing through any intermediary.

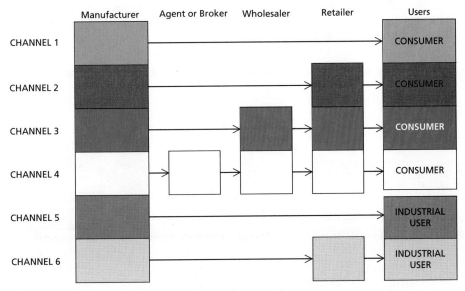

FIGURE 15.3
Channels of distribution: How the product travels from manufacturer to consumer.

Channel 3.   Until the mid-1960s, Channel 2 was a widely used method of retail distribution. But that channel requires a large amount of floor space both for storing merchandise and for displaying it in retail stores. As the cost of retail space rose, retailers found that they could not afford to buy space to store goods. Thus wholesalers have increasingly entered the distribution network. They have taken over more and more of the storage service. A good example of this philosophy in practice is convenience food/gas stores. Approximately 90 percent of the space in these stores is devoted to merchandise displays. Only about 10 percent is used for storage and office facilities.

Wholesalers have always played a role in distributing some products. Many manufacturers only distribute their products in large quantities. Small businesses that cannot afford to purchase large quantities of goods rely on wholesalers to hold inventories of such products and to supply them on short notice. For example, a family-owned grocery store that sells only 12 cases of canned spinach in a year cannot afford to buy a truckload (perhaps 500 cases) in a single order. Instead, it orders one case a month from a local wholesaler, which buys large lots of spinach and other goods from the makers, stores them, and resells them in small quantities to various retailers.

sales agent/broker
An independent businessperson who represents a business and receives a commission in return, but never takes legal possession of the product.

Ernst & Young
http://tax.EY.CA/ey

Channel 4.   This complex channel uses **sales agents**, or **brokers**, who represent manufacturers and sell to wholesalers, retailers, or both. They receive commissions based on the price of goods they sell. Agents generally deal in the related product lines of a few producers, serving as their sales representatives on a relatively permanent basis. Travel agents, for example, represent the airlines, car-rental companies, and hotels. In contrast, brokers are hired to assist in buying and selling temporarily, matching sellers and buyers as needed. This channel is often used in the food and clothing industries. The real estate industry and the stock market also rely on brokers for matching buyers and sellers.

Indirect distribution channels do mean higher prices to the end consumer. The more members involved in the channel, the higher the final price to the purchaser. After all, each link in the distribution chain must charge a markup or commission to make a profit. Figure 15.4 shows typical markup growth through the distribution channel.

Ernst & Young conducted a study of the competitiveness of distribution channels which showed that Canada often has an extra layer of wholesale distribution compared to American distribution channels and higher markups at the retail level. But the Canadian retail sector is becoming more like the U.S., with larger stores, more items, and fewer intermediaries.[7]

Intermediaries add to the visible dollar cost of a product but, in many ways, they save the consumer time and thus money. A manufacturer would not sell you one calculator for the same price it charges wholesalers who buy truckloads of them. In other ways, intermediaries actually save you money.

Consider Figure 15.5, which illustrates the problem of making chili without an intermediary—the supermarket. You would probably spend a lot more time (and a lot of

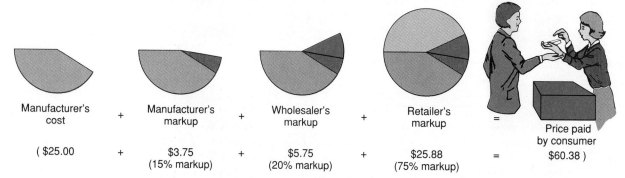

Manufacturer's cost	+	Manufacturer's markup	+	Wholesaler's markup	+	Retailer's markup	=	Price paid by consumer
($25.00	+	$3.75 (15% markup)	+	$5.75 (20% markup)	+	$25.88 (75% markup)	=	$60.38)

FIGURE 15.4

Where your dollar goes in the distribution channel for an electronic calculator.

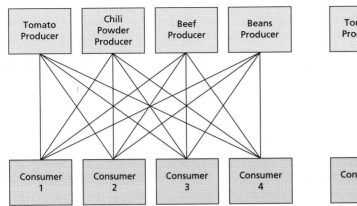

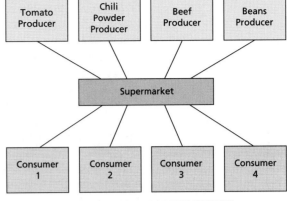

PURCHASE OF GOODS WITHOUT INTERMEDIARIES   PURCHASE OF GOODS WITH INTERMEDIARIES

FIGURE 15.5
Advantages of intermediaries.

money on gas) if you had to get all the necessary ingredients on your own. In fact, intermediaries can add form, place, and time utility by making the right quantities available where and when you need them.

Distribution of Industrial Products

Industrial channels are important because each company is itself a customer that buys other companies' products. The Kellogg Co. buys grain to make breakfast cereals, Stone Container Corp. buys rolls of paper and vats of glue to make corrugated boxes, and Victoria Hospital buys medicines and other supplies to provide medical services. Industrial distribution, therefore, refers to the network of channel members involved in the flow of manufactured goods to industrial customers. Unlike consumer products, industrial products are traditionally distributed through Channels 5 or 6 (refer back to Figure 15.3).

Channel 5. Most industrial goods are sold directly by the manufacturer to the industrial buyer. As contact points with their customers, manufacturers maintain **sales offices**. These offices provide all services for the company's customers and serve as headquarters for its salespeople.

sales offices
Offices maintained by sellers of industrial goods to provide points of contact with their customers.

Steel, transistors, and conveyors are all distributed through Channel 5. Because such goods are usually purchased in large quantities, intermediaries are often unnecessary. In some cases, however, brokers or agents may enter the distribution chain between manufacturer and buyer.

Channel 6. Wholesalers function as intermediaries between manufacturers and users in only a very small percentage of industrial channels. Brokers and agents are even rarer. Channel 6 is most often used for accessory equipment (computer terminals, office equipment) and supplies (floppy disks, copier paper). While manufacturers produce these items in large quantities, companies buy them in small quantities. Few companies, for example, order truckloads of paper clips. As with consumer goods, then, intermediaries help end-users by representing manufacturers or by breaking down large quantities into smaller sales units.

In some areas, however, relationships are changing. In the office-products industry, for instance, Channel 6 is being displaced by the emergence of a new channel that looks very much like Channel 3 for consumer products: Instead of buying office supplies from wholesalers (Channel 6), many users are shopping at office discount stores such as Office Depot. Warehouselike superstores target small- and medium-sized businesses, which generally buy supplies at retail stores, much as they target retail consumers. In these new "discount stores for industrial users," customers stroll down the aisles behind shopping carts, selecting from 7000 items at prices 20 to 75 percent lower than manufacturers' suggested prices.

Distribution Strategies

Choosing a distribution network is a vital consideration for a company. It can make the firm succeed or fail. The choice of distribution strategy determines the amount of market exposure the product gets and the cost of that exposure.

The appropriate strategy depends on the product class. The goal is to make a product accessible in just enough locations to satisfy customers' needs. Milk can be purchased at many retail outlets (high exposure). But there is only one distributor for Rolls-Royce in a given city.

Different degrees of market exposure are available through intensive distribution, exclusive distribution, and selective distribution. **Intensive distribution** means distributing a product through as many channels and channel members (using both wholesalers and retailers) as possible. For example, as Figure 15.6 shows, Caramilk bars flood the market through all suitable outlets. Intensive distribution is normally used for low-cost, consumer goods such as candy and magazines.

In contrast, **exclusive distribution** occurs when a manufacturer grants the exclusive right to distribute or sell a product to one wholesaler or retailer in a given geographic area. Exclusive distribution agreements are most common in high-cost, prestige products. For example, Jaguar automobiles are sold by only a single dealer servicing a large metropolitan area.

Selective distribution falls between intensive and exclusive distribution. A company that uses this strategy carefully selects only wholesalers and retailers who will give

intensive distribution
A distribution strategy in which a product is distributed in nearly every possible outlet, using many channels and channel members.

exclusive distribution
A distribution strategy in which a product's distribution is limited to only one wholesaler or retailer in a given geographic area.

selective distribution
A distribution strategy that falls between intensive and exclusive distribution, calling for the use of a limited number of outlets for a product.

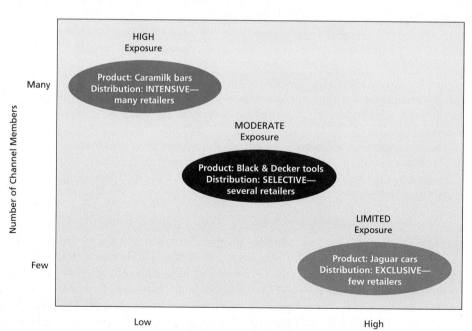

FIGURE 15.6
Amounts of market exposure from three kinds of distribution.

special attention to the product in terms of sales efforts, display position, etc. Selective distribution policies have been applied to virtually every type of consumer product. It is usually embraced by companies like Black & Decker whose product lines do not require intense market exposure to increase sales.

Channel Conflict and Channel Leadership

Manufacturers can choose to distribute through more than one channel or wholesaler. They can also choose to make new uses of existing channels. Similarly, most retailers are free to strike agreements with as many producers as capacity permits. In such cases, *channel conflict* may arise. Conflicts are resolved when members' efforts are better coordinated. A key factor in coordinating the activities of independent organizations is *channel leadership*. Another strategy for improving coordination is known as the *vertical marketing system*.

Channel Conflict.   Channel conflict occurs when members of the channel disagree over the roles they should play or the rewards they should receive. John Deere, for example, would no doubt object if its dealers began distributing Russian and Japanese tractors. Similarly, when a manufacturer-owned factory outlet store discounts the company's apparel or housewares, it runs the risk of alienating the manufacturer's retail accounts. Channel conflict may also arise if one member has more power than the others or is viewed as receiving preferential treatment. Needless to say, such conflicts defeat the purpose of the system by disrupting the flow of goods to their destinations.

Consider the case of IBM, which sells both through wholesalers and retailers and directly to major corporations. When IBM makes a direct sale, its dealers point out that they have lost a chance to earn money by making the sale themselves. If this pattern repeatedly frustrates one particular dealer, that dealer may take action—switching, for example, from IBM to Apple products.[8]

Channel Leadership.   Usually, one channel member is most powerful in determining the roles and rewards of other members. That member is the channel captain. Often, the channel captain is a manufacturer, particularly if the manufacturer's product is in high demand. In some industries, an influential wholesaler or a large retailer like Wal-Mart or Sears may emerge as channel captain because of large sales volumes.

Vertical Marketing Systems.   To overcome problems posed by channel conflict and issues of channel leadership, the **vertical marketing system (VMS)** has emerged. In a VMS, separate businesses join to form a unified distribution channel, with one member coordinating the activities of the whole channel. There are three types of VMS arrangements:

- In a *corporate VMS*, all stages in the channel are under single ownership. The Limited, for example, owns both the production facilities that manufacture its apparel and the retail stores that sell it.
- In a *contractual VMS*, channel members sign contracts agreeing to specific duties and rewards. The Independent Grocers' Alliance (IGA), for example, consists of independent retail grocers joined with a wholesaler who contractually leads—but does not own—the VMS. Most franchises are contractual VMSs.
- In an *administered VMS*, channel members are less formally coordinated than in a corporate or contractual VMS. Instead, one or more of the members emerge as leader(s) and maintain control as a result of power and influence. Although the administered VMS is more fragile than the corporate and contractual forms, it is more unified than channels relying on independent members.

vertical marketing system
A system in which there is a high degree of coordination among all the units in the distribution channel so that a product moves efficiently from manufacturer to consumer.

Independent Grocers' Alliance
www.igainc.com

■ WHOLESALING

Now that you know something about distribution channels, we can consider the broader role played by intermediaries. Wholesalers provide a variety of functions for their customers, who are buying products for resale or for business use. In addition to storing products and providing an assortment of products for their customers, wholesalers offer delivery, credit, and information about products. Not all wholesalers provide all of these functions. The specific services they offer depend on the type of intermediary involved: merchant wholesalers or agents/brokers.

Merchant Wholesalers

merchant wholesaler
An independent wholesaler who buys and takes legal possession of goods before selling them to customers.

full-service merchant wholesaler
A merchant wholesaler who provides storage and delivery in addition to wholesaling services.

limited-function merchant wholesaler
An independent wholesaler who provides only wholesaling—not warehousing or transportation—services.

drop shipper
A type of wholesaler who does not carry inventory or handle the product.

rack jobber
A full-function merchant wholesaler specializing in non-food merchandise who sets up and maintains display racks of some products in retail stores.

Most wholesalers are independent operators who derive their income from sales of goods produced by a variety of manufacturers. All **merchant wholesalers** take title to merchandise. That is, merchant wholesalers buy and own the goods they resell to other businesses. They usually provide storage and a means of delivery.

A **full-service merchant wholesaler** provides credit, marketing, and merchandising services. Approximately 80 percent of all merchant wholesalers are full-service wholesalers.

Limited-function merchant wholesalers provide only a few services, sometimes merely storage. Their customers are normally small operations that pay cash and pick up their own goods. One such wholesaler, the **drop shipper**, does not even carry inventory or handle the product. Drop shippers receive orders from customers, negotiate with producers to supply goods, take title to them, and arrange for shipment to customers. The drop shipper bears the risks of the transaction until the customer takes title to the goods.

Other limited-function wholesalers, known as **rack jobbers**, market consumer goods—mostly nonfood items—directly to retail stores.[9] Procter & Gamble, for example, uses rack jobbers to distribute products like Pampers diapers. After marking prices, setting up display racks, and displaying diapers in one store, the rack jobber moves on to another outlet to check inventories and shelve products.

Agents and Brokers

Agents and brokers serve as sales forces for various manufacturers. They are independent representatives of many companies' products. They work on commissions, usually about 4 to 5 percent of net sales. Unlike merchant wholesalers, they do not take title to—that is, they do not own—the merchandise they sell. Rather, they serve as the sales and merchandising arms of manufacturers who do not have their own sales forces.

The value of agents and brokers lies primarily in their knowledge of markets and their merchandising expertise. They also provide a wide range of services, including shelf and display merchandising and advertising layout. Finally, they maintain product saleability by removing open, torn, or dirty packages, arranging products neatly, and generally keeping them attractively displayed. Many supermarket products are handled through brokers.

■ RETAILING

You probably have had little contact with merchant wholesalers, merchandise brokers, or manufacturers. If you are like most Canadians, you buy nearly all the goods and services you consume from retailers. Most retailers are small operations, often consisting of just the owners and part-time help. But there are a few very large retailers, and these account for billions of dollars of sales each year.

In the past few years, U.S. retailers have become very aggressive in expanding into Canada and Europe. This has created problems for retailers in those countries, but bargains for consumers (see the box "U.S. Discounters Making Waves in Canada and Europe").

Types of Retail Outlets

The major categories of retail stores are department, speciality, discount (bargain), convenience, supermarkets, warehouse clubs, and hypermarkets. Some retailing is also done without stores.

TRENDS & CHALLENGES

U.S. Discounters Making Waves in Canada and Europe

During the last five years, several U.S. retail giants have invaded the Canadian market. Why has this happened now? Most U.S. executives say that the Canada-U.S. Free Trade Agreement had a lot to do with it. Large U.S. retailers feel that the Canadian retail industry is five to ten years behind the U.S. in terms of purchasing, distribution, and technology. Since Canada is no longer a protected market, these retailers see good profit possibilities in Canada.

Since 1985, Price/Costco has opened 47 stores in Canada. Wal-Mart purchased 122 stores from Woolco and opened them as Wal-Marts in 1994. The Gap expanded from 34 outlets to 64.

But U.S. firms are beginning to experience some difficulties in Canada. Home Depot, which came to Canada in 1994, originally planned to open 50 stores within five years. But in 1995, the firm announced that it was scaling back its expansion plans. Several unexpected problems were encountered, including cumbersome zoning procedures for its proposed stores, a drop in housing starts that will reduce demand for the firm's products, and intense competition from existing firms like Revelstoke Home Centres.

Other U.S. chains are also experiencing problems. Eagle Hardware & Garden Inc. pulled out of western Canada after battling stores like Revelstoke for over a year, and pet food superstore Petstuff Inc. closed four of its Toronto-area stores. Even Wal-Mart lost money on its Canadian operations in its first year.

Not only have some U.S. retail giants not done as well as expected, some Canadian retailers are turning out to be unexpectedly aggressive competitors. Canadian Tire, for example, is doing much better than retail analysts predicted. After hiring a new CEO who had a lot of experience in hardware sales in the U.S., it has fought back and sharply expanded its presence in small and medium-sized markets. It has replaced small stores with larger ones, and it has improved its logistical system. And the head office has become much more interested in what is happening in the retail stores, and in getting Canadian Tire dealers to buy into the company's overall strategy. Between 1992 and 1994, profit jumped 25 percent.

Because high prices are the rule rather than the exception in Europe, U.S. discounters like Price/Costco, Toys Я Us, and Kmart are also starting to compete there. Bargain-hungry Europeans are welcoming these discounters with open arms. For example, at the grand opening of England's first factory outlet mall, 25 000 people showed up (some having travelled great distances) to pay discount prices for apparel by Wrangler, Benetton, and Pierre Cardin.

These changes are very threatening to European retailers, and some have already gone out of business. Some have gone to court in an attempt to defend their turf. The three largest grocery chains in Britain took legal action to keep Price/Costco out (they failed). In both Germany and France, merchants have banded together to oppose changes—like late-night hours—that American discounters bring with them. But these responses simply highlight the vulnerability of retail outlets that are not responsive to consumer needs.

U.S. discounters feel that the European market is a place where they can deliver bargains to consumers and in the process make fat profit margins for themselves.

department stores
Large retail stores that offer a wide variety of high-quality items divided into specialized departments.

Department Stores.   As the name implies, **department stores** are organized into specialized departments—shoes, furniture, appliances, etc. Department stores began in the 1800s and were initially located in downtown districts, although most now have suburban branches. Generally, department stores are quite large and handle a wide range of goods. They usually offer a variety of services as well, such as generous merchandise return policies, credit plans, and delivery. The largest department stores—The Bay and Sears—have combined annual sales over $9 billion.

specialty stores
Small retail stores that carry one line of related products.

Specialty Stores.   In sharp contrast to department stores are **specialty stores**, small stores that carry one line of related products. These stores serve a carefully defined market segment by offering a full product line in a narrow product field, along with knowledgeable sales personnel. For example, most golf courses have a pro shop that carries golf clubs, as well as apparel, shoes, and other accessories for golfing. Other examples of specialty stores are The Fishin' Hole, Radio Shack, and Jiffy Lube.

Particularly in the apparel industry, the 1980s were the decade of the specialty store. Between 1980 and 1990, retailers like The Gap, The Limited, and Ann Taylor spearheaded the growth spurt of a multibillion-dollar industry in stylish upscale clothing. More apparel manufacturers are entering the retail industry. Companies like Timberland (outdoor wear), Tommy Hilfiger (casual clothing), OshKosh B'Gosh (children's clothes), and Speedo (swim and athletic wear) have all opened showcase outlets in specialty shopping centres and large malls.

category killers
Retailers who carry a deep selection of goods in a narrow product line.

Retailers who carry an extremely deep selection of goods in a relatively narrow product line and hire technical experts to give customers advice are called **category killers**. They are so named because they carry virtually everything within a certain category. Home Depot, which recently purchased 75 percent of Aikenhead's Home Improvement Warehouse from Molson, is an example of a category killer. It sells building materials, lawn and garden supplies, and home improvement products.

discount houses
Bargain retail stores that offer major items such as televisions and large appliances at discount prices.

Discount Houses.   After World War II, some retailers began offering discounts to certain customers. These **discount houses** sold items like televisions and other appliances at substantial reductions in price in order to sell large volumes of products. As name-brand items became more plentiful in the early 1950s, discounters offered better assortments to customers while still embracing a basic philosophy of low-rent facilities and cash-only sales. But as discount houses became more firmly entrenched in the marketplace, they began moving to better locations, improving in-store decor, and selling better-quality merchandise at higher prices. They also began offering some of the services of a department store, such as credit plans and noncash sales. Kmart, Zellers, and Wal-Mart are discount stores. The box "The Changing Face of Canadian Retailing" describes how these much-publicized retailers operate.

catalogue showrooms
Bargain retail stores in which customers place orders for items described in a catalogue and pick up those items from an on-premises warehouse.

Catalogue showrooms mail catalogues with colour pictures of products, product descriptions, and prices to customers' homes and businesses. In the showroom, customers view samples on display, place orders, and wait briefly while clerks retrieve their orders from the warehouse attached to the showroom.

factory outlets
Bargain retail stores that are owned by the manufacturers whose products they sell.

Factory outlets sell merchandise directly from the factory to consumers, thereby avoiding wholesalers and retailers. The first factory outlets featured products such as apparel, linens, food items, and furniture. Located next to the factories in warehouse-like facilities, their distribution costs were very low. Consequently, they could offer their products at lower costs.

convenience stores
Retail stores that offer high accessibility, extended hours, and fast service on selected items.

Convenience Stores.   While selection is the lure of department stores and price the lure of discount stores, **convenience stores**, as their name implies, offer ease of purchase. They stress an easily accessible location with parking, extended store hours (in many cases 24 hours), and fast service. Neighbourhood gasoline/food retailers like 7-Eleven stores are convenience stores.

TRENDS & CHALLENGES

The Changing Face of Canadian Retailing

In February 1998, Hudson's Bay Co. announced that it had purchased Kmart. Kmart had been the number three player in the discount department store segment in Canada, but it had had a tough time responding to the intense competition that developed after the Wal-Mart invasion. A study by CIBC Wood Gundy showed that in spite of the fact that Wal-Mart had been in Canada only a few years, by 1997 it already held 45 percent of the discount department store market. Zellers held 41 percent, and Kmart had 14 percent.

The Bay plans to combine its 298 Zellers stores with Kmart's 112 stores. About 40 former Kmart stores will be closed and 6000 people will lose their jobs. Retail consultants feel that the merging of Kmart and Zellers will allow Zellers to more effectively compete with Wal-Mart.

The new, bigger Zellers does not intend to compete with Wal-Mart on price (that seems impossible); rather, Zellers will introduce jazzier and more stylish clothing and housewares that are trendier than Zellers customers are accustomed to. Zellers plans to copy the success of Target Stores, a U.S. chain that has adopted a strategy of selling stylish goods at bargain prices to middle- and upper-income consumers.

Discount stores are not the only type of retail outlets that are responding to the Wal-Mart threat. Department stores are also fighting back with better service, more choices, and revamped stores. Sears Canada, for example, plans to spend more than $240 million on store facelifts by 2001. The Bay, meanwhile, is planning to split into two chains. The largest outlets will continue to operate as department stores, while the smaller outlets will evolve into specialty retail outlets like Kohl's in the U.S., a chain that features low prices and guaranteed in-stock apparel on brands like Nike, Levi's, and Jockey.

Wal-Mart is not going to take any of this lying down. It is going to be a formidable competitor because it gives consumers what they want: low prices, convenience, good selection, no stock-outs, and fast in-and-out time. But Wal-Mart is not alone in changing the face of Canadian retailing. Warehouse clubs and "category killers" like Office Depot and Home Depot are also challenging traditional retailing and distribution practices.

Each of these three kinds of retailers has a slightly different strategy. Warehouse clubs keep prices low by offering minimal service, limited selection, and no guarantee that the same brand will be available next week. They pursue high volume and are content with low margins. Category killers offer a deep selection of a narrow range of goods and have higher margins, which allows them to provide much more customer service. Wal-Mart, Kmart, and Zellers lie somewhere in between these two formats, providing a wide range of products at low prices.

The success of these three retailing formats shows just how much Canadian consumers have changed over the years. In the 1960s, Canadian families spent more than 80 percent of their income on consumption; now it is 72 percent. Real disposable income has been falling and is now down to the level it was in 1980. Because of this, consumers are very price-conscious. They are also time-conscious; one study showed that shoppers now spend 20 minutes less on the average trip to a shopping mall than they did in 1982.

The success of Wal-Mart bears looking into. Its annual sales revenue of nearly $120 billion is five times greater than the total of all Canadian department and discount stores combined. How does it achieve this? Wal-Mart has figured out how business operates *and* how consumers think, and it successfully manipulated both of these. A large part of its success is attributed to its inventory and distribution systems. Checkout scanners feed information to distribution centres where products move on high-speed conveyers. Most of its stores are within a day's drive of a distribution centre, and many stores are replenished daily. It is really just-in-time retailing. Information technology allows Wal-Mart's suppliers to better plan their production schedules because they know almost instantaneously what is going on at the retail level.

The system ensures that products will not be out of stock and that they will be the lowest price possible, a big advantage in an industry where small margins are the rule. Wal-Mart has a policy of everyday-low prices; it has no sales except on items that are being closed out. But its big advantage comes with the use of something called variable pricing—maintaining unusually low prices on goods like motor oil, paper towels, and laundry detergent that are frequently purchased by customers. Local Wal-Mart managers have authority to lower prices on these goods to below that of their competitors. Because of the low prices on these sensitive goods, customers often think that Wal-Mart has the lowest prices on everything (it doesn't). Wal-Mart stores have sales of about $300 per square foot, which is about 50 percent higher than discount competitors like Kmart and Zellers.

Wal-Mart
www.wal-mart.com

This furniture shopper has chosen a specialty store that carries a complete line of furnishings and offers interior decorating services.

supermarkets
Large retail stores that offer a variety of food and food-related items divided into specialized departments.

warehouse clubs
Huge, membership-only, combined retail-wholesale operations that sell brand-name merchandise.

Canada Safeway
www.safeway.com

hypermarkets
Large institutions with broad product offerings but with somewhat higher prices than warehouse clubs.

scrambled merchandising
The retail practice of carrying any product expected to sell well, regardless of whether it fits into the store's original product offering.

Supermarkets. Beginning in the last half of the 1930s, a radical shift began to occur in the grocery business from the small corner grocery store to supermarkets. Like department stores, **supermarkets** are divided into departments of related food and household paper and cleaning products. The emphasis is on low prices, self-service, and wide selection. The largest supermarkets are chain stores such as Safeway, Loblaws, and Provigo.

Warehouse Clubs. One of the newer innovations in retailing is the **warehouse club** (also called wholesale clubs). These are huge, membership-only, combination retail-wholesale operations that sell all kinds of brand-name merchandise. They carry groceries, appliances, tires, clothing, and countless other items at very low prices.

Traditional retailers like Canada Safeway generate 80 percent of their sales from just 20 percent of the products they carry. By contrast, warehouse clubs stock only the 20 percent and sell huge volumes of it at low margins. Supermarkets carry about 20 000 items, but warehouse clubs carry only about 3500. The typical warehouse club margin is 8 percent, while at more traditional discount stores the margin can be up to 40 percent. By carrying only the top-selling brands, warehouse clubs have been able to expand their product lines into non-grocery items like appliances, consumer electronics, tools, and office supplies.

Some traditional retailers have also experimented with the "warehouse format." Canadian Tire, for example, opened a warehouse format store in St. Hubert, Quebec, in 1991. The company's strategy is to convince consumers that it can match the low prices at warehouse clubs like Price/Costco.[10]

Hypermarkets. **Hypermarkets** are also large institutions with broad merchandise offerings, but they have somewhat higher prices than warehouse clubs. Hypermarkets may also include service departments such as cafeterias and beauty salons. Meijer's Thrifty Acres near Detroit and Hypermarché Laval near Montreal are examples of hypermarkets. These firms practise **scrambled merchandising**, carrying any product—whether similar or dissimilar to the store's original product offering—they feel will sell.

Other retail variations exist. Liquidation World, with locations in Calgary, Edmonton, and Surrey, B.C., does not carry a standard product line. Instead, it gets deals on merchandise from insurance companies, receivers, and bankruptcy trustees and then sells the products at low prices. And McDonald's opens a mobile outlet during the summer months in Grand Bend, Ontario. The company is thinking of using mobile units at special events like concerts.[11]

Nonstore Retailing

Not all goods and services are offered for sale in stores. In fact, some retailers sell all or most of their products without stores. Examples of nonstore retailing include mail order, vending machines, video marketing, telemarketing, electronic shopping, and direct selling.

Mail Order. Firms that sell by **mail order** typically send out splashy catalogues describing a variety of merchandise. Singer-actress Cher calls her catalogue "a coffeetable book you can order from." Called *Sanctuary*, it features a medieval theme—lamps with chain-mail shades, wrought-iron bedsteads, and velvet pillows with Gothic church designs.[12]

mail order
A form of nonstore retailing in which customers place orders for merchandise shown in catalogues and receive their orders via mail.

Some firms sell solely through the mail. Others, such as Sears and Consumers Distributing, have a combination marketing strategy and distribute merchandise through both catalogue sales and retail outlets. Although mail-order firms have existed for a long time, computer technology and telephone-charge transactions have helped this industry boom in recent years.

Vending Machines. Certain types of consumer goods—most notably candy, soft drinks, and cigarettes—lend themselves to distribution through **vending machines**. Vending machine sales have increased in recent years, but they still represent only a small proportion of retail sales.

vending machine
Machine which dispenses mostly convenience goods like candy, cigarettes, and soft drinks.

Video Marketing. More and more companies have begun using television to sell consumer commodities such as jewellery and kitchen accessories. Many cable systems now offer **video marketing** through home shopping channels that display and demonstrate products and allow viewers to phone in orders. One weekend in 1993, Ivana Trump's appearance on the Home Shopping Club netted $2 million in orders for her high-fashion apparel.

video marketing
Selling to consumers by showing products on television that consumers can buy by telephone or mail.

Telemarketing. **Telemarketing** is the use of the telephone to sell directly to consumers. WATS (Wide Area Telephone Service) lines can be used to receive toll-free calls from consumers in response to television and radio advertisements. Offering live or automated dialling, message delivery, and order taking, telemarketers can use WATS lines to call consumers to promote products and services. Telemarketing is used for both consumer and industrial goods, and it is experiencing rapid growth in Canada, the U.S., and Great Britain.

telemarketing
Use of the telephone to sell directly to consumers.

Electronic Shopping. **Electronic shopping** is made possible by computer information systems that allow sellers to connect into consumers' computers with information about products and services. The member's computer video display shows the available products, which range from plane reservations to consumer goods. Viewers can examine detailed product descriptions, compare brands, send for free information, or purchase by credit card—all at home. Prodigy, a joint venture of IBM and Sears, is the largest of the home networks.

electronic shopping
Using computer information systems to help sellers connect with buyers' computers with information about products and services.

Direct Selling. The oldest form of retailing, **direct selling** is still used by companies that sell door-to-door or through *home-selling parties*. Most of us have talked with salespeople from World Book, Avon, or Fuller Brush as they make their door-to-door sales calls.

direct selling
A form of nonstore selling sometimes called door-to-door sales.

Direct selling is also common in the wholesaling of such industrial goods as commercial photocopying equipment. Although direct selling is convenient and gives customers one-on-one attention, prices are usually driven up by labour costs (salespeople often receive commissions of 40 to 50 cents on every sales dollar). Worldwide, 9 million direct salespeople now generate annual sales of $35 billion. In Japan alone, for instance, 1.2 million distributors have made Amway Corp. second only to Coca-Cola as the most profitable foreign retailer.[13]

Some door-to-door firms use **multi-level marketing**, which attracts both buyers and sellers. The company convinces people to sell the product to anyone they can. In return the salesperson gets a commission. Salespeople also get a commission on the sales of any person they recruit to work for the business. Amway and Mary Kay Cosmetics are two of the most well-known multi-level marketing firms.

■ PHYSICAL DISTRIBUTION

Physical distribution refers to the activities needed to move products efficiently from manufacturer to consumer. The goals of physical distribution are to keep customers satisfied, to make goods available when and where consumers want them, and to keep costs low. Thus physical distribution includes *warehousing* and *transporting operations*.

Warehousing Operations

Storing or **warehousing** products is a major function of distribution management. In selecting a warehousing strategy, managers must keep in mind the characteristics and costs of warehousing operations.

Types of Warehouses.   There are two basic types of warehouses: private and public. Within these categories, we can further divide warehouses according to their use as storage sites or as distribution centres.

The first type, **private warehouses**, are owned by and provide storage for just one company, be it a manufacturer, a wholesaler, or a retailer. Most are used by large firms that deal in mass quantities and need storage regularly.

Public warehouses are independently owned and operated. Companies that use these warehouses pay for the actual space used. Public warehouses are popular with firms that need such storage only during peak business periods. They are also used by manufacturers who want to maintain stock in numerous locations in order to get their products to many markets quickly.

Storage warehouses provide storage for extended periods of time. Producers of seasonal items, such as agricultural crops, most often use this type of warehouse. In contrast, **distribution centres** store products whose market demand is constant and quite high. They are used by retail chains, wholesalers, and manufacturers that need to break large quantities produced or bought into the smaller quantities their stores or customers demand.

Warehousing Costs   All warehouse types involve costs. These costs include obvious expenses such as storage-space rental or mortgage payments (usually computed by square foot), insurance, and wages. They also include the costs of inventory control and materials handling. **Inventory control** is a vital part of warehouse operations. It goes beyond keeping track of what is on hand at any time and involves planning to ensure that an adequate supply of a product is in stock at all times—a tricky balancing act.

Materials handling is the transportation, arrangement, and orderly retrieval of goods in inventory. Most warehouse personnel are employed in materials handling. Keeping materials handling costs down requires managers to develop a strategy for storing a company's products that takes into account product locations within the warehouse. One strategy for managing materials is **unitization**, a method that standardizes the weight and form of materials and makes storage and handling more systematic. To reduce the high costs of materials handling, more and more warehouses are automating. Computerized systems can move, store, and retrieve items from storage in the warehouse.

multi-level marketing
A system in which a salesperson earns a commission on their own sales and on the sales of any other salespeople they recruit.

physical distribution
Those activities needed to move a product from the manufacturer to the end consumer.

warehousing
That part of the distribution process concerned with storing goods.

private warehouses
Warehouses owned and used by just one company.

public warehouses
Independently owned and operated warehouses that store the goods of many firms.

storage warehouses
Warehouses used to provide storage of goods for extended periods of time.

distribution centres
Warehouses used to provide storage of goods for only short periods before they are shipped to retail stores.

inventory control
The part of warehouse operations that keeps track of what is on hand and ensures adequate supplies of products in stock at all times.

materials handling
The transportation and arrangement of goods within a warehouse and orderly retrieval of goods from inventory.

unitization
A materials-handling strategy in which goods are transported and stored in containers with a uniform size, shape, and/or weight.

Transportation Operations

Transportation, for both passengers and freight is big business. In 1993, the world's 50 largest transportation companies had revenues totalling $380 billion.

The major transportation modes are rail, water, truck, air, and pipelines. In the early part of the 20th century, railroads dominated the Canadian transportation system, but by the 1970s, truck and air transportation had become much more important. Using operating revenue as the basis for comparison, in 1993 the most important modes of transportation in Canada were trucks, air, and rail (in that order).

Cost is a major factor when a company chooses a transportation method. The difference in cost among the various transportation modes is directly related to the speed of delivery. The higher the speed of delivery, the greater the cost. But cost is not the only consideration. A company must also consider the nature of its products, the distance the product must travel, timeliness, and customers' needs and wants. A company shipping orchids or other perishable goods will probably use air transport, while a company shipping sand or coal will use rail or water transport.

Trucks. The advantages of trucks include flexibility, fast service, and dependability. Nearly all sections of Canada, except the far north, can be reached by truck. Trucks are a particularly good choice for short-distance distribution and more expensive products. Large furniture and appliance retailers in major cities, for example, use trucks to shuttle merchandise between their stores and to make deliveries to customers. Trucks can, however, be delayed by bad weather. They also are limited in the volume they can carry in a single load.

More and more manufacturers are using **expedited transportation**, which involves paying a higher-than-normal fee for truck delivery in return for guaranteed delivery times. Even this higher fee is still cheaper than air freight.[14]

expedited transportation
Paying a higher-than-normal fee for truck delivery for guaranteed delivery times.

Planes. Air is the fastest available transportation mode. In Canada's far north, it may be the only available transportation. Other advantages include greatly reduced costs in packing, handling, unpacking, and final preparations necessary for sale to the consumer. Also, inventory-carrying costs can be reduced by eliminating the need to store certain commodities. Fresh fish, for example, can be flown to restaurants each day, avoiding the risk of spoilage that comes with packaging and storing a supply of fish. However, air freight is

A container train crosses the Salmon River bridge in New Brunswick.

the most expensive form of transportation. In recent years a whole new industry has evolved to meet the customer's need to receive important business papers and supplies "overnight."

Railroads.   Railroads have been the backbone of our transportation system since the late 1800s. Until the 1960s, when trucking firms lowered their rates and attracted many customers, railroads were fairly profitable. They are now used primarily to transport heavy, bulky items such as cars, steel, and coal.

Water Carriers.   Of all the transportation modes, water transportation is the least expensive. Unfortunately, water transportation is also the slowest way to ship. Boats and barges are mainly used for extremely heavy, bulky materials and products (like sand, gravel, oil, and steel) for which transit times are unimportant. Manufacturers are beginning to use water carriers more often because many ships are now specially constructed to load and store large standardized containers. The St. Lawrence Seaway is a vital link in Canada's water transportation system.

Water transportation is particularly important in Canada's far north. Northern Transportation Co. Ltd. has 90 barges, 9 seagoing tugboats, and 250 employees. The company uses barges to deliver commodities like fuel oil to various isolated hamlets along the western edge of Hudson's Bay during the summer months. Each barge has a capacity of 4000 tonnes.[15]

Pipelines.   Like water transportation, pipelines are slow in terms of overall delivery time. They are also completely inflexible, but they do provide a constant flow of the product and are unaffected by weather conditions. Traditionally, this delivery system has transported liquids and gases. Lack of adaptability to other products and limited routes make pipelines a relatively unimportant transportation method for most industries.

intermodal transportation
The combined use of different modes of transportation.

containerization
The use of standardized heavy-duty containers in which many items are sealed at the point of shipment and opened only at the final destination.

Intermodal Transportation.   **Intermodal transportation**—the combined use of different modes of transportation—has come into widespread use. For example, shipping by a combination of truck and rail ("piggy-back"), water and rail ("fishy-back"), or air and rail ("birdy-back") has improved flexibility and reduced costs.

To make intermodal transport more efficient, **containerization** uses standardized heavy-duty containers in which many items are sealed at points of shipment and opened only at final destinations. On the trip, containers may be loaded onto ships for ocean transit, transferred onto trucks, loaded on railcars, and delivered to final destinations by other trucks. The containers are then unloaded and returned for future use. International Cargo Management Systems has developed a device that is attached to the inside of containers being shipped. The device pulls in signals from global positioning satellites to determine the container's latitude and longitude. The device then transmits this information to computers at a tracking centre. Customers can call the tracking centre to determine where their package is at any moment.[16]

Companies Specializing in Transportation

The major modes of transportation are available from one or more of four types of transporting companies: common carriers, freight forwarders, contract carriers, and private carriers.

common carriers
Transportation companies that transport goods for any firm or individual wishing to make a shipment.

The nation's **common carriers** transport merchandise for any shipper—manufacturers, wholesalers, retailers, and even individual consumers. They maintain regular schedules and charge competitive prices. The best examples of common carriers are truck lines and railroads.

In 1897, the *Crow's Nest Pass Agreement* established the rate that railways could charge for hauling grain. This agreement was essentially a freight subsidy that helped prairie farmers pay some of their transportation costs to distant ports. But in 1995, the

Liberal government abolished the Crow subsidy. Freight rates increased for prairie farmers, which caused them to reduce their emphasis on growing wheat and increase their emphasis on raising livestock.[17] Since the Crow rate was eliminated, livestock production and agricultural processing have increased on the prairies.

Not all transportation companies own their own vehicles. A **freight forwarder** is a common carrier that leases bulk space from other carriers, such as railroads or airlines. It then resells parts of that space to smaller shippers. Once it has enough contracts to fill the bulk space, the freight forwarder picks up whatever merchandise is to be shipped. It then transports the goods to the bulk carrier, which makes delivery to an agreed-on destination, and handles billing and any inquiries concerning the shipment.

freight forwarders
Common carriers that lease bulk space from other carriers and resell that space to firms making small shipments.

Some transportation companies will transport products for any firm for a contracted amount and time period. These **contract carriers** are usually self-employed operators who own the vehicle that transports the products. When they have delivered a contracted load to its destination, they generally try to locate another contract shipment (often with a different manufacturer) for the return trip.

contract carriers
Independent transporters who contract to serve as transporters for industrial customers only.

A few manufacturers and retailers maintain their own transportation systems (usually a fleet of trucks) to carry their own products. The use of such **private carriers** is generally limited to very large manufacturers such as Kraft Foods and Canada Safeway.

private carriers
Transportation systems owned by the shipper.

Distribution as a Marketing Strategy

Distribution is an increasingly important way of competing for sales. Instead of just offering advantages in product features and quality, price, and promotion, many firms have turned to distribution as a cornerstone of their business strategies. This approach means assessing and improving the entire stream of activities—wholesaling, warehousing, transportation—involved in getting products to customers. Its importance is illustrated at Compaq Computer, which registered a loss of nearly $1 billion in sales for 1994 because products were unavailable when and where customers wanted them. To correct the problem, Compaq has placed distribution at the top of its list as the competitive strategy for the future. This commitment entails reworking the company's whole supply chain of distributors and transportation.

A key tool in contemporary distribution strategy is technology. Computers, for example, allow manufacturers to be electronically connected to specific customers. Even while in production, then, every unit in the factory can be already earmarked for a specific destination. This procedure streamlines the supply chain and allows it to be more efficient. The process for filling each customer's order can be customized and unnecessary steps eliminated more easily. Unnecessary waiting is reduced, and in some cases, the need for intermediaries in the distribution network is also eliminated. Because it speeds up delivery times, customers do not go elsewhere for products. Finally, it reduces inventories in the supply chain, thereby lowering inventory costs and freeing up funds for other uses.

Another approach to streamlining is the use of **hubs**—central distribution outlets that control all or most of a firm's distribution activities. This approach, which has emerged in the manufacturing sector, sees distribution from a systems perspective instead of focusing on the *separate steps* in the distribution network. Three types of distribution centres have emerged from this approach: *supply-side* and *"pre-staging," supplier-coordinated*, and *distribution-side hubs*.

hub
Central distribution outlet that controls all or most of a firm's distribution activities.

Supply-Side and "Pre-Staging" Hubs. *Supply-side hubs* make the most sense when large shipments of supplies flow regularly to a single industrial user, such as a large manufacturer. They are used, for example, by automobile factories, where thousands of incoming supplies can arrive by train, truck, and air. The chief job of the hub is to coordinate the customer's materials needs with supply-chain transportation. If the hub is successful, the factory's inventories are virtually eliminated, storage-space requirements are reduced, and long-haul trucks, instead of lining up at the customer's unloading dock, keep moving.

Supplier-Coordinated Hubs.   The reverse practice occurs when a factory's suppliers, rather than the factory itself, set up their own coordinated hub. This is the system that supplies all the components for Compaq Computer's factories in Houston, Texas. Thirty-five suppliers store parts in a warehouse 20 kilometres away and coordinate their trucking so that parts arrive just when needed at Compaq.

National Semiconductor
www.national.com

Distribution-Side Hubs.   While supply-side hubs are located near industrial customers, *distribution-side hubs* may be located much farther away—especially if customers are geographically dispersed. National Semiconductor, one of the world's largest chip-makers, is an example. National's finished products, silicon microchips, are produced in plants throughout the world and shipped to customers such as IBM, Toshiba, Siemens, Ford, and Compaq at factory locations around the globe. National airfreights its microchips worldwide from a single distribution centre in Singapore.

SUMMARY OF LEARNING OBJECTIVES

1. **Identify the various *pricing objectives* that govern pricing decisions and describe the tools used in making these decisions.** A firm's pricing decisions reflect the pricing objectives set by its management. Such objectives as profit maximization and a variety of market share goals may thus be relevant to those decisions. Cost-oriented pricing (recognizing the need to cover costs) and break-even analysis (determining the price level at which profits will be generated) can then be used as tools in determining prices.

2. **Discuss *pricing strategies* and tactics for existing and new products.** Either a price-skimming (pricing very high) or a penetration-pricing strategy (pricing very low) may be effective for new products. Depending on other elements in the marketing mix, existing products may be priced at, above, or below prevailing prices for similar products. Guided by a firm's pricing strategies, managers set prices using tactics such as *price lining* (offering items in certain categories at a limited number of prices), *psychological pricing* (appealing to buyers' perceptions of relative prices), and *discounting* (reducing prices to stimulate sales).

3. **Identify the different *channels of distribution* and explain different *distribution strategies*.** In selecting a *distribution mix*, a firm may use all or any of six distribution channels. The first four are aimed at getting products to consumers, and the last two are aimed at getting products to industrial customers. Channel 1 involves direct sales to consumers. Channel 2 includes a *retailer*. Channel 3 involves a retailer and a *wholesaler*, while Channel 4 includes an *agent* or *broker* who enters the system before the wholesaler and a retailer. Channel 5 involves a direct sale to an industrial user. Channel 6, which is used infrequently, entails selling to industrial users through wholesalers. Distribution strategies include *intensive, exclusive*, and *selective distribution*, which differ in the number of products and channel members involved and in the amount of service performed in the channel.

4. **Explain the differences between *merchant wholesalers* and *agents/brokers*.** *Wholesalers* act as distribution intermediaries. They may extend credit as well as store, repackage, and deliver products to other members of the channel. *Full-service* and *limited-service merchant wholesalers* differ in the number and types of distribution functions they offer. Unlike wholesalers, *agents* and *brokers* never take legal possession of the product. Rather, they function as sales and merchandising arms of manufacturers that do not have their own sales forces. They may also provide such services as advertising and display merchandising.

5. **Identify the different types of *retail stores*.** Retailers can be described according to two classifications: product-line retailers and bargain retailers. *Product-line retailers* include department stores, supermarkets, hypermarkets, and specialty stores. *Bargain retailers* include discount houses, off-price stores, catalogue showrooms, factory outlets, warehouse clubs, and convenience stores. These retailers differ in terms of size, services and products offered, and pricing. Some retailing also takes place without stores. *Nonstore retailing* may use direct-mail catalogues, vending machines, direct selling, telemarketing, or video marketing.

6. **Describe the major activities in the *physical distribution process*.** *Physical distribution* refers to all the activities needed to move a product from manufacturer to consumer, including warehousing and transportation of products. *Warehouses* may be *public* or *private* and may function either as long-term *storage warehouses* or as *distribution centres*. In addition to storage, insurance, and wage-related costs, the cost to warehouse goods also includes *inventory control* (maintaining adequate but not excessive supplies) and *materials handling* (transporting, arranging, and retrieving supplies).

7. **Compare the five basic forms of *transportation* and identify the types of firms that provide them.** *Trucks, railroads, planes, water carriers* (boats and barges), and *pipelines* are the major transportation modes used in the distribution process. They differ in cost, availability, reliability of delivery, speed, and number of points served. Air is the fastest but most expensive mode; water carriers are the slowest but least expensive. Since transport companies were deregulated, they have become more cost-efficient and competitive by developing such innovations as *intermodal transportation* and *containerization*. Transportation in any form may be supplied by *common carriers*, *freight forwarders*, *contract carriers*, or *private carriers*.

STUDY QUESTIONS AND EXERCISES

Review Questions

1. List five objectives a firm might have in setting its prices.

2. Identify four types of discounting and give an example for each that is different from the examples in the text.

3. From the manufacturer's point of view, what are the advantages and disadvantages of using intermediaries to distribute a product? From the end buyer's view?

4. How do the six distribution channels cited in the chapter differ from one another?

5. How do manufacturer-owned, merchant, and agent wholesalers differ? How are they the same?

6. Compare the five types of bargain stores listed in the text. Give an example of each in your town or city.

Analysis Questions

7. Suppose that a book company selling to book distributors has fixed operating costs of $600 000 per year and variable costs of $3.00 per book. How many books must the firm sell to break even if the selling price is $6.00? If the company expects to sell 50 000 books next year and decides on a 40 percent markup, what will the selling price be?

8. Under what competitive conditions would you price your existing product at the prevailing market price for similar products? Above the prevailing price? Below the prevailing price?

9. Give three examples (other than those in the chapter) of products that use intensive distribution. Do the same for products that use exclusive distribution and selective distribution. For which category was it easiest to find examples? Why?

10. If you could own a firm in the business of transporting products, what type of firm would you prefer to own (truck, air, shipping, etc.)? Why?

Application Exercises

11. Interview the manager of a local manufacturing firm. Identify the firm's distribution strategy and the channels of distribution it uses. Where applicable,

describe the types of wholesalers and/or retail stores the firm uses to distribute its products.

12. Choose any consumer item at a supermarket and trace the chain of physical distribution activities that brought it to the store's shelf.

BUILDING YOUR BUSINESS SKILLS

Goal

To encourage students to consider the value of online retailing as an element in a company's distribution system.

Situation

As the distribution manager of a privately owned clothing manufacturer, specializing in camping gear and outdoor clothing, you are convinced that your product line is perfect for online distribution. But the owner of the company is reluctant to expand distribution from a successful network of retail stores and a catalogue operation. Your challenge is to convince the boss that retailing via the Internet can boost sales.

Method

Step 1: Join together with four or five classmates to research the advantages and disadvantages of an online distribution system for your company. Among the factors to consider are

- The likelihood that target consumers are Internet shoppers. Camping gear is generally purchased by young, affluent consumers who are comfortable with the Web.
- The industry trend to online distribution. Are similar companies doing it? Have they been successful?

- The opportunity to expand inventory without increasing the cost of retail space or catalogue production and mailing charges.
- The opportunity to have a store that never closes.
- The lack of trust many people have about doing business on the Web. Many consumers are reluctant to provide credit card data on the Web.
- The difficulty electronic shoppers have in finding a Website when they do not know the store's name.
- The frustration and waiting time involved in Web searches.
- The certainty that the site will not reach consumers who do not use computers or who are uncomfortable with the Web.

Step 2: Based on your findings, write a persuasive memo to the company's owner stating your position about expanding to an online distribution system. Include information that will counter expected objections.

Follow-Up Questions

1. What place does online distribution have in the distribution network of this company?

2. In your view, is online distribution the wave of the future? Is it likely to increase in importance as a distribution system for apparel companies? Why or why not?

New Ways to Buy a Car

You know the routine: You walk into a car dealership, find a car that looks interesting, and then start negotiating with a salesperson. But you feel terribly insecure because you really have no idea of what constitutes a "good deal." Even if you are able to reach an agreement about which car to purchase and what you are willing to pay, there is always that nagging feeling that you paid too much. Is there a solution to this problem?

In the mid-1980s, the Saturn division of General Motors implemented a revolutionary pricing strategy. Saturn would take the hassle and heartache out of the dealer-consumer relationship by selling vehicles for a fixed low price that would make negotiation unnecessary. Pricing experts believed that this "no-haggle" approach to auto pricing would appeal to consumers who hated to dicker and who believed that traditional dealers maximized commissions by keeping prices high. Meanwhile, salespeople working for fixed-price dealers would be paid by the sale, not by a sliding scale commission linked to profit.

Unfortunately, not all good ideas work in the marketplace, and many auto dealers now believe that the fixed-price approach has some basic flaws. For example, although thousands of consumers have embraced the fixed-price concept, many more continue to seek dealers who are willing to negotiate price.

According to a recent survey, 89 percent of customers who visit fixed-price dealers, rather than buying from them, use their quoted prices as starting points from which to negotiate with traditional dealers. This practice, of course, leaves fixed-price dealers with two types of customers—those who are too busy to shop around and want the convenience of one-stop shopping and those who know so little about car buying that they might have been willing to pay more than the averaged fixed price.

Moreover, no-haggle dealers found themselves squeezed by competitors willing to undercut close-to-the-bone fixed prices in order to make sales and reduce inventories. The most aggressive competition is in cities where consumers routinely comparison shop at several dealers. Fixed-price dealers do best in areas—mostly rural—where they face few rivals. The reality, explains Chrysler CEO Robert J. Easton, is that "one price works better when you don't have dealerships selling the same product quite so close together."

A recent survey conducted by the marketing research firm of Dohring Co. found a sharp increase in the number of consumers who want to negotiate prices. According to Dohring's report, "Automotive consumers need to feel that they get a good deal when they purchase a vehicle, and, for most, the only way [to accomplish this] is through negotiation." As a result, the number of haggle-free new car dealerships in the U.S. has plummeted in recent years. From a total of nearly 2000 in 1994, the number had dropped to fewer than 1200 in 1996.

What is the situation in Canada? The Saturn one-price idea has been tried at various places in Canada. For example, you can visit a one-price dealership in Richmond Hill, Ontario. The North York Chevrolet Geo Oldsmobile dealership began offering one-price selling after its general manager visited a one-price dealership in Michigan. When the new system was implemented, the two top salespeople at the dealership left for greener pastures. And sales staff have let some people walk out the door because they were as little as $8 apart on the price. Sales numbers have not risen since the new system was implemented. But the dealership does get a lot fewer calls from dissatisfied customers after the sale is made.

The potential problems with the one-price system have not reduced its popularity with other automobile companies. In an attempt to increase its market share to 10 percent, Toyota Canada Inc. introduced the one-price system in 1998; included in the system is the elimination of sales commissions.

If you want to take a high-tech approach, you can purchase a no-haggle car on the Internet from Auto-By-Tel. You simply click onto Auto-By-Tel's Website and make a purchase order. Within 48 hours, one of the 90 Canadian Auto-By-Tel dealers phones you with a no-haggle price. The system requires that consumers know exactly what they want, but most of those who use this system do know.

In the U.S., there are several Internet sites that give consumers two pieces of crucial information that they need to get a good deal: (1) the dealer's cost to buy

➤

the car from the factory, and (2) how much profit a dealer needs to make on each car. Once this information becomes more widely available in Canada, consumers will have much more power when they are buying.

■ Case Questions

1. What are the various objectives a business might be pursuing when it prices its products? What objective(s) are automobile dealers pursuing when they price their products?

2. What are the advantages and disadvantages of the one-price system for buying automobiles?

3. Would you prefer to buy an automobile from a one-price dealer or from a traditional dealer? Explain the reasons for your choice.

Chrysler
www.chrysler.com

Auto-By-Tel
www.autobytel.com

CBC VIDEO CASE V-1

End in Sight for Eaton's?*

"The strong family connection . . . is always a problem. You can't always necessarily make the best business decisions because so much is tied up with the family name."

—*Richard Talbot, Thomas Consultants International*

Canadians have treasured the traditions, parades, and guarantees of retail giant Eaton's for generations. Such intergenerational trust and treasuring may, however, be a thing of the past. Eaton's, one of the touchstones of Canadian living for almost 130 years, recently admitted that it was in dire financial straits. The company's announcement stunned many longtime customers. For some, the thought of shopping elsewhere was tantamount to "deserting family." While the company was an early industry leader, pioneering such retail practices as catalogue shopping for Canada's rural community, it appears to have not kept pace with a changing world.

Part of the near-demise is attributable to basic shifts in the retail marketplace. According to business historian and University of Toronto professor Michael Bliss, the traditional department store has become a retail dinosaur. While department stores controlled close to half of retail spending in the 1950s, their market has been "eroded at top end by specialty stores and at bottom end by discount semi-department stores," leaving mid-line department stores in a retail endgame. In the past the company refused to dicker on price, inviting customers who wished to squabble to simply go elsewhere; in the 1990s, many former customers have done exactly that.

Prospects for change, and hence survival, are undeniably complex. For a national, privately held concern such as Eaton's, attempting large-scale change is equivalent to trying to make a U-turn with the *Queen Mary*. The core challenge any move must address, however, is how to consistently deliver superior customer value. Another complicating factor is location, with many of Eaton's stores located in the formerly bustling downtown hubs of Canada's cities. With downtown retail environments already battered by the flight of countless retail dollars to suburban discounters such as Wal-Mart and Zellers any turnaround strategy faces a severe set of operating constraints.

In a recent interview, Eaton's family representative George Eaton admitted that some of the company's retail strategies, such as Every Day Value Pricing, have simply not worked. In an effort to keep the company's customers, landlords, and suppliers informed of its plans during this tumultuous time, Eaton stated the family business plans to focus on new formats that emphasize fashion and service. The company also plans to put major dollars into renovating its facilities. The new cost-conscious formats of such players as Wal-Mart affected the traditional U.S. department store in the late 1980s, Eaton also observed. It is only now, 10 years later, that the impact is being felt north of the border. On a hopeful note, Eaton concluded the interview by observing that many U.S. department stores, including J.C. Penney and Sears, are now re-emerging with strong prospects for a new retail era.

➤

STUDY QUESTIONS

1. What is marketing? How well did the managers at Eaton's appear to market their company?

2. What is the external environment? How well did Eaton's managers appear to understand and respond to the external environment?

3. What are the different types of consumer products? Which of these best describes the products sold by Eaton's?

* Source: This case was written by Professor Reg Litz of the University of Manitoba. Video Resource: "Eaton's Tape," *The National Magazine* (February 27, 1997).

CBC VIDEO CASE V-2

Hockey Night in Cajun-ada?*

"There was an entertainment void in this market!"

—hockey promoter Tim Berryman

Lafayette, Louisiana, is a long way from the National Hockey League. Located in the "bayou" of the deep south, this Louisiana city is about as climactically different as could be imagined from the frozen Canadian rivers where hockey originated. However, these long-standing weather barriers show signs of being all but eliminated with the recent expansion of professional hockey into the southern United States.

Enter the Louisiana Ice Gators. The team is but one of several new minor league teams that have formed in the wake of the NHL's southward expansion. The Louisiana franchise plays in the East Coast Hockey League that includes teams from Florida to Pennsylvania. The Ice Gators' roster is made up of players from Ontario and Quebec who want a shot at professional hockey. Operating out of Lafayette's Cajundome, the team is managed by the Berryman brothers. Both brothers are no strangers to professional sports; at one time, Tim played linebacker for the Toronto Argonauts, while Dave once ranked second in Canadian tennis.

The franchise, admittedly a risky venture, became a reality when a number of factors came together at just the right time. First was Lafayette's underused Cajundome. Sitting empty too much of the time, the facility's management was highly motivated to find a tenant. Next came the brothers Berryman. They believed that hockey could compete with basketball even though the locals didn't know a puck from a power play. "There was an entertainment void in this market," Tim observes. The final ingredient was money, and it came in two parts. First was the $1.5 million franchise fee arranged through the help of several venture capitalists—a lawyer and a couple of oil tycoons from California. With the outside financiers contributing 75 per-

cent, Tim and Dave were still able to maintain a 25 percent interest in the team. Second was sponsorship money—$1 million from Pepsi.

One of the Berrymans' priorities is to keep the sponsors happy, which means filling the seats. How? Get the kids in the arena and the parents will follow. Going after families means pricing the evening right. At about $25 for a night of entertainment, the package seems to work. Part of the formula means featuring more than just hockey—in this case, product giveaways and lots of spontaneous off-ice happenings.

The Berrymans' formula appears to be working; the Ice Gators are the league's biggest draw, outdrawing even some NHL teams. The Cajundome wins, too, with concession sales of $800 000 as part of their cut, a figure they hope to double very soon. The future could bring another increase in cash flow—but this one flowing out. The team's players, earning an average salary of only $380 per week, are interested in getting a bigger piece of the action, which could mean a possible unionization drive.

STUDY QUESTIONS

1. What are the different kinds of consumer products and services? How would you categorize the product or service offered by the Louisiana Ice Gators?

2. What is a promotional mix? How does the concept apply to marketing the Ice Gators?

3. What is the difference between a cash, seasonal, trade, and quantity discount? Which, if any, of these discounts is the Ice Gators' management using?

* Source: This case was written by Professor Reg Litz of the University of Manitoba. Video Resource: "Louisiana Hockey," *Venture* #630 (February 16, 1997).

LANDS' END VIDEO CASE V-3

Getting the Product Out at Lands' End

LEARNING OBJECTIVES

The purpose of this video exercise is to help students:

1. See how a specific company conducts its physical distribution operations

2. Understand the interaction of human and technological resources in the design and control of a company's distribution process

3. Appreciate the roles played by customer service and quality assurance in the design and control of a company's distribution process

BACKGROUND INFORMATION

The flow chart accompanying this case outlines the operations that take place at Lands' End's distribution centre. This process enables Lands' End to get products to customers in only two business days (or three if an order needs embroidering or monogramming). The key, according to Phil Schaecher, Senior Vice President for Operations, is the fact that "LE's distribution centre is staffed by the best people available working together with some of the most sophisticated technology in the industry."

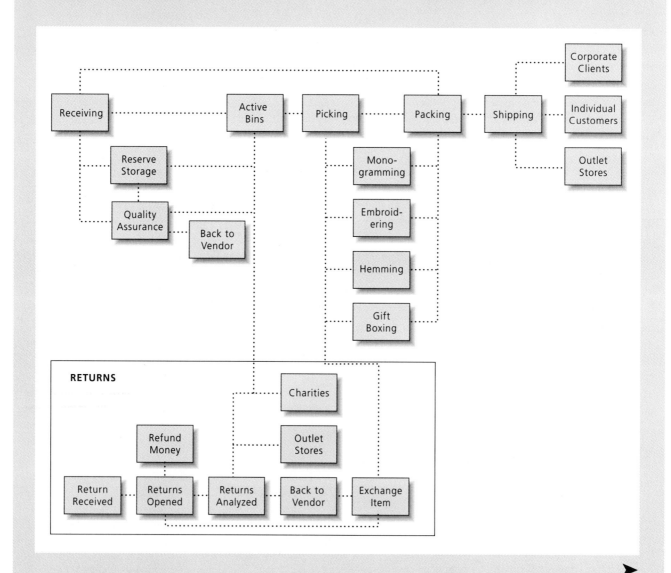

In each major step—receiving, active bins, picking, packing, and shipping—every item is tracked by a bar code prepared the night before it is received at the centre. This bar code enables a computer system to track the item throughout the building. The computer, for example, uses data on current demand to direct merchandise to active bins, quality assurance, shipping, or (as in most cases) reserve storage. The computer also prints out the "pick tickets" used by order-fillers to take items from active bins, which store items that will be needed in the immediate future. Because the bar code on the pick ticket also serves as the packing ticket, all items destined for the same packing bin bear the same three-digit code and are thus delivered by the computer to the same packing bin.

THE VIDEO

Video Source. "Lands' End: Getting the Product Out," *Prentice Hall Presents: On Location at Lands' End*. The video describes in step-by-step detail the computerized operations that enable Lands' End to distribute products to customers within two days of receiving an order. The flow chart accompanying the case is followed carefully as each step in the company's distribution process is illustrated with scenes of the Dodgeville distribution centre at work. Senior Vice President for Operations Phil Schaecher and veteran packer Bill Gantenbein explain how various steps in the system work.

DISCUSSION QUESTIONS

1. Why is Lands' End's physical distribution process particularly appropriate for a mail order retailer?

2. In what areas do you see activities in the video that can be classified as operations management? As operations control?

3. Which activities depicted in the video pertain to the control of warehousing costs? To inventory control? To materials handling?

4. As the video shows, Lands' End attaches considerable importance to *order processing* (the filling of orders as they are received) and *order-cycle times* (the total time elapsed between the customer's placement and receipt

of an order). In what respects does the Lands' End approach to these processes reflect its mission and competitive strategy?

5. In what ways is *total quality management* integrated into Lands' End's distribution operations?

FOLLOW-UP ASSIGNMENT

At the end of the video, the narrator asks, *"With so much technology in place, why does Lands' End place such a high value on employees who work in the warehouse?"* One way to address this question might be to find out exactly why other companies value employees as part of high-tech operations. Contact the Office of the American Workplace (OAW) at **http://www.fed.org/uscompanies/labor**

Using the directories labelled "A-M" and "N-Z," go to the entries on one or more of the following companies:

- Davis Vision Inc.
- Motorola Inc.
- Rhino Foods
- White Storage and Retrieval Systems

By examining each company's description of its activities and goals under such headings as "Employee Participation," "Organizational Structure," "Product/Service Quality," and "Strategic Integration of Business," you should be in a position to draw up an informed answer to the question posed above.

FOR FURTHER EXPLORATION

Contact Land's End at **http://www.landsend.com**

At the Web page, scroll down to the icon labelled "Site Map." From here, you can access the company's description of the various "Services," including "Sizing," "Hemming Info," "Monogramming," "Gift Boxing," and "Care Info," that it offers between the "Picking" and "Packing" operations outlined in the flow chart above. In particular, the feature labelled "Let's Talk" might shed some light on the importance that Lands' End attaches to customer service operations as a component of its distribution process.

MANAGING FINANCIAL ISSUES

Management of the financial transactions of a business firm are absolutely critical to its survival. Whether it involves properly accounting for costs, raising money to start a new firm, having an accurate view of the riskiness of the firm's investments, or monitoring the firm's activities in securities markets, financial management is a key business activity. The opening cases of the chapters in this section are diverse, yet they all deal specifically with the important function of financial management.

Part Six, Managing Financial Issues, provides an overview of how firms raise and manage money, how they define and manage risk, and how they use Canadian securities markets to meet their financial needs.

- In **Chapter 16, Understanding Money and Banking,** we explore the nature of money, its creation through the banking system, and the role of the Bank of Canada in the nation's financial system.

- Next, in **Chapter 17, Financial Decisions and Risk Management,** we look at the reasons businesses need funds and how financial managers raise both long- and short-term funds. We also examine the kinds of risks businesses encounter and the ways in which they deal with such risks.

- Finally, in **Chapter 18, Understanding Securities and Investments,** we consider the markets in which firms raise long-term funds by examining how these markets operate and how they are regulated.

CHAPTER 16

UNDERSTANDING MONEY AND BANKING

WHAT'S THE NEW PRICE?

If you want to find out how much the Iraqi *dinar* is worth, don't check with the Central Bank or the Ministry of Finance. Instead, check the Shorja outdoor market in Baghdad and watch how the black market for the Iraqi currency operates. Exchange rates here are affected by international events that Iraqis hear about on their short-wave radios. A rumoured new missile strike by the U.S., for example, will send the dinar plunging, but a visit to Baghdad by a U.N. weapons-inspection team might send it up if the report is positive (the report usually isn't). There are thousands of illegal money changers in the streets of Baghdad, and their assessment of international news has a big effect on how much the dinar is worth.

The dinar fluctuates so much because its value is determined by the country's oil exports. After the Gulf War of 1991, the UN imposed sanctions on Iraq, limiting the amount of oil it could export. Before the war, the Iraqi government was loaded with cash it received from selling oil, and the official exchange rate was three U.S. dollars per dinar. But in late 1996 on the black market, it took 1190 dinars to buy one dollar. The average Iraqi earns only 5000 dinars a month, and one kilogram of flour costs hundreds of dinars. Thus, there is great economic hardship in Iraq.

Because the dinar's value is so heavily influenced by the actions of foreign governments, retailers operate under almost impossible conditions. The value of the currency changes by the hour (or by the minute if a crisis develops). Retailers have

therefore been forced to become experts in international politics. Retailers call money changers numerous times each day to determine the latest value of the dinar. The standard question is: What's the new price? They also spend a lot of time listening to short-wave radio broadcasts in the hope of hearing some important international news that will help them determine whether the dinar is going up or down in value.

Retailers aren't the only people who have problems. Consumers are also driven to distraction by price changes. One man who wanted to buy two automobile tires noticed a price of 98 000 dinars at the first shop he visited. Thinking that was too high, he kept looking but all he could find was another shop offering the tires for 110 000 dinars. He returned to the first shop to buy the tires, but found that while he was gone, the price there had gone up to 120 000 dinars.

The government of Saddam Hussein has not tried to do away with the black market. Rather, it has set up licensed exchange offices around Iraq to compete with the black market money changers. But the black market still thrives, especially when big transactions are involved or when people who are trading don't want others to know who they are. The official exchange-office managers keep in touch with the black market traders so they know what exchange rates they should charge. These managers may also do some trading on the black market themselves. Generally, the black market offers better rates than either the government's exchange offices or the banks.

The opening case shows just how important money is to each of us as we go about our daily lives. Money is also important to business firms, and in this chapter we describe what money is, the different definitions of the money supply, and why money is essential for every business. We also describe the major financial institutions in Canada, and the way they facilitate business activity. The failures of firms such as Bargain Harold's, Olympia & York, Royal Trustco, and Canadian Commercial Bank underscore the importance of stability in Canada's economic system.

By focusing on the learning objectives of this chapter, you will better understand the environment for banking in Canada, and the different kinds of financial institutions that are important. After reading this chapter, you should be able to:

1. Define *money* and identify the different forms it takes in the nation's money supply.
2. Describe the different kinds of *financial institutions* that make up the Canadian financial system and explain the services they offer.
3. Explain how banks create money and identify the means by which they are regulated.
4. Explain the functions of the *Bank of Canada* and describe the tools it uses to control the money supply.
5. Identify ways in which the financial industry is changing.
6. Understand the importance of international banking and finance in an increasingly global financial system.

■ MONEY

When someone asks you how much money you have, what do you say? Do you count the bills and coins in your pockets? Do you mention the funds in your chequing and savings accounts? What about stocks, bonds, your car? Taken together, the value of everything you own is your personal *wealth*. Not all of it, however, is *money*. In this section, we will consider what money is and what it does.

What Is Money?

The bills and coins you carry every day are money. So are U.S. dollars, British pound notes, French francs, and Japanese yen. Modern money often takes the form of printed paper or stamped metal issued by a government. But over the centuries, items as diverse as stone wheels, salt, wool, livestock, shells, and spices have been used as money. **Money** is any object generally accepted by people as payment for goods and services.

Thousands of years ago, people began to accept certain agreed-upon objects in exchange for goods or services. As early as 1100 B.C., the Chinese were using metal money that represented the objects they were exchanging (for example, bronze spades and knives). Coins probably came into use sometime around 600 B.C. and paper money around A.D. 1200.

money
Any object generally accepted by people as payment for goods and services.

Desirable Characteristics of Money

Any object can serve as money if it is portable, divisible, durable, and stable.[1] To understand why these qualities are important, imagine using as money something valuable that lacks them—a 35 kilogram salmon, for example.

Portability of Money.   If you wanted to use the salmon to buy goods and services, you would have to lug a 35 kilogram fish from shop to shop. Modern currency, by contrast, is lightweight and easy to handle.

Throughout the ages, humans have used many monetary devices. Two interesting ones that were in common circulation are the Iroquois wampum belt (early 19th century) from eastern North America and this ancient Greek coin (circa 375 B.C.).

Divisibility of Money.   Suppose you wanted to buy a hat, a book, and some milk from three different stores—all using the salmon as money. How would you divide the fish? First, out comes a cleaver at each store. Then, you would have to determine whether a kilogram of its head is worth as much as a kilogram from the middle. Modern currency is easily divisible into smaller parts with fixed value for each unit. In Canada, for example, a dollar can be exchanged for 4 quarters, 10 dimes, 20 nickels, 100 pennies, or any combination of these coins. It is easy to match units of money with the value of all goods.

Durability of Money.   Fish seriously fails the durability test. Each day, whether or not you "spend" it, the salmon will be losing value (and gaining scents). Modern currency, on the other hand, does not spoil, it does not die, and, if it wears out, it can be replaced with new coins and paper money.

Stability of Money.   Fish are not stable enough to serve as money. If salmon were in short supply, you might be able to make quite a deal for yourself. But in the middle of a salmon run, the market would be flooded with fish. Since sellers would have many opportunities to exchange their wares for salmon, they would soon have enough fish and refuse to trade for salmon. While the value of the paper money we use today has fluctuated over the years, it is considerably more stable than salmon.

The Functions of Money

Imagine a successful fisherman who needs a new sail for his boat. In a *barter economy—one in which goods are exchanged directly for one another*—he would have to find someone who not only needs fish but who is willing to exchange a sail for it. If no sail-maker wants fish, the fisherman must find someone else—say, a shoemaker—who wants fish and will trade for it. Then the fisherman must hope that the sailmaker will trade for his new shoes. Clearly, barter is quite inefficient in comparison to money. In a money economy, the fisherman would sell his catch, receive money, and exchange the money for such goods as a new sail.

In broad terms, money serves three functions:

- *Medium of exchange.* Like the fisherman "trading" money for a new sail, we use money as a way of buying and selling things. Without money, we would be bogged down in a system of barter.

- *Store of value.* Pity the fisherman who catches a fish on Monday and wants to buy a few bars of candy on, say, the following Saturday. By then, the fish would have spoiled and be of no value. In the form of *currency*, however, money can be used for future purchases and so "stores" value.
- *Unit of account*. Finally, money lets us measure the *relative* values of goods and services. It acts as a unit of account because all products can be valued and accounted for in terms of money. For example, the concepts of "$1000 worth of clothes" or "$500 in labour costs" have universal meaning because everyone deals with money every day.

The Money Supply: M-1

For money to serve as a medium of exchange, a store of value, or a unit of account, buyers and sellers must agree on its value. The value of money, in turn, depends in part on its supply, that is, how much money is in circulation. When the money supply is high, the value of money drops. When the money supply is low, the value of money increases.

Unfortunately, it is not easy to measure the supply of money, nor is there complete agreement on exactly how it should be measured. The "narrow" definition of the money supply is called M-1. **M-1** counts only the most liquid forms of money: currency and demand deposits (chequing accounts) in banks.

M-1
Only the most liquid forms of money (currency and demand deposits).

Currency.   **Currency** is paper money and coins issued by the Canadian government. It is widely used to pay small bills. Canadian currency states clearly: "This note is legal tender." Legal tender is money the law requires a creditor to accept in payment of a debt.

currency
Paper money and coins issued by the government.

Demand Deposits.   The majority of Canadian households have chequing accounts against which millions of cheques are written each year. A **cheque** is an order instructing the bank to pay a given sum to a specified person or firm. Although not all sellers accept cheques in payment for goods and services, many do. Cheques enable buyers to make large purchases without having to carry large amounts of cash. Sellers gain a measure of safety because the cheques they receive are valuable only to them and can later be exchanged for cash. Money in chequing accounts, known as **demand deposits**, is counted in M-1 because such funds may be withdrawn at any time without notice.

cheque
An order instructing the bank to pay a given sum to a specified person or firm.

demand deposit
Money in chequing accounts; counted as M-1 because such funds may be withdrawn at any time without notice.

The Money Supply: M-2

M-2 includes everything in M-1 plus items that cannot be spent directly but that are easily converted to spendable forms: *time deposits, money market mutual funds*, and *savings deposits*. M-2 accounts for nearly all the nation's money supply. It thus measures the store of monetary value that is available for financial transactions. As this overall level of money increases, more is available for consumer purchases and business investment. When the supply is tightened, less money is available; financial transactions, spending, and business activity thus slow down.

M-2
Everything in M-1 plus savings deposits, time deposits, and money market mutual funds.

Time Deposits.   Unlike demand deposits, **time deposits** require prior notice of withdrawal and cannot be transferred by cheque. On the other hand, time deposits pay higher interest rates. Thus the supply of money in time deposits—such as *certificates of deposit* (*CDs*) and *savings certificates*—grew rapidly in the 1970s and 1980s as interest rates rose to levels never before seen in Canada.

time deposit
A deposit that requires prior notice to make a withdrawal; cannot be transferred to others by cheque.

Money Market Mutual Funds.   **Money market mutual funds** are operated by investment companies that bring together pools of assets from many investors. The fund buys a collection of short-term, low-risk financial securities. Ownership of and profits (or losses) from the sale of these securities are shared among the fund's investors.

money market mutual funds
Funds operated by investment companies that bring together pools of assets from many investors.

These funds attracted many investors in the 1980s because of high payoffs and because they often allow investors to write cheques against their shares. Mutual funds pay higher returns than most individuals can get on their own because:

1. Funds can buy into higher-paying securities that require larger investments than most individuals can afford.

2. They are managed by professionals who monitor changing investment opportunities.

Savings Deposits.   In the wake of new, more attractive investments, traditional savings deposits, such as passbook savings accounts, have declined in popularity.

Credit Cards

Although not included in M-1 or M-2, credit—especially credit cards—has become a major factor in the purchase of consumer goods in Canada. The use of MasterCard, Visa, American Express, Discover, and credit cards issued by individual businesses has become so widespread that many people refer to credit cards as "plastic money." Nevertheless, credit cards do not qualify as money. Rather, they are a *money substitute*; they serve as a temporary medium of exchange but are not a store of value. The box "To Catch a Credit Card Thief" describes an interesting development in credit card fraud detection.

Credit cards are big business for two reasons. First, they are quite convenient—and about to become both more convenient and more reliable:

TRENDS & CHALLENGES

To Catch a Credit Card Thief

Imagine a computer technology that could find relationships among hundreds of unrelated variables and, in the process, recognize patterns, make associations, generalize about new problems, and even learn from the experience. This technology, which roughly mimics the activity of the human brain, is currently operational in the form of *neural networks*. Not surprisingly, companies that have incorporated these networks into their computer systems are already experiencing significant productivity gains.

Neural network chips will soon be part of all computers. Over the next five years, neural network chips not only will be integrated into every PC but will also control the ordinary tasks of everyday life, including microwave cookery (the oven will know how long to cook a chicken without being told) and balancing the shifting load in a washing machine.

Meanwhile, banks and other credit card issuers are already using neural networks to detect credit card fraud. Before the development of neural networks, companies relied on specialized computer programs to detect sudden, obvious changes in cardholders' spending patterns.

For example, a cardholder who normally purchased no more than $500 at a time would be notified if thousands of dollars in jewellery and furs were suddenly charged to the account. The relatively crude nature of these early systems often created more problems than solutions, however. Computers often flagged innocent cardholders as well as those who had lost their cards. Consumers who may have altered their spending habits even slightly were notified, a practice that annoyed many and wasted the time and resources of fraud detectors.

Faced with an inefficient system, one bank began using a neural network. Its old system had alerted it to as many as 1000 potential frauds each day (many of which were false alarms), but the neural network flagged only about 100—each of which was likely to signal an actual case of fraud. Using the neural network, bank personnel can now focus on fewer cases and complete investigations within hours rather than days. In one case, the bank notified a customer that her credit card has been stolen only hours after the theft had taken place and before she realized that it was gone.

Visa
www.visa.com

- Visa, for instance, has already modified the software used at its processing centres and can now attach a special "transaction identifier" to every transaction. This digital code stays with the transaction from the time the consumer uses the card until the time everyone in the system has been paid. Visa says that the number of erroneous charges has already been greatly reduced.

- MasterCard is experimenting with real-time auditing of charges filed by merchants: Every transaction will be completed as soon as it is made rather than, as now, at the end of the day with 20 million others. Merchants will be paid more quickly, and chances of both error and fraud will be reduced significantly.[2]

Second, credit cards are extremely profitable for issuing companies. Profits derive from two sources:

1. Some cards charge annual fees to holders. All charge interest on unpaid balances. Depending on the issuer, cardholders pay interest rates ranging from 11 to 20 percent.

2. Merchants who accept credit cards pay fees to card issuers. Depending on the merchant's agreement with the issuer, 2 to 5 percent of total credit-sales dollars goes to card issuers.

Annually, more than 25 million cards are used in Canada, 28 million in the United Kingdom, and over 1 billion in the U.S. The accompanying problems are international in scope. The number of cards issued in Japan, for instance, doubled (to 166 million) from 1985 to 1990—and so did the number of delinquencies. Many younger Japanese have incurred large debts by using credit cards to purchase high-ticket items like travel packages and automobiles. In South Korea, because heavy spending by young people is contributing to higher inflation, the finance minister has actually curbed the issuance of credit cards: No more cards can be issued to college students, to people younger than 20, or to workers holding jobs less than one year.[3]

■ THE CANADIAN FINANCIAL SYSTEM

The financial system is central to business firms in Canada. A financial system is made up of organizations and individuals who are sources and users of funds, and/or who help funds flow from sources to users. (See Figure 16.1.) People or organizations with surplus funds will want to earn a return on them. An individual may put his or her money into a savings deposit, buy a bond or a life insurance policy, or invest in the stock market. A business firm may deposit its money in a bank in the short term, buy treasury bills, or buy long-term securities. Charitable organizations and governments may also have surplus funds they wish to invest for certain periods of time.

All people and organizations are users of funds. Sometimes they are unable to raise all the funds they require from personal or internal sources. Money must then be raised from other people or institutions that have surplus funds. Individuals borrow money for certain purposes. Business firms raise money to finance projects, as do governments.

Financial institutions facilitate the flow of funds from sources to users. Their services are important both to organizations that have surplus funds to invest and to those that are in a deficit position and must raise funds.

Financial Intermediaries

There are a variety of financial intermediaries in Canada. They vary in size, in importance, in the types of sources they appeal to, in the form of the claim they give to sources of funds, in the users they supply credit to, and in the type of claim they make against the users of funds.

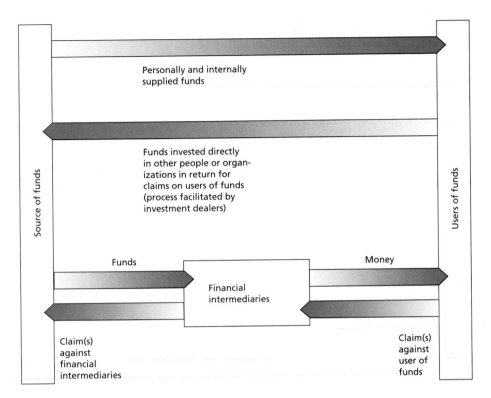

FIGURE 16.1
Sources of funds, users of funds, financial intermediaries, and investment dealers.

Until recently, the financial community in Canada was divided rather clearly into four distinct legal areas. Often called the "four financial pillars," they were: (1) chartered banks; (2) alternate banks, such as trust companies and *caisses populaires* or credit unions; (3) life insurance companies and other specialized lending and saving intermediaries, such as factors, finance companies, venture capital firms, mutual funds, and pension funds; and (4) investment dealers. We will discuss the role of these four financial divisions in a moment, but it is important to understand that so many changes have taken place in the financial services industry that the differences across the four divisions are now very blurred.

The crumbling of the four financial pillars began in 1980 when several changes were made to the *Bank Act*. The process accelerated when additional changes were made in 1987 and 1992. Canadian banks, for example, are now permitted to own securities dealers (in 1996, the Royal Bank purchased investment dealer Richardson Greenshields); they are also permitted to sell commercial paper and to own insurance companies (although they are not allowed to sell insurance in their own bank branches). Banks have also established subsidiaries to sell mutual funds.

The changes to the *Bank Act* have also allowed subsidiaries of U.S. banks to set up business in Canada, and over 40 of them have done so. In 1997, legislation was changed again to allow *branches* of U.S. banks to conduct business in Canada.

Trust companies have declined in importance during the last few years, and many smaller trust companies have been bought by banks or insurance companies. The largest trust company—Canada Trust—now offers services that are similar to those offered by banks. Insurance companies are facing increased challenges since banks can now sell insurance. The mutual fund business is booming and has created many new jobs during the last decade.

All these significant changes must be kept in mind as we now turn to a discussion of the four financial pillars of the Canadian economy.

Canada Trust
www.canadatrust.com

■FINANCIAL PILLAR #1—CHARTERED BANKS

chartered bank
A privately owned, profit-seeking firm that serves individuals, nonbusiness organizations, and businesses as a financial intermediary.

A **chartered bank** is a privately owned, profit-seeking firm that serves individuals, non-business organizations, and businesses as a financial intermediary. Chartered banks offer chequing and savings accounts, make loans, and provide many other services to their customers. They are the main source of short-term loans for business firms.

Chartered banks are the largest and most important financial institution in Canada. They offer a unique service. Their liability instruments (the claims against their assets) are generally accepted by the public and by business as money or as legal tender. Initially, these liability instruments took the form of bank notes issued by individual banks. The *Bank Act* amendments of 1944 removed the right to issue bank notes.

Canada has a branch banking system. Unlike the United States, where there are hundreds of banks, each with a few branches, in Canada there are only a few banks, each with hundreds of branches.

The 1980 *Bank Act* requires Schedule A banks to be Canadian-owned and have no more than 10 percent of voting shares controlled by a single interest. It also permits Schedule B banks, which may be domestically owned banks that do not meet the 10 percent limit or may be foreign-controlled. Schedule B banks are initially limited to one main office and one branch. Since the passing of the Act, several foreign banks have set up Schedule B subsidiaries. The Act limits foreign-controlled banks to deposits that do not exceed 8 percent of the total domestic assets of all banks in Canada.

The five largest Schedule A banks account for about 90 percent of total bank assets. Some of them also have branches in other countries. There are thousands of branch bank offices in Canada, about one for every 3300 people.

Services Offered by Banks

The banking business today is a highly competitive industry. No longer is it enough for banks to accept deposits and make loans. Most, for example, now offer bank-issued credit cards and safe-deposit boxes. In addition, many offer pension, trust, international, and financial advice, and electronic money transfer.

Pension Services. Most banks help customers establish savings plans for retirement. Banks serve as financial intermediaries by receiving funds and investing them as directed by customers. They also provide customers with information on investment possibilities.

trust services
The management of funds left in the bank's trust.

Trust Services. Many banks offer **trust services**—the management of funds left "in the bank's trust." In return for a fee, the trust department will perform such tasks as making your monthly bill payments and managing your investment portfolio. Trust departments also manage the estates of deceased persons.

International Services. The three main international services offered by banks are *currency exchange*, *letters of credit*, and *banker's acceptances*. Suppose, for example, that a Canadian company wants to buy a product from a French supplier. For a fee, it can use one or more of three services offered by its bank:

letter of credit
A promise by a bank to pay money to a business firm if certain conditions are met.

banker's acceptance
Promises that the bank will pay a specified amount of money at a future date.

1. It can exchange Canadian dollars for French francs at a Canadian bank and then pay the French supplier in francs.
2. It can pay its bank to issue a **letter of credit**—a promise by the bank to pay the French firm a certain amount if specified conditions are met.
3. It can pay its bank to draw up a **banker's acceptance**, which promises that the bank will pay some specified amount at a future date.

A banker's acceptance requires payment by a particular date; letters of credit are payable only after certain conditions are met. The French supplier, for example, may not be paid until shipping documents prove that the merchandise has been shipped from France.

Financial Advice.   Many banks, both large and small, help their customers manage their money. Depending on the customer's situation, the bank may recommend different investment opportunities. The recommended mix might include guaranteed investment certificates, mutual funds, stocks, and bonds. Today, bank advertisements often stress the role of banks as financial advisers.

Electronic Funds Transfer.   Chartered banks and some other financial institutions now use electronic funds transfer (EFT) to provide many basic financial services. **Electronic funds transfer** combines computer and communication technology to transfer funds or information into, from, within, and among financial institutions. Examples include the following:

- Automated teller machines (ATMs), or 24-hour tellers, are electronic terminals that let you bank at almost any time of day or night. Generally, you insert a special card and enter your own secret identification number to withdraw cash, make deposits, or transfer funds between accounts.

- Pay-by-phone systems let you telephone your financial institution and instruct it to pay certain bills or to transfer funds between accounts merely by pushing the proper buttons on your phone.

- Direct deposits or withdrawals allow you to authorize in advance specific, regular deposits and withdrawals. You can arrange to have paycheques and social assistance cheques automatically deposited and recurring expenses, such as insurance premiums and utility bills, automatically paid.

- Point-of-sale transfers let you pay for retail purchases with your debit card. A **debit card** is a type of plastic money that immediately reduces the balance in the user's bank account when it is used. For example, if you use a debit card at a grocery store, the clerk simply runs the card through the machine and asks you to punch in a personal identification number on a keypad next to the cash register. The price of the groceries is then deducted electronically from your chequing account, and money moves from your chequing account to the grocery store's account.

- The so-called **smart card** is a credit card-sized computer that can be programmed with "electronic money." Also known as "electronic purses" or "stored-value cards," smart cards have existed for nearly a decade. Shoppers in Europe and Asia are the most avid users, holding the majority of the 33 million cards in circulation at the beginning of 1995.[4]

  Why are smart cards increasing in popularity today? For one thing, the cost of producing them has fallen dramatically—from as much as $10 to as little as $1. Convenience is equally important, notes Donald J. Gleason, president of Electronic Payment Services' Smart Card Enterprise division. "What consumers want," Gleason contends, "is convenience, and if you look at cash, it's really quite inconvenient."[5]

  Smart cards can be loaded with money at ATM machines or, with special telephone hookups, even at home. After using your card to purchase an item, you can then check an electronic display to see how much money your card has left. Analysts predict that in the near future, smart cards will function as much more than electronic purses. For example, travel industry experts predict that people will soon book travel plans at home on personal computers and then transfer their reservations onto their smart cards. The cards will then serve as airline tickets and boarding passes. As an added benefit, they will allow travellers to avoid waiting in lines at car rental agencies and hotel front desks.

electronic funds transfer (EFT)
A combination of computer and communications technology that transfers funds or information into, from, within, and among financial institutions.

debit card
A type of plastic money that immediately on use reduces the balance in the user's bank account and transfers it to the store's account.

smart card
Credit card-sized computer that can be programmed with "electronic money."

Automated Teller Machines (ATMs) have revolutionized the way we do our banking. Now we have access to our money almost everywhere we go—shopping malls, grocery stores, even roadside "minibanks."

E-cash
Money that moves among consumers and businesses via digital electronic transmissions.

• A new, revolutionary world of electronic money has begun to emerge with the rapid growth of the Internet. Electronic money, known as **E-cash**, is money that moves along multiple channels of consumers and businesses via digital electronic transmissions. E-cash moves outside the established network of banks, cheques, and paper currency. How does E-cash work? Traditional currency is used to buy electronic funds, which are downloaded over phone lines into a PC or a portable "electronic wallet" that can store and transmit E-cash. E-cash is purchased from any company that issues (sells) it, including banks. When shopping online—say, to purchase jewellery—a shopper sends digital money to the merchant instead of using traditional cash, cheques, or credit cards. Businesses can purchase supplies and services electronically from any merchant that accepts E-cash. E-cash flows from the buyer's into the seller's E-cash funds, which are instantaneously updated and stored on a microchip.

Although E-cash transactions are cheaper than handling cheques and the paper records involved with conventional money, there are some potential problems. Hackers, for example, may break into E-cash systems and drain them instantaneously. Moreover, if the issuer's computer system crashes, it is conceivable that money "banked" in memory may be lost forever. Finally, regulation and control of E-cash systems remains largely nonexistent; there is virtually none of the protection that covers government-controlled money systems.[6]

Figure 16.2 summarizes the services that chartered banks offer. Banks are chartered by the federal government and are closely regulated when they provide these services. The box "Consumer Satisfaction with Banks" compares Canadian and U.S. banks.

Bank Deposits

Chartered banks provide a financial intermediary service by accepting deposits and making loans with this money. Banks make various types of loans to businesses. When applying for a business loan, it is wise for the manager to remember that the banker is interested in making money for the bank through the loan. The banker is also interested in how the loan will be repaid and how it will be secured. A brief written statement accompanied by a cash-flow analysis is a useful approach when applying for a loan.

Long- and short-term loans

Automated teller machines

Safeguard property entrusted to it

Debit and credit cards

Savings accounts

Guaranteed investment certificates

Chequing accounts

Buy and sell securities for customer accounts

Exchange Canadian dollars for foreign currencies

Exchange foreign currencies for Canadian dollars

Advise customers on financial matters

FIGURE 16.2
Examples of services provided by many chartered banks and trust companies.

TRENDS & CHALLENGES

Consumer Satisfaction with Banks: Canada vs. the U.S.

How satisfied are you with the Canadian banking system? Bank-bashing is the second most popular sport in Canada after politician-bashing. Consumers feel that even while banks are making multibillion dollar profits, they provide poor service and do a poor job of listening to customer concerns. But bank customers are even less happy in the U.S.

A survey by the Gallup Organization and *American Banker* magazine found that:

- only slightly more than half the respondents were satisfied with their bank
- the banks' most desirable customers—young, university-educated people with above-average incomes—are the most unhappy
- the larger the bank, the less satisfied the customers

Why would this be so? One reason is competition. Even though there are far more banks in the U.S. than in Canada, there is typically less competition in a given U.S. market than there is in Canada. Each of the "Big 6" banks in Canada competes in virtually every market, but in the U.S., a given market may have only two or three banks. This means, in effect, that service fees are higher in the U.S. because there is less competition there. The service fees charged for ATMs are illustrative.

Consumer groups in the U.S. are on the warpath over rapidly rising ATM fees. Access to ATMs had been free until 1997, but now most banks—and particularly the large ones—are charging users on both ends of the transaction. Customers pay about $1.25 to their own bank every time they use another institution's ATM, but they also pay up to $2.50 to the machine's owner. That is three or four times higher than what a Canadian customer would pay for a similar transaction.

Other differences exist between the U.S. and Canadian banking systems. For example, Canadians expect that if they write or cash a cheque, it will clear overnight, but in the U.S., it may take a week to clear. And other services that Canadians take for granted—currency exchange or the ability to pay bills at ATMs—may not even be available at a given bank in the U.S.

All of these specific issues are reasons that U.S. customers are unhappy with their banks. But perhaps the most fundamental advantage of the Canadian banking system is its stability. Since the early 1980s, there have been only two bank failures in Canada, while there have been 1600 bank failures in the U.S.

chequable deposit
A chequing account.

term deposit
Money that remains with the bank for a period of time with interest paid to the depositor.

One type of deposit a customer can make in a bank is a chequable, or demand, deposit. A **chequable deposit** is a chequing account. Customers who deposit coins, paper currency, or other cheques in their chequing accounts can write cheques against the balance in their accounts. Their banks must honour these cheques immediately; this is why chequing accounts are also called demand deposits.

The other type of deposit a customer can make in a chartered bank is a term deposit. A **term deposit** is one that remains with the bank for a period of time. Interest is paid to depositors for the use of their funds. There are two types of term deposits. The most popular is the regular passbook savings account. Although banks can require notice before withdrawals can be made, they seldom do. These accounts are intended primarily for small individual savers and non-profit organizations.

Another type of term deposit is the guaranteed investment certificate. This deposit is made for a specified period of time ranging from 28 days to several years. These certificates are available to all savers. The interest rate paid on a guaranteed investment certificate is higher than that paid on a regular savings account, but a depositor must give up interest if the certificate is cashed in before its maturity date.

Bank Loans

Banks are the major source of short-term loans for business. Although banks make long-term loans to some firms, they prefer to specialize in providing short-term funds to finance inventories and accounts receivable. Many loans made to businesses are secured by inventory under section 83 of the *Bank Act*. Section 86 of the *Bank Act* allows banks to make loans against the security of bills of lading and warehouse receipts. Section 82 allows banks to take as security hydrocarbons in store or under the ground.

A secured loan is backed by collateral such as accounts receivable or a life insurance policy. If the borrower cannot repay the loan, the bank sells the collateral. An unsecured loan is backed only by the borrower's promise to repay it. Only the most creditworthy borrowers can get unsecured loans.

prime rate of interest
The lowest rate charged to borrowers.

Borrowers pay interest on their loans. Large firms with excellent credit records pay the prime rate of interest. The **prime rate of interest** is the lowest rate charged to borrowers. This rate changes from time to time owing to changes in the demand for and supply of loanable funds as well as to policies of the Bank of Canada. The so-called "Big 6" Canadian banks (Royal Bank, CIBC, Bank of Montreal, Bank of Nova Scotia, Toronto-Dominion, and National Bank of Canada) typically act in concert with respect to the prime rate.

National Bank of Canada
www.nbc.ca

Banks as Creators of Money

In the course of their activities, financial institutions provide a special service to the economy—they create money. This is not to say that they mint bills and coins. Rather, by taking in deposits and making loans, they *expand the money supply*. We will first look at how this expansion process works, assuming that banks have a **reserve requirement**, that is, that they must keep a portion of their chequable deposits in vault cash or as deposits with the Bank of Canada. (This reserve requirement was dropped in 1991, and the implications of this change are described later.)

reserve requirement
The requirement (until 1991) that banks keep a portion of their chequable deposits in vault cash or as deposits with the Bank of Canada.

Suppose you saved $100, took it to a bank, and opened a chequing account. Some portion of your $100 is likely to stay in your account, so your bank can earn interest by lending some of it to other borrowers. Let's assume that there is a reserve requirement, and that it is 10 percent. Your bank must therefore keep $10 of your $100 deposit in reserve, so it has only $90 to lend.

Now suppose a person named Jennifer Leclerc borrows $90 from your bank. She now has $90 added to her chequing account. Assume that she writes a cheque for $90 payable to Canadian Tire. Canadian Tire's bank ends up with a $90 deposit, and that bank is also required to keep $9 in reserve. It therefore has $81 to lend out to someone else.

This process of deposit expansion can continue as shown in Figure 16.3. As you can see, your original deposit of $100 could result in an increase of $1000 in new deposits for all banks in the system. But, what happens if there is no reserve requirement? At the extreme, it means that banks could (theoretically) create infinite amounts of money because they don't have to keep any in reserve. But banks will not do this because it is risky. So, in practice, the dropping of the reserve requirement simply means that banks will be able to create more money than they did when there was a reserve requirement.

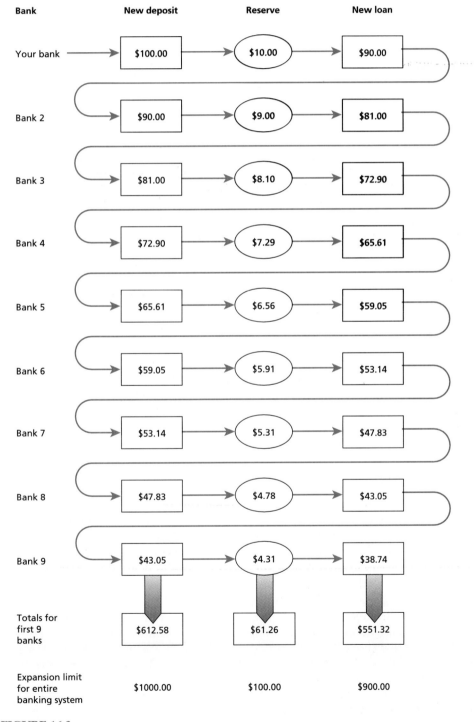

FIGURE 16.3
How the chartered banking system creates money.

Why was the reserve requirement changed? Partly because banks claimed that in the new, deregulated financial services industry it was going to be difficult for them to compete with trust and insurance companies, who have no reserve requirements.

Even though the reserve requirement has disappeared, the chartered banks must still keep clearing balances with the Bank of Canada, which can increase or decrease these balances and thereby continue to influence interest rates as before.

The change in reserve requirements could cost the federal government millions of dollars each year in lost interest; it will also lead to increased bank profits or lower loan rates to consumers, or some combination of both.[7]

Other Changes in Banking

Toronto-Dominion Bank
http://www.tdbank.ca/tdbank

Fundamental changes in addition to those already described are taking place in banking. For example, deregulation has caused banks to shift away from their historical role as intermediaries between depositors and borrowers. Canada's banks are diversifying to provide a wider array of financial products to their clients. Training bankers to be effective in this environment is necessary. For example, over 100 executives at Toronto-Dominion Bank attended a Harvard University course that taught them to think like investment bankers. The Bank of Montreal conducted a similar course for over 400 executives.

In the last few years, large companies have reduced their use of bank loans. To compensate for this loss, banks are setting up money market operations. For example, until deregulation, only securities firms were allowed to sell commercial paper (see Chapter 17), but banks expect to dominate in this area before too long. (Commercial paper is usually issued by blue-chip companies that pay a fee to investment dealers or banks to sell the security.) Banks have been allowed to sell commercial paper since 1987, when deregulation opened up this possibility. The Bank of Montreal and the Toronto-Dominion Bank have been the most active in this new market.

In Canada, about 200 companies have a credit rating good enough for commercial paper. Banks want to use commercial paper more because they do not have to keep capital reserves on hand for commercial paper as they do for acceptances.

Changes are also taking place in banking because consumers are no longer content to simply keep money in a bank when they can get more for it elsewhere. Banks are responding by selling a growing array of corporate and government securities through their branches.

All of this activity is transforming the profit base of banks. In the past, they made most of their money from the spread between interest rates paid to depositors and the rates charged on loans. Investment banking, on the other hand, is fee-based. Banks are making a larger proportion of their profits from fees, and this is blurring the traditional boundary between banks and securities firms.

Another change concerns international banking. Because U.S. and other foreign banks are now allowed to do business in Canada, Canada's banks are going to experience increased competition. Canadian banks are responding with a variety of tactics, including attempts to merge with one another so they can afford the millions in technology investment that will be needed to remain competitive.[8] In 1998, for example, the Canadian Imperial Bank of Commerce and the Toronto-Dominion Bank tried to merge, as did the Royal Bank and Bank of Montreal. But both of these mergers were blocked by the federal government because it feared the mergers would reduce competition and harm consumers. Banks are also trying other things to be more competitive, like cooperating to spread their fixed costs. Syncor Services, for example, is a joint venture between three banks that provides cheque-clearing services across Canada.[9] The Competitive threat from one foreign bank is decribed in the box "Discount Banking: Will it Work?"

T R E N D S C H A L L E N G E S

Discount Banking: Will It Work?

International Nederlanden Groep (ING) is a large Dutch firm (1996 profits of $2.38 billion) that has decided to use Canada as a test market for a new concept: discount banking. One of its banking subsidiaries, called ING Direct, is off to a good start. It hopes to have 35 000 customers and more than $250 million in deposits in its first year.

How does ING propose to achieve these goals? By paying higher interest on deposits than its competitors, by not levying fees or service charges as the Big 6 Canadian banks do, and by charging lower rates on loans than traditional banks do. How can it do all these things and still earn a profit? By using *branchless banking*, and by relying on the latest information processing technologies to serve customers.

A study by the Canadian Imperial Bank of Commerce showed that the cost of paying a bill in person at a bank branch is $1.29; paying the same bill by Internet costs $0.15. If ING has no branches, it may be able to develop a huge cost advantage over Canadian banks. In simple terms, ING is a high-volume, low-margin bank—the Wal-Mart of banking, if you will.

How can ING be sure that Canadians will do business with a bank that has no branches? They can't, but they know that Canadians are famous for their willingness to embrace new technologies such as e-mail, debit cards, and automated teller machines. They are banking on this willingness (no pun intended) to be competitive in the Canadian market. ING's customers will be able to carry out banking transactions with ING without having to go to a bank branch.

If ING can make it in Canada, that will mean that other foreign financial institutions may also get interested. So, Canadian banks aren't concerned just about ING. They are also going to have to contend with giant U.S. financial companies such as Wells Fargo Bank, which offers small business loans to Canadians even though it has no branches in Canada. All the necessary work to complete the transaction is done by direct mail, the Internet, and telemarketing.

Will the new technologies allow foreign banks to enter Canada and put real pressure on the Big 6 Canadian banks? Time will tell.

The Bank of Canada

The **Bank of Canada**, formed in 1935, is Canada's central bank. It has a crucial role to play in managing the Canadian economy and in regulating certain aspects of chartered bank operations.

The Bank of Canada is managed by a board of governors composed of a governor, a deputy governor, and 12 directors appointed from different regions of Canada. The directors, with cabinet approval, appoint the governor and deputy governor. The deputy minister of finance is also a non-voting member of the board. Between meetings of the board, normally held eight times a year, an executive committee acts for the board. This committee is composed of the governor, the deputy governor, two directors, and the deputy minister of finance. The executive committee meets at least once a week.

Bank of Canada
Canada's central bank; formed in 1935.

Bank of Canada
www.bank-banque-canada.ca

Operation of the Bank of Canada. The Bank of Canada plays an important role in managing the money supply in Canada. (See Figure 16.4.) If the Bank of Canada wants to increase the money supply, it can buy government securities. The people selling these bonds deposit the proceeds in their banks. These deposits increase banks' reserves and their willlingness to make loans. The Bank of Canada can also lower the bank rate; this action will cause increased demand for loans from businesses and households because these customers borrow more money when interest rates drop.

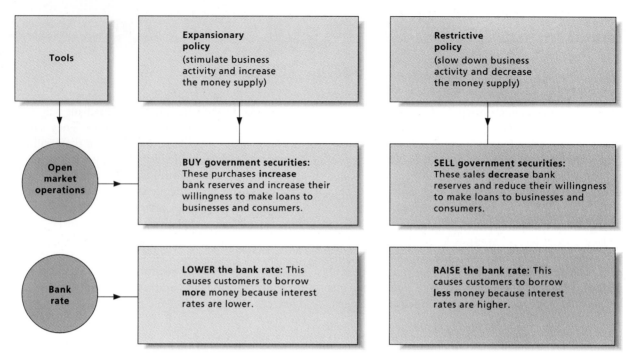

FIGURE 16.4
Bank of Canada monetary policy actions.

If the Bank of Canada wants to decrease the money supply, it can sell government securities. People spend money to buy bonds, and these withdrawals bring down banks' reserves and reduce their ability to make loans. The Bank of Canada can also raise the bank rate; this action will cause decreased demand for loans from businesses and households because these customers borrow less money when interest rates rise.

Member Bank Borrowing from the Bank of Canada.   The Bank of Canada is the lender of last resort for chartered banks. The rate at which chartered banks can borrow from the Bank of Canada is called the **bank**, or rediscount, **rate**. It serves as the basis for establishing the chartered banks' prime interest rates. By raising the bank rate, the Bank of Canada depresses the demand for money; by lowering it, the demand for money increases. In practice, chartered banks seldom have to borrow from the Bank of Canada. However, the bank rate is an important instrument of monetary policy as a determinant of interest rates.

In 1985, two Schedule A Alberta-based banks, Canadian Commercial Bank and Northland Bank, failed. These were the first bank failures in Canada since the Home Bank failed in 1923. Because of these failures, some smaller regional banks had difficulty maintaining their deposit bases. To ease this banking crisis, the Bank of Canada lent over $4 billion to chartered banks.

bank rate
The rate at which chartered banks can borrow from the Bank of Canada.

■ FINANCIAL PILLAR #2—ALTERNATE BANKS

Trust Companies

trust company
Safeguards funds and estates entrusted to it; may also serve as trustee, transfer agent, and registrar for corporations.

Another financial intermediary that serves individuals and businesses is the alternate, or near, bank: the trust company. A **trust company** safeguards property—funds and estates—entrusted to it; it may also serve as trustee, transfer agent, and registrar for corporations and provide other services.

A corporation selling bonds to many investors appoints a trustee, usually a trust company, to protect the bondholders' interests. A trust company can also serve as a transfer agent and registrar for corporations. A transfer agent records changes in ownership of a corporation's shares of stock. A registrar certifies to the investing public that stock issues are correctly stated and comply with the corporate charter. Other services include preparing and issuing dividend cheques to shareholders and serving as trustee for employee profit-sharing funds. Trust companies also accept deposits and pay interest on them.

Credit Unions/Caisses Populaires

Credit unions (called *caisses populaires* in Quebec) are also alternate banks. They are important to business because they lend money to consumers to buy durable goods such as cars and furniture. They also lend money to businesses. **Credit unions** and *caisses populaires* are cooperative savings and lending associations formed by a group with common interests. Members (owners) can add to their savings accounts by authorizing deductions from their paycheques or by making direct deposits. They can borrow short-term, long-term, or mortgage funds from the credit union. Credit unions also invest substantial amounts of money in corporate and government securities.

credit union
Cooperative savings and lending association formed by a group with common interests.

■ FINANCIAL PILLAR #3—SPECIALIZED LENDING AND SAVINGS INTERMEDIARIES

Life Insurance Companies

An important source of funds for individuals, nonbusiness organizations, and businesses is the life insurance company. A **life insurance company** is a mutual or stock company that shares risk with its policyholders in return for payment of a premium. It lends some of the money it collects from premiums to borrowers. Life insurance companies are substantial investors in real estate mortgages and in corporate and government bonds. Next to chartered banks, they are the largest financial intermediaries in Canada. We discuss insurance companies in more detail in Appendix II.

life insurance company
A mutual or stock company that shares risk with its policyholders for payment of premiums.

Factoring Companies

An important source of short-term funds for many firms is factoring companies. A **factoring company** (or factor) buys accounts receivable (amounts due from credit customers) from a firm. It pays less than the face value of the accounts but collects the face value of the accounts. The difference, minus the cost of doing business, is the factor's profit.

A firm that sells its accounts receivable to a factor without recourse shifts the risk of credit loss to the factor. If an account turns out to be uncollectable, the factor suffers the loss. However, a factor is a specialist in credit and collection activities. Using a factor may enable a business firm to expand sales beyond what would be practical without the factor. The firm trades accounts receivable for cash. The factor notifies the firm's customers to make their overdue payments to the factor.

factoring company
Buys accounts receivable from a firm for less than their face value, and then collects the face value of the receivables.

Financial Corporations

There are two types of financial corporations: sales finance companies and consumer finance companies.

A major source of credit for many firms and their customers is the sales finance company. A **sales finance company** specializes in financing installment purchases made

sales finance company
Specializes in financing installment purchases made by individuals or firms.

by individuals and firms. When you buy durable goods from a retailer on an installment plan with a sales finance company, the loan is made directly to you. The item itself serves as security for the loan. Sales finance companies enable many firms to sell on credit, even though the firms could not afford to finance credit sales on their own.

General Motors Acceptance Corporation (GMAC) is a sales finance company. It is a captive company because it exists to finance installment contracts resulting from sales made by General Motors. Industrial Acceptance Corporation is a large Canadian sales finance company.

Sales finance companies also finance installment sales to business firms. Many banks have installment loan departments.

An important source of credit for many consumers is the consumer finance company. A **consumer finance company** makes personal loans to consumers. Often the borrower pledges no security (collateral) for the loan. For larger loans, collateral may be required, such as a car or furniture.

These companies do not make loans to businesses but they do provide the financing that turns many people into actual paying customers. Household Finance Corporation is an example of a consumer finance company.

consumer finance company
Makes personal loans to consumers.

Venture Capital Firms

venture capital firm
Provides funds for new or expanding firms thought to have significant potential.

A **venture capital firm**, or development firm, will provide funds for new or expanding firms thought to have significant potential. Venture capital firms obtain their funds from initial capital subscriptions, from loans from other financial intermediaries, and from retained earnings.

Venture capital firms may provide either equity or debt funds to firms. Financing new, untested businesses is risky, so venture capital firms want to earn a higher-than-normal return on their investment. The ideal situation is an equity investment in a company that becomes very successful and experiences substantial increases in its stock value.

Pension Funds

pension fund
Accumulates money that will be paid out to plan subscribers in the future.

A **pension plan** accumulates money that will be paid out to plan subscribers at some time in the future. The money collected is invested in corporate stocks and bonds, government bonds, or mortgages until it is to be paid out.

■ FINANCIAL PILLAR #4—INVESTMENT DEALERS

Investment dealers (called stockbrokers or underwriters) perform two important financial functions. First, they are the primary distributors of new stock and bond issues (underwriting). Second, they facilitate secondary trading of stocks and bonds, both on stock exchanges and on over-the-counter stock and bond markets (the brokerage function). These functions are discussed in more detail in Chapter 18.

■ OTHER SOURCES OF FUNDS

Government Financial Institutions and Granting Agencies

Industrial Development Bank (IDB)
A subsidiary of the Bank of Canada created to make loans to business firms.

Federal Business Development Bank (FBDB)
Took over operation of the IDB in 1975; particularly active in lending money to small businesses.

In Canada, a number of government suppliers of funds are important to business. In general, they supply funds to new and/or growing companies. However, established firms can also use some of them.

The **Industrial Development Bank (IDB)**, a subsidiary of the Bank of Canada, was created to make loans to business firms. The **Federal Business Development Bank**

(FBDB) took over operation of the IDB in 1975. The IDB was set up to make term loans, primarily to smaller firms judged to have growth potential but unable to secure funds at reasonable terms from traditional sources. Its services were expanded by providing proportionally more equity financing and more management counselling services. The FBDB has been especially active in providing loans for small businesses.

A variety of provincial industrial development corporations provide funds to developing business firms in the hope that they will provide jobs in the province. These were discussed in Chapter 7.

The federal government's Export Development Corporation can finance and insure export sales for Canadian companies. The Canada Mortgage and Housing Corporation (CMHC) is involved in providing and guaranteeing mortgages. The CMHC is particularly important to the construction industry.

A number of federal and provincial programs are specifically designed to provide loans to agricultural operators. Most of these, with the exception of farm improvement loans that guarantee bank loans to farmers, are long-term loans for land purchase.

In addition to these activities, governments are involved in providing grants to business operations. For example, the federal government, through the Department of Regional Industrial Expansion (DRIE), gives grants for certain types of business expansion in designated areas of the country. Other federal government grants are available for activities such as new product development.

Export Development Corporation
www.edc.ca

Canada Mortgage & Housing Corp.
www.cmhc-schl.gc.ca

International Sources of Funds

Not all of the financing requirements of Canadian businesses and governments are met from within Canada. Foreign sources of funds are also important. The financial institutions of Canada play a role in facilitating the flow of funds into the country.

The Canadian capital market is one part of the international capital market. Canadian provinces borrow extensively in foreign markets such as those in London and in New York. Canadian corporations likewise find it attractive to borrow in foreign markets.

Foreign sources of funds have been significant to the economic development of Canada. Although many groups and individuals have expressed concern about foreign ownership of Canadian firms, projections of Canada's future capital requirements indicate that it will continue to need foreign sources of funds. Canadian financial institutions will continue to play a large role in making these funds available.

■ INTERNATIONAL BANKING AND FINANCE

Each nation tries to influence its currency exchange rates for economic advantage in international trade. The subsequent country-to-country transactions result in an *international payments process* that moves money among buyers and sellers on different continents.

Exchange Rates and International Trade

As we saw in both Chapters 4 and 12, every country's currency exchange rate affects its ability to buy and sell on the global market. The value of a given currency—say, the Canadian dollar—reflects the overall supply and demand for Canadian dollars both at home and abroad. This value, of course, changes with economic conditions. Worldwide, therefore, firms will watch those trends. What, for example, is the current exchange rate between their own currencies and that of Canada? Decisions about whether or not to do business in Canada will be affected by more or less favourable exchange rates. How do firms determine when rates are favourable?

The Law of One Price.   When a country's currency becomes *overvalued*, its exchange rate is higher than warranted by its economic conditions. Its high costs make it less competitive. Because its products are expensive to make and buy, fewer are purchased by other countries. The likely result is a *trade deficit*. In contrast, an *undervalued* currency means low costs and low prices. It attracts purchases by other countries, usually leading to a *trade surplus*.

law of one price
The principle that identical products should sell for the same price in all countries.

How do we know if a currency is overvalued or undervalued? One method involves a simple concept called the **law of one price**: the principle that identical products should sell for the same price in all countries. In other words, if the different prices of a Rolex watch in different countries were converted into a common currency, the common-denominator price should be the same everywhere.

But what if prices are not equal? In theory, the pursuit of profits should equalize them: Sellers in high-priced countries will have to reduce prices if they are to compete successfully and make profits. As prices adjust, so, too, should the exchange rates between different currencies until the Rolex can be purchased for the same price everywhere.

A simple example that illustrates over- and undervalued currencies is the "Big MacCurrencies," an index published in the British magazine *The Economist*. The "identical product" here is always McDonald's Big Mac, which is made locally in 68 countries. The first two columns in Table 16.1 list several countries and Big Mac prices in terms of local currencies. Each country's price is then converted into U.S. dollars (based on recent exchange rates). As you can see, while the Swiss price (SFr5.70) is most expensive, the Chinese yuan is the cheapest.

According to the Big Mac index, then, the Swiss franc is the most overvalued currency (against the U.S. dollar), while the Chinese yuan is the most undervalued. In theory, this means that you could buy Big Macs in China (using yuan) and resell them in Switzerland (for Swiss francs) at a handsome profit. In China, therefore, the demand for burgers would increase, driving the price up towards the higher prices in the other countries. In other words, the law of one price would set in. The index also indicates that the exchange rates of Greece, Taiwan, Chile, and Canada are slightly overvalued or undervalued against the U.S. dollar.[10]

Government Influences on Exchange Rates.   What happens when a currency becomes overvalued or undervalued? A nation's economic authorities may take action to correct its balance-of-payments conditions. Typically, they will *devalue* or *revalue* the nation's

■ **TABLE 16.1 The "Big Mac" Currency Index**

Country	Big Mac Prices in Local Currency	Big Mac Prices in Equivalent U.S. Dollars	Local Currency Overevaluation (+) or Undervaluation (–)
United States	$2.30	$2.30	
Switzerland	5.70 francs	3.96	+72%
Denmark	25.75 krone	3.85	+67
Argentina	3.60 pesos	3.60	+57
Belgium	109 francs	3.10	+35
S. Korea	2300 won	2.84	+24
Greece	620 drachma	2.47	+8
Taiwan	$62 Taiwanese	2.35	+2
Chile	948 pesos	2.28	-1
Canada	**$2.86 Canadian**	**2.06**	**-10**
Australia	$2.45 Australia	1.72	-25
Poland	3100 zloty	1.40	-40
China	9.00 yuan	1.03	-55

currency. The purpose of *devaluing*—as Mexico did in 1994—is to cause a decrease in the home country's exchange value. It will then be less expensive for other countries to buy the home country's products. As more of its products are purchased, the home country's payment deficit goes down. The purpose of revaluation is the reverse: to increase the exchange value and reduce the home country's payment surplus.

The International Payments Process

Now we know why a nation tries to control its balance of payments and what, at least in part, it can do about an unfavourable balance. Exactly how are payments made? Transactions among buyers and sellers in different countries are simplified through the services provided by their banks. For example, payments from buyers flow through a local bank that converts them from the local currency into the foreign currency of the seller. Likewise, the local bank receives and converts incoming money from the banks of foreign buyers. The *payments process* is shown in Figure 16.5.[11]

Step 1. A Canadian olive importer withdraws $1000 from its chequing account in order to buy olives from a Greek exporter. The local Canadian bank *converts* those dollars into Greek drachmas at the current exchange rate (230 drachmas per dollar).

Step 2. The Canadian bank sends the cheque for 230 000 drachmas (230 × 1000) to the exporter in Greece.

Steps 3 and 4. The exporter sends olives to its Canadian customer and deposits the cheque in its local Greek bank. While the exporter now has drachmas that can be spent in Greece, the importer has olives to sell in Canada.

At the same time, a separate transaction is being made between a Canadian machine exporter and a Greek olive oil producer. This time, the importer/ exporter roles are reversed between the two countries: The Greek firm needs to *import* a $1000 olive oil press from Canada.

Steps 5 and 6. Drachmas (230 000) withdrawn from a local Greek bank account are converted into $1000 Canadian and sent via cheque to the Canadian exporter.

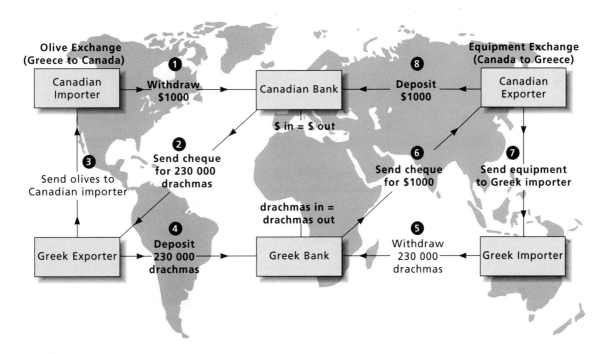

FIGURE 16.5
The international payments process.

Steps 7 and 8. The olive oil press is sent to the Greek importer, and the importer's cheque is deposited in the Canadian exporter's local bank account.

In this example, trade between the two countries is in *balance*: Money inflows and outflows are equal for both countries. When such a balance occurs, *money does not actually have to flow between the two countries*. Within each bank, the dollars spent by local importers offset the dollars received by local exporters. In effect, therefore, the dollars have simply flowed from Canadian importers to Canadian exporters. Likewise, the drachmas have moved from Greek exporters to Greek importers.

Interbank Trading.   To get a true picture, however, we must multiply this simple illustration by the huge number of daily transactions that take place between countries. Obviously, this system of trade involves banks (or other financial institutions) that buy and sell foreign currencies for their customers. Among these currency trades, the U.S. dollar was by far the most active currency, being involved in 89 percent of all transactions. Next most active were the German mark (34 percent), the Japanese yen (23 percent), and the British pound (9 percent).

International Bank Structure

There is no worldwide banking system that is comparable, in terms of policymaking and regulatory power, to the system of any single industrialized nation. Rather, worldwide banking stability relies on a loose structure of agreements among individual countries or groups of countries.

The World Bank and the IMF.   Two United Nations agencies, the World Bank and the International Monetary Fund, help to finance international trade. Unlike true banks, the **World Bank** (technically the International Bank for Reconstruction and Development) actually provides only a very limited scope of services. For instance, it funds national improvements by making loans to build roads, schools, power plants, and hospitals. The resulting improvements eventually enable borrowing countries to increase productive capacity and international trade.

The **International Monetary Fund (IMF)** is a group of some 150 nations that have combined their resources for the following purposes:

- To promote the stability of exchange rates
- To provide temporary, short-term loans to member countries
- To encourage members to cooperate on international monetary issues
- To encourage development of a system for international payments

World Bank
www.worldbank.org

International Monetary Fund
www.imf.org

World Bank
United Nations agency that provides a limited scope of financial services, such as funding national improvements in undeveloped countries.

International Monetary Fund (IMF)
United Nations agency consisting of about 150 nations who have combined resources to promote stable exchange rates, provide temporary short-term loans, and serve other purposes.

SUMMARY OF LEARNING OBJECTIVES

1. **Define *money* and identify the different forms it takes in the nation's money supply.** Any item that is portable, divisible, durable, and stable satisfies the four basic characteristics of *money*. Money also serves three functions: it is a medium of exchange, a store of value, and a unit of account. The nation's money supply is often determined by two measures. *M-1* includes liquid (or spendable) forms of money: currency (bills and coins), demand deposits, and other "chequable" deposits (such as chequing accounts and ATM withdrawals). *M-2* includes M-1 plus items which cannot be directly spent but which can be easily converted to spendable forms: time deposits, money market funds, and savings deposits. *Credit* must also be considered as a factor in the money supply.

2. **Describe the different kinds of *financial institutions* that make up the Canadian financial system and explain the services they offer.** The financial intermediaries that form the "four financial pillars" in Canada are chartered banks, alternate banks, life insurance companies, and investment dealers. The chartered banks, which are at the heart of our financial system, are the most important source of short-term funds for business firms. The chartered banking system creates money in the form of expanding demand deposits. The four kinds of financial institutions offer services like financial advice and brokerage services, electronic funds transfer, pension and trust services, and lending of money.

3. **Explain how banks create money and identify the means by which they are regulated.** By taking in deposits and making loans, banks create money, or more accurately, they expand the money supply. The overall supply of money is controlled by the Bank of Canada.

4. **Explain the functions of the *Bank of Canada* and describe the tools it uses to control the money supply.** The Bank of Canada manages the Canadian economy, controls the money supply, and regulates certain aspects of chartered banking operations. If the Bank of Canada wants to increase the money supply, it can buy government securities or lower the bank rate. If it wants to decrease the money supply, it can sell government securities or increase the bank rate.

5. **Identify ways in which the financial industry is changing**. The clear divisions between the activities of the "four financial pillars" are becoming less obvious. For example, deregulation has allowed banks to begin selling commercial paper. Other financial intermediaries are also beginning to get involved in new financial activities. For example, life insurance companies are starting to take over trust companies so they can get a foothold in the trust business.

6. **Understand the importance of international banking and finance in an increasingly global financial system.** Electronic technologies now permit speedy global financial transactions to support the growing importance of international finance. Country-to-country transactions are conducted according to an international payment process that moves money among buyers and sellers in different nations. Each nation tries to influence its currency exchange rates to gain advantage in international trade. For example, if a nation's currency is overvalued, a higher exchange rate usually results in a trade deficit. Conversely, undervalued currencies can attract buyers and create trade surpluses. Governments may act to influence exchange rates by devaluing or revaluing their national currencies (that is, by decreasing or increasing them). Devalued currencies make it less expensive for other countries to buy the home country's products.

STUDY QUESTIONS AND EXERCISES

Review Questions

1. What is money? What are its ideal characteristics?
2. What are the components of M-1? Of M-2?
3. Describe the structure and operation of the Bank of Canada.
4. List and describe the sources of short-term funds for business firms.

Analysis Questions

5. What kinds of changes in banking are shifting banks away from their historical role?
6. Do we really need all the different types of financial institutions we have in Canada? Could we make do with just chartered banks? Why or why not?
7. Should credit cards be counted in the money supply? Why or why not?

8. Should chartered banks be regulated or should market forces be allowed to set the money supply? Defend your answer.

Application Exercises

9. Beginning with a $1000 deposit and assuming a reserve requirement of 15 percent, trace the amount of money created by the banking system after five lending cycles.

10. Interview the manager of a local chartered bank. Identify the ways in which the Bank of Canada helps the bank and the ways in which it limits the bank.

BUILDING YOUR BUSINESS SKILLS

Goal

To help students evaluate the risks and rewards associated with excessive credit card use.

Situation

Suppose that you've been out of school for a year and are now working in your first job. Your annual $30 000 salary is enough to support your apartment, car, and the basic necessities of life, but the luxuries are still out of reach. You pay cash for everything until one day you get a preapproved credit card solicitation in the mail, which offers you a $1500 line of credit. You decide to take the offer and begin charging purchases. Within a year, five other credit card companies have contacted you, and you accumulate a total credit card line of $12 000.

Method

Step 1: Working with three or four classmates, evaluate the advantages and dangers inherent in this situation, both to the consumer and to credit card issuers. To address this issue, research the current percentage of credit card delinquencies and rate of personal bankruptcies. Find out, for example, how these rates compare with those in previous years. In addition, research the profitability of the credit card business.

Step 2: Evaluate the different methods that credit card companies use to attract new customers. Specifically, look at the following practices:

- Sending unsolicited, preapproved credit card applications to consumers with questionable and even poor credit
- Offering large credit lines to consumers who pay only monthly minimums
- Lowering interest rates on accounts as a way of encouraging revolving payments
- Charging penalties on accounts that are paid in full at the end of every billing cycle (research the GE Rewards MasterCard)
- Sending card holders catalogues of discounted gifts that can be purchased with their charge cards
- Linking credit card use to a program of rewards— say, frequent flier miles linked to amounts charged.

Step 3: Compile your findings in the form of a set of guidelines designed for consumers receiving unsolicited credit card offers. Your guidelines should analyze the advantages and disadvantages of excessive credit card use.

Follow-Up Questions

1. If you were the person in our hypothetical example, how would you handle your credit situation?

2. Why do you think credit card companies continue to offer cards to people who are financially overextended?

3. What criteria can you suggest to evaluate different credit card offers?

4. How do you know when you have enough credit?

Prentice Hall

COMPANION WEBSITE

T A K E   I T   T O   T H E   N E T

Check out our Companion Website

for this chapter's Exploring the Net exercise, featuring three Canadian banks' demonstration sites for electronic banking and other intriguing, annotated destinations. You'll also find practice exercises, updated weblinks from the text, links to newsgroups, updates, and more.

w w w . p r e n t i c e h a l l . c a / e b e r t

BUSINESS CASE 16

The Canadian Dollar: How Low Can It Go?

In the early 1970s, the Canadian dollar was worth about one U.S. dollar. But during the last 25 years or so, the Canadian dollar has moved erratically downwards, and by mid-1998, it had declined to about $0.67 (U.S.). During one period in July 1998 the Canadian dollar set a new record low on eight consecutive days.

The average Canadian probably doesn't pay too much attention to the complexities of currency fluctuations in general, but does pay a lot of attention to the value of the Canadian dollar in terms of the U.S. dollar. Given that the U.S. is close to Canada, is a world power, and is our biggest trading partner, this is not surprising. But the fact is that while the Canadian dollar has *dropped* in value compared to the German mark, the English pound, and the U.S. dollar, it has actually *increased* in value compared to the Indonesian rupiah, the Thai baht, the Malaysian ringgit, and the Japanese yen.

Currency fluctuations create winners and losers. As the value of the Canadian dollar declines, winners are typically exporters (because the prices of our exported goods become cheaper in foreign countries) and tourist operators (more tourists come to Canada since they can get more for their money). Losers are typically importers (who must pay higher prices for foreign goods), Canadians who travel abroad (the cost of their travel will be higher because the value of the dollar is lower), and anyone who has loans that are in foreign currency.

But the creation of winners and losers is not quite that simple. Canadian companies that export their products to the U.S. but get most of their raw materials from within Canada benefit because they pay their bills in Canadian dollars but get revenue in U.S. dollars. MacMillan Bloedel Ltd., for example, gains $3 million a year in increased profits for every one cent drop in the Canadian dollar. On the other hand, companies whose revenues come from Canadians but whose costs are paid in U.S. dollars are hurt when the Canadian dollar declines (for example, professional sports teams in Canada who pay their players in U.S. dollars).

Whether you are a winner or a loser also depends on the foreign country with which you do the most business. Japanese tourists, for example, used to flock to the Canadian Rockies for their vacations. But since 1995, the loonie has increased 51 percent in value compared to the Japanese yen, so far fewer Japanese tourists are now coming to Canada. Conversely, since the loonie has decreased in value compared to the U.S. dollar, more American tourists are coming to Canada. In Toronto, for example, the number of *conventions* increased only 2 percent from 1996 to 1997, but the number of *people* at those conventions increased 43 percent.

But we should not conclude from statistics like these that it will be easy for Canadian tourist operators to entice Americans to visit Canada. The trouble lies with the Americans' legendary ignorance about things Canadian. This translates into a lack of knowledge about the good financial deals Americans can get when they exchange U.S. dollars for Canadian dollars. For example, they might not know that a $100 hotel room will only cost them about U.S.$67.

One other problem: While it is true that Americans will find their dollar worth 6 percent more now than it was worth just a year ago in Canada, they are also finding that their dollar is worth 70 percent more than the Thai baht, 57 percent more than the Malaysian ringgit, and 23 percent more than the Australian dollar. In other words, the U.S. dollar goes further in just about any country an American might want to visit, so we can't assume they will come to Canada to spend their money.

Even when the Canadian dollar increases in value there can be problems. Many Asian students who used to come to universities in Canada no longer can afford to; the Malaysian ringgit, for example, has dropped 40 percent in relation to the Canadian dollar. The same thing has happened to the currencies of Indonesia and Thailand.

■ Case Questions

1. What are the benefits of a "high" Canadian dollar? The drawbacks?

2. What are the benefits of a "low" Canadian dollar? The drawbacks?

3. Compare the level of the Canadian dollar over the last 15 years with Canada's pattern of imports and exports. Is there any relationship among imports, exports, and the level of the Canadian dollar? (The *Bank of Canada Review* contains the information you need to answer this question.)

4. Do you think the government of Canada should intervene to influence the value of the Canadian dollar? Defend your answer.

C H A P T E R

17

FINANCIAL DECISIONS AND RISK MANAGEMENT

WHAT HAPPENED TO BRAMALEA?

For 37 years, Bramalea was one of Canada's largest and most respected builders and property developers. At its peak, it controlled assets worth $6 billion. But it got into trouble in the late 1980s for the same reason so many other firms did—greed and leverage. In 1990, Marvin Marshall was brought in to solve the problems that were developing.

The problems were more serious than most people knew. Bramalea had, for example, bought $1.5 billion of land at highly inflated late 1980s prices. It had also layered debts on every asset the company owned. Insiders knew the firm would need large amounts of new capital if it was to survive. But the Olympia & York failure had made it almost impossible to get that money from public capital markets.

Marshall and his team, therefore, came up with a plan to sell $1.5 billion in assets between 1993 and 1998. They would use this money to repay the company's outstanding loans. The plan was based on the assumption that the market for commercial space would recover and that investors would once again start buying real estate stocks. Many people at Bramalea were skeptical about the feasibility of the plan, but since there didn't seem to be any alternative, they supported it. Several large banks also went along with the plan because they had taken a big hit when Olympia & York failed, and they hoped they could somehow get their money back by keeping Bramalea afloat.

For a while, things seemed to be going according to plan. In late 1993, while addressing a gathering of pension

fund managers and investment funds, Marshall noted that interest rates were low, the company had a positive cash flow, and its stock price had increased.

But apparently this was not enough for Bramalea. The company was determined to grow, in spite of its high debt levels. To accomplish this, several lenders were persuaded to defer interest which was due on loans they had made to Bramalea. This allowed Bramalea to buy still more land and build more new houses. It also allowed the company to tell shareholders that the company was operating according to plan. This was technically true since the lenders had agreed to the plan, but it obscured the fact that Bramalea was still badly in need of money. In the fall of 1994, rumours started circulating that Bramalea management had been sighted in meetings with firms with large amounts of money to invest in real estate. The thought was that the company was trying to get its hands on a lot more cash than the banks would lend it. After numerous complicated discussions with various financiers, no deal could be arranged which would give Bramalea the money it needed. This situation, coupled with the rumours, started the "death spiral" of Bramalea's stock, which lost half its value in one week.

When it became clear that no one was willing to lend Bramalea the amount of money it needed, the company sought the bankruptcy protection that led to its demise. Bramalea had hoped that demand for real estate would increase to the point that it could sell its assets to pay off its debts. When that didn't happen, it gambled that it could build and sell new houses fast enough to generate the money it needed to pay off its loans. It lost.

As the Bramalea case shows, how a company handles its finances can mean the difference between life and death for the firm. It can also affect the level of interest that investors show in the firm. These fundamental facts apply to both established firms and those that are just starting up.

In this chapter, we will examine the role of financial managers and show why businesses need financial management. We will discuss the sources of short-term funds and how they are put to use, as well as sources and uses of long-term financing. As you will see, using funds involves risks and so requires management to protect the firm from unnecessary financial losses.

After reading this chapter, you should be able to:

1. Describe the responsibilities of a *financial manager*.
2. Identify four sources of *short-term financing* for businesses.
3. Distinguish between the various sources of *long-term financing* and explain the risks entailed by each type.
4. Show how financial *returns* to investors are related to *risks* they take.
5. Explain how risk affects business operations and identify the five steps in the *risk-management process*.

■ THE ROLE OF THE FINANCIAL MANAGER

We have seen that production managers are responsible for planning and controlling the output of goods and services. We have noted that marketing managers must plan and control the development and marketing of products. Similarly, **financial managers** plan and control the acquisition and dispersal of the company's financial assets.

The business activity known as **finance** (or **corporate finance**) typically entails four responsibilities:

- determining a firm's long-term investments
- obtaining funds to pay for those investments
- conducting the firm's everyday financial activities
- helping to manage the risks that the firm takes

financial managers
Those managers responsible for planning and overseeing the financial resources of a firm.

finance
The business function involving decisions about a firm's long-term investments and obtaining the funds to pay for those investments.

Objectives of the Financial Manager

The overall objective of financial managers is to increase the value of the firm and thus to increase shareholder wealth. To reach this goal, financial managers must ensure that the company's earnings exceed its costs—in other words, that the company earns a profit. For a proprietorship or partnership, profits translate into an increase in the owners' wealth. For a corporation, profits translate into an increase in the value of its common stock.

The various responsibilities of the financial manager in increasing a firm's wealth fall into three general categories: *cash-flow management*, *financial control*, and *financial planning*.

cash flow management
Managing the pattern in which cash flows into the firm in the form of revenues and out of the firm in the form of debt payments.

Cash-Flow Management.   To increase a firm's value, financial managers must ensure that it always has enough funds on hand to purchase the materials and human resources that it needs to produce goods and services. At the same time, of course, there may be funds that are not needed immediately. These must be invested to earn more money for a firm. This activity—**cash flow management**—requires careful planning. If excess cash balances are allowed to sit idle instead of being invested, a firm loses the cash returns that it could have earned.

financial control
The process of checking actual performance against plans to ensure that the desired financial status is achieved.

Financial Control.   Because things never go exactly as planned, financial managers must be prepared to make adjustments for actual financial changes that occur each day. **Financial control** is the process of checking actual performance against plans to ensure that the desired financial status occurs. For example, planned revenues based on forecasts usually turn out to be higher or lower than actual revenues. Why? Simply because sales are unpredictable. Control involves monitoring revenue inflows and making appropriate financial adjustments. Excessively high revenues, for instance, may be deposited in short-term interest-bearing accounts. Or they may be used to pay off short-term debt. Otherwise earmarked resources can be saved or put to better use. In contrast, lower-than-expected revenues may necessitate short-term borrowing to meet current debt obligations.

Budgets are often the backbone of financial control. The budget provides the "measuring stick" against which performance is evaluated. The cash flows, debts, and assets not only of the whole company but of each department are compared at regular intervals against budgeted amounts. Discrepancies indicate the need for financial adjustments so that resources are used to the best advantage.

financial plan
A description of how a business will reach some financial position it seeks for the future; includes projections for sources and uses of funds.

Financial Planning.   The cornerstone of effective financial management is the development of a **financial plan**. A financial plan describes a firm's strategies for reaching some future financial position. In constructing the plan, a financial manager must ask several questions:

- What amount of funds does the company need to meet immediate plans?
- When will it need more funds?
- Where can it get the funds to meet both its short- and long-term needs?

To answer these questions, a financial manager must develop a clear picture of *why* a firm needs funds. Managers must also assess the relative costs and benefits of potential funding sources. In the sections that follow, we will examine the main reasons for which companies generate funds and describe the main sources of business funding, both for the short and long term.

■ WHY BUSINESSES NEED FUNDS

Every company needs money to survive. Failure to make a contractually obligated payment can lead to bankruptcy and the dissolution of the firm. But the successful financial manager must distinguish between two different kinds of financial outlays: short-term operating expenditures and long-term capital expenditures.

Short-Term (Operating) Expenditures

A firm incurs short-term expenditures regularly in its everyday business activities. To handle these expenditures, financial managers must pay attention to accounts payable and receivable and to inventories.

Accounts Payable.   In drawing up a financial plan, financial managers must pay special attention to accounts payable, for it is the largest single category of short-term debt for most companies. But they must rely on other managers for accurate information about the quantity of supplies that will be required in an upcoming period. Financial managers also need to consider the time period in which they must pay various suppliers. For example, a financial manager for *Maclean's* magazine needs information from production about both the amount of ink and paper needed to print the magazine and when it will be needed. Obviously, it is in the firm's interest to withhold payment as long as it can without jeopardizing its credit rating.

Accounts Receivable.   A sound financial plan requires financial managers to project accurately both the amounts buyers will pay to the firm and when they will make those payments. For example, a manager at Kraft Foods needs to know how many dollars' worth of cheddar cheese Safeway supermarkets will order each month and how quickly it pays its bills. Because they represent an investment in products on which the firm has not yet received payment, accounts receivable temporarily tie up some of the firm's funds. It is in the firm's interest to receive payment as quickly as possible.

Kraft Foods
www.kraft.com

Given that it is in the self-interest of buyers to delay payment as long as possible, how can a financial manager predict payment times? The answer lies in the development of a *credit policy*, the set of rules governing the extension of credit to customers. The credit policy sets standards as to which buyers are eligible for what type of credit. Financial managers extend credit to customers who have the ability to pay and honour their obligations to pay. They deny credit to firms with poor repayment histories.

The credit policy also sets payment terms. For example, credit terms of "2/10; net 30" mean that the selling company offers a 2 percent discount if the customer pays within 10 days. The customer has 30 days to pay the regular price. Thus, on a $1000 invoice, the buyer would have to pay only $980 on days one to ten but all $1000 on days 11 to 30. The higher the discount, the more incentive buyers have to pay early. Sellers can thus adjust credit terms to influence when customers pay their bills. Often, however, credit terms can be adjusted only slightly without giving competitors an edge.

Levi Strauss
www.levi.com

Inventories.   Between the time a firm buys raw materials and the time it sells finished products, it has funds tied up in **inventory**, materials and goods that it will sell within the year. There are three basic types of inventories: raw materials, work-in-process, and finished goods.

The basic supplies a firm buys to use in its production process are its **raw materials inventory**. Levi Strauss' raw materials inventory includes huge rolls of denim. **Work-in-process inventory** consists of goods partway through the production process. Cut-out but not-yet-sewn jeans are part of the work-in-process inventory at Levi's. Finally, the **finished goods inventory** are those items ready for sale. Completed blue jeans ready for shipment to dealers in Levi jeans are finished goods inventory.

Failure to manage inventory can have grave financial consequences. Too little inventory of any kind can cost the firm sales. Too much inventory means that the firm has funds tied up that it cannot use elsewhere. In extreme cases, too much inventory may force a company to sell merchandise at low profits simply to obtain needed cash.

inventory
Materials and goods currently held by the company that will be sold within the year.

raw materials inventory
That portion of a firm's inventory consisting of basic supplies used to manufacture products for sale.

work-in-process inventory
That portion of a firm's inventory consisting of goods partway through the production process.

finished goods inventory
That portion of a firm's inventory consisting of completed goods ready for sale.

Long-Term Expenditures

Companies need funds to cover long-term expenditures for fixed assets. As noted in Chapter 12, fixed assets are items that have a lasting use or value, such as land, buildings, and machinery. The Hudson Bay Oil and Gas plant in Flin Flon, Manitoba, is a fixed asset.

Because they are so crucial to business success, long-term expenditures are usually planned more carefully than are short-term expenditures. But long-term expenditures pose special problems for the financial manager because they differ from short-term expenditures in several ways. First, unlike inventories and other short-term assets, they are not normally sold or converted into cash. Second, their acquisition requires a very large investment in funds. Third, they represent an ongoing tie-up of the company's funds. All these features influence how long-term expenditures are funded.

■ SOURCES OF SHORT-TERM FUNDS

Just as firms have many short-term expenditures, so they can call on many short-term sources for the funds to finance day-to-day operations and to implement short-term plans. These sources include trade credit, secured and unsecured loans, commercial paper, and factoring accounts receivable.

Trade Credit

Accounts payable are not merely an expenditure. They are also a source of funds to the company, which has the use of both the product purchased and the price of the product until the time it pays its bill. **Trade credit**, the granting of credit by one firm to another, is effectively a short-term loan.

The most common forms of trade credit are open-book accounts, promissory notes, and trade drafts and trade acceptances. **Open-book credit** is essentially a "gentlemen's agreement." Buyers receive their merchandise along with an invoice stating the terms of credit. Sellers ship the products on faith that payment will be forthcoming.

When sellers want more reassurance, they may insist on a legally binding written document called a **promissory note**. Buyers must sign a promissory note before the merchandise is shipped. The agreement states when and how much money will be paid to the seller in return for immediate credit.

Another type of credit agreement, the **trade draft**, is written by sellers, not buyers. Attached to the shipment of merchandise, a trade draft states the promised date and amount of repayment due the seller. The buyer must sign the draft to take possession of the merchandise. Once signed by the buyer, the document is called a **trade acceptance**. Trade drafts and trade acceptances are useful forms of credit in international transactions.

Trade credit is not without problems. During the recession of 1990-92, many large firms did not pay their bills for 90 days or more. Much of this money was owed to small firms who were afraid to hound the big firms for the money. But the small firms desperately needed the cash and many of them were pushed to the brink of insolvency.[1]

Secured Short-Term Loans

For most firms, bank loans are a vital source of short-term funding. Such loans almost always involve a promissory note in which the borrower promises to repay the loan plus interest. In **secured loans**, banks also require the borrower to put up **collateral**—to give the bank the right to seize certain assets if payments are not made as promised. Inventories, accounts receivable, and other assets may serve as collateral for a secured loan.

Perhaps the biggest disadvantage of secured borrowing is the paperwork and administrative costs. Agreements must be written, collateral evaluated, and the terms of the loans enforced. But secured loans do enable borrowers to get funds when they might not qualify for unsecured credit. And even creditworthy borrowers benefit by borrowing at lower rates than with unsecured loans.

trade credit
The granting of credit by a selling firm to a buying firm.

open-book credit
A form of trade credit in which buyers receive their merchandise along with an invoice stating the terms of credit, but in which no formal promissory note is signed.

promissory note
A written commitment to pay a stated sum of money on a given date; a form of trade credit in which the buyer signs an agreement regarding payment terms before receiving the merchandise.

trade draft
A form of trade credit in which the seller draws up a statement of payment terms and attaches it to the merchandise; the buyer must sign this agreement to take delivery of the merchandise.

trade acceptance
A trade draft that has been signed by the buyer.

secured loan
A short-term loan in which the borrower is required to put up collateral.

collateral
Any asset that a lender has the right to seize if a borrower does not repay a loan.

Inventory Loans.   When a loan is made with inventory as a collateral asset, the lender loans the borrower some portion of the stated value of the inventory. Inventory is more attractive as collateral when it provides the lender with real security for the loan amount: For example, if the inventory can be readily converted into cash, it is relatively more valuable as collateral. Other inventory—say, boxes full of expensive, partially completed lenses for eyeglasses—is of little value on the open market. Meanwhile, a thousand crates of boxed, safely stored canned tomatoes might well be convertible into cash.

Accounts Receivable.   When accounts receivable are used as collateral, the process is called **pledging accounts receivable**. In the event of nonpayment, the lender may seize the receivables—that is, funds owed the borrower by its customers. If these assets are not enough to cover the loan, the borrower must make up the difference. This option is especially important to service companies such as accounting firms and law offices. Because they do not maintain inventories, accounts receivable are their main source of collateral.

pledging accounts receivable
Using accounts receivable as collateral for a loan.

Typically, lenders who will accept accounts receivable as collateral are financial institutions with credit departments capable of evaluating the quality of the receivables. Loans are granted only when lenders are confident that they can recover funds from the borrower's debtors. (We will discuss the companies that specialize in these loans, called *factors*, later in the chapter.)

Unsecured Short-Term Loans

With an **unsecured loan**, the borrower does not have to put up collateral. In many cases, however, the bank requires the borrower to maintain a *compensating balance*: The borrower must keep a portion of the loan amount on deposit with the bank in a non-interest-bearing account.

unsecured loan
A short-term loan in which the borrower is not required to put up collateral.

The inventory in this auto parts warehouse is good collateral because it is neatly stored, accessible, can be readily evaluated, and is quickly disposable.

The terms of the loan—amount, duration, interest rate, and payment schedule—are negotiated between the bank and the borrower. To receive an unsecured loan, then, a firm must ordinarily have a good banking relationship with the lender. Once an agreement is made, a promissory note will be executed and the funds transferred to the borrower. Although some unsecured loans are one-time-only arrangements, many take the form of *lines of credit, revolving credit agreements,* or *commercial paper*.

Lines of Credit.   A standing agreement with a bank to lend a firm a maximum amount of funds on request is called a **line of credit**. With a line of credit, the firm knows the maximum amount it will be allowed to borrow if the bank has sufficient funds. The bank does not guarantee that the funds will be available when requested, however.

For example, suppose the Toronto-Dominion Bank gives Sunshine Tanning Inc. a $100 000 line of credit for the coming year. By signing promissory notes, Sunshine's borrowings can total up to $100 000 at any time. The bank may not always have sufficient funds when Sunshine needs them. But Sunshine benefits from the arrangement by knowing in advance that the bank regards the firm as creditworthy and will loan funds to it on short notice.

Revolving Credit Agreements.   Revolving credit agreements are similar to bank credit cards for consumers. Under a **revolving credit agreement**, a lender agrees to make some amount of funds available on demand to a firm for continuing short-term loans. The lending institution guarantees that funds will be available when sought by the borrower. In return, the bank charges a *commitment fee*—a charge for holding open a line of credit for a customer even if the customer does not borrow any funds. The commitment fee is often expressed as a percentage of the loan amount, usually 0.5 to 1 percent of the committed amount.

For example, suppose the Toronto-Dominion Bank agrees to lend Sunshine Tanning up to $100 000 under a revolving credit agreement. If Sunshine borrows $80 000, it still has access to $20 000. If it pays off $50 000 of the debt, reducing its debt to $30 000, then it has $70 000 available to it. Sunshine pays interest on the borrowed funds and also pays a fee on the unused funds in the line of credit.

Commercial Paper.   Some firms can raise funds in the short run by issuing commercial paper. Since **commercial paper** is backed solely by the issuing firm's promise to pay, it is an option for only the largest and most creditworthy firms.

How does commercial paper work? Corporations issue commercial paper with a face value. Companies that buy commercial paper pay less than that value. At the end of a specified period (usually 30 to 90 days but legally up to 270 days), the issuing company buys back the paper—*at the face value*. The difference between the price the buying company paid and the face value is the buyer's profit.

For example, if Noranda needs to borrow $10 million for 90 days, it might issue commercial paper with a face value of $10.2 million. Insurance companies with $10 million excess cash will buy the paper. After 90 days, Noranda would pay $10.2 million to the insurance companies.

Commercial paper offers those few corporations able to issue it several advantages. Its cost is usually lower than prevailing interest rates on short-term loans. And it gives the issuing company access to a wide range of lenders, not just financial institutions.

Factoring Accounts Receivable

One way to raise funds rapidly is **factoring**, that is, selling the firm's accounts receivable. In this process, the purchaser of the receivables, usually a financial institution, is known as the *factor*. The factor pays some percentage of the full amount of receivables to the selling firm. The seller gets money immediately.

line of credit
A standing agreement between a bank and a firm in which the bank specifies the maximum amount it will make available to the borrower for a short-term unsecured loan; the borrower can then draw on those funds, when available.

revolving credit agreement
A guaranteed line of credit for which the firm pays the bank interest on funds borrowed as well as a fee for extending the line of credit.

commercial paper
A method of short-run fundraising in which a firm sells unsecured notes for less than the face value and then repurchases them at the face value within 270 days; buyers' profits are the difference between the original price paid and the face value.

factoring
Selling a firm's accounts receivable to another company for some percentage of their face value in order to realize immediate cash; the buyer's profits depend on its ability to collect the receivables.

For example, a factor might buy $40 000 worth of receivables for 60 percent of that sum ($24 000). The factor profits to the extent that the money it eventually collects exceeds the amount it paid. This profit depends on the quality of the receivables, the costs of collecting the receivables, the time until the receivables are due, and interest rates.

■ SOURCES OF LONG-TERM FUNDS

Just as firms need funds to cover their short-term expenditures, so they need to finance long-term expenditures for fixed assets. Firms need funds for buildings and equipment necessary for conducting their business. Companies may seek long-term funds from outside the firm (debt financing), or they may draw on internal financial sources (equity financing).

Debt Financing

Long-term borrowing from outside the company—**debt financing**—is a major component of most firms' long-term financial planning. The two primary sources of such funding are long-term loans and the sale of bonds.

Long-Term Loans.   In some respects, a long-term loan is like a short-term loan. The major difference is that a long-term loan extends for three to ten years, while short-term loans must generally be paid off in a few years or less. Most corporations get their long-term loans from a chartered bank, usually one with which the firm has developed a long-standing relationship. But credit companies, insurance companies, and pension funds also grant long-term business loans.

Interest rates on long-term loans are negotiated between borrower and lender. Although some bank loans have fixed rates, others have *floating rates* tied to the prime rate (see Chapter 16). A loan at "1 percent above prime," then, is payable at 1 percentage point higher than the prime rate. This rate may fluctuate—"float"—because the prime rate itself goes up and down as market conditions change.

Long-term loans are attractive to borrowing companies for several reasons. First, because the number of parties involved is limited, long-term loans can often be arranged quickly. Second, the firm need not make a public disclosure of its business plans or the purpose for which it is acquiring the loan. Third, the duration of a long-term loan can easily be matched to the borrower's needs. Finally, if the firm's needs change, long-term loans usually contain clauses making it possible to change the loan's terms.

Long-term loans also have some disadvantages. Large borrowers may have trouble finding lenders to supply enough funds. Long-term borrowers may also have restrictions placed on them as conditions of the loan. They may have to pledge long-term assets as collateral. And they may have to agree not to take on any more debt until the borrowed funds are repaid.

Corporate Bonds.   Like commercial paper, a **corporate bond** is a contract—a promise by the issuing company or organization to pay the holder a certain amount of money on a specified date. Unlike commercial paper, however, bond issuers do not pay off quickly. In many cases, bonds may not be redeemed for 30 years from the time of issue. In addition, unlike commercial paper, most bonds pay the bondholder a stipulated sum of interest semiannually or annually. If it fails to make a bond payment, the company is in default.

The terms of a bond, including the amount to be paid, the interest rate, and the **maturity** (payoff) **date**, differ from company to company and from issue to issue. They are spelled out in the bond contract, or *bond indenture*. The indenture also identifies which of the firm's assets, if any, are pledged as collateral for the bonds.

debt financing
Raising money to meet long-term expenditures by borrowing from outside the company; usually takes the form of long-term loans or the sale of corporate bonds.

← lowest rate charged to borrowers

corporate bond
A promise by the issuing company to pay the holder a certain amount of money on a specified date, with stated interest payments in the interim; a form of long-term debt financing.

maturity date
The date on or before which a company must pay off the principal of a particular bond issue.

Corporate bonds are the major source of long-term debt financing for most corporations. Bonds are attractive when companies need large amounts of funds for long periods of time. The issuing company gets access to large numbers of lenders through nationwide bond markets and stock exchanges.

But bonds involve expensive administrative and selling costs. They also may require very high interest payments if the issuing company has a poor credit rating. We will return to these characteristics when we consider the market for bonds in more detail in Chapter 18.

Equity Financing

equity financing
Raising money to meet long-term expenditures by issuing common stock or by retaining earnings.

Although debt financing has strong appeal in some cases, looking inside the company for long-term funding is preferable under other circumstances. In small companies, the founders may increase their personal investment in the firm. In most cases, however, **equity financing** takes the form of issuing common stock or of retaining the firm's earnings. As you will see, both options involve putting the owners' capital to work.

Common Stock.   As noted in Chapter 2, when shareholders purchase common stock, they seek profits in the form of both dividends and appreciation. Overall, shareholders hope for an increase in the market value of their stock because the firm has profited and grown. By selling shares of stock, the company gets the funds it needs for buying land, buildings, and equipment.

For example, suppose Sunshine Tanning's founders invested $10 000 by buying the original 500 shares of common stock (at $20 per share) in 1995. If the company used these funds to buy equipment and succeeded financially, by 1999 it might need funds for expansion. A pattern of profitable operations and regularly paid dividends might allow Sunshine to raise $50 000 by selling 500 new shares of stock for $100 per share. This additional paid-in capital would increase the total shareholders' equity to $60 000, as shown in Table 17.1.

It should be noted that the use of equity financing via common stock can be expensive because paying dividends is more expensive than paying bond interest. Why? Interest paid to bondholders is a business expense and, hence, a tax deduction for the firm. Stock dividends are not tax-deductible.

Retained Earnings.   Another approach to equity financing is to use retained earnings. These earnings represent profits not paid out in dividends. Using retained earnings means that the firm will not have to borrow money and pay interest on loans or bonds. A firm that has a history of eventually reaping much higher profits by successfully reinvesting retained earnings may be attractive to some investors. But the smaller dividends that can be paid to shareholders as a result of retained earnings may decrease demand for—and thus the price of—the company's stock.

■ **TABLE 17.1   Shareholders' Equity for Sunshine Tanning Inc.**

Common Shareholders' Equity, 1995:	
Initial common stock (500 shares issued @ $20 per share, 1995)	$10 000
Total shareholders' equity	$10 000
Common Shareholders' Equity, 1999:	
Initial common stock (500 shares issued @ $20 per share, 1995)	$10 000
Additional paid-in capital (500 shares issued @ $100 per share, 1999)	50 000
Total shareholders' equity	$60 000

For example, if Sunshine Tanning had net earnings of $50 000 in 1999, it could pay a $50-per-share dividend on its 1000 shares of common stock. But if it plans to remodel at a cost of $30 000 and retains $30 000 of earnings to finance the project, only $20 000 is left to distribute for stock dividends ($20 per share).

Financial Burden on the Firm.   If equity funding can be so expensive, why don't firms rely instead on debt capital? Because long-term loans and bonds carry fixed interest rates and represent a fixed promise to pay, regardless of economic changes. If the firm defaults on its obligations, it may lose its assets and even go into bankruptcy.

Because of this risk, debt financing appeals most strongly to companies in industries that have predictable profits and cash flow patterns. For example, demand for electric power is steady from year to year and predictable from month to month. So provincial electric utility companies, with their stable stream of income, can carry a substantial amount of debt.

Hybrid Financing: Preferred Stock

Falling somewhere between debt and equity financing is the *preferred stock* (see Chapter 2). Preferred stock is a hybrid because it has some of the features of corporate bonds and some features of common stocks. As with bonds, payments on preferred stock are for fixed amounts, such as $6 per share per year. Unlike bonds, however, preferred stock never matures. It can be held indefinitely, like common stock. And dividends need not be paid if the company makes no profit. If dividends are paid, preferred shareholders receive them first in preference to dividends on common stock.

A major advantage of preferred stock to the issuing corporation is its flexibility. It secures funds for the firm without relinquishing control, since preferred shareholders have no voting rights. It does not require repayment of principal or the payment of dividends in lean times.

Choosing Between Debt and Equity Financing

Part of financial planning involves striking a balance between debt and equity financing to meet the firm's long-term need for funds. Because the mix of debt versus equity provides the firm's financial base, it is called the *capital structure* of the firm. Financial plans contain targets for the capital structure, such as 40 percent debt and 60 percent equity. But choosing a target is not easy. A wide range of debt-versus-equity mixes is possible.

The most conservative strategy would be to use all equity financing and no debt. Under this strategy, a company has no formal obligations for financial payouts. But equity is a very expensive source of capital. The riskiest strategy would be to use all debt financing. While less expensive than equity funding, indebtedness increases the risk that a firm will be unable to meet its obligations and will go bankrupt. Magna International, for example, has had a high debt-to-equity ratio in the recent past. Industry analysts believe increased demand for automobiles will allow the firm to make large profits and pay off much of the debt, causing its debt/equity ratio to fall.[2] Somewhere between the two extremes, financial planners try to find a mix that will maximize shareholders' wealth.

Magna International
www.magnaint.com

The Risk-Return Relationship.   While developing plans for raising capital, financial managers must be aware of the different motivations of individual investors. Why, for example, do some individuals and firms invest in stocks while others invest only in bonds? Investor motivations, of course, determine who is willing to buy a given company's stocks or bonds. Everyone who invests money is expressing a personal preference for safety versus risk. Investors give money to firms and, in return, anticipate receiving future cash flows.

Some cash flows are more certain than others. Investors generally expect to receive higher payments for higher uncertainty. They do not generally expect large returns for

risk-return relationship
Shows the amount of risk and the likely rate of return on various financial instruments.

secure investments such as government-insured bonds. Each type of investment, then, has a **risk-return relationship**. Figure 17.1 shows the general risk-return relationship for various financial instruments. High-grade corporate bonds, for example, rate low in terms of risk on future returns but also low on size of expected returns. The reverse is true of junk bonds, those with a higher risk of default.

Risk-return differences are recognized by financial planners, who try to gain access to the greatest funding at the lowest possible cost. By gauging investors' perceptions of their riskiness, a firm's managers can estimate how much it must pay to attract funds to their offerings. Over time, a company can reposition itself on the risk continuum by improving its record on dividends, interest payments, and debt repayment.

■ RISK MANAGEMENT

Financial risks are not the only risks faced every day by companies (and individuals). In this section, we will describe various other types of risks that businesses face and analyze some of the ways in which they typically manage them.

risk
Uncertainty about future events.

speculative risk
An event that offers the chance for either a gain or a loss.

pure risk
An event that offers no possibility of gain; it offers only the chance of a loss.

Coping with Risk

Businesses constantly face two basic types of **risk**—that is, uncertainty about future events. **Speculative risks**, such as financial investments, involve the possibility of gain or loss. **Pure risks** involve only the possibility of loss or no loss. Designing and distributing a new product, for example, is a speculative risk: The product may fail or it may succeed and earn high profits. The chance of a warehouse fire is a pure risk.

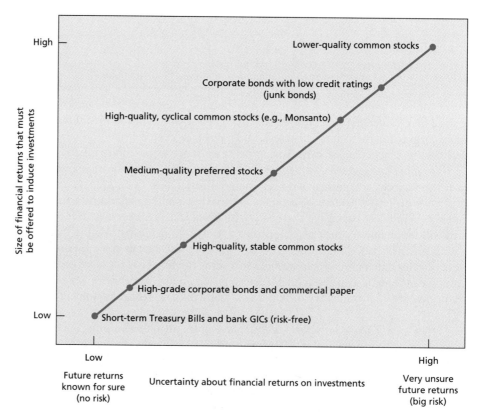

FIGURE 17.1

Investors expect a chance at greater financial returns for riskier investments.

For a company to survive and prosper, it must manage both types of risk in a cost-effective manner. We can thus define the process of **risk management** as "conserving the firm's earning power and assets by reducing the threat of losses due to uncontrollable events."[3] In every company, each manager must be alert for risks to the firm and their impact on profits. The risk-management process usually entails the five steps outlined in Figure 17.2.

Step 1: Identify Risks and Potential Losses.   Managers analyze a firm's risks to identify potential losses. For example, a firm with a fleet of delivery trucks can expect that one of them will eventually be involved in an accident. The accident may cause bodily injury to the driver or others, may cause physical damage to the truck or other vehicles, or both.

Step 2: Measure the Frequency and Severity of Losses and Their Impact.   To measure the frequency and severity of losses, managers must consider both past history and current activities. How often can the firm expect the loss to occur? What is the likely size of the loss in dollars? For example, our firm with the fleet of delivery trucks may have had two accidents per year in the past. If it adds trucks, however, it may reasonably expect the frequency of accidents to increase.

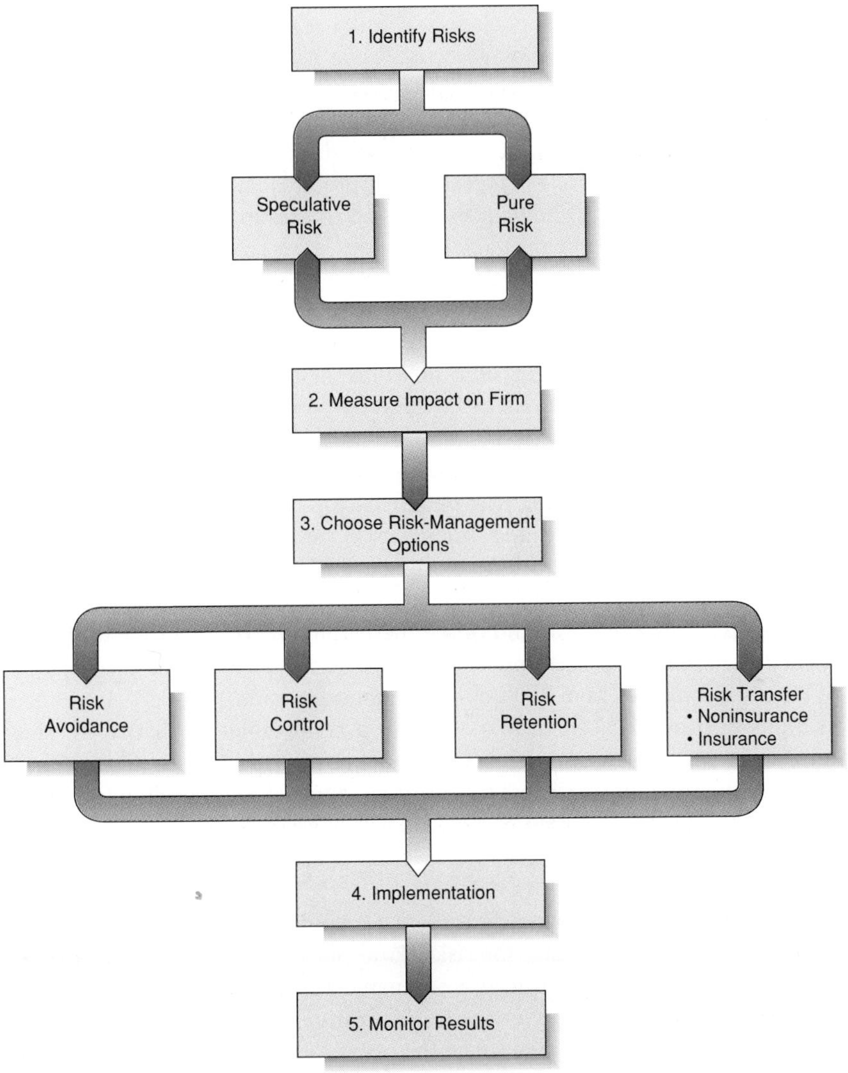

risk management
Conserving a firm's (or an individual's) financial power or assets by minimizing the financial effect of accidental losses.

FIGURE 17.2
The risk-management process.

Step 3: Evaluate Alternatives and Choose the Techniques That Will Best Handle the Losses.   Having identified and measured potential losses, managers are in a better position to decide how to handle them. With this third step, they generally have four choices: *risk avoidance, control, retention,* or *transfer.*

risk avoidance
Stopping participation in or refusing to participate in ventures that carry any risk.

A firm opts for **risk avoidance** by declining to enter or by ceasing to participate in a risky activity. For example, our firm with the delivery trucks could avoid any risk of physical damage or bodily injury by closing down its delivery service. Similarly, a pharmaceutical maker may withdraw a new drug for fear of liability suits.

By definition, risk avoidance is always successful. It is not, however, always practical. A manager who avoids a certain risk may be acting inconsistently with the firm's strategic direction. For example, if a speedy, centrally controlled delivery system gives our company a competitive edge, risk avoidance may be the wrong choice.

risk control
Techniques to prevent, minimize, or reduce losses or the consequences of losses.

When avoidance is not practical or desirable, firms can practice **risk control**—say, the use of loss-prevention techniques to minimize the frequency of losses. A delivery service, for instance, can prevent losses by training its drivers in defensive-driving techniques, mapping out safe routes, and conscientiously maintaining its trucks.

Unfortunately, loss-prevention techniques cannot guarantee that losses will not occur. Rather, they concede that losses may occur while trying to minimize their severity. Seat belts or air bags, for example, can minimize injuries to truck drivers when accidents do happen. Many firms use fire extinguishers, fire alarms, or burglar alarms to reduce loss.

All risk-control techniques involve costs. The risk manager's job, therefore, is to find techniques whose benefits exceed their costs. For example, a new sprinkler system may cost $100 000. However, if it reduces fire losses by $150 000, it is money well spent.

risk retention
The covering of a firm's unavoidable losses with its own funds.

When losses cannot be avoided or controlled, firms must cope with the consequences. When such losses are manageable and predictable, they may decide to cover them out of company funds. The firm is thus said to "assume" or "retain" the financial consequences of the loss: hence the practice known as **risk retention**. For example, the firm with the fleet of trucks may find that vehicles suffer vandalism totalling $100 to $500 per year. Depending on its coverage, the company may find it cheaper to pay for repairs out of pocket rather than to submit claims to its insurance company.

Some large organizations choose to build up their own pools of funds as a reserve to cover losses that would otherwise be covered by commercial insurance. This type of coverage is called **self-insurance**.

self-insurance
Occurs when a company chooses to build up a pool of its own funds as a reserve to cover losses that would otherwise be covered by insurance.

The primary motive for self-insurance is to avoid the high cost of buying coverage from private insurers. For example, part of a firm's paid premiums go to cover the insurer's administrative, advertising, and sales costs. Self-insurance avoids these costs. Suppose, for instance, that an athletic club pays $100 000 in premiums annually but experiences average losses of only $20 000. Let's say, however, that the club decides instead to set up its own reserve fund of $50 000 annually. If it also establishes efficient procedures for handling damages and other losses, it might achieve comparable coverage through self-insurance *and* save $50 000 in annual premiums.

risk transfer
The transfer of risk to another individual or firm, often by contract.

As a practical matter, self-insurance is not a reasonable alternative for smaller or new companies (even large ones) that have not yet built up sizable reserves. What would happen if our athletic club suffers a $1 million fire loss when its reserve fund has grown to only $100 000? It may be forced to close. Had its previous commercial coverage been in effect, however, the entire loss might have been covered. Then it could have resumed operations after the club was renovated.

insurance policy
A written contract between an individual or firm and an insurance company transferring financial liability in the event of some loss to the insurance company in return for a fee.

When the potential for large risks cannot be avoided or controlled, managers often opt for **risk transfer**: They transfer the risk to another firm—namely, an insurance company. In transferring risk to an insurance company, a firm pays a sum called a *premium.* In return, the insurance company issues an **insurance policy**—a formal agreement to pay the policyholder a specified amount in the event of certain losses. In some cases, the insured party must also pay a **deductible**—an agreed-upon amount of the loss that the insured must absorb prior to reimbursement. Thus, our delivery service may buy insur-

deductible
A previously agreed-upon amount of loss the insured must absorb before reimbursement from the insurer.

Losses are reduced or prevented when this security specialist uses electronic surveillance (left), and when workers are reminded to wear safety gear at this construction site (right).

ance to protect itself against theft, physical damage to trucks, and bodily injury to drivers and others involved in an accident. Similarly, retail stores buy protection in case customers are injured on their premises. (We discuss insurance more fully in Appendix II.)

Step 4: Implement the Risk-Management Program. The means of implementing risk-management decisions depends on both the technique chosen and the activity being managed. For example, risk avoidance for certain activities can be implemented by purchasing those activities from outside providers, such as hiring delivery services instead of operating delivery vehicles. Risk control might be implemented by training employees and designing new work methods and equipment for on-the-job safety. For situations in which risk retention is preferred, reserve funds can be set aside out of revenues. When risk transfer is needed, implementation means selecting an insurance company and buying the right policies.

Step 5: Monitor Results. Because risk management is an ongoing activity, follow-up is always essential. New types of risks, for example, emerge with changes in customers, facilities, employees, and products. Insurance regulations change, and new types of insurance become available. Consequently, managers must continually monitor a company's risks, reevaluate the methods used for handling them, and revise them as necessary.

SUMMARY OF LEARNING OBJECTIVES

1. **Describe the responsibilities of a *financial manager*.** The job of the *financial manager* is to increase a firm's value by planning and controlling the acquisition and dispersal of its financial assets. This task involves two key responsibilities: (1) *cash-flow management*—making sure that a firm has enough available money to purchase the materials it needs to produce goods and services; and (2) *financial planning*—devising strategies for reaching future financial goals.

2. **Identify four sources of *short-term financing* for businesses.** To finance short-term expenditures, firms rely on *trade credit*—credit extended by suppliers—and on loans. *Secured loans* require *collateral:* the legal interest in assets that may include

inventories or accounts receivable. *Unsecured loans* may be in the form of *lines of credit* or *revolving credit agreements.* Some very large firms issue *commercial paper*—short-term promises to pay. Smaller firms may choose to *"factor" accounts receivable*—that is, sell them to financial institutions.

3. **Distinguish between the various sources of *long-term financing* and explain the risks entailed by each type.** Long-term sources of funds include debt financing, equity financing, and the use of preferred stock. *Debt financing* uses long-term loans and *corporate bonds* (promises to pay holders specified amounts by certain dates), both of which obligate the firm to pay regular interest. *Equity financing* involves the use of owners' capital, either from the sale of common stock or from retained earnings. *Preferred stock* is a "hybrid" source of funding that has some of the features of both common stock and bonds. Financial planners must choose the proper mix of long-term funding. *All-equity financing* is the most conservative, least risky, and most expensive strategy. *All-debt financing* is the most speculative option.

4. **Show how financial *returns* to investors are related to the *risks* they take.** Financial managers and investors must consider *risk-return relationships:* the risks involved in generating returns from different investments. If future return is certain, investors are willing to accept lower returns. But if the return is uncertain, they typically demand greater potential return before investing. For financial managers, the problem is to secure the greatest possible funding at the least possible cost. They work, then, to reduce the riskiness of investing in their company by compiling a good record of dividend, interest, and debt payment.

5. **Explain how risk affects business operations and identify the five steps in the *risk-management process.*** Businesses operate in an environment pervaded by risk. *Speculative risks* involve the prospect of gain or loss. *Pure risks* involve only the prospect of loss or no loss. Firms manage their risks by following some form of a five-step process: identifying risks, measuring possible losses, evaluating alternative techniques, implementing chosen techniques, and monitoring programs on an ongoing basis. There are generally four methods of handling risk: *risk avoidance, control, retention,* and *transfer.*

STUDY QUESTIONS AND EXERCISES

Review Questions

1. What are the financial manager's three main responsibilities?

2. What are the main short-term sources of funds for businesses? Long-term sources of funds?

3. In what ways do the two sources for debt financing differ from each other? How do they differ from the two sources of equity financing?

4. What is the main source of credit for small businesses? Why?

5. Describe the risk-management process. What role does the risk manager play in the firm?

Analysis Questions

6. Why would a business "factor" its accounts receivable?

7. How would you decide the best mix of debt and equity financing for a company?

8. If you were a financial manager for a large firm, what types of short-term funding would you use most? Why?

Application Exercises

9. Interview the owner of a local small business. Identify the types of short-term and long-term funding used by the firm. As well, ask the owner to describe the risk-management process he or she uses in the business. Determine the reasons behind both these decisions.

10. Choose two well-known firms in different industries and compare their financial structures. Using public records and financial reports, determine each company's short-term debt, long-term debt, common equity, and preferred stock funding.

BUILDING YOUR BUSINESS SKILLS

Goal

To encourage students to better understand the major financial and risk management issues that face large companies.

Background

In 1997–98, all of the following companies reported financial problems relating to risk management:

- Oxford Health Care
- Eastman Kodak
- Apple Computer
- United Parcel Service
- Citibank

Method

Step 1: Working alone, research one of the companies listed here to learn more about the financial risks that were reported in the news.

Step 2: Write a short explanation of the financial and management issues that were faced by the firm that you researched.

Step 3: Join in teams with students who researched other companies and compare your findings.

Follow-Up Questions

1. Were there common themes in the "big stories" in financial management?
2. What have the various companies done to minimize future risks and losses?

Prentice Hall   T A K E   I T   T O   T H E   N E T

Check out our Companion Website
for this chapter's Exploring the Net exercise, featuring the Website of the Federal Business Development Bank of Canada and other intriguing, annotated destinations. You'll also find practice exercises, updated Weblinks from the text, links to newsgroups, updates, and more.

w w w . p r e n t i c e h a l l . c a / e b e r t

BUSINESS CASE 17

Barings Trader's Big Bet Breaks Bank

Twenty-eight-year-old Nicolas Leeson had certainly contributed his share to the bottom line of Barings PLC, the venerable British merchant bank. In less than two years as manager of Barings' futures-trading subsidiary in Singapore, Leeson had boosted profits from $1.2 million in 1992 to $30 million by the first seven months of 1994. Leeson's job involved buying and selling futures contracts, particularly investments known as derivatives. His specialties were trades in three markets: the Japanese stock index, known as the Nikkei 225; the futures market in Osaka, Japan; and the Singapore International Monetary Exchange (Simex). For exam-

ple, Leeson exploited small price differences by buying contracts on Simex and selling them for slightly higher prices in Osaka. He was not, however, engaging in these trades on behalf of Barings' clients; rather, his trades were in-house transactions using the bank's own money. Many of Barings' 4000 employees enjoyed the fruits of Leeson's labours. In 1994, for example, a bonus pool of more than $160 million was paid out. Leeson's own 1994 bonus was more than half a million dollars, twice what he had received in 1993.

As one might expect for a British investment bank founded in 1762, Barings was widely regarded as a conservative institution. Indeed, its clients include the

➤

Queen herself. Thus the financial world was astounded in February 1995, when it was revealed that Leeson had incurred staggering trading losses of nearly $1 billion. In the aftermath of the disclosure, the Bank of England refused to come to the rescue by providing financial backing. Barings had no alternative but to declare bankruptcy. The problem, experts agreed, was a lack of internal risk-management controls. As one British banking official put it: "I always feared that the biggest danger to the banking system would be a rogue derivatives trader, but I never believed it could be on this scale."

What did happen to Barings? Over a three-week period, Leeson apparently bought $27 billion in futures contracts. In doing so, he wagered—very heavily—that the sluggish Japanese stock market would stage a rally. If the Nikkei 225 rose as he predicted, Leeson would cash in and profit. How? The contract price on which he had originally agreed would be lower than the actual level of the index when the contract came due. He would profit by the amount of the difference. In fact, however, the Nikkei fell *below* Leeson's contract price—whereby Barings was obligated to *pay* the difference. The young trader tried desperately to reverse his losses, but he was forced to put up cash for margin calls. In other words, he had to pay to maintain a certain percentage of the daily value of his contract—which was dropping along with the Nikkei.

Where did Leeson get the money? Investigators believe that he convinced Barings officials in London to advance him more cash by claiming that he was trading on behalf of a client who would soon be depositing funds with the bank. The ploy failed. After leaving a note saying simply, "I'm sorry," Leeson disappeared. Several days later, he was apprehended by German police.

How could a single trader have racked up such losses? After all, Leeson's activities were subject to oversight by risk-management officials at Barings. Indeed, computers could have provided a warning when Leeson's trades exceeded pre-set amounts (as one financial expert notes, "There's widely available software for this type of risk management"). Barings officials, however, were slow to catch on, partly because Leeson was, in essence, supervising and settling his own trading activities. Despite warnings about lax controls over Leeson's trading following an internal audit in mid-1994, recommended changes were not made. For one thing, the same audit stressed Leeson's indispensability to the firm: "Without Leeson," advised internal audi-

tors, Barings' Singapore operations "would lack a trader with the right combination of experience in trading sizable lots, a detailed appreciation of trading strategies, familiarity with local traders' limits and practices, and contacts among traders and officials."

Another reason may have been internal rivalries and turf battles pitting Barings' London-based banking operations against the company's trading divisions in other parts of the world. In the weeks following Leeson's arrest, there was a flurry of accusations regarding which Barings executive should have been responsible for preventing the fiasco. "The great shame," lamented one Barings official, "is that we're very conservatively run. The one thing that we were trying to minimize—risk taking—is what blew us out of the water."

Ultimately, the fate of Barings PLC was determined within a matter of days. A Dutch banking and insurance company, Internationale Nederlanden Groep NV (ING), paid a nominal sum of one British pound in exchange for all of Barings' liabilities and assets. The purchase came after ING officials carefully inspected Barings' books. "Don't forget, we're Dutch, after all," explained a spokesperson for ING. "We've got a well-deserved reputation for caution and thriftiness." Still, ING announced that it would provide an immediate cash infusion of more than $1 billion to allow Barings to continue its operations.

What happened to Nick Leeson? After being arrested in Germany, he was kept in jail while awaiting extradition to Singapore. In late 1995, after a trial in Singapore, he was sentenced to six and a half years in prison.

■ *Case Questions*

1. Discuss Leeson's trading activities in terms of the risk-reward relationship.

2. Explain the type of risk that Leeson was facing in his financial dealings.

3. The Bank of England might have intervened to prevent Barings from falling into bankruptcy. What did Bank of England officials hope to achieve by not coming to the rescue?

4. Using the framework developed in the chapter, explain how a proper risk-management plan could help a financial institution prevent a disaster of the magnitude described in this case.

5. What are some of the risks and challenges ING might face as the new owner of Barings?

CHAPTER

18

UNDERSTANDING SECURITIES AND INVESTMENTS

A WHOPPER OF A FRAUD

David Walsh (shown in photo) started a company called Bre-X in the basement of his Calgary home in 1988. He readily admitted that he was looking for the pot of gold at the end of the rainbow. But he had to continually scramble to put deals together and to stay ahead of creditors.

Bre-X was eventually listed on the Alberta Stock Exchange, and the company acquired various mineral claims in the Northwest Territories. But Walsh had trouble raising exploration capital and the company was going nowhere. During this period, the price of Bre-X stock was about 27 cents a share.

In 1993, good fortune descended on David Walsh when John Felderhof, a mining friend, told him about some interesting mining properties in Indonesia, particularly a place called Busang. To get the money he needed to explore the site, Walsh convinced some friends to invest in Bre-X. He was able to raise $200 000 this way.

In September 1993, Bre-X did its first test drilling at the Busang site. Felderhof was convinced that there was about 2 million ounces of recoverable gold there. Eventually, Walsh struck a deal with the Toronto brokerage firm of Loewen Ondaatje McCutcheon Ltd. and received $4.5 million to continue exploration of Busang. By now Bre-X stock was trading at about $2 per share.

Late in 1994, the geologists found what they claimed was a large gold-laden dome of rock containing perhaps 10 million ounces of gold. When this news hit the stock market,

the value of Bre-X stock soared to nearly $15 per share. Over the next few months, estimates of the amount of gold at Busang increased to 100 million ounces, and by early 1996, Bre-X stock had rocketed to $150 per share. The company was now listed on the Toronto Stock Exchange. In May 1996, Bre-X shares split 10-for-1, and the price immediately moved up to $28 per share (a pre-split equivalent of $280 per share).

The good news continued unabated until early 1997. Then it was announced that Michael de Guzman, a Bre-X geologist, had died when he fell out of a helicopter. This immediately created suspicion about what was going on in Busang. Rumours also started circulating that there might not be as much gold as originally thought at the Busang site. What happened, so the rumour said, was that drilling samples had been "salted" (tampered with) to make it appear as if there was significant gold in the samples. This tampering could have easily been achieved by one or two people adding gold to sample bags. As this rumour spread during the next few weeks, the price of the stock gradually dropped from about $28 per share to $3 to $4 per share.

Eventually, an independent study of the Busang core samples was carried out by Strathcona Minerals Services. When that study showed that the Busang samples really had been salted, a panic ensued on the stock market. In one day, the price of the stock dropped from $3 per share to 8 cents per share as frantic investors sold off their holdings.

But most investors couldn't sell their shares at anything close to what they had been worth even the day before, and total losses were in the millions. Losses ranged widely: One investor from Vancouver learned a cheap lesson while losing only $100, but the City of Edmonton's pension fund lost $745 000. Karl Zetmeir, an investor who owned 200 000 shares of Bre-X when it was worth over $28 per share, hung in until the bitter end and lost $5.2 million. And First Marathon Inc., a sophisticated investment company, lost $4.5 million. Some companies actually profited from the debacle. New York–based Oppenheimer & Co. made $100 million by betting that the price of Bre-X was going to fall sharply.

On May 8, 1997, the Toronto Stock Exchange delisted Bre-X, saying that it no longer met the required listing standards. The wild ride was over, but investors filed two class action lawsuits against Bre-X, the TSE, and several brokerage firms that promoted the stock. The investors are trying to recover nearly $3 billion in losses because of the scam. A single organization, the Ontario Teachers Pension Plan Board, lost $300 million, but insiders at Bre-X made more than $100 million on stock options as the stock price rose during 1996. The lawsuits proceeded even though David Walsh died in 1998.

Although sensational, the Bre-X scam is not an isolated case. In early 1996, Timbuktu Gold Corp. stock was trading for $30 per share (up from 30 cents a share the year before), when it was revealed that core samples had been salted and that the gold strike was phoney. And, just a couple of weeks after the Bre-X fiasco, Delgratia Mining Corp. said that promising core samples from a Nevada property that it owned were also salted.

Thousands of Canadians regularly invest their money in stocks and bonds. As the opening case demonstrates, people who buy stocks may make money or they may lose money. Stock prices can rapidly change due to market conditions or the unethical behaviour of certain individuals, and the impact of these factors may be hard to predict. In this chapter, we will consider the types of markets in which stocks and bonds are sold. You will then be better able to understand the nature of interactions between buyers and sellers in these markets and the reasons for government regulation of them.

After reading this chapter, you should be able to:

1. Explain the difference between *primary* and *secondary securities markets*.
2. Discuss the value of *common stock* and *preferred stock* to shareholders and describe the secondary market for each type of security.
3. Distinguish among various types of *bonds* in terms of their issuers, safety, and retirement.
4. Describe the investment opportunities offered by *mutual funds* and *commodities*.
5. Explain the process by which securities are bought and sold.
6. Explain how securities markets are regulated.

■ WHAT ARE SECURITIES MARKETS?

securities
Stocks and bonds (which represent a secured-asset-based claim on the part of investors) that can be bought and sold.

Stocks and bonds are both known as **securities** because they represent a secured (asset-based) claim on the part of investors. But while stocks are a claim on all the assets of a corporation (because they represent a part-ownership of the business), bonds are strictly a financial claim on the business. Collectively, the market in which stocks and bonds are sold is called the *securities market*.

Primary and Secondary Markets for Securities

primary securities market
The sale and purchase of newly issued stocks and bonds by firms or governments.

Primary securities markets handle the buying and selling of new stocks and bonds by firms or governments. New securities are sometimes sold to one buyer or a small group of buyers. These so-called private placements allow the businesses that use them to keep their plans confidential. But because such offerings cannot be resold, buyers demand higher returns from them.

Most new stocks and some bonds are sold to the wider public market. To bring a new security to market, the issuing corporation must obtain approval from a provincial securities commission. It also needs the services of an investment banker. **Investment bankers** serve as financial specialists in issuing new securities. Such well-known firms as RBC Dominion Securities and Wood Gundy provide three types of investment banking services. They advise the company on the timing and financial terms for the new issue. By *under-writing* (buying) the new securities, investment bankers bear some of the risk of issuing the new security. And, finally, they create the distribution network that moves the new securities through groups of other banks and brokers into the hands of individual investors.

New securities represent only a small portion of securities traded, however. The market for existing stocks and bonds, the **secondary securities market**, is handled by organizations like the Toronto Stock Exchange. We will consider the activities of these markets later in this chapter, after you know more about stocks and bonds and who buys them.

investment banker
Any financial institution engaged in purchasing and reselling new stocks and bonds.

secondary securities market
The sale and purchase of previously issued stocks and bonds.

■STOCKS

Each year, financial managers, along with millions of individual investors, buy and sell the stocks of thousands of companies. This widespread ownership has become possible because of the availability of different types of stocks and because markets have been established for conveniently buying and selling them. In this section, we will focus on the value of *common* and *preferred stock* as securities. We will also describe the *stock exchanges* where they are bought and sold.

Toronto Stock Exchange
www.tse.com

Common Stock

Individuals and other companies buy a firm's common stock in the hope that the stock will increase in value, affording them a capital gain, and/or will provide dividend income. But what is the value of a common stock? Stock values are expressed in three different ways: as par value, as market value, and as book value.

Par Value.   The face value of a share of stock, its **par value**, is set by the issuing company's board of directors. But this arbitrary accounting value has almost nothing to do with the real value of the share.

Market Value.   The real value of a stock is its **market value**, the current price of a share in the stock market. Because it reflects buyers' willingness to invest, market value depends on a firm's history of dividend payments as well as expectations of **capital gains**, profits from selling the stock for more than it cost. Investors are primarily concerned with a stock's market value. Attempts are often made to influence the price of a stock (see the box "The Art of Influencing a Company's Stock Price").

Book Value.   Another commonly cited value, **book value**, represents shareholders' equity divided by the number of shares of common stock. Shareholders' equity is the sum of all common stock, retained earnings, and additional paid-in capital. While book value is often published in financial reports, its usefulness is also limited.

Investment Traits of Common Stock.   Common stocks are among the riskiest of securities. When companies have unprofitable years, they cannot pay dividends. Shareholder income—and perhaps share price too—drops. Even companies with solid reputations sometimes have downturns. IBM is an example. Cash dividends have been paid continuously to shareholders every year since 1916. Revenues per share grew steadily from the 1970s to 1990, then began falling until 1993, when IBM showed a financial loss rather than a profit. Along with lower earnings per share during 1990–93, IBM paid smaller dividends to shareholders each year. During this period, IBM's stock price fell steadily, from a 1990

par value
The arbitrary value of a stock set by the issuing company's board of directors and stated on stock certificates; used by accountants but of little significance to investors.

market value
The current price of one share of a stock in the secondary securities market; the real value of a stock.

capital gains
Profits from the sale of an asset (such as stock) for a higher price than that at which it was purchased.

book value
The value of a stock expressed as the total shareholders' equity (assets minus liabilities and preferred stock) divided by the number of shares of common stock outstanding; used by accountants but of little significance to investors.

TRENDS & CHALLENGES

The Art of Influencing a Company's Stock Price

What determines the price of a company's stock? There are some obvious financial things like a company's sales and earnings, or the number of promising new products it is bringing to the market. But other factors like stock market rumours, investor relations, and the activities of individual stockbrokers can also play a part.

Rumours   One of the most well-known stock exchanges in Canada is the Vancouver Stock Exchange, not because it is large or successful, but because numerous charges have been made that stock swindles and market manipulations are not adequately controlled. Overall, the exchange is viewed by many as a place where highly speculative stocks are traded, where rumour and speculation abound, and investors have a good chance of losing their shirt. This is especially true for the so-called "penny mine" stocks—those that cost less than a dollar per share and are very high-risk. A 1994 report (the latest of several which have been critical of the exchange) recommended that investors be given more information about the market, that stock promoters be more tightly regulated, and that more restrictions should be placed on traders' activities.

Investor Relations   This is the art of disseminating information about a company's financial condition through activities like annual meetings, corporate reports, road shows, site tours, contacts with stock analysts, and properly timing the release of financial information. While public relations tries to make the company look good to the general public, investor relations tries to play up the positive aspects of a company's finances to a sophisticated audience of stockbrokers, financial analysts, and financial institutions.

There is a fine line between investor relations and mere hype. Done poorly, it can cause the price of the company's stock to decline, which in turn impacts on the earnings of company executives, since part of their compensation package is made up of stock options. A reduced stock price also makes it harder for the firm to raise funds.

American Barrick Resources Corp. is a Toronto-based company that is well-known for its investor relations. The company's CEO meets with financial analysts over a lunch buffet to spread the good word about his company. He communicates openly with the financial community and conducts a question-and-answer period at the end of the lunch. In addition, the company publishes a detailed account of its various gold mining operations and also conducts site tours for interested analysts.

Stockbrokers   Individuals who buy and sell stock for their clients are also part of the equation that determines stock prices. Positive recommendations to customers can increase the demand for certain stock, and negative recommendations can reduce it. The brokerage industry has something of an image problem at the moment, due in part to the insider trading scandals of the late 1980s.

The general public has always worried that stockbrokers will put their own financial interests ahead of their customers'. Most brokers receive a combination of percentage of gross commissions (usually 30 to 45 percent) plus transaction size. A broker who grosses $150 000 annually in commissions with an average commission of $100 is lucky to take home $45 000. Because of these pressures, many brokers are not interested in customers with less than $20 000 in their account. To increase their earnings, brokers may be tempted to pursue a "churn and burn" strategy (buying and selling stocks frequently) to increase their commissions.

Customers who have large accounts may be able to negotiate discounts. A full-service broker (one that buys and sells stocks and performs other services like conducting research on companies) will charge an average of 2 percent of the total share price per trade. But a good customer could ask for a 10 percent discount on a $10 000 transaction, and a 20 percent discount on a $50 000 transaction. Discount brokers (those who provide few services beyond buying and selling shares of stock) charge about $40 per transaction.

IBM
www.ibm.net

high of $123 per share to a 1993 low of $41.[1] By 1995, however, profits had again increased, and IBM's stock price rose in 1996 to a high of $135. In 1996, things got even better, as IBM enjoyed a significant increase in its core business (selling computers and information technology to major corporations). In November 1996, IBM stock hit a nine-year high of $158.50.

Common stocks offer high growth potential for investors. In particular, the common stocks of pollution control, medical technology, natural gas, financial services, and high-technology firms can yield high returns. And the "blue-chip" stocks of some well-established firms like General Electric and Imperial Oil offer investors a history of secure income.

Preferred Stock

Preferred stock is usually issued with a stated par value, such as $100. Dividends paid on preferred stock are usually expressed as a percentage of the par value. For example, if a preferred stock with a $100 par value pays a 6 percent dividend, shareholders would receive an annual dividend of $6 on each share.

Some preferred stock is *callable*. The issuing firm can require the preferred shareholders to surrender their shares in exchange for a cash payment. The amount of this cash payment, known as the *call price*, is specified in the agreement between the preferred shareholders and the firm.

Investment Traits of Preferred Stock.   Because of its preference on dividends, preferred stock's income is less risky than the common stock of the same company. Moreover, most preferred stock is cumulative. With **cumulative preferred stock**, any dividend payments the firm misses must be paid later, as soon as the firm is able. Typically, the firm cannot pay any dividends to its common shareholders until it has made up all late payments to preferred shareholders. If a firm with preferred stock having a $100 par value and paying a 6 percent dividend fails to pay that dividend for two years, it must make up the arrears of $12 per share before it can pay dividends to common shareholders.

cumulative preferred stock
Preferred stock on which dividends not paid in the past must first be paid up before the firm may pay dividends to common shareholders.

Nevertheless, even the income from cumulative preferred stock is not as certain as the corporate bonds of the same company. The company cannot pay dividends if it does not make a profit. The purchase price of the preferred stock can also fluctuate, leading to a capital gain or loss for the shareholder. And the growth potential of preferred stock is limited due to its fixed dividend.

Stock Exchanges

Most of the secondary market for stocks is handled by organized stock exchanges. In addition, a so-called "dealer," or the over-the-counter, market handles the exchange of some stocks. A **stock exchange** is an organization of individuals formed to provide an institutional setting in which stock can be bought and sold. The exchange enforces certain rules to govern its members' trading activities. Most exchanges are non-profit corporations established to serve their members.

stock exchange
A voluntary organization of individuals formed to provide an institutional setting where members can buy and sell stock for themselves and their clients in accordance with the exchange's rules.

To become a member, an individual must purchase one of a limited number of memberships—called "seats"—on the exchange. Only members (or their representatives) are allowed to trade on the exchange. In this sense, because all orders to buy or sell must flow through members, they have a legal monopoly. Memberships can be bought and sold like other assets.

Brokers.   Some of the people working on the trading floor are employed by the exchange; others trade stocks for themselves. But a large number of those working on the trading floor are brokers. A **broker** receives buy and sell orders from those who are not members of the exchange and executes the orders. In return, the broker earns a commission from the order placer.

broker
An individual licensed to buy and sell securities for customers in the secondary market; may also provide other financial services.

More and more investors are starting to bypass brokers and buy stocks on the Internet. The box "The Brave New World of Cyberspace Brokerage" describes this trend.

The Toronto Stock Exchange.   The largest stock exchange in Canada is the Toronto Stock Exchange (TSE). It is made up of about 100 individual members who hold seats. The

TRENDS CHALLENGES

The Brave New World of Cyberspace Brokerage

People who trade securities are in it to make money. Therefore, it should come as no surprise that thousands of computer-savvy investors are trying to maximize profits by doing business with discount brokers on the Internet. The following figures tell a story about how much investors can save by executing their own buys and sells in cyberspace.

- Merrill Lynch, a full-service broker offering extensive investment research, personal service, and order execution, charges $100 to $1100 to trade 100 to 5000 shares of stock.

- Fidelity Investments, a traditional discount broker that executes orders over the phone but provides no research, charges between $55 and $270 for the same trade.

- E*Trade Securities, an electronic discount broker that lets customers handle their own account activities, charges a flat $15 to $20 for most trades.

Ed Harrison, a small investor from Santa Clarita, California, makes several trades a week on the Internet and sees cyberspace investing as an opportunity to save money. "My broker was so nice, but boy, he was robbing me," reports Harrison. "All he ever did was place my trades. I can do that for myself." And he can do it simply. "Anyone who feels comfortable picking up the phone and telling a broker, 'Buy me 100 shares of such and such' would find this just as easy," maintains Frederick Roehm, a Portland, Oregon, student.

Although investors are happy doing business with Internet-based discount brokers, full-service brokers are worried that this newest investment trend may undermine their customer base. As investors realize that they can tap into investment research sites on the Web, obtain stock quotes and mutual fund rankings, and execute orders via

an Internet broker at any time of the day or night, they are likely to question whether full-service brokers are worth premium prices.

This skepticism is likely to become more pronounced as Internet brokers add a variety of services to help guide investment decisions. Lombard Institutional Brokerage, for example, offers graphs showing the movement of stocks and options as well as a free quotation service that gives investors the ability to track, via their own computers, the movement of up to 50 stocks. By the middle of 1996, more than one million investors had visited Lombard's Website, and activity in the company's 7000 Internet accounts tripled in a three-month period.

The pressure from Internet brokers is already changing traditional brokers. For the first time, Prudential is allowing customers to access their accounts on the Web, although trades are not yet permitted. Fidelity Investments will allow individuals to review their personal retirement accounts on the Web and plans to implement its own electronic trading system some time in the near future.

How do investors reach Web-based brokers? Here are three addresses:

E*Trade
www.etrade.com

**Lombard Institutional
Brokerage Inc.**
www.lombard.com

Pawws Financial Network
www.pawws.com

securities of most major corporations are listed here. A company must pay a fee before it can list its security on the exchange. In addition to the TSE, there are stock exchanges in Winnipeg, Calgary, Vancouver, and Montreal.

New York Stock Exchange
www.nyse.com

The New York Stock Exchange.   For many people, "the stock market" means the New York Stock Exchange (NYSE). Founded in 1792 and located at the corner of Wall and Broad Streets in New York City, the largest of all U.S. exchanges is in fact the model for exchanges worldwide. With an average of 345 million shares changing hands each day, about 45 percent of all shares traded on U.S. exchanges are traded there.

The Toronto Stock Exchange is one of several in Canada where shares of stock in Canadian companies are bought and sold.

Only firms meeting certain minimum requirements—earning power, total value of outstanding stock, and number of shareholders—are eligible for listing on the NYSE. In 1995, about 2700 listings were traded on the NYSE with a total market value of about $3.1 trillion. Exxon Corp.'s common shares had the highest value in 1995—$145 billion. NYSE trading volume in 1995 was over 87 billion shares.[2]

The Montreal Stock Exchange.   In recent years, the Montreal Exchange has been aggressively promoting itself and improving its trading systems. It now accounts for nearly 24 percent of the combined Montreal-Toronto trading value. The Montreal Exchange has a sizable market share in many of Canada's blue-chip companies. It handles more than 50 percent of the shares traded in companies like Bombardier, Provigo, Memotec Data, and Power Corporation.

Foreign Stock Exchanges.   In 1980, the U.S. stock market accounted for over half the market value of the world market. In 1975, the equity of IBM alone was greater than the national market equities of all but four countries! Market activities, however, have shifted as the value of shares listed on foreign exchanges continues to grow. The annual dollar value of trades on exchanges in London, Tokyo, and other cities is in the trillions. In fact, the London exchange exceeds even the NYSE in number of stocks listed; in market value, transactions on U.S. exchanges are now second to those on Japanese exchanges.

New exchanges are beginning to flourish in cities from Shanghai, China, to Warsaw, Poland. Founded in 1991, for example, the Chinese exchange now trades about $350 million in shares on a good day—more than the bustling Hong Kong exchange on a slow day. China now has about 2 million shareholders in various companies, with the number growing about 50 000 every week.

Meanwhile, many analysts currently regard the Polish exchange as the world's strongest-performing market. Although it lists only 22 stocks, the Polish index increased in volume by 700 percent in 1993. In countries like both China and Poland, thriving stock exchanges have contributed, among other things, to more efficient, profit-conscious companies (many of them once or still state-owned).[3]

Foreign stock exchanges have become increasingly important to portfolio managers. Foreign exchanges allow investors to *diversify* (spread investable funds among a variety of investments to reduce risk). Astute managers have also been able to achieve higher returns by investing internationally.

The Over-the-Counter (OTC) Market.   Many securities are not listed on any of the organized securities exchanges. Making a market in these securities is one of the functions of investment dealers. These securities are traded in the over-the-counter (OTC) market. (In reality, it is an over-the-telephone market.) The **over-the-counter market** is a complex of dealers in constant touch with one another. Stocks and bonds of some smaller corporations are traded on the OTC market as well as all fixed-income securities, including bonds and debentures. The Canadian Dealing Network (CDN), a subsidiary of the Toronto Stock Exchange, is an over-the-counter network. In 1997, the value of shares traded throught CDN was worth $12.6 billion, an amount almost equal to the value of shares traded on the Vancouver and Alberta stock exchanges combined.[4]

Security dealers in the OTC market often buy securities in their own names. They must maintain an inventory of securities to make a market in them. They hope to sell them to their clients at a higher price. These dealers also buy shares at the request of their clients for a commission. Dealers selling to one another charge a wholesale price and sell to their customers at a retail price.

■ BONDS

A **bond** is a written promise that the borrower will pay the lender, at some stated future date, a sum of money (the principal) and a stated rate of interest. Bondholders have a claim on a corporation's assets and earnings that comes before the claims of common and preferred shareholders. Bonds differ from one another in terms of maturity, tax status, and level of risk versus potential yield (the interest rate). Potential investors must take these factors into consideration to evaluate which particular bond to buy.

To help bond investors make assessments, several services rate the quality of bonds from different issuers. Table 18.1 shows ratings by three principal rating services: Standard & Poor's, Moody's, and the Canadian Bond Rating Service. The rating measures the bond's *default risk*—the chance that one or more promised payments will be deferred or missed altogether. Credit ratings by Canadian agencies are often more lenient than the ratings given by U.S. agencies. While the differences are not great, on various occasions they are enough to make a company's bonds classified as "investment" grade rather than "junk."[5]

Although all corporations issue common stock, not all issue bonds. Shareholders provide equity (ownership) capital, while bondholders are lenders (although they are also considered "investors" as far as the securities market is concerned). Stock certificates represent ownership, while bond certificates represent indebtedness. Federal, provincial, and city governments as well as non-profit organizations also issue bonds.

over-the-counter (OTC) market
A complex of dealers in constant touch with one another who trade stocks and bonds of some smaller corporations and all fixed-income securities (bonds and debentures).

Canadian Dealing Network
tse.com/investor/cdnwhat.html

bond
A written promise that the borrower will pay the lender, at a stated future date, the principal plus a stated rate of interest.

Canadian Bond Rating Service
www.cbrs.com

■ TABLE 18.1   Bond Ratings

	High Grade	Medium Grade (Investment Grade)	Speculative	Poor Grade
Moody's	Aaa Aa	A Baa	Ba B	Caa to C
Standard & Poor's	AAA AA	A BBB	BB B	CCC to D
Canadian Bond Rating Service	A++	B++	C	B

Government Bonds

Government bonds—for example, New Canada Savings Bonds—are among the safest investments available. However, securities with longer maturities are somewhat riskier than short-term issues because their longer lives expose them to more political, social, and economic changes. All federal bonds, however, are backed by the Canadian government. Government securities are sold in large blocks to institutional investors who buy them to ensure desired levels of safety in portfolios. As their needs change, they may buy or sell government securities to other investors.

Provincial and local governments also issue bonds (called municipal bonds) to finance school and transportation systems and a variety of other projects. The most attractive feature of municipal bonds is the fact that investors do not pay taxes on interest received. Banks invest in bonds nearing maturity because they are relatively safe, liquid investments. Pension funds, insurance companies, and private citizens also make longer-term investments in municipals.

Corporate Bonds

Corporate bonds are a major source of long-term financing for Canadian corporations. They have traditionally been issued with maturities ranging from 20 to 30 years. In the 1980s, 10-year maturities came into wider use. As with government bonds, longer-term corporate bonds are somewhat riskier than shorter-term bonds. Bond ratings of new and proposed corporate issues are published to keep investors informed of the latest risk evaluations on many bonds. Negative ratings do not preclude a bond's success, but they do raise the interest rate that issuers must offer.

Corporate bonds may be categorized in one of two ways: (1) according to methods of interest payment and (2) according to whether they are *secured* or *unsecured*.

Private corporations are not the only organizations that issue bonds. The government of Canada issues New Canada Savings Bonds to finance its debt.

registered bond
Names of holders are registered with the company.

bearer (coupon) bonds
Require bondholders to clip coupons from certificates and send them to the issuer in order to receive interest payments.

secured bonds
Bonds issued by borrowers who pledge assets as collateral in the event of nonpayment.

debentures
Unsecured bonds.

callable bond
A bond that may be paid off by the issuer before the maturity date.

sinking-fund provision
A clause in the bond indenture (contract) that requires the issuing company to put enough money into a special bank account each year to cover the retirement of the bond issue on schedule.

serial bond
A bond issue in which redemption dates are staggered so that a firm pays off portions of the issue at different predetermined dates.

convertible bond
Any bond that offers bondholders the option of accepting common stock instead of cash in repayment.

Interest Payment: Registered and Bearer Bonds. **Registered bonds** register the names of holders with the company, which simply mails out cheques. Certificates are of value only to registered holders. **Bearer** (or **coupon**) **bonds** require bondholders to clip coupons from certificates and send them to the issuer in order to receive payment. Coupons can be redeemed by anyone, regardless of ownership.

Secured Bonds. Borrowers can reduce the risk of their bonds by pledging assets to bondholders in the event of default. **Secured bonds** can be backed by first mortgages, other mortgages, or other specific assets. If the corporation does not pay interest when it is due, the firm's assets can be sold and the proceeds used to pay the bondholders.

Unsecured Bonds. Unsecured bonds are called **debentures**. No specific property is pledged as security for these bonds. Holders of unsecured bonds generally have claims against property not otherwise pledged in the company's other bonds. Accordingly, debentures have inferior claims on the corporation's assets. Financially strong corporations often use debentures.

The Retirement of Bonds

Maturity dates on bonds of all kinds may be very long. But all bonds must be paid off—*retired*—at some point. Most bonds are callable, but others are serial or convertible.

Callable Bonds. Many corporate bonds are callable. The issuer of a **callable bond** has the right at almost any time to call the bonds in and pay them off at a price stipulated in the bond indenture (contract). Usually the issuer cannot call the bond for a certain period of time after issue, but some are callable at any time.

Issuers are most likely to call in existing bonds when the prevailing interest rate is lower than the rate being paid on the bond. But the price the issuer must pay to call in the bond, the *call price*, usually gives a premium to the bondholder. For example, a bond might have a $100 face value and be callable by the firm for $108.67 anytime during the first year after being issued. The call price and the premium decrease annually as the bonds near maturity.

A Notice of Redemption calls for certain bonds to be turned in and paid off by the issuer. The accrual of interest on the selected bonds stops upon the redemption date.

Sinking Funds. Bonds are often retired by the use of a **sinking-fund provision** in the bond indenture. This method requires the issuing company to put a certain amount of money into a special bank account each year. At the end of a number of years, the money in this account (including interest) is sufficient to redeem the bonds. Failure to meet the sinking-fund provision places the bond issue in default. Bonds with sinking funds are generally regarded as safer investments than bonds without them.

Serial and Convertible Bonds. As an alternative to sinking funds, some corporations issue serial or convertible bonds. In a **serial bond** issue, the firm retires portions of the bond issue at different predetermined dates. In a $100 million serial bond issue maturing in 20 years, for example, the company may retire $5 million of the issue each year.

Convertible bonds can be paid off in (converted to) common stock of the issuing company, at the option of the bondholder, instead of in cash. Since bondholders have a chance for capital gains, the company can offer lower interest rates when issuing the bonds. However, since bondholders cannot be forced to accept stock in lieu of money, conversion will work only if the corporation is considered a good investment.

To draw a clearer picture of how convertible bonds work, let's consider the following example. In 1993, Lowe's Companies Inc. sold a $250 million issue of 4 1/2 percent convertible bonds. The bonds were issued in $1000 denominations; they mature in 2003 and are called after 1996. At any time before maturity, each debenture of $1000 is convertible into 19 1/8 shares of the company's common stock. Between October 1993 and March 1994, the stock price ranged from a low of $28 to a high of $67. In that time, then, 19 1/8 common shares had a market value ranging from $535 to $1281.[6] In other words, the holder could have exchanged the $1000 bond in return for stock to be kept or sold at a possible profit (or loss).

Secondary Securities Markets for Bonds

Unlike stocks, nearly all secondary trading in bonds occurs in the over-the-counter market rather than on any organized exchange. As a result, precise statistics about annual trading volumes are not recorded.

Like stocks, however, market values and prices of bonds change from day to day. Prices of bonds with average risks tend to move up or down until the interest rate they yield generally reflects the prevailing interest rate of the economy. That is, the direction of bond prices moves opposite to interest rate changes—as interest rates move up, bond prices tend to go down. The prices of riskier bonds fluctuate more than those of higher-grade bonds and often exceed the interest rate of the economy.

■ OTHER INVESTMENTS

Although stocks and bonds are very important, they are not the only marketable securities for businesses. Financial managers are also concerned with investment opportunities in mutual funds, commodities, and options.

Mutual Funds

Companies called **mutual funds** pool investments from individuals and other firms to purchase a portfolio of stocks, bonds, and short-term securities. Investors are part-owners of this portfolio. For example, if you invest $1000 in a mutual fund that has a portfolio worth $100 000, you own 1 percent of the portfolio. Mutual funds usually have portfolios worth many millions of dollars.

Like stocks and bonds, there are many types of mutual funds. Investors in **no-load funds** are not charged a sales commission when they buy into or sell out of the mutual fund. **Load funds** carry a charge of between 2 and 8 percent of the invested funds.

Mutual funds vary by the investment goals they stress. Some stress safety. The portfolios of these mutual funds include treasury bills and other safe issues that offer immediate income (liquidity). Short-term municipal bond funds emphasize tax-exempt immediate income.

Other funds seek higher current income and are willing to sacrifice some safety. Long-term municipal bond mutual funds, corporate bond mutual funds, and income mutual funds (which invest in common stocks with good dividend-paying records) all fall into this category.

Still other funds stress growth. Examples include balanced mutual funds, which hold a mixture of bonds, preferred stocks, and common stocks. Growth mutual funds stress common stocks of established firms. Aggressive growth mutual funds seek maximum capital appreciation. To get it, these funds sacrifice current income and safety. They invest in stocks of new companies, troubled companies, and other high-risk securities.

Mutual funds give small investors access to professional financial management. Their managers have up-to-date information about market conditions and the best large-scale investment opportunities. The box "Are Pension and Mutual Funds Too Powerful?" describes a potential problem in this area

mutual fund
Any company that pools the resources of many investors and uses those funds to purchase various types of financial securities, depending on the fund's financial goals.

no-load fund
A mutual fund in which investors are not charged a sales commission when they buy into or sell out of the fund.

load fund
A mutual fund in which investors are charged a sales commission when they buy into or sell out of the fund.

TRENDS & CHALLENGES

Are Pension and Mutual Funds Too Powerful?

Institutional investors such as pension and mutual funds invest money in the stock market for themselves and for their clients. During the past decade, the activities of institutional investors have increased so much that by early 1995 they accounted for 72 percent of the volume on the Toronto Stock Exchange. In the mid-1980s, the figure was less than 60 percent.

John Hart, the president of the Canadian Shareholders Association, says that pension and mutual funds have formidable power to control the activities of corporate Canada by investing (or not investing) in certain stocks. Over the past decade, these funds have acquired large blocks of shares in many publicly traded Canadian companies.

Why has this shift taken place? Because mutual funds are growing in popularity with investors who want professionals to invest their money. The stock market crash in October 1987 drove many individual investors from the market, and they have not returned. Observers of the stock market worry that with so few organizations dominating the daily trading on the exchange, that an oligopoly effectively exists and this is not consistent with traditional ideas about stock markets.

In order to work efficiently, a stock market should have many small investors, each investing in a variety of companies. But in the current situation, there are relatively few investors, so the market is not very "liquid." This may make it difficult to determine what the real value of a stock is. It also makes it difficult for smaller firms to obtain equity capital because stock market analysts focus all their concern on the bigger firms.

The recent activities of the Ontario Teachers Pension Plan Board (OTPPB) illustrate the concerns that many observers have about the impact of institutional investors on the stock market. The OTPPB invests pension contributions from over 200 000 Ontario teachers. The market value of its investments is currently about $35 billion.

The power of the OTPPB can be seen if we consider the move by Wallace McCain (recently ousted from McCain Foods) to convince Hillsdown Holdings PLC to sell him a controlling stake in Maple Leaf Foods Inc. While McCain did take the usual contingent of investment bankers to the takeover discussions, he also took along George Engman, the vice president of Ontario Teachers. Engman was at the meeting because he was carrying a commitment from Teachers to invest $150 million in the Maple Leaf Foods bid. Without this commitment, McCain would probably have found it difficult to interest banks in lending money for the takeover. (The strategy worked and McCain now owns Maple Leaf Foods.)

Pension funds became more active in the stock market after the province of Ontario relaxed the strict investment rules that had formerly applied to pension funds. The OTPPB set up a merchant banking team, which oversees the pension fund's purchases of shares to help acquirers finance corporate takeovers or restructuring. In just a few years, the OTPPB has spent about $500 million on corporate acquisitions; more than $1 billion of additional money is authorized.

This active involvement in acquisitions by pension funds is a new development. Some large U.S. pension funds *indirectly* finance acquisitions by investing in acquisition funds, but they are not directly involved in this kind of activity. The Ontario Municipal Employees Retirement Board (OMERS) has also directly invested some of its $21 billion in acquisitions, but most of those are low-profile ventures.

Commodities

futures contract
An agreement to purchase a specified amount of a commodity at a given price on a set date in the future.

commodities market
The market in which investors can buy and sell contracts for a variety of goods.

In addition to buying and selling bonds, individuals and businesses may elect to buy and sell commodities as an investment. **Futures contracts**—agreements to purchase a specified amount of a commodity at a given price on a set date in the future—can be bought and sold in the **commodities market**. Futures contracts are available for commodities ranging from coffee beans and live hogs to propane and platinum, as well as for stocks. Since selling prices reflect traders' beliefs about the future, prices of such contracts are very volatile, and futures trading is very risky. The Chicago Board of Trade is the world's largest commodity exchange. The Winnipeg Commodity Exchange is the largest commodity exchange in Canada.

To clarify the workings of the commodities market, let's look at an example. On April 29, 1996, the price of gold on the open market was U.S.$392.40 per ounce. Futures contracts for October 1996 gold were selling for $397.10 per ounce. This price reflected investors' judgment that gold prices would be higher the following October. Now suppose that you purchased a 100-ounce gold futures contract in April for $39 710 ($397.10 × 100). If in June 1996 the October gold futures sold for $422.10, you could sell your contract for $42 210. Your profit after the two months would be $2500.

Winnipeg Commodity Exchange
www.wce.mb.ca

Margins.   Usually, buyers of futures contracts need not put up full purchase amounts. Rather, the buyer posts a smaller amount—the **margin**—that may be as small as $3000 for contracts up to $100 000. Let's look again at our gold futures example. As we saw, if you had posted a $3000 margin for your October gold contract, you would have earned a $2500 profit on that investment of $3000 in only two months.

However, you also took a big risk involving two big *ifs*:

1. If you had held onto your contract, and
2. if gold had dropped to a value of only $377 in October 1996,

you would have lost $2010. If you had posted a $3000 margin to buy the contract, you would receive only $990. In fact, between 75 and 90 percent of all small-time investors lose money in the futures market. For one thing, the action is fast and furious, with small investors trying to keep up with professionals ensconced in seats on the major exchanges. Although the profit potential is also exciting, experts recommend that most novices retreat to safer stock markets. Of course, as one veteran financial planner puts it, commodities are tempting: "After trading commodities," he reports, "trading stocks is like watching the grass grow."[7]

Most investors in commodities markets never intend to take possession of the commodity in question. They merely buy and sell the futures contracts. But some companies buy futures to protect the price of commodities important to their businesses, as when Canada Packers trades in hog futures.

More than 400 "commodity exchanges" have opened up in the former Soviet Union. These exchanges bring together buyers and sellers of many different types of goods. Although they call themselves commodity exchanges, they are in fact far more primitive than commodity exchanges in Canada and the U.S. One trader says they are more like flea markets than commodity exchanges.[8]

margin
The percentage of the total sales price that a buyer must put up to place an order for stock or a futures contract.

Gold is one of the many commodities for which futures contracts can be bought.

■ BUYING AND SELLING SECURITIES

The process of buying and selling stocks, bonds, and other financial instruments is complex. To start, you need to find out about possible investments and match them to your investment objectives. Then you can select a broker and open an account. Only when you have a broker can you place different types of orders and make different types of transactions.

Using Financial Information Services

Have you ever looked at the financial section of your daily newspaper and found yourself wondering what all those tables and numbers mean? If you cannot read stock-and-bond quotations, you probably should not invest in these issues. Fortunately, this skill is easily mastered. More complicated but also important is some grasp of market indexes.

Stock Quotations.   Figure 18.1 shows the type of information newspapers give about daily market transactions of individual stocks. The corporation's name is shown along with the number of shares sold (expressed in board lots). Prices are quoted in dollars and fractions of a dollar ranging from 1/8 to 7/8. A quote of 50 5/8 means that the price per share is $50.625.

Company	Sales	High	Low	Close	Change
H Bay Co	347 106	34.500	32.000	32.250	-2.500
Humbird	196 310	50.250	47.250	48.850	-2.900
Hy Zels	1 500	4.700	4.700	4.700	-0.100
IBEX T	3 500	5.600	5.250	5.400	-0.200
IITC A	7 000	1.000	1.000	1.000	0.000
IPL eng	38 329	53.000	52.000	52.650	+0.150
ISG Tech	6 583	4.050	3.900	3.950	-0.150
Imasco L	439 447	44.800	44.000	44.250	-0.500
Imax	46 058	35.000	34.000	35.000	+0.500
Imp Metal	22 879	1.630	1.530	1.590	-0.020
Imperial Oil	311 141	87.700	84.750	87.100	+1.100
Inco	**376 030**	**29.150**	**28.500**	**28.600**	**-0.400**
Indochin o	6 100	5.700	5.500	5.500	-0.100
Inex Ph o	8 800	5.250	5.000	5.250	-0.100
Infocorp o	24 400	0.750	0.660	0.740	-0.010
Innova T o	15 000	0.870	0.870	0.870	-0.030
Insulpro	12 000	1.180	1.080	1.130	+0.020

- *Stock*
  Inco (Name of Company)
- *Sales*
  376 030
  Total number of shares traded on this date. There were 376 030 shares sold.
- *High*　　　　*Low*
  29.150　　　28.500
  During the trading day, the highest price was $29.15 and the lowest price was $28.50.
- *Close*
  28.600
  At the close of trading on this date, the last price paid per share was $28.60.
- *Net Change*
  -0.400
  Difference between today's closing price and previous day's closing price. Price decreased by $0.40.

FIGURE 18.1
How to read a stock quotation.

Bond Quotations. Bond prices also change from day to day. These changes form the *coupon rate*, which provides information for firms about the cost of borrowing funds.

Prices of domestic corporation bonds, Canadian government bonds, and foreign bonds are reported separately. Bond prices are expressed in terms of 100, even though most have a face value of $1000. Thus, a quote of 85 means that the bond's price is 85 percent of its face value, or $850.

A corporation bond selling at 155 1/4 would cost a buyer $1552.50 ($1000 face value × 1.5525), plus commission. The interest rate on bonds is also quoted as a percentage of par, or face, value. Thus "6 1/2s" pay 6.5 percent of par value per year. Typically, interest is paid semiannually at half of the stated interest or coupon rate.

The market value (selling price) of a bond at any given time depends on its stated interest rate, the "going rate" of interest in the market, and its redemption or maturity date. A bond with a higher stated interest rate than the going rate on similar quality bonds will probably sell at a premium above its face value—its selling price will be above its redemption price. A bond with a lower stated interest rate than the going rate on similar quality bonds will probably sell at a discount—its selling price will be below its redemption price. How much the premium or discount is depends largely on how far in the future the maturity date is. The maturity date is shown after the interest rate. When more than one year is given, the bond is either retractable or extendible.

Figure 18.2 shows the type of information daily newspapers give about bond transactions.

	Issuer	Coupon	Maturity	Price	Yield	Change
■ *BC Tel* Company name is British Columbia Telephone.	**GOVERNMENT OF CANADA**					
	Canada	4.00	Mar 15-99	100.175	3.865	+0.158
	Canada	7.75	Sep 1-99	105.627	4.514	+0.124
■ *Coupon* The annual rate of interest at face value is 9.65 percent.	Canada	5.50	Feb 1-00	101.897	4.600	+0.155
	Canada	8.50	Mar 1-00	108.417	4.648	+0.164
	Canada	7.50	Sep 1-00	107.122	4.780	+0.199
■ *Maturity* The maturity date is April 8, 2022.	**PROVINCIALS AND GUARANTEED**					
	Alta	8.00	Mar 1-00	107.242	4.673	+0.130
■ *Price* On this date, $138.48 was the price of the last transaction.	BC	9.00	Jan 9-02	114.729	5.046	+0.250
	Hy Que	7.00	Jun 1-04	108.100	5.514	+0.460
	Man	7.75	Sep 14-00	107.604	4.868	+0.172
	Ont Hy	7.75	Nov 3-05	114.086	5.546	+0.493
	PEI	8.50	Oct 27-15	123.663	6.285	+0.845
■ *Yield* This is computed by dividing the annual interest paid by the current market price.	**CORPORATE**					
	Bell	8.80	Aug 24-04	119.790	5.491	+0.490
■ *Change* The closing price on this day was up $1.11 from the closing price on the previous day.	**BC Tel**	**9.65**	**Apr 8-22**	**138.489**	**6.488**	**+1.118**
	Cdn Util	8.43	Jun 1-05	117.385	5.583	+0.475
	Nova Gas	8.30	Jul 15-03	113.508	5.503	+0.386
	Royal Bk	5.40	Sep 7-02	100.461	5.289	+0.297
	Suncor	6.10	Aug 7-07	100.959	5.967	+0.515

FIGURE 18.2
How to read a bond quotation.

Bond Yield. Suppose you bought a $1000 par-value bond in 1980 for $650. Its stated interest rate is 6 percent, and its maturity or redemption date is 2000. You therefore receive $60 per year in interest. Based on your actual investment of $650, your yield is 9.2 percent. If you hold it to maturity, you get $1000 for a bond that originally cost you only $650. This extra $350 increases your true, or effective, yield.

Market Indexes. Although they do not indicate how particular securities are doing, **market indexes** provide a useful summary of trends in specific industries and the stock market as a whole. Such information can be crucial in choosing appropriate investments. For example, market indexes reveal bull and bear market trends. **Bull markets** are periods of upward-moving stock prices. The years 1981 to 1989 featured a strong bull market. Periods of falling stock prices, such as 1972 to 1974, are called **bear markets**.

The most widely cited market index is the **Dow Jones Industrial Average**. The "Dow," as it is sometimes called, is the sum of market prices for 30 of the largest industrial firms listed on the NYSE. By tradition, the Dow is an indicator of blue-chip stock price movements. Because of the limited number of firms it considers, however, it is a limited gauge of the overall stock market.

The Dow has been very volatile during the mid-1990s. On February 23, 1995, it topped 4000 for the first time ever. On April 24, it went over 4300. On November 20, 1996, it broke the 6400 barrier for the first time, and on February 13, 1997, it topped 7000. In July 1997, the index rose above 8000, by March 1998 it rose above 8600 and by April 1998 it rose above 9000.

market index
A measure of the market value of stocks; provides a summary of price trends in a specific industry or of the stock market as a whole.

bull market
A period of rising stock prices; a period in which investors act on a belief that stock prices will rise.

bear market
A period of falling stock prices; a period in which investors act on a belief that stock prices will fall.

Dow Jones Industrial Average
An overall market index based on stock prices of 30 of the largest industrial, transportation, and utility firms listed on the New York Stock Exchange.

Why was there such optimism on the part of investors? What does the Dow's performance say about attitudes towards the economy? Though unable to pinpoint one single reason for the Dow's performance, experts cite three factors that have been important: continued growth in corporate profits, continued merger and acquisition activity, and continued low inflation and low interest rates.

But with the Dow rising so far so fast, experts also expect that there will be some major downturns. In October 1997, for example, the Dow dropped over 550 points in one day. That was an all-time record drop. The next day, however, the Dow rebounded by over 300 points.

Selecting a Broker

In choosing a broker, you must consider what services you need. All brokerages execute customers' orders for securities purchases and sales. **Discount brokerage houses** do little beyond this minimum. But their low commissions make them popular with some investors.

In contrast, **full-service brokerages** offer a variety of services, including investment advice to meet individuals' financial goals. They suggest the best mix of debt versus equity for corporate investors. One service that some brokerages use as a tool in competing with other houses is research. Firms that offer research services provide clients with assessments on the quality and investment prospects of different industries, companies, and securities. Such reports are supplied free of charge, but brokerage fees are higher at these houses.

Placing an Order

Based on your own investigations and/or recommendations from your broker, you can place many types of orders. A **market order** requests the broker to buy or sell a certain security at the prevailing market price at the time. For example, your broker would have sold your Alcan stock for between $37.62 and $38.00 per share on April 5, 1995. When you gave the order to sell, however, you did not know exactly what the market price would be.

In contrast, both limit and stop orders allow for buying and selling of securities only if certain price conditions are met. A **limit order** authorizes the purchase of a stock only if its price is less than or equal to a given limit. For example, a limit order to buy a stock at $80 per share means that the broker is to buy it if and only if the stock becomes available for a price of $80 or less. Similarly, a **stop order** instructs the broker to sell a stock if its price falls to a certain level. For example, a stop order of $85 on a particular stock means that the broker is to sell it if and only if its price falls to $85 or below.

You can also place orders of different sizes. A **round lot** order requests 100 shares or some multiple thereof. Fractions of a round lot are called **odd lots**. Trading odd lots is usually more expensive than trading round lots, because an intermediary called an odd-lot broker is often involved, which increases brokerage fees.

Financing Securities Purchases

When you place a buy order of any kind, you must tell your broker how you will pay for the purchase. You might maintain a cash account with your broker. Then, as stocks are bought and sold, proceeds are added into the account and commissions and costs of purchases are withdrawn by the broker. In addition, as with almost every good in today's economy, you can buy shares on credit.

discount brokerage house
A stock brokerage that charges a minimal fee for executing clients' orders but offers only limited services.

full-service brokerage
A stock brokerage that offers a variety of services, including investment advice, to help clients reach their financial goals.

market order
An order to a broker to buy or sell a certain security at the current market price.

limit order
An order to a broker to buy a certain security only if its price is less than or equal to a given limit.

stop order
An order to a broker to sell a certain security if its price falls to a certain level or below.

round lot
The purchase or sale of stock in units of 100 shares.

odd lots
The purchase or sale of stock in units other than 100 shares.

Margin Trading.   As with futures contracts, you can buy stocks on *margin*—putting down only a portion of the stock's price. You borrow the rest from your broker, who, in turn, borrows from the banks at a special rate and secures the loans with stock.

Margin trading offers clear advantages to buyers. Suppose you purchased $100 000 worth of stock in Alcan, paying $50 000 of your own money and borrowing the other $50 000 from your broker at 10 percent interest. If, after one year, the shares have risen in value to $115 000, you could sell them, pay your broker $55 000 ($50 000 principal plus $5000 interest), and have $60 000 left over. Your original investment of $50 000 would have earned a 20 percent profit of $10 000. If you had paid the entire price of the stock from your own funds, your investment would have earned only a 15 percent return.

Brokerages benefit from margin trading in two ways. First, it encourages more people to buy more stock, which means more commissions to the brokerage. And, second, the firm earns a profit on its loans, since it charges buyers a higher interest rate than it pays the bank.

Short Sales.   In addition to money, brokerages also lend buyers securities. A **short sale** begins when you borrow a security from your broker and sell it (one of the few times it is legal to sell what you do not own). At a given time in the future, you must restore an equal number of shares of that issue to the brokerage, along with a fee.

For example, suppose that in June you believe the price of Alcan stock will soon fall. You order your broker to sell short 100 shares at the market price of $38 per share. Your broker will make the sale and credit $3800 to your account. If Alcan's price falls to $32 per share in July, you can buy 100 shares for $3200 and give them to your broker, leaving you with a $600 profit (before commissions). The risk is that Alcan's price will not fall but will hold steady or rise, leaving you with a loss.

short sale
Selling borrowed shares of stock in the expectation that their price will fall before they must be replaced, so that replacement shares can be bought for less than the original shares were sold for.

■ SECURITIES REGULATION

Canada, unlike the United States with its Securities and Exchange Commission (SEC), does not have comprehensive federal securities legislation or a federal regulatory body. Government regulation is primarily provincial and there is a degree of self-regulation through the various securities exchanges.

In 1912, the Manitoba government pioneered in Canada laws applying mainly to the sale of new securities. Under these **"blue-sky laws,"** corporations issuing securities must back them up with something more than the blue sky. Similar laws were passed in other provinces. Provincial laws also generally require that stockbrokers be licensed and securities be registered before they can be sold. In each province, issuers of proposed new securities must file a prospectus with the provincial securities exchange. A **prospectus** is a detailed registration statement that includes information about the firm, its operation, its management, the purpose of the proposed issue, and any other data helpful to a potential buyer of these securities. The prospectus must be made available to prospective investors.

Ontario is regarded as having the most progressive securities legislation in Canada. The *Ontario Securities Act* contains disclosure provisions for new and existing issues, prevention of fraud, regulation of the Toronto Stock Exchange, and takeover bids. It also prohibits **insider trading**, which is the use of special knowledge about a firm to make a profit in the stock market.

The Toronto Stock Exchange provides an example of self-regulation by the industry. The TSE has regulations concerning listing and delisting of securities, disclosure requirements, and issuing of prospectuses for new securities.

U.S. Securities and Exchange Commission
www.sec.gov

blue-sky laws
Laws regulating how corporations must back up securities.

prospectus
A detailed registration statement about a new stock filed with a provincial securities exchange; must include any data helpful to a potential buyer.

insider trading
The use of special knowledge about a firm to make a profit on the stock market.

SUMMARY OF LEARNING OBJECTIVES

1. **Explain the difference between *primary* and *secondary securities markets*.** *Primary securities markets* involve the buying and selling of new securities, either in public offerings or through *private placements* (sales to single buyers or small groups of buyers). *Investment bankers* specialize in trading securities in primary markets. *Secondary markets* involve the trading of existing stocks and bonds through such familiar bodies as the New York and Toronto Stock Exchanges.

2. **Discuss the value of *common stock* and *preferred stock* to shareholders and describe the secondary market for each type of security.** *Common stock* affords investors the prospect of capital gains, dividend income, or both. Common stock values are expressed in three ways: as *par value* (the face value of a share when it is issued), *market value* (the current market price of a share), and *book value* (the value of shareholders' equity compared with that of other stocks). Market value is the most important value to investors. *Preferred stock* is less risky than common stock; for example, cumulative preferred stock entitles holders to receive missed dividends when the company is financially capable of paying. It also offers the prospect of steadier income than common stock. Shareholders of preferred stock must be paid dividends before shareholders of common stock.

   Both common and preferred stock are traded on *stock exchanges* (institutions formed to conduct the trading of existing securities) and in *over-the-counter (OTC) markets* (dealer organizations formed to trade securities outside stock exchange settings). "Members" who hold seats on exchanges act as *brokers*—agents who execute buy-and-sell orders—for nonmembers. Exchanges include the New York Stock Exchange, the Toronto Stock Exchange, and regional and foreign exchanges. In the OTC market, licensed traders serve functions similar to those of exchange members.

3. **Distinguish among various types of *bonds* in terms of their issuers, safety, and retirement.** The safety of bonds issued by various borrowers is rated by such services as Moody's and the Canadian Bond Rating Service. *Government bonds* are the safest investment because they are backed by the federal government. *Municipal bonds*, which are offered by provincial and local governments to finance a variety of projects, are also usually safe, and the interest is frequently tax-exempt. *Corporate bonds* are issued by businesses to gain long-term funding. They may be *secured* (backed by pledges of the issuer's assets) or unsecured *(debentures)* and offer varying degrees of safety. *Serial bonds* are retired as portions are redeemed at preset dates; *convertible bonds* are retired by conversion into the issuer's common stock. Government and corporate bonds are *callable*; that is, they can be paid off by the issuer prior to their maturity dates.

4. **Describe the investment opportunities offered by *mutual funds* and *commodities*.** Like stocks and bonds, *mutual funds*—companies that pool investments to purchase portfolios of financial instruments—offer investors different levels of risk and growth potential. *Load funds* require investors to pay commissions of 2 to 8 percent; *no-load funds* do not charge commissions when investors buy in or out. *Futures contracts*—agreements to buy specified amounts of commodities at given prices on preset dates—are traded in the *commodities market*. Commodities traders often buy on *margins*, percentages of total sales prices that must be put up to order futures contracts.

5. **Explain the process by which securities are bought and sold.** Investors generally begin with some homework to study such *financial information services* as newspaper stock, bond, and OTC quotations. *Market indexes* like the Dow Jones Industrial Average and Standard & Poor's Composite Index provide useful summaries of trends, both in specific industries and in the market as a whole. Investors can then place different types of orders. *Market orders* are orders to buy or sell at

current prevailing prices. Because investors do not know exactly what prices will be when market orders are executed, they may issue *limit orders* or *stop orders* that are to be executed only if prices rise to or fall below specified levels. *Round* and *odd lots* are purchases ordered, respectively, in multiples or fractions of 100 shares. Securities can be bought on margin or as part of *short sales*—sales in which investors sell securities that are borrowed from brokers and returned at a later date.

6. **Explain how securities markets are regulated.** To protect investors, provincial securities commissions regulate the public offering of new securities and enforce laws against such practices as *insider trading* (using special knowledge about a firm for profit or gain). Many provincial governments prosecute the sale of fraudulent securities and enforce *blue-sky laws* that require dealers to be licensed and registered where they conduct business.

STUDY QUESTIONS AND EXERCISES

Review Questions

1. What are the purposes of the primary and secondary markets for securities?

2. Which of the three measures of common stock value is most important? Why?

3. What is the difference between callable and convertible bonds?

4. How might an investor lose money in a commodities trade?

5. How do the provincial securities commissions regulate securities markets?

Analysis Questions

6. Which type of stock or bond would be most appropriate for your investment purposes at this time? Why?

7. Which type of mutual fund would be most appropriate for your investment purposes at this time? Why?

8. Choose from a newspaper an example listing of a recent day's transactions for each of the following: a stock on the NYSE; a stock on the TSE; an OTC stock; a bond on the NYSE. Explain what each element in the listing means.

Application Exercises

9. Interview the financial manager of a local business or your school. What are the investment goals of this organization? What mix of securities does it use? What advantages and disadvantages do you see in its portfolio?

10. Contact a broker for information about setting up a personal account for trading securities. Prepare a report on the broker's requirements for placing buy/sell orders, credit terms, cash account requirements, services available to investors, and commissions/fees schedules.

BUILDING YOUR BUSINESS SKILLS

Goal

To encourage students to understand how a company's internal and external environment affects the price of its common stock.

Method

Step 1: Research the activity of one of the following common stocks during 1998. In addition, research the internal and external events that affected the company during the year:

- IBM
- Canadian National Railway
- Bank of Montreal
- Viacom
- General Motors of Canada
- Air Canada
- Apple Computer
- Borden

Step 2: Based on your analysis, answer the following sets of questions:

- What happened to the stock price during the period? What was the high during the year? What was the low?

- What events affected the stock price?
- Which of these events involved internal changes—say, reorganizations, layoffs, a new CEO, a new labour contract, dramatic changes in sales? What were the effects of these events?
- Which of these events involved external factors—say, changes in the competitive environment or an economic downturn? What were the effects of these events?

Follow-Up Questions

1. What were the main factors that influenced the company's stock price?
2. Based on what you learned, can you predict how well the stock will perform over the coming year?

Prentice Hall ◄ **T A K E   I T   T O   T H E   N E T**

Check out our Companion Website
for this chapter's Exploring the Net exercise, featuring the Website of the Toronto Stock Exchange and other intriguing, annotated destinations. You'll also find practice exercises, updated Weblinks from the text, links to newsgroups, updates, and more.

COMPANION WEBSITE   **w w w . p r e n t i c e h a l l . c a / e b e r t**

BUSINESS CASE 18

Institutional Investors Are Getting More Demanding

Thomas Taylor runs TMI-FW Inc., a company that invests money from a variety of sources, including the Ontario Teachers Pension Plan Board (OTPPB). Taylor's company has invested more than $600 million to acquire major stakes in six Canadian companies that he considers to be undervalued. Taylor's strategy is to boost the value of a company's stock by motivating reluctant managers to downsize and sell assets. Taylor is an "activist investor" who is part of a shift in power away from corporations and towards mutual and pension fund managers in Canada.

Taylor sounds the alarm on a company by first acquiring a big block of stock. Then he visits the top managers in the company and tries to convince them that they need to make some changes that will "unlock shareholder values." Two of the companies he targeted—Moore Corp. and MacMillan-Bloedel—removed their CEOs shortly after Taylor acquired a major stake in those companies.

A fundamental power struggle is being fought between management and the agents who invest the savings of millions of Canadians. The capital pool controlled by organizations such as Jarislowsky Fraser & Co., Canadian National Pension Trust Fund, and the Ontario Municipal Employees Retirement System (OMERS) keeps growing. It now totals over $1 trillion.

Because takeovers and mergers have reduced the number of companies they can invest in, institutional investors have taken to watching their investments very closely.

The institutions win some fights and lose others. OMERS holds 6 percent of the common shares of Xerox Canada Inc. When the U.S. head office decided to exchange one common share of the U.S. company for three of the Canadian company, OMERS complained that the price was too low. The plan was approved anyway and OMERS sued Xerox. Since then, the Ontario Securities Commission (OSC) has developed more stringent rules on directors' responsibilities to shareholders during takeovers.

Sometimes institutional investors have had their representatives elected to the board of directors of companies they are concerned about. Royal Trust Energy Corp. nominated two of its officials to sit on the board of the near-bankrupt Oakwoods Petroleum Ltd. When it became clear that two pension funds—CN's and Central Trust's—would support the Royal Trust nominees, two incumbent management-supported nominees withdrew their names.

Major battles between pension funds and company management often shape up over the issue of poison pills. Poison pills usually give shareholders the right to buy

►

company stock at a below-market price if a would-be purchaser's holdings go beyond a certain level. Management favours poison pills, but institutional investors usually oppose them. In the case of Inco, the institutional investors were major losers when the company persuaded shareholders to adopt the poison pill by offering them a $10 dividend if they would approve the plan.

Management often resents institutional investors, arguing that they do not know how a specific company should be run yet they insist on input anyway. They want institutional investors simply to pick stocks for their clients, not try to tell company management what to do. They point out that institutions generally have no positive advice to offer; rather, they just veto management plans. When the pension funds of CBC and Investors Group torpedoed a restructuring plan at Unicorp Canada Ltd., they did not offer an alternative. Instead they insisted that the company come up with proposals for them to accept or reject. Unicorp finally abandoned the restructuring.

Pension fund managers counter by stressing that they are preventing company management from taking advantage of small investors. Companies, they argue, too often view small shareholders as a source of cheap money rather than as equal partners in the enterprise.

Not too many years ago, experts said that activist investing was not likely to work in Canada as it has in the U.S. But the explosive increase in money that is managed by pension and mutual funds has given these money managers a lot more clout. The leading pension funds in Canada such as OMERS are planning to become more aggressive in their activist investing.

■ Case Questions

1. What motivates pension fund managers to try to influence the management decisions of companies they hold stock in?

2. What are the pros and cons of pension fund managers trying to influence management decisions of the companies the pension fund holds stock in?

3. Why do institutional investors such as pension funds oppose "poison pills"?

4. Imagine that you are a top manager in a company whose stock is often bought by institutional investors. What kinds of complaints about institutional investors are you likely to have?

CBC VIDEO CASE VI-1

Mutual Funds, Mutual Problems?*

"We've got a number of people who started a business about nine years ago from nothing . . . they've built it up to something that is extremely valuable."

—Peter Brewster, editor of Canadian Mutual Fund Advisor

A few years ago, Andrew Gates began saving for his future by stashing his money away in Altamira mutual funds. The 34-year-old was attracted by the company's no-load policy. The absence of fees, Gates reasoned, meant higher returns for investors. For several years, his expectations were validated, with the mutual fund company providing its investors, which included over 300 000 Canadians, with industry-leading returns.

Lately, however, the story has been quite different, with Altamira's senior management enmeshed in intense internal political infighting. The fighting appears to have come at a price. With attention increasingly pulled away from the market and redirected towards a Toronto courtroom, returns have slumped, with the company recently

winding up in twelfth spot within the industry. After working together for years to develop one of the country's hottest investment companies, the founders are now more intent on directing their competitive prowess against each other.

The key issue is whether the senior partners will hold or sell the company. One of the company's principals, Altamira's chief executive officer Ronald Bead, wants to cash out. He has initiated discussions with Canada's five chartered banks to see if any of them might be interested. His overtures produced one serious offer; the Toronto-Dominion Bank offered almost $800 million for control of the company. However, the company's other senior partners want to continue working there. The tragedy of cases such as this one is that the same forces that built the company could now tear it apart.

Part of Altamira's drop in performance may also be attributable to its large size. In its earlier years, it was comparatively less conservative and cautious. Now, with all the expectations that go along with investors looking to the

➤

fund for solid and reliable returns, it seems sentenced to a more conservative investment strategy. Some predict that the company may never lead the pack again. The infighting and general maturation of the company haven't resulted in Andrew Gates taking money out of the company . . . yet. Conversely, he hasn't invested more money.

STUDY QUESTIONS

1. What is the difference between par value and market value? Are both, only one, or neither of these affected by the political infighting going on at Altamira?

2. What is a mutual fund? What is the difference between a no-load and a load fund? Which is Altamira?

3. What is book value? How is the book value of Altamira being affected by the internal politics there?

* Source: This case was written by Professor Reg Litz of the University of Manitoba. Video Resource: "Altamira," *Venture* #633 (March 9, 1997).

Altamira
www.altamira-group.com

CBC VIDEO CASE VI-2

*Auto Lotto**

"If I can get out of this by writing out a cheque for $10 000, it's easier than spending $5000 to investigate."

—Allan Wood, insurance company executive

Insurance company executives report that questionable auto insurance claims are on the rise. The "crash for cash" mentality involves people intentionally staging minor automobile accidents in order to rake in cash from insurance companies that would rather settle out of court than fight in court. The strategy involves staging a low, or even no, speed fender bender, with little, if any, damage to either vehicle or occupants. The incident later gets reframed as a "major accident." In Alberta alone, the "auto lotto" pay-out arising from such accidents was estimated at $125 million in 1995.

Why does this happen? Part of the problem, insurance investigators report, is a "got nothing to lose" mentality. Part is also attributable to the incentive structure of the legal system. The use of contingency fee-based lawyering means that attorneys only get paid if their clients do, which means either winning their case in court or settling out of court. Part is also related to the system's acceptance of difficult-to-substantiate "soft tissue" injuries. What makes the increase of these cases particularly interesting, however, is that the number of collisions appears to be actually declining.

In one case, an alleged victim was driving a van along an Edmonton street. Suddenly, he stopped for no apparent

reason, only to suffer a low speed rear-end collision from the car behind. The van received only minor damages. The driver, however, sued for chronic pain to his neck and lower back. Complicating the lawsuit further, the driver's wife sued for permanent disabilities to neck, back, shoulder, and lower jaw areas, even though it was later determined that only the husband and his four-year-old had been in the van at the time of the accident. An investigator later claimed it was impossible for the driver to have suffered the type and degree of injuries claimed.

The eventual settlement ordered the driver to stay away from manual labour; later, he was observed working as a machine operator and operating a vehicle while displaying a range of movement in his neck. Likewise, the driver's wife was seen lifting heavy bags of groceries, hoisting boxes, and cleaning their van. The claimants of this accident seem particularly suspect, however, by virtue of the sheer volume of accidents they seem to find themselves involved in; the husband reports involvement in no fewer than three other accidents, while his spouse reported being involved in five accidents in three years.

To be alert to the possibility of being taken for a ride on the "auto lotto," insurance companies recommend that people keep a disposable camera and notebook in their vehicle. Immediately after an accident, take notes and pictures of the accident and all apparent damage. Second, ask the other driver(s) about their previous insurance claim history. Finally, pressure the insurance company to investigate the accident thoroughly rather than just cave in to get out of the "auto lotto" game.

STUDY QUESTIONS

1. What is the difference between speculative and pure risk? How do they apply to the "auto lotto"?

2. What is risk control? How does it relate to the tactics of the insurance companies?

3. What is risk avoidance? What could an insurance company do if it wanted to practise risk avoidance regarding the "auto lotto"?

* Source: This case was written by Professor Reg Litz of the University of Manitoba. Video Resource: "Insurance Fraud," *Marketplace* #24 (March 25, 1997).

THE LEGAL ENVIRONMENT FOR BUSINESS IN CANADA

■ THE ROLE OF LAW IN CANADIAN SOCIETY

law
The set of rules and standards that a society agrees upon to govern the behaviour of its citizens.

Law is the set of rules and standards that a society agrees upon to govern the behaviour of its citizens. Both the British and the French influenced the development of law in Canada. In 1867, the *British North America (BNA) Act* created the nation of Canada. The *BNA Act* was "patriated" to Canada in 1982 and is known as the *Constitution Act*. This act divides legislative powers in Canada between the federal and provincial governments.

Sources of Law

The law in Canada has evolved and changed in response to our norms and values. Our laws have arisen from three sources: 1) customs and judicial precedents (the source of common law), 2) the actions of provincial and federal legislatures (the source of statutory law), and 3) rulings by administrative bodies (the source of administrative law).

common law
The unwritten law of England, derived from precedents and legal judgments.

  Common law is the unwritten law of England, derived from ancient precedents and judges' previous legal opinions. Common law is based on the principle of equity, the provision to every person of a just and fair remedy. Canadian legal customs and traditions derive from British common law. All provinces except Quebec, which uses the French *Civil Code*, have laws based on British common law, and court decisions are often based on precedents from common law. That is, decisions made in earlier cases that involved the same legal point will guide the court.

statutory law
Written law developed by city councils, provincial legislatures, and parliament.

  Statutory law is written law developed by city councils, provincial legislatures, and parliament. Most law in Canada today is statutory law.

administrative law
Rules and regulations that government agencies develop based on their interpretations of statutory laws.

  Administrative law is the rules and regulations that government agencies and commissions develop based on their interpretations of statutory laws. For example, Consumer and Corporate Affairs Canada develops regulations on false advertising using federal legislation.

The Court System

In Canada, the judiciary branch of government has the responsibility of settling disputes among organizations or individuals by applying existing laws. Both provincial and federal courts exist to hear both criminal and civil cases. The Supreme Court of Canada is the highest court in Canada. It decides whether or not to hear appeals from lower courts.

■BUSINESS LAW

business law
Laws that specifically affect how businesses are managed.

Business firms, like all other organizations, are affected by the laws of the country. **Business law** refers to laws that specifically affect how business firms are managed. Some laws affect all businesses, regardless of size, industry, or location. For example, the *Income Tax Act* requires businesses to pay income tax. Other laws may have a greater impact on one industry than on others. For example, pollution regulations are of much greater concern to Inco than they are to Lawson Travel.

Business managers must have at least a basic understanding of seven important concepts in business law:

- contracts
- agency
- bailment
- property
- warranty
- torts
- negotiable instruments

Contracts

contract
An agreement between two parties to act in a specified way or to perform certain acts.

Agreements about transactions are common in a business's day-to-day activity. A **contract** is an agreement between two parties to act in a specified way or to perform certain acts. A contract might, for example, apply to a customer buying a product from a retail establishment or to two manufacturers agreeing to buy products or services from each other. A valid contract includes several elements:

- *an agreement*—All parties must consciously agree about the contract.
- *consideration*—The parties must exchange something of value (e.g., time, products, services, money, etc.)
- *competence*—All parties to the contract must be legally able to enter into an agreement. Individuals who are below a certain age or who are legally insane, for example, cannot enter into legal agreements.
- *legal purpose*—What the parties agree to do for or with each other must be legal. An agreement between two manufacturers to fix prices is not legal.

breach of contract
When one party to an agreement fails, without legal reason, to live up to the agreement's provisions.

The courts will enforce a contract if it meets the criteria described above. Most parties honour their contracts but, occasionally, one party does not do what it was supposed to do. **Breach of contract** occurs when one party to an agreement fails, without legal reason, to live up to the agreement's provisions. The party who has not breached the contract has three alternatives under the law in Canada: 1) discharge, 2) sue for damages, and 3) require specific performance.

An example will demonstrate these three alternatives. Suppose Barrington Farms Inc. agrees to deliver 100 dozen long-stemmed roses to the Blue Violet Flower Shop the week before Mother's Day. One week before the agreed-upon date, Barrington's informs Blue Violet that it cannot make the delivery until after Mother's Day. Under the law, the owner of the Blue Violet can choose among any of the following:

Discharge. Blue Violet can also ignore its obligations in the contract. That is, it can contract with another supplier.

Sue for Damages. Blue Violet can legally demand payment for losses caused by Barrington's failure to deliver the promised goods. Losses might include any increased price Blue Violet would have to pay for the roses or court costs incurred in the damage suit.

Required Specific Performance.   If monetary damages are not sufficient to reimburse Blue Violet, the court can force Barrington's to live up to its original contract.

Agency

In many business situations, one person acts as an agent for another person. Well-known examples include actors and athletes represented by agents who negotiate contracts for them. An **agency-principal relationship** is established when one party (the agent) is authorized to act on behalf of another party (the principal).

The agent is under the control of the principal and must act on behalf of the principal and in the principal's best interests. The principal remains liable for the acts of the agent as long as the agent is acting within the scope of authority granted by the principal. A salesperson for IBM, for example, is an agent for IBM, the principal.

agency-principal relationship
When one party (the agent) is authorized to act on behalf of another party (the principal).

Bailment

Many business transactions are not covered by the agency-principal relationship. For example, suppose you take your car to a mechanic to have it repaired. Because the repair shop has temporary possession of something you own, it is responsible for your car. This is a **bailor-bailee relationship**. In a bailor-bailee relationship, the bailor (the car owner) gives possession of his or her property to the bailee (the repair shop) but retains ownership of the item. A business firm that stores inventory in a public warehouse is in a bailor-bailee relationship. The business firm is the bailor and the warehouse is the bailee. The warehouse is responsible for storing the goods safely and making them available to the manufacturer upon request.

bailor-bailee relationship
When a bailor, a property owner, gives possession of the property to a bailee, a custodian, but retains ownership of the property.

property
Anything of tangible or intangible value that the owner has the right to possess and use.

The Law of Property

Property includes anything of tangible or intangible value that the owner has the right to possess and use. **Real property** is land and any permanent buildings attached to that land. **Personal property** is tangible or intangible assets other than real property. Personal property includes cars, clothing, furniture, money in bank accounts, stock certificates, and copyrights.

real property
Land and any permanent buildings attached to that land.

personal property
Tangible or intangible assets other than real property.

Transferring Property.   From time to time, businesses and individuals need to transfer property to another person or business. A **deed** is a document that shows ownership of real property. It allows the transfer of title of real property.

A **lease** grants the use of an asset for a specified period of time in return for payment. The business or individual granting the lease is the lessor and the tenant is the lessee. For example, a business (the lessee) may rent space in a mall for one year from a real estate development firm (the lessor).

A **title** shows legal possession of personal property. It allows the transfer of title or personal property. When you buy a snowmobile, for example, the former owner signs the title over to you.

deed
A document that shows ownership of real property.

lease
A document that grants the use of an asset for a specified period of time in return for payment.

title
A document that shows legal possession of personal property.

Warranty

When you buy a product or service, you want some assurance that it will perform satisfactorily and meet your needs. A **warranty** is a promise that the product or service will perform as the seller has promised it will.

There are two kinds of warranties—express and implied. An **express warranty** is a specific claim that the manufacturer makes about a product. For example, a warranty that

warranty
A promise that the product or service will perform as the seller has promised it will.

express warranty
A specific claim that a manufacturer makes about a product.

implied warranty
An assumption that a product will perform as the manufacturer claims it will.

a screwdriver blade is made of case-hardened steel is an express warranty. An **implied warranty** suggests that a product will perform as the manufacturer claims it will. Suppose you buy an outboard motor for your boat and the engine burns out in one week. Because the manufacturer implies by selling the motor that it will work for a reasonable period of time, you can return it and get your money back.

Because opinions vary on what is a "reasonable" time, most manufacturers now give limited time warranties on their products. For example, they will guarantee their products against defects in materials or manufacture for six months or one year.

Torts

tort
A wrongful civil act that one party inflicts on another.

intentional tort
A wrongful act intentionally committed.

negligence
A wrongful act that inadvertently causes injury to another person.

product liability
The liability of businesses for injuries caused to product users because of negligence in design or manufacture.

strict product liability
The liability of businesses for injuries caused by their products even if no evidence of negligence in the product's design or manufacture exists.

A **tort** is a wrongful civil act that one party inflicts on another and that results in injury to the person, to the person's property, or to the person's good name. An **intentional tort** is a wrongful act intentionally committed. If a security guard in a department store suspects someone of shoplifting and uses excessive force to prevent him or her from leaving the store, the guard might be guilty of an intentional tort. Other examples are libel, embezzlement, and patent infringement.

Negligence is a wrongful act that inadvertently causes injury to another person. For example, if a maintenance crew in a store mops the floors without placing warning signs in the area, a customer who slips and falls might bring a negligence suit against the store.

In recent years, the most publicized area of negligence has been product liability. **Product liability** means that businesses are liable for injuries caused by product users because of negligence in design or manufacturing. **Strict product liability** means that a business is liable for injuries caused by their products even if there is no evidence of negligence in the design or manufacture of the product.

Negotiable Instruments

negotiable instruments
Types of commercial paper that can be transferred among individuals and business firms.

Negotiable instruments are types of commercial paper that can be transferred among individuals and business firms. Cheques, bank drafts, and certificates of deposit are examples of negotiable instruments.

The *Bills of Exchange Act* specifies that a negotiable instrument must

- be written
- be signed by the person who puts it into circulation (the maker or drawer)
- contain an unconditional promise to pay a certain amount of money
- be payable on demand
- be payable to a specific person (or to the bearer of the instrument)

endorsement
Signing your name to a negotiable instrument making it transferable to another person or organization.

Negotiable instruments are transferred from one party to another through an endorsement. An **endorsement** means signing your name to a negotiable instrument; this makes it transferable to another person or organization. If you sign only your name on the back of a cheque, you are making a *blank* endorsement. If you state that the instrument is being transferred to a specific person, you are making a *special* endorsement. A *qualified* endorsement limits your liability if the instrument is not backed up by sufficient funds. For example, if you get a cheque from a friend and want to use it to buy a new stereo, you can write "without recourse" above your name. If your friend's cheque bounces, you have no liability. A *restrictive* endorsement limits the negotiability of the instrument. For example, if you write "for deposit only" on the back of a cheque and it is later stolen, no one else can cash it.

INSURANCE

The reason why companies often find insurance appealing is clear—in return for a sum of money, they are protected against certain potentially devastating losses. But why are insurance companies willing to accept these risks for other companies?

Like all firms, insurance companies are in business to make a profit. They do so by taking in more premiums than they pay out to cover policyholder losses. They profit because they have many policyholders paying them for protection against the same type of loss, yet not all policyholders will experience a loss. As the box "Risky Decisions in the Insurance Business" shows, sometimes insurance companies take on too much risk.

The Statistical Basis of Insurance

For example, consider a town with 5000 insured houses. Based on past history, insurers know that about 50 of these will be involved in a fire each year and that damages will average $40 000 per house involved. That is, insurance companies can expect to pay $2 million ($40 000 × 50) to cover their policyholders. By charging each household in the town $500 a year for fire insurance, the company effectively spreads out the risk. It also earns a gross profit of $500 000 ($2.5 million in premiums versus $2 million in damages). This is the insurer's gain for providing risk-spreading services.

To earn a profit, insurance companies must know the likelihood of a particular loss. The more they know, the better their predictions and the fairer the rates they set will be. Insurance companies also benefit from a statistical principle called the **law of large numbers**. As the number of people who seek insurance rises, so does the chance that the actual loss rate will be the same as the statistically calculated rate.

law of large numbers
The statistical principle that the larger the number of cases involved, the more closely the actual rate will match the statistically calculated rate.

To help them properly price insurance policies, insurers use a system of classification that rates possible losses based on certain characteristics. The frequency of loss from an automobile accident varies with the number of kilometres driven per year, whether the driving is done in a rural or urban area, and the driver's experience. An individual driving under 5000 kilometres per year on uncongested roads with many years of experience will probably have fewer accidents than someone in the opposite situation. Therefore, individuals with a lower probability of accidents as determined by these classification characteristics should pay a relatively lower premium. If insurance companies did not try to make rates equitable, so few customers might buy policies that the insurance company could not cover its costs.

The ultimate purpose of insurance is to *indemnify* policyholders. That is, policyholders should be brought back to their financial position before the loss. No policyholder should gain financially from insurance. To remain financially viable, an insurance company must be sure never to pay for losses not covered by the policy nor to pay too much for each loss.

Insurable versus Uninsurable Risks

Like every business, insurance companies avoid certain risks. Towards this end, insurers divide potential sources of loss into insurable risks and uninsurable risks and issue policies only for insurable risks. While some policies provide certain exemptions, in general, to qualify as an insurable risk, the risk should be predictable, outside the control of the insured, spread geographically, and verifiable.

Predictable.   The insurance company must be able to use statistical tools to forecast the likelihood of a loss. For example, the insurer needs information about the number of car accidents in the past year to estimate the expected accidents for the following year. Translating the expected level of accidents into expected dollar losses helps to determine the premium.

Outside the Control of the Policyholder.   The loss must result from an accident, not from an intentional act by the policyholder. Insurers do not have to cover the damages if a policyholder deliberately sets fire to an office building. To avoid paying in cases of fraud, insurers may refuse to cover losses when they cannot determine whether the policyholder's action contributed to the loss.

Spread over a Large Geographic Area.   One insurance company would not want to have all of the hail coverage in Saskatchewan or all of the earthquake coverage in Vancouver. Through selective underwriting of risks, the insurance company can dilute its chances of a large loss.

Verifiable.   Did an employee develop emphysema due to a chemical he worked with in his job or because he smoked two packs of cigarettes a day for 30 years? Did the policyholder pay the renewal premium *before* the fire destroyed her home? Were the goods stolen from company offices or the president's home? What was the insurable value of the destroyed inventory?

Types of Insurance Companies

Insurance firms can be either private or public (government).

Private Insurance Companies.   Private insurers may be shareholder-owned or mutually owned. **Stock insurance companies**, as the former are known, are like any other corporation. They sell stock to the public, which hopes to earn a profit on its investment. Shareholders can be, but do not have to be, policyholders of the insurance company.

Mutual insurance companies are owned by their policyholders, for whom they seek to provide insurance at lower rates. As *cooperative* operations, they divide profits among policyholders, either by issuing dividends or by reducing premiums. In other words, the company's profits are generated for the direct benefit of policyholders rather than for outside shareholders. As non-profit operations, they divide any profit among policyholders at the end of the year.

Two of the most important activities of private insurers are the underwriting and marketing of insurance offerings. **Underwriting** involves two basic tasks:

1. determining which applications for insurance to accept and which ones to reject
2. deciding what rates the insurer will charge.

These decisions are made by *underwriters*—experts who gather information and tabulate data, assess loss probabilities, and decide which applications will be accepted. The purpose of all these functions, of course, is to maximize the insurer's profits.

Agents and brokers are the people who market insurance. An **insurance agent** represents and is paid a commission by an insurance company. The agent, then, represents the insurance seller. An **insurance broker**, on the other hand, is a freelance agent who represents insurance buyers rather than sellers. Brokers work for clients by seeking the best coverage for them. They are then paid commissions by the insurers whom they recommend to their clients. Some brokers also offer risk-management advice for clients.

Public Insurers.   Most insurance that businesses buy is written by private insurance companies. But some—and a great deal of individual insurance—is issued by government agencies.

stock insurance company
Any insurance company whose stock is held by members of the public, who may or may not be policyholders of the company.

mutual insurance company
Any insurance company that is owned by its policyholders, who share in its profits.

underwriting
Determining which applications for insurance to accept and deciding what rates the insurer will charge.

insurance agent
A person who markets insurance and is paid a commission by the insurance company.

insurance broker
A freelance agent who represents insurance buyers rather than insurance sellers.

Provincial governments administer workers' compensation insurance and the federal government administers the employment insurance program. Employers, employees, and the government share the cost of these programs. The federal government also operates the Social Insurance program. It has become an important part of our economic life and is a major means of protecting older, disabled, and poor citizens from economic hardship.

■ INSURANCE PRODUCTS TO MEET DIVERSE NEEDS

Insurance companies are often distinguished by the types of insurance coverage they offer. While some insurers offer only one area of coverage—life insurance, for example—others offer a broad range. In this section, we describe three major categories of business insurance: *liability*, *property*, and *life*. Each of these broad categories includes a wide variety of coverage plans and options.

Liability Insurance

As we saw in Chapter 3, *liability* means responsibility for damages in case of accidental or deliberate harm to individuals or property. Who, for example, might be financially responsible—liable—for the medical expenses, lost wages, and pain and suffering incurred by an individual temporarily or permanently disabled because of another's actions? **Liability insurance** covers losses resulting from damage to people or property when the insured party is judged liable.

Workers' Compensation.   A business is liable for any injury to an employee when the injury arises from activities related to occupation. When workers are permanently or temporarily disabled by job-related accidents or disease, employers are required by law to provide **workers' compensation** coverage for medical expenses, loss of wages, and rehabilitation services.

Property Insurance

Firms purchase **property insurance** to cover injuries to themselves resulting from physical damage to or loss of real personal property. Property losses might result from fire, lightning, wind, hail, explosion, theft, vandalism, or other destructive forces. Many different forms of property insurance exist to cover the many types of property losses.

Business Interruption Insurance.   In some cases the loss to property may be minimal in comparison to the loss of income suffered as a result of the property damage. A manufacturer may be required to close down for an extended period of time while repairs are being completed. During that time the company is not generating income. However, certain expenses—taxes, insurance premiums, and salaries for key personnel—may continue to accrue. The company may also need to keep running advertisements to make customers aware that repairs are progressing so they do not take their business elsewhere permanently. To cover these potential losses, a firm may buy **business interruption insurance**.

Life Insurance

Insurance can protect not only a company's physical and capital assets but its labour assets as well. As part of their benefits packages, many businesses buy **life insurance** for their employees. Life insurance companies accept premiums from policyholders in return for the promise to pay a **beneficiary** after the death of the policyholder. A portion of the premium is used for current losses and expenses. The remainder is invested in various types of financial instruments such as corporate bonds and stocks. A portion of the investment income generated offsets the premium paid by the policyholder. Therefore, an insurance company with a high investment return theoretically should

liability insurance
Insurance covering losses resulting from damage to persons or property of other people or firms.

workers' compensation
A business's liability for injury to its employee(s) resulting from any activities related to the occupation.

property insurance
Insurance covering losses resulting from physical damage to real estate or personal property.

business interruption insurance
Insurance to cover potential losses incurred during times when a company is unable to conduct its business.

life insurance
Insurance that pays benefits to survivors of a policyholder.

beneficiary
The person to whom benefits of a life insurance policy are paid.

charge less than one with a lower investment return, assuming that both companies have similar loss experience and expenses.

Life insurance is a profitable business in Canada. In 1994, the top 10 insurance companies received over $28.9 billion in premiums from policyholders; net profit for the top 10 firms combined was almost $1.4 billion.[9] Among the many products life insurance companies offer are whole life, term insurance, universal life, and group life insurance.

whole life insurance
Insurance coverage in force for the whole of a person's life, with a buildup of cash value.

Whole Life Insurance.   In **whole life insurance**, a business or individual pays a sum that is sufficient to keep the policy in force for the whole of the person's life. This sum can be paid every year for life or for a stated period of years (such as 20 years). For example, Evita Guard may pay $115 each year and be assured that her beneficiary, her husband, will receive the stated face value upon her death. Alternatively, she could pay $198 each year for 20 years and receive the same benefit. In both cases, the policy is said to be paid up.

term insurance
Insurance coverage for a fixed period of time, often one, five, 10, or 20 years.

Term Insurance.   As its name suggests, **term insurance** provides coverage for a term (a temporary time period) stated in the policy. The term can be for one, five, 10 or 20 years. Term insurance has no cash value and is less expensive than any of the other forms discussed in this section. A policyholder receives maximum death protection for the premium paid. An individual who has a limited insurance budget but a significant need for death protection should consider term insurance. Term insurance is also the form of life insurance companies supply most often to their employees.

universal life policy
A term insurance policy with a savings component.

Universal life policies combine a term insurance product with a savings component. Although this product may require a high initial premium, premium payments are flexible and interest earned on the savings component is competitive with other money market instruments.

group life insurance
Life insurance written for a group of people rather than an individual.

Group Life Insurance.   Most companies buy **group life insurance**, which is underwritten for groups as a whole rather than for each individual member. The insurer's assessment of potential losses and its pricing of premiums are based on the characteristics of the whole group. Johnson & Johnson's benefit plan, for example, includes group life coverage with a standard program of protection and benefits—a master policy purchased by J&J—that applies equally to all employees.

Key Insurance.   Many businesses choose to protect themselves against the loss of the talents and skills of key employees. If a salesperson who brings in $2.5 million in sales every year dies or takes a new job elsewhere, the firm will suffer loss. Moreover, the firm will incur recruitment costs to find a replacement and training expenses once a replacement is hired. *Key person insurance* can offset the lost income and the additional expenses.

A related matter is who takes control of a business when a partner or associate dies. At issue is whether the surviving business partners are willing to accept an inexperienced heir as a management partner in the business. Business continuation agreements are traditionally used to plan for this situation. The business owners can plan to buy the ownership interest of the deceased associate from his or her heirs. The value of the ownership interest is determined when the agreement is made. Special business insurance policies can provide the funds needed to make the purchase.

NOTES, SOURCES, AND CREDITS

■ REFERENCE NOTES

Chapter 1

1. Larry Peppers and Dale G. Gails, *Managerial Economics: Theory and Applications for Decision Making* (Englewood Cliffs, NJ: Prentice-Hall, 1987).
2. Howard W. French, "On the street, Cubans fondly embrace capitalism," *The New York Times*, February 3, 1994, p. A4.
3. Richard I. Kirkland, Jr., "The death of socialism," *Fortune*, January 4, 1988, pp. 64–72.
4. Page Smith, *The Rise of Industrial America* (New York: Viking Penguin, 1990).
5. Barrie McKenna, "The heat is on for Hydro Quebec," *The Globe and Mail*, November 24, 1993, pp. B1, B9.
6. John Stackhouse, "Missing the market," *Report on Business Magazine*, January 1992, p. 38; also Karen Lynch, "Wave of privatization sweeps the globe," *The Financial Post*, November 11, 1991, p. 42.
7. "Privatization bug bites in France as leaders try to prime economy," *The Financial Post*, November 27, 1993, p. 22; also "Privatization a global revolution," *The Globe and Mail*, September 3, 1993, p. B2.
8. Adam Smith, *The Wealth of Nations* (New York: Modern Library, 1937; originally published in 1776).
9. Nicholas C. Siropolis, *Small Business Management*, 4th ed. (Boston: Houghton Mifflin, 1990).
10. "Big G is growing fat on oat cuisine," *Business Week*, September 18, 1989, p. 29.
11. John Partridge and Lawrence Surtees, "Rogers faces assault from Telcos," *The Globe and Mail*, March 28, 1994, pp. B1–B2.
12. "Where global growth is going," *Fortune*, July 31, 1989, pp. 71–92.
13. Peter Cook, "Nation's living standards under growing pressure," *The Globe and Mail*, August 31, 1991, pp. B1–B2.
14. Andrew Nikiforuk, "Putting a Price Tag on the Planet," *Canadian Business*, August 1997, p. 83.
15. *World Development Report 1997*, pp. 215, 237.

Chapter 2

1. Madelaine Drohan, "Ottawa targets interprovincial barriers," *The Globe and Mail*, May 14, 1991, p. B5.
2. U.S. Small Business Administration, "Selecting the legal structure for your firm," *Management Aid No. 6.004* (Washington, D.C.: U.S. Government Printing Office, 1985).
3. Quoted in Lowell B. Howard, *Business Law* (Woodbury, NY: Barron's Woodbury Press, 1965), p. 332.
4. John Heinzl, "The battling McCain's show signs of softening," *The Globe and Mail*, August 27, 1994, p. B1.
5. Dennis Slocum, "Mutual Life Goes Public," *The Globe and Mail*, December 9, 1997, pp. B1, B6.
6. Scott Kilman, "Giant Cargill Resists Pressure to Go Public As It Pursues Growth," *The Wall Street Journal*, January 9, 1997, pp. A1, A4.
7. Ann Gibbon, "Pattison Keeps Deals Spinning," *The Globe and Mail*, June 9, 1997, pp. B1, B5.
8. See "A seat on the board is getting hotter," *Business Week*, July 3, 1989, p. 72.
9. John Heinzl, "Dual Share Structures Targeted," *The Globe and Mail*, January 9, 1997, pp. B1, B10.
10. David Berman, "Feeling Oppressed? Call Izzy," *Canadian Business*, April 24, 1998, pp. 49–51.
11. "A seat on the board is getting hotter." See note 8.
12. Stratford P. Sherman, "How Philip Morris diversified right," *Fortune*, October 23, 1989, pp. 120–128.
13. "Beyond Marlboro country," *Business Week*, August 8, 1988, pp. 54–58.
14. "Board Feat," *The Globe and Mail*, August 15, 1995, p. B8.

Chapter 3

1. Michael Stern, "Ethical standards begin at the top," *The Globe and Mail*, November 11, 1991, p. B4.
2. Richard P. Nielsen, "Changing unethical organizational behavior," *Academy of Management Executive*, May 1989, pp. 123–130.
3. Mark Schwartz, "Heat's on to Get an Effective Code," *The Globe and Mail*, November 27, 1997, p. B2.
4. Jeremy Main, "Here comes the big new cleanup," *Fortune*, November 21, 1988, pp. 102–118.

5. Catherine Collins, "The race for zero," *Canadian Business*, March 1991, pp. 52–56.
6. Allan Robinson and Allan Freeman, "Mining's Dam Problem," *The Globe and Mail*, May 16, 1998, pp. B1–B2.
7. Geoffrey Scotton, "Cleanups can hurt, companies warned," *The Financial Post*, June 25, 1991, p. 4.
8. Marc Huber, "A double-edged endorsement," *Canadian Business*, January 1990, pp. 69–71.
9. John Saunders, "Polar plastic plot flops," *The Globe and Mail*, June 10, 1994, p. B1.
10. Shona McKay, "Willing and able," *Report on Business*, October 1991, pp. 58–63.
11. "Why business is hiring the mentally abled," *Canadian Business*, May 1991, p. 19.
12. J. Southerst, "In pursuit of drugs," *Canadian Transportation*, November 1989, pp. 58–65.
13. "Is Ivan Boesky just the tip of the insider iceberg?" *Dun's Business Month*, January 1987, p. 22.
14. Daniel Stoffman, "Good behavior and the bottom line," *Canadian Business*, May 1991, pp. 28–32.

Chapter 4

1. Bill Saporito, "Where the global action is," *Fortune*, Autumn/Winter 1993, pp. 62–65.
2. John Tagliabue, "Coca-Cola reaches into impoverished Albania," *New York Times*, May 20, 1994, pp. D1, D3; Joseph B. Treaster, "Kellogg seeks to reset Latvia's breakfast table," *New York Times*, May 19, 1994, pp. D1, D8.
3. Brenton R. Schlender et al., "Special Report/Pacific Rim: The battle for Asia," *Fortune*, November 1, 1993, pp. 126-156; Philip Shenon, "Missing out on a glittering market," *New York Times*, September 12, 1993, Sec. 3, pp. 1, 6; Steven Greenhouse, "New tally of world's economies catapults China into third place," *New York Times*, May 20, 1993, pp. A1, A8.
4. John Heinzl, "Conference Board Warns of Pitfalls in Chinese Ventures," *The Globe and Mail*, November 5, 1996, p. B8.
5. Michael Porter, "Why nations triumph," *Fortune*, March 12, 1990, pp. 94–108.
6. Jeffrey Taylor and Neil Behrmann, "Coffee prices surge after frost hits Brazil," *Wall Street Journal*, June 28, 1994, pp. C1, C16; Dori Jones Yang with Bill Hinchberger, "Trouble brewing at the coffee bar," *Business Week*, August 1, 1994, p. 62.
7. Janet McFarland, "Canada Keeps Rank in World Survey," *The Globe and Mail*, April 22, 1998, p. B7.
8. "Canada Moves Up the Competitiveness Scale," *Winnipeg Free Press*, May 21, 1997, p. B8.
9. Madelaine Drohan, "Dependency on U.S. Leaves Canada 'Vulnerable:' WTO," *The Globe and Mail*, November 20, 1996.
10. Anthony DePalma, "G.M. gives Mexico its own 'Chevy'" *The New York Times*, May 12, 1994, pp. D1, D6; James B. Treece et al., "New worlds to conquer," *Business Week*, February 28, 1994, p. 51.
11. Peggy Berkowitz, "You say potato, they say McCain," *Canadian Business*, December 1991, pp. 44–48.
12. "50 Top Exporters," *Report on Business*, July 1995, p. 89.
13. Daniel Stoffman, "Cross-border selling," *Report on Business Magazine*, November 1991, pp. 61–68.
14. John Stackhouse, "Missing the market," *Report on Business Magazine*, January 1992, p. 38.
15. "In hot pursuit of international markets," *Innovation*, Summer 1990, pp. 11–13.
16. Jeremy Main, "How to go global—and why," *Fortune*, December 17, 1990, pp. 70–73; see p. 72.
17. Randall Litchfield, "The pressure on prices," *Canadian Business*, February 1992, pp. 30-35.
18. Konrad Yakabuski, "Quebec Courts Margarine War," *The Globe and Mail*, October 14, 1997, pp. B1, B4.
19. Peter Cook, "Can Anyone Anywhere Ban Bribery?" *The Globe and Mail*, October 1, 1997, p. B2.
20. Nicholas Bray, "OECD Ministers Agree to Ban Bribery As Means for Companies to Win Business," *The Wall Street Journal*, May 27, 1997, p. A2.
21. Barrie McKenna, "Aluminum Producers Whispering Dirty Word," *The Globe and Mail*, March 5, 1994, pp. B1, B5.
22. Jalil Hamid, "Coffee Rally Reignited," *The Globe and Mail*, May 22, 1997, p. B9.
23. Anna Wilde Mathews, "As U.S. Trade Grows, Shipping Cartels Get a Bit More Scrutiny," *The Wall Street Journal*, October 7, 1997, pp. A1, A8.
24. Madelaine Drohan, "OECD Trumpets Cartel Crackdown," *The Globe and Mail*, March 27, 1998, p. B7.
25. "Bike Makers Win Dumping Case," *The Globe and Mail*, December 11, 1997, p. B6.
26. "New global trade regulator starts operations tomorrow," *Winnipeg Free Press*, December 31, 1994, p. A5.
27. Andrew Purvis, "Super Exporter," *Time*, April 28, 1997, p. 36.

Chapter 5

1. Robert Williamson, "Motivation on the Menu," *The Globe and Mail*, November 24, 1995, p. B7.
2. Charles W. L. Hill and Gareth Jones, *Strategic Management: An Analytical View*, 2nd ed. (Boston: Houghton Mifflin, 1992).
3. David Berman, "Hold the Fries," *Canadian Business*, January 30, 1998, pp. 32-34.
4. Dave Ulrich and Dale Lake, "Organizational Capability: Creating Competitive Advantages," *The Academy of Management Executive*, February 1991, pp. 77–83.
5. "Cruise-Ship Delays Leave Guests High and Dry," *Wall Street Journal*, October 24, 1997, pp. B1, B10.
6. Alex Taylor III, "How a top boss manages his day," *Fortune*, June 19, 1989, pp. 95–100.
7. John Lorinc, "Managing when there's no middle," *Canadian Business*, June 1991, pp. 86–94.
8. Paul M. Eng and Evan I. Schwartz, "The games people play in the office," *Business Week*, October 11, 1993, p. 40.
9. Terrence Deal and Allen Kennedy, *Corporate Cultures: The Rites and Rituals of Corporate Life* (Reading, MA: Addison-Wesley, 1982).
10. Bruce McDougall, "The thinking man's assembly line," *Canadian Business*, November 1991, pp. 40–44.
11. Marina Strauss, "Baker's brassy style may rub off on McKim," *The Globe and Mail*, January 27, 1992, pp. B1, B6.

Chapter 6

1. See John A. Wagner and John R. Hollenbeck, *Management of Organizational Behavior* (Englewood Cliffs, NJ: Prentice Hall, 1992), pp. 563–565.
2. Alan Deutschman, "How H-P Continues to Grow and Grow," *Fortune*, May 2, 1994, pp. 99–100; Stratford Sherman, "Secrets of H-P's 'Muddled' Team," *Fortune*, March 18, 1996, pp. 116–20.
3. Jay Diamond and Gerald Pintel, *Retailing*, 6th ed. (Upper Saddle River, NJ: Prentice Hall, 1996), pp. 83–84.
4. Jacquie McNish, "A chairman with worries lots of others would like," *The Globe and Mail*, April 14, 1990, p. B6.
5. Peter Larson, "Winning strategies," *Canadian Business Review*, Summer 1989, p. 41.
6. Ian Allaby, "The search for quality," *Canadian Business*, May 1990, pp. 31-42.
7. Donna Fenn, "The Buyers," *Inc.*, June 1996, pp. 46–48+.
8. Brian Dumaine, "Payoff from the New Management," *Fortune*, December 13, 1993, pp. 103–104.
9. J. Galbraith, "Matrix organization designs: How to combine functional and project forms," *Business Horizons*, 1971, pp. 29-40; also H.F. Kolodny, "Evolution to a matrix organization," *Academy of Management Review*, 4, 1979, pp. 543-553.
10. Lawton R. Burns, "Matrix management in hospitals: Testing theories of matrix structure and development," *Administrative Science Quarterly*, 34, 1989, pp. 48-50.
11. Glenn Rifkin, "Digital dumps matrix management," *The Globe and Mail*, July 21, 1994, pp. B1, B4.
12. Barnaby J. Feder, "The Tech exec who also brings home the bacon," *New York Times*, August 21, 1994, Sec. 3, p. 4.
13. James P. Sterba, "At the Met Opera, It's Not Over Till The Fat Man Folds," *The Wall Street Journal*, January 5, 1998, pp. 1, 6.
14. Thomas Peters and Robert Waterman, *In Search of Excellence* (New York: Harper & Row, 1982).
15. Shawn Tully, "Why to Go for Stretch Targets," *Fortune*, November 14, 1994, pp. 145–46+; Larry Armstrong, "Nurturing an Employee's Brainchild," *Business Week*, Enterprise 1993, p. 196.

Chapter 7

1. *Small Business Profiles*, Statistics Canada, 1998.
2. Peter Waal, "Robocorp," *Canadian Business*, January 16, 1998, pp. 57–60.
3. Murray McNeill, "Women step out on their own," *Winnipeg Free Press*, December 8, 1994, p. C10; also *The State of Small Business 1989, Annual Report on Small Business in Ontario* (Toronto: Ministry of Industry, Trade and Technology, 1990), p. 8.
4. Alan M. Cohen, "Entrepreneur and Entrepreneurship: The Definition Dilemma," Working Paper Series No. NC89–08, National Centre for Management Research and Development, The University of Western Ontario, London, February 1989.
5. *The State of Small Business*, pp. 24–27. See note 3.
6. *The State of Small Business*, p. 29. See note 3.
7. Andrew Willis and Donn Downey, "Pezim's Death Marks End of an Era," *The Globe and Mail*, April 23, 1998, pp. B1, B8.
8. David Berman, "Carving Up Cuddy," *Canadian Business*, March 27, 1998, pp. 39–44.
9. Gordon Pitts, "East Coast Clan Defies the Odds," *The Globe and Mail*, May 18, 1998, p. B9.
10. The statistics in this section are from *Small Business in Canada: Growing to Meet Tomorrow* (Ottawa: Supply and Services Canada), Cat. No. C28–12 1989E; also *The State of Small Business*, see note 3.
11. Paul Waldie, "Small business hits out," *The Financial Post*, September 4–6, 1993, pp. 1, 10–11.

Chapter 8

1. Udayan Gupta, "Keeping the Faith," *Wall Street Journal*, November 22, 1991, p. R16; Greg Moorhead and Ricky W. Griffin, *Organizational Behavior*, 5th ed. (Boston: Houghton Mifflin, 1998).
2. Ronald Lieber, "Why Employees Love These Companies," *Fortune*, January 12, 1998, pp. 72–74.
3. Michael Stern, "Empowerment empowers employees," *The Globe and Mail*, December 9, 1991, p. B4.
4. Margot Gibb-Clark, "Canadian workers need some respect," *The Globe and Mail*, September 4, 1991, pp. B1, B6.
5. Margot Gibb-Clark, "Frustrated workers seek goals," *The Globe and Mail*, May 2, 1991, p. B7.
6. Margot Gibb-Clark, "Family ties limit workers," *The Globe and Mail*, January 22, 1991, pp. B1–B2.
7. Frederick W. Taylor, *Principles of Scientific Management* (New York: Harper and Brothers, 1911).
8. Fritz J. Roethlisberger and William J. Dickson, *Management and the Worker* (Cambridge, MA: Harvard University Press, 1939).
9. Douglas McGregor, *The Human Side of Enterprise* (New York: McGraw-Hill, 1960).
10. Abraham Maslow, "A theory of human motivation," *Psychological Review*, July 1943, pp. 370–396.
11. Frederick Herzberg, Bernard Mausner, and Barbara Bloch Snydeman, *The Motivation to Work* (New York: Wiley, 1959).
12. Victor Vroom, *Work and Motivation* (New York: Wiley, 1964); Craig Pinder, *Work Motivation* (Glenview, IL: Scott, Foresman, 1984).
13. J. Stacy Adams, "Toward an understanding of inequity," *Journal of Abnormal and Social Psychology*, Vol. 75, No. 5 (1963), pp. 422–436.
14. Edwin Locke, "Toward a theory of task performance and incentives," *Organizational Behavior and Human Performance*, Vol. 3 (1968), pp. 157–189.
15. Madelaine Drohan, "What Makes a Canadian Manager?" *The Globe and Mail*, February 25, 1997, p. B18.
16. Gregory Moorhead and Ricky W. Griffin, *Organizational Behavior*, 3rd ed. (Boston: Houghton and Mifflin, 1992).
17. Margot Gibb-Clark, "BC Telecom managers get an overhaul," *The Globe and Mail*, July 23, 1994, p. B3.
18. Wilfred List, "On the road to profit," *The Globe and Mail*, July 10, 1991, pp. B1, B3.
19. Ricky Griffin, *Task Design* (Glenview, IL: Scott, Foresman, 1982).
20. Richard J. Hackman and Greg Oldham, *Work Redesign* (Reading, MA: Addison-Wesley, 1980).

21. Robert White, "Changing needs of work and family: A union response," *Canadian Business Review*, Autumn 1989, pp. 31–33.
22. Margot Gibb-Clark, "Banks' short work week improves service," *The Globe and Mail*, September 23, 1991, p. B4.
23. "Escape from the office," *Newsweek*, April 24, 1989, pp. 58–60.
24. Margot Gibb-Clark, "Satellite office a hit with staff," *The Globe and Mail*, November 18, 1991, p. B4.
25. "Slaves of the New Economy," *Canadian Business*, April 1996, pp. 86–92.
26. Dawn Walton, "Survey Focuses on Job Sharing," *The Globe and Mail*, June 10, 1997, p. B4.

Chapter 9

1. "More firms use personality tests for entry-level blue collar jobs," *Wall Street Journal*, January 16, 1986, p. 25.
2. Bruce McDougall, "The thinking man's assembly line," *Canadian Business*, November 1991, p. 40.
3. "Testing for drug use: Handle with care," *Business Week*, March 28, 1988, p. 65.
4. Malcolm MacKillop, "An Employer's Guide to Drug Testing," *The Globe and Mail*, April 9, 1998, p. B13.
5. Jacquie McNish, "Akers out as IBM CEO," *The Globe and Mail*, January 27, 1993, pp. B1–B2.
6. Joseph B. White and Carol Hymowitz, "Watershed Generation of Women Executives Is Rising to the Top," *The Wall Street Journal*, February 10, 1997, pp. A1, A6.
7. I.L. Goldstein, *Training in Organizations: Needs Assessment, Development, and Evaluation*, 2nd ed. (Monterey, CA: Brooks/Cole, 1986).
8. Jerry Zeidenberg, "Extra-curricular," *Canadian Business*, February 1991, pp. 66–69.
9. Charles Davies, "Strategy session 1990," *Canadian Business*, January 1990, p. 50.
10. Scott Feschuk, "Phi Beta Cuppa," *The Globe and Mail*, March 6, 1993, pp. B1, B4.
11. "Well-paid workers, low-paid bosses?" *Canadian Business*, December 1992, p. 17.
12. David Roberts, "A long way from Cambodia," *The Globe and Mail*, July 5, 1994, p. B18.
13. C.D. Fisher, L. Schoenfeldt, and B. Shaw, *Personnel/Human Resources Management* (Boston: Houghton-Mifflin, 1990).
14. Bob Cox, "Women gaining on men's wages," *The Globe and Mail*, January 18, 1994, p. B4.
15. *Statistics Canada Survey of Labour and Income Dynamics: Moving out of Low-paid Work, 1993-1995*.
16. "Ouch! The squeeze on your health benefits," *Business Week*, November 20, 1989, pp. 110–116.
17. McDougall, "The thinking man's assembly line." See note 2.
18. "Canadians Are Retiring Earlier," *Winnipeg Free Press*, June 12, 1997, p. B12.
19. Michael Moss, "For Older Employees, On-the-Job Injuries Are More Often Deadly," *The Wall Street Journal*, June 17, 1997, pp. A1, A10.
20. Russell Mitchell and Michael Oneal, "Managing by Values," *Business Week*, August 1, 1994, pp. 46–52.
21. Kathleen Murray, "The Unfortunate Side Effects of 'Diversity Training,'" *New York Times*, August 1, 1995, p. 37.

22. Faye Rice, "How to Make Diversity Pay," *Fortune*, August 8, 1994, p. 84.
23. Randall S. Schuler, *Managing Human Resources*, 4th ed. (St. Paul: West, 1992).
24. Stephen Bluen and Vanessa Jubiler-Lurie, "Some Consequences of Labor-Management Negotiations: Laboratory and Field Studies," *Journal of Organizational Behavior*, September 1990, pp. 105–111.
25. Madelaine Drohan, "Steel hands try velvet gloves," *The Globe and Mail*, p. B26.
26. Margot Gibb-Clark, "Wounds left by strike require healing," *The Globe and Mail*, September 30, 1991, p. B4.
27. Robert Frank, "UPS and downs," *The Globe and Mail*, June 7, 1994, p. B24.

Chapter 10

1. *StatsCan Household Spending on Services Report*, released October 15, 1998.
2. *Ibid.*
3. Roger G. Schroeder, *Operations Management: Decision Making in the Operations Function*, 3rd ed. (New York: McGraw-Hill, 1989), pp. 234–64.
4. Theodore Levitt, "Marketing Intangible Products and Product Intangibles," *Harvard Business Review*, May–June 1981, pp. 94–102.
5. Shawn Tully et al., "20 Companies on a Roll," *Fortune*, Autumn/Winter 1993, pp. 28–29.
6. Richard B. Chase, "Where Does the Customer Fit in a Service Organization?" *Harvard Business Review*, November–December 1978, p. 137–42.
7. John R. Dorfman, "Deere's stock is attractive to those who see farmers about to splurge on new equipment," *Wall Street Journal*, July 1, 1991, p. C2; Steven Weiner, "Staying on top in a tough business in a tough year," *Forbes*, May 27, 1991, p. 38.
8. Alex Taylor III, "Ford's $6 billion baby," *Fortune*, June 28, 1993, pp. 76–77+; Richard W. Stevenson, "Ford sets its sights on a world car," *New York Times*, September 27, 1993, pp. D1, D4; James B. Treece, "Motown's struggle to shift on the fly," *Business Week*, July 11, 1994, pp. 111–112.
9. Don Marshall, "Time for just in time," *P&IM Review*, June 1991, pp. 20–22. See also Gregg Stocker, "Quality function deployment: Listening to the voice of the customer," *APICS: The Performance Advantage*, September 1991, pp. 44–48.
10. Richard J. Schonberger and Edward M. Knod, Jr., *Operations Management*, 5th ed. (Burr Ridge, IL: Irwin, 1994), Chapter 11.
11. Bruce McDougall, "The thinking man's assembly line," *Canadian Business*, November 1991, p. 40.
12. Alan Freeman, "Why firms avoid taking inventory," *The Globe and Mail*, December 12, 1994, pp. B1, B4.
13. Thomas A. Stewart, "Brace for Japan's Hot New Strategy," *Fortune*, September 21, 1992, p. 64.

Chapter 11

1. Estimated from *Survey of Current Business* (Washington, DC: U.S. Dept. of Commerce, August 1997), p. 42; *Monthly Labor Review* (Washington, DC: U.S. Dept. of Labor, August 1997), p. 76; Carl G. Thor, *Perspectives '94*

(Houston: American Productivity and Quality Center, 1994), p. 17.

2. Bruce Little, "Canada Seen Lagging in Productivity Race," *The Globe and Mail*, October 17, 1997, pp. B1, B22.

3. *StatsCan Labour Productivity Report*, released July 21, 1998.

4. "50 Top Employers," *Report on Business*, July 1995, p. 81.

5. Bruce McDougall, "The next battleground," *Canadian Business*, February 1992, pp. 52–57.

6. Marina Strauss, "Canada rated 6th in quality of its manufactured goods," *The Globe and Mail*, February 10, 1994.

7. "A feisty domestic with a chip on its shoulder," *Canadian Business*, November 1991, p. 15.

8. Bruce McDougall, "The thinking man's assembly line," *Canadian Business*, November 1991, p. 40.

9. William Carley, "To Keep GE's Profits Rising, Welch Pushes Quality-Control Plan," *The Wall Street Journal*, January 13, 1997, pp. A1, A8.

10. Jeremy Main, "How to steal the best ideas around," *Fortune*, October 19, 1992, pp. 102–106; also Otis Port and Geoffrey Smith, "Beg, borrow—and benchmark," *Business Week*, November 30, 1992, pp. 74–75; also Howard Rothman, "You need not be big to benchmark," *Nation's Business*, December 1992, pp. 64–65.

11. Gordon Pitts, "Stepping on the quality ladder," *The Globe and Mail*, June 30, 1992, p. B20; also Timothy Pritchard, "Big three adopt new standard," *The Globe and Mail*, March 28, 1994, p. B3.

12. Michael Hammer and James Champy, "The promise of reengineering," *Fortune*, May 3, 1993, pp. 94–97; also Thomas A. Stewart, "Reengineering: The hot new managing tool," *Fortune*, August 23, 1993, pp. 41–48; also Ronald Henkoff, "The hot new seal of quality," *Fortune*, August 23, 1993, pp. 116–118.

13. Cathryn Motherwell, "How to fix a model of a muddle," *The Globe and Mail*, November 22, 1994, p. B30.

14. Janet McFarland, "How a Business Fad Went Wrong," *The Globe and Mail*, January 31, 1996, p. B13.

15. John Kotter, "Leading Change: Why Transformation Efforts Fail," *Harvard Business Review*, March-April 1995, p. 66.

16. Joseph White, "Re-Engineering Gurus Take Steps to Remodel Their Stalling Vehicles," *The Wall Street Journal*, November 26, 1996, pp. A1, A13.

17. "Customer service you can taste," *Canadian Business*, July 1991, pp. 19–20.

18. *Business Week*, Special 1989 Issue: "Innovation in America," p. 177.

19. Leonard L. Berry, A. Parasuraman, and Valarie A. Zeithaml, "Improving service quality in America: Lessons learned," *Academy of Management Executive*, Vol. 8, No. 2, 1994, pp. 32–45.

Chapter 12

1. Ronald Hilton, *Managerial Accounting*, 2nd ed. (New York: McGraw-Hill, 1994), p. 7.

2. Mark Heinzl, "Noranda to Shed Interests in Forestry and Energy, Refocusing on Mining," *Wall Street Journal*, November 19, 1997, pp. A3, A6.

3. M. Rothkopf, "No more easy questions on the uniform CPA examination," *Accounting Horizons*, Vol. 1, No. 4, December 1987, pp. 79–85.

4. L.A. Nikolai, J.D. Bazley, and J.C. Stallman, *Principles of Accounting*, 3rd ed. (Boston: PWS-Kent, 1990).

5. C.T. Horngren and G.I. Sundem, *Introduction to Financial Accounting* (Englewood Cliffs, NJ: Prentice-Hall, 1987).

6. Douglas Lavin, "GM would have to cut 20,000 workers to match Ford efficiency, report says," *Wall Street Journal*, June 24, 1994, p. C22.

7. Terrence P. Paré, "How to Find Out What They Want," *Fortune*, Autumn/Winter 1993, pp. 39–41.

8. Larry Long and Nancy Long, *Computers*, 3rd ed. (Englewood Cliffs, NJ: Prentice Hall, 1993), pp. 57–59.

9. Peter Nulty, "When to Murder Your Mainframe," *Fortune*, November 1, 1993, pp. 109–10; Long and Long, *Computers*, pp. 117–18, 216–17.

10. Bruce Nussbaum et al., "Winners: The Best Product Designs of the Year," *Business Week*, June 7, 1993, p. 68; Long and Long, *Computers*, pp. 27–29, 473–74.

11. Gary McWilliams, "Computers Are Finally Learning to Listen," *Business Week*, November 1, 1993, pp. 100–101; Gene Bylinski, "At Last! Computers You Can Talk To," *Fortune*, May 3, 1993, pp. 88–91; Larry Schmitt, "Neural Networks Solve Complex Vision Problems," *Automation*, August 1991, p. 38.

12. Andrzej J. Taramina, "Expert Systems in Manufacturing," *P & IM Review with APICS News*, December 1990, pp. 42, 45.

13. Deidre A. Depke and Richard Brandt, "PCs: What the Future Holds," *Business Week*, August 12, 1991, pp. 58–64.

14. Joshua Macht, "The Ultimate Head Trip," *Inc. Technology*, no. 3, 1997, p. 77.

15. Mary J. Cronin, "Using the Web to Push Key Data to Decision Makers," *Fortune*, September 29, 1997, p. 254; Brent Schlender, "A Conversation with the Lords of Wintel," *Fortune*, July 8, 1996, pp. 42–44.

16. Robert D. Hoff, Kathy Rebello, and John W. Verity, "Java's Cup Runneth Over," *Business Week*, May 20, 1996, pp. 103–104.

17. John W. Verity, "What Hath Yahoo Wrought?" *Business Week*, February 12, 1996, pp. 88–90.

18. Amy Cortese, "Here Comes the Intranet," *Business Week*, Feburary 26, 1996, pp. 76–79; Alison Sprout, "The Internet Inside Your Company," *Fortune*, November 27, 1995, pp. 161–62.

19. Robert D. Hof, Seanna Browder, and Peter Elstrom, "Internet Communities," *Business Week*, May 5, 1997, pp. 64–76, 70, 74, 76, 78.

Chapter 13

1. From "AMA board approves new marketing definition," *Marketing News*, March 31, 1985, p. 1, published by the American Marketing Association.

2. *Harley-Davidson Inc.: 1995 Annual Report* (Milwaukee: Harley-Davidson, 1995), p. 33. See Philip Kotler, *Marketing Management: Analysis, Planning, Implementation, and Control*, 9th ed. (Upper Saddle River, NJ: Prentice Hall, 1997), pp. 12–13, 48–51.

3. Jonathan Kapstein, Thaine Peterson and Lois Therrien, "Look out world, Philips is on a war footing," *Business Week*, January 15, 1990, pp. 44–45.

4. Margot Gibb-Clark, "Customers have a say on IBM managers' pay," *The Globe and Mail*, April 1, 1991, p. B4.

5. "Above the crowd," *Canadian Business*, April 1990, p. 76.
6. Philip Kotler, *Marketing Management: Analysis, Planning, Implementation, and Control*, 7th ed. (Englewood Cliffs, NJ: Prentice-Hall, 1991).
7. "Microwaves, VCRs Seen as Comforts of Home Now," *Winnipeg Free Press*, March 20, 1998, p. A15.
8. David Kirkpatrick, "Now Everyone in PCS Wants To Be Like Mike," *Fortune*, September 8, 1997, pp. 91–92.
9. Stephen Barr, "Trading places: Barter re-enters corporate America," *Management Review*, August 1993, p. 30; John J. McDonald, "Barter can work," *Chief Executive (U.S.)*, June 1994, p. 40.
10. John Heinzl, "Crayon Maker Draws in an Older Kid," *The Globe and Mail*, March 5, 1998; also Shawna Steinberg, "Have Allowance, Will Transform Economy," *Canadian Business*, March 13, 1998, pp. 59–71.
11. John Morton, "How to spot the really important prospects," *Business Marketing*, January 1990, pp. 62–67.
12. Paul Sutter, "How to succeed in bubble gum without really trying," *Canadian Business*, January 1992, pp. 48–50.
13. Marjorie Sorge, "Good-Bye World Cars; Honda Boosts Local Engineering," *Automotive Industries*, April 1996, p. 29.
14. Marina Strauss, "First you have to get their attention," *The Globe and Mail*, July 12, 1991, p. B1.
15. Terence Pare, "How to find out what they want," *Fortune*, Autumn/Winter 1993, pp. 39–41.
16. Oliver Bertin, "John Deere reaps the fruits of its labors," *Globe and Mail*, September 2, 1991, pp. B1, B3.
17. Stephen Barr, "Trading places: Barter re-enters corporate America," *Management Review*, August 1993, p. 30; John J. McDonald, "Barter can work," *Chief Executive (U.S.)*, June 1994, p. 40.
18. William J. Stanton, Michael J. Etzel, and Bruce J. Walker, *Fundamentals of Marketing*, 10th ed. (New York: McGraw-Hill, 1994), Chapter 5.
19. Thomas Russell, Glenn Verrill, and W. Ronald Lane, *Kleppner's Advertising Procedure*, 11th ed. (Englewood Cliffs, NJ: Prentice-Hall, 1990; also James Engel, Martin Warshaw, and Thomas Kinnear, *Promotional Strategy*, 6th ed. (Homewood, IL: Richard D. Irwin, 1987).

Chapter 14

1. Bill Richards, "Nike Plans to Swoosh into Sports Equipment but It's a Tough Game," *The Wall Street Journal*, January 6, 1998, pp. A1, A10.
2. Todd Vogel, "Will GE's new jet engine ever get off the ground?" *Business Week*, February 4, 1991, pp. 98–99; Tim Smart et al., "Clash of the flying titans," *Business Week*, November 22, 1993, pp. 64–66.
3. Rebecca Blumenstein, "Auto Industry Reaches Surprising Consensus: It Needs New Engines," *The Wall Street Journal*, January 5, 1998, pp. A1, A10.
4. Kyle Pope and Evan Ramstad, "HDTV Sets: Too Pricey, Too Late?," *The Wall Street Journal*, January 7, 1998, p. B1.
5. Cyndee Miller, "Little relief seen for new product failure rate," *Marketing News*, June 21, 1993, p. 1; Nancy J. Kim,

"Back to the drawing board," *The Bergen (New Jersey) Record*, December 4, 1994, pp. B1, B4.
6. David Square, "Mouse Pad Gets Oodles of Nibbles," *The Winnipeg Free Press*, July 26, 1997, p. B10.
7. Marina Strauss, "Packaging is a marketer's last chance to say 'Buy me'," *The Globe and Mail*, September 17, 1991, p. B4.
8. William Pride and O.C. Ferrell, *Marketing*, 5th ed. (Boston: Houghton Mifflin, 1987).
9. John B. Clark, *Marketing Today, Successes, Failures, and Turnarounds* (Englewood Cliffs, NJ: Prentice Hall, 1987), p. 32.
10. Michael Allen, "Developing new line of low-priced PCs shakes up Compaq," *Wall Street Journal*, June 15, 1992, pp. A1, A4.
11. Marina Strauss, "This billboard wants to pass you by," *The Globe and Mail*, February 27, 1992, p. B4.
12. Laurie Ward, "Big rock brews strong U.S. growth," *The Financial Post*, September 25, 1993, p. 7.
13. Cynthia Reynolds, "Click Here for Hype," *Canadian Business*, June 12, 1998, pp. 67–69.
14. Lisa Napoli, "Direct Sellers Hold Fast to Ideals," *The Globe and Mail*, February 24, 1998, p. B14.
15. Patrick Brethour and Mark Evans, "Builders of the Electronic Mall," *The Globe and Mail*, July 11, 1998, pp. B1, B5.
16. "Regulators wary of ads rapping rivals," *The Globe and Mail*, May 23, 1991, p. B4.
17. William Bulkeley, "Rebates' Secret Appeal to Manufacturers: Few Consumers Actually Redeem Them," *The Wall Street Journal*, February 10, 1998, p. B1.
18. "Point-of-purchase rush is on," *Advertising Age*, February 8, 1988, p. 41.
19. Lois Therrien, "Want shelf space at the supermarket? Ante up," *Business Week*, August 7, 1989, pp. 60–61.
20. Jennifer Lawrence, "Free samples get emotional reaction," *Advertising Age*, September 30, 1991, p. 10.
21. "Pageant Runner-Up Looks for Compensation," *Winnipeg Free Press*, February 3, 1998, p. A4.
22. Joseph Periera, "Toy Story: How Shrewd Marketing Made Elmo a Hit," *The Wall Street Journal*, December 16, 1996, pp. B1, B8.
23. Pam Weisz, "Border Crossings: Brands Unify Image to Counter Cult of Culture," *Brandweek*, October 31, 1994, p. 26.
24. "Does the 'Special Relationship' Include Ketchup and Cola?" *Adweek*, December 13, 1993, p. 17.
25. Shelley Garcia, "Philips Seeks Shop," *Adweek*, December 5, 1994, pp. 1, 46; Rosalyn Retkwa, "T1 Buys $10 Million Facelift," *Business Marketing*, 78, 4 (April 1993), p. 6.

Chapter 15

1. Stephen Kindel, "Tortoise gains on hare," *Financial World*, February 23, 1988, pp. 18–20.
2. Bruce Nussbaum, *Good Intentions* (New York: Atlantic Monthly Press, 1990), pp. 176+; Brian O'Reilly, "The inside story of the AIDS drug," *Fortune*, November 5, 1990, pp. 112+; Julia Flynn with John Carey, "Wellcome's

AZT faces attacks on two fronts," *Business Week*, July 26, 1993, p. 36.

3. Stewart A. Washburn, "Establishing Strategy and Determining Cost in the Pricing Decision," *Business Marketing*, July 1985, pp. 64–78.

4. John Saunders, "Retailer's Pricing Strategies Seen As Confusing," *The Globe and Mail*, February 28, 1997, p. B6.

5. Scott McCartney, "Gap Grows Between Business, Leisure Fares," *The Globe and Mail*, November 12, 1997, pp. A16, A18.

6. "Odd prices hurt image of prices," *Business Month*, July 1987, p. 23.

7. Randall Litchfield, "The pressure on prices," *Canadian Business*, February 1992, pp. 30–35.

8. Stephanie Anderson Forest, "The education of Michael Dell," *Business Week*, March 22, 1993, pp. 82–86; Lois Therrien, "Why gateway is racing to answer on the first ring," *Business Week*, September 13, 1993, pp. 92–93; Peter Burrows, "The computer is in the mail (really)," *Business Week*, January 23, 1995, pp. 76–77; Scott McCartney, "Michael Dell—and his company—grow up," *Wall Street Journal*, January 31, 1994, pp. B1, B2.

9. Dale M. Lewison, *Retailing*, 5th ed. (New York: Macmillan, 1994), p. 454; Louis Stern and Adel I. El-Ansary, *Marketing Channels*, 4th ed. (Englewood Cliffs, NJ: Prentice Hall, 1992), pp. 129–130.

10. Kenneth Kidd, "Canadian Tire opts for austerity," *The Globe and Mail*, July 17, 1991, pp. B1–B2; also John Heinzl, "Canadian Tire treads new ground in warehouse stores," *The Globe and Mail*, October 7, 1991, pp. B1–B2.

11. Barnaby Feder, "McDonald's makes a comeback," *The Globe and Mail*, January 22, 1994, p. B8.

12. Julie Iovine, "Cher's gothic look, by mail," *New York Times*, September 8, 1994, p. C8.

13. Philip Kotler and Gary Armstrong, *Marketing: An Introduction*, 3rd ed. (Englewood Cliffs, NJ: Prentice Hall, 1993), p. 362; Scott Donaton and Joe Mandese, "GM, Hachette to test TV show," *Advertising Age*, September 13, 1993, p. 1.

14. Andrew Tausz, "Getting there fast—by truck," *The Globe and Mail*, March 1, 1994, p. B23.

15. Andrew Allentuck, "Arctic delivery tough sailing," *The Globe and Mail*, March 1, 1994, p. B23.

16. Rick Tetzeli, "Cargo that phones home," *Fortune*, November 15, 1993, p. 143.

17. Bill Redekop, "The crow subsidy is history," *Winnipeg Free Press*, February 28, 1995, p. 1.

Chapter 16

1. P.S. Rose and D.R. Fraser, *Financial Institutions*, 3rd ed. (Plano, TX: Business Publications, Inc., 1988).

2. Robert E. Calem, "Taking the worry out of paying with plastic," *New York Times*, November 14, 1993, Sec. 3, p. 9.

3. William Cantrell, "Why are all of those Canadian issuers selling?" *Credit Card Management*, December 1991, pp. 26–31; Thomas Holden, "The Japanese discover the perils of plastic," *Business Week*, February 10, 1992, p. 42; Richard L. Holman, "Korea curbs credit cards," *Wall Street Journal*, December 22, 1994, p. A10.

4. Russell Mitchell, "The Smart Money Is on Smart Cards," *Business Week*, August 14, 1995, pp. 68–69; Nikhil Deogun, "The Smart Money Is on 'Smart Cards,' but Electronic Cash Seems Dumb to Some," *Wall Street Journal*, August 5, 1996, pp. B1, B8.

5. Kelly Holland and Greg Burns, "Plastic Talks," *Business Week*, February 14, 1994, pp. 105–107; Saul Hansell, "An End to the 'Nightmare' of Cash," *New York Times*, September 6, 1994, pp. D1, D5; Thomas McCarroll, "No Checks. No Cash. No Fuss?" *Time*, May 9, 1994, pp. 60–62; Marla Matzer, "Plastic Mania," *Forbes*, October 24, 1994, pp. 281–82.

6. Kelly Holland and Amy Cortese, "The Future of Money," *Business Week*, June 12, 1995, pp. 66–72+.

7. Grep Ip, "Ottawa Set to Lose Millions When Reserve Rules Dropped," *The Financial Post*, July 17, 1991, p. 3.

8. John Heinzl, "Face of Banking Changing," *The Globe and Mail*, April 17, 1998, pp. B1, B7.

9. Karen Horcher, "Reconstruction Zone," *CGA Magazine*, June 1997, p. 19.

10. "Big MacCurrencies," *The Economist*, April 9, 1994, p. 88.

11. Robert J. Carbaugh, *International Economics*, 5th ed. (Cincinnati: South-Western, 1995), Chapter 11.

Chapter 17

1. Jerry Zeidenberg, "Suppliers at mercy of big companies," *The Globe and Mail*, June 10, 1991, p. B10.

2. John Heinzl, "Good strategy gone awry, top retailer's tale of woe," *The Globe and Mail*, March 7, 1992, pp. B1, B4.

3. Thomas P. Fitch, *Dictionary of Banking Terms*, 2nd ed. (Hauppauge, NY: Barron's, 1993), p. 531.

Chapter 18

1. *The Value Line Investment Survey*, January 28, 1994, p. 1095.

2. *NYSE Fact Book: 1995 Data* (New York: New York Stock Exchange, 1996), pp. 7, 43.

3. Nicholas D. Kristof, "Don't joke about this stock market," *New York Times*, May 9, 1993, Sec. 3, pp. 1, 6; Jane Perlez, "Warsaw's exuberant exchange," *New York Times*, December 25, 1993, pp. 47–48.

4. Peter Shawn Taylor, "Pennies from Hell," *Canadian Business*, February 27, 1998, pp. 69–71.

5. Greg Ip, "Are Canadian Bond Raters Biased?" *The Globe and Mail*, December 13, 1995, pp. B1, B8.

6. *Moody's Bond Survey*, August 2, 1993, p. 4138.

7. Amey Stone, "Futures: Dare you defy the odds?" *Business Week*, February 28, 1994, pp. 12–13.

8. Steven Greenhouse, "Exchanges thrive as Russians pursue market economy," *Winnipeg Free Press*, November 3, 1991, p. B13.

9. *The Financial Post*, July 1995, p. 172.

Appendix III

1. Alex Markels, "Job Hunting Takes Off in Cyberspace," *Wall Street Journal*, September 20, 1996, p. B1.

■ SOURCE NOTES

Chapter 1

Voisey's Bay: Field of Dreams or Nightmare? Summarized from Gary Lamphier, "Diamond Fields' Dream," *The Globe and Mail*, April 22, 1995, pp. B1, B4; also Tim Falconer, "Boomtown Jitters," *Report on Business*, November 1995, pp. 122–34; also "The Big Nickel," *The Financial Post*, June 8, 1996, p. 33; also Jacquie McNish, "Inco Digs Deep with Gamble on Voisey's Bay," *The Globe and Mail*, December 22, 1997, pp. B1, B8; also Allan Robinson, "Inco Delays Voisey's Bay," *The Globe and Mail*, September 20, 1997, pp. B1, B7; also Terence Corcoran, "Killing the Voisey's Bay Goose," *The Globe and Mail*, September 20, 1997, p. B2; also Allan Robinson, "Inco Chairman Defends Actions," *The Globe and Mail*, April 23, 1998, p. B3; also Brian Hutchinson, "A Plugged Nickel," *Canadian Business*, April 24, 1998, pp. 43–46. **Raising Rhinos for Horns and Profits** Summarized from Ken Wells, "African Game Ranchers See a New Way to Save Endangered Species," *The Wall Street Journal*, January 7, 1997, pp. A1, A11. **Figure 1.3** *Bank of Canada Review*, Summer 1997, Table A1, p. S7. **Coping with Inflation** Summarized from Peter Cook, "Brazil campaigns against inflation," *The Globe and Mail*, May 16, 1994, p. B1; also Katherine Ellison, "Heart attacks price of Brazil's chaotic economy," *The Financial Post*, January 17, 1994, p. C8; also Peter Cook, "Brazil's inflation fight gets real," *The Globe and Mail*, July 4, 1994, p. B1; also Isabel Vincent, "Argentina's miracle more of a paradox," *The Globe and Mail*, March 17, 1994, p. B1; also Bruce Little, "Deflation returns after 40 years," *The Globe and Mail*, June 18, 1994, pp. B1, B3; also Barrie McKenna, "Is it the last gasp for inflation?" *The Globe and Mail*, February 17, 1994, pp. B1, B8. **Figure 1.4** *Bank of Canada Review*, Summer 1997, Table H5, p. S89. **Improved Productivity at Canadian National Railways** Summarized from Geoff Kirbyson, "CN Boss Delivers the Good News to Shareholders," *Winnipeg Free Press*, April 29, 1998; also Geoffrey Rowan, "CN Productivity Right Off the Tracks," *The Globe and Mail*, October 9, 1991, pp. B1, B4. **Business Case 1** Summarized from Brent Jang, "An Oil Boom Dawns on Newfoundland," *The Globe and Mail*, March 7, 1997, pp. B1, B6; also Allanna Sullivan, "Four Decades Later, Oil Field Off Canada Is Ready to Produce," *The Wall Street Journal*, April 1, 1997, pp. A1, A6; also Brent Jang, "The Economics of Hibernia," *The Globe and Mail*, May 17, 1997, pp. B1, B3.

Chapter 2

Employee Buyouts—Good News and Bad News Summarized from Gail Lem, "Algoma chief shares pain, gives up $400,000 bonus," *The Globe and Mail*, May 4, 1994, pp. B1–B2; also Patricia Commins, "United Airlines unions bet on success," *The Globe and Mail*, December 24, 1993, p. B5; also Robin Sidel, "Employee ownership seen as industry trend," *The Globe and Mail*, December 24, 1993, p. B5; also David Roberts, "The brew crew takes over," *The Globe and Mail*, December 21, 1993, p. B20; also Hugh McBride, "How to lose freedom and gain the world," *The Globe and Mail*, January 25, 1994; also Kimberley Noble, "Can the workers make a go of it?" *The Globe and Mail*, August 17, 1991, p. B18; also Nattalia Lea, "Study of a Spinoff: Workers to Owners," *The Globe and Mail*, April 3, 1995, p. B6. **Unlimited Liability at Lloyd's of London** Adapted from

Madelaine Drohan, "Lloyd's ends tradition of unlimited liability," *The Globe and Mail*, April 30, 1993, pp. B1, B8; also "Investors revel in Lloyd's suit win," *Winnipeg Free Press*, October 5, 1994, p. C12; "Lloyd's Offers $6 Billion Solution," *The Globe and Mail*, May 24, 1995, p. B8; also "Lloyd's Rings Bell to Celebrate Rescue," *The Globe and Mail*, September 5, 1996, p. B9. **Going Public** Summarized from Patrick Brethour, "The Price of Going Public," *The Globe and Mail*, April 30, 1997, p. B12. **Mountain Equipment Co-op** Summarized from Ann Gibbon, "Mountain Equipment Blazes New Trail," *The Globe and Mail*, January 30, 1998, p. B27. **Business Case 2** Summarized from Robert Tomsho, "Costly Funerals Spur a Co-op Movement to Hold Down Bills," *The Wall Street Journal*, November 12, 1996, pp. A1, A5.

Chapter 3

Problems at the Better Business Bureau Summarized from Kimberley Noble and Dan Westell, "Better Business Bungle," *The Globe and Mail*, September 23, 1995, pp. B1, B4; Tamsen Tillson, "Thumbs Down for the Critic," *Canadian Business*, August 1995, pp. 66–67; John Heinzl, "Tuz Charged with Defrauding BBB," *The Globe and Mail*, December 12, 1996, p. B5; Janet McFarland, "Former BBB President Cleared," *The Globe and Mail*, April 3, 1998, p. B6; Peter Verburg, "For Better or For Worse," *Canadian Business*, June 12, 1998, pp. 56–62. **To Bribe or Not to Bribe** Summarized from Madelaine Drohan, "To bribe or not to bribe," *The Globe and Mail*, February 14, 1994, p. B7; see also Margaret Shapiro, "A Country on the Take," *Winnipeg Free Press*, November 21, 1994, p. A7. **Recycling Financial Results** Summarized from Janet McFarland, "Philip Shares Plunge Amid Controversy," *The Globe and Mail*, January 7, 1998, pp. B1, B6; also Janet McFarland and Paul Waldie, "A Breach in the House of Philip," *The Globe and Mail*, February 14, 1998, pp. B1, B6; also Janet McFarland, "Philip Services Denies It Leaked Insider Data," *The Globe and Mail*, February 18, 1998, pp. B1, B11; also Janet McFarland, "Philip Restates Earnings Again," *The Globe and Mail*, April 24, 1998, pp. B1, B4; also Janet McFarland, "Investors Desert Philip," *The Globe and Mail*, April 25, 1998, pp. B1, B4; also Mark Stevenson, "Waste Not," *Canadian Business*, January 1994, pp. 20–26; also Sean Silcoff, "Something's Missing," *Canadian Business*, May 13, 1998, pp. 72–80; also Sean Silcoff, "New Face, Same Mess," *Canadian Business*, June 12, 1998, pp. 41–44. **What To Do in a Mad Cow Crisis** Lawrence K. Altman, "U.S. Officials Confident That Mad Cow Disease of Britain Has Not Occurred Here," *New York Times*, March 27, 1996, p. A12; Gina Kolata, "Study Questions Top Theory on Cause of Mad Cow Disease," *New York Times*, January 17, 1997, p. A19; Patrick Barrett, "Beef Industry Takes Stock," *Marketing*, March 28, 1996, p. 14; John Darnton, "British Beef Banned in France and Belgium," *New York Times*, March 22, 1996, p. A8; Darnton, "For the British Beef War: A Truce but No Victory," *New York Times*, June 24, 1996, p. A9; Mary Kay Melvin, "Food Managers in England Report on Impact of Mad Cow Disease," *Amusement Business*, April 15, 1996, p. 16; Richard L. Papiernik, "U.S. Chains Switch Beef Sources in U.K.," *Nation's Restaurant News*, April 8, 1996, p. 1. **Business Case 3** Kevin Kelly and Kathleen Kerwin, "There's another side to the López saga," *Business Week*, August 23, 1993, p. 26; John Templeman and Peggy Salz-Trautman, "VW figures its best defense may be a good offense," *Business Week*, August 9, 1993, p. 29; Templeman and

David Woodruff, "The aftershock from the López affair," *Business Week*, August 19, 1993, p. 31; Doron Levin, "Executive who left G.M. denies taking documents and sues," *The New York Times*, May 25, 1993, pp. A1, D21; Ferdinand Protzman, "VW hums tightfisted López tune," *The New York Times*, April 30, 1994, pp. 39, 47; Gabriella Mitchener, "VW Agrees To Big Settlement with GM," *The Wall Street Journal*, January 10, 1997, p. A3.

Chapter 4

Purdy's Goes International Summarized from Gayle MacDonald, "Purdy's Test Asia's Sweet Tooth," *The Globe and Mail*, June 9, 1997, p. B7; also Elizabeth Church, "Chocolate Maker Resists Asian Flu," *The Globe and Mail*, February 2, 1999, p. B15. **The Asian Crisis: A Worldwide Threat** Based on information contained in the followng sources: Jim Rohwer, "Asia's Meltdown: It Ain't Over Yet," *Fortune*, July 20, 1998, pp. 93–95; also Joji Sakurai, "Japan's Economy Needs First Aid, GDP Data Reveal," *Winnipeg Free Press*, June 13, 1998, p. B19; also Karene Witcher, Darren McDermott, and Jay Solomon, "Tensions Rise as IMF, Indonesia Lock Horns," *The Globe and Mail*, February 16, 1998, p. B6; also Darren McDermott, "Predictions Grow Dire as Won and Rupiah Erode," *The Globe and Mail*, December 17, 1997, p. B6; also Bob Davis, "South Korea Played The Reluctant Patient to IMF's Rescue Team," *The Wall Street Journal*, March 2, 1998, pp. A1, A12; also Steve Glain, "From Alaska Fisheries to Australian Outback, Asian Crisis Hits Home," *The Wall Street Journal*, March 16, 1998, pp. A1, A8. **Table 4.1** *Market Research Handbook*, 63-224, 1995, p. 37. **A Tale of Three Currencies** Summarized from David Rocks, "Czech Currency Falls on Hard Times," *The Globe and Mail*, June 10, 1997, p. B7; also Craig Torres and Paul Carroll, "Mexico Reverses Currency Policy," *The Wall Street Journal*, December 21, 1994, pp. A3, A6; also Paul Carroll and Craig Torres, "Mexico Unveils Program of Harsh Fiscal Medicine," *The Wall Street Journal*, March 10, 1995, pp. A3, A11; also Craig Torres, "Mexican Markets Are Hit by Fresh Blows," *The Wall Street Journal*, February 16, 1995, p. A11; also Michael Urlocker and Frances Misutka, "Russians Learn to Love the Greenback," *The Financial Post*, September 11, 1993, p. 9; also "Russia Tumbles, Russia Reels," *The Globe and Mail*, October 12, 1994, pp. B1, B20. Laura Eggertson, "Peso Crisis Lingers for Many Mexicans," *The Globe and Mail*, October 7, 1997, pp. B1, B12. **The Pleasures and Perils of International Business** Summarized from Jonathan Kaufman, "Tethered to Pittsburgh for Years, an Engineer Thrives on Trips to Asia," *The Wall Street Journal*, November 19, 1996, pp. A1, A8. **Figure 4.2** Griffin/Ebert, *Business*, Fourth Edition (Englewood Cliffs, NJ: Prentice Hall, 1996). **Table 4.2** *International Trade Statistics*, Volume II, 1995, pp. S2–S16. **Faux Pas in Foreign Lands** Summarized from Phillip Day, "A-OK? Not for this Moscow Crowd, after Clinton Gives 'em the Finger," *Winnipeg Free Press*, June 18, 1994, p. C6; also Tamsen Tillson, "The art of the deal in China," *The Globe and Mail*, September 5, 1994, pp. B1-B2. **The Cavalier Attitude Towards Murky Tea** Norihiko Shirouzu, "Snapple in Japan: How a Splash Dried Up," *Wall Street Journal*, April 15, 1996, p. B1; Edith Hill Updike, "Is Cavalier Japanese for Edsel?" *Business Week*, June 24, 1996, p. 39. **Business Case 4** Marcus W. Brauchli, "The Outlook: China's Big Advantage Is a Young Population," *Wall Street Journal*, April 14, 1996, p. A1; Kathy Chen, "Young Chinese Loosen the Purse Strings," *Wall Street Journal*, July 15, 1996, p. A9; Pete Engardio, "Microsoft's Long March," *Business Week*, June 24, 1996, pp. 52–54; Seth Faison, "U.S. and China Agree on Pact to Fight Piracy," *New York Times*, June 18, 1996, p. A6; David E. Sanger, "Software Pirates Growing in Number in China, U.S. Says," *New York Times*, May 8, 1996, pp. A1, A9; Jarie H. Lili, "Boom-at-a-Glance," *New York Times Magazine*, February 16, 1996, pp. 26–27.

Chapter 5

Planning and Strategy at Seagram Summarized from Allan Swift, "Polygram Bid Heats Up," *Winnipeg Free Press*, November 5, 1998, p. B12; also Brian Milner, "Seagram's Top Gun Shoots for the Stars," *The Globe and Mail*, June 6, 1998, pp. B1, B6; also "Investors Expected to Snap Up Tropicana IPO," *The Globe and Mail*, June 12, 1998, p. B12; also Brian Milner, "Seagram Snares Polygram," *The Globe and Mail*, May 22, 1998, pp. B1, B4. **What Do Managers Actually Do?** Summarized from Henry Mintzberg, *The Nature of Managerial Work* (New York: Harper and Row, 1973), Chapter 3. **The Downsizing Craze** Summarized from Greg Ip, "Jobs Cut Despite Hefty Profits," *The Globe and Mail*, February 6, 1996, pp. A1, A4; also Greg Ip, "Shareholders vs. Jobholders," *The Globe and Mail*, March 23, 1996, pp. B1, B4. **Changing the Culture of a Manufacturing Plant** Summarized from Gabriella Stern, "How a Young Manager Shook Up the Culture at Old Chrysler Plant," *The Wall Street Journal*, April 21, 1997, pp. A1, A6. **Business Case 5** Summarized from "A Message from Mudville," *Canadian Business*, March 1996, pp. 36–37; also Scott Taylor, "Baseball Develops Class Systems," *Winnipeg Free Press*, December 15, 1996, p. A8; also David Napier, "Beeston Plays Hardball," *The Financial Post Magazine*, September 1992, pp. 28–32.

Chapter 6

Restructuring at Canadian Pacific Summarized from Ann Gibbon, "CP Rail Moving to Calgary," *The Globe and Mail*, November 21, 1995, pp. B1, B19; also Ann Gibbon, "Reorganization of CP Draws Applause," *The Globe and Mail*, November 22, 1995, p. B2. **Project Management at Genstar Shipyards Ltd.** Interview with Tom Ward, Operations Manager for Genstar Shipyards Ltd. **Heard It Through the Grapevine** Summarized from Owen Edwards, "Leak soup," *GQ*, April 1989, pp. 224+; see also Beatryce Nivens, "When to Listen to the office grapevine," *Essence*, March 1989, p. 102; John S. Tompkins, "Gossip: Silicon Valley's secret weapon," *Science Digest*, August 1986, pp. 58+; see also "Why you need the grapevine," *Glamour*, August 1986, pp. 126+. **Business Case 6** Susan Chandler, "United We Own," *Business Week*, March 18, 1996, pp. 96–100; Perry Flint, "The Buck Stops Lower," *Air Transport World*, September 1995, pp. 28–32.

Chapter 7

Zepf Technologies Inc. Awards for Business Excellence, *1989 Winners' Profiles*, Industry, Science and Technology Canada; also Rod McQueen, "Jobless in recovery," *The Financial Post*, October 14, 1995, p. 14. **Figure 7.1** *Quality of Work in the Service Sector*, Statistics Canada, 11-612E, No. 6, 1992. **Jimmy Pattison—**

Canadian Entrepreneur Extraordinaire Diane Francis, "What makes Jim Pattison run—and whistle," *The Financial Post*, March 5, 1994, p. S3. **Figure 7.2** Allan J. Magrath, "The thorny management issues in family-owned business," *Business Quarterly*, Spring 1988, p. 73. Reprinted with permission of *Business Quarterly*, published by the Western Business School, The University of Western Ontario, London, Ontario. **Just Like Home** Summarized from Richard T. Ashman, "Born in the U.S.A.," *Nation's Business*, November 1986, pp. 41+; see also "Canadian franchisees start to fight abuses," *Wall Street Journal*, October 6, 1988, p. B1; see also Ted Holden et al., "Who says you can't break into Japan?" *Business Week*, October 16, 1989, p. 49; see also Joann S. Lublin, "For U.S. franchisers, a common tongue isn't a guarantee of success in the U.K.," *Wall Street Journal*, August 16, 1988, p. 25; see also Matt Moffitt, "For U.S. firms, franchising in Mexico gets more appetizing, thanks to Michael Selz," *Wall Street Journal*, January 3, 1991, p. A6; see also Michael Selz, "Europe offers expanding opportunities to franchisers," *Wall Street Journal*, July 20, 1991, p. B2; see also Jeffrey A. Tannenbaum, "Franchisers see a future in East Bloc," *Wall Street Journal*, June 5, 1990, pp. B1+; see also Jeffrey A. Tannenbaum, "Small businesses join franchise push in Japan," *Wall Street Journal*, May 17, 1989, p. B1; see also Andrew Tanzer, "A form of flattery," *Forbes*, June 2, 1986, pp. 110+; see also Russell G. Todd, "U.S. fast-food franchises go East in American international venture," *Wall Street Journal*, November 15, 1988, p. B2; see also Meg Whittemore, "International franchising," *Inc.*, April 1988, pp. 116+. **Table 7.4** Starke/Sexty, *Contemporary Management in Canada*, Scarborough: Prentice Hall Canada (1995). **Business Case 7** Summarized from John Southerst, "Ontario Proposals Hit Sore Point with Franchisors," *The Globe and Mail*, November 25, 1996, p. B6; also Ellen Roseman, "Flowering Firm Faces Branch Battles," *The Globe and Mail*, November 28, 1995, p. B13; also John Lorinc, "War and Pizza," *Canadian Business*, November 1995, pp. 87–97; also John Lorinc, *Opportunity Knocks*. Scarborough: Prentice-Hall Canada Inc., 1995.

Chapter 8

Working on Long-Standing Problems Summarized from Patricia Lush, "MacBlo Slashes Operations," *The Globe and Mail*, January 22, 1998, pp. B1, B8; also Paul Waldie, "MacBlo Appoints New CEO," *The Globe and Mail*, September 17, 1997, pp. B1, B6; also Mark Stevenson, "Be Nice for a Change," *Canadian Business*, November, 1993, pp. 81–85. **Does Every Worker Want To Be Empowered?** Summarized from Timothy Aeppel, "Not All Workers Find Idea of Empowerment as Neat as it Sound," *The Wall Stree Journal*, September 8, 1997, pp. A1, A13. **Workplace Blues** Summarized from Arthur Bragg, "Should you make a lateral move?" *Sales & Marketing Management*, June 1989, pp. 70+; Carey W. English, "Money Isn't Everything," *U.S. News & World Report*, June 23, 1986, pp. 64+; see also "Family Ties," *Inc.*, August 1989, p. 112; see also Curtis Hartman and Steven Pearlstein, "The joy of working," *Inc.*, November 1987, pp. 61+; see also John Naisbitt and Patricia Aburdene, "When companies are great places to work," *Reader's Digest*," January 1987, pp. 141+. **Incentives and Motivation** Summarized from Bruce McDougall, "Perks with pizzazz," *Canadian Business*, June 1990, pp. 78–79; see also Don Champion, "Quality—a way of life at B.C. Tel," *Canadian Business Review*, Spring 1990, p. 33; see also Margot Gibb-Clark, "Companies find merit in using pay as a carrot," *The Globe and Mail*, May 9, 1990, p. B1; also Margot Gibb-Clark, "The right reward," *The Globe and Mail*, August 10,

1990, p. B5; see also Peter Matthews, "Just rewards—the lure of pay for performance," *Canadian Business*, February 1990, pp. 78–79; also Ian Allaby, "Just Rewards," *Canadian Business*, May 1990, p. 39; see also David Evans, "The myth of customer service," *Canadian Business*, March 1991, pp. 34–39; also Bud Jorgensen, "Do bonuses unscrupulous brokers make?" *The Globe and Mail*, May 28, 1990, p. B5; also Wayne Gooding, "Ownership is the best motivator," *Customer Business*, March 1990, p. 6. **The Japanese Management System** Summarized from Brenton Schlender, "Japan's white collar blues," *Fortune*, March 21, 1994, pp. 97–100; also Brenton Schlender, "Japan: Is it changing for good?" *Fortune*, June 13, 1994, pp. 124–134; also Edith Terry, "Japan lives with tradition," *The Globe and Mail*, May 14, 1994, pp. B1, B4; also William Ouchi, *Theory Z* (Reading, Mass.: Addison-Wesley, 1981); also Suzanne McGee, "How Japanese managers are trained," *The Financial Post*, June 1, 1985, p. 25; also Chalmers Johnson, "Japanese-style management in America," *California Management Review*, Summer 1988, pp. 34–45; N. Coates, "Determinants of Japan's business success: Some Japanese executives' views," *Academy of Management Executive*, February 1988, 2, pp. 69–72. **Business Case 8** Stratford Sherman, "Levi's: As Ye Sew, So Shall Ye Reap," *Fortune*, May 12, 1997, pp. 104–116; also Ralph King, "Levi's Factory Workers Are Assigned to Teams, and Morale Takes a Hit," *The Wall Street Journal*, May 20, 1998, pp. A1, A6.

Chapter 9

Breaking Through the Glass Ceiling Summarized from John Heinzl, "Women Take Charge at Canadian Units," *The Globe and Mail*, November 29, 1996, p. B10; also Greg Keenan, "Ford Canada Gets New CEO," *The Globe and Mail*, April 9, 1997, p. B1; also Joseph White and Carol Hymowitz, "Watershed Generation of Women Executives is Rising to the Top," *The Globe and Mail*, February 10, 1997, pp. A1, A6; also Greg Keenan, "Woman at the Wheel," *The Globe and Mail*, July 8, 1995, pp. B1, B6. Greg Keenan and Janet McFarland, "The Boys' Club," *The Globe and Mail*, September 27, 1997, pp. B1, B5. **Mismatch in Jobs and Skills** Bruce Little, "Employment sweepstakes requires flexible ticket," *The Globe and Mail*, January 13, 1993, pp. B1, B6. **Screen Test** Summarized from Rose Fisher, "Screen Test," *Canadian Business*, May 1992, pp. 62–64. **What?! A Union at Wal-Mart?** Summarized from John Heinzl and Marina Strauss, "Wal-Mart's Cheer Fades," *The Globe and Mail*, February 15, 1997, pp. B1, B4; also Margot Gibb-Clark, "Why Wal-Mart Lost the Case," *The Globe and Mail*, February 14, 1997, p. B10. Susan Bourette, "Organized Labour Lures Growing Number of Youth," *The Globe and Mail*, July 4, 1997, pp. B1, B4; also Susan Bourette, "Women Make Strides in Union Movement," *The Globe and Mail*, August 29, 1997, pp. B1–B2; also Susan Bourette, "Wal-Mart Staff Want Out of Union," *The Globe and Mail*, April 23, 1998, p. B9. **Figure 9.4** *Labour Organizations in Canada*, 1996, p. xiv. **Strike Was No Ball for Business** Summarized from Marina Strauss and Harvey Enchin, "Strike is no ball for business," *The Globe and Mail*, August 22, 1994, pp. B1, B5; also Marina Strauss, "Broadcasters bodychecked," *The Globe and Mail*, October 1, 1994, pp. B1, B2; also Scott Feschuk, "Hockey shutout costs provinces millions," *The Globe and Mail*, December 8, 1994, pp. B1, B10; also Marina Strauss, "Broadcasters worry: When the games return, will advertisers follow?" *The Globe and Mail*, December 3, 1994, pp. B1, B7; also Harvey Enchin, "Hockey loss crosschecks Maple Leaf Gardens," *The Globe and Mail*, November 11, 1994, p. B1,

B4. **Business Case 9** Summarized from Mark Brender, "Free isn't easy," *The Globe and Mail*, August 9, 1994, p. B18; also Margot Gibb-Clark, "Temps take on new tasks," *The Globe and Mail*, December 22, 1993, p. B1; also Merle MacIsaac, "New broom sweeps schools," *The Globe and Mail*, March 22, 1994, p. B22; also Robert Williamson, "Tradition gives way to world of freelancers," *The Globe and Mail*, January 15, 1993, pp. B1, B4; also Sally Ritchie, "Rent-a-manager," *The Globe and Mail*, August 17, 1993, p. B22.

Chapter 10

Toyota's Production System: Still the Standard Summarized from Alex Taylor, "How Toyota Defies Gravity," *Fortune*, December 8, 1997, pp. 100–108. **Just-in-Time to the Hospital** Bruce Little, "Stock Answers," *The Globe and Mail*, June 6, 1995, p. B12. **Robots: Mixed Success** Summarized from Gordon Bock, "Limping along in robot land," *Time*, July 13, 1987, pp. 46+; see also Gene Bylinsky, "Invasion of the service robots," *Fortune*, September 14, 1987, pp. 81+; "*Ecce* Robo," *The Economist*, October 15, 1988, pp. 19+; see also Bill Lawren, "Humans make a comeback," *Omni*, August 1987, pp. 32+; see also "Living with smart machines," *The Economist*, May 21, 1988, pp. 79+; see also Wally Dennison, "Robotics paint system makes splash at CN," *Winnipeg Free Press*, October 6, 1988, p. 30; see also "Robots aren't for burning," *Canadian Business*, September 1984, p. 45; see also Renate Lerch, "More firms finding place for robots on factory floor," *The Financial Post*, June 29, 1985, p. C6; see also Carolyn Leitch, "When boxes have brains," *The Globe and Mail*, April 12, 1994, p. B26. **Business Case 10** Valerie Reitman, "Honda Sees Performance and Profits from New Accord," *Wall Street Journal*, August 27, 1997, p. B4; Keith Naughton et al., "Can Honda Build a World Car?" *Business Week*, September 8, 1997, pp. 100–108.

Chapter 11

Dell Speeds Its Way to Quality Summarized from Joan Magretta, "The Power of Virtual Integration: An Interview with Dell Computer's Michael Dell," *Harvard Business Review*, March–April 1998, pp. 73–84; also Gary McWilliams, "Whirlwind on the Web," *Business Week*, April 7, 1997, pp. 132–36; Andrew E. Serwer, "Michael Dell Turns the PC World Inside Out," *Fortune*, September 8, 1997, pp. 76–86; David Kirkpatrick, "Now Everyone in PCs Wants To Be Like Mike," *Fortune*, September 8, 1997, pp. 91–92; Stephanie Anderson Forest et al., "And Give Me an Extra-Fast Modem with That, Please," *Business Week*, September 29, 1997, p. 38. **Suggestions for Improving Canada's International Competitiveness** Summarized from Harvey Enchin, "Canada urged to stop living off fat of the land," *The Globe and Mail*, October 25, 1991, pp. B1, B6. **TQM at Standard Aero Ltd.** Summarized from Ted Wakefield, "No Pain, No Gain," *Canadian Business*, January 1993, pp. 50–54. **ISO 9000: Seeking the Standard in Quality** Ronald Henkoff, "The Hot New Seal of Quality," *Fortune*, June 28, 1993, pp. 116–20; Todd Leeuwenburgh, "Quality Standards That Can Open Doors," *Nation's Business*, November 1992, pp. 32–33; Johan B. Levine, "Want EC Business? You Have Two Choices," *Business Week*, October 19, 1992, pp. 58–59; Otis Port, "More Than a Passport to European Business," *Business Week*, November 1, 1993, pp. 146H, 146J. **SABRE-Toothed Tiger of the Skies** "Air reservation merger is off," *The New York Times*,

October 16, 1991, p. D3; "Best practice companies," *Financial World*, September 17, 1991, pp. 36+; "The computer network that keeps American flying," *Fortune*, September 24, 1990, p. 46; Max D. Hopper, "Rattling SABRE—New ways to compete on information," *Harvard Business Review*, May–June 1990, pp. 188+; "Hotels find better lodging in airline reservation systems," *Business Week*, July 10, 1989, p. 84E; Kenneth Lambich, "American takes on the world," *Fortune*, September 24, 1990, pp. 40+. **Business Case 11** Louis Kraar, "Behind Samsung's High-Stakes Push into Cars," *Fortune*, May 12, 1997, pp. 119–120.

Chapter 12

Information Processing Under Pressure Robert Williamson, "Cyber Seadogs," *The Globe and Mail*, July 18, 1995, p. B18. **Who Can We Blame for This Mess?** Summarized from Edward Clifford, "Big Accounting Firms Face Insurance Crunch," *The Globe and Mail*, November 13, 1993, p. B3; also "Cooperants' Auditors Sued," *The Financial Post*, October 30, 1993, p. 8; also Patricia Lush, "Gap widens between views on auditor's role in Canada," *The Globe and Mail*, February 14, 1986, p. B3; also Chris Robinson "Auditors' Role Raises Tough Questions," *The Financial Post*, June 22, 1985. **Can You Believe It?** Summarized from Geoffrey Rowan, "Date Digit Glitch Bedevils Computers," *The Globe and Mail*, April 9, 1996, p. B8; Lee Gomes, "Why Prepping Mainframes for 2000 Is So Tough," *The Wall Street Journal*, December 9, 1996, pp. B1, B8; Patrick Brethour, "Report Warns of '2000 crisis'," *The Globe and Mail*, October 8, 1997, pp. B1, B14; Murray McNeill, "Firm Cashing in on Millenium," *Winnipeg Free Press*, June 11, 1997; Thomas Petzinger, "Programmer Attacks the Millennium Bug," *The Globe and Mail*, June 20, 1997, p. B6. **Business Case 12** Joel Brinkley, "PC Makers Challenge Broadcasters over Format for Digital Television," *New York Times*, April 8, 1997; Joel Brinkley, "Who Will Build Your Next TV? Industries Fight for $150 Billion Prize," *New York Times*, March 28, 1997; Neil Gross, "Defending the Living Room: How TV Makers Intend to Fend Off Cyberlopers," *Business Week*, June 24, 1996, pp. 96–98; Frank Rose, "The End of TV as We Know It," *Fortune*, December 23, 1996, pp. 58–68; Robert D. Hof and Gary McWilliams, "Digital TV: What Will It Be?" *Business Week*, April 21, 1997; Kyle Pope and Mark Robichaux, "Waiting for HDTV? Don't Go Dumping Your Old Set Just Yet," *Wall Street Journal*, September 12, 1997, p. 1; David Bank, "Changing Picture," *Wall Street Journal*, September 11, 1997, p. R15.

Chapter 13

How Good Is Market Research Information? Summarized from Elizabeth Jensen, "Networks Blast Nielsen, Blame Faulty Ratings For Drop in Viewership," *The Wall Street Journal*, November 22, 1996, pp. A1, A8; also R. Turner and J.R. Emshwiller, "FlimFlam? Movie Research Czar Is Said by Some to Sell Manipulated Findings," *The Wall Street Journal*, December 17, 1993, pp. A1, A7. **Teenagers: An International Market Segment** Summarized from Shawn Tully, "Teens: The most global market of all," *Fortune*, May 16, 1994, pp. 90–97. **Romancing The Profits** Summarized from Gina Mallet, "Greatest romance on earth," *Canadian Business*, August 1993, pp. 19–23. **Pitfalls in Global Promotion** Griffin/Ebert, *Business*, Third Edition. **Business Case 13** Summarized from

William M. Bulkeley, "Wring in the New: Washers That Load from Front Are Hot," *The Wall Street Journal*, April 29, 1997, pp. A1, A5.

Chapter 14

Promoting Athletes and Sales Summarized from John Heinzl, "Logos an Olympic Event," *The Globe and Mail*, October 20, 1997, pp. B1, B6; also John Heinzl, "How Roots Plants Its Products," *The Globe and Mail*, May 28, 1998, p. B10. **Developing and Promoting a New Product** Richard Siklos, "Dogfight at 51,000 Feet," *The Financial Post*, May 17, 1997, pp. 6–7; also Daniel Stoffman, "Bombardier's Billion-Dollar Space Race," *Canadian Business*, June 1994, pp. 91–101. **Predicting the Success of New Products** Summarized from Jared Mitchell, "Wonders and Blunders," *Report on Business*, September 1995, pp. 152–162. **Building Brands at Nestlé** Summarized from Carla Rapaport, "Nestlé's brand building machine," *Fortune*, September 19, 1994, pp. 147–156. **Figure 14.4** *Media Digest*, 1996, p. 11. **Business Case 14** Ian Fisher, "A New Jordan Sneaker Inspires a Frenetic Run," *New York Times*, July 4, 1996, pp. B1, B4; Leigh Gallagher, "Industry Retailers See Swoosh as Double-Edged Sword," *Sporting Goods Business*, April 1996, p. 8; Robert McAllister, "Jordan Fever Is Heating Up Retailers," *Footwear News*, March 20, 1995, pp. 2–3; Catherine Salfino, "Pro Name Game Gives Nike, Reebok Foothold in Apparel Arena," *Daily News Record*, February 28, 1996, p. 3; Bill Richards, "Nike Takes Off on New Marketing Track," *The Globe and Mail*, March 3, 1998, p. B10.

Chapter 15

Big Changes at Canada's Most Famous Retailer Summarized from Ian McGugan, "Eaton's on the Brink," *Canadian Business*, March 1996, pp. 38–48, 65–73; also "Eaton's Stuns Nation," *Winnipeg Free Press*, February 28, 1997, pp. A1, A3; John Heinzl and Paul Waldie, "Eaton's Drowning in Red Ink," *The Globe and Mail*, February 28, 1997, p. B1; John Heinzl, Carolyn Leitch, John Saunders, Marina Strauss, and Paul Waldie, "Inside the Debacle at Eaton's," *The Globe and Mail*, March 1, 1997, pp. B1, B4; Rob Ferguson, "Eaton's Gets on With It," *Winnipeg Free Press*, September 9, 1997, p. B3; Casey Mahood, "Wal-Mart Claims Another Victim," *The Globe and Mail*, February 7, 1998, pp. B1, B5; Geoff Krbyson, "Eaton's Makes Its Pitch to Brokers," *The Winnipeg Free Press*, May 12, 1998, p. B7. **How Much Should a Movie Ticket Cost?** Summarized from Brian Milner, "Charge More for Movies, Bronfman Urges Industry," *The Globe and Mail*, April 1, 1998, pp. B1, B4; also Bruce Orwall, "Bronfman's 'Real-World' a Tough Sell in Hollywood," *The Wall Street Journal*, April 3, 1998, p. B9. **U.S. Discounters Making Waves in Canada and Europe** Summarized from John Heinzl, "Canadian Tire pulls out of U.S.," *The Globe and Mail*, December 2, 1994, pp. B1, B6; also William C. Symonds, "Invasion of the retail snatchers," *Business Week*, May 9, 1994, pp. 72–73; also Carla Rapaport, "The new U.S. push into Europe," *Fortune*, January 10, 1994, pp. 73–74; also Marina Strauss, "Imasco sells stores," *The Globe and Mail*, June 26, 1990, pp. B1–B2; also Karen Howlett, "Once bitten in the U.S. market, Canadian Tire not shy about re-entering," *The Globe and Mail*, May 6, 1988, p. B3; also Kenneth Kidd, "Success breeds prudence as Canadian Tire peers over 49th parallel," *The Globe and Mail*, January 31, 1990, p. 36; also Frances Phillips, "Canadian Tire finds Texas trails a bit bumpy," *The Financial Post*, March 26, 1983, p. 18; also Jean Matthews and Greg Boyd, "Can Lionel Robbins rescue Dylex?" *Canadian Business*, November 1990, pp. 106–114; also Beppi Crosariol, "What makes the U.S. so tough," *Financial Times of Canada*, October 8, 1990, p. 14; also *The Financial Post* Information Service, History Sections on Canadian Tire Corporation and Dylex Ltd.; also John Heinzl, "Home Depot Finds Canada Chilly," *The Globe and Mail*, June 23, 1995, pp. B1, B17; also John Lorinc, "Road Warriors," *Canadian Business*, October 1995, pp. 26–43. **The Changing Face of Canadian Retailing** Summarized from Casey Mahood, "Wal-Mart Claims Another Victim," *The Globe and Mail*, February 7, 1998, pp. B1, B5; also Sean Silcoff, "Boutique Z," *Canadian Business*, May 8, 1998, pp. 62–66; also Mark Stevenson, "The Store to End All Stores," *Canadian Business*, May 1994, pp. 20–29; also Sean Silcoff, "The Emporiums Strike Back," *Canadian Business*, September 26, 1997, pp. 53–61. **Business Case 15** Keith Bradsher, "Sticker Shock: Car Buyers Miss Haggling Ritual," *New York Times*, June 13, 1996, pp. D1, D23; Bradley J. Fikes, "Haggling Over Price Is No Longer Automatic," *San Diego Business Journal*, October 3, 1994, pp. 17–18; Greg Keenan, "Revolution on the Car Lot," *The Globe and Mail*, March 22, 1997, pp. B1, B4; Greg Keenan, "Toyota Embarks on Dealership Overhaul," *The Globe and Mail*, September 1997, pp. B1, B20.

Chapter 16

What's the New Price? Summarized from Anne Reifenberg, "Dialing for Dinars: Iraqis Turn on Radio To Set Exchange Rate," *The Wall Street Journal*, September 20, 1996, pp. A1, A4. **To Catch a Credit Card Thief** Gene Bylinsky, "Computers That Leard by Doing," *Fortune*, September 6, 1993, pp. 96–102; Robert E. Calem, "Taking the Worry out of Playing with Plastic," *The New York Times*, November 13, 1993, Sec. 3, p. 9. **Consumer Satisfaction with Banks: Canada vs. the U.S.** Summarized from Barrie McKenna, "U.S. Banking Industry Riles Consumers," *The Globe and Mail*, October 13, 1997, pp. B1, B6. **Discount Banking: Will It Work?** Summarized from Sean Silcoff, "No Frills. Unbeatable Prices. It Worked for Wal-Mart," *Canadian Business*, August 1997, pp. 34–42. **Business Case 16** Summarized from Bruce Little and Chad Skelton, "The Flip Side of the Languishing Loonie," *The Globe and Mail*, June 20, 1998, pp. B1, B7.

Chapter 17

What Happened to Bramalea? Summarized from Kimberly Noble, "How Bramalea Gambled—and Lost," *The Globe and Mail*, April 1, 1995, pp. B1, B4. **Business Case 17** Sara Webb et al., "A royal mess: Britain's Barings PLC bets on derivatives—and the cost is dear," *The Wall Street Journal*, February 27, 1995, pp. A1, A6; Marcus W. Brauchli, Nicholas Bray, and Michael R. Sesit, "Broken bank: Barings PLC officials may have been aware of trader's position," *The Wall Street Journal*, March 6, 1995, pp. A1, A7; Richard W. Stevenson, "Markets shaken as a British bank takes a big loss," *The New York Times*, February 27, 1995; pp. A1, D5; Paula Dwyer et al., "The lesson from Barings' straits," *Business Week*, March 13, 1995, pp. 30–32. Glenn Whitney, "Dutch concern agrees to buy Barings assets," *The Wall Street Journal*, March 5, 1995, pp. A3, A5; "Leeson's Six-and-a-half Year Sentence Greeted with Mixed Reviews," *The Globe and Mail*, December 4, 1995, pp. B1, B10.

Chapter 18

A Whopper of a Fraud Summarized from Brian Hutchinson, "The Prize," *Canadian Business*, March 1997, pp. 26–48 and 65–72; also Andrew Willis, "Bre-X's Winners and Losers," *The Globe and Mail*, May 7, 1997, pp. B1, B6; also Karen Howlett, "David Walsh: Naive or Scandal-Plagued?," *The Globe and Mail*, May 31, 1997, pp. B1, B6; also Philip Mathias, "The Sad, Twisted Tale," *The Financial Post*, October 19, 1996, pp. 6–7; also Paul Waldie, Michael Den Tandt, "How Bre-X Samples Were Salted," *The Globe and Mail*, May 8, 1997; also Stephen Northfield, "Delgratia Says Gold Results Fake," *The Globe and Mail*, May 20, 1997, pp. B1, B9; James McCarten, "Lawsuits Proceed Despite Coma," *Winnipeg Free Press*, June 4, 1998, p. B11; Paul Waldie, "Bre-X Suit Passes Hurdle in Ontario," *The Globe and Mail*, December 16, 1997, p. B7; also Paul Waldie, "Report Deepens Bre-X Fiasco," *The Globe and Mail*, February 19, 1998, pp. B1, B10. **The Art of Influencing a Company's Stock Price** Summarized from Patricia Lush, "Matkin lowers the boom on VSE," *The Globe and Mail*, January 26, 1994, pp. B1, B7; also Douglas Gould, "Who needs brokers?" *Report on Business Magazine*, June 1990, pp. 35–37; also John Lorinc, "Making your firm a stock market star," *Canadian Business*, January 1992, pp. 51–54. **The Brave New World of Cyberspace Brokerage** Vanessa O'Connell, "Stock Answer," *Wall Street Journal*, June 17, 1996, p. R8; "With the World Wide Web, Who Needs Wall Street?" *Business Week*, April 29, 1996, pp. 120–21. **Are Pension and Mutual Funds Too Powerful?** Summarized from Karen Howlett and Susan Bourette, "Pension, Mutual Funds Dominate TSE Trading," *The Globe and Mail*, July 21, 1995, pp. B1, B6; also Jacquie McNish, "Pension Fund Power," *The Globe and Mail*, June 17, 1995, pp. B1, B3. **Business Case 18** Summarized from Daniel Stoffman, "Look who's calling the shots," *Canadian Business*, July 1990, pp. 45–47; Jacquie McNish, "CEOs Whistling Tommy's Tune," *The Globe and Mail*, January 30, 1998, pp. B1, B10.

■PHOTO CREDITS

Chapter 1
Page 2, Diamond Fields Resources Inc.;
Page 8, Susan McCartney; Bettmann
Archives; Junebug Clark; David R.
Frazier, Paolo Koch/Photo Researchers;
Page 9 Ontario Ministry of Agriculture
and Food; Page 14, Prentice Hall
Archives/R. Craig

Chapter 2
Page 22, Spruce Falls Mill; Page 26,
The Granger Collection; Page 34,
Imperial Oil Limited

Chapter 3
Page 43, Canada Wide; Page 48,
Canapress/AP Photo/Emilio
Morenatti/EFE; Page 52, David R.
Frazier/Photo Researchers; Page 55,
McDonald's Restaurants; Pablo
Bartholomew/Gamma Liaison

Chapter 4
Page 60, Purdy's Chocolate Stores; Page
62, Tomasz Tomaszewski Photography;
Page 72, Kevin Peterson/Parallel
Productions, General Mills;
Nortel/M.A. Malfavon Y. Associates;
Page 77, Canapress/Jacques Boissinot;
Page 81, Greg Baker/AP Wide World
Photos

Chapter 5
Page 88, Canapress; Page 93, AP Wide
World Photos/Ed Andrieski; Page 97,
Will McIntyre, Blair Seitz, Hank
Morgan/Photo Researchers; Page 99
Henley & Savage/The Stock Market Jan
Feingersh/The Stock Market Al
Harvey/The Slide Farm Federal Express
Customer Service; Page 103, Mainframe
Entertainment Inc.

Chapter 6
Page 109, CP Rail System; Page 113,
Lois Psyhoyos/Matrix International;
Page 115, First Light/Jose L. Peirez;

Page 123, Renee Lynn/Photo
Researchers

Chapter 7
Page 128, Lawrence Zepf; Page 131,
Prentice Hall Archives; Page 137, Midas
Canada Inc.

Chapter 8
Page 150, Canapress/Chuck Stoody;
Page 156, Courtesy Western Electric;
Page 158, Financial Post/Peter Redman;
Page 165, The Slide Farm/Al Harvey;
Page 166, Image Network/Chip
Henderson

Chapter 9
Page 173, Canapress/Andre Forget;
Page 178, Hunt Personnel; Page 182,
Canapress/Jacques Brinon; Page 187,
Canapress/Fred Chartrand; Page 192,
The Province/Colin Price; Page 197,
Canapress

Chapter 10
Page 208, Toyota Motor Manufacturing
Canada Inc.; Page 213, The Slide
Farm/Al Harvey; Page 217, Dick
Hemingway; Page 221, Jay Freis/ The
Image Bank; Courtesy Jervis B. Webb;
Courtesy Atlantic Container Line; Page
227, Courtesy Calma Company

Chapter 11
Page 231, Clark Jones/AP Wide World
Photos; Page 236, Hank Morgan/Photo
Researchers; Page 240, Chris Jones/The
Stock Market; Page 248, Dofasco
Canada

Chapter 12
Page 253, Photo by Wayne Farrar; Page
258, The Slide Farm/Al Harvey; Page
264, Courtesy The Coca Cola
Company; Page 272, Louis
Psihoyos/Matrix International

Chapter 13
Page 286, Dick Hemingway; Page 289,
Loblaws Brands Limited; Toronto
Zoo/Chiat Day/Illustrator Doug
Martin; Page 294, Created by Atlantic
Progress Magazine; Harley Davidson;
Reprinted with permission of Johnson &
Johnson; Courtesy of Nokia; Page 303,
The Body Shop

Chapter 14
Page 311, Canapress/Chuck Stoody;
Page 325, Prentice Hall Archives; Boy
Scouts of Canada; Canapress/Paul
Chiasson; Page 327, The Globe and
Mail

Chapter 15
Page 336, Canapress/Frank Gunn; Page
344, Richard Hutchings/Photo
Researchers; Page 354, Larry
Mulvehill/Photo Researchers; Page 357,
Canadian National

Chapter 16
Page 369, Canapress/Jassim
Mohammed; Page 371, The Granger
Collection (both); Page 378, Kathleen
Bellisles

Chapter 17
Page 394, The Financial Post; Page 399,
David Pollack/The Stock Market; Page
407, Photo Researchers (both)

Chapter 18
Page 411, Canapress/Jim Wells; Page
417, Toronto Star/D. Lock; Page 419,
Canada Investment and Savings; Page
423, Canapress Photo Services

INDEX

■ COMPANY, NAME AND PRODUCT INDEX

The page on which a weblink appears is printed in boldface.

■ SUBJECT INDEX

The page on which the key term is defined is printed in boldface.